GROWTH OF THE
AMERICAN REVOLUTION

1766–1775

As indicated by the dates in the title of this book, the revolution described in it is not the Revolutionary War. It is, in fact, in the familiar words of John Adams, the revolution "in the minds and hearts of the [American] people" toward Great Britain. If eighteenth-century usage as to titles prevailed, a fitting title for this book would be:

GROWTH OF THE AMERICAN REVOLUTION 1766–1774

Being an Account of the Change in the Minds and Hearts of a Majority of the People of the Thirteen Colonies Who Rebelled against Great Britain in 1775, together with a description of the Provocative Conduct of the British Parliament and Government Accounting for this Change and the Colonists' Responses to the said Conduct.

BERNHARD KNOLLENBERG

GROWTH
of the
AMERICAN
REVOLUTION
1766–1775

THE FREE PRESS
A Division of Macmillan Publishing Co., Inc.
NEW YORK

Collier Macmillan Publishers
LONDON

The Free Press
A Division of Macmillan Publishing Co., Inc.,
866 Third Avenue, New York, N.Y. 10022

Collier–Macmillan Canada Ltd.

Library of Congress Catalog Card Number: 74-7716

Printed in the United States of America

printing number
1 2 3 4 5 6 7 8 9 10

Library of Congress Cataloging in Publication Data

Knollenberg, Bernhard, 1892–1973.
  Growth of the American Revolution: 1766–1775.

  Bibliography: p.
  1. United States—History—Revolution, 1775–1783—
Causes. 2. United States—Politics and government—
Colonial period, ca. 1600–1775.
I. Title.
E210.K64 1975   973.3'11   74-7716
ISBN 0-02-917110-5

Photos from The John Carter Brown Library, Brown University

CONTENTS

Acknowledgments ix

Chronology: 1766–1775 xi

Introduction 1

1. The Rockingham Ministry and the Stamp Act 14

2. Repeal of the Stamp Act and Passage of the Declaratory Act 21

3. Colonial Grievances Remaining after Repeal of the Stamp Act 26

4. The Chatham Ministry and Its Inherited Colonial Problems 35

5. The Townshend Act Duties of 1767 42

6. The Farmer's Letters 48

7. Protests, Non-Importation Agreements, and Hillsborough's Provocative Letters 54

8. The American Customs Board and the *Liberty* Riot 61

9. The Treason Resolution: Proposed Revision of the Townshend Act 66

10. Revision of the Townshend Act and Dilution of Non-Importation 70

11. British Troops at Boston and the "Boston Massacre" 75

12. The *Gaspee* Affair and the Judges' Salary Controversy 82

13. The Tea Act of 1773 90

14. Colonial Opposition to the Tea Act and the Boston Tea Party 95

15. The Boston Port Act and British Troops to Boston 103

16. Proposals for a Tighter Rein on Massachusetts 109

17. The Massachusetts Petition of 1773 and Its Consequences 113

18. The Massachusetts Regulating and Administration of Justice Acts 117

19. The Quebec Act   121

20. Calls for a General Congress and Instructions to the Delegates   126

21. Unifying and Divisive Elements in the Congress   132

22. The Continental Congress: First Steps   138

23. Statement of Grievances and Approval of the Suffolk Resolves   146

24. The Association and the Memorial to the Colonists   151

25. Petition to the King and Other State Papers of the Congress   156

26. Developments in Massachusetts: May–September, 1774   163

27. The British Government and the Colonies: June, 1774–April, 1775   169

28. The Colonial Response to the Congress   175

29. Massachusetts Prepares for War: October, 1774–April, 1775   179

30. Gage's Military Activities While Awaiting Orders from England   184

31. Dartmouth's Letter Galvanizes Gage into Action   188

32. The Day of Lexington and Concord: April 19, 1775   191

APPENDIXES

Introduction (1)   Irritants before 1765   197
             (2)   Colonial Tories and Whigs   199

Chapter 1   George III and Establishment of the Rockingham Ministry   204

Chapter 2   The Act of 1696 and the Declaratory Act of 1766   206

Chapter 3   (1)   The Act of 1663 and Colonial Admiralty Courts   208
             (2)   The Free Port Act of 1766   211

Chapter 5   General Writs of Assistance   212

Chapter 7   Project for Anglican Bishops in the Colonies   217

Chapter 9   The Admiralty Court at Halifax and Its Successors   222

Chapter 10   Uneven Observance of the Non-Importation Agreements   223

Chapter 11 (1) Impressment and the Case of Michael Corbet   225
            (2) Clashes between Civilians and British Troops in New
                 York   227

Chapter 13 The Refund of Duty on Tea   228

Chapter 14 Was the *Dartmouth* Ordered to Enter Port?   229

Chapter 20 (1) Election of Delegates from Pennsylvania   231
            (2) New York Politics and the New York Delegation to the
                 Congress   233
            (3) Members of the First Continental Congress   239
            (4) Samuel Adams' Conduct as Collector of Taxes   242

Chapter 22 Galloway's Plan of Union   246

Chapter 23 (1) Grievances against the Crown   247
            (2) The Suffolk County Resolves   249

Chapter 26 The Solemn League and Covenant   250

Chapter 27 (1) Who Furnished the Information about Proceedings of
                 the Congress?   252
            (2) Peace Negotiations of Benjamin Franklin   254

Chapter 28 New York and the Continental Congress: 1775   258

Chapter 29 Colonial Whigs and Negro Slavery: 1765–1775   261

Chapter 32 April 19th: The Conflict of Evidence   264

Notes 269
Bibliography 493
Index 535

ACKNOWLEDGMENTS

CERTAINLY the happiest years of Bernhard Knollenberg's life, which ended suddenly the sixth of July, 1973, were the years since 1945, when he was able to give full time to his research into the origin and growth of the revolutionary spirit in this country and the writing of his two books covering the years from 1759 up to the actual outbreak of hostilities in 1775. This was a totally absorbing task to which he devoted an average of fourteen hours a day. The second and final volume was virtually complete when he died.

It was his express wish that I call on John R. Alden for help, should he be unable to see his book through its publication. An old friend and a fellow historian, Professor Alden undertook this task with eagerness, generosity, and devotion. He was firm in insisting that nothing be changed. In addition to proofreading, he has been helpful in every possible way. I cannot overstate my appreciation and gratitude.

Thanks also are due to all those friends, historians, and members of the staffs of Yale University Library and all other libraries and archives whose cheerful, prompt, and intelligent assistance made this book possible.

For the past thirteen years our friend and neighbor, Mrs. Marian Renehan, has typed and retyped B.K.'s chapters with a zeal second only to his zeal in writing them. Her knowledge of his working methods and her help in countless ways have been invaluable.

Finally, a word must be said about our indebtedness to Wilmarth S. Lewis, whose role in the appointment of my husband as Librarian of Yale University in 1938 gave him his start on the way to this life of study, research, and writing in which he found such satisfaction. "Lefty" Lewis' never failing encouragement, understanding, and perceptive advice have been inextricably woven into our lives all these years and I can only offer for us both my heartfelt thanks.

Mary Tarleton Knollenberg

Chester, Connecticut
December, 1973

CHRONOLOGY: 1766–1775

1766

January 1. George III, who succeeded his grandfather, George II, as King in 1760, is on the throne. The Cabinet members of the Ministry, which succeeded the Grenville Ministry in July, 1765, are Lord Rockingham, First Lord of the Treasury and head of the Ministry; the Duke of Newcastle, Lord Privy Seal; General Henry Seymour Conway, Secretary of State for the Southern Department (in charge of colonial affairs) and Leader of the House of Commons; the Duke of Grafton, Secretary of State for the Northern Department; Lord Northington, the Lord Chancellor; Lord Egmont, head of the Admiralty; and Lord Winchilsea, President of the (Privy) Council. William Dowdeswell has the important office of Chancellor of the Exchequer, but is not of the Cabinet.

Most of the thirteen colonies that later rebelled, hereafter sometimes referred to simply as the colonies, are in an uproar over the colonial Stamp Act passed a few months before the Rockingham Ministry took office.

January 14. William Pitt, out of office since 1762 but still influential, speaks forcefully in the Commons for repeal of the Stamp Act.

January 20. Rockingham, Conway, and other leading members of the Rockingham party decide to sponsor repeal of the Stamp Act, but with an accompanying act declaring the authority of Parliament to legislate for the colonies "in all cases whatsoever."

February. Benjamin Franklin, most distinguished American in Great Britain and London Agent for the Pennsylvania Assembly, testifies in the Commons that colonists dispute the right of Parliament to levy a stamp tax or other "internal" tax on the colonies, but not its right to levy import duties or other "external" taxes.

March. Repeal of the Stamp Act and passage of the Declaratory Act.

April. Rejoicing in the colonies over repeal of the Stamp Act; little notice taken there of the Declaratory Act.

April. Renewal of a Quartering Act requiring colonies in which British troops are quartered to furnish them with certain supplies.

May. Grafton resigns; Conway switches from the Southern to the Northern Department of the Secretaryship of State; the Duke of Richmond becomes Secretary of State for the Southern Department.

June. Passage of an act imposing additional restrictions on colonial trade and levying a duty for revenue (as distinct from a duty to regulate trade) on colonial imports of molasses.

July–December. The molasses duty excites little opposition in the colonies.

July. William Pitt (elevated to the House of Lords as Earl of Chatham) succeeds Newcastle as Lord Privy Seal and Rockingham as First Minister. Grafton returns to office as First Lord of the Treasury. Lord Granby, Master General of the Ordnance, is now included in the Cabinet. Lord Shelburne replaces Richmond as Secretary of State for the Southern Department and in the Cabinet. Sir Charles Pratt (elevated to the peerage as Lord Camden) replaces Northington as Lord Chancellor. Charles Townshend succeeds William Dowdeswell as Chancellor of the Exchequer and is soon included in the Cabinet. Northington, Conway, and Egmont retain office and remain in the Cabinet, with Northington switching to President of the Council in place of Winchilsea.

September. Egmont resigns and is succeeded (in December) by Sir Edward Hawke as First Lord of the Admiralty and a member of the Cabinet.

September. British customs officers armed with a "general writ of assistance" empowering them to enter private premises to search for contraband attempt to enter a cellar in the home of Daniel Malcom to search for contraband suspected to be hidden there. Malcom, challenging the legality of such a writ and supported by a gathering crowd, intimidates the officers so that they do not enter.

October. The Attorney-General of England gives an opinion that colonial courts have no authority to issue general writs of assistance under existing law.

December. The New York Assembly declines to vote funds for the supplies for British troops stationed in the colony, as required by the Quartering Act.

December. New York merchants petition the King, complaining of various British restrictions on colonial trade.

1767

January–December. Friction between British customs officers and colonial merchants over enforcement of British restrictions on colonial trade.

January. Townshend announces in the Commons that he will later present a plan for raising additional revenues in the colonies.

May. Townshend presents to the Commons his proposal for an act levying duties on colonial imports of tea, paper, glass, and paint.

June. Passage of the so-called Townshend Act levying these duties to take effect in November and also authorizing the issue by colonial courts of general writs of assistance to British customs officers in the colonies.

June. Passage of an act providing for the establishment of an American Customs Board to tighten enforcement of British acts of trade and customs in the colonies.

June. Passage of the New York Suspending Act forbidding the passage of any other laws by the New York Legislature until it passed a law providing for the supplies for British troops in the colony required by the Quartering Act.

June. Alarmed by news of the proposed Suspending Act, the New York Assembly passes an act for the supplies required by the Quartering Act.

July. Chatham has a mental breakdown; Grafton succeeds him as acting head of the Ministry.

July–December. Little protest in the colonies against the Townshend Act duties.

September. Townshend dies; Frederick North (called Lord North as a courtesy title) succeeds Townshend as Chancellor of the Exchequer.

November. Establishment of the new American Customs Board at Boston.

December. Northington dies and is succeeded as President of the Council and a member of the Cabinet by Lord Gower, a leading member of the party headed by the Duke of Bedford, which consistently favors stern measures to suppress colonial insubordination.

1768

January–December. Continuing friction between British customs officers and colonial merchants over enforcement of British restrictions on colonial trade.

January–May. Publication throughout the colonies of a series of letters, the so-called "Farmer's Letters," by John Dickinson of Pennsylvania, denying the right of Parliament to levy any kind of duties for revenue on the colonies. These letters arouse widespread opposition to the Townshend Act duties.

January. Responsibility for colonial affairs is assigned to a third Secretary of State, Secretary of State for the Colonies. Lord Hillsborough is appointed the new Secretary.

January. Conway is succeeded as Secretary of State by Lord Weymouth, another leading Bedfordite. Conway is succeeded as Leader of the Commons by North, but remains in the Cabinet in the politically unimportant office of Lieutenant-General of the Ordnance.

February. The Massachusetts House of Representatives adopts resolutions denying the right of Parliament to levy any kind of tax for revenue on the colonies and sends a circular letter to the Assemblies of the other colonies inviting them to take similar action.

March. Demonstrations in Boston against members of the American Customs Board. The Board appeals for British warships and troops for its protection and to assist in enforcing the British acts of trade and customs imposed on the colonies.

April. Hillsborough sends a circular letter to colonial Governors instructing them to try to prevent the Assembly of their respective colonies from taking action similar to that of Massachusetts, and, if unsuccessful, to dissolve the Assembly.

May. The British warship *Romney* arrives in Boston from the British naval base at Halifax, Nova Scotia, in response to the American Customs Board's appeal.

May. A new House of Commons is elected, without material change in the political complexion of the House or any immediate change of Ministry.

June–December. The Assemblies of most of the colonies adopt resolutions similar to those of the Massachusetts House, in defiance of Hillsborough's circular letter. Also the Massachusetts House refuses to accede to a demand by Hillsborough to rescind its February resolutions.

June. Attack on customs officers in Boston following seizure by the customs of John Hancock's sloop *Liberty* for alleged evasion of customs duties.

August–September. Merchants of Boston and New York City adopt agreements to cease importing from Great Britain all except a few specified articles until the Townshend Act duties are repealed.

October. Arrival in Boston of British troops in response to the American Customs Board's appeal.

October. Shelburne retires and is replaced as Secretary of State and in the Cabinet by Lord Rochford.

November. Chatham retires and is replaced as Lord Privy Seal by Lord Bristol, who is not included in the Cabinet.

1769

January–December. Continuing friction between British customs officers and colonial merchants over enforcement of British restrictions on colonial trade.

January–December. Friction between the British troops stationed in Boston and residents of Boston and neighboring towns.

January. The Duke of Bedford denounces the unruly conduct of Boston and the Massachusetts House of Representatives and successfully moves for an address to the King to have the ringleaders in Massachusetts identified and tried in England for treason.

February. Merchants of Philadelphia adopt a non-importation agreement similar to those of Boston and New York City.

March–October. Non-importation agreements adopted in most of the other colonies.

May. The Cabinet, at a meeting attended by all except Hawke, votes to sponsor repeal of the Townshend Act duties, except the duty on tea, at the next meeting of Parliament. Grafton, Conway, Camden, and Granby favor total repeal; they are outvoted by North, Gower, Hillsborough, Weymouth, and Rochford, who favor retention of the tea duty.

May. Hillsborough sends a circular letter to colonial Governors announcing the Cabinet's decision to propose at the next meeting of Parliament repeal of most of the Townshend Act duties.

May–December. The Virginia House of Burgesses denies the right of Parliament to tax the people of Virginia and denounces the proposal to send for trial in England persons accused of treason or other crimes in the colonies. Several other colonial Assemblies adopt similar resolutions.

1770

January–December. Continuing friction in various colonies between British customs officers and colonial merchants over enforcement of British restrictions on colonial trade.

January–March. Continuing friction between British troops and residents of Boston.

January. Grafton resigns; North succeeds him as head of the Treasury and First Minister. Camden resigns his place as Lord Chancellor, which is filled by commissioners. Granby resigns as Master General of the Ordnance and withdraws from the Cabinet.

February. James Otis, long the outstanding but erratic leader of the popular party in Boston and the Massachusetts House of Representatives, becomes unmistakably insane. Samuel Adams is now the foremost leader of the party in Massachusetts.

March. British troops shoot and kill several Bostonians in the so-called Boston Massacre.

March. Adams and other popular leaders in Boston secure withdrawal of all British troops from Boston.

April. The Townshend Act duties on paper, glass, and paint manufactured in Great Britain are repealed; the duty on tea is retained, avowedly to maintain Parliament's claim of authority to tax the colonies.

July. New York City merchants revise their non-importation agreement to apply only to imports from Great Britain that are subject to duties levied by Parliament.

September–December. Non-importation agreements in the other colonies are revised along the same lines as in New York City.

November. George Grenville, father of the Stamp Act, dies.

December. Weymouth resigns as Secretary of State. Lord Sandwich, another leading Bedfordite, replaces Weymouth as Secretary of State and in the Cabinet.

1771

January–December. North, with the King's steady support, establishes a strong, stable administration. Continuing friction between British customs officers and colonial merchants over enforcement of British restrictions on colonial trade. Easing of tension between the British government and the colonists over the issue of taxation; the Townshend Act duty on tea remains on the British statute books but is largely evaded by smuggling of tea, winked at by customs officers.

January. Lord Apsley becomes Lord Chancellor and a member of the Cabinet. Lord Sandwich succeeds Hawke (last remaining member of the Cabinet in the Chatham Ministry) as First Lord of the Admiralty. Lord Halifax succeeds Sandwich as a Secretary of State.

January. Bedford dies, but his party remains united and influential.

June. Lord Suffolk, a follower of the late George Grenville, succeeds Halifax as a Secretary of State and in the Cabinet.

1772

January–December. Continuing friction in the colonies between British customs officers and colonial merchants over enforcement of restrictions on colonial trade.

June. Unidentified men in Rhode Island burn the *Gaspee,* an armed schooner in the British customs service, and seriously wound its commander.

July. Hillsborough issues an order that salaries of judges of the Massachusetts Superior (Supreme) Court, heretofore paid by the province, be paid by the Crown.

August. Hillsborough is succeeded as Secretary of State for the Colonies and a member of the Cabinet by North's stepbrother, Lord Dartmouth.

September. The King appoints a Commission of Inquiry to discover culprits in the *Gaspee* affair and issues order that they be brought to England to be tried for treason.

November. On motion of Samuel Adams, a Boston town meeting denounces the payment of the judges' salaries by the Crown and other British innovations endangering colonial liberties and sends a circular letter to other towns in the province inviting them to communicate their sentiments.

December. Formation of network of Committees of Correspondence throughout Massachusetts in response to the Boston letter.

December. News of the Crown order in the *Gaspee* affair is published in newspapers throughout the colonies.

1773

March. The Virginia House of Burgesses elects a standing Committee of Correspondence, including Peyton Randolph, Richard Henry Lee, Patrick Henry, and Thomas Jefferson, to correspond with the Assemblies of the other colonies concerning the proposed sending of persons accused of crimes in the colonies to England for trial and other British measures affecting the colonies.

March–December. Most of the colonial Assemblies respond favorably to the circular letter from Virginia, thus establishing a network of intercolonial Committees of Correspondence.

May. Passage of the Tea Act of 1773 designed to enable the British East India Company to increase the sale of its teas in the colonies and to increase revenues from the Townshend Act duty on tea, by authorizing the Company to ship tea to the colonies and sell it there on its own account.

June. Publication in Boston of letters from Thomas Hutchinson of Massachusetts and other Crown officers in Massachusetts to prominent members of Parliament, recommending the tightening of British rule over the province.

June. The Massachusetts House of Representatives petitions the King to dismiss Hutchinson from the Governorship of the colony.

August–November. The Company's agents other than in Boston resign under pressure from local popular leaders.

September–October. The East India Company ships tea to merchants appointed its agents in Boston, New York City, Philadelphia, and Charleston.

November–December. Popular leaders in Boston try in vain to have the Company's tea returned to Great Britain without payment of the tea duty.

December 16. A band of men disguised as Indians throws overboard the tea on the *Dartmouth* and other ships that had later entered Boston harbor with Company tea on board.

1774

January 19. News of the destruction at Boston of the Company's tea reaches London.

January 29. Many leading members of Parliament attend a meeting of a committee of the Privy Council summoned to consider the petition of the Massachusetts House for dismissal of Hutchinson, and hear a Philippic against the people of Massachusetts for their alleged flaunting of British authority over the past ten years. The committee recommends rejection of the petition as "scandalous and calculated only for the seditious purpose of keeping up a spirit of clamor and discontent in the said province."

February 7. The King, with the advice of the Privy Council, rejects the petition.

February 19. The Cabinet—North, Gower, Sandwich, Suffolk, Rochford, Apsley, and Dartmouth—votes to propose a bill closing the port of Boston.

March. The Cabinet votes to propose a bill amending the charter and laws of Massachusetts.

March. Passage of the Boston Port Act.

April. The King appoints General Thomas Gage, Commander-in-Chief of the British army in North America, Governor of Massachusetts.

May. Passage of the Massachusetts Regulating Act amending the charter and laws of Massachusetts.

May. General Gage arrives in Boston.

May. The Virginia House of Burgesses passes a resolution denouncing the Boston Port Act and calling for the observance of a Fast Day to implore divine guidance to prevent civil war.

May. Lord Dunmore, Crown-appointed Governor of Virginia, dissolves the House for passing this resolution and does not reconvene the House until June, 1775.

May. Members of the dissolved House pass a resolution calling for an intercolonial congress.

June 1. The Boston Port Act, shutting the port of Boston to nearly all commercial traffic, goes into effect.

June. Passage of the Quebec Act vastly extending the boundaries of the province and providing for its government by a Governor and Council appointed by the Crown, without any elected Assembly.

June. The Massachusetts House sends a circular letter to the Assemblies of the other colonies inviting them to send delegates to an intercolonial congress to meet at Philadelphia in September, and elects its own delegates to the proposed congress.

June–July. Several regiments of British troops and British warships are assembled at Boston to assist Gage in enforcing the Boston Port Act and Massachusetts Regulating Act.

June–August. All the colonies except Georgia elect delegates to the proposed intercolonial congress.

June–December. Contributions of food and money from all the colonies pour into Boston, by land, for the relief of the Bostonians.

July. George Washington, shortly before his election as one of the Virginia delegates to the projected congress, writes forcefully of the necessity to do more than merely petition for redress of colonial grievances.

September 5. The First Continental Congress, hereafter referred to simply as the Congress, assembles at Philadelphia, with the cream of the colonial patriot leadership in attendance.

September 6. A committee of delegates from the towns of Suffolk County, Massachusetts, of which Boston is county seat, adopts a set of fiery resolutions, known as the Suffolk Resolves, advising immediate military preparations and remaining on the defensive only so long as consistent with self-preservation.

September–October. Gage, in Boston, writes Dartmouth that Massachusetts is in a state of rebellion and that Connecticut and Rhode Island, too, are preparing for war.

September 17. The Massachusetts delegates lay the Suffolk Resolves before the Continental Congress. The Congress implies approval of the Resolves by ordering their publication in the newspapers.

September 27. The Congress resolves that the colonists stop importing anything from Great Britain or Ireland beginning December 1, 1774.

September 28. Joseph Galloway, a Pennsylvania delegate, proposes to the Congress a so-called plan of union with Great Britain.

September 30. The Congress resolves that the colonists stop exporting anything to Great Britain, Ireland, or the West Indies beginning September 10, 1775, unless the grievances of America are redressed before that time.

October–November. Election of a new House of Commons. Little change in the political complexion of the House, and no change in the Cabinet.

October 11. A Massachusetts congress attended by delegates from most of the towns of the province meets in Concord, Massachusetts.

October 14. The Continental Congress adopts a Statement of Rights and Grievances. The stated grievances include taxation of the colonies for revenue; denial of trial by jury in the colonies in cases involving alleged violation of British acts of trade and customs; restriction of colonial trade; and the Boston Port, Massachusetts Regulating, and Quebec Acts of 1774.

October 20. The Congress adopts an Association calling for non-importation and non-exportation along the lines of its resolutions of September 27 and 30 and for non-consumption of goods imported in violation of the ban on importation.

October 21. The Congress rejects Galloway's plan.

October 22. The Congress calls for a second congress to meet in Philadelphia, May 1, 1775, if colonial grievances are not redressed before then.

October 25. The Congress adopts a petition to the King for help in securing redress of colonial grievances, but expressly disclaiming any desire for a diminution of the Crown's prerogative, including the very important right of the Crown to disallow acts passed by the Legislatures of Pennsylvania and of Virginia, Massachusetts, New York, the Carolinas, and all the other royal colonies.

October 25. The Massachusetts Congress votes over £10,000 for the purchase of military supplies.

October 26. The Continental Congress dissolves itself.

October 26–28. The Massachusetts Congress recommends that men of the provincial militia elect officers to replace those appointed by the Crown-appointed Governor and that at least a quarter of the men of every militia company ("minute men") be ready to march instantly. It also chooses a Committee of Safety (virtually a Board of War), headed by

John Hancock, and a Receiver General of taxes to receive the taxes payable to the Tory provincial Treasurer.

November 18. The King writes North on receipt of Gage's alarming letters, "I am not sorry that the line of conduct seems now chalked out; . . . blows must decide whether they [the New Englanders] are to be subject to this Country or independent. . . ."

November–December. Committees are formed throughout the colonies to obtain signatures to the non-importation, non-exportation, and non-consumption agreements recommended by the Continental Congress and to enforce observance of the agreements.

November–December. The Assembly or a convention in four of the colonies represented at the First Continental Congress approves its proceedings and elects delegates to the proposed Second Congress.

November–December. Several military companies in Virginia prepare for war and invite Washington to command and drill them.

November 30. The King, in his speech opening the new Parliament, refers to the "violence of a very criminal nature in Massachusetts" and declares his resolution "to withstand every attempt to weaken or impair the supreme authority of this Legislature over all the Dominions of my Crown."

December 4. Franklin begins talks with influential English acquaintances in the hope of finding an acceptable compromise of the conflicting claims of Parliament and the colonies.

December 10. The Massachusetts Congress proposes that all towns in the province fully equip their minute men and provide them with thirty rounds of ammunition each.

1775

January–April 5. The Assembly or a convention in all the other colonies represented at the First Continental Congress, except New York, approves its proceedings and elects delegates to the Second Congress.

January–February. The New York Assembly refuses to approve the proceedings of the First Continental Congress or to elect delegates to the proposed Second Congress.

January 13 and 21. The Cabinet decides to reinforce Gage. The Cabinet decides also to propose the adoption of a declaration by both Houses of Parliament stating that they would desist from taxing the colonies if the colonists themselves "made sufficient and permanent provision for their civil governments and defense," but without indicating what would be accepted as "sufficient."

January 19. Chatham moves in the House of Lords for withdrawal of the British troops from Boston; the motion is defeated 61 to 18.

January 22. London merchants and others petition the Commons to adopt "healing measures"; the petition is rejected 187 to 81.

January 27. Dartmouth writes Gage informing him of reinforcements being sent him; he also recommends vigorous action by Gage, including seizure of the leading men in the Massachusetts Congress, even at the risk of this being "a Signal for Hostilities."

February–April. The Massachusetts Congress further prepares for war.

February 1. Chatham presents in the House of Lords a plan of conciliation; the plan is rejected 61 to 32.

March 1. Franklin's negotiations for a possible peaceful settlement terminate fruitlessly.

March 22. Edmund Burke, a leading member of the Rockingham party and London Agent for New York, presents to the Commons and speaks eloquently in support of a plan for conciliating the colonies. His plan is rejected 270 to 78.

April 14. Gage receives Dartmouth's long-delayed, fateful letter of January 27.

April 15. The Massachusetts Congress, sitting at Watertown, adjourns until May 10, and its members disperse.

April 18 (night). Gage sends an expeditionary force to seize military stores of the Massachusetts rebel government collected at Concord.

April 19. British troops, en route to Concord, fire on and kill Massachusetts troops at Lexington; war begins.

INTRODUCTION

I N my *Origin of the American Revolution: 1759–1766* I described measures of the British Parliament and British officials in charge of colonial administration that drove most of the British North American colonies to the brink of rebellion in 1765–1766.[1]

Repeal of the most disturbing of these measures, the Stamp Act of 1765,[2] averted a collision.[3] But passage and subsequent implementation of the Declaratory Act of 1766, declaring that Parliament had "full power and authority" to legislate for the colonies "in all cases whatsoever"[4] laid the basis for a second crisis. This time, the crisis culminated in the rebellion of the colonies hereafter referred to as the thirteen colonies.

The resolution for the fateful Declaratory Act passed with remarkable ease. In the House of Lords the vote was 125 to 5. In the Commons there was so little opposition to the proposed act that its opponents did not even call for a division when, on a voice vote, there were not more than ten nays. A few members of Parliament continued to challenge the doctrine set forth in the act, but there is no evidence that the number ever was large.[5]

Fortified by the Declaratory Act and the overwhelming majorities in both Houses of Parliament in favor of it, successive British Ministries proposed and easily secured the passage of the acts levying taxes on the colonies, acts imposing additional restrictions on colonial trade, and acts providing for rigorous enforcement of these new restrictions and of the many other restrictions on colonial trade previously imposed. No party in Parliament, after passage of the Declaratory Act, challenged the right of Parliament to tax the colonies. Many of the Rockingham party challenged the policy of taxing colonials, but even this party strongly supported the policy of tightly restricting colonial trade for the benefit or supposed benefit of British merchants and manufacturers.

British voters (probably fewer than 200,000 out of a population of around 8,000,000)[6] seem to have heartily supported Parliament on both these major points; I have found no evidence that any candidate for election to the House of Commons from 1766 to 1774 lost his seat for voting with the majority on them.

The correspondence of the King, George III, evidences that he, too, was in sympathy with Parliament on the questions of taxing the colonies;[7] and there is no evidence that he disagreed with Parliament on restricting colonial trade.

As to the attitude of the non-voting rank and file in Great Britain concerning the British measures objected to in the colonies, I have found little basis for judgment; apparently, however, most of them either had no opinion or favored the action of Parliament.

At one time, I thought the many letters in London newspapers denouncing Parliament's taxing the colonists indicated much popular British sympathy for them on this issue. But Verner Crane's masterly *Benjamin Franklin's Letters to the Press* reveals that many, if not most, of these sympathetic letters were contributed, under various pseudonyms, by Benjamin Franklin, in London as Agent for the Pennsylvania Assembly. Franklin wrote from London in 1770 that "we have for sincere friends and well-wishers the body of Dissenters throughout England,"[8] but, even if he were right, the Dissenters were, after all, only a small minority of the people of England.

As will be seen in the course of this book, my sympathies are with the colonial Whigs in their opposition to British taxation of the colonies.[9] But it must be recognized that at the time of the adoption of the fateful Townshend Act of 1767, which levied colonial import duties, a distinction drawn by colonial spokesmen between "internal" and "external" taxes gave reason for members of Parliament to suppose that the levy of colonial import duties was not opposed in principle by most of the colonists.

From the very beginning of the controversy over British taxation of the colonies there was general agreement among the colonists that Parliament's levy of a colonial stamp tax or other "internal" tax, such as a land tax, was unconstitutional and should be opposed on principle. But prior to passage of the Townshend Act, many of the colonists had stated or clearly implied that the colonists recognized the authority of Parliament to levy "external" taxes, including import duties, on the colonies.

In the spring of 1764, the British Ministry, headed by George Grenville, proposed, and Parliament passed, the American Act of 1764, levying import duties for revenue (as distinguished from duties to regulate trade) on several articles imported into the colonies and adopted a resolution for a stamp tax to be levied at the next session of Parliament.

The following October, the Connecticut Legislature approved a pamphlet protesting against the resolution for a colonial stamp tax on the ground that such a tax was an "internal" tax and that levying an internal tax on the colonies was an invasion of colonial rights and privileges. However, far from challenging the right of Parliament to levy duties for revenue on colonial imports, classified as an "external" tax, the pamphlet implied that such duties were acceptable in principle. It even suggested that if Parliament considered it necessary and proper to raise a revenue in the colonies, the revenue be raised by levying duties on "the Importation of Negroes, and on the Fur Trade etc."[10]

This pamphlet was sent by the Governor to the colony's London Agent, Richard Jackson, a member of Parliament, for his guidance.[11]

A month later, the Massachusetts Legislature (the House of Representatives and Council jointly) took similar action. It adopted a petition to the House of Commons, signed on behalf of both branches of the Legislature, protesting against the proposed stamp tax as encroaching on the Legislature's exclusive right to levy "internal taxes" on the colony. The Legislature also protested against the duty on molasses imported into the colonies, levied by the recent American Act of 1764, but only on the ground that the duty was excessively high, and the Legislature did not protest at all against the other duties levied by the act.[12]

True, the Speaker of the House, in sending the petition to the House's London Agent, advised him to "collect the sentiments of the Representative Body of the People" from an earlier letter from the House protesting against Parliament's levying any kind of tax on the colony.[13] But there is no evidence that this communication was made known to the members of the House of Commons, and, even if it was, the House was justified in giving superior weight to the petition.

In 1765, the colonial Stamp Act Congress and the Assemblies of most of the colonies, including Connecticut and Massachusetts, adopted resolutions denying the right of Parliament to levy any kind of taxes on the colonies.[14] But this action was counterbalanced by the subsequent testimony (February, 1766) of Franklin in hearings in the House of Commons concerning the proposed repeal of the Stamp Act. As London Agent for the Pennsylvania Assembly and the most distinguished colonial in Great Britain, his testimony carried weight.

Franklin stated that, though the colonists denied the right of Parliament to levy the recently imposed colonial stamp tax, they did not object in principle to Parliament's levying duties for revenue on colonial imports and exports. The difference, he explained, was that "an internal tax [such as a stamp tax or a tax on property] is forced from the people without their consent, if not laid by their own representatives," whereas a duty on exports "is added to the first cost and other charges on the commodity, and when it is offered to sale, makes a part of the price. If the people do not like it at that price, they . . . are not obliged to pay it."

Furthermore, said Franklin, "the sea is yours; you maintain by your fleets the safety to navigation in it . . . ; you may have therefore a natural and equitable right to some toll or duty on merchandizes carried, . . . towards defraying the expense you are at in ships to maintain the safety of that carriage."[15]

Franklin's testimony seemed to be confirmed by the absence of opposition in the colonies to an act passed a few months later levying a duty for revenue on molasses imported into the colonies.

It was not until after the publication throughout the thirteen colonies in 1767–1768 of John Dickinson's famous "Farmer's Letters," denying the right of Parliament to levy any kind of colonial taxes for revenue, that the Whigs united in taking this stand.

The position of colonial Whigs concerning the other chief point in dispute, Parliament's regulation (restriction) of colonial trade, also changed between 1764 and 1774.

Initially, all the colonial petitions conceded, expressly or by implication, the unlimited authority of Parliament to regulate, i.e., restrict, colonial trade. But long before 1774, some of the Whig leaders denied that Parliament had authority to legislate in any way with respect to the colonies, and, in 1774, the First Continental Congress challenged the earlier Whig concession as to regulation of colonial trade by maintaining that Parliament's authority over colonial trade extended only to passing acts designed to benefit the empire as a whole, not to passing acts designed to promote British interests at the expense of colonial.

The colonists' change of position as to the extent of Parliament's authority to levy taxes for revenue on the colonies and to regulate colonial trade is understandable. As will be seen in later chapters, the Whig leaders were feeling their way toward a position on which they and their followers were prepared to take a firm stand. But the failure to take this stand at the very beginning of the controversy had the unfortunate consequence of giving rise to, and confirming, the widespread fear in Great Britain that Whig leaders in the colonies were aiming at complete independence from British rule.

This fear was in fact not well founded. The private correspondence, as well as the public professions, of the Whig leaders evidence their recognition until the eve of the Declaration of Independence in 1776 of the authority of *the Crown* over the colonies in many important respects. This included recognition of the Crown's control over the colonies' relations with foreign nations; the authority of the Crown to use the colonies as a base for military operations against the colonial possessions of France and Spain in America; to hear appeals from, and reverse on points of law, the decision of colonial courts; and to disallow acts passed by the Legislatures of all the royal colonies (including Virginia, Massachusetts, and the Carolinas) and of Pennsylvania.

This recognized right of the Crown to disallow all colonial laws enabled the British government to enforce the extremely important standing order of the Crown against the enactment of any law putting inhabitants of the colonies "on a more advantageous footing than those of this kingdom" or levying any duties "upon British shipping or upon the product or manufactures of Great Britain. . . ."[16] Though British trade with foreign nations might be and often was severely discriminated against or even absolutely prohibited by foreign laws or decrees, the ports and markets of the British colonies were always open to British ships and products and on the most favorable terms.

If from the very beginning of the controversy the leaders of the colonial Whigs had taken the stand they eventually took as to the very limited authority of Parliament and had stressed their clear-cut recognition of the authority of the Crown with respect to the matters described above and the importance to Great Britain of this recognition, would a rupture have been averted, at least for many years? Who can say?

In considering, as we are about to do, the proceedings in the thirteen

British North American colonies with which this book is chiefly concerned, it is well to have in mind their great differences in population and commensurate political influence.

The estimated population of these colonies (including areas in their boundaries which later became separate states) in 1770, as given in *Historical Statistics of the United States* was:

	Whites	Blacks (chiefly slaves)
Virginia	273,000	190,000
Massachusetts	261,000	5,000
Pennsylvania	234,000	6,000
Connecticut	178,000	6,000
New York	154,000	19,000
Maryland	139,000	64,000
North Carolina	128,000	70,000
New Jersey	109,000	8,000
New Hampshire	62,000	1,000
Rhode Island	54,000	4,000
South Carolina	49,000	75,000
Delaware	34,000	2,000
Georgia	13,000	11,000
Total	1,688,000	461,000[17]

Chapters 1–12 deal chiefly with the provisions of acts of Parliament, 1763–1773, laying taxes for revenue on the colonies, imposing new restrictions on colonial trade, and providing for rigorous enforcement of both the new and old restrictions, and with the opposition to these acts.[18]

With one exception, the other acts of Parliament contributing to colonial discontent, described and discussed in these chapters, were relatively unimportant. The exception was an Act of 1772 authorizing trial in Great Britain of persons accused of destroying arsenals or dockyards of the British government in the colonies or ships of the royal navy under construction or repair there. Alarming in itself, this act was all the more so because it intensified colonial fear that the British Government might carry out its threat to transport colonists to Great Britain to be tried there for treason under an ancient but not obsolete English act of 1543.

For a time, there was reason to hope that, despite the unresolved issues over Parliament's taxation of the colonies and the measures to expand and rigorously enforce British restrictions on colonial trade, a rupture would be avoided.

Repeal in 1770 of all the major Townshend Act duties, except the duty on tea, ushered in a three-year period of relative calm. The strong opposition of colonial Whigs to the Townshend Act had been inspired chiefly by the fear that the act was intended primarily to establish a precedent for levying heavier taxes in the future. By repealing most of the duties imposed by that act and refraining from levying any other taxes, Parliament largely allayed this fear.

Furthermore, most of the Whig leaders, as men of property and conservative instincts, had been alarmed by the violence incidental to the colonial opposition to recent British measures and welcomed a restoration of "law and order" so long as Parliament showed no sign of further encroachment on colonial liberty.

Samuel Adams, who had succeeded James Otis as the leader of the Whigs in Massachusetts, continued to agitate against British measures endangering or seeming to endanger colonial liberties, but the tide was against him.

There was a flare-up in 1772 over the Act of 1772 just cited and a proposal to send to England for trial the participants in an attack in Rhode Island waters on a British naval vessel, the *Gaspee,* stationed there. But this blew over when a special commission of enquiry established by the Crown failed to identify any of the culprits.

This respite was broken by the revival of the issue of colonial taxation through passage of the Tea Act of 1773.

Chapters 13–19 deal chiefly with this act; the shipment of tea to the colonies by the East India Company as authorized by the act; destruction of the tea shipped by the Company to Boston; the ensuing Boston Port, Massachusetts Regulating, and other so-called "Intolerable Acts" of 1774; and the sending of British troops from the British Isles to Boston to help enforce the Boston Port and the Massachusetts Regulating Acts.

To understand the significance of the Tea Act of 1773, the reader must have in mind two earlier acts: an act of 1698 granting the British East India Company the exclusive right to import tea into Great Britain but providing that it could sell its tea only by public auction; and an act of 1721 forbidding the importation of tea into the colonies from any place but Great Britain.

The Tea Act of 1773 amended the Act of 1698 to authorize the Company, which was in financial difficulties, to export and sell tea on its own account in the colonies. This, it was hoped, would help the Company undersell foreign competitors, whose tea was smuggled on a vast scale into the colonies, and at the same time enhance the yield from the Townshend Act duty on tea. (The Company could, of course, be counted on to pay the duty on the tea imported by it into the colonies).

The act was obnoxious to all colonial Whigs in principle because it was evidently designed to make the Townshend Act duty on tea more effective; and to colonial importers of tea, other than the fortunate few chosen to act as the Company's colonial agents, because the act threatened to deprive them of a valuable article of trade. Mass meetings were held in all four of the cities—Boston, New York, Philadelphia, and Charleston—

to which the Company was reported to be shipping tea under the new dispensation, and pressure was put on the Company's agents to resign their agencies.

Boston, where the agents had refused to resign, was the first port at which a ship, the *Dartmouth*, carrying the Company's tea, arrived. The local agents did not dare unload or pay duty on the tea; however, after twenty days from the arrival of the tea it would be seizable by the local British customs officers to secure payment of duty. To prevent this, a body of men disguised as Indians, two days before the tea on the *Dartmouth* became seizable for non-payment of duty, boarded the ship and other later arrived ships carrying the Company's tea, and threw the tea overboard.

In the light of developments at Boston, opponents of the landing of the tea in Philadelphia and New York managed to have the tea destined for these cities sent away without payment of duty. Charleston permitted landing of the tea on condition that the tea would not be sold until receipt of further word from the Company.

Soon after news reached England of the destruction of the tea at Boston, Parliament, under the leadership of Lord North, passed the first of the so-called Intolerable Acts of 1774. This was the Boston Port Act, prohibiting any ship, except government vessels and coasting vessels carrying food and fuel to supply the local inhabitants, to enter or leave the port of Boston.

The act was to take effect June 1, 1774, and remain in force until the King and Privy Council were satisfied on two points. Payment must be made by, or on behalf of, the inhabitants of the town for the damage sustained by the East India Company and for losses sustained by others in riots in Boston arising out of opposition to the landing of the tea. Furthermore, proof must be given that "obedience to the laws shall be so far restored in the said town of Boston that the trade of Great Britain may be safely carried on there and his Majesty's customs duly collected."

This act was followed by a second, even more alarming, act, the Massachusetts Regulating Act.

This act annulled clauses of the Massachusetts charter relating to the provincial Council (the Upper House of the Legislature and the Crown-appointed Governor's advisors) and of an important, long-established Massachusetts law relating to town meetings.

The Massachusetts charter provided for the election of the Council and also subjected the Governor's appointment and removal of judges and sheriffs to the approval of this elected Council. The Massachusetts Regulating Act provided for appointment of the Council by the Crown and gave the Governor unrestricted power to appoint and remove judges and sheriffs subject solely to the proviso that judges of the Massachusetts Superior Court could be dismissed only with the approval of the King.

A Massachusetts law of 1692 authorized the popularly elected town selectmen to call a meeting for business "of publick concernment to the town" at any time. The Regulating Act prohibited them from calling more than one town meeting a year without the Governor's consent.

In 1774, Parliament passed several other so-called "Intolerable Acts" relating to the colonies, of which the most disturbing was the Quebec Act, confirming a form of government for the Province of Quebec that included no elected Assembly and greatly extending the boundaries of the province thus constituted.

To understand the extreme alarm not only in Massachusetts but throughout the thirteen colonies to the Massachusetts Regulating Act, the reader must have in mind the long-established system of government in all the older British colonies in North America.

The non-charter colonies, including New Hampshire, New York, New Jersey, Virginia, North Carolina, South Carolina, and Georgia, had a Legislature consisting of a Crown-appointed Governor and Council and an elected Assembly. Bills having passed both the Assembly and Council were subject, in most of the colonies, to absolute veto by the Governor and even if consented to by him were subject to disallowance by the Privy Council (the King in Council) in England. But, once an act was approved by the Privy Council, it could not be repealed or amended except through a new law passed by the same process as the existing law.

Under this system, the colonists had, over the years—one hundred fifty in Virginia—built up a body of laws covering matters of basic importance to their inhabitants which they had thought were secure from any change —except on the initiation of their own Legislatures.

Thus, in passing the Massachusetts Regulating Act, Parliament struck a blow at the very foundation of their government as understood by the colonists. If Parliament could strike down an act of Massachusetts of over eighty-years' standing as to town meetings and replace it by a more restrictive provision, it could and might strike down any existing act of any of the colonies and replace it by some other provision, no matter how odious to the people of the colony.

As Franklin said in March, 1775 to an influential English acquaintance with whom he was trying to find a basis for peaceful settlement, any British proposal that failed to provide for immediate repeal of the Massachusetts Regulating Act was unthinkable. This act, he pointed out, "set us all adrift, and left us without a privilege we could depend upon, but at their [Parliament's] Pleasure."[19]

The fears aroused by this and the other Intolerable Acts were intensified by the Crown's appointment of the Commander-in-Chief of the British troops in North America, General Thomas Gage, as Governor of Massachusetts and the sending of troops to Boston to help Gage enforce the acts he was called upon to execute.

These troops, together with a regiment already stationed at Castle William near Boston, gave the new Governor a force of nearly thirty-five hundred men in and near Boston.

At its first session following receipt of news of the Boston Port Act, the Massachusetts House of Representatives appealed to the Assemblies of the other twelve colonies to send delegates to an intercolonial congress to meet at Philadelphia in September. All the colonies except Georgia responded in one way or another to the appeal.

Chapters 20–26 describe the convening of this congress, the so-called First Continental Congress, and the measures adopted by it to secure redress of colonial grievances.

The Congress, sitting in Philadelphia from September 5 to October 25, 1774, adopted many important measures, of which the so-called Association was crucial.

The Association, signed by nearly all fifty-six delegates to the Congress, called for a boycott of commerce with Great Britain and Ireland and a partial boycott of commerce with the British West Indies until the following colonial demands were met:

Repeal of all acts of Parliament passed since 1763 levying duties for revenue on colonial imports.

Repeal of all acts extending the jurisdiction of colonial admiralty courts, sitting without jury, beyond their ancient limits, authorizing colonial admiralty judges to issue certificates of probable cause for seizure, thereby depriving persons injured by illegal seizure of their property of damages for the seizure, and requiring oppressive security from the owner in suits for condemnation of his ship or goods as a condition to his entering a defense.

Repeal of the act of 1772 authorizing trial in Great Britain of persons alleged to have destroyed royal arsenals, dockyards, or ships in the colonies or vessels of the royal navy under construction there.

Repeal of the Intolerable Acts of 1774.

Additional state papers adopted by the Congress, described in Chapters 23–25, called for the redress of a number of other colonial grievances, but these were evidently regarded as negotiable.

The most important of these additional papers was a petition to the King, stating: "We wish not a diminution of the prerogative. . . . Your royal authority over us . . . we shall always carefully and zealously endeavour to support and maintain."

This explicit recognition of the Crown's prerogative with respect to the colonies confirmed the repeated assertions of leading colonial Whigs that they were not aiming at complete independence. For the Crown's prerogative unquestionably included control over all foreign relations of the colonies; use of the colonies as bases for British military operations against foreign powers; and authority to review on points of law the decisions of the highest courts of all the colonies.

The prerogative also included authority to prevent the Legislatures of the royal colonies, including Virginia, Massachusetts, New York, New Jersey, New Hampshire, the Carolinas, and Georgia, from passing laws adversely affecting British interests by instructing the Crown-appointed Governors of these colonies to refuse consent to, i.e., veto, any such law. (An especially important example of this was the Crown's instruction to colonial Governors to refuse assent to any law imposing "duties . . . upon British shipping or upon the product or manufactures of Great Britain,"[20] thus providing against discriminatory duties in favor of local shipowners, merchants, or manufacturers against British.)

The last seven chapters describe the response in the colonies and Great Britain to the measures of the Continental Congress and the assembling of a Massachusetts provincial congress which proceeded to establish a rebel government in Massachusetts.

This Congress, meeting off and on at Salem, Concord, and Cambridge from October to December, 1774, set up several committees of which the most important, the Committee of Safety, was authorized to call into the field "so many of the militia of this province as they shall judge necessary" to oppose any attempt to execute the Massachusetts Regulating Act by force.

In preparation for this contingency, the Congress voted that officers of the provincial militia, appointees of the royal Governor, be superseded by elected officers. The company officers were to be elected by the men of the company, field officers by the officers of the companies, and general officers by the Congress. One-quarter at least of the men were to be enlisted as "minute men," to "equip and hold themselves in readiness on the shortest notice . . . to march to the [appointed] place of rendezvous."

A Committee of Supplies was chosen to provide for "the reception and support" of men called into service and to purchase a wide range of military supplies.

To provide funds for these purposes, the Congress directed all collectors of provincial taxes to turn over their collections to a Receiver General elected by the Congress, instead of to the provincial Treasurer, who was a Tory.

Though informed by Governor General Gage of the situation in Massachusetts, the British Cabinet decided to wait for word of the outcome of the Continental Congress. Hopefully, a body composed chiefly of persons distinguished for wealth, family, success at the law, or a combination of the three could be counted on to avoid extremes likely to endanger the favorable status acquired by them under British rule.

When word reached England of the spirited measures adopted by the Continental Congress, the British Cabinet, headed by Lord North, adopted a plan (January 13 and 21, 1775) to reinforce Gage with three regiments of infantry, a regiment of cavalry, and six hundred marines, and to put severe economic pressure on most of the twelve colonies represented at the Congress.

On the other hand, Lord Chatham, long out of the Cabinet but still influential, now made moves for peace. On January 19, he introduced a motion in the House of Lords for immediate withdrawal of all British troops from Massachusetts "to open the way towards an happy settlement of the dangerous troubles in America" and, on February 1, presented a plan that might well have been acceptable to all but a few of the most fiery colonial Whigs.

The plan envisaged taxation of the colonies by Parliament only with the consent of the Assemblies of the colonies; repeal of the provisions denying trial by jury in cases involving alleged violation of British acts restricting colonial trade; and suspension of all the Intolerable Acts of 1774. But Chatham's motion for withdrawal of the troops was defeated 61 to 18, and his plan by a vote of 61 to 32.

In the House of Commons a petition for "healing measures" from merchants and others concerned in commerce with North America was defeated 187 to 81.

North did, indeed, move and secure adoption of a resolution for Parliament to "forbear" taxing all colonies whose legislatures would agree to contribute "their proportion to the common defence." But since no method for determining how much this "proportion" was to be, the proposal was almost meaningless. (Franklin wrote in disgust that the resolution reminded him of a highwayman who, with pistol in hand, kindly offered not to take all your money provided you handed over enough to satisfy him.)[21] Furthermore, and of even greater moment, North's resolution gave no promise of the repeal of the Intolerable Acts, without whose repeal or drastic amendment there was no possibility of a settlement.

Why—after it had become clear that determined colonial opposition to British measures was general and not limited to a relatively few hotheads of little or no local standing—were these efforts for peace so decisively defeated in both Houses? Pride, hauteur, arrogance, call it what you will, of many of the members was doubtless an important factor; no one would be allowed, cost what it might in men and money, to challenge Great Britain without fighting. But probably even more persuasive was the common, though not universal, illusion in Great Britain that it would be easy to bring the colonists to book; that, when put to the test, they would be too cowardly to fight, or, if they did fight, would be easily subdued.

Had not General James Wolfe, hero of the British taking of Quebec in the French and Indian War, written in 1758 to Lord George Sackville (now about to succeed Lord Dartmouth as Secretary of State for the Colonies) that the colonial rangers sent to his support appeared "little better than *canaille*": "The Americans are in general the dirtiest most contemptible cowardly dogs that you can conceive. . . . Such rascals as these are rather an encumbrance than any real strength to an army."[22]

Had not Colonel Lord Percy written from Boston to his father, the Duke of Northumberland, as recently as July, 1774: "The people in this part of the country are in general made up of rashness & timidity. Quick & violent in their determinations, they are fearful in the execution of them (unless indeed, they are quite certain of meeting little or no opposition, & then like all other cowards, they are cruel and tyrannical.) To hear them talk, you would imagine they would attack us & demolish us every night; and yet, whenever we appear, they are frightened out of their wits."[23]

Even more impressive were the assurances given by speakers in Parliament itself. Colonel James Grant, who had fought in the colonies during the French and Indian War and served as Governor of East Florida, stated on the floor of the House of Commons that he "knew the *Americans* well; was certain they would not fight. They would never dare to face an *English* army. . . ."[24] And Lord Sandwich, First Lord of the Admiralty, in the House of Lords, said: "Supposing the Colonies do abound in men, what does that signify? They were undisciplined, cowardly men. I wish instead of forty or fifty thousand of these *brave* fellows, they would produce in the field at least two hundred thousands, the more the better, the easier would be the conquest. . . ."[25]

Colonel Grant's assurance that the colonists would not dare resist was shared by the King, who wrote: "I have not the smallest doubt . . . when once vigorous measures appear to be the only means left of bringing the Americans to a due Submission to the Mother Country that the Colonies will submit."[26]

A letter that was to put the King's confidence to the test was already on its way to Gage in Boston. On January 27, 1775, Lord Dartmouth, Secretary of State for the Colonies, had instructed him "to arrest and imprison the principal actors & abettors" in the Massachusetts Congress "if they should presume again to assemble for . . . rebellious purposes," even though their arrest be "a Signal for Hostilities."

By the time Dartmouth's letter, long delayed in transit, reached Gage on April 14, it was too late for him to seize members of the Massachusetts Congress, but the letter clearly implied that he was to take the offensive even though this might precipitate war.

Spies had informed Gage that the rebel Congress had collected a large quantity of military stores at Concord, twenty miles inland from Boston. Acting on this information he ordered Lieutenant-Colonel Francis Smith to lead a detachment on the night of April 18, 1775, "with the utmost expedition and Secrecy to Concord, where you will seize and destroy" the "Ammunition, Provision, Artillery, Tents and small Arms . . . collected . . . for the avowed purpose of raising and supporting a Rebellion against His Majesty."

When, early in the morning of April 19, an advance party of Smith's detachment, led by Major John Pitcairn of the marines, reached Lexington, on the way to Concord, it encountered a group of Massachusetts soldiers assembled on the village green. One side or the other fired a shot, the evidence as to which fired first is hopelessly conflicting, and in the ensuing firing, eight Americans were killed.

By the time the detachment reached Concord, hundreds of Massachusetts soldiers had gathered there. The detachment succeeded in destroying some of the military supplies stored in and near Concord, but not without some hard fighting. On the return of the detachment to Boston, thousands of Americans dogged their march, killed over fifty British officers and men, and wounded many more, not without heavy losses of their own.

News of the casualties at Lexington and Concord and false reports of the wanton butchery by British troops of helpless old men, women, and children hardened the hearts of colonial Whigs against Britain. Though over a year was to pass before the Congress adopted the Declaration of Independence, the rebellion, ripening into the American War for Independence, was soon in full swing.[27]

CHAPTER 1

THE ROCKINGHAM MINISTRY
AND THE STAMP ACT

DESPITE colonial petitions and protests against the proposed tax, the British Parliament, in March, 1765, passed an act levying a stamp tax in the colonies on newspapers, newspaper advertising, playing cards and dice, and a wide range of documents.[1] The Stamp Act was approved in May by commissioners representing George III, who was ill,[2] and, soon afterward stamp distributors were appointed for the several colonies, and stamped paper was shipped to America for distribution and sale. But in all of the thirteen old colonies of North America, except Georgia, the act, scheduled to take effect November first, was nullified. The distributors were forced by threats of violence to resign, and the colonists proceeded to use unstamped paper for newspapers and other articles in defiance of the act.[3]

Furthermore, at an intercolonial congress, held at New York City in October, 1765, petitions to the King and both Houses of Parliament were adopted denying the right of Parliament to levy any kind of taxes for revenue in the colonies.[4] And merchants in Boston, New York, and Philadelphia made concerted efforts to put pressure on British merchants and manufacturers to seek repeal of the Stamp Act by subjecting their orders for British goods to the condition that the act be repealed.[5]

If George Grenville, whose Ministry introduced and secured passage of the Stamp Act, had still been in office when news of these developments reached England, he probably would have had the British army in North America try to enforce the act. (At his final interview with the King before leaving office, Grenville told the King that "if any man ventured to defeat the regulations laid down for the Colonies, by a slackness in the execution, he should look upon him as a criminal and the betrayer of his country.")[6] If the army had been so employed, the American Revolution might well have been precipitated in 1766 instead of nine years later.

But in July, 1765, after months of political jockeying (described in the appendix to this chapter), the Grenville Ministry had been replaced by the Ministry of the Marquis of Rockingham, First Lord of the Treasury and First Minister, as the head of the Ministry was then called.

One of the most striking aspects of the British Cabinet in the eighteenth century is that, as a rule, the overwhelming majority of its members were drawn not from the relatively large House of Commons, but from the smaller House of Lords. Historians have frequently pointed out that the House of Commons represented only a small percentage of the people of Great Britain. Less noticed has been the fact that so few of the members of the Commons were represented in the Cabinet. The Cabinet in the

Rockingham Ministry was no exception to the rule. Of its eight members only one, Henry Seymour Conway, was a member of the House of Commons—and even he was the younger brother of an English earl.

Still comparatively young (thirty-five), Rockingham had never before held ministerial office, nor Court office higher than a Lord of the Bedchamber. But he had long been one of the most powerful political figures in the wealthy and populous County of York and an important ally of Newcastle, who was First Lord of the Treasury, 1757–1762, and leader of the then most influential group of Whigs. Following the resignation in 1762 of Newcastle and his important ally, the Duke of Devonshire, Rockingham resigned his Court office and took a leading part in the councils and activities of the opposition led by Newcastle.[7]

It is not clear why Newcastle, who replaced Marlborough as Lord Privy Seal, was not asked to head the new Ministry. Perhaps he had ruled himself out as too old (he was nearly seventy-two);[8] perhaps it was thought that giving him chief place would antagonize Pitt, from whom the Ministry hoped for support[9] and who had long been openly cold to Newcastle.[10]

Next to Rockingham and Newcastle probably the most important member of the new Ministry was Conway, appointed a Secretary of State (with responsibility for the Southern Department, the department in charge of colonial affairs) and Leader in the House of Commons.

A brother of the Earl of Hertford and nephew of the great Sir Robert Walpole, Conway had excellent political connections. He was commissioned in the army long before he was of age, and, by 1760, after considerable active service, had become colonel of the crack first regiment of dragoons and attained the rank of lieutenant general. Furthermore, from the time he came of age in 1742, he had been a member of Parliament, and in 1755 was appointed Secretary to the Duke of Devonshire, Lord Lieutenant of Ireland, and, in 1757, a Groom of the King's Bedchamber.

But in 1764 he was dismissed from his place in the King's household and also from the colonelcy of his regiment for having voted against the Ministry on important issues in the House of Commons.[11] He thereupon became one of the leaders of the opposition to the Grenville Ministry. In 1765, he not only opposed the proposed Stamp Act, but was one of the very few members of Parliament, and a highly important one, to base his opposition on the ground that Parliament had no right to tax the colonies.[12]

The other Cabinet members were Conway's fellow Secretary of State, the Duke of Grafton, a follower of Pitt; Rockingham's uncle, Lord Winchilsea, and two holdovers from the old Ministry, the Lord Chancellor (Lord Northington) and Lord Egmont,[13] First Lord of the Admiralty. Also, the King's uncle, the Duke of Cumberland, though holding no ministerial office, was an active member of the new Cabinet until his death in October, 1765.[14]

On receipt of word of the alarming anti-stamp tax disturbances in several of the North American colonies, Conway wrote a circular letter

(October 24) to their Governors to call on the commanders of the British army and navy in North America to help enforce the Stamp Act, but only after the Governors had taken "every Step, which the utmost Prudence and Lenity can dictate" to restore order without military assistance.[15] The tenor, if not the exact wording, of the letter had been agreed upon at a recent meeting of the Privy Council Committee on Plantation (Colonial) Affairs, attended by Winchilsea, Grafton, Egmont, Conway, William Dowdeswell, Chancellor of the Exchequer, and Newcastle's follower, Lord Grantham, joint Postmaster-General.[16]

The Ministry's plan seems to have been to avert bloodshed until Parliament met and then to propose modification of the Stamp Act or repeal depending upon the attitude of Pitt. On December 5, Newcastle sent a message to Pitt that Rockingham, Grafton, Conway, and Egmont had made a "hearty resolve to determine the question about the stamp act in favour of the West Indies [i.e., the colonies], and exactly conformable" to Pitt's ideas.[17] But Pitt refused to commit himself, replying icily that "When his Grace does me the honour to say that anything is 'exactly conformable to *my ideas*', he is pleased to use the name of a man, who has never communicated his ideas to the Duke of Newcastle upon the present state of affairs. . . . Whenever my ideas, in their true and *exact* dimensions, reach the public, I shall lay them before the world myself."[18]

Perplexed by Pitt's refusal to commit himself and by news of a recent particularly violent outbreak against the Stamp Act in New York,[19] which was received on December 10,[20] the Cabinet, though in general opposed to enforcement of the act as it stood, was undecided as to what course to take.[21] Hence the King's speech to the joint Houses at the opening of Parliament on December 17, and the Houses' replies were noncommittal. The speech referred to "Matters of Importance [that] have lately occurred in some of My Colonies in America, which will demand the most serious Attention of Parliament." The proposed replies assured the King that (quoting the Commons' reply) "we will not fail . . . to apply ourselves with the utmost Diligence and Attention to those important Occurences in America . . . and to exert our most zealous Endeavours for the Honour of His Majesty's Government . . . in all parts of His extended Empire."[22]

Grenville immediately moved that this reply be amended by adding a clause "to express our just Resentment and Indignation at the outrageous Tumults and Insurrections which have been excited and carried on in North America, and . . . to assure His Majesty that His faithful Commons . . . will firmly and effectually support His Majesty in all such Measures as shall be necessary for preserving and securing the legal Dependence of the Colonies upon this their Mother Country. . . ."[23]

After some discussion, Grenville withdrew his motion,[24] and a similar motion in the Lords by one of Grenville's followers, Lord Suffolk,[25] was defeated by a vote of 80 to 24.[26]

But division in the Ministry itself over enforcement of the act was revealed when, in the course of debate on Suffolk's motion, Northington said "give up the Law & Great Britain would be Conquered in America & become a Province to her own Colonies. America must submit."[27] Furthermore, in the House of Commons, the Paymaster-General, Charles Townshend, declared that he approved of the Stamp Act and of enforcing it and that "sooner than make our Collonies our Allies [instead of subject provinces] he would wish to see them returned to their Primitive Desarts."[28]

The division in the Ministry is further known from letters between Newcastle and Rockingham during the holiday recess of Parliament. On January 1, 1766, Newcastle wrote Rockingham complaining of the latter's failure to report to him an important dinner meeting on December 27, at Rockingham's house, attended by Rockingham, Egmont, Conway, Lord Dartmouth, President of the Board of Trade, Dowdeswell, and Attorney-General Charles Yorke. At this meeting (according to Newcastle's informant) Yorke had proposed and a majority present agreed to a "Strong Motion . . . for an Act of Parliament declaring the Right of the Parliament of England [over the colonies] & also an Address to the King promising to support His Majesty to the utmost extent"; the latter of which, at least, was "strongly objected to by Lord Egmont and Mr. Conway."[29]

Rockingham replied the next day, in no way challenging the accuracy of Newcastle's information as to the meeting on December 27, and telling him of another recent meeting. This was a dinner meeting on December 31, attended by Rockingham, Dowdeswell, Dartmouth, Conway, Barlow Trecothick, a merchant trading to North America, and two other London businessmen, Sir William Baker and George Aufrère, who had important colonial interests and were members of Parliament.[30] "Upon the whole that has yet passed," said Rockingham, "either at the former or this latter Dinner, I think one thing seems to be the General Opinion—that is that the Legislative Right of this Country over the Colonies should be declared—& upon the Plan of Act 6th of Geo. I relating to Ireland. . . .[31]

"The Grave Matter in which as yet I can not see where & how the different Opinions can be brought to agree is—what must finally be done upon the Stamp Act. *All* would agree to various Amendments[32] & Curtailings of the Act—*Some,* as yet not very many to a Suspension & *very few* to a Repeal.

"Yesterday," Rockingham continued, it had been decided to have Thomas Townshend (a junior member of the Treasury Board, on friendly terms with Pitt) "talk with Mr. Pitt on the present important matter . . . & Mr. Townshend set out for Bath early this morning. . . .

"I called at the Chancellor's [Northington's] today; he is got back & well but I did not see him. I hope he will become more moderate. I think Charles Yorke does."[33]

Newcastle replied on January 3, thanking Rockingham for his letter, and adding, "I own, I fear, (as I should have said if I had been present at the Consultation) that the Idea of *Authority* & *Relief* going Hand-in-Hand . . . will be found very Difficult. And for one, I shall incline rather to be Deficient in that which is only a Declaration in Words than in the Other, on which depend the most Material Interests of this Country, viz., the Recovery or Enjoyment of our Trale & Commerce . . . to America. . . . The other Branches of Trade to Foreign Countries is at present so low & depends so much on the Will & Caprice of the Powers with whom we trade, that there is no great Dependence to be had upon it. . . .

"I am extremely glad to Find that the King & his Ministers have thought proper to learn Mr. Pitt's Sentiments upon this great Question; and I hope Regard will be paid to them."[34]

Townshend's mission proved abortive. Pitt said he would not give his opinion as to what to do concerning the Stamp Act to anyone but the King or the public. He expressed his willingness to take office, but only if his brother-in-law, Lord Temple, were offered Rockingham's place (Rockingham to have some other office) and Newcastle dismissed for "there could not be Two Ministers [and] that wherever the Duke of Newcastle was, he must be *Minister* to a certain Degree . . . ." On hearing of Pitt's statement, Newcastle immediately offered to resign, but apparently neither the King nor Rockingham cared to pursue the matter further on Pitt's terms,[35] and Newcastle remained in office.

When Parliament reconvened on January 14, 1766, the Ministry was still in the dark concerning Pitt's stand. Consequently, the Speech by the King and the prepared replies of the two Houses[36] were again noncommittal as to the Stamp Act. But in the debate that day in the House of Commons on the proposed reply to the King's Speech, Pitt chose to state his position.

Replying to Robert Nugent, former member of the Grenville Ministry, who insisted that "the honour and dignity of the Kingdom obliged us to compel the execution of the Stamp Act, except the right was acknowledged and the repeal solicited as a favour," and that "a pepper-corn, in acknowledgment of the right, was of more value than millions without,"[37] Pitt declared:

"It is my opinion that this kingdom has no right to lay a tax upon the colonies. . . . They are the subjects of this kingdom, equally entitled with yourselves to all the natural rights of mankind and the peculiar privileges of Englishmen. Equally bound by its laws, and equally participating of the constitution of this free country. The Americans are the sons, not the bastards, of England.

"Taxation is no part of the governing or legislative power. The taxes are a voluntary gift and grant of the Commons alone . . . , and this House represents those Commons, the proprietors of the lands, and those proprietors virtually represent the rest of the inhabitants. . . . There is an idea in some that the colonies are [likewise] virtually represented in this House. I would fain know by whom. . . . The idea of virtual representation of America in this House, is the most contemptible idea that ever entered into the head of a man; it does not deserve a serious refutation. The Commons of America, represented in their several assemblies, have ever been in possession of the exercise of this, their constitutional right, of giving and granting their own money. They would have been slaves if they had not enjoyed it. . . ."[38]

Pitt was followed by Grenville, who defended the stamp tax, complained of the ingratitude of the colonists, protected by Great Britain and favored by the grant of bounties to many of their products, and denounced those in England who had encouraged the colonists in their obstinate resistance to the tax.

This response brought Pitt to his feet again. "The gentleman," he said, "tells us, America is obstinate; America is almost in open rebellion. I rejoice that America has resisted. Three millions of people so dead to all the feelings of liberty, as voluntarily to submit to be slaves, would have been fit instruments to make slaves of the rest. . . . The gentleman boasts of his bounties to America! Are not those bounties intended finally for the benefit of this kingdom? If they are not, he has misapplied the national treasures. . . . I will be bold to affirm, that the profits to Great Britain from the trade of the colonies through all its branches is two millions a year. This is the fund that carried you triumphantly through the last war. The estates that were rented at two thousand pounds a year, three score years ago, are at three thousand pounds at present. . . . You owe this to America. This is the price that America pays you for her protection.

"The Americans have not acted in all things with prudence and temper. They have been wronged. They have been driven to madness by injustice. Will you punish them for the madness you have occasioned? Rather let prudence and temper come first from this side. I will undertake for America, that she will follow the example. . . . [Let] the Stamp Act be repealed absolutely, totally and immediately. . . . At the same time, let the sovereign authority over the colonies, be asserted in as strong terms as can be devised, and be made to extend to every point of legislation whatsoever—that we may bind their trade, confine their manufactures, and exercise, every power whatsoever, except that of taking their money out of their pockets without their consent."[39]

The following day Rockingham wrote the King, "The events of yesterday . . . have shown the amazing power and influence which Mr. Pitt has, whenever he takes part in debate."[40]

Fortified by Pitt's support of repeal of the Stamp Act, Rockingham evidently decided to take the plunge in favor of introducing a bill for repeal, as evidenced by a letter of January 20, 1766, from him to Yorke, stating, "Charles Townshend and General Conway, Dowdeswell and the Duke of Grafton were here this evening. The ideas we join in are nearly what I talked of to you this morning, that is—a declaratory Act in General Terms—afterwards to proceed to *Considerations of Trade* etc.—and finally Determination on the Stamp Act—i.e. a *Repeal,* & which its own Demerits & Inconvenience *felt here* will justify."[41]

Following this meeting, a set of resolutions was drafted to be presented to Parliament before introduction of the proposal for repeal.

The most important of these was "Resolved, That the Parliament of

Great Britain, had, hath, and of a right ought to have, full power and authority to make laws and statutes of sufficient force and validity to bind the Colonies and people of America in all cases whatsover."[42]

On receiving a copy of this statement, Yorke proposed that "in all cases whatsoever" be expanded to read "as well in cases of Taxation, as in all other cases whatsover,"[43] thus making it clear beyond question that the assertion of Parliament's authority to legislate for the colonies included authority to tax them. But Rockingham vetoed this proposed change,[44] and, as we shall see in Chapter 2, the resolution as initially drafted was adopted with only trifling changes.[45]

The omission of a specific reference to taxation proved to be of no consequence; the debates in Parliament on the resolution for the Declaratory Act clearly recognized that the words asserting the authority of Parliament to legislate for the colonies "in all cases whatsoever" were intended to include authority to tax them.

The King would have preferred amendment to repeal of the Stamp Act;[46] but, when informed by Rockingham of the Ministry's plan, including repeal of that act, he indicated his intention to use his influence to support adoption of the plan by Parliament.[47]

CHAPTER 2

REPEAL OF THE STAMP ACT
AND PASSAGE OF THE
DECLARATORY ACT

BEFORE the program summarized in Rockingham's letter to Yorke had been launched, the issue of colonial taxation was raised briefly in Parliament on presentation to the House of Commons of the petition to the House from the intercolonial Stamp Act Congress at New York denying the right of Parliament to tax the colonies for revenue.[1] Pitt spoke strongly in support of accepting the petition, but the Ministry gave him no support, and the House voted, without a division, not to receive it.[2]

The Ministry's program for repeal of the Stamp Act was launched on February 3, by proposing in each House a resolution for a bill declaring that "the Parliament of Great Britain had, hath and of right ought to have, full power and authority to make laws and statutes of sufficient force and validity to bind the colonies and people of America Subjects of the Crown of Great Britain in all cases whatsoever."[3]

In the House of Lords, Lord Camden, Chief Justice of the Court of Common Pleas, attacked the proposed resolution on the ground that it was based on a doctrine that Parliament was not bound by any constitutional limitations, whereas it must be recognized that there were such limitations, as, for example, that Parliament "cannot take away any man's private property without making him a compensation," or "condemn any man by bill of attainder without hearing him."[4] But Lord Chancellor Northington, Lord Mansfield, Chief Justice of the King's Bench, and others maintained the contrary,[5] and the resolution was carried by a vote of 125 in favor, to 5 opposed.[6] (The four supporting Camden were Lords Shelburne, Torrington, Paulet, and Cornwallis.)[7]

In the Commons, Secretary of State Henry S. Conway, Leader of the House,[8] William Dowdeswell, Chancellor of the Exchequer, Attorney-General Yorke, and at least ten other members (including several of those usually in opposition to the Ministry) spoke in favor of the proposed declaratory resolution. Only four members—two followers of Pitt (William Beckford, a leading representative of the City of London, and James Hewitt), Isaac Barré, a follower of Shelburne, and Pitt himself spoke against it.[9] Barré made and Pitt seconded a motion to strike out the words "in all cases whatsoever,"[10] but they mustered so few voice votes in favor of their motion that they did not even call for a division. Whereupon the resolution as proposed by the Ministry was adopted without a division.[11]

On February 4–7, there were skirmishes in both Houses on various resolutions collateral to the question of the proposed Declaratory Act.[12]

On February 26, the bill for the Declaratory Act was introduced by the Ministry in the House of Commons, thereafter had the usual readings and was passed by the Commons on March 4, all without any division.[13]

On the following day, the bill was introduced in the House of Lords and thereafter had the usual readings.[14] In the course of these readings, Camden again insisted that British taxation of the unrepresented colonies was "illegal, absolutely illegal, contrary to the fundamental laws of nature, contrary to the fundamental laws of this constitution."[15] But he spoke in vain; the bill passed the Lords, without a division, on March 11.[16]

The next step in the Ministry's program was to lay before the Commons evidence of the damage from the Stamp Act to British trade with the colonies which could be restored only by repeal of the act.[17]

Spurred by fear of loss of trade from a colonial boycott of British exports and of inability to collect debts owed them in the British North American colonies,[18] a large group of London and Bristol merchants engaged in colonial trade adopted a petition to the House of Commons in December, 1765. Calling attention to the drastic curtailment of trade with the colonies due to the Stamp Act and the prospective loss of debts owed to them, they begged the House to take measures to conciliate the colonists.[19] They also, with Rockingham's collaboration, sent a circular letter, enclosing a copy of their petition, to the Lord Mayors of cities, towns, and boroughs throughout Great Britain appealing for similar action by merchants and manufacturers in their several communities.[20]

Furthermore, according to Henry Cruger, Jr., a leading Bristol merchant engaged in colonial trade, the merchants took steps to ensure the support of the manufacturers from whom they bought their supplies, by refraining from giving "a single order for Goods on purpose to compel all Manufacturers to engage with us in petitioning Parliament for a Repeal of the Stamp Act by which thousands were out of employ, and in a starving condition."[21] These efforts were successful; petitions for repeal poured into the House of Commons from manufacturers throughout Great Britain.[22]

But to leave no stone unturned, a number of leading British merchants engaged in colonial trade and Benjamin Franklin appeared in the House of Commons to testify in favor of repeal.[23]

As brought out in the Introduction, Franklin testified that the colonists objected in principle only to Parliament's levying direct taxes on the colonies,[24] thus implying that Parliament might comfortably obtain a revenue from the colonies merely by changing the method of taxing them. He was supported in this by Richard Jackson, a member of the House, who, as joint London Agent with Franklin for Pennsylvania and sole London Agent for Connecticut and the Massachusetts House, presumably also spoke with knowledge.[25]

Other methods to secure repeal are disclosed in the unpublished diary of Thomas Hollis of London, which reveals that he was paying the publisher of the London *St. James Chronicle* to print the strong pro-repeal items appearing in it,[26] and by the statement of Major Thomas James, who, though one of the chief sufferers in the anti-Stamp Tax riots in New York, surprisingly testified in favor of repeal. He later stated privately that "he had 400 Guineas given him [and] a paper of directions . . . how to answer on his examination before the House of Commons."[27]

Grenville, the Duke of Bedford, and Lord Bute, acting through the King's brother, the Duke of York, made a last minute effort to enlist the King's support to block repeal,[28] but the King refused to intervene, stating in a letter of February 18 to York, "I do not think it Constitutional for the Crown personaly to interfere in Measures which it [the Ministry] has thought proper to refer to the advise of Parliament."[29]

Finally, on February 21, the Ministry, with Conway as its spokesman, introduced in the House of Commons a resolution for a bill to repeal the Stamp Act.[30] The resolution was vigorously supported by members of the Ministry and their followers (among whom Rockingham's secretary, Edmund Burke, particularly distinguished himself)[31] on grounds of expediency and by Pitt and his followers chiefly on grounds of the unfairness and unconstitutionality of taxing persons not represented in Parliament. Opponents of the resolution argued that the Stamp Act was constitutional, and that giving way to colonial opposition would be undignified and productive of future controversy.[32]

The King, who had told Rockingham he could report him as favoring repeal, caused considerable difficulty for the administration by later telling Lord Strange he preferred modification of the Stamp Act, rather than repeal.

"His M," wrote Conway to his brother Lord Hertford on February 12, "had told L Rockm & the D of G [Duke of Gloucester] that he *was for the Repeal,* but he on Tuesday [Feb. 11] told *Lord Strange* that he *was not so now;* that he wish'd his opinion to be known & his L [Lordship] *might declare it;* his M has been pleas'd to explain himself to us, that he always was *for the Repeal,* when contrasted with *Inforcing the whole* Act, but not as compared with *Modification;* we told his M this distinction was unfortunately not explain'd to us; and that in consequence we had (as he had allow'd L R particularly to do) declar'd his M to be for the Repeal, & that on all accounts we were engag'd & oblig'd to push that measure."[33]

No wonder (as William Rouet wrote his friend Baron Mure) that "many who wish to know the King's secret wishes, and act accordingly, are quite puzzled what to believe."[34]

In the end, sixty-eight placemen (men holding Crown office) in the House of Commons voted against repeal;[35] but enough of them supported the Ministry[36] to carry the resolution for repeal by the handsome majority of 275 to 167.[37]

On February 24, a motion to recommit the resolution and other dilatory motions by opposition members were easily defeated.[38]

The bill for repeal was introduced in the House of Commons on February 26,[39] and after the usual readings was passed March 4, by a vote of 250 to 122.[40]

The following day the bill was presented to the House of Lords.[41]

Newcastle led off for the Ministry in favor of repeal[42] on the ground that it was inexpedient to retain an act which so greatly antagonized the colonists as to jeopardize British trade with them.[43] Northington also spoke in favor of repeal, but solely on the narrow ground that the Stamp Act evidently could not be executed without armed force; that the House of Commons presumably would decline to vote funds for the enforcement of an act which it had just voted overwhelmingly to repeal; and that the King should not be left by the Lords in the position of being responsible for the execution of a law that he did not have power to enforce.[44]

The argument most strongly pressed by the Lords opposing repeal was that if Parliament gave way on the Stamp Tax, this would serve to encourage the colonists to oppose other acts of Parliament distasteful to them, particularly the acts imposing restrictions on colonial trade.

"The Americans," said Lord Sandwich, "want to get loose from the Act of Navigation. All the complaints made against the ships stationed on their Coasts to prevent illicit trade tend to this purpose. The Stamp Act [is] not the Object of their Sedition but to try their ground whether by Resistance they can get themselves loose from other Acts more disagreeable and detrimental to them."

Lord Lyttelton: "Your Lordships have upon the present Occasion your own Constancy and Dignity to maintain. . . . When this great Concession is made We are, 'tis said, to be firm in maintaining all the Laws there, particularly those for regulating their Commerce, which very laws . . . are the [real] Ground of the present Opposition. . . . The repealing the Law is such an Encouragement to the Plan of Intimidation taken up by the Americans as may make them much more unreasonable in future Demands. Their Insolence will increase by Concessions and where it will stop is not to be known."

Lord Mansfield: "The Americans have adopted on the fatal Occasion a New Principle that they are not subject to the Legislative Authority of Great Britain. . . . In this Situation what is the Effect [of] repealing this Act? It is the giving up the total Legislature of this Kingdom . . . and will put us in the Situation of being dictated to by the Americans who may think they have a Right to an Open Trade and Establishment of Manufactures. What then will become of us?"[45]

This same argument was also stressed in a protest signed by thirty-three of the Lords, including the politically powerful Duke of Bedford and all his outstanding followers in the House of Lords, against the bill for repeal.[46]

This aspect of the opposition to the repeal of the Stamp Act is of particular importance because of its bearing on the prospect of possible redress of another colonial grievance carried over from the Grenville administration, the American Act of 1764 restricting colonial trade (discussed in Chapter 3).

In the Lords, opposition to the bill for repeal was so strong that if the King had not come to the rescue of the Ministry, it is doubtful that the bill would have passed. But he now let it be known that he definitely favored repeal,[47] and at the first reading of the bill on March 11, 1766, the Lords divided 105 to 71 in favor of it.[48] Six days later the bill was passed, without a further division.

On March 18, both the Declaratory Act and the Repeal Act were assented to by commission from the King.[49]

Later in the session, the Repeal Act was supplemented by an act canceling penalties incurred for violation of the Stamp Act and validating documents requiring stamps which were executed without stamps while the Stamp Act was in force.[50]

Although repeal of the Stamp Act restored order in the colonies, adoption of the Declaratory Act paved the way for a future stamp tax or any other kind of tax that Parliament might see fit to impose. Indeed, as is brought out in Chapter 3, before the current session was over, Parliament levied a duty for revenue on one of the principal imports of the British North American colonies, West Indian molasses, which was still in force at the time of the Declaration of Independence.

Theoretically the unlimited legislative authority of Parliament to legislate for the colonies asserted in the Declaratory Act was limited by the prerogative of the Crown to disapprove (veto) acts of Parliament. Thus, the Declaratory Act states in form "the King's majesty, by and with the advice and consent of the lords spiritual and temporal, and commons of Great Britain, in parliament assembled, had, hath, and of right ought to have," etc. But by 1766, the royal prerogative of veto had become obsolete, having last been exercised as far back as 1708.[51]

Thus, under prevailing practice, the Declaratory Act was in effect an assertion by members of Parliament of their right to legislate for the colonies as they saw fit without the colonists having the protection of any constitutional limitation or the veto of the Crown.

CHAPTER 3

COLONIAL GRIEVANCES REMAINING
AFTER THE REPEAL OF
THE STAMP ACT.

AS soon as repeal of the stamp tax seemed assured, thirty-nine English merchants trading with the North American colonies sent a circular letter to their American correspondents reporting the prospective repeal. The merchants added the following admonition.

"You must be sensible," they wrote, "what Friends the Colonies have had in the present Ministry, and are doubtless informed what pains they have taken to serve them. It is justice likewise to them to inform you that they have had great difficulties to encounter in the Cause, the principal of which were unhappily thrown in by the Colonies themselves, we mean the intemperate proceedings of various Ranks of People on your side the Water . . . [which] awakened the Honour of Parliament, and thereby involved every Friend of the Repeal in the Imputation of betraying the Dignity of Parliament. . . .

"If therefore you would make the proper returns to your Country, if you have a Mind to do credit to your Friends and strengthen the hands of your Advocates, hasten, we beseech you, to express filial Duty and Gratitude to your Parent Country. Then will those who have been . . . your Friends, plume themselves on the restoration of Peace to the Colonies. . . . But if . . . it [repeal of the stamp tax] is talked of as a Victory, If it is said the Parliament have yielded up the Right [to tax the colonies] then indeed your Enemies here will have a Complete Triumph. Your Friends must certainly lose all power to serve you. Your Taxmasters probably be restored and such a train of ill consequences follow as are easier for you to imagine than for us to describe. . . ."[1]

This circular letter is quoted at length because its tone explains the unfavorable reaction to the letter in the colonies, described in a letter of Benjamin Franklin to his friend Joseph Galloway.[2] Most important, it strikingly illustrates the view among many Englishmen who, on the whole, were friends of the colonists, that Parliament unquestionably had the right to tax them and that any non-exercise or restraint on the exercise of this right was a favor to the colonists for which they should be duly grateful. If the colonists' English friends held this view, what, the colonists asked themselves, must they expect if and when their "Enemies" (to use the merchants' own term) were again in power?

On reading this letter (a copy of which was published in Hunter's

Virginia Gazette of May 16, 1766), George Washington's friend and neighbor, George Mason, replied:

"Gentlemen:

"There is a letter of yours dated the 20th [should be 28th] of February in the public papers here . . . upon a very interesting subject. I shall, without further preface or apology, exercise the right of a freeman in making such remarks upon it as I think proper.

"The epithets of parent and child have been so long applied to Great Britain and her colonies that . . . we rarely see anything from your side of the water free from the authoritative style of a master to a schoolboy.

"We have [you say in effect] with infinite difficulty and fatigue got you excused this one time; pray be a good boy for the future; do what your papa and mama bid you, and hasten to return them your most grateful acknowledgements for condescending to let you keep what is your own; and then all your acquaintance will love you, and praise you and give you pretty things; . . . but if you are a naughty boy, and . . . pretend to judge for yourselves; when you are not arrived at the years of discretion or capable of judging between good and evil, then everybody will hate you, and say you are a graceless and undutiful child; your parents and masters will be obliged to whip you severely, and your friends will be ashamed to say anything in your excuse; nay, they will be blamed for your faults.

"See your work [it will be said]—see what you have brought the child to. If he had been well scourged at first for opposing our absolute will and pleasure, and daring to think he had any property of his own, he would not have had the impudence to repeat the crime. . . .[3]

"Is not this a little ridiculous when applied to three millions of as loyal and useful subjects as any in the British dominions, who have been only contending for their birth-right, and have now only gained, or rather kept what could not, with common justice or even policy, be denied them? . . ."[4]

The exasperating circular letter, however, was not the only reason that, though repeal of the Stamp Act was hailed with relief and joy by the colonists,[5] they remained discontented.

The most obvious reason for the continuing discontent was the evidence that repeal of the Stamp Act was not to be construed as a relinquishment by Parliament of its claim of right to tax the colonists as it pleased. This was made perfectly clear not only by Parliament's adoption of the Declaratory Act as a corollary to the act of repeal, but by its passage, before rising in 1766, of two acts levying taxes on the colonies. One levied a duty, clearly for revenue (and not, as before, a regulation of trade) on all imports of molasses into the colonies;[6] the other, in effect levying a tax on the colonies in which British troops were quartered in barracks for partial maintenance of these troops.[7]

A second reason was continuance of a colonial currency act passed in 1764 severely restricting the issuance of paper money by all but the New

England colonies,[8] which were already covered by a similar, though some-what less restrictive, act.[9]

A third was continuance of an act (4 Geo. III ch. 15, hereafter referred to as the Act of 1764, or the American Act of 1764) passed in 1764 levying duties for revenue on several colonial imports[10] and imposing additional restrictions on colonial exports and imports.[11]

The Navigation Act of 1660 and later British acts prohibiting the exportation of colonial tobacco, sugar, fur, and a number of other colonial products to any overseas countries except Great Britain had left many important colonial products untouched.[12] The American Act of 1764 extended the restriction on exportation by prohibiting the exportation of colonial lumber and iron to Ireland or any part of continental Europe and of colonial hides, potash, whalebone, coffee, pimento, and cocoa to Ireland or any part of continental Europe north of Cape Finisterre in Spain.[13] Any of these articles consigned to these areas must first be brought to a British port and be unloaded and reloaded there before the carrying vessel could legally proceed to its destination.

An act of 1663 prohibiting the importation into the colonies of most of the products of continental Europe and adjacent islands other than Great Britain excepted wine of Madeira and the Azores.[14] Thanks to this exception, the colonists had built up a flourishing direct trade with these islands, sending out cargoes of foodstuffs, barrel staves, and other colonial products and bringing back return cargoes of wine.[15] The American Act of 1764 struck a blow at this direct trade by levying a much heavier duty on wine imported directly from these islands than imported by way of Great Britain.[16]

An act of 1721 further restricting colonial trade by forbidding the importation of any East Indian product into the colonies except via Great Britain, had been somewhat alleviated by allowing a refund of part of the British import duties on East Indian goods reexported to the colonies.[17] The American Act of 1764 repealed the refund, thus making this restriction more burdensome.[18]

A fourth reason for continuing colonial discontent was the rigorous enforcement of all British restrictions, old and new, on colonial trade, the basis for which was laid by the so-called Hovering Act of 1763 and new enforcement provisions of the American Act of 1764.

The Hovering Act of 1763 provided for the seizure of dutiable or prohibited goods in vessels of fifty tons or less hovering off the coast of the colonies;[19] for the use of vessels of the British navy to help enforce all British acts of trade and revenue applying to the colonies; and for the division among the officers and men of these vessels of part of the net proceeds from the sale of condemned cargo and vessels seized by them.[20]

Soon after the act was passed, twenty British naval vessels were sent to the North American coast,[21] whose commanders were to be commissioned by the English Customs Board[22] as customs officers.[23] British naval vessels had long been authorized to seize foreign vessels forbidden to enter colonial ports for purposes of trade,[24] and the navy was, of course, empowered to seize vessels engaged in trade with an enemy in time of war;[25] but apparently the navy had never before been used, at least in colonial waters, in time of peace as a general arm of the English customs service.

Furthermore, as contemplated by the act, the King promptly held out a strong financial incentive to naval officers to act energetically in their new office by issuing an order for payment to them of a substantial part of the net proceeds from the sale of vessels or cargo seized by them and duly condemned[26]—an order promptly followed by several seizures.[27]

To round out the new enforcement program, all customs officers on leave were ordered to their posts and colonial Governors and the Commander in Chief of the British army in North America were ordered to assist in preventing illegal trade in the colonies.[28]

The enforcement provisions of the American Act of 1764 were even more grievous.

It is a challenge to the reader's attention and patience to follow these provisions; but a comprehension of them is essential to an understanding of the attitude of colonial merchants and shipowners, not only immediately after repeal of the Stamp Act, but throughout the remaining years of the pre-Revolutionary period.

In many respects, North American colonial merchants and shipowners were greatly and obviously benefited by the inclusion of the American colonies in the British Empire. Their vessels were given unrestricted access to British, Irish, and British West Indian ports. They shared on an equal footing with British and Irish vessels the monopoly of the British colonial trade established by a British act of 1660 excluding foreign vessels from colonial ports. Their trade with the Mediterranean was protected by the issuance of passes protecting their vessels and cargo from seizure by raiders from the Barbary Coast. The expansion of their overseas trade was encouraged by the long-term credits allowed by British merchants.

It is reasonable to suppose that, however ready the colonists in general might be to risk a break with Great Britain over the issue of British taxation of the colonies, the merchants, out of strong self-interest, would have hesitated to do so but for the harassment of them pursuant to the enforcement provisions of the American Act of 1764.

Sections 36 and 37 provided an added penalty for violating any of the British restrictions on colonial trade of three times the value of the condemned property, payable by each of the participants.

Section 44 provided that the owner of goods seized for alleged violation of British acts of trade or revenue could not enter a defense in suits for forfeiture of the goods, no matter how small their value, without putting up a bond of £60 to answer the costs and charges of the suit, thus discouraging the owner from even trying to recover the seized goods unless they were of considerable value.

Section 45 provided that if any "goods shall be seized for any cause of forfeiture and any dispute shall arise . . . whether the same have been lawfully imported or exported or concerning the growth, product or manufacture of such goods . . . in such cases the proof thereof shall be upon the owner . . . and not upon the officer who shall . . . seize the same, any law, custom or usage to the contrary notwithstanding."[29]

Sections 43 and 46 made it possible in many cases for the seizing officer to escape any cost or penalty if the owner, despite the obstacles placed in his way by the provisions of the act just described, won the suit. Section 43 authorized the British Customs Board to indemnify any officer for his costs in bringing an unsuccessful suit, and section 46 provided that the owner of a seized vessel or cargo could not recover more than two pence in damages, for the seizure and detention of his property, no matter how great his actual damage, if the presiding judge certified there had been "probable cause" for the seizure.

Heretofore, customs officers were of course tempted to make seizures and bring suits for forfeiture by the lure of sharing in the proceeds from sale if the seized property were condemned; yet they had wisely been deterred from reckless seizure and suit by the fear of heavy court costs and recovery of damages by the owner if the suit for condemnation were dismissed. This deterrent was now greatly weakened by sections 43 and 46 of the American Act of 1764.

Furthermore, sections 29 and 23 now, for the first time, imposed a heavy burden on colonial coastwise and river traffic, most of which had previously been exempt, except in time of war,[30] from customs clearance.[31]

Section 29 (as amended in 1765) provided that vessels carrying cargo from one colony to another must, unless undecked and of twenty tons or less in burden, obtain from the customs authorities a "cocket . . . expressing the quantity and quality of the goods that are liable to the payment of any duty, either upon the importation into, or upon exportation from the said colonies or plantations, [and] the said cocket or cockets shall likewise distinctly specify that the duties have been paid for the same, referring to the terms or dates of entry and payment of such duties, and by whom they were paid," under penalty of forfeiture of all goods not covered by the required cocket.[32]

Section 23 provided that the master of "every ship or vessel" (without excepting even small undecked vessels) must, before taking aboard any non-enumerated colonial products, give bond to the customs authorities of £1,000 if the vessel were under a hundred tons, £2,000 if the vessel were a hundred tons or over, "with condition that in case any molasses or syrups . . . of foreign colonial production shall be laden on board such ship or vessel, the same shall (the danger of the seas and enemies excepted) be brought, without fraud or willful diminution, by the said ship or vessel to some of his Majesty's colonies or plantations in America or to some port in Great Britain."

The penalty for failure to give the required bond was forfeiture of the entire cargo "together with the ship or vessel and her furniture. . . ." The bond must be given for each voyage in which any "non-enumerated" product, including lumber, wheat, flour, corn, vegetables, fish, meat, and dairy products of all kinds, were to be shipped.

Bearing in mind that, because of wretched roads and the absence of any bridges on the lower reaches of the principal colonial rivers, carriage along the whole Atlantic seaboard was then chiefly by water,[33] the reader will appreciate the extreme burdensomeness of this new requirement for bonds for shipments even in small vessels and from place to place within the same colony.

The most disturbing feature of the act was, however, section 41, providing that all suits for forfeitures or other penalties "inflicted by this or any other act or acts of parliament relating to the trade and revenue" of the colonies, might be brought in colonial admiralty courts, in which the judge sat without jury.

As shown in the first appendix to this chapter, this provision laid the foundation for rigid enforcement not only of the new restrictions on colonial trade imposed by the Act of 1764, but of those, heretofore little enforced, imposed by earlier acts.

Moreover, if acquiesced in by the colonists, the provision for the trial without jury of suits under acts of Parliament relating to the trade and revenue of the colonies would establish a precedent for denying trial by jury under all acts of Parliament relating to them.[34] Section 41 of the Act of 1764 was, therefore, a threat not only to colonial merchants, but to the colonists in general.

Warned by colonial pamphlets,[35] letters, [36] and legislative protests[37] of the indignation throughout the colonies over the trade provisions of the American Act of 1764, Henry S. Conway, Secretary of State for the Southern Department in the Rockingham administration, wrote a circular letter to colonial Governors dated March 31, 1766, stating, "A Revision of the late American Trade Laws is going to be the immediate Object of Parliament: Nor will the late Transactions there [resistance to the Stamp Act], however provoking, prevent I dare say, the full Operation of that kind & indulgent Disposition prevailing both in His Majesty & His Parliament, to give to the Trade & interests of America every Relief which the true State of their Circumstances demanded or admits."[38]

But this promise proved to be illusory. The act of Geo. III ch. 52, hereafter referred to as the Act of 1766, did, indeed, reduce the duty of three pence a gallon on British colonial imports of foreign colonial molasses imposed by the American Act of 1764 to a penny a gallon,[39] and waive import duties levied by that act on colonial imports of several West Indian products provided they were reexported.[40] But these favorable changes relating to the importation of West Indian products were partly offset by extending the colonial duty on molasses to include molasses imported from one British colony into another,[41] and by providing that a tariff preference in favor of British West Indian sugar imported into Great Britain heretofore allowed whether the sugar were shipped directly from the West Indies or by way of the British continental colonies should henceforth be allowed only if the sugar were shipped directly from the British West Indies.[42]

Also, and more important, the Act of 1766, which apparently passed without any division,[43] still further restricted the exportation of colonial products directly to Europe.

The Act of 1764, as we have seen, prohibited the export of colonial lumber and iron directly to any part of continental Europe and of a number of other colonial products to any part of continental Europe north of Cape Finisterre. Sections 30 and 31 of the Act of 1766 now prohibited the shipment of any colonial products, including wheat, flour, fish, meat, dairy products, and a number of other less important "non-enumerated"[44] products, the export of which was hitherto unrestricted, to Ireland or any part of continental Europe north of Cape Finisterre except the Spanish ports on the Bay of Biscay.[45] Henceforth, a vessel carrying such products to northern continental Europe or Ireland[46] must first put into a British port and there be unloaded and reloaded before it could legally continue to its destination.

Furthermore, section 29 of the Act of 1766, repealing the onerous requirement of the Act of 1764 for molasses bonds, which, at first glance, appeared to afford relief to the colonies from one of the most galling provisions of the Act of 1764, in fact afforded no relief whatever; the next two sections of the Act of 1766 provided for a new type of bond which was just as onerous as the old. These sections required the master of "every" ship or vessel without regard to size, taking aboard any non-enumerated colonial products in the colonies to furnish a bond ($£1,000$ for vessels if under a hundred tons, $£2,000$ if a hundred tons or over) not to land these products in Ireland or any part of continental Europe north of the Spanish ports in the Bay of Biscay.[47]

The London Agent for the South Carolina Legislature tried to have the bill for the Act of 1766 amended to permit small vessels regularly plying between ports within a single colony to give bond only once a year not to leave for any port outside the colony. But he failed to secure even this reasonable concession.[48]

Some relief from the requirement of bonds seems to have been granted in practice to undecked vessels engaged exclusively in coastwise and river trade;[49] but the failure to legalize this exemption gave countenance to the harassment of small vessels in coastwise trade such as that leading to the *Gaspee* incident (described in Chapter 12).[50]

Two additional factors contributing to continued colonial discontent in 1766 must be briefly noted.

The first was the publication in 1765 and early 1766 of several editions of an exceptionally able and popular pamphlet, *Considerations on the Propriety of Imposing Taxes in the British Colonies,* by Daniel Dulany, a leading Maryland lawyer and planter.[51] Though aimed primarily against the Stamp Act, this pamphlet gave figures indicating that the provision in the Navigation Act of 1660 forbidding the export of colonial tobacco to any place outside the colonies, excepting Great Britain,[52] was costing colonial planters, on tobacco shipped from Virginia and Maryland alone, around £270,000 sterling a year.[53] Thus, though the new British restrictions on exports imposed by the Act of 1766 affected chiefly the northern colonies, southern tobacco planters had recently been alerted to the heavy burden imposed on them by this earlier act restricting colonial exports.

The other was the Free Port Act of 1766, sponsored by the Rockingham administration. Though, at first glance, this act seemed designed to carry out Conway's promise of relief to colonial trade, it was in fact calculated, as brought out in the second appendix to this chapter, to benefit British and British West Indian interests to the detriment of those of the British North American colonies.[54]

Curiously, the most dangerous act of all, the Declaratory Act of 1776, asserting the "full power and authority" of Parliament "to make laws . . . to bind the colonies . . . in all cases whatsoever," gave rise to comparatively little colonial protest.[55] The probable explanation is that, assured by English correspondents that the act was a mere gesture,[56] and eager to reestablish peaceful relations with Great Britian, the colonists, as Samuel Adams later wrote, "chose to treat this act with silence, at least till necessity should oblige them to remonstrate the ill effects of it."[57]

CHAPTER 4

THE CHATHAM MINISTRY AND ITS
INHERITED COLONIAL PROBLEMS

IN April, 1766, the Duke of Grafton, one of the Secretaries of State in the Rockingham Ministry, begged Lord Rockingham to press the King to send for William Pitt and give him carte blanche to come into the present Ministry or form a new one. Rockingham refused, whereupon Grafton told the King he must resign since he had joined the Ministry on the understanding that "any time Mr. Pitt chose to accept," the members of it would "act under him or retire whichever He directed," implying that Pitt was now ready to accept.[1]

Three days later (May 1), Lord Egmont, First Lord of the Admiralty, by direction of the King,[2] proposed to Rockingham and Henry S. Conway, the other Secretary of State and Leader of the House of Commons, "a thorough coalition" with friends of Lord Bute, including Bute's son-in-law, Lord Northumberland. Rockingham and Conway replied that they would not consider going further than to give a place to Bute's brother, James Stuart Mackenzie,[3] whom, as we saw in Chapter 1, the King had dismissed under heavy pressure from a majority of the Cabinet in the Grenville Ministry.

The Lord Chancellor, Lord Northington, who assured the King that "he was alone attach'd to me and would support whatever men I chose to entrust in Government,"[4] presumably was prepared to adopt the King's proposal in full. But the other two members of the Cabinet, Rockingham's father-in-law, Lord Winchilsea, President of the Council, and the Duke of Newcastle, Lord Privy Seal, backed up Rockingham and Conway, declaring with them that "if they were to go farther now than taking in Mr. Mackenzie, their own Friends would all Leave them."[5]

The King thereupon (May 3) asked Bute whether "if I call on those who call themselves attached to you, I cannot form something out of that chosen band that will stand by me. I find," he continued, that "Lord North [a former member of the Treasury Board and an able speaker] is ready to quit opposition; in short I am willing to take any but the men that us'd me so infamously last year . . . , Mr. Greenville and the late Secretarys,"[6] i.e., Secretaries of State Lord Halifax and Lord Sandwich.

On Bute's replying that there were no "hopes of any formation without either Mr. Pitt of Mr. Greenville at the head of it,"[7] the King apparently laid aside or put on ice the thought of a change. Grafton, who resigned on May 23, was replaced by the Duke of Richmond,[8] and the Ministry not only carried on successfully during the brief remainder of the current session of Parliament, which closed June 6,[9] but seemed in a fair way to continue at least until Parliament met again in the fall.[10]

This, however, was not to be. Grafton, without consulting Conway (who, as Leader of the House of Commons would have to bear the brunt of carrying the measure through that House) had promised the King to bring in a bill at the current session of Parliament to settle £8,000 a year more on each of the King's three brothers, and the King had so informed them. Upon learning of this plan, Conway "objected to so considerable a donation being hurried through the remnant of a thin house,"[12] and Rockingham gave way; he told the King that the proposed bill must be deferred until the next session of Parliament.[13] Rockingham managed to soothe the King's brothers by agreeing to present to Parliament before it rose a resolution for a grant to them at the next session.[14] But the King was determined to use Rockingham's breach of promise as an excuse to rid himself of the Rockingham administration as soon as Parliament rose.

"On the strange scene concerning the money for my brothers," he wrote Bute, "I thought the moment was come that I should be able with honour to get rid of my administration; nay I had already sent for the Chancellor [Northington] that he might have sounded Lord Cambden [Pitt's most important follower] with regard to Mr. Pitt when my brothers made the proposal that compromised the affair; this disappointed me but did not remove my resolution of encouraging the Chancellor to continue to get lights from the Chief Justice [Camden] whilst I rely'd on Providence to point out the minute when I could best dismiss my Ministry."[15]

The King had reason to turn to Pitt, since he knew that Pitt had recently gone on record in the House of Commons that "he thought it shameful to proscribe his [Bute's] relations and his friends,"[16] and also had said that (expressing a sentiment dear to the King's heart)[17] "if ever he was again admitted . . . into the Royal presence, it should be independent of any personal [i.e., party] connections whatsoever."[18]

There remained the necessity of Providence affording a better excuse for throwing out the Rockingham Ministry than its refusal to ally itself with the friends of so unpopular a character as Bute[19] or than the King's vexation over the affair of the proposed settlement on his brothers. This came shortly (July 6), when Northington, long dissatisfied with his fellow Cabinet ministers[20] and apparently hoping to curry favor with the King,[21] asked his permission to cease attending Cabinet meetings and if his colleagues asked the reason for thus absenting himself "to declare the little confidence shewed him was the cause of it added to his opinion that he could not with honour continue in the station unless a stronger Administration was formed."[22]

Seizing this opening "to bring things to an issue very honourably to myself" the King had Northington sound out Camden as to "what would be the best channel of getting at Mr. Pitt," who replied that Northington himself was the person.[23] Whereupon the King wrote Pitt July 7,

"Your very dutiful and handsome conduct the last summer makes me desirous of having your thoughts to how an able and dignified ministry may be formed. I desire, therefore, you will come, for this salutory purpose, to town.

"I cannot conclude without expressing how entirely my ideas concerning the basis on which a new administration should be erected, are consonant to the opinion you gave on that subject in parliament a few days before you set out for Somersetshire.

"I convey this through the channel of the Earl of Northington, as there is no man in my service on whom I so perfectly rely, and who, I know, agrees with me perfectly in the contents of this letter."

"George R"[24]

Pitt replied,

"Sire,

"Penetrated with the deepest sense of your Majesty's boundless goodness to me, and with a heart overflowing with duty and zeal for the honour and the happiness of the most gracious and benign Sovereign, I shall hasten to London as fast as I possibly can; wishing that I could change infirmity[25] into wings of expedition, the sooner to be permitted the high honour to lay at your Majesty's feet, the poor but sincere offering of the little services of

"Your Majesty's
most dutiful subject
and devoted servant,
William Pitt."[26]

Pitt's brother-in-law, Lord Temple, offered the place of First Lord of the Treasury as he had been the year before (Chapter 1), again refused to accept, saying he declined to be "a capital cypher, surrounded by cyphers of quite a different complexion, the whole under the guidance of that great Commoner with the Privy Seal in his hand."[27] But this time Pitt proceeded to form a Ministry without Temple, and by the end of the month was ready to take over, as appears from the following letter of July 29, from the King to him:

"I am . . . glad we are now come to a final end of all quid pro quos. I have signed this day the Warrant for creating you an Earl[28] & shall with pleasure receive You in that Capacity tomorrow as well as entrust You with my Privy Seal, as I know the Earl of Chatham will zealously give his aid to destroying all party distinctions and restoring that subordination to Government which alone can preserve that inestimable Blessing Liberty from degenerating into Licentiousness."[29]

The King had informed Rockingham, Newcastle, Conway, and Richmond on July 9 that he had "sent for Mr. Pitt" and on July 23 that Pitt was taking over soon, which he did on July 30.[30]

Thus, without a vote of no confidence in Parliament on any important issue or even the loss of a single by-election, two successive Ministries were dismissed within but little more than a year, at the will, not to say whim, of the King.

Pitt, now Lord Chatham,[31] elected, as indicated by the King's letter last quoted, to take the office of Lord Privy Seal previously held by Newcastle, and three of the most important Cabinet offices were given to Pitt's followers: Rockingham was replaced by Grafton as First Lord of the Treasury, Northington by Lord Camden as Lord Chancellor, and Richmond by Lord Shelburne as a Secretary of State.[32] Three members of the Rockingham Ministry were retained—Conway as a Secretary of State and Leader of the House of Commons,[33] Egmont as First Lord of the Admirality, (but only until September, 1766, when he resigned and was replaced by Admiral Sir Charles Saunders, who in December, 1767, was succeeded by Admiral Sir Edward Hawke),[34] and Northington, who replaced Winchilsea as President of the Council.

The Cabinet was enlarged by adding one of Pitt's friends, Lord Granby, Master General of the Ordnance, who had held that place in the Rockingham Ministry but without a seat in the Cabinet,[35] and Charles Townshend,[36] the new Chancellor of the Exchequer.[37]

Good will was shown toward Bute by restoring his brother, James Stuart Mackenzie, to his former office of Lord Privy Seal for Scotland.[38]

From the standpoint of relations with the colonies, the change in Ministry was dangerous.

Chatham's heading the new Ministry might, at first glance, seem to ensure that during his administration, taxation of the colonies would not be revived, since he had favored repeal of the Stamp Act not only as a matter of policy but, as stated in his great speech of the preceding January, on the ground that "this kingdom has no right to lay a tax upon the colonies."[39]

But what if the colonists failed to behave with "the prudence and temper"[40] he had, in that same speech, declared they would if the Stamp Act were repealed? What if they now opposed other British acts disrelished by them? Wounded in pride by the colonists' repudiation of his assurance as to how they would behave,[41] and notorious for his abrupt shifts of stand,[42] might not Chatham now take a very different position as to colonial taxation? His earlier position that Parliament had no right to pass the proposed stamp Act would be no bar, since apparently it was now accepted British doctrine that the constitution could be changed by mere act of Parliament.[43]

Furthermore, the dismissal of Newcastle from, and inclusion of, Granby and Townshend in the Cabinet were ill omens for the colonies.

Newcastle, the only leading British statesman of the period with long experience in colonial administration,[44] had strongly supported repeal of the Stamp Act and was the only member of the Rockingham Cabinet known to have questioned the proposed Declaratory Act asserting Parliament's unlimited legislative authority over the colonies.[45] Granby, on the other hand, had taken a conspicuously anti-colonial stand by speaking and voting against repeal of the Stamp Act;[46] and Townshend, though generally regarded as extremely erratic,[47] "a meer Weather Cock," as one of his critics called him,[48] had long adhered to at least one political policy —the policy of Parliament's levying taxes for revenue on the colonies.

As early as 1754, Townshend had disapproved a plan to finance colonial defense out of a fund to be raised voluntarily by the colonies because it "begins a great work in a wrong manner," i.e., by having the fund raised by the colonial Assemblies or deputies representing them, instead of by act of Parliament.[49] In 1761, he proposed that Parliament raise funds toward the support of the British army in America by changing the British duty on colonial imports of foreign molasses from a protective tariff to a duty primarily for revenue,[50] and in 1765, when the resolution for a colonial Stamp Act was before Parliament, he spoke strongly in favor of it.[51] Furthermore, though Townshend later supported repeal of the stamp tax, he took pains to point out that he did so only on the ground of immediate expediency.[52]

One of the first problems confronting the new Ministry was the opposition in New York, where more British troops were stationed than in any other of the old thirteen colonies,[53] to an act, the Quartering Act of 1765, requiring every colony in which troops were housed in barracks to furnish the men with fire, candles, vinegar, salt, bedding, cooking utensils, and a daily ration of five pints of beer or cider or half a pint of rum.[54]

In December, 1765, the New York Assembly gave an evasive reply to a demand to provide the supplies required by the act.[55] At this time New Yorkers were inflamed against Great Britain, not only by the Stamp Act, but by the threat to the finality of verdicts of juries involved in the pending case of *Forsey* v. *Cunningham*.[56] Both these irritants had been eliminated by the following June, when compliance with the Quartering Act again was demanded.[57] But even so, the Assembly in effect challenged the act by voting only part of the supplies required by it.[58]

Apparently hopeful that the Assembly could be won over by a conciliatory response, Secretary of State Shelburne wrote Sir Henry Moore, Governor of New York that "it cannot be doubted that His Majesty's Province of New York, after the Lenity of Great Britain so recently extended to America, will not fail to carry into execution the Act of Parliament past last Session for quartering His Majestys Troops in the full extent and meaning of the Act. . . . I must only Sir in general add that I hope and believe that a very little time . . . will allay whatever remains of those Heats which have so unhappily for America prevailed. . . ."[59]

But at its next (December, 1766) session, the Assembly not only refused to vote any of the supplies required by the act, but clearly indicated it had no intention ever of obeying it by sending a message to Governor Moore declaring that "we find it impossible to comply with what is now demanded, consistent with our obligations to our constituents; . . . the objections against making the provisions required are of a nature the most serious and weighty imaginable."[60]

Moore, of course, informed Shelburne of this,[61] and he passed along the information to Chatham in a letter of February 1, 1767,[62] which also referred to and probably enclosed a petition from a large group of New York merchants to the House of Commons complaining of the additional restrictions on colonial trade imposed by the Acts of 1764 and 1766 (described in Chapter 3).[63]

Chatham, laid up at Bath with the gout, replied in a blistering letter (February 3),[64] stating, "A spirit of infatuation has taken possession of New York; their disobedience to the mutiny [Quartering] Act will justly create a great ferment here, open a fair field to the arraigners of America, and leave no room to any to say a word in their defence. . . . The petition of the merchants of New York is highly improper; in point of time, most absurd;[65] in the extent of their pretensions, most excessive; and in the reasoning, most grossly fallacious and offensive. What demon of discord blows the coals in that devoted [i.e., doomed] province I know not, but they are doing the work of their worst enemies themselves. The torrent of indignation will be irresistable, and they will draw upon their heads national resentment by their ingratitude, and ruin, I fear, upon the whole state, by the consequences."

It was Chatham, as we saw in Chapter 1, who, only a year earlier, pointing out that the colonists were without representation in Parliament, had declared, "I rejoice that America has resisted. Three millions of people so dead to all the feelings of liberty, as voluntarily to submit to be slaves, would have been fit instruments to make slaves of the rest." The colonists were still unrepresented in Parliament. Why then should the New York Assembly not refuse to obey the Quartering Act, obviously imposing taxes on the colony,[66] and he of all men not be sympathetic to their disobedience?

Nor was Chatham's denunciation of the merchants' petition much more defensible. One of the grievances complained of, the ban on direct shipment of non-enumerated colonial products to Ireland,[67] was, indeed, about to be repealed[68] and another alleged grievance was apparently based on a misreading of the Free Ports Act of 1766.[69] But the rest of the petition deserved careful and temperate consideration.

Shelburne, Northington, and some other members of the Ministry thought it best to take no notice of the New York merchants' petition unless Grenville, scourge of the colonies, moved that it be laid before the House of Commons.[70] But Chatham sensibly rejected this plan on the ground that any attempt by the government to smother the petition would be vulnerable to attack by the opposition,[71] and his view prevailed. On February 16, 1767, the petition was presented to the House, but apparently received no support.[72]

On this same day, Shelburne wrote Chatham, who still was laid up with the gout, that "the government appears called upon for some measure of vigour, to support the authority of Parliament and the coercive power of this country," and that, though the Cabinet had come to no decision as to what plan to propose, he himself favored dealing with New York by replacing Governor Moore with "some one of a Military Character who might . . . be entrusted . . . to act with Force or Gentleness, as circumstances might make necessary, and with the colonies in general by "giving the Governor Power in case the Assemblys refuse to provide [for] the Troops . . . to billet on Private Houses. . . ."[73]

On March 13, Grafton reported to Chatham that the Cabinet had tentatively decided to deal with the matter by act of Parliament,[74] but no decision as to details was reached until April 24, when, as we learn from a letter of April 26 from Shelburne to Chatham, the Cabinet adopted a plan, subject to Chatham's consideration, embodying a basic idea of Townshend's[75] for an act of Parliament to suspend the authority of the New York Legislature to pass any other law until it had passed one complying with the Quartering Act.[76]

No reply to Shelburne's letter has been found, but there is nothing to indicate that Chatham disapproved of the general idea of enforcing obedience to the Quartering Act[77] or of the particular plan for this described in Shelburne's letter of April 26.

Resolutions for a bill to carry out the Cabinet's plan were outlined to the House of Commons sitting in Committee of the Whole on May 13, and formally submitted to the House two days later.[78]

In debating the resolutions, friends of the colonies, including Conway,[79] Rose Fuller and William Beckford, West Indians by birth, Charles Garth, London Agent for South Carolina, Thomas Pownall, former Governor of Massachusetts, and William Dowdeswell, Edmund Burke, and several other members of the Rockingham party, opposed the resolutions on various grounds; but they were carried on May 15, 180 to 98.[80] Grenville, who had denounced the resolutions as "too feeble," failed to have the proposed bill made more stringent, but he secured the adoption of a motion for an address to the King "to bestow some marks of his favor upon the Governors and officers who had suffered by their obedience to the acts of this legislature. . . ."[81]

A bill embodying the resolutions was introduced in the House of Commons on May 27, passed that House without further opposition on June 15, was slightly amended by the House of Lords, and on July 2, was assented to by the King.[82] The act thus adopted, the New York Restraining Act, provided that all acts passed by the New York Legislature after October 1, 1767, were "to be null and void" until provision was made by the New York Assembly to furnish the King's troops in the colony all the items required by the Quartering Act.[83]

The Ministry also showed its determination to support and perpetuate the Quartering Act by securing passage of an act extending the existing law until March 24, 1769,[84] and similar acts, amended somewhat in 1769,[85] were passed from year to year until after the outbreak of the Revolutionary War.[86]

Massachusetts luckily escaped involvement at the time in the controversy with the British government over the Quartering Act and British restrictions of colonial trade.

The Massachusetts House, in January, 1767, questioned the action of the Governor Francis Bernard and Council in having provided, out of provincial funds, supplies for a company of British artillery temporarily stationed in barracks near Boston.[87] But on Bernard's pointing out that "the provision . . . consisted of fuel and candles only, which . . . always have been allowed in these barracks, and did not include several articles prescribed by the act of Parliament,"[88] the objection apparently was dropped. Furthermore, a petition to the House of Commons from a group of Boston merchants, similar to the one from New York merchants which so provoked Chatham,[89] with the addition of a complaint of interference with New England fishermen by British naval vessels,[90] was not presented. The London Agent of the Massachusetts Assembly to whom the petition was sent for presentation to the House of Commons did not receive it until after the New York merchants' petition had in effect been rejected by the House and, therefore, he prudently abstained from presenting it.[91]

Even so, opposition members in the House of Lords tried to have Massachusetts punished or at least censured[92] for having included in an act to indemnify sufferers in the Stamp Tax riots a provision pardoning offenses committed in the colony during the riots,[93] thus usurping, it was said, the pardoning power of the Crown. But this move, opposed by the Ministry, failed.[94]

Evidently alarmed, as they had reason to be, over the punishment in store for New York because of defiance of the Quartering Act, members of the New York Assembly took steps, even before the bill for the Restraining Act had finally passed, to comply with the Quartering Act. The Assembly passed a bill which became law on June 6, "granting unto His Majesty the Sum of Three thousand Pounds for furnishing necessaries for the Troops Quartered within this Colony," and ordering the Treasurer of the colony to pay General Thomas Gage, Commander-in-Chief of the British forces in North America, up to £3,000 "to be applied for furnishing Necessaries for His Majesty's Troops" quartered in New York. This grant, fully covering the cost of all the supplies required by the Quartering Act,[95] was held by the Crown's chief legal advisers to constitute compliance with the act.[96]

Thus, the immediate controversy over the Quartering Act was quieted, and, though several of the colonies other than New York[97] failed from time to time to comply with the act,[98] it never again became a leading issue, perhaps because the controversy over it was overshadowed by the Townshend Act of 1767, to which we now turn.

CHAPTER 5

THE TOWNSHEND ACT DUTIES OF 1767

DURING the consideration by the House of Commons in January, 1767, of the estimated cost of maintaining the British army in the colonies for the current year,[1] amounting to over £400,000,[2] George Grenville, one of the leaders of the Opposition, moved "That the troops to be kept up in America shou'd be Paid by the Colonies respectively for whose defence & benefit they were Employ'd."[3] The motion was overwhelmingly defeated (106 to 35),[4] but it drew from the Chancellor of the Exchequer, Charles Townshend, an extremely important statement. He, too, he said, "approved of our taxing the Colonies so as to provide for their own safety and preservation," and at this very session would propose a bill "by which the Colonys should be taxed conformable to their abilities, in a manner that should be least burdensome and most efficacious."[5] He had no thought, he added, of raising a sufficient revenue from the colonies immediately to cover all colonial expense, but would "plan by degrees" to "form a revenue in time to bear the whole."[6]

Townshend did not state what kind of tax he had in mind, but on February 1, Secretary of State Lord Shelburne wrote Lord Chatham, who was laid up with the gout,[7] of having heard "from general conversation" that Townshend planned "a new regulation of the tea duty here and some other alterations to produce a revenue on imports there."[8] In this same letter, Shelburne also described Townshend's plan for dealing with the East India Company which differed from the one favored by Chatham and most members of the Cabinet.[9]

In reply (February 3) Chatham denounced Townshend's plan concerning the East India Company, but said nothing as to Townshend's proposal for colonial taxation, thereby tending to indicate that he had no objection to it.[10]

For some weeks following Townshend's statement of January 26 as to colonial taxation he apparently said nothing further on this point, but at a Cabinet meeting on March 12, he outlined his plan for colonial taxation, reported by Grafton to Chatham the next day.

"The vote of supply for the American extraordinaries" wrote Grafton, "were then considered; when Mr. Townshend declared that if the reduction of them was not determined the closing of the [sittings of the] committee of supply by drawing the troops nearer the towns,[11] laying the Indian charges upon the provinces[12] and by laying a tax on the American ports, he would not remain chancellor of the exchequer. His behavior, on the whole, was such as no cabinet will, I am confident, ever submit to."[13]

Chatham replied the same day (March 12): "Lord Chatham's best respects attend the Duke of Grafton. . . . Lord Chatham not being yet well enough to engage in business, is particularly directed by Dr. Addington,[14] to desire to be excused from Conversations of that sort for the present. He begs to express his best acknowledgements to the Duke of Grafton for the honor of His Grace's Note, and hopes His Grace will have the goodness to pardon an Invalid for not writing with his own hand.

"Lord Chatham is unable to suggest any new Plan for the Disposition of the Troops in America, and submits that it may be more advisable to postpone it for this year, for further Consideration. The Indian Trade, will be most safely and properly settled, by the opinion of The Lords of Trade.[15]

"Upon the whole, Lord Chatham will acquiesce with pleasure, to the Opinions of the Cabinet; and thinks those Opinions when taken, and approved by the King, ought to be communicated to the rest of the King's Servants and to the Friends of Government. Lord Chatham must beg leave for the present to be excused entering into business, till he is somewhat stronger."[16]

In the light of this letter from Chatham, indicating no disapproval of Townshend's project of colonial taxation, it is not surprising that the Cabinet did not take a stand against the project.[17]

In presenting his budget as Chancellor of the Exchequer to the House of Commons on April 15, Townshend barely mentioned an undescribed "American tax,"[18] but in a debate in the House, May 13, on the proposed New York Restraining Act (discussed in Chapter 4), he finally outlined what he had in mind.

He proposed, he said, to lay taxes upon America but not internal taxes, because, though he looked upon "the distinction between external and internal taxes as ridiculous"[19] it was accepted by "the Americans," and this was sufficient for his purposes.[20]

Pointing out that Crown officials in several of the colonies were dependent on the local legislatures for their salaries and that "the Authority of the executive Power" would be strengthened by their being "no longer dependent upon the pleasure of any Assembly,"[21] he promised to offer "in the Committee of Supply, . . . a Duty upon [colonial imports of] Raisins . . . Oranges, Lemons and Oil [olive oil] and a Duty upon Port Wine, [and] . . . allow to America the Importation thereof direct from Portugal and from any part of Spain." He also would propose a reduction of the drawback (refund) of British duties allowed on reexportation to the colonies of several foreign products, thus increasing the net revenue from existing British import duties.[22] "All these together," he said, "might produce between £30 and £40,000 per annum."[23]

This plan, it will be observed, differed radically from the one suggested by Townshend in January. The amount to be collected was a small fraction of the sum then indicated, and, as brought out later in this chapter, the revenue was to be applied not toward payment of British troops stationed in America, but to payment of the salaries of civil officials there.

The act was to be sweetened for the colonists by amending the Act of

1663, forbidding importation of European products into the colonies except by way of Great Britain, to permit colonial importation of fruit, olive oil, and port wine directly from continental Europe. But when Grenville protested against such "subversion of the Act of Navigation"[24] and was widely supported,[25] this article of Townshend's program was dropped.

The plan finally presented to the House of Commons sitting in Committee of the Whole on June 1, and to the House in regular session the following day provided for the following import duties payable in the colonies: four shillings a hundredweight on crown, plate, flint, and white glass; one shilling two pence a hundredweight on green glass; two shillings a hundredweight on paint and lead; a flat rate of three pence a pound on teas of all grades;[26] three pence to twelve shillings (thirty-six pence) a ream on sixty-six grades of paper.[27] Townshend estimated that the duty on tea would produce an annual revenue of about £20,000 and the duties on glass, paint, lead, and paper, about £17,000.[28]

Unlike the British Acts of 1764 and 1766 levying duties for revenue on colonial imports and the Stamp Act of 1765, which provided that the revenue was to be applied "towards defraying the expences of defending, protecting and securing the British colonies and plantations in America,"[29] the revenue from the proposed new act was to "be applied, in the First Place, in making a more certain and adequate Provision for the Charge of the Administration of Justice, and the Support of Civil Government in such of the said Colonies and Plantations, where it shall be found necessary." Only the residue, if any, was to be applied "towards defraying the necessary Expences of defending, protecting and securing the said Colonies and Plantations."[30]

This feature of the proposed act made it particularly dangerous to colonial liberty. The act would not only further implement Parliament's assertion of authority to tax the colonists without their consent, but would, if productive of the estimated revenue, enable the British government to make some Crown-appointed Governors and judges in the colonies dependent on the British government not only for their appointment and continuance in office but for their salaries. By voting their salaries for only a year at a time, colonial Legislatures had retained an influence over them balancing that of the British government derived from the Crown's power to dismiss them at pleasure. By paying the salaries of the colonial Governors and judges, the British government would gain greater if not exclusive power of influencing them.

This object, long held in view by British ministers,[31] could, of course, be attained by the Crown's payment of the officials from revenue raised from British taxpayers; but apparently no Ministry thought it expedient to ask Parliament for taxes payable by British taxpayers to pay colonial judges and Governors heretofore supported by funds voted by colonial Legislatures.

A bill incorporating Townshend's plan passed quickly through both the Commons and the Lords,[32] apparently without opposition[33] or a division[34] at any stage of the proceedings, and was assented to by commissioners for the King on June 29.[35] This act, the act of 7 Geo. III ch. 46, commonly known as the Townshend Act, was to take effect November 20, 1767.

Many factors contributed to the easy passage of this potentially explosive act.

One of the most important was Chatham's failure to take a stand against the proposed duties. His distinguished biographer, Basil Williams, states that Chatham was indignant with Townshend over his "threat to tax America."[36] But Williams cites no evidence for this assertion, and there is reason to believe he was mistaken.

In the first place, Chatham's letters of February 3 and March 13 to Shelburne and Grafton, quoted earlier in this chapter, give no sign of indignation over Townshend's proposal for duties on colonial imports. Furthermore, Chatham's wrath over the New York Assembly's opposition to the Quartering Act, virtually imposing a tax on the colonies in which British troops were quartered, indicates that he was now not opposed to colonial taxes of all kinds. Indeed, if Lord George Sackville's letter concerning Chatham's (Pitt's) speech against the Stamp Act in January, 1766 (quoted in Chapter 1), correctly reported him, he had indicated even then that he was not opposed in principle to duties on colonial imports and exports.[37]

A second important factor in the lack of opposition to the proposed duties was that, in view of the Rockingham Ministry's sponsorship in 1766 of the duty for revenue on colonial imports of molasses (described in Chapter 3), Rockingham's party could not now consistently attack in principle the similar duties on colonial imports to be levied by the Townshend Act.[38]

Another important factor was the flood of newspaper articles and pamphlets published in England after repeal of the Stamp Act playing up the light financial burdens of the colonies compared with those of Great Britain; the colonists' alleged ingratitude and lawlessness; and the necessity of compelling them to recognize their subordination to British rule.[39] Despite the counter propaganda of Franklin,[40] this anti-colonial campaign had apparently made much impression; letter after letter from England during the spring of 1767 spoke of the recent striking change in public sentiment concerning the colonists.[41]

Yet another factor was the passivity at this time of British merchants trading with the colonies, whose support of repeal of the Stamp Act had been an important contribution toward securing repeal. Offended by the failure of their colonial correspondents to express gratitude for their successful efforts for repeal,[42] they offered no opposition to passage of the Townshend Act.

Finally, and perhaps most important of all, was the fact that Franklin, chief spokesman for the colonies in the proceedings in Parliament for repeal of the Stamp Act, had testified that the colonists were not opposed in principle to Parliament's levying duties for revenue on colonial imports and exports.

At the beginning of his testimony, Franklin said merely that he had never heard any colonial objections in principle to Parliament's levying duties on colonial imports and exports "to regulate commerce," leaving open the question whether they would object to such duties if imposed for revenue.[43] But when pressed for his opinion on this further, vital point, he stated, as quoted earlier in this volume, that the colonists objected in principle only to "internal" taxes (such as stamp or excise taxes) and not to "external" taxes, i.e., duties on imports and exports, even though these were for revenue, rather than for the regulation of trade.[44]

You cannot conceive, wrote Franklin's London friend, William Strahan, to a correspondent in Philadelphia, "what impression his Replies made upon the House . . . ," and others wrote in similar vein concerning the great influence of Franklin's testimony.[45]

Again, on April 12, 1767, only about a month before Townshend's plan for colonial taxation was laid before the House of Commons, Franklin (writing in the guise of an Englishman in an article in the *London Chronicle*) stated, "The colonies submit to pay all external taxes laid on them by way of duty on merchandizes imported into their country and never disputed the authority of Parliament to lay such duties. The distinction indeed between internal and external taxes is here looked upon as groundless and frivolous. . . .[46] However, whether there be validity in this distinction or not, seems to be immaterial; since if they are willing to pay *external* though not internal taxes, . . . 'tis then the same thing to us, provided we get the same money. . . ."[47]

Moreover, Franklin's statements had seemingly been confirmed by the colonists' general acceptance, without protest, of the duty on molasses levied by the Act of 1766 (described in Chapter 3).[48]

Since, as Townshend pointed out, the colonists themselves apparently accepted in principle the authority of Parliament to levy duties on colonial imports,[49] and the proposed rates of duty were not immoderate,[50] could English friends of the colonies in Parliament justify themselves in objecting to Townshend's plan? Would they not lay themselves open to the charge, which Opposition members of Parliament were at all times anxious to avoid, that they were merely trying to embarrass the administration for party reasons?

Two other important measures relating to the colonies, enacted by Parliament in 1767, must be noted.

The first, embodied in section 10 of the Townshend Act, required colonial superior courts to grant writs of assistance to British customs officers in the colonies to aid them in searching warehouses, homes, and other buildings for smuggled goods.

Section 10 apparently was intended to require the superior courts of all the other colonies to issue so-called "general" writs, giving the customs officers a blanket warrant for searches,[51] such as the Massachusetts Superior Court was granting customs officers stationed in Massachusetts. But, as brought out in the appendix to this chapter, most of the colonial courts narrowly construed section 10 to require the granting of only so-called particular or special writs. Thus, in spite of section 10 of the Townshend Act, the commotion over general writs of assistance in Massachusetts, described in the second appendix to this chapter, did not spread to the other colonies.

The other new measure was an act (7 Geo. III ch. 41) authorizing an American Customs Board,[52] whose establishment and activities are described in Chapter 8.

CHAPTER 6

THE FARMER'S LETTERS

THE Townshend Act duties, though complained of,[1] went into effect on November 20, 1767, without any attempt in the colonies to prevent their enforcement.

The *Boston Gazette,* organ of the Boston radicals, was the only colonial newspaper that conducted anything approaching a campaign against the act,[2] and it failed to arouse massive opposition even in Boston. A movement for non-consumption of many foreign imports launched at a Boston town meeting of October 28 made considerable headway, but it was so little directed specifically against the Townshend Act that not one of the articles taxed by the act was included in the thirty-odd items that signers of the agreement promised not to purchase.[3] Furthermore, when handbills tending to provoke resistance to the act were posted around the city, another Boston town meeting (November 20) denounced the "scandalous and threatening Papers . . . posted up in various parts of the Town . . . tending to excite Tumults and Disorders."[4]

According to Governor Francis Bernard of Massachusetts, the former leading firebrand, James Otis, had taken a forward part in encouraging acquiescence, advising the town meeting of October 28, "to tread warily for fear of offending G.B." and stating at the meeting on November 20 that, "as to the New Duties . . . it would be very imprudent in this Town to make an opposition when every other Town in the Province and every other Province in America seemed to acquiesce in them and be contented."[5]

Several factors contributed to the initial colonial acquiescence in the Townshend Act, so strikingly in contrast to the immediate and widespread colonial opposition to the Stamp Act.

First was the fear that opposition to the Townshend Act was likely to get out of hand, as had the opposition to the Stamp Act. The frightening riots in New York, Boston, Newport, Philadelphia, and Charleston[6] and the tenants' uprising on the Hudson[7] growing out of opposition to that act were still fresh in the minds of many.[8]

The second was the testimony of Franklin[9] and other responsible spokesmen for the colonists that they recognized the right of Parliament to levy duties for revenue on the colonies and the colonists' subsequent acquiescence in the duty for revenue on molasses levied by the Act of 1766. How could the colonists justly now oppose in principle the duties levied by the Townshend Act?[10] If any of these duties were excessively heavy, let the colonists petition for a reduction of these particular duties, as Franklin had said they would do if they considered any duty too high.[11]

A third factor was the difference in severity and immediate impact between the Stamp Act and the Townshend Act.

Though some of the Townshend Act duties might perhaps be considered too high, none of them was conspicuously so. But this was not true of some of the taxes levied by the Stamp Act. In the case of Franklin and Hall's *Pennsylvania Gazette,* for example, the stamp tax on advertisements would come to around 80% of the paper's advertising revenue[12] and to around 70% of its revenue from subscribers.[13] The percentage of tax on copies of cheaper newspapers (the *Gazette* was a relatively high-priced newspaper) would be even greater,[14] and on almanacs, another important resource of colonial printers, greater still.[15]

David Hall, Franklin's partner in publishing the *Gazette,* wrote him from Philadelphia in June, 1765, that "there is the greatest Reason to fear that the Number of our Customers from the First of November next [when the Stamp Act was to take effect] will be very trifling, and the Two Shillings Duty on any Advertisement will knock off the greater Part of them [advertisers] likewise." In October he added, "To shew you my fears were not groundless with respect to our Customers . . . , I am sorry to tell you that we have already lost at least 500 of them, and if so many have dropped before, what may we not expect after the first of November."[16] Franklin's printer friend James Parker wrote in similar vein from New York.[17]

Furthermore, the taxes levied by the Stamp Act[18] were payable directly by tens of thousands of colonists in all walks of life throughout all parts of the colonies. The Townshend Act duties, on the other hand, were payable directly by relatively few of the colonists—the great planters in the southern colonies, who imported many articles directly from merchants in Great Britain, and the merchant importers in the principal colonial ports. Besides, only the former would have to bear the entire burden of the Townshend Act duties payable by them; the merchants could shift to their customers part of, if not the entire, burden of the duties.[19]

The colonies finally were aroused to action against the Townshend Act by a series of twelve weekly letters signed "A Farmer" published in the *Pennsylvania Chronicle,* beginning December 2, 1767. At least twenty of the other twenty-six newspapers published in the thirteen colonies during the first five months of 1768[20] reprinted all or some of these letters,[21] and they also were reprinted as pamphlets in Philadelphia (two editions), Boston (two editions), and New York.[22] The letters had an influence beyond that of any other political writing in the Revolutionary period except Paine's *Common Sense,* published eight years later.[23]

The "Farmer," as it soon became known, was John Dickinson, a thirty-five-year-old lawyer in Philadelphia, whose *The Late Regulations Respecting the British Colonies in America . . . ,*[24] published in the winter of 1765–1766, was one of the ablest of the colonial pamphlets attacking the Stamp Act and recent additional British restrictions on colonial trade and currency.

Son of a well-to-do Delaware farmer and judge, Dickinson had come to Philadelphia in 1750, spent three years there as a law clerk, then studied law for several years at the Middle Temple in London and in 1757 entered practice in Philadelphia.[25] He was elected a member and Speaker of the Delaware Assembly in 1760. Transferring to Pennsylvania, he served from 1762 to 1765 as one of the representatives of Philadelphia County in the Pennsylvania Assembly, where he was an outstanding opponent of the so-called Quaker Party of which Franklin was a leading member,[26] and was a delegate from Pennsylvania to the intercolonial Stamp Act Congress of 1765.[27] However, defeated for a fourth term in the fall of 1765, Dickinson was no longer in the Assembly when the Farmer's Letters, which made him famous, appeared.[28]

The first of the letters denounced the New York Restraining Act as an effort to compel New York's submission to taxation by Parliament and called upon the other colonies to unite in protesting against the Restraining Act. The New York Legislature, as we have seen, had yielded to the act before this letter was published, but the very fact of New York, unsupported by her sister colonies, having yielded, gave point to the chief message in Dickinson's opening letter that *"To divide, and thus to destroy, is the first political maxim in attacking those who are powerful by their union"* and that only by recognizing "the cause of *one* is the cause of *all"* could the colonists preserve their liberty.[29]

The succeeding eleven letters were devoted primarily to arousing united opposition to the Townshend Act.[30]

In his second letter Dickinson wisely went to the heart of his campaign against the act. Without attempting to defend or reconcile earlier statements of Franklin and other colonists to the contrary, he insisted that there was no difference in principle between "internal" and "external" taxes, when, as in the case of the Townshend Act, the "external" taxes were imposed not to regulate trade, but to raise a revenue.[31] Both, he maintained, were unconstitutional.

Observing that Parliament's authority not only to forbid the colonists to import articles needed from abroad from any place but Great Britain, but also to forbid colonial manufacturing[32] had long been established, Dickinson pointed out that if Parliament now succeeded in establishing its asserted authority to impose duties on imports from Great Britain, it could milk the colonies just as effectively by "external" taxes as by stamp or other "internal" taxes. The colonies were, Dickinson declared, "in the situation of a city besieged, which is surrounded by the works of the besiegers in every part *but one.* If *that* is closed up, no step can be taken, *but to surrender at discretion.* If Great Britain can order us to come to her for necessities we want, and can order us to pay what taxes she pleases before we take them away, or when we land them here, we are as abject slaves as France and Poland can shew in wooden shoes, and with uncombed hair."[33]

The third letter was a blast against colonial defeatists "who shake their heads with solemn motion" saying, "when we are strong enough to resist, we shall attempt it, but now we are not strong enough, and . . . if we should get into riots and tumults against it [the Townshend Act], it will only draw down heavier displeasure upon us."

"Are these men," Dickinson exclaimed, "ignorant that usurpations, which might have been successfully opposed at first, acquire strength by continuance, and thus become irresistible?" Nor were "riots and tumults" necessary to the assertion of colonial rights. Other measures to secure redress were open and should initially be pursued.[34]

The first step was to petition for redress, the second would be to prevent *"the oppressors reaping advantage from their oppressions,"* that is, by boycotting goods from Great Britain until the taxes protested against were repealed. Only if both of these measures failed and it finally "became UNDOUBTED, that an inveterate resolution is formed to annihilate the liberties of the governed" would resort to "force" be warranted.[35]

In the fourth letter, Dickinson, reaffirming his stand that there was no "material difference between the *Stamp-Act* and the *late Act* for laying a duty on paper, etc.," recognized that such a distinction had indeed been made by some of the colonists, but he pointed out that the Stamp Act Congress of 1765 had been with him in denouncing as unconstitutional any kind of tax for revenue levied by Parliament on the colonies.[36]

The fifth letter took up the argument that the colonists ought in fairness pay some taxes to compensate Great Britain for her fostering and protecting the colonies. Dickinson's reply to this was that Great Britain was already more than compensated for the benefits she bestowed on the colonies by the commercial advantages she derived from her restrictions on colonial trade and manufacturing. Quoting one British writer after another on the value to Great Britain of its colonial trade, he exclaimed, "How many British authors have demonstrated, that the present wealth, power and glory of their country are founded upon these colonies?" And they were right, for "as constantly as streams tend to the ocean, have they [the colonists] been pouring the fruits of all their labors into their mother's lap."[37]

The sixth letter dealt with the argument that the distinction noted in the second letter between duties for the regulation of trade and duties for revenue was illusory because Parliament could elude the distinction simply by describing duties actually for revenue as being laid for the regulation of trade. Granting, said Dickinson, that Parliament might describe as a regulation of trade a duty or set of duties which were in fact designed primarily for revenue, and that in some cases it might be difficult to distinguish one from the other, yet "names will not change the nature of things"; the true object could be perceived. Furthermore, any argument based on the possible difficulty of drawing the distinction was pointless in the present case, since the Townshend Revenue Act was "formed *expressly* FOR THE SOLE PURPOSE OF RAISING A REVENUE."[38]

The seventh and eighth letters warned the colonists not to let themselves be lulled by the moderateness of the duties imposed by the act. "*That* is the very circumstance," said Dickinson, "most alarming to me. For I am concerned that the authors of this law would never have obtained an act to raise so trifling a sum as it must do, had they not intended by *it* to establish a *precedent* for future use. . . ." "The people of Great Britain will be told," he continued, "that *they* are sinking under an immense debt—that great part of this debt has been contracted in defending the colonies—that *these* are so ungrateful and undutiful that they will not contribute one mite to its payment—not even to the support of the army now kept up for their 'defence and security' . . . that the only way to retain them in 'obedience', is to keep a strict watch over them, and to draw off part of their riches in taxes—and that every burden laid upon *them,* is taking off so much from *Great* Britain. These assertions will be generally believed, and the people will be persuaded that they cannot be too angry with the colonies, as that anger will be profitable to themselves."[39]

The ninth and tenth letters were among the most meaty and important of the series.

The ninth brought out the danger to the colonists of the provision in the act for applying the revenue from the act to the "charge of the administration of justice, and the support of civil government," in the colonies, including payment of the salaries of colonial judges and Governors. In the past, the colonists had been able to counterbalance the influence of the Crown over many Crown-appointed colonial judges and Governors by their dependence on the colonial Legislatures for their salaries. By making these officials independent of the colonial Legislatures for their pay, the act would destroy this important source of colonial influence. "Is it possible," Dickinson exclaimed, "to form an idea of slavery more *compleat,* more *miserable,* more *disgraceful,* than that of a people where *justice is administered, government exercized* . . . AT THE EXPENCE OF THE PEOPLE, and yet WITHOUT THE LEAST DEPENDENCE AMONG THEM." "If," he declared, "we can find no relief from this infamous situation . . . we may bow down our necks, with all the stupid serenity of servitude, to any drudgery which our lords and masters shall please to command."[40]

The tenth letter pointed to Ireland as a timely object lesson of what might be expected to befall the colonists if they should submit to the yoke of British taxation. Following the establishment of a permanent revenue for the Crown in Ireland, the revenue had been applied not chiefly to the benefit of the people of that nation, but to the support of a horde of British pensioners and holders of sinecure offices. To the extent of around £15,000 a year—the private revenue of the King—the pensions were not subject to criticism; but they had long far exceeded that amount and in two recent years alone had been increased by more than £158,000. "Besides the burdens of *pensions* in Ireland," Dickinson pointed out, "almost all the *offices* in that poor kingdom have been . . . bestowed upon strangers. . . . In the same manner shall we unquestionably be treated, as soon as the late taxes levied upon us shall make posts in the 'government' and the 'administration of justice' [quoting the Townshend Act] *here* worth the attention of people of influence in *Great-Britain*.[41]

"Some persons," he continued, reverting to the theme of his seventh and eighth letters, "may imagine the sums to be raised by the Townshend Act are but small, and therefore may be inclined to acquiesce under it. A conduct more dangerous to freedom, as before has been observed, can never be adopted. Nothing is wanted at home but a PRECEDENT, the force of which shall be established by the tacit submission of the colonists."[42]

The eleventh letter brilliantly elaborated this theme by showing how in England seemingly innocuous precedents had been used as the basis for extremely oppressive measures, ending with expression of Dickinson's conviction that the Townshend Act was "an *experiment made of our disposition* . . . , a bird sent out over the waters, to discover whether the waves that lately agitated this part of the world with such volume, are yet subsided."[43]

The twelfth and last letter, published February 15, 1768, was devoted to recapitulating and stressing the main points presented in the preceding eleven.[44]

Governor Bernard wrote his friend Richard Jackson, former London Agent for the Massachusetts House and a member of Parliament, enclosing "a compleat Set of the Pennsylvania Farmer's Letters," with the warning that if the "System of American Policy" set forth in these letters, "artfully wrote and . . . universally circulated, should receive no Refutation . . . it will become a Bill of Rights in the Opinion of the Americans."[45]

No refutation of any consequence appeared, and the Farmer's Letters became, as Bernard predicted, a kind of colonial Bill of Rights.[46]

CHAPTER 7

PROTESTS, NON-IMPORTATION AGREEMENTS, AND HILLSBOROUGH'S PROVOCATIVE LETTERS

ON December 5, 1767, Dickinson wrote James Otis, "The Liberties of our Common Country appear to me to be at this moment exposed to the most imminent Danger; and this Apprehension has engag'd me to lay my Sentiments before the Public in Letters of which I send you a Copy. . . . Only one has yet been publish'd and what there Effect may be, cannot yet be known, but whenever the Cause of American Freedom is to be vindicated, I look towards the Province of Massachusetts Bay. She must, as she has hitherto done, first kindle the Sacred Flame, that on such occasions must warm and illuminate the Continent. . . ."[1]

Otis' reply[2] has not been found; but he evidently took prompt action.

On December 21, Boston newspapers published the first two of the Farmer's Letters,[3] and the following day, a Boston town meeting, presided over by Otis, instructed the town's members in the Massachusetts House of Representatives to propose a petition to the King for repeal of the Townshend Act.[4]

On January 20, 1768, the House adopted a petition to the King denouncing Parliament's taxation of the colonists for revenue as violating their "sacred right" as Englishmen "of being taxed only by representatives of their own free election," and begging for relief.[5]

Furthermore, pursuant to a resolution of the House, its Speaker, Thomas Cushing, sent a circular letter, dated February 11, 1768, to the Speakers of the other colonial Assemblies in North America, describing the House's proceedings and expressing the hope that the other Assemblies would likewise take "such constitutional measures . . . as are proper" in the matter.[6]

At the opening of the spring session of the Virginia Legislature, Peyton Randolph, Speaker of the House of Burgesses, laid the Massachusetts letter before the House,[7] which promptly (April 14), adopted, without a dissenting voice, a Petition to the King, a Memorial to the House of Lords, and a Remonstrance to the House of Commons, maintaining that any tax levied by Parliament on the colonies primarily for revenue, rather than for the regulation of trade, was unconstitutional.[8]

The House requested the Acting Governor, John Blair, to send these protests to the Secretary of State in charge of colonial affairs for presentation to the King and the respective Houses of Parliament. It also directed the Speaker to report its proceedings to other colonial Assemblies in North America, with the suggestion that the colonies "unite in a firm but decent

Opposition to every Measure which may affect the Rights and Liberties of the British Colonies in America."[9]

New Jersey and Connecticut were the next colonies to act. On May 6, the New Jersey Assembly adopted a Petition to the King, referring to the duties recently imposed by Parliament on the colonies for revenue, declaring that one of the "Rights and Liberties vested in the People of this Colony is the Privilege of being exempt from any Taxation but such as is imposed on them by themselves or their Representatives,"[10] and, early in June, the Connecticut Assembly adopted a similar Petition to the King.[11]

Before discussing the action of the Assemblies of the other thirteen colonies on the Massachusetts circular letter, we turn to another recent development in Great Britain. This was the establishment of a third Secretary of State, a Secretary to deal exclusively with colonial affairs, and the appointment of Lord Hillsborough to the new office. Because of the very important part played by Hillsborough in colonial affairs from 1768 to 1772 and the absence of any biography of him, a sketch of his background will be given.

In December, 1767, the King and Cabinet decided to carry out a project previously considered, but dropped several times in the past, to appoint a third Secretary of State, a Secretary for the Colonies and transfer the direction of colonial affairs from the Secretary for the Southern Department to the new Secretary.[12]

Lord Shelburne, Secretary for the Southern Department, was offered the new Department,[13] but he rejected the offer, stating, "I see so many difficulties in the framing and modelling any such new office, that I cannot think of taking it upon me."[14] Whereupon the new Secretaryship was given (January 20, 1768) to Hillsborough,[15] who, soon afterward was also appointed President of the Board of Trade,[16] thus closely linking the two offices which had most to do with the details of colonial administration.[17]

Hillsborough had been in political life for many years. He had sat in the House of Commons from 1741 to 1756, and since then in the House of Lords. He was an officer of the King's household from 1754 to 1756 during the Newcastle Ministry, President of the Board of Trade from 1763 to 1765 in the Grenville Ministry, President of the Board again in the first few months of the Chatham Ministry, and thereafter joint Postmaster General until his appointment as Secretary of State.[18]

His close attention to business as President of the Board of Trade gave promise that he would faithfully apply himself to the administration of colonial affairs,[19] but what stand he would take in matters of broad colonial policy was unpredictable. Though apparently closer to Grenville than to any other outstanding political leader,[20] Hillsborough was not classified as one of his followers ("friends" in eighteenth-century political parlance)[21] and people, including Grenville himself, were much puzzled as to what his colonial policy was likely to be.[22]

In March, 1768, Hillsborough wrote General Thomas Gage denouncing the reported efforts in the colonies "to lessen the Importation of British manufactures" as showing "a malevolent & ungrateful Disposition," and in a conversation with Benjamin Franklin, he censured "the doctrines' set forth in the *Farmer's Letters* "as extremely wild etc."[23] He therefore probably approved, if he did not initiate, the following important letters signed by him as Secretary of State, dated April 21 and 22, 1768.[24]

The first, a circular letter to colonial Governors in North America, stated:

"I have his Majesty's commands to transmit to you the inclosed copy of a letter from the speaker of the House of Representatives of the colony of Massachusetts Bay, addressed by order of that House to the Speaker of the Assembly of each colony upon the continent of North America.

"As his Majesty considers this measure to be of a most dangerous & factious tendency, . . . it is his Majesty's pleasure that you should immediately upon receipt hereof exert your utmost influence to defeat this flagitious attempt to disturb the public peace by prevailing upon the Assembly of your province to take no notice of it, which will be treating it with the contempt it deserves. . . . But if, notwithstanding these expectations and your most earnest endeavours, there should appear in the Assembly of your province a disposition to receive or give any countenance to this seditious paper, it will be your duty to prevent any proceeding upon it by an immediate prorogation or dissolution."[25]

The second, a letter to Governor Francis Bernard of Massachusetts, stated:

"It gives great concern to his Majesty to find that . . . [the Massachusetts House] have presumed to . . . resolve upon a measure of so inflammatory a nature as that of writing to the other colonies on the subject of intended representations against some late acts of parliament . . . and therefore it is the King's pleasure that . . . you should require of the House of Representatives, in his Majesty's name, to rescind the resolution which gave birth to the circular letter . . . [and if] the new assembly should refuse to comply . . . it is the King's pleasure that you should immediately dissolve them. . . ."[26]

The demand for rescission, when presented by Bernard to the Massachusetts House of Representatives, was rejected June 30, 1768, by a vote of 92 to 17. In reporting this to Hillsborough, Bernard stated that those voting against rescission included "many members who were scarce ever known, upon any other occasion, to vote against the government-side of a question."[27] Of the seventeen who voted for rescission, twelve held offices under appointment by Bernard or his predecessors as Governor of the province.[28]

Bernard, of course, dissolved the House, as required by Hillsborough's letter.[29] At the next election, a large majority of those who had voted against rescission were returned to the House, but only five of the seventeen so-called Rescinders were reelected.[30] Bernard reported to Hillsborough that the threat of Massachusetts Whigs to "clear the [provincial] Council of Tories" had also been carried out.[31]

The favorable response to the Massachusetts letter by the Assemblies of Virginia, New Jersey, and Connecticut, mentioned above, had been voted before Hillsborough's letter arrived. Following the arrival of this letter the Assemblies of Maryland, Rhode Island, Pennsylvania, Delaware, New Hampshire, South Carolina, North Carolina, and Georgia spurned the letter and followed their sister colonies in adopting petitions to the King denying or questioning the right of Parliament to levy taxes for revenue of any kind on the colonies.[32]

For some weeks it appeared that the New York Assembly, which met on October 27, 1768,[33] would not fall into line.[34] But finally, in December, the Assembly adopted, without any record of dissent, a Petition to the King, a Memorial to the House of Lords, and a Representation to the House of Commons denouncing the Townshend Act as unconstitutional and urging its repeal,[35] and voted that a favorable response be made to the Massachusetts circular letter.[36]

The action of the Virginia House of Burgesses was particularly impressive. As we have seen, it had already adopted a Petition to the King protesting against the Townshend Act duties as an infringement of the constitutional rights of the colonists. But on learning of Hillsborough's circular letter, the House adopted, without a dissenting voice, resolutions reaffirming the stand taken in the Petition and asserting the right of every colony "to procure the Concurrence of his Majesty's other Colonies, in dutiful Addresses, praying the royal Interposition in Favour of the Violated Rights of America."[37]

The protests of the colonial Assemblies were fortified by a movement for non-importation agreements to put pressure on British merchants and manufacturers to work for repeal of the Townshend Act.[38]

On August 1, 1768, sixty "Merchants and Traders of the Town of Boston"[39] signed an agreement "that we will not from and after January 1, 1769, import into the province any tea, paper, glass, or painters' colours until the acts imposing duties on these articles are repealed." The agreement further provided that the signers would not import "any kind of goods or merchandize from Great Britain . . . from January 1, 1769, to January 1, 1770, except salt, coals, fish-hooks and lines, hemp, duck, barlead and shot, wool-cards and card-wire."[40]

Additional signatures were obtained the next day, and by August 10, all but sixteen of the Boston merchants, shopkeepers, and other importers of British goods were reported to have signed the agreement.[41]

The merchants of Salem, Massachusetts, next to Boston the most important commercial town of Massachusetts, followed suit on September 6.[42]

On August 27, the merchants in New York City entered into a pact somewhat similar to Boston's, but differing in several important respects.

The New York agreement applied to goods shipped from Great Britain after November 1, 1768, no matter when they arrived; called for the exemption of a somewhat different list of articles from those specified in the Boston agreement; and decreed that any subscribers violating the agreement "be deemed enemies to this country." Even more important, it provided that the ban on importation of all the goods specified in the agreement, not merely the goods (tea, etc.) taxed by the Townshend Act, should continue until that act was repealed.[43]

Furthermore, the New York agreement was fortified by an agreement of New York City "tradesmen" (in the sense of those following a trade such as carpenter, shoemaker, weaver, baker, and tailor) to boycott any "merchant, store-keeper or retailer" who refused to sign the merchants' agreement and publicize them as "an enemy to the true interest of Great Britain and her colonies."[44]

What induced the majority of the merchants of Boston, New York, and Salem to take a step that would entail so severe a sacrifice of immediate self-interest? Along with the colonists in general, they doubtless were influenced by Hillsborough's provocative circular letter and the logic of Dickinson's persuasive *Farmer's Letters*. But they in particular were the ones who suffered the direct impact of the harassing trade restrictions imposed by Parliament in the Acts of 1764 and 1766 and the measures to enforce them (described in Chapters 3 and 5 and the appendices to these chapters). The vicissitudes of Daniel Malcom, John Hancock, and Henry Laurens, described in other chapters of this book, are illustrative of what merchants all along the American seaboard had been experiencing during the past few years.

Philadelphia merchants (though urged to fall in line by a broadside written by John Dickinson, pointing out that Hillsborough's circular letter evidenced British determination to try "to enslave us"),[45] long hesitated to join the movement.[46] But at last, on February 6, 1769, they agreed to suspend further orders until March 10,[47] and when that date arrived without any favorable word from England, they signed an agreement, similar to New York's, not to import goods shipped from Great Britain after April 1, 1769, until the Townshend Act duties were repealed.[48]

After Philadelphia joined the movement, the merchants of New Haven and New London, Connecticut, and New Castle County, Delaware, came in.[49] Last of the important northern ports to join was Newport, Rhode Island, whose merchants did not agree until October 30, 1769, and even then only after heavy pressure from the merchants in other colonies and under an agreement which was not to take effect until January 1, 1770, and contained a larger number of exemptions than that of New York, Boston, and Philadelphia.[50] So far as is known, the merchants of New Hampshire and New Jersey did not adopt any agreement at all.[51]

For a few weeks there was danger of the movement's foundering, when in October, 1769, the Boston merchants, without consultation with those elsewhere, decided to maintain the boycott until all British duties for revenue on the colonies, including those imposed by acts prior to 1767,[52] were repealed. But the merchants of New York and Philadelphia refused to enlarge the scope of the boycott, and in December the Boston merchants receded.[53]

The movement in Virginia, first of the southern colonies to ently was initiated by George Washington, who in April, 1769, w friend and neighbor George Mason, enclosing a copy of the recent delphia agreement and stating, "At a time when our lordly Masters Great Britain will be satisfied with nothing less than the deprivation of American freedom, it seems highly necessary that [petitioning having failed] some thing shou'd be done to avert the stroke and maintain the liberty which we have derived from our Ancestors. . . . How far then their attention to our rights and priviledges is to be awakened or alarmed by Starving their Trade and manufactures remains to be tryed. . . . That there will be difficulties attending the execution of it every where, from clashing interests and selfish designing men, cannot be denied; but in the Tobacco Colonies where the Trade is so diffused, and in a manner wholly conducted by Factors for their principals at home, these difficulties are certainly enhanced, but I think not insurmountably increased, if the Gentlemen in their several Counties wou'd be at some pains to explain matters to the people, and stimulate them to a cordial agreement to purchase none but certain innumerated Articles out of any of the Stores . . . nor import nor purchase any themselves."[54]

Mason replied that he, too, favored a non-importation agreement,[55] and sent Washington a draft of a proposed form of agreement[56] in time for him to take it with him to Williamsburg, where he was to attend the spring session of the House of Burgesses as a representative of Fairfax County.[57] After sitting only ten days, the House was dissolved on May 17 by Governor Lord Botetourt for adopting resolutions asserting that no one but Virginia's own Legislature had the right to impose taxes on the inhabitants of the colony and denouncing as unconstitutional Parliament's recent Address to the King (discussed in Chapter 9), for sending persons in the colonies accused of treason or misprision of treason to England for trial.[58] But the members, including Washington, immediately reassembled at the Raleigh Tavern,[59] and there, on May 18, 1769, adopted a non-importation agreement, known as "the Association," effective immediately except as to goods already ordered.[60]

The agreement, initially signed by eighty-eight members of the House and later by many other subscribers,[61] was more drastic than the northern agreements in several respects. Though some goods proscribed under the northern agreements were not included in the boycott, the boycott of the proscribed goods applied whether the proscribed goods were imported from Great Britain or the European continent and it included wine, slaves, and "any manner of Goods taxed by Act of Parliament, for the Purpose of Raising a Revenue in America" no matter where they came from.[62]

Furthermore, the agreement banned not only future importation of the proscribed goods, but, after September 1, 1769, the purchase of such goods even if imported at an earlier date;[63] and pledged the subscribers (presumably to increase the supply of wool available for local manufacture)

killed any Lambs that shall be weaned before
any year . . . ; and, unless and until otherwise
subscribers held after due notice, the agreement
merely until the Townshend Act was repealed
levying duties for revenue in the colonies were

importation agreement along the general lines of
was adopted by a large group of "Merchants,
Mechanics and other Inhabitants" of Maryland
meeting at Annapolis.

Agitation for a non-importation agreement by the merchants of Charleston, South Carolina, began as early as February, 1769, but no action was taken until July 20, when a group of Charleston merchants adopted an agreement which, two days later, was approved at a mass meeting and signed by over two hundred subscribers including planters and mechanics, as well as merchants.[66] Similar in many respects to the Virginia and Maryland agreements, it went further in providing for continuance until repeal not only of the Townshend Act but of the "acts lately passed . . . [by which] we are . . . deprived of those invaluable Rights, Trial by our Peers and the Common Laws"[67]—evidently referring to the provisions in the Acts of 1764 and 1769 (discussed in Chapter 3 and the appendix to Chapter 9), providing for trial in colonial admiralty courts, sitting without jury.

In September and November, agreements along the general lines of the South Carolina agreement were adopted in Georgia and North Carolina, respectively,[68] thus establishing a boycott, nominally at least, of most imports from Great Britain in nearly all of the thirteen colonies that later rebelled.

Two other important developments in 1769 must be briefly noted.

The publication in New York in 1769 of a pamphlet urging the settlement of one or more Church of England bishops in the colonies brought to a head the fear of northern Congregationalists and Presbyterians that an Anglican episcopate was about to be established in the colonies. This fear was quieted by assurances from trusted correspondents in England that the British Ministry was giving no support to the project and there was no immediate danger of its success. But for a time it appeared that another serious colonial grievance was to be added to those already accumulated.[69]

The other was the flat refusal of the Massachusetts House of Representatives to vote funds for the supply of British troops quartered in the colony required by the colonial Quartering Act (discussed in Chapter 3 and 4).[70] Parliament did not retaliate as it had in the case of the similar action by the New York House; but the refusal of the Massachusetts House to comply with the colonial Quartering Act was another black mark against the colony contributing to the passage of the fateful Massachusetts Regulating Act of 1774 (described in Chapter 18).

CHAPTER 8

THE AMERICAN CUSTOMS BOARD
AND THE *LIBERTY* RIOT

O UTBREAKS against enforcement of the restrictions and duties on colonial trade, described in earlier chapters, began in 1765, when the Collector of Customs at Pokomoke, Maryland, was fiercely assaulted while in the execution of his office.[1] Not long afterward, a mob of some forty men at Dighton, Massachusetts, boarded the sloop *Polly*, which had been seized along with its cargo by customs officers, and carried away the cargo and all the sloop's fittings.[2] In 1766 came the brush between customs officers and Daniel Malcom at Boston (described in the second appendix to Chapter 5), and in the same month, a band of men rescued goods seized by customs officers at Newbury, Massachusetts.[3]

A few months later, the Collector and Comptroller at Falmouth, Massachusetts, were held prisoners while a mob carried away contraband which had been seized by the officers in the storehouse of Enoch Ilfley.[4]

In Charlestown, South Carolina, a whole series of bitter controversies between customs officials, including the commander of H.M.S. *Sardoine* stationed there, developed in 1766 and 1767, involving among others Henry Laurens, prominent South Carolina merchant and planter and later President of the Continental Congress.[5]

However, the most sensational and consequential of these was the *Liberty* incident at Boston in June, 1768, involving the local customs officers, the commander of the warship *Romney*, and the American Customs Board, whose headquarters was in Boston.

This Board consisted of five Commissioners—Henry Hulton, former official in the English Customs Board in London, John Temple, former Surveyor General of Customs for the Northern District of North America, William Burch, whose background is obscure, Charles Paxton, former Surveyor of Customs for the Port of Boston, and John Robinson, former Collector of Customs at Newport, Rhode Island.[6] Commissioned in September, 1767[7] pursuant to the act of 7 Geo. III ch. 41 (described in Chapter 7), the Board began to officiate two months later.[8]

The decision to seat the Board at Boston (rather than at the more centrally located New York City or Philadelphia) was said to be attributable to Paxton's influence with Charles Townshend,[9] and this report perhaps contributed to the particular animus against Paxton that appeared even before the Board began to sit.

Referring to the report that Boston was to be the Board's headquarters and Paxton a member of it, Governor Francis Bernard of Massachusetts wrote in September to Secretary of State Lord Shelburne that "the Faction [radical faction at Boston] or their underlings give out that they intend to do something when the Commissioners of Customs come; and particularly threaten Mr. Paxton who is understood to be one of them."[10]

Though Bernard's fear that Paxton and perhaps the other Commissioners might be molested did not immediately materialize, members of the Board were given notice from the very beginning that the Board was unwelcome in Boston. On the arrival of Hulton, Burch, and Paxton from England on November 5, Guy Fawkes or Pope's Day, a procession celebrating the day carried "Devils, Popes & Pretenders thro' the Streets, with Labels on their breasts, Liberty & Property and no Commissioners." Paxton was singled out for special notice by one of the devils carrying the label "Charles" affixed to his breast.[11] "Furthermore, a few months later, he "Suffered the Indignitie of being burnt in Effigie,"[12] and on the anniversary of the repeal of the Stamp Act, March 18, effigies both of him and of the Inspector-General of Customs, John Williams, were carried to the celebrated Boston Liberty Tree, where they were "exhibited on the Tree" and left "hanging a few Hours."[13]

Some weeks later, hostility to the Board as a whole was evidenced at a Boston meeting by the adoption of a resolution not to permit the use of Faneuil Hall, owned by the town, for the Governor's annual election day dinner if the Commissioners were invited[14] and by the developments described in an indignant statement of the Commissioners in May, 1768, denouncing John Hancock, a "Merchant of the largest property in this Town" and "the Idol of the Mob."[15]

"Early this winter," wrote the Commissioners, Hancock, one of Boston's representatives in the Massachusetts House,[16] had declared in the House that "he would not suffer our Officers to go even on board of any of his London Ships, and now he carries his Opposition to Government to a still higher pitch.

"Being Major of the Company of Cadets . . . and it being usual for the Governor to invite all the servants of the Crown to dine with him on the day of their [the Province's] Election . . . a Majority of his Corps met together a few days ago, and came to a Resolution to acquaint the Governor that they would not attend him on that occasion as usual if he invited the Commissioners of the Customs to dine with him, and this being signified to his Excellency, he . . . positively required their attendance. Mr. Hancock thereupon tore the Seal off his Commission, and all the rest of the Company except nine declared they would not continue longer in the Service. This infatuated man now gives out in public that if we the Commissioners are not recalled, he will get rid of us before Christmas."[17]

The Commissioners' imprudence in putting on a good deal of show in private life[18] and the arrogance or seeming arrogance of some of them doubtless contributed to their extreme unpopularity. "You can't think how we are treated by these Bashaws," exclaimed the Boston lawyer, John

Palfrey, and Governor John Wentworth of neighboring New Hampshire wrote an English friend, "You can scarcely credit the absurd, inflammatory and contumelious conduct of that new . . . Board sent hither last year. . . . All the paper imported since their arrival would not suffice to record their arrogance. . . ."[19] Similar comments were made by others,[20] including some of the officers in the customs service.[21]

But the decisive reason for the Board's extreme unpopularity almost certainly was its zeal in carrying out its duty to supervise the enforcement of British acts imposing duties on colonial imports and restrictions on colonial trade,[22] with special attention to Boston, which was under the Board's immediate surveillance. Chief Justice Thomas Hutchinson wrote from Boston in August, 1768, that the root of the Board's extreme unpopularity there was its "vigilance in carrying the acts of trade into execution[23] . . . particularly in this port where the Board is constantly held,"[24] and the denunciation of the Board in a protest prepared by a group of Boston merchants[25] and published, with a few omissions, in *Observations on Several Acts of Parliament . . . [and] on the Conduct of . . . the Board of Commissioners . . .* (Boston, 1769) boils down to a denunciation of the Board's efforts strictly to enforce these acts.[26]

In any case, the Commissioners were soon convinced that to carry out their duties effectively and to secure protection for themselves, they must have the assistance of the British naval and military forces in America.

As early as February 12, 1768, they wrote the Treasury Board in London, stating that they could not carry out their duties "untill the hand of Government is properly strengthened" and that "At present, there is not a Ship of War in the province,[27] nor a company of Soldiers nearer than New York which is two hundred and fifty miles distant from this place." On March 4, they wrote Commodore Samuel Hood at Halifax, Nova Scotia, requesting that, in view of the "conduct and temper" of the people of Boston, he send "two or more ships of war there."[28] Soon afterward, Governor Bernard wrote Secretary of State Lord Shelburne of the need for troops.[29]

Hood, stationed at Halifax, responded promptly by sending two armed schooners and the fifty-gun warship, the *Romney*,[30] which reached Boston about the middle of May.[31]

Soon after the *Romney's* arrival, her commander, Captain John Corner, began to impress merchant seamen,[32] a practice which was particularly inhumane and embittering in the colonies. As long since pointed out by Governor Trelawney of Jamaica, most colonial sailors were only part-time seamen, with "small familys and propertys at home," who were so homesick "to return to their familys and the life they were used to" that, if unable to escape, they were likely to die.[33] Furthermore, under a British act relating to impressment in the colonies, there was strong ground for the position that impressment of any persons other than deserters from the British navy was illegal there.[34]

The unrest in Boston over the Board's strict enforcement of the British acts of trade and revenue, coupled with Captain Corner's impressments, came to a head a few weeks after his arrival.

As noted in Chapter 3, the Act of 1764 levied a much heavier duty on wine imported into the colonies directly from Madeira, the Azores, and the Canary Islands than if imported by way of Great Britain. Until recently, the customs officers at Boston had tempered this act by indulging the continued import of wine directly from the wine islands.[35] Just what the "indulgence" was is not clear. But whatever it may have been,[36] it was now stopped.[37] When the Commissioners were informed that Hancock's sloop *Liberty* had imported more wine directly from Madeira than the amount entered for duty,[38] they ordered the Collector of the Port of Boston, Joseph Harrison, formally to seize the sloop as a preliminary to suit in the local admiralty court for her condemnation.[39]

After arranging with Captain Corner to send a party to his assistance if needed, Harrison, accompanied by the Comptroller of the Port, Benjamin Hallowell, carried out the Commissioners' order on the evening of June 10, by "putting the King's mark [a broad arrow] on the Main Mast" of the *Liberty*.[40] No opposition was made to this legal,[41] formal seizure,[42] but when, on a signal from Hallowell, a boat from the *Romney* was sent ashore, whose crew began to cut the *Liberty* from her moorings with the evident intention of carrying her away, hell broke loose.

The affair was vividly described in a letter written a few days later by Hutchinson to a friend in England.

"In the evening [of June 10]," wrote Hutchinson, "the Custom House Officers seized a Sloop belonging to Mr. Hancock . . . for making a false entry. . . . The Officers differed in Opinions, the Collector thinking she might lay at the wharffe after she had the broad arrow but the Comptroller thot it best to move her under the Guns of the *Romney* which lay a quarter of a mile from the Shoar and made a signal for the man of war boats to come ashoar.

"The people upon the wharffe said there was no occasion; she would ly safe and no Officer had a right to move her; but the master of the Man of War cut her moorings and carried her off. A Mob presently gathered and insulted the Custom House Officers . . . , tore their cloaths and bruised and otherwise hurt them until one after another [including Harrison's son, who also was assaulted] they escaped. The mob increased to 2 or 3,000, chiefly sturdy boys and negroes, and broke the windows of the Comptroller's house and then the Inspector Williams," and concluded its outrages by burning a boat belonging to Harrison.[43]

The indication in Hutchinson's letter that the landing party's illegal cutting of the *Liberty*'s moorings and taking her from her berth, and not her seizure by the customs officers, provoked the attack on the customs officers[44] is affirmed by numerous affidavits and eyewitnesses made soon after June 10.[45]

Fearing for their lives, the Commissioners fled to the *Romney,* from which they wrote the Customs Board in London on June 13:

"In the evening [of June 10] the Collector and Comptroller made seizure of the said vessel, and delivered her into the charge of the Master [at Arms] of his Majesty's ship *Romney,* which lay near the wharf where the seizure was made, who immediately carried her along side the said ship, as there was a mob assembled, who attempted to rescue her.

"The Collector and Comptroller, with the son of the Collector, on their return from the wharf into town were attacked by a numerous and outrageous mob; Mr. [Thomas] Irving, Inspector of imports and exports, who happened to be passing . . . was likewise attacked by the mob, who cried out, He is a Commissioner, kill him, kill him; these persons were grossly insulted and much bruised, and escaped with the utmost hazard of their lives. . . ."[46]

This report, it will be observed, was misleading, as was also a similar report by Governor Bernard,[47] in omitting one of the most important aspects of the affair—that the fury of the mob was aroused not by formal seizure of the *Liberty,* but by the high-handed and illegal[48] conduct of the party from the hated *Romney* in cutting the moorings of the *Liberty* and towing her away from her berth.

Soon after the *Liberty* incident, Captain Corner eased the tension in Boston over impressment by promising the Massachusetts Council to refrain from impressing residents of Massachusetts.[49] But subsequent proceedings for condemnation of the *Liberty* and suits against Hancock and others for heavy penalties for alleged participation in illegal importation of wine in the vessel continued to keep the *Liberty* and Hancock in the public eye for many months. (The vessel was condemned, and the suits against Hancock and others were eventually dismissed.)[50]

Furthermore, accounts of the *Liberty* riot, dispatched by the American Customs Commissioners and Bernard to officials in England led to a measure which spread extreme alarm throughout the colonies: the adoption by both Houses of Parliament of the treason resolution (described in Chapter 9).

CHAPTER 9

THE TREASON RESOLUTION: PROPOSED REVISION OF THE TOWNSHEND ACT

B Y the time the 1767–1768 session of Parliament opened in November, 1767, Lord Chatham, who had long been mentally ill,[1] though still retaining his lucrative sinecure of Lord Privy Seal, was wholly incapacitated from giving any attention to public affairs.[2] The post of First Minister passed to his follower and colleague, the Duke of Grafton, First Lord of the Treasury, who, "immature, sensitive and uncertain,"[3] was little fitted by ability, temperament, or experience for this responsibility.

Well aware of the need to strengthen the Ministry politically and in experienced personnel, Grafton, as early as July, 1767, had offered important places to followers of Lord Rockingham and of the Duke of Bedford.[4] But the negotiations for a "broad-bottom" Ministry, including followers of Bedford's temporary ally, George Grenville, failed, when Bedford refused to accept Rockingham's demands that Henry Seymour Conway be continued as Leader in the House of Commons.[5] Grafton's subsequent negotiations solely with the Rockinghams were likewise unsuccessful because Rockingham refused to enter the Ministry, even as its head, unless authorized by the King to form a wholly new Ministry.[6] Finally, in December, 1767, Bedford and Grafton struck a bargain pursuant to which two of Bedford's followers, his son-in-law, Lord Gower, and Lord Weymouth were given Cabinet office, Gower as President of the Council, in place of Lord Northington, and Weymouth as Secretary of State for the Northern Department, in place of Conway.[7]

Conway, however, remained in the Cabinet and also continued to act as Leader in the House of Commons until February, 1768, when he was succeeded as Leader by the Chancellor of the Exchequer, Frederick North[8] (usually called by his courtesy title of Lord North accorded him as eldest son of the Earl of Guilford). North had been appointed to this important office, with admission to the Cabinet, following the death of Charles Townshend in September, 1767.[9]

Another major change (described in Chapter 7) was the transfer of colonial affairs from the office of the Secretary of State for the Southern Department to a new, third Secretary, a Secretary of State for the colonies, and the appointment of Lord Hillsborough to the new office.

Parliament itself, in its 1767–1768 session during which this important change in colonial administration was made, passed only two acts affecting the colonies, a further extension of the colonial Quartering Act and a provision for several new colonial admiralty courts, discussed in an appendix to this Chapter.

In May, 1768, there was a general election for a new House of Commons, but the complexion of the House was little altered[10] and there was no immediate change in the Cabinet.

However, shortly before the opening in November, 1768, of the first session of the new Parliament, Lord Shelburne, Secretary of State for the Southern Department, who had long been at loggerheads with most of the Cabinet ministers,[11] resigned.[12] He was replaced by Lord Rochford, a career diplomat, apparently not attached to any political group.[13] Chatham, too, now resigned his office of Lord Privy Seal[14] and was replaced by one of his followers, Lord Bristol, who, however, was not admitted to the Cabinet.[15]

Thus, when the new Parliament assembled in November, 1768, the Cabinet consisted of five Chathamites—Grafton, Conway, Lord Camden, Lord Granby, and Sir Edward Hawke; two Bedfordites—Gower and Weymouth; and Hillsborough, North, and Rochford, not closely identified with any political party.[16]

The King's speech at the opening of the 1768–1769 session of Parliament and the replies of both Houses implied that Massachusetts was to be dealt with sternly,[17] and, after the holiday recess, resolutions were introduced in the House of Lords denouncing the conduct of Boston and Massachusetts.[18] Moreover, Bedford successfully moved in the Lords for an address to the King asking him to secure information as to treason or misprision (concealment) of treason in Massachusetts, with a view to bringing the chief offenders to trial in England—under an old act of Henry VIII, providing for punishment of these crimes committed outside, as well as within, the realm.[19]

The House of Commons, led by North,[20] concurred[21] and the King replied that he would take the requested action.[22] This was done by a letter of February 20, 1769, from Hillsborough to Governor Francis Bernard of Massachusetts directing him to procure and transmit "the fullest information that can be obtained, touching all treasons and misprision of treason committed within your Government since the 30th day of December 1767."[23]

Furthermore, at a Cabinet meeting on February 13, Hillsborough proposed an act of Parliament to deprive Massachusetts immediately of its charter right to an elective Council and to provide that "the passing or entering upon the Journal of the House of Representatives of said Province, any Note, Resolution or Order, by which the Power and Authority of Parliament to make Laws and Statutes of sufficient Force and Validity to bind the said Province in all Cases Whatsoever, are denied or drawn into question, shall be ipso facto an avoidance and forfeiture of the Charter granted for the government of said Province."[24] But when Camden and Conway opposed these proposals[25] and were supported by the King,[26] the proposals were dropped.[27]

In April, Thomas Pownall, former Governor of Massachusetts and now a member of the House of Commons, moved that the House consider the repeal of the Townshend Act duties. Spokesmen for the Ministry opposed the motion, but they indicated they might favor consideration of repeal at the next session of Parliament, and Conway even went so far as to propose that the House commit itself to consider this at its next session.[28]

Futhermore, at a meeting on May 1, 1769, attended by all the members of the Cabinet except Hawke, the following resolution was adopted:

"It is the unanimous opinion of the lords present to submit to His Majesty as their advice that no measure should be taken which can any way derogate from the legislative authority of Great Britain over the colonies. But that the Secretary of State [Hillsborough] in his correspondence and conversation be permitted to state it as the opinion of the king's servants that it is by no means the intention of Administration nor do they think it expedient or for the interest of Great Britain or America to propose or consent to the laying any further taxes upon America for the purpose of raising a revenue, and that it is at present their intention to propose in the next session of Parliament to take off the duties upon paper, glass and colours imported into America, upon consideration of such duties having been laid contrary to the true principles of commerce."[29]

In an autobiography written many years later, Grafton stated that he himself, Camden, Granby, and Conway voted in favor of total repeal of the Townshend Act duties, but were outvoted by other members of the Cabinet—North, Gower, Weymouth, Rochford, and Hillsborough.[30]

No contemporary evidence has come to light clearly supporting this statement;[31] but remarks by Grafton and Weymouth in debate in the House of Lords in 1776 support its credibility. Grafton said "In 1769 . . . I moved in the Cabinet for a repeal, and was out-voted (if I recollect right) by a majority of one." Weymouth replied, "The noble Duke is very right; I was present, and am free to declare that I was one of the members of the Cabinet who gave my vote for having the tea duty retained, and am not ashamed to own it. . . ."[32]

The administration let the colonists know of the Cabinet's decision quoted above by spreading word of it among merchants in London,[33] who were worried over the loss of trade from the colonial non-importation agreements, and by a circular letter from Hillsborough to colonial Governors.

Hillsborough wrote, "the whole legislature concur in the opinion . . . that no measure ought to be taken which can any way derogate from the legislative authority of Great Britain over the colonies, . . . [but] I can take it upon me to assure you, notwithstanding intimations to the contrary from men with factious and seditious views, that His Majesty's present Administration have at no time entertained a design to propose to Parliament to lay any further taxes upon America for the purpose of raising a revenue, and that it is at present their intention to propose in the next session of Parliament: to take off the duties upon glass, paper and colours upon consideration of such duties having been laid contrary to the true principles of commerce."[34]

The Cabinet presumably hoped that the announcement of its intention to support revision of the Townshend Act would allay the colonial antagonism manifested by the spirited legislative protests against the act, the non-importation agreements, and the *Liberty* incident at Boston. But if so, it failed to take into account the foreseeable colonial reaction to the report of the resolution in Parliament proposing that Bostonians accused of treason be shipped to England to be tried for treason and the evident intention to retain the duty for revenue on tea.

On May 9, 1769, the Virginia House of Burgesses passed resolutions declaring that "the seizing any Person or Persons, residing in this Colony, suspect of any Crime whatsoever, committed therein, and sending such Person or Persons, to Places beyond the Sea, to be tried, is highly derogatory of the Rights of British subjects; as thereby the inestimable Privilege of being tried by a Jury from the Vicinage, as well as the Liberty of summoning and producing Witnesses on such Trial, will be taken away from the Party accused."[35] The House also passed a resolution again denying the right of Parliament to tax the people of Virginia, and directed its Speaker to send a copy of both resolutions to Speakers of the other Assemblies in British North America requesting their concurrence.[36]

By the end of the year similar protests were passed by the Assemblies of all thirteen colonies[37] except New Hampshire, Pennsylvania, and Georgia.[38] Those of the Massachusetts Houses were especially vigorous. They included protests not only against British taxation of the colonists and the threatened sending of colonists to England for trial, but against "the establishment of a standing army in the colony in time of peace, without the consent of the General Assembly of the same. . . ."[39]

In the event, no one was arrested in Massachusetts to be sent to England for trial.[40] But the fact that Parliament proposed to have the government apply the ancient treason act of Henry VIII to the colonies was alarming enough. Furthermore, since Hillsborough's circular letter said nothing about repeal of the Townshend Act duty on tea, the letter implied that the Ministry was determined to maintain Parliament's claim of authority to tax the colonies by retaining this duty. Consequently, the colonial non-importation agreements were retained.

CHAPTER 10

REVISION OF THE TOWNSHEND ACT AND DILUTION OF NON-IMPORTATION

WHEN Parliament reconvened in January, 1770, the Ministry, still headed by the Duke of Grafton, faced the combined opposition of the Rockingham group and of Lord Chatham (sufficiently recovered in health to resume political activities) and his small group of followers.

The chief point on which the two groups were united was condemnation of the recent action by the House of Commons, influenced by the King,[1] in refusing John Wilkes a seat in the House for Middlesex County, to which he had been elected by a great majority, and seating his leading opponent, Colonel Henry Luttrell.[2]

But the Ministry's colonial policy was evidently under fire, too, as indicated by the language of motions in both Houses of Parliament for amendment of a proposed address of thanks to the King for his speech at the opening of Parliament. On January 9, 1770, Chatham moved in the Lords that the address be amended to call for inquiry into the causes of discontent "in so many parts of Your Majesty's dominions," obviously referring to discontent in the colonies, as well as in England. William Dowdeswell (Chancellor of the Exchequer in the Rockingham Ministry) made a similar motion in the Commons.[3]

The motions were defeated in both Houses, in the Lords by 203 to 35, in the Commons by 254 to 138.[4] Thereupon Lord Chancellor Camden, who supported Chatham in the Lords, was dismissed,[5] and Lord Granby, Master General of the Ordnance, who supported Dowdeswell in the Commons, resigned.[6] Soon afterward, Grafton, pilloried unmercifully in the London *Public Advertiser* by the brilliant "Junius"[7] and bereft of two of the three remaining Cabinet ministers who had served with him under Chatham, also resigned.[8]

The office of Master General of the Ordnance was left vacant, the office of Lord Chancellor was put into commission, and, on January 28, 1769, Grafton was succeeded as head of the Treasury and First Minister by the Chancellor of the Exchequer and Leader of the House of Commons, Lord North.[9]

The new First Minister had long been in public life. He had sat in the House of Commons for fifteen years as a member for the borough of Banbury controlled by his father, Lord Guilford. Appointed a member of the Treasury Board in 1759 during the Newcastle–Pitt Ministry, he had continued in this office throughout the Bute and Grenville Ministries. He followed Grenville into retirement in 1765; but, on formation of the

Chatham Ministry, at Chatham's particular request, was appo[...] lucrative office of joint Paymaster-General of the Army, which [...] until appointed Chancellor of the Exchequer in November, 1767.[10]

Writing of North's appointment to the latter office, William Samuel Johnson, the able and well-informed London Agent for Connecticut, said, "Lord North . . . is esteemed a man of good abilities . . . [and] it is said he understands the business of the finances very well. . . . He did not speak very often in the House [the last session] but when he did, he was well heard, and has a dignity in his manner that gives weight to his sentiments, which were generally sensible, cool and temperate."[11] Johnson made no comment on North's attitude toward the colonies, but the fact that he had voted against repeal of the Stamp Act[12] would tend to identify him with those favoring inflexible support of Parliament's asserted authority to tax the colonies.

Soon after becoming head of the Ministry, North informed Johnson, still in London as Agent for Connecticut, that the Ministry planned to carry out the commitment made in 1769 for revision of the Townshend Act.[13] This assurance was carried out in large measure when, on March 5 (after presenting to the House of Commons a "Petition of the Merchants and Traders of the City of London trading to North America" begging for some relief from the injury to their trade attributable to that act),[14] North moved for leave to bring in a bill to repeal the duties on paper, glass, and paint manufactured in Great Britain.[15]

In introducing his motion for partial repeal, North said he favored repeal of the duties on British-made glass, paper, and paint because the duties ran counter to the long-established policy of encouraging the exportation of British manufactures;[16] but that the other duties could not be repealed "without giving up that just right which I shall ever wish the mother country to possess, the right of taxing the Americans."[17] Moreover, yielding on the point of taxation, far from satisfying the colonists would, North declared, simply encourage them to demand the repeal of other British acts which they disliked.[18]

North was challenged by Thomas Pownall, former Governor of Massachusetts,[19] who moved for complete repeal on the ground that the duty on tea, by encouraging the smuggling of Dutch tea into the colonies, occasioned heavy losses to the British East India Company. The Company itself, so far as is known, gave Pownall no support;[20] but he was supported by Conway and Colonel Isaac Barré, not only on commercial grounds, but because total repeal would, they pointed out, be the most decisive way of convincing the colonists that Parliament did not mean to tax them for purposes of revenue.

Welbore Ellis, who had been in the Grenville Ministry, opposed both North and Conway on the ground that all the Townshend Act duties, whether commercially sound or not, should be retained lest even partial repeal be considered as yielding to colonial threats. Lord Barrington[21]

Importation

ined to the
he held

71

a whole in the colonies that had submitted
ange in the colonies that had not.[22]

ed amendment was finally brought to a vote,
42; and North's original motion was adopted,
vision.[23] A bill along the lines of this motion was
of Commons on April 6.[24] The bill was passed by
a few days later, without a division, and on April 12,
proved by the King.[25]

t of news of the partial repeal of the Townshend Act,
a c.. ew York merchants took action to secure revision of the
non-imp agreements. They sent a circular letter dated June 2,
1770, to merchants in Boston, Philadelphia, Connecticut, and Rhode
Island, proposing a consultation as to the advisability of relaxing the
existing non-importation agreements to cover only such articles as were
subject to colonial import duties imposed by Parliament.[26] On rejection
of this proposal,[27] they voted, July 10,[28] immediately to modify their own
agreement (whatever others might do) along the line suggested in their
circular letter.[29]

There was a great outcry in the other colonies against the New Yorkers'
desertion of the common cause.[30] But, as shown in the appendix to this
chapter, the New York merchants had much justification for their action
in that they had more faithfully observed their agreement than the
associators elsewhere, and hence had suffered more severely in trade than
the others, a justification which they naturally were quick to point out.[31]

With so important a competitive port as New York open to importation
from Great Britain of all except duties articles, the merchants of Philadelphia and Boston probably would have followed suit under any circumstances. But there was another important factor in the breakdown of
the non-importation agreements: the unfairness in operation of each
agreement among the signatory merchants of the particular port to which
it applied.

There was much specialization among colonial merchants; one might
engage chiefly in trade with Great Britain, another with Ireland, another
with the West Indies, and still another in illegal trade with the continental
countries, particularly in smuggling tea and other goods from Holland.
In the short run, if the agreement was faithfully kept, an importer
ordinarily engaged chiefly in importing British goods might not find the
agreement onerous, since the general drying up of the supply of new
goods would give him the opportunity profitably to unload out-of-style or
shopworn goods which he must otherwise have sold at a loss. But in the
long run he would be hit hard by the agreement; whereas those engaged
chiefly in smuggling or in legal trade with Ireland or the West Indies
would be comparatively little affected.

The merchants of Philadelphia on September 20, and those of Boston on
October 12, voted to revise their agreements to harmonize with the modi-

fied New York agreement.[32] On October 25, the merchants of Baltimore announced that they, too, would henceforth limit their boycott to dutied articles from Great Britain,[33] and, two months later, the merchants of South Carolina took similar action.[34]

There is no evidence of any formal termination of the agreements in North Carolina and Georgia, probably because the agreements there had been so little observed[35] that formal termination was regarded as superfluous. The Virginians did not formally modify their agreement until July, 1771,[36] but efforts made in June, 1770, to tighten its enforcement had signally failed.[37]

The poor observance of the non-importation agreement in some of the colonies[38] and the virtual collapse of the movement gravely weakened the most important source of colonial influence on the British government and Parliament: the fear among the politically powerful merchants and manufacturers of Great Britain that if the British government seriously antagonized America, they might lose the colonial market for their wares.

Furthermore, the virtual failure of the movement tended to discourage all British sympathizers with the colonies and encourage their opponents. William Temple, for example, wrote in 1771 that the recent "pusilanimity & mean acquiescence [of the colonists] . . . has in some measure sacrificed every friend they had here . . . , and from such experience I believe it will be with some caution that any person of rank or consequence will ever again step forth in their cause. . . ."[39] And three years later, Ralph Izard of South Carolina, writing from England to a friend at home, remarked on the "wonderful confidence" that the collapse of the colonial non-importation movement of 1768–1770 had since given to those in Great Britain favoring stern measures against the colonies.[40]

One of the most interesting aspects of the colonial non-importation movement is evidence of the part played by skilled manual workmen, called variously tradesmen, mechanics, craftsmen, artisans, artificers, and manufacturers,[41] in connection with the non-importation agreements in New York, Charleston, Philadelphia, and Boston.

As brought out in Chapter 7, immediately after adoption of the New York City merchants' non-importation agreement in August, 1768, New York City "tradesmen" agreed to boycott and publicize any "merchant, storekeeper or retailer" who refused to sign the merchants' non-importation agreement.

In Charleston, the tradesmen (referred to there as "mechanics") took an active part in the adoption and provision for enforcement of the local non-importation agreement.[42]

In Boston, when the local non-importation agreement was tottering in September, 1770, "the most respectable Tradesmen of the Town" were among those attending a meeting[43] which voted in favor of an intercolonial congress of merchants to devise means for continuing and strengthening non-importation.

In Philadelphia, when it became known in May, 1770, that some of the local merchants proposed to relax their non-importation agreement, a mass meeting of "the artisans, manufacturers, tradesmen and others" voted to sustain the local non-importation agreement "by all prudential ways and means." And the subsequent decision of the local merchants on June 5 not to relax their agreement was said to have been effected by intrusion into the meeting of a "body of disaffected Mechanics."[44]

In considering the clash between merchants and tradesmen over continuation of the non-importation agreement, it must be borne in mind that, as soon as colonial merchants engaged chiefly in the importation and sale of goods from Great Britain sold their existing stock, they were hard hit by stoppage of new supplies. Whereas colonial tradesmen—shoemakers ("cordwainers"), tailors, hatters, potters, weavers, cabinet makers, iron-workers, braziers, ropemakers, soap boilers, coachmakers, etc.—who made things competing with British imports from material available in the colonies,[45] stood to benefit from prolonging the non-importation agreements; the agreements operated as a kind of prohibitively high protective tariff in their favor.

Though immediately successful, the Ministry's plan was, in the long run, calamitous, and forseeably so. For retention of the duty on tea, avowedly as a symbol of Parliament's continuing assertion of the right to tax the colonists as it pleased, was almost certain, sooner or later, to result in a collision between the British government and the colonies.

CHAPTER 11

BRITISH TROOPS AT BOSTON
AND THE "BOSTON MASSACRE"

AS brought out in Chapter 8, as early as February and March, 1768, the American Customs Board and Governor Bernard of Massachusetts had suggested sending British troops to Boston. But orders for this were not given until June 8, 1768, when Lord Hillsborough instructed General Thomas Gage, Commander in Chief of the British army in North America, to dispatch "such Force as You shall think necessary to Boston, to be Quartered in that Town, and to give every legal assistance to the Civil Magistrate in the Preservation of the Public Peace; and to the Officers of the Revenue."[1]

On receipt of this order, which was long in arriving, Gage ordered two regiments to be sent to Boston from the British garrison at Halifax, Nova Scotia,[2] and on September 8, Governor Bernard let it be known in Boston that troops were on their way.[3]

There was immediate talk by local radicals of preventing the troops from landing,[4] and those attending a Boston town meeting on September 13 seemed prepared to back them up. The "Inhabitants of the Town of Boston," it was resolved, "will at the utmost peril of their Lives and Fortunes take all legal and constitutional measures to defend . . . all and singular the rights . . . belonging to us as British subjects," and, "as by a good and wholesome Law of this Province, every listed Soldier and other House-holder . . . shall always be provided with a well fixed Fire Lock, Musket, Accoutrement and Ammunition . . . and as there is at this Time a prevailing apprehension in the minds of many, of an approaching War with France, . . . those of the said Inhabitants who may at present be unprovided be and hereby are requested fully to observe the said Law at this Time."[5] (The reference to preparation for fighting the French was, of course, a subterfuge, as was made clear by the moderator of the meeting, James Otis, who, when asked "to be more explicit," pointed to a large chest of arms stored in the town hall where the meeting was held and said, "There are the arms; when an attempt is made against your liberties, they will be delivered.")[6] The keeping of a standing army in the colony without the consent of the people also was denounced as unconstitutional.[7]

At this meeting, the town elected a committee consisting of its members in the Massachusetts House of Representatives to meet with similar committees from other towns in the province and directed its selectmen to write those of the other towns enclosing copies of the proceedings at Boston and proposing a general convention to be held at Faneuil Hall on

September 22.[8] But if Boston radical leaders hoped to secure province-wide support for resistance to the landing of the expected British troops, they must have been sorely disappointed. For, while there was a good turnout in response to the Boston invitation (nearly a hundred towns, or about two-thirds of the total in the province were represented),[9] the convention, which sat for just a week, was very moderate in its resolves.[10]

It did, to be sure, complain of "the late acts of Parliament for an American revenue" and the introduction of a "standing army . . . among the people, contrary, as we apprehend, to the Bill of Rights," but a majority of those present were evidently more eager to record their specific intentions than to encourage armed resistance. Disclaiming "all pretence to any authoritative or governmental acts," they declared, as individual citizens, that they wished "no irregular steps" to be taken by the people; that "the gracious attention of his sacred Majesty to the cause and grounds of our complaints, is the only regular source of relief from our present distresses," and that "We think ourselves happy in being connected with the parent state in that subordination which forms the happiest bond of union between the colonies themselves."[11]

On October 1, 1768, three days after the convention was disbanded, the British troops from Halifax, drawn chiefly from the Fourteenth and Twenty-ninth Infantry Regiments and numbering about seven hundred men,[12] landed at Boston without opposition.[13] Six weeks later the Sixty-fourth and Sixty-fifth Regiments, of about five hundred men each, began to arrive from Ireland,[14] and remained at Boston until transferred to Halifax the following July.[15]

Reassured by the presence of the troops sent for their protection, the Commissioners of Customs, who, as we saw in Chapter 8, fled after the Boston riot of June, 1768, now returned to town.[16]

Even before the first soldiers arrived, Governor Bernard and the Massachusetts provincial Council quarreled over the latter's refusal to prepare quarters for the troops in Boston on the ground that adequate barracks were already available for them at Castle William[17] near the mouth of Boston harbor.[18] There was also a clash later between Bernard and the Massachusetts House of Representatives over his request for funds to cover the cost of supplies for the troops required by the British Quartering Act (described in Chapter 3). Flatly refusing to vote the required funds, the House denounced this and all other British acts taxing the colonies as "acts for raising a tribute in America, for . . . disposition among placemen and pensioners" reminiscent of the period when imperial Rome, having drawn to itself "all the treasures of the East, . . . fell a sacrifice to the unbounded corruption and venality of its grandees."[19]

According to a series of articles concerning events in Boston, published in the *New-York Journal* from October 13, 1768, to November 30, 1769, clashes between the troops and civilians began within a few weeks of the arrival of the British troops in Boston.[20] But the reports of these clashes before the one in July, 1769, apparently were either concocted or greatly exaggerated.[21] The only serious incident during this period involved the British warship *Rose* cruising near Boston, one of whose officers was killed in April, 1769, by a merchant seaman, Michael Corbet, in resisting impressment.[22] (This incident and Corbet's ensuing trial at Boston by a special court consisting exclusively of Crown officers is described in the first appendix to this chapter.)

The earliest well-authenticated incident of a serious nature between British troops and civilians in or near Boston occurred in July, 1769.

On July 19, John Riley, a grenadier in the Fourteenth Regiment, taunted by a butcher, Jonathan Winship, knocked him down.[23] Winship complained to Riley's commanding officer, Col. William Dalrymple, but the latter, far from reprimanding Riley, said he was glad that Riley had taught Winship a lesson.[24] Furthermore, when haled before a justice of the peace and fined for his assault on Winship, Riley refused to pay the fine and slashed and wounded a constable who tried to arrest him.[25]

In September, there was a further ugly incident, this time between James Otis and John Robinson, of the American Customs Commission, in which some British officers also were involved.[26]

In October, another serious clash took place between soldiers and civilians, stemming from the alleged trespass by the British military in building a guard house and stationing a guard of British soldiers on land on Boston Neck leased by the town of Boston to Robert Pierpont.[27] On October 24, Pierpont and a crowd of supporters attacked with bricks, stones, and sticks a detachment of soldiers under Ensign (Second Lieutenant) John Ness while they were marching back from the guard house to their barracks. In the course of this attack two of the soldiers were injured.[28]

Quarrels continued between Boston civilians and British soldiers during the fall and winter of 1769–1770;[29] but no other serious incident disturbed the peace of the town until late in February, 1770, when Boston was set ablaze by the killing of a twelve- or thirteen-year-old boy, Christopher Snider (or Seider), under the following circumstances.

At a meeting of the so-called "body" of merchants on December 4, 1769, a majority voted to change the local non-importation agreement (described in Chapter 7), which banned the importation of articles subject to duty under the Townshend Act until that act was repealed, but of other articles only until the end of 1769. The new agreement continued the ban on these articles, too, until the Townshend Act was repealed.[30]

Despite heavy pressure,[31] eight local merchants or mercantile firms refused to sign the new agreement,[32] and, on January 23, 1770, in the teeth of orders from Acting Governor Thomas Hutchinson to disperse,[33] the body of merchants took drastic action against the holdouts. They published a broadside, naming and denouncing the latter as traitors.[34]

Among these was Theophilus Lillie, who not only was one of the earlier Boston holdouts, referred to in Chapter 10, but had recently made himself particularly conspicuous by publishing a letter complaining of those who in the name of liberty were trying to deprive him and others of their liberty to do business as they pleased.[35]

On February 22, a crowd of boys made sport of Lillie by planting a large sign in front of his store, displaying caricatures of him and other holdouts and a hand pointing to his store.[36] A neighbor, Ebenezer Richardson, who, as a notorious customs informer,[37] was as unpopular as Lillie himself, tried to tear down the sign. The boys thereupon turned their attention to him; they chased him to his house and threw rocks through the windows, some of which hit Richardson, his wife, and one of his daughters. They were soon joined by several men, including one who came to the door, shouting "Come out you damn Son of Bitch, I'll have your Heart out. . . ." At this point, Richardson fired a charge of bird shot into the crowd, fatally wounding young Snider and injuring another boy, John Gore.[38]

Richardson was dragged before a justice of the peace, committed to jail, and, on Snider's death eight hours later, was held on a charge of murder.[39]

The anti-British feeling aroused by young Snider's death rose to fever pitch on the day of the boy's funeral. "My Eyes never beheld such a funeral," wrote John Adams in his diary for February 26. "A vast Number of Boys walked before the Coffin, a vast Number of Women and Men after it . . . This Shewes there are many more Lives to spend if wanted in the Service of their Country . . . , that the Ardor of the People is not to be quelled by the Slaughter of one Child and the Wounding of another."[40]

The British troops in Boston had no part in the killing of Snider, but the friction between them and the citizens of Boston over the past year made them a natural target for the outburst of anti-British feeling over the boy's death and funeral.

Also, here again, as we find repeatedly in the progress of the Revolution, the proceedings in one colony influenced those of another.

On February 19, the *Boston Gazette* and the *Boston Evening-Post* published accounts drawn from New York newspapers of recent clashes between civilians and British soldiers in New York City, which (quoting John Adams once more) had "excited the resentment of the soldiers here as well as exultation among some sorts of the inhabitants."[41]

Apparently inspired by the accounts from New York, a workman at John Gray's rope-walk, called out to a passing British soldier on March 2, "Soldier, will you work." "Yes," said the soldier. "Then go and clean my shit house," replied the workman. Swearing by the Holy Ghost that he would be revenged for this insult, the soldier returned first with eight or nine, later with thirty or more, soldiers armed with clubs and cutlasses and headed by a tall negro drummer. Workmen at the rope-walk, wielding the formidable tools of their trade known as wouldring sticks, succeeded in driving the soldiers away.[42] But it was rumored that the soldiers would seek revenge the following Monday night, March 5,[43] and there were in fact several clashes between soldiers and civilians that moon-lit night before the affair known to history as the Boston Massacre took place.[44]

The testimony concerning this tragedy is conflicting, but the following account is supported by what seems to be the weight of evidence.

Hugh White, a soldier of the Twenty-ninth Regiment, stationed as a sentry before the Customs House, provoked by Edward Garrick or Gerrish, a young barber's apprentice, struck him with his gun.[45] Soon afterward the boy returned with a sizable crowd, chiefly boys and youths, and, pointing at White, said, "There is the son of a bitch that knocked me down."[46] Whereupon some of the crowd shouted "Kill him, kill him, knock him down," and pelted White with snowballs, ice, and other missiles.[47]

Learning of the sentry's predicament, Captain Thomas Preston of the Twenty-ninth, officer of the day at the so-called "Main Guard" stationed near the Customs House, marched with a party of six privates and a corporal,[48] with guns unloaded but with fixed bayonets,[49] to White's relief. A large crowd, led by Crispus Attucks, "a mulatto fellow,"[50] soon gathered and pelted Preston and his men with snowballs, pieces of ice, oyster shells, and sticks.[51] The men loaded their guns,[52] but the crowd, far from drawing back, came close, calling out, "Come on you rascals, you bloody backs, you lobster scoundrels, fire if you dare, G——d damn you, fire and be damned, we know you dare not," and striking at the soldiers with clubs and a cutlass.[53] Whereupon they fired—whether with or without orders from Preston is not clear.[54] Attucks, Samuel Gray, and James Caldwell were killed on the spot; Samuel Maverick, a youth of seventeen, and Patrick Carr died of wounds soon afterward; and six others were wounded but survived.[55]

Preston, the soldiers, and four men in the Customs House alleged to have fired shots from it were promptly arrested, indicted for murder, and held in prison pending trial for murder in the Massachusetts Superior Court,[56] which prudently postponed trial until fall, thus giving the people of Boston and vicinity from whom the jury would be drawn, time to cool off.[57]

Three witnesses had signed affidavits soon after the "Massacre" that they heard Preston order his men to fire,[58] and, on March 30, Acting Governor Thomas Hutchinson wrote Governor Francis Bernard, "I am afraid poor Preston has but little chance. Mr. Auch [Robert Auchmuty] who is his Counsel tells me the evidence is very strong that the firing upon the Inhabitants was by his order. . . ."[59]

Auchmuty was joined by John Adams and Josiah Quincy, Jr., as counsel for Preston. Adams and Quincy, but not Auchmuty, also represented the soldiers.[60] Samuel Quincy and Robert Treat Paine were the prosecuting attorneys.[61]

Under the common law rules of evidence then prevailing in Massachusetts, as well as in England, a person accused of a felony could not testify as a witness in a prosecution for the crime, but had the right to question witnesses at his trial.[62] It was, therefore, of great concern to the accused soldiers to be tried at the same time as Preston, since they would thus have the opportunity to confront witnesses whom the latter might call to testify that he had not ordered the men to fire.[63] Doubtless this was what three of the soldiers had in mind in petitioning the trial court to "have our Trial at the same time with our Captain, for we did our Captains Orders and . . . it is very hard, he being a Gentleman should have more chance to save his life than we poor men that is Obliged to Obay his command."[64]

However, presumably at Preston's request, the court ordered that he be tried separately, and his trial, which lasted from October 24 to October 30, 1770, preceded that of the men.[65]

The jury brought in a verdict of "Not Guilty," without qualification, thereby acquitting him not only of murder, but of the lesser crime of manslaughter.[66]

The superiority of Preston's lawyers (of whom he wrote soon after the trial, "The Counsel for the Crown, or rather the town were but poor and managed badly; my Counsel on the contrary were men of parts, & exerted themselves with great spirit and cleverness, particularly Judge Auchmuty")[67] and his reputation as an exceptionally discreet and humane officer[68] doubtless weighed in his favor. But more important, the evidence, on the whole, called for a favorable verdict. The testimony clearly showed that Preston had come to the Customs House on a legal mission, and had not fired any of the fatal shots. On the question of whether he had ordered the men to fire, the testimony was conflicting. Some witnesses testified that he gave the order, others of no less apparent credibility testified he had not.[69]

The trial of the eight soldiers took place November 27 to December 5, with the same counsel on both sides as in Preston's trial, except that Sampson S. Blowers instead of Auchmuty joined Adams and Josiah Quincy as lawyers for the defense.[70] The voluminous testimony of over fifty witnesses[71] was well and fully summarized in the charges to the jury by Justice Edmund Trowbridge and Peter Oliver. It showed that the soldiers had assembled at the Customs House legally, from which it followed that the illegal act of one could not be held against the group as a whole. Only two of the soldiers, Hugh Montgomery and Matthew Killroy, could be identified as having fired shots resulting in death;[72] and it was clear that even they had fired only under great provocation.[73]

The charges to the jury by the trial judges pointed to verdicts that none of the accused was guilty of murder and that Montgomery and Killroy, because of the provocation under which they fired, were, if guilty at all, guilty at most of manslaughter.[74] The jury brought in unqualified verdicts of "Not guilty" in favor of all the accused except Montgomery and Killroy and "Not guilty of murder but guilty of manslaughter" in the cases of these two.[75] Pleading benefit of clergy, they escaped with burning on the hand.[76]

The evidence against the men in the Customs House accused of participation in the "Massacre" apparently was so weak that on December 12 the jury acquitted all four "without going from their seats."[77]

Samuel Adams (who, after James Otis, Jr., suffered a mental breakdown, [78] had become the unrivaled leader of the Boston radicals) tried to whip up popular resentment over the acquittals by a series of articles in the *Boston Gazette* from mid-December, 1770, through January, 1771.[79] But he was unsuccessful; the letters and diary entries of many observers record that the town remained remarkably quiet.[80] Even the harried Customs Commissioners, who, following the Boston Massacre had again fled to Castle William,[81] ventured to return to Boston. (They remained until the commotion in Boston over the Tea Act of 1773, described in Chapter 13, sent them scurrying for a third time to the shelter of the Castle.)[82]

The calm with which the outcome of the trials was accepted doubtless was attributable in large measure to the evidence at the trials that the soldiers had not fired until they were attacked. But another important factor was the withdrawal of the troops from Boston immediately after the "Massacre." On the following day, a committee of leading Bostonians[83] prevailed upon the provincial Council and Acting Governor Hutchinson to pray Colonel William Dalrymple, commander of the British troops at Boston,[84] to remove all of them to Castle William.[85] Dalrymple acceded to this request,[86] and, a few weeks later, the tension in Boston was further reduced by sending the Twenty-ninth Regiment to New Jersey, thus leaving only the Fourteenth, which had not been directly involved in the "Massacre," even in the vicinity of Boston.[87]

The sending of British warships and troops to Boston for the protection of the American Customs Board and the "Massacre" resulting from the presence of the troops there were, however, ultimately of great significance in the movement toward revolution.

Year after year from 1771 to 1775, the day of the "Massacre" was memorialized in public orations[88] by such notables as Dr. Joseph Warren[89] and John Hancock, who, expanding on the horror of the "unprovoked murders" of March 5,[90] helped keep alive the spirit of opposition to British encroachments on colonial home rule. The dead of that day were made a symbol of alleged British ruthlessness as the death of Edith Cavell was to become a symbol of alleged German "Schrecklichkeit" in World War I.

Perhaps even more significant was the unfavorable effect of the "Massacre" on public opinion in Great Britain. The assault on the British sentries at the Customs House leading to the "Massacre" contributed to the ill repute of Boston as the hotbed of colonial insubordination, and thus helped lay the foundation for the fateful Boston Port Act and Massachusetts Regulating Acts of 1774 (described in later chapters).

CHAPTER 12

HE *GASPEE* AFFAIR AND THE
DGES' SALARY CONTROVERSY

FOR more than two years following 1770, there was an easing of the controversy over the principal issue between Great Britain and the colonies—taxation. The revised non-importation agreements continuing the boycott on tea and other dutied imports from Great Britain were apparently observed only in so far as they applied to tea, and even as to it only if smuggling from Holland or other non-British sources of supply was more lucrative than legal importation.[1]

There was a long-drawn controversy between the Massachusetts Legislature (general court) and the Crown-appointed Governor of the colony over the latter's removal of the meetings of the Legislature from Boston to Cambridge.[2] There was another between the Crown-appointed Governor and Council of South Carolina and the provincial Assembly over the latter's dubious claim of right to appropriate public funds without the concurrence of the Governor and Council.[3] But these both were localized.

The same was true of an insurrection, the Regulator Insurrection, in North Carolina[4] and a controversy over fees in Maryland,[5] both of which, moreover, only remotely involved the British government.

There also were clashes during this period[6] (as before)[7] between colonial merchants and customs officers, including commanders of British warships acting as an arm of the British customs service. But, though these clashes arose from a common source, enforcement of British restrictions and duties on colonial trade, they led to no united opposition until the latter part of 1772. Steps then taken by the British government to send persons involved in the burning of one of the ships, the *Gaspee,* from Rhode Island to England for trial again united the colonies in common indignation and alarm.

In the years before 1770, Rhode Island had been the scene of several clashes involving British men of war,[8] and, soon after his arrival in February, 1772, Lieutenant William Dudingston, commander of the *Gaspee,*[9] began to lay the foundation for another.[10] He illegally sent to Boston rum seized by him in Rhode Island[11] and stopped and searched with "intemperate, if not reprehensible zeal to aid the customs service" (as the Royal Commission of Inquiry, described later in this chapter, put it)[12] vessel after vessel in Narragansett Bay, a nearly landlocked bay extending from Newport many miles into the very heart of Rhode Island.[13] He also evaded letters from Governor Joseph Wanton of Rhode Island requiring him to produce a commission authorizing him to act as a customs officer.[14]

Dudingston sent Wanton's letters to Admiral John Montagu,[15] commanding the British fleet in North American waters, who, far from discountenancing his lieutenants's conduct, wrote an insolent letter to Wanton on April 8, 1772, stating:

"Lieutenant Dudingston, commander of His Majesty's armed schooner, and a part of the squadron under my command, has sent me two letters he received from you,[16] of such a nature, I am at a loss what answers to give them, and ashamed to find they came from one of His Majesty's governors. . . .

"He sir, has done his duty, and behaved like an officer; and it is your duty, as a governor, to give him your assistance, and not endeavor to distress the King's officers for strictly complying with my orders. I shall give them directions, that, in case they receive any molestation in the execution of their duty, they shall send every man so molesting them to me. . . . I shall report your two insolent letters to my officer, to His Majesty's secretaries of state, and leave them to determine what right you have to demand a sight of all orders I shall give to all officers of my squadron; and I would advise you not to send your sheriff on board the King's ship again, on such ridiculous errands."[17]

Wanton replied temperately to Montagu's letter,[18] and on May 20, sent copies of it and his reply to Secretary of State Lord Hillsborough with a covering letter pointing out the lawlessness of Dudingston's conduct and the injustice and impropriety of some of Montagu's statements.[19] But long before orders could be given to Montagu to put a stop to Dudingston's galling activities, they were violently terminated when the *Gaspee* ran aground[20] on the afternoon of June 9[21] near Pawtuxet, Rhode Island, in Narragansett Bay a few miles south of Providence.

About the middle of the following night a party of over a hundred men in six or eight boats boarded the *Gaspee,* shot and seriously wounded Dudingston, bound the members of the crew, put them and Dudingston ashore at Pawtuxet, and burned the vessel to the water's edge.

On learning of the attack, Lieutenant-Governor Darius Sessions hastened to Pawtuxet from Providence and secured affidavits from three members of the crew concerning the attack. However, none of them could identify any members of the attacking party and Dudingston himself declined to talk, both because of his "indisposition of body" and because it was his duty, he said, to say nothing until he could give his testimony at a court martial, which he expected to face because he had lost a ship. Sessions wrote Wanton an account of the attack, enclosing the affidavits he had procured, and advising the Governor to issue a proclamation offering a large reward for the arrest of the offenders.[22]

Wanton promptly acted on Sessions' advice by issuing a proclamation strongly denouncing the attack, commanding all officials in the colony to exert themselves to the utmost to discover and arrest the attackers, and offering a reward of one hundred pounds sterling to any one identifying one or more of them, the reward to be paid immediately on his or their conviction.[23] But no claimants for the reward appeared.

However, early in July, an indentured servant, Aaron Briggs, coming aboard the *Beaver*, another patrol ship stationed at Newport, was identified as one of the attackers by a sailor formerly of the *Gaspee*. When questioned by the *Beaver*'s commanding officer, Captain John Linzee, Briggs "confessed" that he had taken part in the attack. He also named two leading men of Rhode Island, John Brown of Providence and Simeon Potter of Bristol, as members of the attacking party.[24]

Admiral Montagu sent a copy of Briggs' confession to Governor Wanton with a covering letter of July 11.[25] But when Wanton had a warrant sworn out for Briggs' arrest, Linzee illegally and "in a most contemptuous . . . manner" refused to permit the deputy sheriff holding the warrant to come aboard. After this (to quote further from the report of the Royal Commission) "the civil magistrates ceased their endeavors to discover the offenders."[26]

In the meantime, Montagu's report on the attack to British officials in London[27] had led to meetings of the Cabinet and of the Privy Council,[28] following which the King issued a proclamation in September, 1772, offering a reward of five hundred pounds per person for the discovery and conviction of persons participating in the attack.[29] The King also appointed a Commission of Inquiry, consisting of Governor Wanton, the Chief Justices of New York, New Jersey, and Massachusetts and the judge of the New England Admiralty District, to go into the whole affair and to collect evidence on the basis of which the accused were to be arrested by the civil authorities of Rhode Island and turned over to Montagu to be shipped to England for trial.[30]

The original plan was to try the offenders in Great Britain under a recent act, the so-called Dockyards Act of 12 Geo. III ch. 24 (1772).[31] The act imposed a sentence of death for maliciously setting afire, burning, or otherwise destroying British men of war, and, if the offense were committed outside the realm, for indictment and trial of the offender or offenders, at the option of the Crown, either in the place where the offense was committed, or "in any shire or county in this realm . . . any law, usage or custom notwithstanding."[32] But the destruction of ships covered by this act related exclusively to ships in dockyards, and, since the *Gaspee* clearly was not in a dockyard when attacked, the chief legal officers of the Crown held that its attackers could not be prosecuted under this act.[33]

They advised, however, that "the attack was an act of high treason, viz. of levying war against His Majesty, and the offenders may be indicted either here or in Rhode Island. . . ."

Guided by this opinion, the Privy Council decided that the Crown should proceed under the Treason Act of 35 Henry VIII ch. 2 (1543), described in Chapter 9.[34]

Pursuant to this decision, Lord Dartmouth,[35] who had recently succeeded Hillsborough as Secretary of State for the Colonies, wrote Wanton (September 4) that "the offence is, in the opinion of the law servants of the Crown, . . . an act of high treason, viz. levying war against the King."

"It is His Majesty's intention," he continued, "that the persons concerned in the burning the *Gaspee* schooner, and in the other violences which attended that daring insult, should be brought to England, to be tried; and I am therefore, to signify to you His Majesty's pleasure, that such of the offenders as may have been or shall be arrested and committed within the colony of Rhode Island, be delivered to the care and custody of Rear Admiral Montagu . . . or to such officers as he shall appoint to receive them, taking care that you do give notice to the persons accused, in order that they may procure such witnesses on their behalf as they shall think necessary, which witnesses, together with all such as may be proper to support charges against them, will be received and sent here with the prisoners."[36]

The penalty for treason was even more terrifying than for burning a war vessel. A convicted traitor's family, as well as he, was punished by forfeiture of his entire estate to the King[37] and he himself was subject to a most horrible death. The penalty (quoting Blackstone) was: "1. That the offender be drawn to the gallows. . . . 2. That he be hanged by the neck, and then cut down alive. 3. That his entrails be taken out and burned, while he is yet alive. 4. That his head be cut off. 5. That his body be divided into four parts . . . [and] his head and quarters be at the king's disposal."[38]

The Commissioners sat for several weeks at Newport in January, May, and June, 1773,[39] but the only person implicated besides Aaron Briggs and those named by him was a "tall, slender man wearing his own hair, of a brown color," whose family name was Greene[40]—one of the commonest names in the colony.[41] Thus, all substantial hope of discovery and conviction centered on Briggs, and when he was examined by the Commissioners they found that his testimony not only had been extorted under duress, but could not possibly be true.

"We humbly conceive it our duty to declare to Your Majesty," they wrote in their report to the King, "that the conduct of Capt. Linzee [who had threatened to whip and then hang Briggs if he did not confess] tended too strongly to extort from a weak or wicked mind, declarations not strictly true; that some parts of his [Briggs'] depositions falsify others; that allowing the account he gave of leaving . . . his residence, on the night the *Gaspee* was burnt, to be true or even near the truth, must render his being at the taking and destroying her, totally impossible. . . . In addition to all which, there is full and satisfactory evidence, to prove him, the whole of that night, to have been at home . . . and therefore we are most humbly of opinion, no credit is due to said Aaron's testimony."[42]

The Commissioners turned over the depositions they had taken covering the attack to the judges of the Rhode Island Superior Court for action, but the judges informed them that "we are all of opinion that the several matters and things contained in said depositions do not induce a probable suspicion that the persons mentioned therein, or either or any of them are guilty of the crime, aforesaid."[43] The judges added that "if the honorable commissioners are of a different sentiment, we should be glad to receive their opinion, for our better information," but the latter produced nothing further.[44]

The Commissioners' report to the King, dated June 22, 1773, set forth their findings of fact concerning the attack on the *Gaspee*, told of their futile efforts to identify the offenders, and censured the Rhode Island government for its failure to continue efforts to discover and arrest the attackers after Captain Linzee's refusal to turn over Briggs to the deputy sheriff. But they also criticized Linzee and Dudingston, pointing out that Linzee not only had refused to surrender Briggs when legally called upon to do so, but had "treated the civil authority in a most contemptuous and unjustifiable manner" and that Dudingston had unduly delayed acquainting Governor Wanton "with his power and authority" and had apparently "from an intemperate, if not reprehensible zeal to aid the revenue service, exceeded the bounds of his duty."[45]

Following receipt of this report, the British government let the matter drop.[46] (Dartmouth, if his sentiments were correctly reported,[47] almost certainly welcomed the occasion for this.) So, in the end, no one was sent to England for trial for alleged complicity in the attack on the *Gaspee*.

But this outcome was unforseeable when, in December, 1772, Governor Wanton laid Dartmouth's letter of September 4, quoted above, before the Rhode Island General Assembly.[48]

Soon afterward (December 19) the *Providence Gazette* reported that "commissioners are to sit at Newport, and examine such persons as Admiral Montagu shall direct to be apprehended . . . [who] are to be sent to England where they are to be tried for high treasons."[49] This alarming report was, of course, picked up by newspapers throughout the colonies.[50]

In March, the Virginia House of Burgesses took steps (as it had under the similar circumstances in 1769, described in Chapter 9) to secure united colonial opposition to this new British threat.

The House elected "a standing Committee of Correspondence," including the Speaker, Peyton Randolph, Richard Henry Lee,[51] Patrick Henry, and Thomas Jefferson, "whose business it shall be to obtain the most early and Authentic intelligence of all such Acts and Resolutions of the British Parliament, or proceedings of Administration, as may relate to or affect the British Colonies in America, and to keep up and maintain a Correspondence and Communication with our sister Colonies, respecting these important Considerations . . . and that they do, without delay, inform themselves particularly of . . . a *Court of inquiry,* said to have been lately held in Rhode Island with Powers to transmit Persons accused of Offences committed in America to places beyond the Seas, to be tried."[52]

The Speaker was ordered to transmit copies of these proceedings to the Speakers of the other Assemblies in British North America with the request that they appoint similar committees. This he promptly did in a circular letter of March 19, enclosing the Virginia proceedings and asking the other Speakers to "lay them before your Assembly as early as possible, and request them to appoint some of their body to communicate from time to time with the corresponding committee of Virginia."[53]

Within the next year, the Assemblies of all twelve colonies adopted Virginia's suggestion,[54] thus establishing a network of committees representing the popular Assemblies of all thirteen colonies to cooperate in matters of common concern.

At the time the colonists in general were disturbed by the proposed proceedings against participants in the attack on the *Gaspee,* the people of Massachusetts were further alarmed over a move by the British government to pay the judges of the Superior Court of the province out of the duties for revenue levied by Parliament on the colonies.

In England, an act of 1701 provided for judicial tenure during good behavior and for permanent, fixed salaries for the judges,[55] but this act did not extend to the colonies. There, the tenure of judges was either unregulated or, in the royal colonies other than Massachusetts, was regulated by commissions[56] and instructions[57] issued to successive Governors of the colony. The usual practice was for the Governor to grant judicial commissions revocable at the pleasure of the Crown.[58] But for some years prior to 1761 the Governors of New York and New Jersey had granted good behavior commissions,[59] leading to bitter controversy in New York when the Crown insisted on the abandonment of this local practice.[60]

In Massachusetts, which alone among the royal colonies still had a charter, the appointment of judges was governed by a provision in the charter empowering the Crown-appointed Governor of the colony, with the advice and consent of the provincial Council, "to constitute and appoint judges," without any restriction as to the kind of tenure to be granted.[61] Furthermore, the commission and instructions from the Crown to successive Governors of the colony did not impose any restriction on their freedom to grant judges tenure on such terms as they chose.[62]

The practice in Massachusetts was to appoint judges without any reference in their commissions as to tenure.[63] There was a difference of opinion as to whether such a commission gave the judges tenure during good behavior or only during the pleasure of the Crown; but in a series of learned letters to the press, John Adams established that such a commission gave the judges the latter kind of tenure.[64]

However, until 1772, the influence of the Crown over judges in the colony through retention of power to dismiss them at pleasure had been balanced by the influence over them retained by the people of the colony through the practice of the Massachusetts House of Representatives to vote the judges' salaries for only a year at a time.[65]

Shortly before leaving office, Lord Hillsborough issued an order (July 26, 1772) to the British Treasury to pay the salaries for the current year of Peter Oliver, Chief Justice of the Massachusetts Superior (Supreme)

Court, and the associate judges of the court.[66] Ten days later the Treasury carried out this order by issuing warrants for payment of these salaries "from the Duties on Tea imported into America."[67]

Rumors of this move to make the judges of the Supreme Court of Massachusetts dependent exclusively on the Crown were afloat in Boston as early as the end of August, and in October, Samuel Adams was told by an unidentified member of the Massachusetts Council that Governor Hutchinson had recently received authentic word of it.[68] The Massachusetts Legislature was not in session; but on October 28, a Boston town meeting chose a committee headed by Adams to ask the Governor if the report were true.[69]

Hutchinson evaded the question, stating that it would not be proper for him to inform the people of Boston whether or not he had "received any advice relative to the public Affairs of the Government," whereupon the town chose another committee to take further action in the matter.[70] This second committee, the famous Boston Committee of Correspondence, prepared a statement reciting many alleged infringements by Parliament and the Crown of the "Rights, Liberties and Privileges" of the people of Massachusetts, including the recent innovation concerning payment of the judges' salaries, and a proposed circular letter to all the towns of the province urging a "free communication of your sentiments to this Town of our common danger."[71]

This statement and the accompanying letter, approved at a Boston town meeting on November 20, were sent by the town clerk (William Cooper) to the selectmen of every town in the colony,[72] and over a hundred towns, including nearly all of those in the vicinity of Boston, responded favorably.[73] Thus was launched a network of Committees of Correspondence throughout the province, headed by the Boston Committee, of which Samuel Adams was the driving force.

Worried by this development, Governor Hutchinson delivered a speech at the opening of the winter session of the Massachusetts Legislature in January, 1773, declaring the right of Parliament to legislate in all respects for the colonies, insisting that he knew "of no line that can be drawn between the supreme authority of Parliament and the total independence of the colonies" and pointing out that if "there should be two independent Legislatures in one and the same state . . . the two Legislative bodies will make two governments as distinct as the kingdoms of England and Scotland before the union. . . ."[74]

The provincial Council replied that, granting Parliament had "*supreme* authority" throughout the empire, it did not have "*unlimited* authority," and that, however difficult it might be to determine just where the line was to be drawn, Parliament had no authority to levy taxes on the people of Massachusetts without their consent given directly or through representatives elected by them.[75]

The House of Representatives, on January 29, went further. Agreeing with Hutchinson as to the difficulty of drawing "a line between the universal authority of Parliament [over the colonies] and no authority at all," it declared that this difficulty did not really present itself in Massachusetts because, under the charter of the province properly construed, Parliament had no authority there of any kind. Having two legislative bodies, each independent of the other, would, indeed, as Hutchinson said, "make two governments as distinct as the kingdoms of England and Scotland" before the union, but there was nothing amiss with this since the two governments were still "united in one head and common Sovereign. . . ."[76]

No action was currently taken by the British Ministry on this bold reply.[77] But it was among the documents laid before Parliament in 1774 in support of the Ministry's resolution for the fateful Massachusetts Regulating Act of 1774, revising the charter and laws of Massachusetts to tighten Crown control over the government of the province.[78]

CHAPTER 13

THE TEA ACT OF 1773

Passage of the Tea Act of 1773, the East India Company's action authorized by it, and the ensuing Boston Tea Party led directly to the American Revolution. Consequently, the background and adoption of the act demand close examination.

Under an act of 1698, the Company of English merchants trading to the East Indies, (hereinafter called the East India Company or simply the Company) had the exclusive right to import East Indian products, including tea, into Great Britain, with the proviso that they must be sold by the Company to all comers at auction.[1] In 1721 Parliament passed the act, referred to in earlier chapters, prohibiting the importation of East Indian products into the British colonies from any place but Great Britain.[2] Under these two acts, the only tea that could legally be imported into the British colonies in 1773 (with a minor exception as to tea imported into Great Britain under special Treasury license)[3] was tea imported into Great Britain by the Company.

The Act of 1721 was widely evaded by smuggling tea into the colonies from foreign countries,[4] estimated to average at least 900,000 pounds a year.[5] Even so, customs records show large exports of tea each year from England to the thirteen old British colonies in North America. For example, in the years from 1764 through 1768, immediately preceding the operation of the colonial non-importation agreements (described in Chapters 10 and 12), the exports of tea from England to these colonies averaged 562,281 pounds a year.[6]

In the years 1769–1772, during which the non-importation agreements were in force, the export of tea to the thirteen colonies dropped to an average of 213,417 pounds a year.[7] Due in part to this severe decline, the Company was in serious financial difficulty by the end of 1772.[8]

On January 7, 1773, the stockholders ("General Court") of the Company voted to have the directors petition for "an Act of Parliament . . . taking off the three pence per Pound Duty in America."[9] But on February 25, the stockholders changed their earlier vote to petition "that leave may be given to export teas duty free to America,"[10] and the petition presented by the Company to the House of Commons on March 2 conformed to this vote.[11]

The relief proposed by this vote and the ensuing petition by the Company to the House of Commons differed from the relief proposed by the stockholders on January 27. The earlier proposal was for repeal of the Townshend Act duty on tea; the relief now requested was for refund of the entire British import duty on tea reexported to the colonies. Under an act of 1772, the Company was entitled to a refund of three-fifths of the British import duty.[12] The relief now requested was for refund of the remaining two-fifths.

The duty on imports of tea into Great Britain was about 24% ad valorem.[13] The additional refund now requested was, therefore, two-fifths of about 24%, or about 9.6% ad valorem. As shown in an appendix to this chapter, this requested refund would probably just about offset the import duty of three pence per pound payable in the colonies under the Townshend Act. But, though this refund would enable the Company to sell its tea in the colonies for about the same price as if the Townshend Act duty were repealed, the Company would still be faced with the barrier imposed by the colonial non-importation agreements on the importation of tea subject to the Townshend Act duty.

Why the stockholders of the Company decided to request this less favorable form of relief has not come to light; but it is reasonable to suppose that the Ministry let it be known it would refuse to support repeal of the Townshend Act duty.

An obvious reason for such a refusal was that repeal of this duty would be construed as a victory for the colonists tending to weaken Parliament's claim of right to tax them. Another probable reason was that, as pointed out in Chapter 5, the Townshend Act provided for the application of the revenue from this act primarily to "defraying the charges of the administration of justice and the support of civil government" in the colonies. This duty thus laid the foundation for giving the British government exclusive control over colonial Governors and judges by having them depend on the Crown, rather than on the colonial Legislatures for their salaries.

It was the latter reason that Lord North apparently had in mind in stating to the House of Commons in April, 1773, "I am unwilling to give up that [the tea] duty upon America. . . . If the East India Company will export tea to America they will very much increase the duty, and consequently very much facilitate the carrying of Government in that part. . . . I must see a very substantial reason before I part with a fund so applicable to the support of Civil [government in the colonies.]"[14]

On April 26, North proposed resolutions in the House of Commons sitting in Committee of the Whole that, if enacted into law would not allow a refund of the entire British import duty on tea reexported to the colonies, but would amend the act of 1698 to permit the Company, under license from the Treasury, to export tea on its own account to the colonies. The resolutions stated:

"That upon all teas, which shall be sold at any of the East India Company's public sales or be imported under license after the 10th Day of May 1773, and shall be exported to any of the British Plantations in America, a Drawback [refund] be allowed of all the Duties of Customs paid upon the Importation of such Teas.

"That Provision be made for impowering the Commissioners of the

Treasury to grant Licenses to the East India Company to export Teas to the British Plantations in America, or to Foreign Parts; provided that, at the Time of taking out such Teas for Exportation, there be left remaining in the Company's Warehouses a Quantity of Tea not less than Ten millions of Pounds Weight; and that upon all Teas which shall be so exported, a Drawback be allowed of all the Duties of Customs paid upon the Importation of such Teas, and an Exemption from the Inland Duties charged thereupon."[15]

So far as appears from the two known reports of the debate on the resolutions, no one opposed granting the Company relief. But five members—William Dowdeswell, Barlow Trecothick, George Johnstone, his brother William Johnstone, who had changed his name to Pulteney, and Charles Wolfram Cornwall[16]—spoke in favor of repeal of the Townshend Act duty as a method more likely to induce the colonists to buy the Company's tea.

Dowdeswell, Chancellor of the Exchequer in the Rockingham administration and one of the leading members of the Rockingham party in the House of Commons, said to North, "I tell the Noble Lord now if he don't take off the [Townshend Act] duty they won't take the tea."[17]

Dowdeswell was followed by Trecothick, one of four members for London in the House and London Agent for New Hampshire. His speech was reported in a letter from Charles Garth, a member of the House and London Agent for South Carolina, to the South Carolina Committee of Correspondence.

Garth wrote, "In the Committee upon East India matters, after Lord North had proposed the Resolutions . . . relative to the encrease of Consumption of Tea in North America, Mr. Trecothick observed that the most effectual Method to obtain this Point would be to take off the Import Duty in America of 3d per pound," through which, without affecting the revenues any more than the proposed refund of British import duty, "the Company would be . . . benefited to a much greater Degree, by a larger Consumption when the People in America should find themselves relieved of this import Duty." However, "The Ministry refused to alter their Plan, being of Opinion that America would, when this Law passes, to be able to buy Tea at a lower Rate from the Company than from any other European Nation, and that Men will always go to the Cheapest Market. . . ."[18]

Johnstone, Pulteney, and Cornwall concurred in what Dowdeswell and Trecothick had said.[19]

According to Garth, the Ministry "declined any political Argument touching the Right of Parliament to impose Taxes on the Americans;"[20] but, as Dowdeswell pointed out, the obvious reason for proposing the allowance of an additional refund of British import duty, instead of repeal of the Townshend Act duty on tea, was to maintain the asserted right of Parliament to tax the colonies.[21]

There is no indication that Dowdeswell, in proposing amen[?] the resolutions to repeal the Townshend Act duty on tea, spoke on[?] of the Rockingham party. Apparently none of the other members of[?] party, including Edmund Burke, who customarily spoke against an[?] measure opposed by the party, said anything on this occasion.[22]

The following day (April 27), the resolutions approved in the Committee of the Whole were adopted by the House, and on May 5 the bill incorporating them was passed by the House without a division at any stage of the proceedings.[23]

The bill was adopted without opposition in the House of Lords on May 7 and assented to by the King three days later.[24]

Thus, one of the most important bills ever passed by Parliament was adopted without serious opposition at any stage.

Some months later, Arthur Lee wrote Samuel Adams that he thought the Tea Act was "a ministerial trick of Lord North's . . . to stir up again some violence on your [the colonies'] part, which might justify them [the Ministry] in continuing the present impositions by coercive measures,"[25] and many years later John Almon accused the King of having refused to permit the Ministry to consider any change in plan to avoid provoking the colonies because he was determined to try "the question [of taxation] with America."[26] But no evidence of any such sinister motives was adduced by Lee or Almon or has been found.[27]

The true explanation seems to be that the Ministry expected that the Tea Act would afford relief to the Company[28] and at the same time increase the revenue from the Townshend Act duty by increasing colonial consumption of legally imported, duty-paid tea.[29]

In July, 1773, the Company, which had more than the required ten million pounds of tea in reserve,[30] decided to ask the Treasury for a license to export tea to the colonies on its own account,[31] and, a month later, applied for and promptly obtained a license to export up to 600,000 pounds.[32] During the succeeding two months, the Company shipped 598,659 pounds in seven ships, four to Boston, and one each to New York, Philadelphia, and Charleston.[33]

The Company appointed thirteen firms of colonial merchants as its distributing agents: Richard Clarke and Sons, Thomas and Elisha Hutchinson (sons of Governor Thomas Hutchinson), Benjamin Faneuil and John Winslow in Boston; Henry White, Abraham Lott and Co. and Pigou and Booth in New York; Thomas and Isaac Wharton, Abel James and Henry Drinker, Jonathan Brown and Gilbert Barkly in Philadelphia; and Peter Leger and William Greenwood and Roger Smith in Charleston.[34]

The agents were to be allowed a commission of six percent of the proceeds from their sales of tea at prices suggested by the Company,[35] out of which they were to pay for cartage, warehousing, and other expenses in the colonies.[36] They were to sell the tea at public sale, the buyers to

of the purchase price immediately, the balance in

to arrange for payment of the duty on behalf
ring the customs officers security to pay at a later
the tea was sold) or giving them bills of exchange
, or, if neither of these methods could be arranged,
d using the proceeds to pay the duty.[38]

ea Act was passed, William Bollan, London Agent
Council, warned the Council, "Unlimited authority
is the great fact which they appear determined to defend; and, as that
comprises a power to take money out of your pockets at the discretion
of others, to be applied to purposes you do not approve; . . . [a power
which] is capable of such exercise in future as will subject you to pay
dear. . . ."[39]

If safely landed and sold, the Company's shipments of tea would
immediately yield over £7,000 duty under the Townshend Act,[40] and
more important, lay the foundation for other duty-paid shipments in
years to come. Would the colonists submit to this new effort to strengthen
the act?

CHAPTER 14

COLONIAL OPPOSITION TO THE TEA ACT AND THE BOSTON TEA PARTY

THERE is no evidence that news of the Tea Act initially aroused much excitement in the colonies, probably because it was thought for some time that the new act repealed the Townshend Act duty on tea.[1]

But this misunderstanding was pointed out in the *Pennsylvania Journal* of September 29, 1773, quoting a letter from a colonist in London asserting that the Tea Act was a scheme of Lord North to establish the Townshend Act duty on tea, which, if effective, "will for ever after be pleaded as precedent for every imposition the Parliament of Great Britain shall think proper to saddle with us. It is much to be wished," the writer added, "the Americans will convince Lord North that they are not *yet ready* to have the yoke of slavery riveted about their necks and send back the tea whence it came." A week later (October 7) the *New-York Journal* published another letter from London, making clear that the Tea Act did not repeal the Townshend Act duty on tea and adding, "I have told several of the [East India] Company that the Tea and Ships will all be burnt . . . as I think you will never suffer an Act of Parliament to be so crowded down your Throats; for if you do, it is all over with you."[2]

There followed a strong attack on the Tea Act and the Company's plan to ship tea on its own account to the colonies. The act was denounced by "Scaevola" (Thomas Mifflin)[3] in the *Pennsylvania Chronicle* of October 11, and soon afterward in newspapers throughout the colonies.[4] Furthermore, a mass meeting at Philadelphia on October 15 passed resolutions denouncing the measure as an attack "upon the liberties of America which every American was in duty bound to oppose," and the Committee of Correspondence of the Massachusetts House sent a letter to the Committees in other colonies pointing out the necessity for every colony to take "effectual methods to prevent this measure from having its designed effects."[5]

The act was attacked not only because it was designed to implement collection of the Townshend Act duty on tea, but because of its threat to give the East India Company a monopoly of the colonial market for tea.[6] Moreover, once a monopoly of tea was established, the Company, it was said, could be expected to secure legislation enabling it to establish a monopoly of the colonial market for all East Indian products.[7]

Schlesinger's well-known statement that even if the act had exempted tea shipped by the Company from the Townshend Act duty on tea, "there is every reason to believe that the course of American opposition would have developed unchanged and the tea would have then been dumped into the Atlantic as an undisguised and unmixed protest against a grasping trade monopoly"[8] almost certainly goes too far; there is massive evidence that the threat of the colonial duty on tea was at least as important as the threat of monopoly in arousing American opposition to the act.[9] But, apparently, the threat of monopoly was an essential ingredient of the explosion of colonial opposition about to be described.

The plan to nullify the act adopted by Whig leaders was to secure the resignation of the East India Company's local agents before the tea arrived, a plan similar to that successfully employed in 1765 to nullify the Stamp Act by securing resignation of the Stamp Distributors before arrival of the stamps.[10]

As brought out later in the chapter, this plan was successful at Philadelphia, Charleston, and New York. But at Boston, the consignees, including two sons of Governor Thomas Hutchinson,[11] encouraged by Hutchinson to stand fast,[12] refused to resign.[13]

On October 23, a group of Boston Whigs, known as the North End Caucus, resolved to "oppose the vending any tea, sent by the East India Company, . . . with our lives and fortunes,"[14] and on November 3, a group of men, headed by William Molineux,[15] tried to frighten the agents into resigning, but the effort failed.[16]

Next, the town of Boston at a meeting held November 5, elected a committee consisting of the selectmen of the town, headed by John Hancock, and three other leading citizens to wait on the consignees and "request them from a regard of their own characters and the peace and good order of this Town and Province immediately to resign their appointment."[17] Three of them replied immediately that they must defer decision until they were informed "what obligations either of a moral or pecuniary nature we may be under to fulfill the trust that may be devolved on us;" the next day, November 6, a similar reply was received from the fourth.[18]

Here the matter rested until November 18, when, on the return from England of Jonathan Clarke,[19] son and partner of the agent Richard Clarke, another town meeting was held: a new committee was chosen to request from the consignees an immediate answer to the question of whether or not they would resign their agencies. Their initial answer, delivered the same afternoon, was a categorical "No."[20] In the afternoon of November 27, Jonathan Clarke arranged a meeting with the selectmen of the town at which he promised them that when the tea arrived, none of it would be unloaded or disposed of and that, on receipt of further orders from the Company which were expected with the tea, he would "immediately hand in proposals to the Selectmen to lay before the town."[21] But, as we shall see, this promise was not kept.

On the very night following this meeting, the *Dartmouth,* first of the tea ships to reach America, anchored off Boston harbor and the next day

(November 28) entered the harbor.[22] Three days later she docked at Griffin's wharf.[23]

Many years later Hutchinson wrote that, following instructions from the Boston tea consignees, the *Dartmouth* anchored outside the Port of Boston awaiting word if the tea could be safely landed, but that a Boston town committee, including Samuel Adams, ordered the master "to bring the ship up to land."[24] The implication is that the committee sought to provoke an incident. But, as brought out in an appendix to this chapter, no contemporary evidence has been found supporting Hutchinson's statement, and there is strong evidence of its being untrue.

On learning of the *Dartmouth*'s arrival the Boston selectmen sent Clarke a message requesting that he let them have his promised proposals, only to be told that he was out of town, his whereabouts unknown.[25] Where he was that day has not come to light. However, the following day Clarke and the other consignees fled to the protection of the British troops stationed on Castle Island since the Boston Massacre in 1770, where Governor Hutchinson had arranged for their reception.[26] The frightened Commissioners of the American Customs Board went with them.[27]

The Boston Committee of Correspondence, organized a year earlier (as told in Chapter 12), immediately met,[28] and, presumably under its auspices, early the following morning (November 29) handbills were distributed reporting the arrival of a ship with East India Company tea on board and calling for a mass meeting (as distinguished from a formal town meeting) at Faneuil Hall at nine that morning, to arrange to prevent the landing of the tea.[29] So large a number appeared that the meeting, after voting that the tea must be returned, was adjourned to meet that afternoon in a larger room, the auditorium of the Old South Meeting House. There, the crowd, estimated at around twenty-five hundred, voted unanimously that the tea must be sent back without payment of duty and chose a watch of twenty-five men to guard the vessel and cargo, headed by Captain Edward Proctor of the North End Caucus and including Paul Revere and several other members of the Caucus.[30]

On November 30, there was a second mass meeting, at which Francis Rotch, part owner of the *Dartmouth,* promised, under pressure, to send his ship back to London with the tea on board.[31] To this latter meeting the Boston tea agents, through Richard Clarke's son-in-law, the artist John Singleton Copley, sent an offer to store the tea and submit it to a committee of inspection until they heard from the Company what to do with it. But since this premised the agents' retaining their agencies, the offer was, of course, unacceptable and was promptly rejected.[32]

In the early part of December two more of the Boston-bound tea ships, the *Eleanor* and the *Bruce,* arrived and were ordered by a committee of local Whigs to dock beside the *Dartmouth.*[33] (The tea on the fourth of the Boston-bound tea ships, the *William,* accidentally wrecked on Cape

Cod on December 10, was taken to Castle Island a few weeks later.)[34] But attention was centered on the *Dartmouth* because, under British law, goods subject to customs duty could be seized to secure payment of duty twenty days after the carrying vessel entered port,[35] and the deadline with respect to the tea on the *Dartmouth* would expire December 18.[36]

Finding that Rotch was not making arrangements for the return of the *Dartmouth*'s cargo of tea, before the deadline,[37] the Boston Committee of Correspondence arranged for a mass meeting at Old South Meeting House on December 14, which was attended by over five thousand inhabitants of Boston and neighboring towns. The meeting passed a resolution requiring Rotch to apply immediately to the Collector of Customs for clearance of the *Dartmouth* and its tea to leave Boston. The Collector declined to give an answer until he had talked over the matter with the local Comptroller of Customs, whereupon the meeting was adjourned for two days.[38]

By the time the people assembled at Old South Church for the adjourned meeting on December 16, two days before the tea on the *Dartmouth* would become subject to seizure, there had been important developments. The Collector, after consulting with the Comptroller, had refused clearance,[39] and a report had spread that the tea on all three of the tea ships in port was about to be taken under the protection of the British war vessels stationed at Boston and deposited at Castle Island.[40] Having thus secured the safety of the tea, the consignees, it was feared, would pay the duty and then secretly market the tea.[41]

There still remained two possibilities of avoiding seizure of the *Dartmouth*'s tea and payment of the duty: sailing the vessel secretly out of the harbor with the tea on board or sailing her out openly under a clearance from the customs officers or, as a last resort, a pass from Governor Hutchinson.

The first was eliminated by messages from Hutchinson to the commander of the British troops at Castle William, at the mouth of the main channel of Boston harbor,[42] not to let any vessel leave the harbor without clearance or a pass and to Admiral John Montagu to keep watch over less-used channels of the harbor through which the ship might try to slip out.[43]

The second was eliminated by the refusal of the customs officers to grant a clearance and of Hutchinson to grant Rotch a pass. The failure of this last resort was reported by Rotch to the adjourned mass meeting in the late afternoon of December 16.[44]

What followed was described by Hutchinson in a letter to an English correspondent giving an account of the whole affair.[45]

"The owner [of the *Dartmouth*]," said Hutchinson, "was first to apply to the Custom House for a clearance and that being refused, to me for a pass which you may easily suppose I did not grant. All this time nobody suspected they wou'd suffer the Tea to be destroyed,[46] there being so many men of property active at these meetings as Hancock, Phillips, Rowe,

Dennie and others besides the Select men and the Town Clerk [William Cooper] who was Clerk of all the meetings. [Samuel] Adams never was in greater glory.

"In the afternoon of the last day of the meeting the owner of the *Dartmouth* came to Milton to demand or desire a pass for his vessel; after I had told him when his vessel was regularly cleared out and not before he shou'd have a pass, I asked him what he imagined the intentions of the people to be with respect to the Tea; he said he had always supposed they had no other intention than forcing it back to England and he believed they wished to have the vessel go down and be stopped by a shot from the Castle that they might say they had done all in their power. . . .[47]

"The Speakers in the meeting kept the people together until he returned with the answer which I had given, when Dr. Y——g [Young][48] pronounced him a good man who had done all in his power to gratify the people and charged them to do no hurt to his person or property, and immediately after, the meeting was declared to be dissolved and the wharffs were surrounded with the greatest part of the same people whilst a select number, prepared for the purpose, were unloading the vessels and emptying 340 Chests into the Dock which was done completely in two or three hours. Nobody seriously pretends to separate the meeting in Doctor Sewalls [Old South] meeting house from the meeting at Griffins wharf where the three ships lay but they say all is to be justifyed. . . .

"Upon Information of an Intention to go down with the Ships without a clearance I renewed to Colonel Leslie the orders to stop all vessels without a pass[49] and gave notice to Admiral Montagu who disposed his ships to prevent their passing thro' the other channels as Captain Hall suspected they shou'd.[50] This was all in my power, unless the owners of the Ships wou'd have hauled them off under the protection of the men of war, even if I had known of the design to have destroyed the Tea."

Hutchinson was later criticized for not himself having asked Montagu to take the tea ships under his protection;[51] it was even said or intimated that he had failed to do so in order to provoke an incident. But this was unfair. As his contemporary letters show, the destruction of the tea took him by surprise; he thought the tea would be safe because of the numerous "men of property" who had taken an active, public part in the meetings to compel return of the tea to England, and to protect themselves from being forced to pay for the tea would seek to preserve it.[52] For him to call on Montagu[53] or on the commander of the troops at Castle William[54] for help when apparently none was needed to preserve the tea would subject him to bitter denunciation, if nothing worse, by the Boston radicals.

Though Hutchinson's account of the destruction of the tea gives most of the essential facts, additional interesting bits of information are available from other contemporary sources.

The *Dartmouth*'s log of December 16 records that the crowd at the wharf numbered about a thousand and consisted in part of men "dressed and whooping like Indians;"[55] John Andrews, a Boston merchant, wrote his brother-in-law, William Barrell of Philadelphia, on December 18 that the meeting at the Old South did not break up until "the candles were light," that the party boarding the tea ships were "cloath'd in Blankets with the head muffled, and copper color'd countenances, being each arm'd with a hatchet or axe, and pair pistoles . . .," and that "before *nine* o'clock . . . every chest [of tea] . . . was knock'd to pieces and flung over the sides."[56] The Massachusetts *Gazette* of December 23 adds that this party, as it passed the meetinghouse on the way to the wharf, gave a war-whoop, which was answered by some of those inside.[57]

At a meeting of a committee of the Privy Council held the following February, John Dean Whitworth, an onlooker at the Tea Party,[58] testified that the boarding party consisted of between forty and fifty men[59] and Rotch contributed the well-known detail that when he reported the Governor's refusal to give him a pass, Samuel Adams, who was presiding at the adjourned meeting in the Old South Meeting House, said he "did not see what more they could do to save their Country."[60]

A petition from the Board of Directors of the British East India Company to John Pownall, Under Secretary of State, dated February 16, 1774, furnishes the information that the destroyed tea was worth £9,659.[61]

One of the impressive aspects of the Tea Party was the orderliness with which it was conducted. No one plundered or injured the rest of the cargo on any of the tea ships.[62]

Much has been written about mob violence in the colonies in the pre-Revolutionary period;[63] but from 1766 until the outbreak of war, most of the colonial resistance to unpopular British measures was, as in the case of the Boston Tea Party, remarkably restrained. The occasional tarring and featherings[64] were, indeed, a shockingly cruel form of vengeance or intimidation, but even these were not lethal.[65]

The rioting, plundering, and wanton destruction of property in Boston, Newport, and New York incident to opposing enforcement of the Stamp Act in 1765 apparently caused Whig leaders throughout the colonies to try to prevent a recurrence of this.[66]

Another striking aspect of the Boston Tea Party was the perfect concealment of the identity of those who threw the tea overboard. Sixty years after the event a man in his nineties named himself and fifty-seven others as members of the Party, and, still later, fifty-five names "derived principally from family tradition," were added to the list.[67] Hancock was currently said to have led the boarding party;[68] a barber named Eckley was arrested at the time for alleged participation, but he was discharged for lack of evidence; and Hutchinson wrote in 1778 that "Will Moore" was reputed to be "Captain of the Men who destroyed the tea."[69] But even as late as 1819, John Adams wrote that he did not know and never had known the name of a single participant,[70] and no reliable evidence has ever come to light as to who was in the Party.

Probably, as Drake suggests in his well-known *Tea Leaves,* the lead was taken by members of the North End Caucus,[71] who are known to have taken the initiative in resolving that the tea must be sent back and furnished the initial watch over the tea in December.[72]

Turning to the other ports to which the Company shipped tea, we find that before December 2, when the *London,* bringing the Company's tea to Charleston, reached port, the consignees there had been "prevailed upon by threats and flattery" to resign their agency.[73] Since no one claimed the tea at the end of the twenty-day period for payment of duty, the tea was seized by the local customs officers and stored in a warehouse,[74] where it remained until seized and sold by the South Carolina revolutionary government in July, 1776.[75]

The Company's agents at Philadelphia had also resigned before the *Polly,* bringing the Company's tea to Philadelphia, reached port.[76] When, on December 26, it arrived at Gloucester Point on the Delaware, a little down river from Philadelphia, its master, Samuel Ayres, was warned by a crowd on the river bank to proceed no further. He anchored his vessel there, and the next morning was haled before an immense mass meeting in the square before the State House. At this meeting resolutions were passed thanking the people of Boston for not allowing the tea to be landed there, and demanding that Ayres return to England with the tea on board.[77]

Gloucester Point was within the Port of Philadelphia,[78] and hence the tea had become liable for duty; but the local customs officers apparently made no effort to detain the *Polly,* which, before the day was over, set sail for England with the tea aboard.[79]

In New York City, 1,500 copies of "an instrument of association" dated November 29, 1773, was circulated throughout the city inviting the inhabitants "to associate together under the name and state of the *Sons of Liberty of New York*" and to bind themselves to brand as "an enemy to the liberties of America" anyone who "shall aid or abet . . . the introduction of tea . . . into this Colony, while it is subject, by a British act of Parliament, to the payment of a duty for the purpose of raising a revenue."[80] Two weeks later, local newspapers reported that the instrument had been signed by "a vast number of the inhabitants, including most of the principal lawyers, merchants, landowners, masters of ships and mechanics of the city."[81]

Following the destruction of the Company's tea at Boston, the New York tea consignees wrote a letter, dated December 27, to the master of the tea ship headed for New York, to be delivered to him before he entered port, stating that "we can neither receive the tea or pay the duty . . . [and] give you our opinion that . . . it will be most prudent for you to return [without attempting to land the tea] as soon as you can be supplied with such necessaries as you may have occasion for on the voyage."[82]

Due to foul weather, the New York tea ship, the *Nancy,* Benjamin Lockyer, master, did not arrive at Sandy Hook outside New York harbor until April 18 or 19, 1774.[83]

On receipt from the pilot who came out to meet him with letters from the consignees, presumably similar to the one of December 27 just quoted Lockyer halted his ship outside the port and came ashore in the pilot boat.[84] He delivered a letter dated April 20 to Henry White, addressed to him and the other consignees, stating that, "Having considered the circumstances mentioned in your letters . . . I have left the ship and cargo at Sandy Hook for their safety" and making a formal "tender of the cargo of tea" consigned to them, to which the consignees replied formally, declining to receive the tea.[85]

Lockyer had promised a committee, which met him on his landing, that "as the consignees would not receive his cargo, he would not go to the custom-house and would make all the dispatch he could to leave the city," and, on April 24, he sailed back to London with the tea on board.[86]

Thus, when all returns were in, the Company found that at Boston it still had agents but no tea, at Charleston, tea (held by the customs officers) but no agents, and at Philadelphia and New York neither agents nor tea.[87]

CHAPTER 15

THE BOSTON PORT ACT AND
BRITISH TROOPS TO BOSTON

NEWS of the destruction of the East India Company's tea at Boston reached London on or before January 20,[1] and was considered at a Cabinet meeting on January 29, 1774. At this meeting, attended by all members of the Cabinet—North and Lords Gower, Rochford, Apsley, Sandwich, Suffolk, and Dartmouth[2]—it was resolved, apparently without dissent, that "in consequence of the present disorders in America, effectual steps . . . be taken to secure the Dependance of the Colonies on the Mother Country."[3] Just what steps to take was left for future decision; but, considering the complexion of the Cabinet, they were likely to be drastic.

North, for reasons indicated in Chapter 10, would presumably favor strong measures of punishment for an act violently opposing collection of the British duty on tea, and, except possibly Dartmouth, none of the other members of the Cabinet could be expected to oppose drastic measures against Boston.

Gower and Sandwich, who had succeeded Sir Edward Hawke as First Lord of the Admiralty in January, 1771, were leading members of the Bedford party, which had consistently favored stern measures to suppress colonial insubordination. Suffolk, appointed one of the Secretaries of State in June, 1771, had been a faithful follower of George Grenville, father of the Stamp Act, until the latter's death in November, 1770. Rochford, though not connected with the Bedford or Grenville parties probably had been among the Cabinet members who voted in 1769 against Grafton's proposal for total repeal of the Townshend Act duties. Apsley, Lord Chancellor since January, 1771, had long been on the bench and out of politics; but his father was a prominent Tory and he himself had been a Tory member of the House of Commons before becoming a judge. Besides, having been appointed Lord Chancellor during the Ministry of North, he presumably could be counted on to support North's policies.[4]

At a Cabinet meeting on February 4, Dartmouth proposed, and the Cabinet approved, a resolution to request the King to direct the Governor of Massachusetts "to remove the seat of Government [from Boston] to such other place in the province as he shall think least likely to be influenced by the town of Boston," and to remove the officers of the customs "to such other port as shall be judged most convenient."[5]

It was also decided at this meeting to ask the Attorney-General, Edward Thurlow, and the Solicitor-General, Alexander Wedderburn, for an opinion whether the proceedings against landing the Company's tea at

Boston amounted to "the crime of High Treason, and if so against whom [to proceed], and what will be the proper and legal method of proceeding against such persons."[6]

In response to a "case" submitted to them by Dartmouth,[7] Thurlow and Wedderburn gave an opinion (February 11) that "the Acts and Proceedings, stated in the above mentioned case, do amount to the Crime of High Treason, namely, to the levying of War against His Majesty"; that "Molyneux, Denny, Warren, Church and Johonat, who in the Character of a Committee went to the length of attacking Clarke,[8] are chargeable with the Crime of High Treason"; that Jonathan Williams, Samuel Adams, John Hancock, Edward Proctor, and many other unnamed persons who had participated in the proceedings at Boston against landing the tea were apparently guilty of high treason or at least of "high misdemeanour";[9] and that the accused might be proceeded against either "by prosecuting Them for their Treason" in Massachusetts or by "transmitting them hither to be tried in some County of England."

However, the law officers concluded that "Upon perusing the State of the Evidence of Mr. Scott,[10] the only Person now in England who can give evidence,[11] We think that, as it stands, it is scarce sufficient to affect any person with the crime of High Treason unless the resolutions, taken at the meeting which he speaks of,[12] can be more distinctly established, and referred to the persons He mentions."[13]

On receipt of this opinion, Dartmouth rounded up a dozen persons who had been in Boston during the preceding November and December, and secured depositions from them at a meeting of the Privy Council on February 19.[14] But after considering this testimony, the law officers informed the Cabinet on February 28, that, in their opinion, "the charge of High Treason cannot be maintained against any individuals on the ground of the depositions taken at the Council Board."[15]

Initially, the Cabinet seems to have planned to take executive action only against Boston and the leaders of the opposition there,[16] but a resolution adopted at a Cabinet meeting on February 19 discloses that, by this time, the Ministry had decided to ask for the intervention of Parliament. The resolution states:

"That it be moved [in Parliament] for leave to bring in a Bill to take away from the Town & district of Boston the privileges of a Port until the East India Company shall have been indemnified in the Loss they have sustained by the Destruction of their Teas, either by the said Town at large or by the Committee of the Body of the people which conducted the Measures that led to that Act of Violence."[17]

At a meeting on February 28, the Cabinet came to a decision as to the procedure to be followed in launching the Boston Port bill.[18] Pursuant to this decision, the King, on March 7, presented to both Houses of Parliament a message laying before them copies of over a hundred documents describing the opposition to the landing of the tea at Boston and elsewhere, with the request that he be enabled "effectually to take such Measures as may be most likely to put an immediate Stop to the present Disorders, . . . and [secure] the Execution of the Laws, and the just Dependence of the Colonies upon the Crown and Parliament of Great Britain."[19]

Both Houses promptly adopted addresses thanking the King for submitting the papers and assuring him that appropriate action would be taken in accordance with his request,[20] and a week later (March 14), North moved in the House of Commons for leave "to bring in a Bill to discontinue the Landing and Discharging, Lading and Shipping of Goods, Wares, and Merchandise, at the said Town of Boston, or within the Harbour thereof. . . ."[21]

Speaking in support of his motion, North stated that, since this was "the third time the officers of the customs had been prevented from doing their duty in the harbour of Boston,"[22] he thought "the inhabitants of the town deserved punishment" and that, while some individuals might be made to suffer unjustly, there was ample precedent,[23] "where the authority of a town had been, as it were asleep and inactive, . . . for the town to be fined for such neglect. . . ."[24]

Again there was but little opposition, and the motion was adopted without a division.[25]

The bill as introduced by North March 18 provided for closing the Port of Boston[26] on and after June 1, 1774, to all commerce except importation of military or other supplies for the Crown and "fuel or victual brought coastwise . . . for the necessary use and sustenance of the inhabitants of the said town of Boston," until the following conditions were met:

First: The King in Council must find and declare that "peace and obedience to the laws shall be so far restored in the said town of Boston, that the trade of Great Britain may safely be carried on there and his Majesty's customs duly collected. . . ."

Second: The King must be convinced that "full satisfaction hath been made by or on behalf of the said town of Boston to the united company of merchants of England trading to the East Indies, for the damages sustained by the said Company by the destruction of their goods sent to Boston, on certain ships or vessels as aforesaid."

Third: The Governor or Lieutenant Governor of Massachusetts must certify to the King in Council that "reasonable satisfaction hath been made to the officers of his Majesty's revenue, and others, who suffered by the riots and insurrections, above mentioned"[27] in November and December, 1773, and January, 1774.

Furthermore if and when Boston were reopened to general commerce, vessels were to load and unload their cargo only "upon such wharfs, quays and places" as "his Majesty, his heirs or successors shall judge necessary and expedient. . . ."[28]

The bill obviously envisaged more than payment to the East India Company of the value of the destroyed tea, but just what else was far from clear. What would be required to satisfy the Privy Council that "obedience to the laws" had been so far restored at Boston as to give assurance that British trade could be safely carried on there and customs duties be duly collected?

What customs officers and others must be compensated and what was to be "reasonable" satisfaction? Even the amount to be paid the East India Company was indefinite. Was the amount to be limited to the value of the tea destroyed—about £9,000[29]—or did the "full" satisfaction to be given include satisfaction for incidental damages such as the anticipated profits on the sale of the destroyed tea?

Futhermore, the bill authorized the Crown to select particular wharfs within the Port of Boston as the only ones at which goods could be legally landed. Presumably the purpose of this provision was to facilitate enforcement of the British customs duties and restrictions on colonial trade; but it would obviously enable the Crown to favor wharf owners who were Tories and punish, perhaps bankrupt, those who were Whigs.[30]

Apparently there was no debate on either the first or second reading of the bill on March 18 and 21,[31] but it was extensively debated in the Commons sitting in Committee of the Whole on March 23, and again on the third and final reading of the bill two days later.

Rose Fuller, member for Rye, long a resident of Jamaica but now living in England, maintained that Boston ought not be punished unless and until demand was made for a fixed indemnity, say £25,000, to be paid within a reasonable, specified time, and the demand was not met.[32] A number of other speakers also opposed on various grounds the bill as it stood. George Byng, a staunch follower of Rockingham, proposed an amendment to except trade with British merchants; Charles James Fox moved to amend the bill in various ways; and George Dempster, William Dowdeswell, Edmund Burke, Lord John Cavendish, Thomas Townshend, John Sawbridge, and George Johnstone, former Governor of West Florida, flatly opposed the bill or sought to have its operation deferred.[33]

Among the numerous supporters of the bill, Charles Van, member for the Welsh borough of Brecon, made himself conspicuous by declaring that "the town of Boston ought to be knocked about their ears, and destroyed; *Delenda est Carthago*," and that Great Britain would "never meet with that proper obedience in the colonies to the laws of this country, until you have destroyed that nest of locusts."[34] The most striking aspect of the debate was, however, the conduct of two usual champions of the colonists, Henry S. Conway and Isaac Barré, who spoke not against, but in support of, the bill.[35]

There was no call for a division on either day,[36] because, according to Edmund Burke, opponents of the bill "made so little impression that it was not thought advisable to divide the House."[37] But a related motion to accept a petition against the bill from William Bollan, London Agent for the Massachusetts Council, was defeated 170 to 40.[38]

The Boston Port bill passed the Commons on March 25 and was promptly laid before the House of Lords, where it was supported by a number of speakers, including Lord Mansfield, Chief Justice of the King's Bench, who declared the recent event at Boston an overt act of high treason.[39] The bill was opposed by the Duke of Richmond, Lord Shelburne, Lord Camden, and several other peers,[40] but passed the Lords, apparently without a division at any stage, on March 30 and was assented to by the King the next day.[41]

Shelburne wrote Lord Chatham March 15 that Dartmouth had recently told him he was determined "to cover America from the present storm to the utmost of his power,"[42] but there is no evidence of Dartmouth's having opposed the measures taken against Boston and Massachusetts, either in the Cabinet or in Parliament.[43] Indeed, Benjamin Franklin seems to have sized Dartmouth up pretty accurately in writing his son, William Franklin, that Dartmouth "is truly a good Man, and wishes sincerely a good Understanding with the Colonies, but does not seem to have Strength equal to his Wishes" and that "with Dispositions for the best Measures, is easily prevail'd with to join in the worst."[44]

Some of the members of the House of Commons who had refrained from opposing the Boston Port bill said they had done so under the impression that, if this bill were passed, the Ministry would propose repeal of the colonial tea duty.[45] But there apparently had been a misunderstanding; when Fuller moved for repeal of the duty, North opposed the motion, and, though Edmund Burke and others strongly supported Fuller, his motion was defeated 182 to 49.[46]

To ensure enforcement of the Act, Governor Thomas Hutchinson was to be replaced as Governor of Massachusetts by General Thomas Gage, Commander in Chief of the British army in North America, who was to be supported at Boston by four regiments. These, he had told the King, would be "sufficient to [deal with] any disturbance."[47]

On April 2, orders were given to send the Fourth, Fifth, Thirty-eighth, and Forty-third Regiments from England and Ireland to Boston,[48] and, five days later, Gage, in England on leave of absence, was appointed Governor under a commission and instructions giving him greater authority than that of former Governors of Massachusetts.[49] Previously, the Governor had had authority to reprieve (subject to review by the King), but not to pardon, persons accused of willful murder or treason; Gage's commission empowered him to pardon persons convicted of these, as well as of lesser, offenses.[50] Previous instructions directed the Governor not to declare martial law "without the advice and consent of our Council"; this limitation was omitted in the instructions to Gage.[51]

Furthermore, at a Cabinet meeting on April 7, attended by Gage and the law officers of the Crown, it was decided that "in case of dangerous tumult and insurrection . . . it will be the duty of the Governor of the Province to . . . repel force and violence by every means within his reach."[52] This would, of course, include the use of the British troops at Boston under Gage's orders in his capacity as Commander in Chief of all British troops in North America.

Gage also was furnished with a copy of the law officers' opinion as to treason in Boston (quoted earlier in this chapter), with instructions "to employ your utmost Endeavours to obtain sufficient Evidence against the principal Actors [named] therein; and in case . . . you shall be of opinion that upon Indictment of them there is a probability of their being brought to punishment, it is His Majesty's Pleasure that you . . . direct the proper Steps to be taken for their Prosecution."[53]

In his covering letter, Dartmouth wrote, "His Majesty trusts that no opposition will, or can, with any Effect, be made to the carrying the Law into Execution . . . but Should it happen otherwise your Authority as the first Magistrate, combined with your Command over the King's Troops, will, it is hoped, enable You to meet every opposition, and fully to preserve the public peace, by employing those Troops with Effect should the madness of the People on the one hand or the timidity or want of Strength of the peace officers on the other hand, make it necessary to resort to their assistance. . . .

"Sovereignty of the King in his Parliament over the Colonies," Dartmouth continued, "requires a full and absolute submission, and His Majesty's Dignity demands that, until that submission be made, the Town of Boston, where so much anarchy and confusion have prevailed, should cease to be the place of the Residence of his Governor, or of any other Officer of Government who is not obliged by Law to perform his functions there." Hence, Gage and all other officials not thus excepted, until otherwise ordered, were "to make the Town of Salem the place of your residence. . . ."[54]

The Boston Port Act was only the first of several colonial measures projected by the North Ministry, the most important of which was the Massachusetts Regulating Act altering the charter and laws of the province.[55]

CHAPTER 16

PROPOSALS FOR A TIGHTER
REIN ON MASSACHUSETTS

THE proposal and adoption of the Massachusetts Regulating Act of 1774 is understandable only in the light of letters over many years from important officials in the colonies to officials in England, declaring that the whole of Massachusetts, not Boston alone, was singularly unruly and suggesting alterations in the form of government of the colony to make it more tractable.

These came not only from members of the harassed American Customs Board,[1] thrice driven to seek safety at Castle William, but from others who wrote presumably with more detachment.

In June, 1768, following the recent *Liberty* riot (described in Chapter 8), Gage, then as now Commander in Chief of the British army in North America,[2] wrote Lord Barrington, Secretary at War[3] and one of the so-called "King's Friends,"[4] that the riot portended "open Revolt, not only of the City of Boston but of the whole Province of Massachusetts Bay." "Quash this Spirit at a Blow,"[5] he said, "without too much regard to the Expence, and it will prove oeconomy in the End. Such Resolute and determined Conduct will Astonish the rest of the Provinces and damp the Spirit of Insurrection that may lurk amongst them. . . ." "If," Gage added, "the Principles of Moderation and Forbearance are again adopted [as they had been in dealing with colonial opposition to the Stamp Act], . . . There will be an End to these Provinces as British Colonies, give them what Name you please."[6]

In May, 1769, deploring the fact that Parliament had taken no action to punish those responsible for assembling the extra legal convention at Boston (described in Chapter 11), Gage wrote Barrington recommending "Impeachment[7] of those who signed the Letters of Convention";[8] "Abolition of the Town Meetings of Boston";[9] establishment of "a Corporation in lieu thereof, as in other Citys . . .";[10] and "Appointment of the Council by the King." (In all the royal colonies except Massachusetts, the provincial Council or Upper House was appointed by mandate of the King.[11] In Massachusetts, the Council was chosen annually by joint ballot of the newly elected House of Representatives and the outgoing Council,[12] subject to rejection by the Governor of any or all of the members so chosen.)[13]

Again deploring the weakness of the British government in dealing with the colonies in general and Massachusetts in particular, Gage wrote Barrington in September, 1770, "I think it must be plain to every Man, that no Peace will ever be established in that Province till the King Nominates his Council, and Appoints the Magistrates, And that all Town-Meetings are absolutely abolished. . . ."[14]

Two months later, he wrote Barrington, "I declare to your Lordship my private Opinion, that America is a mere Bully, from one End to the Other. . . ."[15]

Extreme unrest at home, marked by the Wilkes riots, and the imminent threat of war with Spain over the Falkland Islands[16] discouraged action by the British government or Parliament against the colonies in 1770–1771; all British military resources were needed elsewhere. But soon after quiet was restored at home and the Falkland Island dispute was peacefully settled, Gage wrote Barrington (April, 1772), "The profound Tranquillity you enjoy at present is a happy Circumstance . . . [in which] to regulate the Affairs of this Country. . . . It is necessary . . . that Great Britain should not only assert but also support that Supremacy which she claims over the Members of the Empire, or she will Soon only be supreme in Words. . . ." And in the next to last private letter he wrote Barrington before leaving for England on leave in June, 1773, Gage stressed the importance of not yielding to any colonial demands. It was, he pointed out, "an Axiom in Politicks that a Government when forced into one Concession to the People lays the Foundation of . . . Pretensions before unthought of. . . ."[17]

As might be expected, Barrington passed on Gage's letters, or the more important passages from them, to members of the Cabinet and to the King.

In 1768, Barrington wrote Gage that he had shown his recent letter as to the advisability of keeping the colonies as weak as possible, to Secretary of State Lord Hillsborough, who would "not fail to remember the very material things contain'd in it."[18] In 1769 he informed Gage that the King "sees most of your private letters to me."[19] In September, 1772, Barrington wrote Gage that, in view of the "weight and importance" of a recent letter from Gage opposing establishment of a new colony on the Ohio because it was good policy "to keep the Settlers within reach of the Sea-Coast as long as we can, and to cramp their Trade as far as it can be done prudentially," he had shown extracts from it to Lord North, Lord Dartmouth, and the President of the Council, Lord Gower.[20]

Gage's views were strongly reinforced by Governor Francis Bernard of Massachusetts, related by marriage to Barrington,[21] in letters to him and other government officials in England, urging changes in the form of government of the colony.

Exasperated by the refusal of the Massachusetts Council and House to reelect to the Council a number of persons whom he wished reelected[22] and by the Council's failure to support him in several other matters,[23] Bernard wrote various British officials urging appointment of the Council by the King.[24] He also partially supported Gage's view that the commissions of magistrates in Massachusetts be revoked,[25] and made the additional suggestion that grand juries in Massachusetts be chosen by the county sheriffs (who were appointees of the Governor), instead of by the existing mode of popular election.[26]

Perhaps even more influential were the letters of Lieutenant Governor (later Governor) Thomas Hutchinson to members of Parliament and government officials in England. Coming from a native of Massachusetts who had repeatedly been chosen to elective offices there before appointment to Crown office,[27] Hutchinson's letters would naturally be thought less subject to possible bias against the people of the province than those of outsiders.

Soon after passage of the Declaratory Act of 1766, Hutchinson wrote Richard Jackson, member of Parliament and a secretary to George Grenville, "A bare declaration that we are subject, though in an act of Parliament, does not, in fact, make us so. . . . Something further is therefore necessary in order to secure their [the colonists'] obedience. Is it not very necessary they should explicitly acknowledge a general subjection? Every person in publick office, every member of the legislature especially, in every colony, should understand this subjection. . . . I wish to see known established principles, one general rule of subjection, once acknowledged, any attempts in opposition to them will be more easily resisted and crushed."[28]

In letter after letter to correspondents in England, Hutchinson insisted that the very nature of government required a supreme authority, that the British Parliament had this authority throughout the British Empire, which the colonies in general and Massachusetts in particular must be compelled to recognize.

Writing John Pownall, Under Secretary of State, in April, 1770, concerning the colonial non-importation agreement (described in Chapter 7), Hutchinson declared that the colonists would never "return to a state of order until they are compelled to it and kept in awe by a power superior to them."

A few days later, he wrote Secretary of State Lord Hillsborough on the same subject. "It will," he said, "be happy for the colonies if Parliament shall have gone into such measures as his Majesty has been pleased to recommend for suppressing the Confederacies [i.e., the non-importation agreements] against the authority of Parliament. Until this is done I see no prospect of the recovery of any degree of vigour in the Government of this Province. . . . The longer we go on in this way without check from the Supreme Authority the farther the Infection spreads."[29]

Learning that Parliament had not taken the action expected by him to punish the signers of the non-importation agreements, Hutchinson wrote Pownall in July, 1770, "Parliament's rising without any notice of us is discouraging to the Servants of the Crown but . . . if in the next Session they make thorough work it will be a happy delay." And, when the next session of Parliament opened, Hutchinson wrote Hillsborough, "A firm persuasion that Parliament is determined, at all events, to maintain its supreme authority is all we want; few or none are now so weak [foolish] as to question their power to do it. . . . An act to enable the King to alter the bounds of the Province [of Massachusetts] . . . , the

Charter notwithstanding, by making . . . Main and country East of it a distinct and separate Province . . . might be kept as a rod over us, and a security for our good behaviour until the King's pleasure should be determined; or if it should be executed immediately . . . would be a striking instance of the power and authority of Parliament."[30]

A few months later Hutchinson suggested to Pownall that Parliament pass an act making it "High Treason" to write or print that "an Act of Parliament is of no validity, in any case whatsoever. . . ."[31]

Hutchinson also buttressed the recommendations of Gage and Bernard for an act of Parliament to change the form of government of Massachusetts. He suggested legislation to abolish or restrict town meetings in Boston,[32] to correct the alleged "great abuse in the choice of juries, more especially grand juries," in Massachusetts by having juries appointed as they were in England,[33] and to change the method of selecting the Massachusetts Council. His initial suggestion concerning the Council was for passage of an act of Parliament (similar to the New York Suspending Act of 1767, described in Chapter 4) invalidating all current acts of the Massachusetts Legislature until the Legislature elected a full panel of Council members approved by the Governor. But in January, 1771, Hutchinson swung over to support of the recommendation of Gage and Bernard for appointment of the members of the Council by the Crown.[34]

Thus, when the destruction of the East India Company's tea at Boston aroused the North Ministry to action, it had before it a mass of testimony from leading Crown officials in the colonies recommending drastic changes in the government of Massachusetts.

Furthermore, at this critical time, a petition from the Massachusetts House of Representatives to the Crown for the removal of Hutchinson from office gave his lawyer an opportunity to present to a meeting of the Privy Council attended by many leading members of Parliament a review of the alleged iniquities of Massachusetts over the past ten years, buttressing the recommendations of Gage, Bernard, and Hutchinson for reorganization of the government of Massachusetts.

CHAPTER 17

THE MASSACHUSETTS PETITION OF 1773 AND ITS CONSEQUENCES

THE background of, and proceedings on, the petition of the Massachusetts House of Representatives, referred to in Chapter 16, were as follows:

In December, 1772, Benjamin Franklin, London Agent for the Massachusetts House,[1] wrote its Speaker, Thomas Cushing, "There has lately fallen into my Hands part of a Correspondence, I have reason to believe laid the Foundation of most if not all our present grievances . . . [and] I send you enclosed the original letters, to obviate every Pretence of Unfairness in Copying, Interpolation, or Omission. . . .

"As to the writers, I can easily as well as charitably conceive it possible that a Man educated in Prepossessions of the unbounded Authority of Parliament, etc. may think unjustifiable every Opposition even to its unconstitutional Exercize. . . . But when I find . . . [men] bartering away the Liberties of their native Country for Posts, and negotiating for Salaries and Pensions extorted by the People, and, conscious of the Odium these might be attended with, calling for Troops to protect and secure the Enjoyment of them . . . I cannot but . . . deem them mere Time servers, seeking their own private Emolument thro' Any Quantity of Public Mischief. . . ."[2]

The letters, dated May, 1767, to October, 1769, were addressed to, or came into the hands of, Thomas Whately, formerly Secretary to the Treasury during the administration of George Grenville and one of Grenville's leading followers in the House of Commons.[3] The most important were from Governor Thomas Hutchinson, his brother-in-law Lieutenant-Governor Andrew Oliver (Lieutenant-Governor and Secretary of Massachusetts, respectively, at the time the letters were written), and Charles Paxton, Boston-born member of the American Customs Board. How Franklin obtained these letters has never been disclosed.[4]

Hutchinson's letters did not include any of those quoted in Chapter 16; these more damaging letters did not come to light until 1775.[5] But those from Hutchinson in the batch sent by Franklin to Cushing describe leaders of the Boston town meetings as "Ignorant," members of the Massachusetts Convention of 1768, discussed in Chapter 8, as "ridiculous," and several members of the Provincial Council as of "low cunning." The letters further suggest that Parliament show "marks of resentment . . . upon the province in general or particular persons" for the opposition in Massachusetts to recent acts of Parliament, and that all who would not renounce the non-importation agreements of 1768 be subjected "to penalties adequate to the offence."

The next to the last of Hutchinson's letters declared that "if no measures still have been taken to secure this dependence [of the colonies on Great Britain] or nothing more than some declaratory acts or resolves, it is all over with us. The friends of government will be utterly disheartened, and the friends of anarchy will be afraid of nothing, be it ever so extravagant. . . ."[6] There must, he said, be an "abridgement of what are called English liberties," and he added, "I doubt whether it is possible to project a system of government in which a colony 3,000 miles distant from the present state shall enjoy all the liberties of the parent state. I am certain I have never yet seen the projection."[7]

The most damaging passages of Oliver's letters were those in a letter to Whately dated May 7, 1767, written "in confidence of my name not being used on the occasion," urging the very measure that had most disturbed the colonists—passage of an act of Parliament for raising a colonial revenue and applying the revenue to pay the salaries of Crown-appointed officials in the colonies. Oliver also suggested a plan for defeating any colonial non-importation agreements that might be entered into to secure repeal of such an act.

"As the trade is now managed," Oliver wrote, "the dealer here sends to the merchant in England for his goods;[8] upon these goods the English merchant puts a profit of 10, or more probably 15 per cent when he sends them to his employer in America. The merchant is so jealous of foregoing this profit that an American trader cannot well purchase the goods he wants of the manufacturer; for should the merchant know that the manufacturer had supplied an American, he would take off no more of his [the manufacturer's] wares.

"The merchants . . . know the goods which the American market demands and may therefore safely take them off from the manufacturer though they [the merchants] should have no orders for shipping them this year or perhaps the next; and I dare say it would be no longer before the Americans would clamor for a supply, for it is vain to think they can supply themselves. The merchant might then put an advanced price upon his goods, and possibly be able to make his own terms, or if it should be thought the goods would not bear an advanced price to indemnify him, it might be worth while for the government to agree with the merchants beforehand to allow them a premium equivalent to the advance of their stock, and then the game would be over."[9]

Most damaging of all was a letter from Paxton to Whately of June 20, 1768, stating, "Unless we have immediately two or three regiments, tis' the opinion of all the friends to Government that Boston will be in open rebellion."[10]

In his letter to Cushing, Franklin said he had engaged that the letters were not to be printed nor generally shown.[11] But in spite of this restriction, copies of them were laid before the Massachusetts House of Representatives, which, in June, 1773, adopted a Petition to the King for dismissal of Hutchinson and Oliver.

These men, the Petition declared, had sought "to excite the resentment of the British Administration against this province, to defeat the endeavours of our agents and friends to serve us by a fair representation of our state of facts, to prevent our humble and repeated petitions from reaching the ear of your Majesty. . . ." Having thus "rendered themselves justly obnoxious to your loving subjects and entirely lost their confidence . . . ," they should be removed and replaced by persons in whom the people of the province could confide.[12]

On June 25, Cushing wrote Franklin enclosing the Petition for presentation to the King, together with attested copies of the letters on which the Petition was based, and a resolution of the House for the Petition.[13] Cushing instructed Franklin to employ "Arthur Lee our counsel on this occasion and any other counsel you may think proper,"[14] thus indicating that the House supposed the King would order a hearing on the Petition.

On August 24, Franklin wrote Cushing that he had sent the Petition to Secretary of State Lord Dartmouth at his country seat in Staffordshire,[15] and, on or before December 3, Dartmouth delivered the Petition to the King.

The latter directed that it be laid before the Privy Council,[16] and Dartmouth promptly notified Franklin that the King would probably refer the consideration of it to "a committee of council."[17] The committee to which Dartmouth referred was the Privy Council's important Committee for Plantation Affairs whose recommendations to the King in Council were invariably adopted.[18]

On January 8, Franklin was notified that the hearing was to be held on the eleventh at the Cockpit,[19] but on his request for postponement, it was put off until January 29.[20] Arthur Lee was ineligible to represent the House at the hearing because he had not yet been admitted to the English bar.[21] But Franklin promptly retained an experienced solicitor, Thomas Life, who in turn retained two eminent barristers, John Dunning and John Lee, to represent the House at the hearing.[22]

Franklin's plan was to support the Petition at the hearing by showing, passage by passage, how falsely the letters had represented the conduct of the people of Massachusetts, and to this end he prepared a brief for submission to the barristers.[23] But then came a severe blow.

The barristers pointed out (quoting a letter from Franklin to Cushing) that "we wanted [lacked] evidence to prove these passages false . . . and as to the political reflections of the writers, though these might appear in the letters and need no other proof, yet they would never be considered here as offences, but as virtues and merits." The barristers, therefore, decided it would be advisable merely "to state as facts the general discontent of the people, that the governor had lost all credit with them . . . , of which the petition was itself full proof, . . . and then show that it must in such a situation be necessary for his Majesty's service, as well as the peace of the province to remove them."[24]

The hearing before the Committee on January 29, was remarkable for the number who attended it. "There never was such an appearance of privy councillors on any occasion," wrote Franklin, "not less than thirty-five, besides an immense crowd of other auditors."[25] Edmund Burke made a similar comment.[26]

As previously decided, Dunning and John Lee argued that "the matter rested wholly on their Lordships' Opinion of the Propriety or impropriety of continuing persons in Authority" who had, "(whether on sufficient or insufficient Grounds) entirely forfeited the confidence of those Assemblies with whom they were to act, and of that people whom they were to govern," and that the "materials on which the prudence of the Council was to operate . . . were fully sufficient for that prudential consideration, however inadequate they might prove for the support of a criminal charge. . . ."[27]

Solicitor-General Alexander Wedderburn, who in his private capacity as barrister represented Hutchinson and Oliver at the hearing, declined to confine the case to this issue. The Petition charged his clients with having written misleading statements as to the alleged misconduct of people in Massachusetts; he therefore claimed and was granted permission to review the conduct of the people of the province to show that their behavior was in fact as bad as his clients had described it to be.[28] So far as is known, the barristers for Massachusetts presented nothing in reply to this.

The text of the part of Wedderburn's speech denouncing the province of Massachusetts is missing;[29] but, according to Franklin, Wedderburn "went into what he called a history of the province for the last ten years, and bestowed plenty of abuse upon it."[30]

Thus, a Petition designed to vindicate the people of Massachusetts enabled the Solicitor-General, at this critical time, to present a damning case against them before many of the most influential members of Parliament.

Following the hearing, the Committee recommended dismissal of the Petition as "groundless, vexatious and scandalous, and calculated only for the seditious purposes of keeping up a spirit of clamor and discontent in the said province."[31] Soon afterward (February 7), the King in Council, quoting with approval the Committee's recommendation, dismissed the Petition.[32]

In his argument against granting the Petition, Wedderburn savagely attacked Franklin, who had sparked the Petition by procuring and sending the Hutchinson and other letters to Cushing. The following day Franklin was dismissed from his Crown office of Joint Deputy Postmaster in the British colonies on the continent of North America north of North Carolina.[33]

CHAPTER 18

THE MASSACHUSETTS REGULATING AND ADMINISTRATION OF JUSTICE ACTS

ON March 1, 1774, the Cabinet made its momentous decision (referred to in Chapter 15) to introduce a bill "to alter the Constitution of the province of Massachusetts Bay." The Cabinet had considered such a bill at a meeting on February 19, but at that time, it had left open the question of whether the bill should be "put forward in the present Session or suspended till the next" in order to give the Massachusetts Legislature an opportunity "to shew cause . . . why such an Alteration should not be made."[1] The decision to press for immediate passage[2] was made because, quoting Lord North, it seemed prudent "to seize this opportunity when all persons of all parties were of the same mind" to present the bill at the current session of Parliament.[3]

Pursuant to the Cabinet's decision, North secured leave from the House of Commons, on March 28, to bring a bill "for regulating the government of the province of Massachusetts Bay in New England,"[4] and, on April 15, he introduced the bill.[5]

This bill struck at the very roots of local self-government long enjoyed in Massachusetts, by providing for changes in choosing members of the provincial Council, appointing important provincial officials, holding town meetings, and selecting juries.

Under the Massachusetts Charter of 1691, the provincial Council—the Upper House of Legislature and an advisory council to the royal Governor —was elected annually by joint vote of the incoming members of the Massachusetts House of Representatives and the outgoing members of the Council. The Massachusetts Regulating bill provided that beginning August 1, 1774, the Council was to be appointed by the King.[6]

Under the charter, the Governor could commission provincial judges, justices of the peace, county sheriffs, and the Attorney-General only with the advice and consent of the Council. The Regulating bill provided that beginning July 1, these officers were to be appointed by the royal Governor independently of the Council,[7] and also might be removed without consent of the Council.[8]

Under a Massachusetts act dating back to 1692, the popularly elected town selectmen were empowered to call a meeting at any time for any business "of publick concernment to the town." The Regulating bill provided that beginning August 1, town meetings could not be called more than once a year without written permission from the Governor.[9]

Under various other Massachusetts acts approved by the Crown, grand jurors were elected at town meetings and panels of petty jurors were drawn by lot at such meetings from a list of persons prepared by the selectmen of the towns within the jurisdiction of court in which they were to serve. The Regulating bill provided that beginning October 1, jurors should be chosen by the Crown-appointed county sheriffs.[10]

This bill, debated at length on its second reading, April 22, met with stronger opposition than the Boston Port bill. Most of those who had spoken against the earlier bill spoke also against the second, and they now were joined by Henry S. Conway, Isaac Barré, Thomas Pownall, former Governor of Massachusetts,[11] John Dunning, Solicitor-General in the Grafton Ministry, Charles James Fox, and three leading followers of Lord Rockingham—Edmund Burke, Sir Edward Astley, and Sir George Saville.[12] But even so, on a call for a division, opponents of the bill mustered only 64 votes, while 239 votes were cast in favor of the bill, which was passed without further division on May 11.[13]

Taken up the next day by the House of Lords, the bill was opposed by much the same peers as had opposed the Boston Port bill, but again in vain.[14] On the call for a division, the opponents numbered only 20 or 21, as compared with at least 57 in favor of the bill.[15] After some unimportant amendments, the bill passed the Lords on May 11 without further division, was promptly accepted as amended by the House of Commons, and was assented to by the King on May 20.[16]

This act was extremely menacing not only to the other charter colonies —Connecticut, Rhode Island, Pennsylvania, and Maryland—the threat to whose charters from Parliament's amendment of the Massachusetts charter was obvious, but also to the colonies having no charters.

The very foundation of government of these colonies rested on the long-established rule that once a provincial act had been approved by the Crown, the Crown had no authority thereafter to repeal or amend it.[17] The Massachusetts Regulating Act, as we have seen, changed not only the Massachusetts charter, but provincial acts approved by the Crown. If Parliament had power to do this with respect to the laws of Massachusetts, what was to prevent it from doing what it pleased with the laws of all the colonies?

While the bill for the Massachusetts Regulating Act was pending, Rose Fuller moved in the House of Commons (April 19) for the repeal of the Townshend Act duty on tea,[18] and was supported by Edmund Burke in his famous speech on American taxation.[19] However, the motion was defeated 182 to 49.[20]

In opposing Fuller's motion, North said, "Convince your Colonies that you are able and not afraid to controul them, and, depend upon it, obedience in them will be the result . . . ; let us conduct ourselves with firmness and resolution throughout the whole of these measures, and there is no doubt but peace and quietude will soon be restored."[21]

The expectation that four regiments, supported by a number of warships, would suffice to enable General Gage to enforce the Boston Port Act was perfectly reasonable. But to expect, as North and a great majority in Parliament apparently did, that four regiments would suffice to enforce the Massachusetts Regulating Act throughout the province evidenced an egregious misconception of the temper of the people of Massachusetts.

Governors Francis Bernard and Hutchinson had contributed to the dangerous misconception in British governmental circles. As we saw in Chapter 16, their letters urging British action to enforce Parliament's asserted unlimited authority over the colonies repeatedly implied that, once the government had the firmness to use a little force, the colonists would submit.

But Gage himself was chiefly responsible for the misconception. In letter after letter to members of the British Ministry (quoted and discussed in Chapter 16), he indicated that there would be no serious resistance in the colonies to the coercive measures suggested by him. Furthermore, in a recent audience with the King, Gage had assured him that the colonists "will be Lyons, whilst we are Lambs but if we take the resolute part they will undoubtedly prove very meek."[22]

The Boston Port and Massachusetts Regulating Acts were supplemented by a third act: an act for "the impartial administration of justice in . . . Massachuset's Bay . . ." commonly called in the colonies, "the Murdering Act."

The act provided that if any person "acting under the direction and order of any magistrate, for the suppression of riots or for the carrying into effect the laws of revenue," was indicted in Massachusetts for murder or other capital offenses and it appeared that an impartial trial could not be had there, the Governor might, with the consent of the provincial Council, shift the trial from Massachusetts to Great Britain or such other British colony as he chose.[23] The act was to take effect June 1, 1774, and run for three years.

Introduced in the House of Commons on April 21, the bill for the act passed with relatively little opposition there or in the House of Lords.[24] Eight of the peers, including Lord Rockingham and the Duke of Richmond, filed a protest against it, pointing out that the Ministry had presented no evidence tending to show the accused would not be given a fair trial and that the only British officer, civil or military, tried for murder in Massachusetts (Captain Thomas Preston) had in fact received a fair trial and was acquitted. But the bill was promptly assented to by the King.[25]

One other act passed in 1774 must be noticed, an act to supplement the annual colonial Quartering Act, by providing that if, after due demand, any colony failed to furnish barracks for British troops stationed in the colony at places where their "presence may be necessary and required," the Governor of the colony could requisition "so many uninhabited . . . or other buildings" as he considered necessary for quartering the troops, allowing reasonable allowance for their use.[26]

Apparently, no one in the House of Commons spoke against the bill for this act, which rapidly passed all stages there without a division.[27] In the House of Lords, on the third reading of the bill, Chatham, appearing publicly for the first time in two years,[28] spoke against it.[29] But, though his surprising appearance lent a dramatic touch to the proceedings, he was able to muster only 16 votes against the administration's 57 in support of the bill.[30]

CHAPTER 19

THE QUEBEC ACT

WHILE the Massachusetts Regulating bill was pending in Parliament, Lord Dartmouth introduced a bill in the House of Lords for government of the province of Quebec, which, since its cession by France in 1763, had been essentially under military government.[1] The bill also provided for extension of the boundaries of the province to include a large part of the vast region reserved as Indian territory by the famous Royal Proclamation of 1763.[2]

Introduced in the Lords on May 2, the Quebec bill quickly passed that House without even a division.[3] When laid before the House of Commons for concurrence on May 18, the bill was attacked by much the same members as had recently opposed the Massachusetts Regulating bill;[4] but, after some amendment, it easily passed there, too—by a majority of 56 to 20.[5] On return of the amended bill to the Upper House, Lord Chatham, who had not been present when the bill was initially before that House, appeared and bitterly denounced it,[6] but in vain; the bill was adopted in the Lords, 26 to 7.[7]

The Lord Mayor and Alderman of London thereupon petitioned the King to withhold his assent, on the ground that the act was unconstitutional.[8] But this failed; on June 22 the act was assented to by the King.[9]

This act, unlike the Boston Port Act and the Massachusetts Government Acts, was projected before destruction of the East India Company's tea at Boston, and a bill along the general lines of the act probably would have been introduced and passed at the 1774 session of Parliament even if there had been no Boston Tea Party.

As early as August 4, 1773, the Lord Chancellor, Baron Apsley, wrote Lord Dartmouth, "The Chancellor's Compliments to Lord Dartmouth; takes the liberty to send him some Papers relative to Canada, which, together with the Reports of the Kings Advocate, the Attorney-General & the Solicitor-General, will, he believes, enable his Lordship to form a plan of Government for that Province fit to be laid before Parliament; & the Chancellor is happy in having received assurance from his Lordship that He means to undertake it."[10]

A few weeks later, Francis Maseres, former Attorney-General of Quebec, who had just seen Lord North, wrote that the latter was apparently "fully determined to do something towards the settlement of that Province [Quebec] in the next session of parliament . . . ," and on December 3, Under Secretary of State, John Pownall, wrote of North's pressing him for "a precis of the affairs of Quebec."[11]

Furthermore, on December 1, Dartmouth himself wrote Hector

Cramahé, Lieutenant-Governor of Quebec, that "arrangements . . . [concerning] the Civil Government of the Colony . . . will probably be settled in a very short Time"; that he would "urge the Justice and Expediency of giving all possible Satisfaction to the new [French Canadian] subjects on the Head of Religion"; and that "The Limits of the Colony" also would be considered, since "the existence of settlements in the interior Country" and "a variety of other Considerations . . . induce a doubt both of the Justice and Propriety of restraining the Colony to the narrow limits prescribed in the Proclamation [of 1763]."[12]

As foreshadowed by Dartmouth's letter, the bill for the government of Quebec (Canada) contained not only provision for the future government of the province but a vast extension of its boundaries.

The most important provisions for the government of the province were embodied in sections 5, 7, 8, 11, 12, 13, and 14 of the Quebec Act.

Section 5 gave the Roman Catholic clergy of Quebec the right to receive from all professing Roman Catholics in the province the "dues and rights" to which they had been entitled under the old French regime in Canada.[13]

Section 7 amended the act of 1 Elizabeth ch. 1 (1558) to enable Roman Catholic residents of Quebec to hold Crown offices in the province by substituting a simple oath of allegiance on taking office for the oath denying the "ecclesiastical or spiritual" authority of the Pope previously required.[14]

Section 8 confirmed or restored property rights in the province established under French rule,[15] and restored trial of civil cases without jury as had been the practice under French rule.

Section 11 provided that trial by jury in criminal cases introduced under British rule should be retained

Sections 12 and 13 provided for appointment by the Crown of a Council consisting of not more than twenty-three, nor less than seventeen, residents of the province[16] authorized "to make ordinances for the good government of the said province," but having no power to tax except to authorize towns or districts in the province to levy taxes "respecting the local convenience and oeconomy of such town or district." (A provincial revenue was provided by a supplementary act, the Quebec Revenue Act of 1774, discussed later in this chapter.) The act was silent as to the councilor's tenure of office, thus empowering the King to ensure control over them by granting them commissions revocable at his pleasure, which is what he did.[17]

Sections 12 and 14 provided that ordinances passed by the provincial Council were subject to veto by the Crown-appointed Governor of the province and if approved by him were still subject to disallowance by the King in Council.[18]

A statement in Section 12 that "it is at present inexpedient to call an assembly" tended to imply that government of the province without an elected Assembly was temporary, but, in the event, no provision was made for this until 1791.[19]

The Quebec Act also in effect (by silence) confirmed the old French system of land grant by fief or seigneurie," which the British government had reestablished in Quebec in 1771. The system imposed semi-feudal servitude such as requiring that on a re-sale of land the purchaser render homage and fealty on bended knee to the Governor as representative of the King[20] and that the vendor pay the King part of the proceeds from the sale ("Fines and Dues") for the privilege of selling it.[21]

When the province was ceded to Great Britain in 1763, the system of granting Crown land prevailing under the old French regime was abolished in favor of the liberal English system of grant in so-called free and common socage prevailing in the old British colonies.[22] But Colonel Guy Carleton, Governor of Quebec, was in favor of restoring the system of grant in fief and seigneurie because of the "Fines and Dues" that would come to the Crown and because, under this form of tenure "the Vassals" were required to take an oath to the King binding them "to appear in Arms for his Defence, in case His Province is ever attacked" and ensuring "a proper subordination" to him.[23]

Carleton's view prevailed; in 1771, the King instructed him hereafter to grant Crown land in the province "in Fief or Seigneurie, as hath been practiced heretofore antecedent to the Conquest thereof, omitting however in such Grants, so to be made by you, the reservation of the exercise [by the grantee] of such judicial Powers as hath been long disused within Our said Province."[24]

The other principal provision of the act, the provision for extension of the boundaries of the province, was embodied in Sections 1 and 2. The province as established in 1763 comprised roughly the present province of Quebec and the eastern part of the present province of Ontario.[25] Sections 1 and 2 enlarged the boundaries of Quebec to include the vast territory extending from the western boundary of Pennsylvania west to the Mississippi River and from the Ohio River north to the Hudson Bay Territory, with the proviso that "nothing herein contained, relative to the boundary of the province of Quebec, shall in anywise affect the boundaries of any other colony."[26] Just what this proviso meant is uncertain,[27] but it seems to have been generally understood in the colonies that, whatever the meaning of this proviso, the addition to the province comprised most of so-called Northwest Territory, including the present states of Ohio, Indiana, Illinois, Michigan, Wisconsin, and the eastern part of Minnesota.[28] This apparently was the understanding in Great Britain, too.[29] A major reason for the new boundary was that it permitted the establishment of civil government over French settlements in that region.

Even if the Quebec Act had been passed at a less troubled time, incorporation of much of the Northwest Territory in a province having so

autocratic a form of government and so un-English a form of land tenure
would have been unpalatable to residents of the old British colonies, who
were looking forward to the opening up of this rich territory to settlement.[30] But the timing of the act made it particularly objectionable.

John Sullivan, a delegate from New Hampshire to the Continental
Congress, in session when news of the act reached the colonies, wrote
that "the Canada Bill in my opinion [is] the most dangerous to American
Liberties among the whole train [of the Intolerable Acts], for when we . . .
Contemplate that by the late Act their [the French Canadians'] Territory
is so far extended as to include by far the greater part of North America;
that this will be a City of Refuge for Roman Catholics,[31] who will ever
appear in favor of the Prerogative of the Crown, . . . aided by the whole
force of Great Britain & . . . the same Indian Nations [that fought us in
the late war], we must suppose our Situation be Infinitely more Dangerous
now than it was then. . . ."[32]

Richard Henry Lee denounced the act on the floor of Congress as "the
worst grievance" of all,[33] and Joseph Reed wrote Dartmouth from Philadelphia that "the Quebec Bill added [such] fuel to the fire . . . that all
those deliberate measures of petitioning previous to opposition [initially
contemplated] were laid aside as inadequate to the apprehended mischief
and danger, and now the people are generally ripe for any plan the
Congress advise, should it be war itself."[34] It may be said that the act was
condemned because it favored Roman Catholics and because it injured
them.

Suspicion that the Quebec Act was cooked up at this particular time as
a threat to the old British colonies was, as we have seen, unjustified.
Nevertheless, the idea of pleasing the French Canadians in order to enlist
their help against the old British colonies in case of rebellion certainly
was present in the minds of some of the framers and supporters of the
Quebec bill.

Governor Carleton, in England on leave of absence from his government, and consulted by the Ministry on the bill,[35] had written General
Gage in 1767 that "no. Pains, Address nor Expence" would be too great
to attach the French Canadians to Great Britain. This, he pointed out,
would help secure a strong line of military communication between
Quebec and New York City that would "separate the Northern from
the Southern Colonies." The following year (at the height of the colonial
non-importation movement), Carleton wrote Hillsborough of the desir-
ability of gaining "the affections of the Canadians," who were "not united
in any common principle, interest or wish with the other Provinces. . . ."[36]

Furthermore, in pamphlets concerning the Quebec Act, Under Secretary of State William Knox, who also was consulted by Dartmouth concerning the bill,[37] wrote that "the avowed purpose of the old colonies to
oppose the execution of the laws of England" was one of the inducements
for adopting "a plan of lenity and indulgence" toward the Canadians and

that one of the advantages of the act was giving "a politic check to the independence of our American children."[38]

In similar vein, Lord Lyttelton, in supporting the Quebec bill in the House of Lords, remarked that "if British America was determined to resist the lawful power . . . of Great Britain, he saw no reason why the loyal inhabitants of Canada should not co-operate . . . in subduing them" and thought it fortunate that, "from their local situation, they might be some check to those fierce fanatic spirits . . . who pretended to be contending for liberty. . . ."[39]

The Quebec Revenue Act of 1774,[40] mentioned earlier in this chapter, was an added grievance to the people of the old British North American colonies, not only because of its fresh assertion of Parliament's claim of right to tax the colonies, but because it discriminated against the business interests of the old North American colonies in favor of the British West Indies, Great Britain, Ireland, and Quebec.

Rum or spirits distilled in the British North American colonies was taxed nine pence a gallon, while rum distilled in the British West Indies was taxed only six pence, and brandy and spirits distilled in Great Britain only three pence a gallon. The duty on molasses and syrups imported in ships owned in the North American colonies was six pence a gallon; if imported in ships owned in Quebec, Great Britain, or Ireland, only three pence.[41]

Even more seriously discriminatory was a provision in the Quebec Revenue Act providing that articles subject to duty, including rum, a staple of the Indian trade, unless imported by way of the St. Lawrence River, must be entered for duty at St. John's, Quebec. Thus, a merchant of, say, New York City, Philadelphia, or Baltimore engaged in trade with the Indians on the Ohio, in territory now tentatively included in the province of Quebec, must send his rum for customs entry to a point over two hundred miles from his place of business, whereas his competitor in Quebec or Montreal could make customs entry at a customs house within a few blocks of his warehouse.[42] This provision of the Quebec Act was amended in May, 1775,[43] but by that time the Revolutionary War had begun.

CHAPTER 20

CALLS FOR A GENERAL CONGRESS AND INSTRUCTIONS TO THE DELEGATES

NEWS of the King's assent to the Boston Port Act reached Boston May 10, 1774.[1] Three days later, a Boston town meeting resolved that general agreement in the British North American colonies to stop all imports from and exports to Great Britian and every part of the West Indies "till the Act for Blocking up this Harbor be repealed the same will prove the Salvation of North America & her Liberties." The moderator of the meeting, Samuel Adams, was instructed to send a copy of this resolution, with a covering letter, to "all our Sister Colonies." The town also approved sending out a circular letter by the Boston Committee of Correspondence (the establishment of which was described in Chapter 12) "to the other Colonies and the several Towns in this Province . . . relative to shutting up this Harbour etc."[2]

On May 14, "Mr. Riviere" (Paul Revere) was speeding southwestward with the resolution, Adams' covering letter, and a letter from the Boston Committee of Correspondence to correspondents in the chief ports of the other colonies.[3]

The first to respond to Boston's appeal was Providence, Rhode Island. On May 17, a Providence town meeting instructed the town's Committee of Correspondence to assure Boston that Providence considered all the colonies as "equally concerned" over "the present alarming conduct of the British Parliament" and that "a universal stoppage of trade" would be the best method of securing relief. But the Committee added that the first step should be the convention of a Congress of representatives of the assemblies of the colonies in North America to reach an agreement for united action[4]—a project which had been suggested by a number of writers during the past year.[5]

The next response was from Philadelphia. On May 21, a committee of nineteen, chosen at a mass meeting held the day before,[6] wrote the Boston Committee that it had "reasons to think" the people of Pennsylvania would not favor a non-importation and non-exportation agreement until an effort had been made for "reconciliation and future harmony with our mother country" by the convocation of a general congress "to state what we conceive our rights and to make a claim or petition of them to his Majesty, in firm, but decent and dutiful terms, so as that we may know by what lines to conduct ourselves in future. . . ."[7]

New York City also rejected the Boston Committee's proposal of an immediate non-importation and non-exportation agreement. A committee of Correspondence (the so-called Committee of Fifty-One), chosen at a mass meeting held in New York some days earlier,[8] wrote the Boston Committee on May 23, "We lament our inability to relieve your anxiety by a decisive opinion. The cause is general and concerns a whole Continent, who are equally interested with you and us; and we forsee that no remedy can be of avail unless it proceeds from the joint act and approbation of all. . . . Upon these reasons we conclude that a Congress of Deputies from the Colonies in general . . . ought to be assembled without delay, and some unanimous resolution formed. . . . Such being our sentiments it must be premature to pronounce any judgment on the expedient [non-importation and non-exportation] you have suggested. . . ."[9]

Before Boston's appeal reached Virginia, the Virginia House of Burgesses, in session when news of the Boston Port Act reached Williamsburg, immediately (May 24) passed a resolve that the first day of June, the day on which the act was to take effect, "be set apart, by the Members of this House, as a day of Fasting, Humiliation and Prayer, devoutly to implore the divine interposition for averting the heavy Calamity which threatens destruction to our Civil Rights and the Evils of civil War, [and] to give us one heart and one Mind firmly to oppose, by all just and proper means, every injury to American Rights. . . ."[10]

Lord Dunmore, royal Governor of the colony, retaliated by promptly dissolving the House.[11] But the next day (May 27) the members of the dissolved House met at the Raleigh Tavern and passed resolutions denouncing the Boston Port Act as "a most dangerous attempt to destroy the . . . rights of all North America" and calling for a boycott of all East Indian products except saltpeter and spices.[12] They also directed the House's Committee of Correspondence to write the similar committees of other colonies proposing an annual intercolonial congress to deliberate on "those general measures which the united interests of America may from time to time require."[13]

By the time the Boston circular letter reached Williamsburg, most members of the dissolved House had left for home. But Peyton Randolph, member for Williamsburg and Speaker of the House, was able to collect twenty-five of the former members. They published a broadside inviting all members of the dissolved House to meet in Williamsburg on August 1 to discuss adoption of non-importation and possible non-exportation, and, in the meanwhile, to collect "the Sense" of their respective counties.[14]

Nearly all of Virginia's sixty-one counties and its three boroughs responded to this letter by sending at least one delegate (chosen in nearly all cases from the members of the recently dissolved House) to the proposed provincial convention.[15] Furthermore, over half of the county conventions passed resolutions for guidance of their delegates.[16]

Particularly notable were the bold and comprehensive resolutions attributed to George Washington's neighbor and friend, George Mason, adopted by the convention of Fairfax County presided over by Washington.

Denouncing the "system formed and pursued by the British Ministry to introduce an arbitrary Government into His Majesty's American Dominions," the resolutions proposed "a Congress of Deputies from all the Colonies to concert a general and uniform plan for the defence and preservation of our common rights, which should include the stoppage of imports, with a few specified exceptions, of goods shipped from Great Britain or Ireland after September 1, 1774, and of all exports to Great Britain after November 1, 1775, until Parliament repealed the Boston Port Act and all acts "for raising a revenue from the people of America without their consent . . . taking away our trials by jury and ordering persons upon criminal accusations to be tried in another county." Furthermore, since the stoppage of exports to Great Britian would disable the people of the colonies from paying their debts, "no judgments should be rendered by the Courts in the said Colonies for any debt" if non-exportation were agreed upon.[17]

The resolutions of Westmoreland County, in which Richard Henry Lee was the leader, were in some respects even stronger. They proposed the stoppage without delay of all imports from or exports to Great Britain and the West Indies until the Boston Port Act and all British acts levying taxes on the colonies were repealed; and that "the gentlemen of the law" should not bring or pursue any actions for debt as long as the proposed "non-exportation agreement subsists. . . ."[18]

On June 3, the Connecticut House of Representatives likewise proposed a general congress, and authorized its Committee of Correspondence, previously established pursuant to the proposal of the Virginia House of Burgesses (described in Chapter 12) to appoint delegates to the congress.[19]

Twelve days later, the Rhode Island General Assembly resolved that "a Convention of Representatives from all the Colonies ought to be holden in some suitable place; as soon as may be . . . ," and chose the colony's two outstanding political leaders, former Governors Stephen Hopkins and Samuel Ward, to represent the colony.[20]

The project for a general congress was finally[21] brought to a head on June 17, when the Massachusetts House of Representatives instructed its Speaker, Thomas Cushing, to write the Speakers of the Assemblies of the other British colonies in North America inviting them to send delegates to a congress to assemble at Philadelphia on September 1,[22] Cushing immediately carried out this instruction.[23]

The Massachusetts House elected as its own delegates Cushing himself, a Boston merchant and for many years one of the town's four representatives in the House;[24] Samuel Adams, another of the Boston representatives, of whom more, later; his second cousin, John Adams, lawyer of Braintree and Boston;[25] Robert Treat Paine, a lawyer of Taunton and one of his town's representatives in the House; and James Bowdoin, a Boston capitalist and former member of the provincial Council, who, alone of the five, declined to serve.[26] All of them were Harvard graduates;[27] all had been born and lived in or within forty miles of Boston.[28]

Even before the proposal of the Massachusetts House for an inter-colonial meeting reached Maryland, a convention of delegates from all the counties of that colony, meeting at Annapolis on June 22–25, chose a strong delegation, headed by Matthew Tilghman, Speaker of the Maryland Assembly, three other of its leading members (Thomas Johnson, Jr., William Paca, and Samuel Chase), and Robert Goldsborough, a former member, to attend any intercolonial congress that might be called.[29]

The Virginia Convention, which assembled at Williamsburg on August 1, chose an outstanding delegation to the proposed intercolonial Congress: Peyton Randolph, Speaker of the dissolved House of Burgesses, and six other of its leading members—Richard Henry Lee, George Washington, Benjamin Harrison, planters; and Richard Bland, Patrick Henry, and Edmund Pendleton, lawyers. It also adopted spirited resolutions relating to the Congress, including resolutions for an agreement not to import anything except medicines from Great Britain after November 1, 1774, and not to export anything whatsoever to Great Britain after August 10, 1775, unless colonial grievances were redressed by that date.[30]

The other thirteen colonies, except Georgia, also sent delegates, chosen in one way or another, to the Congress.

Those from Pennsylvania were chosen by the regular Assembly (under pressure from a provincial convention, described in the first appendix to this chapter); those from New Hampshire, New Jersey, Delaware, and North Carolina by conventions;[31] and those from Connecticut by a Committee of Correspondence authorized by the resolution of the Connecticut House quoted earlier in this chapter.[32]

In South Carolina, the delegates were chosen initially by a mass meeting in Charleston on July 6–8 but were confirmed by the provincial assembly a few weeks later.[33]

In Georgia, efforts were made to secure the election of delegates to the proposed Congress, but without success,[34] nor is this surprising, since Georgia, relatively new and sparsely populated, was still heavily dependent on Great Britain. The Governor and other chief provincial officials were paid from funds voted by Parliament,[35] and its people relied largely for protection against Indian incursions on the influence of the Southern Indian Department, supported and controlled by the British government.[36]

In New York, the proceedings for the election of delegates to the Congress and the composition of the delegation were strikingly different from those in the other colonies represented at the Congress. The election of the delegates was initiated not by the New York Assembly nor its Speaker, but by the New York City Committee of Fifty-One. And of the delegates chosen—Isaac Low, John Alsop, Philip Livingston, James Duane, John Jay, John Haring, Henry Wisner, and Simon Boerum—only Boerum was a member of the Assembly.

(The long, bitter struggle for political hegemony in New York between the so-called Livingston and De Lancey parties which was largely responsible for this peculiarity is discussed in the second appendix to this chapter.)

Among the delegations not previously mentioned, the one from South Carolina, consisting of Thomas Lynch, Henry Middleton, John Rutledge, his young brother, Edward Rutledge, and Christopher Gadsden, was particularly distinguished. But the delegations from the remaining six— Joseph Galloway, Samuel Rhoads, Charles Humphreys, Thomas Mifflin, John Morton, George Ross, and Edward Biddle of Pennsylvania; Eliphalet Dyer, Silas Deane, and Roger Sherman of Connecticut; William Hooper, Joseph Hewes, and Richard Caswell of North Carolina; Caesar Rodney, Thomas McKean, and George Read of Delaware; John Sullivan and Nathaniel Folsom of New Hampshire; and William Livingston, James Kinsey, John Dehart, Stephen Crane, and Richard Smith of New Jersey— also were composed of men well-known at least in their respective colonies and several of them more widely.[37]

The most notable persons missing from the delegations were John Hancock, politically indispensable at home,[38] Benjamin Franklin, who was in England, and John Dickinson. The last, however, on his election to the Assembly six weeks after the Congress opened, was immediately added to the Pennsylvania delegation.[39] "A Shadow, tall but slender as a Reed, pale as ashes," yet looking "as if the Springs of Life were strong enough to last many Years," to quote John Adams' description of him, Dickinson promptly (October 17) joined the Congress[40] and, as we shall see in Chapter 24, played a prominent part in its subsequent proceedings.

Except for most of the delegates from New York and Sullivan of New Hampshire, all fifty-five members of the Congress (as the delegates decided to call their meeting) were currently or had been members of the representative Assemblies of their several colonies. Nine of them were currently or had been Speaker.[41] Nearly half of the delegates were lawyers: most of the others were farmers, planters, or businessmen. (A list of the delegates, with the principal occupation of each, is given in the third appendix to this chapter.)

Edward Rutledge, youngest of the delegates was not quite twenty-five, Hopkins, the oldest, was sixty-seven;[42] most of them were middle-aged. Though several were born in colonies other than where they now resided,[43] all were born in America. None of the delegates was Catholic; but six of the Protestant denominations—Church of England, Presbyterian, Congregational, Quaker, and Baptist—were represented.[44]

Hopkins had been a delegate to the Albany Congress of 1754, and Dyer, Philip Livingston, Morton, McKean, Rodney, John Rutledge, and Gadsden to the Stamp Act Congress of 1765;[45] but the great majority would now for the first time be attending an intercolonial gathering.

If British ministers consulted persons in London familiar with the colonies represented at the congress, they must have learned how little truth there was in the frequent depiction of the leaders of the colonial opposition as agitators of ambiguous character having everything to gain and little or nothing to lose by a revolution. For nearly all the delegates were prosperous businessmen, planters, farmers, or lawyers of outstanding position in their respective colonies.[46]

Indeed, the only delegate who fitted into the picture of unprosperous agitator of ambiguous character was Samuel Adams. There is evidence that he was hard-up,[47] had possibly been guilty as charged of embezzling public funds,[48] and certainly had spent a large part of his time for many years in agitating against British measures threatening colonial liberty.[49]

All the colonies except New York represented at the Congress passed resolutions or gave instructions to guide or restrict their delegates.[50] Most demanded repeal of the Boston Port Act, the Massachusetts Government Act, and all British acts levying taxes for revenue on the colonies, but as to other grievances and the method or methods to secure relief, they disclosed a wide diversity of opinion.

CHAPTER 21

UNIFYING AND DIVISIVE ELEMENTS
IN THE CONGRESS

THE delegates to the Congress, with possibly a few exceptions, apparently were united in the conviction that Parliament's claim of right to tax the colonies as it pleased struck at the very root of colonial liberty and that the Congress must take some action beyond mere petitioning in order to secure the abandonment of this claim.

The prevailing feeling was well expressed by George Washington, not long after his election as one of Virginia's delegates to the Congress. Replying to letters from an old friend and neighbor, Bryan Fairfax, urging that the Congress confine itself to petitioning for redress,[1] Washington wrote:

"As . . . I observe or think I observe that government is pursuing a regular plan, at the expence of law and justice, to over-throw our constitutional rights and liberties, how can I expect any redress from a measure which has been ineffectually tried already? For, Sir, what is it we are contending against? Is it paying the duty of three pence per pound on tea because burthensome? No, it is the right only we have all along disputed, and to this end we have petitioned his Majesty in as humble and dutiful manner as subjects could do. . . .

"The conduct of the Boston people could not justify the rigor of their [Parliament's] measures [against Boston] nor . . . require an act to deprive Massachusetts Bay of their charter or to exempt persons from trial in the place where offences were committed. . . . Are not all these things self evident proofs of a fixed and uniform plan to tax us? If we want further proofs, do not all the debates in the House of Commons serve to confirm this. . . .

"I could wish, I own, that the dispute had been left to posterity to determine, but the crisis is arrived when we must assert our rights or submit to every imposition that can be heaped upon us, till custom and use shall make us as tame and abject slaves as the blacks we rule over with such arbitrary sway."[2]

The underlying ground for the colonists' fear had long since been pointed out by Stephen Hopkins, one of the Rhode Island delegates to the Congress. "If the people in America are to be taxed by the representatives of the people in Britain," said Hopkins, "their malady . . . must always grow greater by time. Whatever burdens are laid upon the Americans will be so much taken off the Britons; the doing this will soon be extremely popular, and those who put up to be members of the House of Commons must obtain the votes of the people by promising to take more and more taxes off of them by putting it on the Americans. This must assuredly be the case. . . ."[3]

The prospect was all the more alarming, as several colonial writers pointed out, because of the known profligacy of the British government in granting exorbitant salaries and undeserved sinecures and pensions.[4] "If places, pensions and dependencies shall be ever increased in proportion to new resources," wrote James Otis, "the game may truly be infinite." "If a set of men [i.e., members of Parliament] have been so profane and lavish of their constituents," said Charles Carroll of Carrollton, "will they be more sparing of ours?"[5]

Nor was the fear of colonial Whigs that the relatively mild duties levied by the Townshend Act would be mightily increased once Parliament had firmly established its asserted right to tax the colonies based solely on general reasoning.

In telling Parliament of his project for colonial taxation "to give Relief to Great Britain from bearing the whole of the Expence of securing, defending and protecting America and the West India Islands," Charles Townshend said he would "in time" do everything to form a revenue "to bear the whole" but "by degrees" and "with great delicacy."[6]

Besides, what was the sense of Parliament's antagonizing the colonists by keeping alive its claim of right to tax them unless it intended later to extract a greater revenue from colonial taxation? There was, to be sure, talk of maintaining this right for use solely in time of emergency. But no emergency existed at the time the Townshend Act was passed. Indeed, during the very session in which this act passed, Parliament *reduced* British taxes by lowering the British land tax from four to three shillings in the pound.[7]

Furthermore, the record of Parliament in restricting colonial trade was a dire warning of what to expect if Parliament established its claim of right to tax the colonies.

In 1660 and 1663 Parliament passed acts prohibiting the export of colonial sugar, tobacco, and several other colonial products, known as "enumerated" products, to any place outside the colonies except England or Ireland and the importation into the colonies of any product of continental Europe, other than salt, except from England.[8]

Having secured colonial acquiescence in these acts, Parliament proceeded to add restriction after restriction.

In 1696, it prohibited the export of the enumerated colonial products to Ireland.[9]

In 1698, it prohibited any kind of trade (import or export) between the colonies and the East Indies, which were defined to include all of the vast region extending from the east coast of Africa to the west coast of the Americas.

In 1699, it prohibited the export of colonial wool and woolen goods to any place outside the colony in which produced.

In 1704, it prohibited overseas export of colonial molasses, tar, turpentine, masts, and naval stores to any place but England. (The Union with Scotland in 1707 put Scotland on the same favorable footing as England after that date.)

In 1721, Parliament prohibited importation into the colonies of any East Indian products, including tea, pepper, spices, drugs, silk and cotton cloth, (which the colonists had hitherto been permitted to import from Holland and other countries of continental Europe) from any place but Great Britain, i.e., England and Scotland.

In 1722, it prohibited the overseas export of colonial fur and copper to any place but Great Britain.

In 1732, it prohibited the export of colonial-made felt or hats to any place outside the colony in which manufactured and the export of colonial hops to Ireland.

In 1733 (under pressure from owners of the great British West Indian sugar plantations many of whom lived in Great Britain), Parliament severely restricted importation into the British North American colonies of products from the foreign West Indies.

In 1750, it struck at colonial manufacturing and trade by prohibiting the erection of any new colonial mill for slitting, rolling, or planting iron or of any new furnace for making steel.

In 1764, it prohibited the overseas export of colonial hides, skins, potash, and several other colonial products to any place but Great Britain and the export of colonial iron and lumber[10] to any part of continental Europe.

In 1766, it prohibited the exportation of any British colonial product whatsoever to any place in continental Europe north of the Spanish ports on the bay of Biscay.[11]

In the light of this record in the field of restricting colonial trade, could there be any reasonable doubt as to what Parliament would do in the field of taxation if it established its claim of right to tax the colonists as it pleased?

The hope, earlier entertained by colonial Whigs, that a change in Ministry might result in the tacit recognition of their claim to freedom from British taxation had by this time faded. This hope had been aroused by the repeated election in 1768 and 1769 of the popular agitator, John Wilkes, as a member of Parliament for Middlesex County and by a movement in England for political reform,[12] widely known in the colonies through English correspondents and newspapers.[13] But when the Duke of Grafton, First Lord of the Treasury and head of the Ministry, resigned in January, 1770, he was succeeded as First Minister by Lord North, who, as Leader of the House of Commons, had strongly supported the exclusion of Wilkes from the House[14] and now explicitly supported retention of the Townshend Act duty on tea to maintain Parliament's claim of right to tax the colonies.[15]

For some months after establishment of the new Ministry, it appeared that the Ministry was about to fall. But by the end of 1770, it was firmly in the saddle, and in succeeding years, with the steady support of the King, it consistently carried its measures by overwhelming majorities in both Houses of Parliament. Consequently, by the time the Continental Congress met in September, 1774, there was little hope of relief through a change in Ministry.

As brought out in the admirable studies of Clinton Rossiter, Caroline Robbins, H. Trevor Colbourn, Bernard Bailyn,[16] and others,[17] one of the powerful forces in unifying colonial sentiment was invocation of the writings of classical authors and earlier English writers in praise or defense of liberty. These were known to the reading public throughout the colonies at first hand or through the heavy borrowing from them in current pamphlets,[18] newspapers, sermons, and almanacs.[19] (The meager colonial stage apparently did not contribute significantly toward arousing and unifying the colonists in opposing the British threat to colonial liberty. But Addison's popular play, *Cato,* evidently did.[20] Patriotic songs also were a contributing influence.[21])

One of the points particularly stressed in the writings in defense of liberty was that liberty, once enjoyed but lost, had commonly been lost because leaders of the people, who ought to have taken timely action to preserve it, had failed in their duty. Would not the history of lost liberties repeat itself if the Congress, to whom the people of America now looked for the preservation of their liberty, failed to unite in taking effective action to this end?

But what should this action be? Here was the rub.

Probably a majority in all the delegations, if not every delegate, would agree that something more than further petitioning was required; that some form of commercial pressure should be applied; and that this pressure should include an agreement not to import from Great Britain anything subject to colonial duty levied by Parliament or in the nature of luxuries.

But should the agreement include such almost indispensable items as equipment for the New England fishing industry, blankets for the Indian trade, and Osnaburgs (pieces of coarse linen cloth) to clothe the southern plantation slaves, all goods which were not manufactured in the colonies, could legally be imported only from Great Britain, and could not easily be smuggled into the colonies from other countries?

Should non-importation be confined to goods from Great Britain or should it be extended to products of Ireland and the West Indies? If not so extended, merchants engaged chiefly in importing from Great Britain would be compelled to make a much greater sacrifice than those engaged chiefly in trade with Ireland or the West Indies.

Furthermore, the instructions to the delegates from some of the provincial Assemblies or conventions called for a ban on exportation, as well as on importation. Assuming (as was far from certain)[22] that all the delegations would support a non-exportation agreement of some kind, questions of whether the ban should apply to Great Britain only, and the exemptions, if any, would be at least as divisive with respect to exportation as with respect to importation.

But even before the Congress got down to decisions on these foreseeable issues, the question must arise as to the method of voting on the decisions to be made. Would the delegations from such rich and populous colonies as Virginia, Massachusetts, and Pennsylvania agree to be put on the same footing as colonies so disproportionately small in population and wealth as New Hampshire, Rhode Island, and Delaware? And if this question could somehow be resolved, would the delegations agree to be bound by the vote of a bare majority, or would some greater percentage or even unanimity be demanded?

Another divisive question was almost certain to arise: the question of the stand to be taken by the Congress concerning the British acts restricting colonial trade.

Probably there would be little, if any, dissent to a demand that trial by jury in cases involving alleged violations of British acts restricting colonial trade be restored. From 1764 onward, colonial Whigs had been united on this point. But how about the authority of Parliament to impose these restrictions, the enforcement of which had been the source of so much and such continuous friction over the past decade?

When the controversy over colonial taxation first arose in 1764, the petitioning of the colonial Assemblies protesting against colonial taxation had, implicitly at least, recognized the authority of Parliament to impose restrictions on colonial trade,[23] and many of the delegates to the Congress had been members of the Assemblies which had adopted these petitions (In the case of Virginia, all of its delegates to the Congress except Henry had been members of the House of Burgesses at the time the Virginia petition—"remonstrance"—of December, 1764, was adopted, and Randolph, Lee, Pendleton, and Harrison were of the committee that drafted it.)[24] Furthermore, at least two of the delegates—Cushing of Massachusetts and Hopkins of Rhode Island—had at that time expressly recognized the authority of Parliament to regulate, i.e., restrict, colonial trade.[25]

But by 1774, this view had been seriously challenged.

In 1771, Samuel Adams, now one of the Massachusetts delegates to the Congress, had denied the authority of Parliament to legislate in any way for the colonies.[26] Two years later, as noted in Chapter 12, the Massachusetts House of Representatives questioned the authority of Parliament to legislate in any way for Massachusetts. In July, 1774, one of the resolves adopted by the Fairfax County convention, chaired by Washington, declared it to be a "fundamental principle" of the British constitution, to whose protection the people of Virginia no less than those of Great Britain were entitled, that people were to be governed "by no laws to which they have not given their consent by Representatives freely chosen by themselves. . . ."[27] And shortly before the Congress assembled, Roger Sherman, one of the Connecticut delegates, told John Adams that, in his opinion, Parliament had no authority whatever over the colonies.[28]

A clash over the question of challenging the authority of Parliament to restrict colonial trade was, therefore inevitable, some of the delegates supporting a resolution denying the authority of Parliament to restrict colonial trade, others opposing such a resolution on principle or as needlessly provocative.

CHAPTER 22

THE CONTINENTAL CONGRESS:
FIRST STEPS

THE Massachusetts delegates—Cushing, Paine, Samuel Adams, and John Adams—set out together for Philadelphia by "coach and four" on August 10, 1774.[1] Diaries of John Adams and Paine enable us to follow their route and reception and to share Adams' impressions of several delegates from other colonies whom they encountered along the way.

Starting from Cushing's home in Boston, they traveled through Framingham, Worcester, and Springfield, Massachusetts, and Hartford, Wethersfield, and Middletown, Connecticut,[2] to New Haven, where they spent two nights at the well-known tavern of Isaac Beers. At Wethersfield they were entertained with punch, wine, and coffee at the home of one of the Connecticut delegates, Silas Deane, a prosperous merchant and lawyer, and at New Haven had a good talk with his fellow delegate, Roger Sherman, "a solid, sensible Man."[3]

Leaving New Haven early in the morning of the 18th, they proceeded by way of Stratford, Norwalk, and Stamford, Connecticut, to New York City, where they arrived on the 20th and put up for nearly a week at an unidentified tavern near the City Hall. At New York they met most of the leading local Whigs, including all but John Jay of the New York City delegates to the Congress—Alsop, "a soft, sweet man," but said to be "unequal to the Trust in point of abilities"; Duane, "a little squint Eyed," who struck Adams as being "very sensible" but also "very artfull"; Philip Livingston, "a down right, strait forward . . . rough, rappid Mortal"; and Low, of whom Adams gave no description but recorded the report that he "will profess Attachment to the Cause of Liberty but his Sincerity is doubted."

On August 26, the Massachusetts delegates resumed their journey to Philadelphia, taking the ferry to Paulus Hook, New Jersey, and traveling by way of Newark, Brunswick, Princeton, and Trenton. So far as is known, they encountered none of the New Jersey delegates but had a glass of wine with the president of Princeton, the Reverend John Witherspoon, whom they found to be "as high a Son of Liberty as any Man in America." Arriving August 29 at Frankfort, then about five miles from, now a part of, Philadelphia, they were met by a line of carriages and "dirty, dusty and fatigued," were escorted to the sumptuous City Tavern, where they were welcomed by a multitude of Philadelphians and treated to a "Supper . . . as elegant as ever was laid upon a table." It was eleven o'clock before they finally got away to Mrs. Sarah Yard's boardinghouse, where (except for a few days' unexplained move to other lodgings) they stayed throughout their nearly two months' residence in Philadelphia.

All the other New England delegates and all from South Carolina had reached Philadelphia by August 31,[4] and those from New Jersey and two from New York arrived on September first.[5] But, perhaps because of a diversity in the resolutions of the provincial conventions as to the date for assembling,[6] so many of the delegates were then still missing that the opening of the Congress was necessarily deferred.

On September 2, four of the delegates from Virginia—Randolph, Lee, Bland, and Harrison—arrived,[7] and on the following day, the Massachusetts delegates had a chance to meet and talk with Lee, who was to play an outstanding role in the Congress. After he "had dined with Mr. [John] Dickinson and drank Burgundy the whole afternoon," wrote Adams in his diary, Lee had supper with the Massachusetts delegates at the home of Thomas Mifflin, where, "very high," he joined them and other guests in drinking "Sentiments till 11 O Clock," including "Wisdom to Britain and Firmness to the Colonies . . . Union of the Colonies . . . Union of Britain and the Colonies, on a Constitutional Foundation—and many other such Toasts."[8]

On the third of September, most of the Maryland delegates and Washington, Henry, and Pendleton (who, leaving Mount Vernon on August 31, had made a rapid trip by way of Annapolis and Chestertown, Maryland, Newcastle, Delaware, and Chester, Pennsylvania) reached Philadelphia,[9] and by the 4th nearly all the delegates from the participating colonies, except North Carolina (whose delegates did not reach Philadelphia until the middle of the month), were on hand.[10]

The following day, September 5 (quoting the opening entry of the official records of the Congress), "A number of the Delegates chosen and appointed by the Several Colonies and Provinces in North America to meet and hold a Congress at Philadelphia assembled at the Carpenters' Hall."[11]

Thanks again to Adams' diary and to letters from him and Silas Deane of Connecticut to family and friends at home, we get glimpses of several more of the delegates.

Those from Virginia particularly impressed Deane. Randolph, he wrote, was of "noble appearance," "affable, open and . . . large in size though not out of proportion," Pendleton, "of easy and cheerful countenance, polite in address, and elegant . . . in Style and diction," Bland, "a plain sensible man," and Henry the "completest [i.e., most perfect] speaker" Deane had ever heard; "the music of his voice" and the "natural elegance of his style and manner" were almost beyond description. Washington was "nearly as tall a man as Col. Fitch and almost as hard a countenance; yet with a very young look, and an easy, soldier like air and gesture."[12] Deane gives no picture of Lee; but Adams describes him as "a tall, spare . . . masterly Man."[13]

Rodney of Delaware found the Massachusetts delegates "moderate men when compared to Virginia, South Carolina and Rhode Island,"[14] and Deane wrote that Gadsden of South Carolina "leaves all New England Sons of Liberty far behind" in fire.[15]

Though Washington was not on a single Congressional committee and apparently took little part in the debates on the floor of Congress,[16] myths had already begun to gather about him. Adams wrote that he was reported to have said at the recent Virginia convention, "I will raise one thousand men, subsist them at my own expense, and march myself at their head to the relief of Boston,"[17] and Deane that he "was the means of saving the remains of that [Braddock's] unfortunate army" in the French and Indian War,[18] neither of which seems to have been true.[19]

Deane and Adams both were also very favorably impressed by Lynch of South Carolina. Despite his "immense fortune," said Deane, Lynch was "plain, sensible, above ceremony" and "carries with him more force in his very appearance than most powdered folks in their conversation," and Adams wrote, "We are all vastly pleased with Mr. Lynch. He is a solid, firm judicious Man." Adams was also favorably impressed by Caesar Rodney of Delaware, who, though "the oddest looking Man in the world . . . his Face . . . not bigger than a large Apple" had "Sense and Fire, Spirit, Wit and Humour in his Countenance." But, as we learn from his diary, Adams had little use for two of Lynch's fellow delegates from South Carolina. Edward Rutledge was "a perfect Bob o'Lincoln, . . . a Peacock—excessively vain . . . jejune, inane and puerile," and his elder brother, John, had "No Depth in his Countenance. Nothing of the profound, sagacious, brilliant or sparkling. . . ."[20] (Unfortunately, no one, so far as is known, described Adams himself.)[21]

I shall have frequent occasion to refer not only to Adams' diary, but also to his notes of debates since they, along with some notes of debates by Duane of New York and Deane of Connecticut and the laconic diary of Ward of Rhode Island, are the chief means of fleshing out the official journals of the Congress. These tell us what proposed resolves were adopted, but nothing of those that were rejected or of the debates and maneuvers that lay behind the decisions. The correspondence of the members is of little help, for all of them apparently observed with remarkable fidelity the resolution adopted almost immediately after the opening of the Congress that "the members consider themselves under the strongest obligations of honour, to keep the proceedings secret untill the majority shall direct them to be made public."[22]

The Congress got off to a rather awkward start not only because of the delay in opening its sessions, but because of pre-convention discord over choice of the place where the Congress should sit. Galloway, as Speaker of the Pennsylvania Assembly, offered the Assembly's commodious chamber in the Pennsylvania State House, and several of the delegates wished to accept this offer.[23] But the majority supported the proposal of

Lynch to accept an offer of the Carpenters' Hall,[24] which, as indicated in the opening record of the Congress, quoted above, was selected.[25] The Hall had the advantage of "an excellent Library, a long Entry where Gentlemen may walk, and a convenient Chamber opposite to the Library."[26] But, according to Deane, it really was chosen over the Assembly Chamber, which was "evidently the best place," only out of pique against Galloway for having secured the exclusion of Charles Thomson, "the Sam Adams of Phyladelphia,"[27] from the colony's delegation to the Congress.[28]

The convention promptly voted to call itself "the Congress"[29] and apparently to call its presiding officer "President," not "the President."[30] Lynch nominated Randolph, long Speaker of the Virginia House, for this office and Thomson, though not a member of the Congress, for Secretary, and both were chosen.[31]

The New York delegates, the peculiarity of whose election was described in Chapter 20, were readily accepted as representing the colony as a whole,[32] and a couple of points of procedure were also promptly decided,[33] apparently without debate. There also seems to have been little difficulty in deciding that the voting should be by colonies and not by individual members.[34] Indeed, since there was no limitation on the number of delegates each colony might send, a vote by individual members would have been almost unthinkable. But the question whether each colony should have a single vote or whether some should have more than one vote on the basis of population,[35] property value, or a combination of the two, was warmly debated.

Patrick Henry of Virginia, most populous of the colonies, declared that "it would be a great injustice if a little Colony should have the same weight in the councils of America as a great one," and argued that each should have a number of votes "in proportion to its opulence and number of inhabitants, its exports and imports,"[36] slaves to be excluded in computing population.[37] Harrison of Virginia also "insisted strongly on the injustice that Virginia should have no greater Weight . . . than one of the smallest colonies," but apparently did not indicate any proposed basis for apportionment.[38] Lynch of South Carolina also favored proportionate voting, yet he maintained that apportionment should be based on "a compound of numbers and property,"[39] presumably with the inclusion of slaves in the estimate either of numbers or of property.

Sullivan of New Hampshire, one of the least populous of the colonies, insisted that each colony should have the same vote, since "a little Colony had its all at stake as well as a great one," and was supported by delegates from two of the other small colonies, Samuel Ward of Rhode Island and Christopher Gadsden of South Carolina.[40]

The delegates from Massachusetts, second most populous of the colonies, wisely remained silent throughout the debate on this potentially explosive question of representation.[41] The peculiar situation of "our embassy," as John Adams aptly described the Massachusetts delegation, was summed up in letters from him to his wife and to his law associate, William Tudor, stating: "We have a delicate course to steer between too much activity and too much insensibility in our critical, interested [i.e., self-interested] situation."[42] "We have been obliged to act with great delicacy and caution, . . . to keep ourselves out of sight . . . , to insinuate our sentiments, designs and desires by means of other persons, sometimes of one province, and sometimes of another."[43]

The question of voting was settled in favor of the small colonies when Lee and Bland of Virginia conceded that the Congress did not have at hand the materials to work out a just method of proportionate voting.[44] However, the resolution that "each Colony or Province[45] shall have one Vote" was qualified by adding "the Congress not being possess'd of, or at present able to procure proper materials for ascertaining the importance of each colony,"[46] to provide against the resolution being "drawn into precedent in future."[47] (This initial victory of the small colonies, nevertheless, was indicative of decisions to come: the draft of the Articles of Confederation submitted to the Second Continental Congress in 1776 and the Articles finally adopted by the Congress in 1777 provided that "each State shall have one vote."[48]

Curiously, the question of whether a bare majority of the participating colonies should suffice to bind the whole—one of the most controversial in formulating the Articles of Confederation adopted by the Second Continental Congress—was decided in the affirmative, apparently without controversy.[49]

The receipt on September 6 of an erroneous report of the British having cannonaded Boston and killed six of its inhabitants[50] prompted a motion that the Congress be opened the next morning with prayer. This led briefly to a threat of a division along ecclesiastical lines, which happily was averted by a motion by Congregationalist Samuel Adams that the Congress be opened the next morning (September 7) with prayer by the Reverend Jacob Duché, a Church of England clergyman. The motion was adopted,[51] and, Duché read the lesson of the day and prayed most acceptably.[52]

The first item of business adopted by the Congress was the establishment on September 6 of a committee,[53] hereafter referred to as the Committee on Rights, composed of two members from each colony,[54] "to State the rights of the Colonies in general, the several instances in which these rights are violated or infringed, and the means most proper to be pursued for obtaining a restoration of them."[55]

On September 17 the Congress took action, described in Chapter 23, on the famous "Suffolk Resolves," adopted at a meeting of delegates from towns in Suffolk County, Massachusetts, of which Boston was the county seat.[56]

A few days later (September 22), the Congress took another important step by resolving unanimously "to request the Merchants and others in the several colonies, not to send to Great Britain, any orders for goods, and to direct the execution of all orders already sent, to be delayed or suspended until the sense of the Congress on the means to be taken for the preservation of the liberties of America is made public,"[57] and on September 26, took up a motion by Lee for "a non-importation."[58]

Galloway, who was opposed to a non-importation agreement,[59] apparently had hoped to form a party in the Congress of members from New York, New Jersey, and Pennsylvania strong enough to stave off the adoption of such an agreement until other efforts to secure relief were tried. But by the time the Congress met, he had lost hope of this,[60] the recent news of the King's assent to the Quebec Act[61] having convinced even the most cautious or conservative Whigs that measures other than mere petitioning were needed. Joseph Reed of Philadelphia wrote Lord Dartmouth on September 25 that on receipt of this news "those deliberate measures of petitioning previous to opposition were laid aside as inadequate to the apprehended mischief and danger," and, on the following day, he wrote his brother-in-law, Denny De Berdt, "No man dares open his mouth against non-importation."[62] Another prominent Philadelphian, James Allen, wrote Ralph Izard in similar vein. The Quebec Act, revealing an "inveterate design of subjugating America," had, Izard said, "aroused the most inattentive and given us but one mind."[63]

It is therefore not surprising that, so far as is known, not a single delegate now spoke in opposition to Lee's motion for non-importation.

Debate apparently was confined to three questions: what the effective date should be; should reference be to the time of shipment or to the time of arrival—in either case, what should be the cut-off date; and whether or not the non-importation agreement should include articles, such as molasses from the West Indies, not imported from Great Britain or Ireland but subject to British duties on importation into the colonies.

Bland proposed that the effective date be fixed with reference to when the goods were shipped rather than when they arrived "because a ship may have a long Voyage," i.e., goods shipped well before non-importation was generally thought of might be penalized because of an unforeseeable long passage of the carrying vessel. But Gadsden and Lee objected to this and favored time of arrival because the other would invite fraudulent antedating of invoices, and this view prevailed.[64]

As to the date for the cut-off, Mifflin favored November 1, 1774, and Cushing and Edward Rutledge an immediate one.[65] But, in spite of the fact that the Virginia convention had proposed November 1, Henry spoke in favor of December 1, and his view prevailed.[66]

Mifflin next proposed that the ban on importation be extended to all "dutied articles" even if not exported from Great Britain or Ireland,[67] but his proposal on this point also failed.

The resolution adopted unanimously September 27 states: "That from and after the first day of December next, there be no importation into

British America from Great Britain or Ireland, of any goods, wares or merchandizes whatsoever, or from any other place, of any such goods, wares or merchandizes, as shall have been exported from Great-Britain or Ireland; and that no such goods, wares or merchandizes imported after the said first day of December next, be used or purchased."[68]

This resolution, it will be observed, went further than the instructions to the delegates for a non-importation agreement (discussed in Chapter 20) in that it included Ireland as well as Great Britain.[69] Since many members of Parliament had large land holdings or other economic stakes in Ireland, the Congress doubtless reasoned that including imports from Ireland in the ban would put additional pressure on members of Parliament to grant the colonists' demands.

The resolution, it will be noted, also included a ban on the "use or purchase of goods," as well as on their importation, thus envisaging direct participation in the boycott not only by importing merchants and planters as in the non-importation agreements of 1768–1770, but by every one in the colonies.[70]

The day following adoption of this non-importation and non-consumption resolution, Galloway moved the adoption of a resolution: "That the Congress will apply to his Majesty for a redress of grievances under which his faithful subjects in America labour; . . . and, as the Colonies from their local circumstances cannot be represented in the Parliament of Great-Britain, they will humbly propose to his Majesty and his two Houses of Parliament, the following plan under which the strength of the whole Empire may be drawn together on any emergency, the interest of both countries advanced, and the rights and liberties of America secured."[71]

The Congress voted (September 28) that the plan (which is outlined and discussed in an appendix to this chapter) be "considered, not committed, but ordered to lie on the table," and, a few weeks later, voted that it be "dismissed."[72]

Two days after Galloway presented his plan, the Congress resolved, over his strong opposition,[73] "That from and after the 10th day of September 1775, the exportation of all merchandize and every commodity whatsoever to Great Britain, Ireland and the West Indies, ought to cease, unless the grievances of America are redressed before that time."[74]

Inclusion of Ireland and the British West Indies in the non-exportation boycott can be readily explained on the same ground as the inclusion of Ireland in the non-importation agreement, namely, to put economic pressure on members of Parliament having economic interests in Ireland and the British West Indies. Inclusion of the foreign West Indies in the boycott presumably was prompted by the known ease with which the ban on exports to the British West Indies could be evaded by ostensibly clearing for a foreign island and actually unloading in one of the British.

Gadsden and Edward Rutledge of South Carolina and Cushing of Massachusetts spoke in favor of having the non-exportation agreement take effect without delay;[75] but, as shown by the provision for deferment in the resolution, their view was not adopted. The long deferment of the date for banning non-exportation presumably was due to instructions to the delegates of Maryland, Virginia, and North Carolina as to the non-exportation of tobacco, described in Chapter 20.[76]

Unlike the resolution for non-importation, the non-exportation resolution was not passed unanimously,[77] but no evidence has been found as to which colony or colonies did not approve it and whether disapproval was manifested by a negative vote or by not voting at all.[78]

To increase the pressure on British merchants and manufacturers to secure the redress of colonial grievances, Gadsden of South Carolina moved that "from & after the 20th September 1774 no remittances to be made to G. Brittain"; he was supported by Ward of Rhode Island and Ross of Pennsylvania. But the motion was opposed by Edward Rutledge and Galloway and was voted down without a dissenting voice.[79]

Thus, by the end of September, the Congress had taken one of the most important of its steps. Redress was to be sought by putting a stop, beginning December 1, 1774, to the importation into the colonies represented at the Congress of all goods from Great Britain or Ireland; to the consumption of any such goods imported after that date; and to the exportation, beginning September 10, 1775, of all products of these colonies to Great Britain, Ireland, and the West Indies.

CHAPTER 23

STATEMENT OF GRIEVANCES AND APPROVAL OF THE SUFFOLK RESOLVES

THE Committee for the Statement of Rights did not submit its draft to the Congress until Steptember 22, and the latter had the statement under consideration for over three weeks before adopting it, after amendment, on October 14.[1]
Judging from John Adams' acid comments, the extreme delay in the submission and adoption of this basic state paper was due chiefly to immoderate speechmaking, both in the committee, of which he was a member, and on the floor of the Congress. The complaint in his diary, October 10, that "The Deliberations of the Congress are spun out to an immeasurable Length. There is so much Wit, Sense, Learning, Acuteness, Subtilty, Eloquence, etc. among fifty Gentlemen, each of whom has been habituated to lead and guide in his own Province, that an immensity of Time is spent unnecessarily," is but one of several of this character made by him.[2] His fellow New Englanders, Dyer and Sherman of Connecticut, who spoke "often and long, . . . very heavily and clumsily,"[3] were, he indicates, among the worst offenders. But the round of heavy eating and drinking that went on after hours,[4] with its inevitable consequence of fatigue and clouded brains, must have contributed materially to the slow pace.

Washington's diary records that he dined at a different house every day but three from September 5 to 24, and, even on one of these he was a guest at what Paine of Massachusetts described as "a grand Dinner to the Congress in the State House," where "almost 500 din'd at once."[5] Washington gives no details,[6] but, thanks again to Adams' diary, we get a pretty good idea of what kind of dinners they were.

On September 7, Adams dined with a large company, including delegates McKean and Rodney of Delaware and Hopkins and Ward of Rhode Island, at the home of Miers Fisher and his "pretty wife," who, with all her simple "Thee's and Thou's," had provided a great variety of tempting dishes—"Ducks, Hams, Chickens, Beef, Pigg, Tarts, Creams, Custards, Gellies, fools, Trifles, floating Islands"—and "Beer, Porter, Punch, Wine and a long Etc."

The following evening, dining with delegates Goldsborough and Johnson of Maryland at the home of Samuel Powell, Adams again found "Everything which could delight the Eye or allure the Taste, curds and Creams . . . 20 sorts of Tarts, fools,[7] Trifles,[8] floating Islands, whipped Sillabubs[9] . . . Parmesan Cheese, Punch, Wine, Porter, Beer Etc. Etc."[10]

Similar entries continue day after day. Indeed, even as late as September 29, Adams wrote of its still being part of the daily routine to dine with some of "the Nobles of Pennsylvania at four O Clock and feast upon ten thousand Delicacies, and sitt drinking Madeira, Claret and Burgundy till six or seven and then go home, fatigued to death. . . ."[11]

But even had the delegates had clear heads and brevity of speech, the preparation and adoption of the Statement of Rights would have consumed much time. As the Connecticut delegation wrote in explaining the unexpected length of their stay, "coming from remote colonies, each of which has some modes of transacting publick business peculiar to itself, some particular provincial rights and interests to guard and secure, [we] must take some time to become acquainted with each one's situations and connexions, as to be able to give an united assent to the ways and means for effecting, what all are desirious of."[12]

The statement finally adopted[13] declared that "by the immutable laws of nature, the principles of the English constitution, and the several charters or compacts," the colonists were "entitled to life, liberty and property"; that "the foundation of English liberty, and of all free government, is a right in the people to participate in their legislative council"; and that, since "the English colonists are not represented, and from their local and other circumstances, cannot properly be represented in the British parliament," they were "entitled to a free and exclusive power of legislation in their several provincial legislatures" subject only to "the negative of their sovereign in such manner as had been heretofore used and accustomed."[14]

As foreshadowed by the instructions to delegates (discussed in Chapter 20), the grievances recited in the statement were all the British acts levying duties for revenue in the colonies:[15] the provisions of the Acts of 1764 and 1766 restricting colonial trade and colonial currency (described in Chapter 3 of this book); the Acts of 1767 authorizing establishment of the American Customs Board (discussed in Chapters 5 and 8) and concerning writs of assistance (discussed in Chapter 5);[16] the Act of 1768 providing for establishment of colonial district courts of admiralty and defining their jurisdiction (described in Chapter 10); the Act of 1772 providing for trial in England of persons accused of destroying royal dockyards, ships, etc., in the colonies (referred to in Chapter 12); and the Intolerable Acts of 1774.[17]

The statement also recited as grievances the Crown's abridging the right of the colonists "to assemble, consider of their grievances and petition the King"; "keeping a Standing army in these colonies, in times of peace, without the consent of the legislature of that colony in which such army is kept"; and exercising "legislative power in several colonies by a council appointed, during pleasure, by the crown."[18]

The Delaware convention had recited as one of the colonial grievances to be dealt with by the Congress "the several acts of the British Parliament for restraining manufactures" in the colonies.[19] Parliament's policy of restricting colonial manufacturing that threatened to compete with British manufacturing doubtless would prove a source of extreme friction when colonial manufacturing skills and natural resources should become more fully developed. But the restrictions had as yet not seriously troubled the colonies, and the Congress was, therefore, probably wise in abstaining, as it did, from including the restriction of colonial manufacturing in its recital of colonial grievances.

To secure redress of the recited grievances, the statement proposed the following measures:

"1st. To enter into a non-importation, non-consumption and non-exportation agreement or association; 2. To prepare an address to the people of Great-Britain, and a memorial to the inhabitants of British America, etc.; 3. To prepare a loyal address to his Majesty. . . ."[20]

So far as is known from the meager evidence of the deliberations on the statement, the members' differences of opinion were confined chiefly, if not exclusively, to two points: the ground or grounds on which the claim of colonial rights should be based; and whether or not the statement should include an acknowledgment of a limited authority of Parliament to regulate colonial trade.

On the first point, Lee favored grounding the colonial claim of rights "on a fourfold foundation; on nature, on the British constitution, on charters, and on immemorial usage." Jay apparently argued that the claim should be rested only on the first two bases. John Rutledge agreed that the claim was "well founded on the British constitution," but "not on the law of nature"; and he was seconded by Duane, who favored "grounding our rights on the laws and constitution of the country from whence we spring, and charters, without recurring to the law of nature, because this will be a feeble support."[21]

As appears from the passage concerning colonial rights quoted above, the decision was to base the claim of rights on "the immutable laws of nature, the principles of the English constitution, and the several charters or compacts."

The chief controversy seems to have been over the second point—what, if anything, should be said in the Statement of Rights concerning Parliament's regulation of colonial trade.

The evidence concerning this controversy, though confusing, indicates that Duane was the leading proponent of some kind of recognition of Parliament's authority to regulate colonial trade;[22] that he made a motion to this end;[23] and that his motion was lost by a tie vote, five to five,[24] with the Massachusetts and Rhode Island delegations not voting because equally divided.[25] (The line-up of the ten delegations that did vote is obscure.)[26]

The controversy was resolved (October 14) through a compromise: it was agreed to include a statement concerning Parliament's regulation of colonial trade but only to declare that "from the necessity of the case, and a regard to the mutual interest of both countries, we cheerfully consent to the operation of such acts of the British parliament as are bona fide restrained to the regulation of our external commerce, for the purpose of securing the commercial advantages of the whole empire to the mother country, and the commercial benefits of its respective members; excluding every idea of taxation, internal or for raising a revenue on the subjects in America, without their consent."[27]

So far as is known, the only British regulation of colonial trade meeting this test was the restriction of the colonial carrying trade to British, Irish, and colonial vessels,[28] which put colonial shipping on the same favored footing as British.

In his *Mutual Claims,* Galloway denounced the passage just quoted as displaying "more art and finesse than an honest mind would wish to find in the conduct of any man, much less in those of character," pointing out that the "concessions" concerning Parliament's regulation of colonial trade in fact "concede nothing." "They have taken especial care," he observed, "that what they have consented to in one breath should be blasted by the next. For there is no law of trade that I know of, nor can such a law be formed, as shall *secure* the commercial advantages *of all the external American commerce* to the mother country . . . and yet 'secure to the colonies' . . . their commercial benefit. . . . Surely they could not mean those statutes which enumerate American commodities and compel us to land them in Britain before they can be exported to foreign markets, nor those which oblige us to purchase their manufactures and forbid us to get them from other countries. These are so far from 'securing' that they greatly diminish the commercial benefits of the colonies. . . ."[29]

There obviously was much force in Galloway's remarks, and the Congress would have been wise to say nothing at all as to the regulation of colonial trade, rather than make an ostensible concession so greatly limited as to be practically meaningless.

While the Statement of Rights was under consideration, the Congress took action (September 17) on the so-called "Suffolk Resolves" laid before it by the Massachusetts delegation.[30] It resolved unanimously "That this assembly deeply feels the suffering of their countrymen in the Massachusetts-Bay, under the late unjust, cruel and oppressive acts of the British Parliament—that they most thoroughly approve the wisdom and fortitude with which opposition to these wicked ministerial measures has hitherto been conducted, and they earnestly recommend to their brethren a perseverance in the same firm and temperate conduct as expressed in the resolutions determined upon at a meeting of the delegates for the county of Suffolk. . . ."[31]

The Congress also voted that this resolution and the Suffolk Resolves themselves be published in the newspapers,[32] thus giving public notice of its action.[33]

To appreciate the impact (described in later chapters) of the Congress' action on the Suffolk Resolves,[34] the reader should have before him the high points of their fiery contents. These are summarized in a second appendix to this chapter.

Furthermore, in response to a letter of September 29 from the Boston Committee of Correspondence, reporting Gage's menacing activities at Boston and requesting the Congress' advice,[35] it was voted (October 8) "That this Congress approve of the opposition by the inhabitants of Massachusetts-Bay, to the execution of the late acts of Parliament, and if the same shall be attempted to be carryed into execution by force all America ought to support them in their opposition."[36]

This resolution, probably introduced by one of the Virginia delegates[37] (unlike that of September 17) did not pass unanimously.[38] What colony or colonies voted against it or did not vote at all is unknown. Only Galloway of Pennsylvania and Duane of New York are known definitely to have opposed the resolution,[39] but the remark of Henry soon after it was adopted that if Galloway, Jay, and the Rutledges had their way, they would "ruin the cause of America,"[40] suggests that Jay and the Rutledges voted with Galloway and Duane on this question.

The Boston Committee probably hoped that their letter might even spur the Congress to vote money, men, and arms for defense. But, if so, in this hope they must have been disappointed.

The day after the Committee's letter of September 29 reached Philadelphia, John Adams wrote William Tudor in Boston (October 7): "If it is a secret hope of many, as I suspect it is, that the congress will advise to offensive measures, they will be mistaken. I have had opportunities enough, both public and private, to learn with certainty the decisive sentiments of the delegates and others on this point. They will not, at this session, vote to raise men or money or arms or ammunition. Their opinions are fixed against hostilities and rupture, except they should be come absolutely necessary; and this necessity they do not yet see. They dread the thought of action because it would . . . render all hopes of reconciliation with Great Britain desperate; it would light up the flames of war, perhaps through the whole continent, which might rage for twenty years, and end in the subduction of America as likely as in her liberation."[41]

Adams' appraisal proved to be correct; the Congress rose on October 26, without having taken any action, open or secret, to prepare for war. It had gone far in measures to exert pressure for redress of colonial grievances; but, as Adams indicated, nearly all of its members were opposed to action that would almost certainly preclude a peaceful settlement.

CHAPTER 24

THE ASSOCIATION AND THE
MEMORIAL TO THE COLONISTS

IMMEDIATELY following the adoption of the non-importation and non-exportation resolutions described in Chapter 22, the Congress (September 30) "Agreed, That Mr. Cushing, Mr. Low, Mr. Mifflin, Mr. Lee and Mr. Johnson be a committee to bring in a plan for carrying into effect, the non-importation, non-consumption and non-exportation agreed upon."[1] Cushing, Low, and Mifflin were merchants in Boston, New York, and Philadelphia, respectively; Lee was a Virginia planter; and Johnson, a Maryland lawyer.

The committee brought in its plan, called the Association, on October 12; and six days later, "after sundry amendments," it was adopted.[2]

The Association, most important of the Congress' state papers, demanded the following redress of colonial grievances:

Repeal of "such parts of the several acts of parliament passed since the close of the last war" as "impose or continue duties on tea, wine, molasses, sugar, syrups, paneles [unrefined sugar], coffee, pimento, indigo, foreign paper, glass and painters' colours imported into America;[3] extend the powers of the admiralty courts beyond their ancient limits . . . [depriving] the American subject of trial by jury; authorize the judge's certificate to indemnify the prosecutor from damages, that he might otherwise be liable to from a trial by his peers; [and] require oppressive security from a claimant of ships or goods seized, before he shall be allowed to defend his property."[4]

Repeal of "that part of the act of 12 G. 3 ch. 24, entitled 'An Act for the better securing his majesty's dock-yards, magazines, ships, ammunition and stores', by which any persons charged with committing any of the offences therein described in America, may be tried in any shire or county within the realm [Great Britain]."

Repeal of "the four acts passed the last session of parliament, viz. that for stopping the port and blocking up the harbour of Boston; that for altering the charter and government of the Massachusetts-Bay; and that which is entitled 'An act for the better administration of justice etc.'[5] and that 'for extending the limits of Quebec etc.'"

Other grievances recited in the documents described in Chapters 23 and 25 presumably were negotiable; those specified here were not. The measures about to be described were to remain in force until every one of the grievances stated in the Association was redressed.

The measures for redress to be pursued by the members of the Congress and their constituents were:

Beginning immediately, not to export sheep to any place;[6]

Beginning December 2, 1774,[7] not to import "any goods, wares or merchandize whatsoever" exported from Great Britain and Ireland,[8] East India tea from any part of the world,[9] molasses, syrups, paneles (raw sugar),[10] coffee or pimento from the British West Indies,[11] wine from Madeira or the Western Isles (the Azores), and foreign indigo;[12]

Beginning December 2, 1774, not to import or purchase any slaves or engage, directly or indirectly, in the slave trade;[13]

Beginning March 1, 1775, "not to purchase or use any East-India tea whatever . . . [or] any of those goods, wares or merchandizes we have agreed not to import, which we shall know, or have cause to suspect, were imported after the first day of December [1774] except such as come under the rules and directions of the tenth article hereafter mentioned";[14] and

Beginning September 10, 1775, not to "directly or indirectly export any merchandize or commodity whatsoever to Great-Britain, Ireland, or the West-Indies, except rice to Europe."[15]

Hardship to persons who received forbidden goods after December 1, was alleviated by providing, in Article 10 of the Association, that goods arriving between December 2, 1774, and January 31, 1775, might be stored or sold and the proceeds applied to reimbursement of the importer's costs, the profit, if any, "to be applied towards relieving and employing such poor inhabitants of the town of Boston as are immediate sufferers by the Boston port-bill. . . ."[16]

The Association called for the election of committees of inspection in every county, city, and town throughout the participating colonies by those qualified to vote for representatives in the several colonial Legislatures. The members of these committees were to keep an eye on their neighbors and publish the names of anyone violating the agreement, after which those loyal to the Association were to break off all dealings with the offender.

A central Committee of Correspondence in each of the participating colonies was to inspect the custom house entries in its colony, and, from time to time, report to the other central Committees its findings concerning these entries and other material circumstances.

Furthermore, to induce the other British colonies in North America to adhere to the Association, the twelve subscribing colonies were to cut off all trade and intercourse with any other that failed to adopt the Association.[17]

Thus, this time the people as a whole, not, as in the case of the non-importation agreements of 1768–1770 merely importers, were to be responsible for enforcing the agreement.

The Association also contained commitments to not raise the price of goods made scarce by observance of the Association,[18] promote local manufacturing, especially of woolen goods, discountenance horse-racing, cock-fighting, plays, and other diversions, and discourage expensive mourning.

The Association's ban on imports was more comprehensive than that envisaged by the non-importation resolution of September 27, quoted in Chapter 22, in that the Association banned not only articles produced in, or exported from, Great Britain or Ireland, but also molasses, coffee, pimento, syrups, and paneles from the British West Indies, wines from Madeira and the Azores, East India tea, foreign indigo wherever produced, and slaves.[19] Some member, probably Lee,[20] moved extension of the non-importation agreement to cover all dutied imports, including molasses and sugar from the foreign West Indies.[21] But this proposal was opposed by Pendleton and Chase and probably by Low, who queried, "Will, can the people bear a total interruption of the West India trade? Can they live without rum [distilled from molasses], sugar and molasses? Will not this impatience and vexation defeat the measure?"[22] The motion failed; importation of dutied molasses and sugar from the foreign West Indies was not banned.

The most striking addition to the ban on importation was of slaves, which, though favored by a resolution of the Virginia Convention of August, 1774,[23] referred to in Chapter 20, was not included in the Congress' non-importation resolution of September 27. Sentiments of humanity and the incongruity of denouncing British "enslavement" of the colonies without at least banning the slave trade probably were the dominant reasons for now adding this.

But practical considerations may well have contributed to this measure, which apparently was adopted without opposition. Shipment of slaves from Africa to America was so important a branch of the British shipping industry that banning their importation into the colonies was an obvious way to put additional pressure on Parliament to meet colonial demands for redress. Furthermore, the inclusion in the Association of a ban on the slave trade would please the Quakers, who were highly influential in Pennsylvania and to a lesser extent in several other colonies.

Turning to non-exportation, some unidentified member moved that the non-exportation resolution of September 30 (quoted in Chapter 22) be revised in the Association to ban the exportation of flaxseed and lumber immediately, instead of September 10, 1775.[24] (Ireland was so dependent on British colonial flaxseed and the British West Indies on British colonial lumber that cutting off the supply of these articles would put particular pressure on members of Parliament and their constituents having Irish or West Indian interests.)

Ward of Rhode Island and Lynch of South Carolina supported the motion, but Ross of Pennsylvania, whose colony exported flaxseed, objected to singling out flaxseed, observing that to ban the export of flaxseed ahead of other items would be "quarrelling with Ireland before We begin with G. Britain"; Sullivan of New Hampshire, whose colony was a large exporter of lumber, objected to singling out lumber; and Galloway

of Pennsylvania, Dyer of Connecticut, and Johnson of Maryland, whose
colonies were exporters of flaxseed, objected to subjecting any kind of
exports to particular hardship.[25]

The opponents of the motion prevailed; it was "Negatived Nem. Con."[26]

The Association, however, revised the non-exportation resolution of
September 30 in one respect, an important one, by exempting the export
of "rice to Europe,"[27] a term broad enough to permit export of rice to
Great Britain and Ireland, as well as to the continent of Europe.

The reasons for exempting rice, as given by the South Carolina delegates upon their return home, were that "while other colonies had the
exportation of wheat, flour, oil, fish and other commodities open [to the
continent of Europe] Carolina would (without the exception of rice) have
had no sort of article to export at all;"[28] that "Carolina having no
manufactures was under a more immediate necessity of some means to
purchase the necessaries of life, particularly negro clothing;" and that
"the lands which produce rice can be turned to no other use; . . . [and]
rice is a perishable article."[29]

Edward Rutledge tried also to secure the exception of South Carolina's
other chief export crop, indigo,[30] but failed; rice alone was excepted.

Another important proposal, moved by Gadsden and supported by
Ward and Ross, was to put additional pressure on Parliament for redress
by stopping all remittances to creditors in Great Britain.[31] But they were
opposed by Edward Rutledge and Galloway, and this proposal was defeated.[32]

The only known argument concerning the grievances to be set forth in
the Association as demanding redress was over the Quebec Act.

Duane, who had unsuccessfully opposed inclusion of this act among the
grievances to be recited in the proposed Address to the King about to be
discussed, now made a similar move concerning the Association. "If we
demand *too much*," he argued, "we . . . may get nothing." "Will it not,"
he added, "be said that we go beyond our sphere, and, while we contend for an exclusive internal legislature [for ourselves] intermeddle with
the police of other governments?"[33]

Duane was supported by his colleague Jay, but McKean of Delaware
and Lee opposed him,[34] and he was defeated;[35] the Quebec Act was
among the acts whose repeal was to be demanded in the Association.[36]

On October 20, a fair copy of the Association was signed by, or on
behalf of, all the members of the Congress except Goldsborough, Rhoads,
Haring, and Randolph,[37] and it was voted to print 120 copies of the
Association,[38] thus providing ten copies for each of the delegations.

On the following day the Congress adopted, and ordered printed a like
number of copies of a Memorial to the inhabitants of the colonies represented at the Congress, prepared by Lee, William Livingston, and Jay,[39]
justifying the Association and appealing for general adoption of, and
firm adherence to, it.[40]

This impressive Memorial begins with the recital of eight acts passed by Parliament from 1764 to 1768, which, together with other unnamed acts, "compared with one another, will be found, not only to form a regular system, in which every part has great force, but also a pertinacious adherence to that system, for subjugating these Colonies (that are not, and from local circumstances cannot be represented in the House of Commons) to the uncontroulable and unlimited power of Parliament, in violation of their undoubted rights and liberties, in contempt of their humble and repeated petitions."

The Memorial proceeds to a vindication of the province of Massachusetts, which, according to the Memorial, had acted with moderation considering the extreme provocation to which it had been subjected during the past decade.

Then follows a masterly summary of evidence in support of the declaration that "Severe as the Acts of Parliament before mentioned are, yet the conduct of Administration hath been equally injurious, and irritating. . . ."

Stationing British troops and ships of war among the colonists "to assist in taking their money without their consent"; making judges "entirely dependent on the Crown for their commissions and salaries"; Lord Hillsborough's letter to Governor Bernard in April, 1768, censuring the Massachusetts House for its resolution to invite the Assemblies of other colonies to join in protesting against the Townshend Act and ordering him to dissolve the House if it refused to rescind this resolution; pouring troops into Boston in 1768 to compel obedience to laws which its people together with those of the other colonies had vainly protested against; and, finally, the recent "outrageous proceedings" against Massachusetts of a severity calculated to frighten the other colonies "to desert their brethren in a common cause" and thus create division that "all may be subdued."

In conclusion, the Memorial appealed for general and steady support of the Association as the only alternative to "either a more dangerous contest, or a final, ruinous and infamous submission," but warned that "the schemes agitated against these colonies have been so conducted, as to render it prudent . . . [to] extend your views to the most mournful events, and be in all respects prepared for every contingency," meaning, of course, war.[41]

On the same day the Congress also adopted an Address to the People of Great Britain following in a general way the Memorial, but emphasizing the iniquity of the Quebec Act in promoting the Catholic religion, a religion which had "dispersed impiety, bigotry, murder and rebellion through every part of the world," and warning the British people, "if you are determined that your Ministers shall wantonly sport with the rights of Mankind . . . we must tell you, that we will never submit to be hewers of wood or drawers of water for any ministry or nation in the world."[42]

CHAPTER 25

PETITION TO THE KING AND OTHER STATE PAPERS OF THE CONGRESS

I N its closing week the Congress pushed through a large number of measures including a resolution of thanks "to those truly noble, honourable and patriotic advocates [in Great Britain] of civil and religious liberty, who have so generously and powerfully, tho' unsuccessfully, espoused & defended the cause of America, both in and out of parliament";[1] a Petition to the King; a circular letter to the inhabitants of St. John's (present-day Prince Edward Island), Nova Scotia, Georgia, East Florida, and West Florida; and an address to the inhabitants of the province of Quebec.

The most important of these papers was the Address (later called Petition) to the King submitted to the Congress on October 21, by a committee consisting of Lee, John Adams, Henry, Johnson, and John Rutledge.[2]

As with the Statement of Rights, the proposed Address gave rise to much debate.

On the very day (October 1) the committee was chosen, two proposals for instructions as to statements to be included in the Address were warmly contested.

The first, moved by Jay, was that the committee be instructed to include an offer to pay for the tea destroyed at Boston. He was supported by his New York colleagues Duane and Low, Ross and (with the proviso that the offer be made conditional on repeal of the Boston Port Act) Pendleton. But Lee and Henry, Gadsden (who had written Samuel Adams in June that Charlestonians were trusting the Bostonians' "Firmness . . . not [to] pay for an ounce of the damn'd Tea"),[3] Lynch, both Rutledges, Goldsborough, Ward, and John Adams opposed the motion, and it was defeated unanimously when Jay failed to muster the support of a majority even of the New York delegates.[4]

The second, moved by Duane, was that the committee be instructed to include in the Address a statement affirming that the colonies, "zealous for the safety and glory of the British Empire, will readily concur in any plan consistent with constitutional Liberty for drawing forth the united Councils, Aid and Strength . . . of his Majesty's Dominions whenever it shall be found necessary."[5]

Lee moved to amend this declaration to include a statement that, since one of the reasons given by Parliament for taxing the colonies was the necessity of defending them, and since "North America is able, willing and, under Providence, determined to defend, protect and secure itself, the Congress do most earnestly recommend to the several colonies, that a militia be forthwith appointed and well disciplined, and that it be well provided with ammunition and proper arms."[6]

Lee's proposed amendment was warmly supported by Henry, who said that "a preparation for Warr is Necessary to obtain peace; that America is not Now in a State of peace; that all the Bulwarks of Our Safety, of Our Constitution are thrown down; that We are Now in a State of Nature; that We ought to ask Ourselves the Question should the planns of Nonimportation & Nonexportation fail of Success, in that Case arms are Necessary & if then . . . [why] are We to hesitate providing them Now whilst in Our power." Sherman and Dyer of Connecticut and Lynch also supported Lee.

But Harrison opposed the proposed amendment on the ground that it would "tend only to irritate, whereas Our business is to reconcile," and he was supported by his colleagues, Pendleton and Bland, both Rutledges, Duane, Low, and Hooper of North Carolina.[7]

The resolution finally adopted (October 3), instructed the committee to state the following: "Whereas the parliamentary taxes on America have been laid, on pretence of defraying the expenses of . . . defending, protecting, and securing the Colonies that they do assure his Majesty that . . . the [colonial] milita, if put upon a proper footing would be amply sufficient for their defence in time of peace; that they are desirous to put it on such a footing immediately; and that in case of war the colonies are ready to grant supplies for raising any further forces that may be necessary."[8]

On October 4, another debate arose, this time over a motion by an unidentified member for an instruction to the committee on the Address to the King apparently to state that harmony between the colonies and Great Britain would be restored if the colonial grievances arising since the late war (1763) were redressed.[9]

The motion was supported by Read of Delaware,[10] but was strongly opposed by Lynch on the ground that it would "leave some of the worst acts in force—the Rice being enumerated, the Hatt Act, the Act for extending Land in America to the payment of Debts,[11] the Act of [7 and 8] Wm. & Mary & the 5th [6th] George 2nd extend[ing] the power of Jurisdiction of Admiralty invidiously,[12] the Governor or the Crown appointing Councillors to act as Legislators in the respective Colonies,[13] . . . all of them Grievances to be remonstrated against."[14]

So far as his objections to the motion concerned the power of colonial admiralty courts, Lynch was supported by his colleague, John Rutledge, who pointed out that these had been unduly "extended before [as well as after] the year 1763," a grievance conceded by him to be "the most enormous of any Whatever . . . as . . . destroying all privileges in the destruction of trial by jury."[15] Biddle of Pennsylvania and Edward Rutledge also opposed the proposed limitation.[16]

John Adams, while not denying that extension of the power of colonial admiralty courts was a major grievance, supported the motion on the ground that it "does not imply that We are to submit to all preceding Acts, but [only] that We shall by such repeal be in the State We were in 1763 as to harmony."[17]

This brought Low of New York to his feet in opposition to the motion because "it is not sufficiently explicit that We ought to speak out, complains of being misapprehended, etc. . . . ,"[18] meaning apparently that the motion was calculated to mislead the King by giving assurance that the colonists would be satisfied with withdrawal of the objectionable British measures taken since 1763, whereas in fact they would not be.

Various amendments were proposed,[19] one of which was adopted,[20] but no copy of this amendment or of the original motion has been found. All we have is the text of the amended motion as adopted, which instructs the committee "to assure his majesty, that in case the colonies shall be restored to the state they were in at the close of the late war, by abolishing the system of laws and regulations for raising a revenue in America, for extending the powers of courts of admiralty, for the trial of persons beyond the sea for crimes committed in America, for affecting the colony of the Massachusetts bay, and for altering the government and extending the limits of Canada, the jealousies [distrusts], which have been occasioned by such acts and regulations of parliament, will be removed and commerce again restored."[21]

The resolution for the instruction to limit the appeal for redress to grievances arising since the late war was carried (October 5) by only a very narrow margin: Massachusetts, Virginia, North Carolina, Connecticut, New Hampshire, and Rhode Island voted yes; South Carolina, Maryland, New York, New Jersey, and Delaware no; the Pennsylvania delegation, equally divided, cast no vote.[22]

South Carolina's dissent presumably was from confining the protest to British measures adopted since "the close of the late war."[23] No evidence has been found as to the reason or reasons for the dissent of Maryland, New Jersey, and Delaware or how the divided Pennsylvania delegation lined up.

On October 21, the committee submitted to the Congress a draft of the proposed address. No copy has been found, but evidently it was unsatisfactory since it was "re-committed,"[24] and John Dickinson (who had recently been elected to the Pennsylvania House and promptly chosen as one of its delegates to the Congress)[25] was added to the committee.[26] A new draft, apparently prepared chiefly by him,[27] was submitted a few days later and promptly adopted.[28]

What changes were made is unknown. Many years later, Dickinson wrote that they were merely to eliminate "language of asperity,"[29] and no evidence to the contrary has come to light. Probably one of the changes in phraseology was to call the document "Petition," rather than "Address." In the previous resolutions of Congress, the proposed document was uniformly referred to as an Address[30] to the King, whereas the document adopted used the more deferential word "Petition."[31]

The Petition to the King was adopted on October 25, signed by all but five of the members of the Congress,[32] and sent to the London Agents of the colonies for presentation to him.[33]

The most striking feature of the Petition to the King (as it was now usually called)[34] was its declaration, "We wish not a diminution of the prerogative. . . . Your royal authority over us . . . we shall always carefully and zealously support and maintain."[35]

This statement by the Congress strongly confirms the repeated denial by practically all the Whig leaders that they were seeking complete independence of British rule.[36] For the royal prerogative unquestionably included control over the foreign relations of the entire empire; the right to use the colonies as bases for military operations against the French, Spanish, and other foreign possessions in America; the authority of the King in Council to review and reverse on points of law the decisions of highest courts of all the colonies[37] and to disallow all acts passed by the legislatures[38] of Pennsylvania, Delaware, and all the royal colonies, including Virginia and Massachusetts.[39] Furthermore, the Whigs had not challenged a long-standing instruction from the King to all colonial Governors forbidding them to assent "to any law wherein the natives or inhabitants" of his colony "are put upon a more advantageous footing than those of this kingdom and that "no duties shall be laid in the province . . . under your government upon British shipping or upon the product or manufacturers of Great Britain. . . ."[40]

This instruction, which had been well observed,[41] secured the access of British ships and goods into the already vast and steadily expanding colonial market, free from local legislation banning or discriminating against them. In the case of foreign countries, British ships and goods often were, and might at any time be, excluded or severely discriminated against; in the colonies they were at all times sure of a free, open market.[42] In short, the habitual assertion of British politicians and publicists that if Parliament could not tax the colonies or at least effectively restrict their trade with foreign countries for the benefit of British merchants, the British people would have no compensation for the cost of protecting the colonies, simply was not true.

The circular letter to the inhabitants of St. John's, Nova Scotia, Georgia, and the Floridas, prepared by a committee composed of Cushing, Lee, and Dickinson, merely enclosed copies of the printed proceedings of the Congress accompanied by a recommendation that "the measures contained in the enclosed papers . . . be adopted with all the earnestness that a well directed zeal for American Liberty can prompt."[43]

The more expansive address to the inhabitants of Quebec drafted by this same committee was adopted after debate and revision just before Congress rose on October 26,[44] with an accompanying resolution that the address be translated into French, printed and distributed through the agency of the delegates from New Hampshire, Massachusetts, and New York.[45]

This address pointed out to the people of Quebec the iniquity of the British government's denial to them of the most basic rights enjoyed by the people of Great Britain—"having a share in their own government by their representatives chosen by themselves"; trial by jury; the writ of habeas corpus; holding land "by the tenure of easy rents and not by rigorous and oppressive services"; freedom of the press. It also invited them to join the "federation" designed to secure these rights to all the British subjects in America and to send representatives to another continental congress,[46] which, as brought out later in the chapter, was to be held the following May.

Fearing that the British government might try to "lay hold of as many delegates as possible and have them carried to England and tried as rebels,"[47] the Congress resolved on October 21, that "seizing or attempting to seize any person in America, in order to transport such person beyond the sea for trial of offences committed within the body of a county in America . . . ought to meet with resistance and reprisal."[48]

The immediate cause of the fear prompting this resolution presumably was the receipt of an affidavit of Samuel Dyer, recently returned from England, relating that he had been seized in Boston and shipped to England for having allegedly tried to induce British soldiers to desert.[49] In London, the government closely examined him to try to obtain incriminating evidence against Whig leaders in Boston, but he had been released when (quoting Secretary of State Lord Dartmouth) "there did not appear to be, in the opinion of the King's Law Servants, the least shadow of ground for detaining him. . . ."[50]

On the same day (October 21) it passed the resolution as to reprisal, the Congress chose a committee consisting of Galloway, McKean, John Adams, and Hooper "to revise the minutes of the Congress."[51] If, as seems probable, the committee's chief mission was to eliminate everything that might be used as evidence to charge any particular member of the Congress with treason, the committee carried out its duty with impressive efficiency; nothing remains in the revised minutes (*Journals*) of the Congress that would not equally implicate every member of the Congress except Dickinson, a latecomer, and Randolph, Rhoads, Haring, and Goldsborough, who, as noted in Chapter 24, did not sign the Association.[52] Galloway and Duane, who tried to absolve themselves,[53] were in no better state than the rest on the record.

On October 22, the Congress recognized that further united action might be required even before the non-exportation agreement was to go into effect, by resolving that "it will be necessary that another Congress should be held on the tenth day of May next, unless the redress of the grievances we have desired be obtained before that time. And we recommend that the same be held at the city of Philadelphia, and that all the Colonies in North-America chuse deputies, as soon as possible, to attend such Congress."[54]

Finally, on October 26, after adopting a vote of thanks to the Pennsylvania House "for their politeness to this Congress," the Congress dissolved itself.[55]

A well-known letter of Governor Cadwallader Colden of New York to Lord Dartmouth, soon after the Congress rose, implies that the Virginia, Maryland, and New England delegations, supported by some of the members from South Carolina, constituted a bloc against which the other delegations could make little headway.[56] But the notes of debates in the Congress give little indication of a division into blocs. The only known vote showing the line-up by colonies—the vote of October 5 on the motion to include in the Address to the King only grievances arising since 1763—does not support Colden's view. Maryland and South Carolina, far from supporting the Virginia and the New England delegations, voted against them.[57] Furthermore, though we do not know the line-up in the five-to-five vote (October 10) on a motion to concede some authority of Parliament to regulate trade (discussed in Chapter 23), we know that Massachusetts and Rhode Island lost their votes on this motion because their delegates were equally divided,[58] thus proving that on this question, at least, there was no solid bloc of New England votes.

Judging from the importance of their committee appointments, Lee of Virginia and Johnson of Maryland (both of whom had long taken leading parts in opposing objectionable British measures in their respective colonial Assemblies) were the leaders in the Congress.[59] Lee was a member of all four of the most important committees—Statement of Rights, the Association, Address to the King, and Memorial to the colonists—and Johnson of all but the last.[60]

Lee's leadership also is indicated by the records of debates, in which he is more frequently referred to than any other member.[61] Johnson is referred to less frequently, but John Adams' well-known diary entry characterizing various members of Congress singled out Johnson for particular commendation, as being "sensible and learned" and having "a clear and cool head [and] an extensive knowledge of trade as well as law."[62]

Even though the Congress' plan to secure redress of colonial grievances by exerting commercial pressure on British merchants and manufacturers failed, the significance of the Congress in the history of the American Revolution can hardly be exaggerated.

In the first place, its resolution for another congress to be held May 10, 1775, laid the basis for the assembling of a second intercolonial congress after the outbreak of hostilities at Lexington and Concord[63] at least a month earlier than would otherwise have been possible—a month of critical importance in the Second Continental Congress' preparations for war.

The First Congress also paved the way for united action in the Second more rapidly than would otherwise conceivably have been possible. As the Connecticut delegates wrote to Governor Trumbull in their letter of October 10, 1774, quoted in Chapter 22, it had given the delegates from the twelve colonies, each having "particular provincial rights and interests to guard and secure," the opportunity "to become so acquainted with each one's situations and connexions as to be able to give an united assent to the ways and means for affecting what all are ardently desirous of."[64]

This was particularly important in influencing the attitude of delegates from the other colonies toward Massachusetts. Many outside Massachusetts, even of those most devoted to the Whig cause, were repelled by the supposed object of Whigs in Massachusetts to become completely independent of British rule. By their temperateness at the Congress, the Massachusetts delegates were able to convince their fellow members that the people of Massachusetts were not fanatics bent on independence; that their objects were the same as those of colonial Whigs in general; and that, therefore, in backing Massachusetts, the members from other colonies were supporting a common cause.

But most important of all was the resolution for enforcement of the non-importation, non-exportation, and non-consumption provisions of the Congress' Association by local committees. When war came, these committees formed a preestablished network of local enforcement agencies which were invaluable in implementing the war measures adopted by the Second Continental Congress.[65]

The formation of these committees will be described in due course. But, before proceeding to the reception in the several colonies of the resolutions of the First Congress, we turn to developments in Massachusetts during the summer of 1774, and their repercussions in Great Britain.

CHAPTER 26

DEVELOPMENTS IN MASSACHUSETTS:
MAY–SEPTEMBER, 1774

BEARING his commission as the new Governor of Massachusetts, General Thomas Gage, Commander-in-Chief of the British Army in North America reached Castle William at the mouth of Boston harbor on May 13, 1774. Four days later, Gage proceeded to Boston and officially succeeded Thomas Hutchinson as Governor of Massachusetts.[1]

Gage's responsibilities included enforcement of the Boston Port Act, which was to take effect June first,[2] enforcement of the Massachusetts Regulating Act, which was to take effect at various dates beginning July first,[3] and execution of his instructions from the Crown (described in Chapter 15). These instructions required him to shift the place of meeting of the Massachusetts ("General Court") Legislature[4] to Salem from its customary place of meeting at Boston and to prosecute for treason the leaders of the opposition to the landing of the British East India Company's tea at Boston.[5]

To support Gage in executing the new acts and his instructions, a squadron of British warships was already stationed at Boston when he arrived, and four British infantry regiments were sent from the British Isles, reaching Boston at various times between June 1 and July 6.[6]

Gage had no difficulty in closing the Port of Boston and in removing the Legislature to Salem,[7] where it sat until dissolved by him on June 17, for having passed the resolution calling for an intercolonial congress (described in Chapter 20).[8]

On the advice of Peter Oliver, Chief Justice of the Massachusetts Superior Court, that "the Times are not favorable for Prosecutions,"[9] Gage deferred action on his instruction to initiate prosecutions for treason, a deferment which proved to be permanent.

For a time, it appeared that a number of Bostonians who favored indemnifying the East India Company and others for losses sustained from the Boston Tea Party, in the hope of securing early repeal or suspension of the ruinous Port Act, might be successful. On May 18, John Andrews, a Boston merchant, wrote his brother-in-law in Philadelphia, "we have many among us who are for compromising matters, and put forward a subscription to pay for the Tea. George Erving has declar'd this day . . . he is prepared to put down two thousand sterling towards it. . . ."[10]

Ten days later, over a hundred persons, mainly Bostonians, signed a farewell address to Hutchinson,[11] in which they deplored the damage to

the property of the East India Company and others, and declared themselves "fully disposed to bear our share of those damages whenever the
sum and manner of laying it can be ascertained."[12] But at a Boston town
meeting on June 17, those favoring payment for the tea remained silent.[13]

On June 27 (quoting Gage), "the better Sort of People" gathered in
force at another town meeting "with Design to make a Push to pay for
the Tea."[14] But they again apparently remained silent on this point, after
which little more is heard of the project.

Boston conservatives moved at this meeting to censure and "annihilate"
the Boston Committee of Correspondence[15] for having exceeded its authority in promoting a so-called Solemn League and Covenant (described
in an appendix to this chapter) binding signers of the covenant not to
purchase any British goods after August 31, 1774; however, this group was
overwhelmingly defeated. Yet the meeting did not sanction the covenant
and thus, in effect, squelched a movement which, for a time, threatened
serious dissension among Massachusetts Whigs.[16]

As we have seen in earlier chapters, several months elapsed between
the effective date of the Boston Port Act and the adoption by the Continental Congress of measures designed to put pressure on Parliament for
repeal of the act. In the meanwhile, the morale of the Bostonians was
sustained by gifts pouring into Boston from all the colonies represented
at the Congress for those suffering from the closing of the Port of Boston,
accompanied by letters of warm sympathy and support.[17]

By June 28, a flock of over 200 sheep was on its way to Boston from
Windham, Connecticut, accompanied by a letter from a committee of
the town to the selectmen of Boston assuring them, "This Town is very
sensible of the obligations we, and with us, all British America, are
under to the Town of Boston who . . . are the generous defenders of our
common rights and liberties. . . ." "We have," the committee continued,
"procured a small flock of sheep . . . [to which] the people of this Town
were almost unanimous in contributing . . . [for] the relief of those honest,
industrious poor who are most distressed by the late arbitrary and oppressive Acts. And rest assured that if Parliament does not soon afford
you relief, and there should in future be any need of our assistance, we
shall, with the utmost cheerfulness, exert our influence to that purpose."

On the same day, a similar message was sent by a committee of the
town of Groton, Connecticut, accompanied by forty bushels of rye and
corn, to which, some weeks later, Groton added two further gifts each of
over 100 sheep and some cattle.[18]

By the end of September, town after town in Connecticut had sent
generous gifts: Farmington, Wethersfield, Brookfield, Norwich, Brooklyn,
Preston, Killingly, East Haddam, Woodstock, Hartford, and Lebanon (the
last topping the list with nearly 400 sheep and a later gift of some cattle),
often accompanied by letters assuring the Bostonians they were regarded
as suffering in a common cause and promising additional help if needed.[19]

Other colonies gave similar encouragement. On August 4, Baltimore sent 1,000 bushels of corn and other produce, with assurances, faithfully carried out, of further support.[20] During the next few months, relief committees in several more colonies followed suit,[21] and by the day of Lexington and Concord all thirteen of the old British colonies in North America, including Georgia, were helping to feed and clothe the people of Boston by gifts either of provisions or money or both.[22]

The Port Act not only laid no restraint on shipments into Boston by land, but permitted importation into the town by water of "fuel and victuals brought coastwise from any part of the continent of America for the necessary use and sustenance of the inhabitants," provided the carrying vessel first cleared customs at Marblehead. Consequently, there was no insuperable difficulty in delivering supplies to the town.

To deal with the unemployment incident to closing the port, a Boston town meeting of May 13 chose an emergency committee headed by Samuel Adams, called variously the Committee of Ways and Means and the Committee on Donations.[23] This committee, later enlarged,[24] used or planned to use the donations or proceeds from them to mend the town's pavements, operate a brickyard, build ships, set up looms for weavers, and buy and distribute wool, flax, cotton, leather, nail-rods, and hemp to spinners, shoemakers, blacksmiths, and rope-makers.[25] The construction of a town wharf and the digging of a town well also were authorized[26] and presumably undertaken.

Another important office of the committee was establishing contact with supporters throughout the colonies by thanking the donors for their gifts and encouraging messages, and assuring them that the people of Boston could be counted on to continue to struggle and suffer for "the common liberties of America" so long as they were "aided and supported by their friends. . . ."[27]

This assurance was fulfilled. When war broke out ten months after the Port Act took effect, the people of Boston still had made no move to secure reopening of their port by offering to pay for the destroyed tea.

But, though the Bostonians made no offer to pay for the tea, they made no move to oppose enforcement of the act, thereby giving Gage a sense of optimism reflected in his earlier letters to Secretary of State Lord Dartmouth.

On May 19, soon after his arrival at Boston, Gage wrote Dartmouth, "I hear from Many that the [Boston Port] Act has staggered the most Presumptious . . . and I may find the Assembly in a better temper than usual . . ."; May 30, "The violent Party seems to break and People fall off from them; . . . many are Impatient for the Arrival of the Troops, And I am told that People [favoring obedience] will then speak and act openly . . ."; June 26, the Boston "Demagogues," though said to be "spiriting up the People throughout the Province to resistance," would, Gage trusted, "want Power to effect it"; July 5, "there is now an open

Opposition to the Faction, carried on with a Warmth and Spirit unknown before; . . . the Terror of Mobs is over, and the Press is becoming free."[28]

But developments following the receipt of news of the passage of the Massachusetts Regulating Act quickly chilled Gage's optimism.

On July 20, he wrote Dartmouth, "I have not yet [officially] received the new Act for the Government of this Province [the Massachusetts Regulating Act], but "it is printed here, and many tell me I must expect all the Opposition to the Execution of it that can be made. . . . The fast day appointed by the Faction was kept in this Town . . . as generally and as punctually as if it had been appointed by Authority [and] I might say the same of most other Places."[29] A week later Gage repeated his apprehension of widespread opposition to the act, adding, "Your Lordship will be inclined to think that if the Opposers of Government may be called only a Faction in this Province [as he himself and Dartmouth had heretofore called them] they are at least a very numerous and powerfull Faction."[30]

The Regulating Act, it will be recalled from Chapter 18, provided for radical changes in the framework of government of the province. Town meetings, which heretofore could be called at any time by the selectmen of the town, could now be called not more than once a year (and then only in March or May) without written permission of the Crown-appointed Governor. The provincial Council, heretofore elective, was now to be appointed by the King. Judges of the county courts and county sheriffs, whose appointment and dismissal by the Governor was heretofore subject to approval of the elected Council, could now be appointed and dismissed by him without such approval. Petty jurors, heretofore drawn by lot from lists prepared by popularly elected selectmen, were now to be chosen by the Crown-controlled sheriffs. As his letters of July 20 and 27 to Dartmouth foreshadowed, Gage found himself powerless to enforce this act outside the immediate radius of the fleet and army occupying Boston.

On August 22, an unauthorized meeting at Salem, called by the local Committee of Correspondence, was held under Gage's very nose,[31] and ten days later he wrote Dartmouth that town meetings were being held throughout the province and "no Persons I have advised with can tell what to do. . . ."[32]

The provision for a Crown-appointed Council also was virtually nullified. Though twenty-five of the thirty-six Crown appointees (known as mandamus councilors because appointed by mandamus of the King) initially accepted,[33] nine of them soon resigned.[34] Six of the remaining lived in Boston. Of the ten who lived elsewhere, every one was driven to Boston or if there already, did not dare return to his home.[35]

Their situation is illustrated by the case of Councilor John Murray of Rutland. In a letter of August 28 to Murray shortly after he left for Boston, never to return, his son Daniel wrote him of recent happenings at his home.[36] Just after his departure, a "rabble," as the son called them, descended on his home, and, on being told Murray was not there, insisted on searching the house and outbuildings to verify this report. After parleying, it was agreed to have a committee of seven make the search. On the committee's finding that the elder Murray had in fact left, "every one dispersed without doing the least damage," but threatened to return and destroy every building on the estate if he did not "make a Public Recantation" of his councilorship.

"Upon the whole, Sir," the son continued, "the temper of the People is worked up to such a pitch, that every person . . . that will not join them are considered as enemies to their country. . . . Tell them the consequences of their proceedings will be Rebellion, Confiscation and Death, and it only serves as oil to the flame; they can draw no consequence to be equally dreadful to a Free People (as they say) like that of being made Slaves, and this is not the language of the common People only you may be assured, as those who have heretofore in life sustained the fairest characters in every respect, are the warmest in this matter . . . so that among the many friends you have heretofore had, I can scarcely mention any to you now; and the very few that remain so, dare not say it, looking upon themselves in the greatest danger."[37]

Daniel Murray's letter is of particular interest for its documentation of the attitude of the farmers of the neighborhood toward the Massachusetts Regulating Act. Thousands of contemporary letters and diary entries of colonial merchants, lawyers, clergymen, and the great planters expressing their reaction to the British measures affecting the colonies considered in this book have come down to us. We also have some, though much more limited, documentation of the reaction to these measures of the tradesmen (mechanics) in the principal colonial cities. But very few letters and diaries of ordinary small-scale farmers, who constituted a great majority of the white population of the thirteen colonies, have come to light,[38] and these few speak almost exclusively of the weather, state of the crops, prices, births, deaths, marriages, ailments, and other non-political topics.[39]

Daniel Murray was, to be sure, not himself a "dirt" farmer, but most of the men referred to in his letter were. These men had annually, for many years, elected his father, John Murray, representative of the town of Rutland and contiguous districts in the Massachusetts House of Representatives. But when Murray now lent his support to the Massachusetts Regulating Act by accepting office under the act, we have his son's word for it that only a very few of his neighbors supported or condoned his conduct.

The reaction of the farmers of Rutland, described in Daniel Murray's letter, was apparently typical of farmers throughout New England.

On August 27, Gage had assured Dartmouth that the courts sitting under the new act "can and will be protected in many places."[40] But on coming to Boston from Salem a few days later, Gage changed his mind upon hearing from the provincial Council that "the Flames of Sedition had spread [so] universally throughout the Country" as to make it "very improper to weaken the troops here by Detachments, whatever, as they could not be of any use to the Courts, as no Jurors would appear." (Even the Superior Court, meeting under the protection of British forces at Boston, proved to be powerless, since "no Jurors would swear in.")[41] The following day (September 3) he wrote Dartmouth that Lieutenant Governor Thomas Oliver had been forced by "great numbers of People," assembled from the surrounding countryside at Cambridge, to resign his commission as one of the mandamus councilors.[42]

Most ominously, the "People," as Gage pointed out, were "not a Boston Rabble but the Freeholders and Farmers of the Country."[43]

Gage's next letter to Dartmouth was even more alarming. On September 12, he wrote, "It is needless to trouble your Lordship with daily Publications of determined Resolutions not to obey the late Acts of Parliament. . . . The Country People are exercizing in Arms in this Province, Connecticut and Rhode Island, and getting Magazines of Arms and Ammunition . . . and such Artillery as they can procure, good or bad. . . . People are resorting to this Town for Protection . . . even [from] Places always esteemed well affected . . . and Sedition flows copiously from the Pulpits. The Commissioners of Customs have thought it no longer safe or prudent to remain at Salem . . . and are amongst others come into the Town [Boston], where I am obliged likewise now to reside on many accounts."[44]

Thus, by mid-September, Gage recognized and informed Dartmouth that his (Gage's) initial optimism was ill-founded and that he was faced not with small, scattered mobs, but with preparations for a general uprising throughout most of New England.

Painted by T. Stothard Esq.r R.A.   Pub.d by G. Tertelini, Cornhill.   Engraved by G. Tertelini.

His Most Gracious Majesty
GEORGE THE THIRD

George III

In Gotham once the Story goes
A Set of Wise-acres arose
Skill'd in the great Politic Wheel
Could pound a Maopie, drown an Eel
With many Things of worthy Note
At present much too long to quote,
Their District was both far and wide
Which not a little swell'd their Pride
But above all that they possess'd
Was a fine Goose, by all confess'd
A Rara Avis to behold
Who laid each Day an Egg of Gold
This made them grow immensely rich
Gave them an avaritious Itch,
The Case belongs to many more

They not contented with their Store
Would Methods vague and strange pursue
To make the Harmless Bird lay Two,
This Glorious purpose to obtain
About her Neck they put a Chain,
And more their Folly to complaint
They Stampt upon her Wings & Feet,
But this had no Effect at all,
Yet made her struggle, flutter, squall,
And do what every Goose would do
That had her Liberty in view.
When one of more distinguish'd Note
Cry'd D--n her, let us slit her Throat,
They did, but not an Egg was found
But Blood came pouring from y Wound.

THE WISE MEN of GOTHAM and their GOOSE

Pub.d 16.th Feb.y 1776. by W. Humphrey Gerrard Street Soho.

A Jibe at British Politicians

George Grenville in Statesmanlike Pose

The Imperious William Pitt the Elder

D. BENIAMIN FRÆNCKLIN.

Grand Comiſſaire plenipotentiaire du Congres d'Amerique en France
né a Boston 1706. en 17. Ianvier.

Se vend a Londres chez Thom Hart.

A French View of Benjamin Franklin

Bostonians Starving Because of the Port Bill Being Fed by Fellow Americans

A New Method of MACARONY MAKING, as practised at BOSTON in NORTH AMERICA.

217

Printed for Carington Bowles, Nº 69 in Sᵗ Pauls Church Yard, London.

Tar-and-Feathering of a Supporter of Britain

Lord George Germain, Defender of British Authority

CHAPTER 27

THE BRITISH GOVERNMENT AND THE COLONIES: JUNE, 1774–APRIL, 1775

FOR more than two months following the adjournment of Parliament in June, 1774, the King and his ministers judged from General Gage's letters of May to early July, quoted in Chapter 26, that all was going smoothly in Massachusetts.[1]

The receipt early in September of Gage's letters of July 20 and 27, reporting the reaction in Massachusetts to news of the Regulating Act, gave the administration some warning of what was to follow. But it was not until the receipt on October 1 of Gage's alarming letters of August 27 and September 2 and 3, that the administration became aware of the seriousness of the situation in Massachusetts.[2]

On reading these letters, the three members of the Cabinet then in London, Lord Dartmouth, Lord North, and the Lord Chancellor Apsley, promptly agreed, that "it will be advisable that the Admiralty should be consulted whether two or three more ships of war with as large a detachment from the marines as can be conveniently accommodated may be sent to Boston immediately without any material hazard or difficulty."[3]

On hearing favorably from Lord Sandwich, First Lord of the Admiralty, Dartmouth wrote Gage (October 17) that the government was sending three additional warships from England to Boston with about 600 marines who were available for land service, if required.[4] Furthermore, the King issued a proclamation forbidding the export of arms or ammunition from Great Britain and sent orders to colonial Governors and British naval officers in colonial waters to prevent the importation of these articles from any place.[5]

On November 18, the even more alarming letters from Gage to Dartmouth of September 12 and 25, also quoted in Chapter 26, were received.[6] Letters from Gage to ex-Governor Thomas Hutchinson of Massachusetts and Lord Barrington, Secretary at War, and from Admiral Samuel Graves to the Admiralty Board, corroborating those to Dartmouth,[7] left no room for doubt that most of New England was in rebellion.

The King immediately sent a note to North: "I am not sorry that the line of conduct seems now chalked out . . . ; the New England Governments are in a State of Rebellion; blows must decide whether they are to be subject to this Country or independant. . . ."[8] The following day, North spoke in similar vein to Hutchinson. Massachusetts, he said, "was in Rebellion and must be subdued."[9]

However, nothing was done pending the assembling of a new Parliament and the receipt of word of the decisions of the Continental Congress.[10]

Under the Septennial Act of 1715,[11] the term of the Thirteenth Parliament, elected in the spring of 1768, would not expire until the spring of 1775. But on August 24, the King wrote North that he wished to dissolve the existing Parliament and hold elections for a new as soon as practicable. The King thought that calling for elections before the expected time would "fill the House [of Commons] with some Gentlemen of landed Property, as the Nabobs [West Indian] Planters and other Volunteers are not ready for the Battle . . ."; furthermore, "the general Congress now assembling in America, the Peace of Russia with the Turks and unsettled state of the French Ministry,"[12] made it "admissable" to do this.[13]

The Cabinet approved, and on September 30, the King issued a proclamation dissolving the existing Parliament and calling for elections to the new.[14]

The elections, tainted with the widespread corruption usual in British elections of the period,[15] were highly favorable to the administration.[16] The problem of colonial policy played little part in the elections (it was an issue in only ten of the 314 constituencies);[17] but its importance was recognized by the administration, which, immediately after the opening of the new Parliament, on November 29, took steps to secure practically carte blanche in dealing with colonial unrest.

The King, speaking for the administration the day after Parliament opened, and referring to the "violences of a very criminal nature in Massachusetts," said that "you may depend on my firm and steadfast resolution to withstand every attempt to weaken or impair the supreme authority of this Legislature over all the Dominions of my Crown." To which assertion the House of Lords replied that "we will cheerfully co-operate in all such measures as shall be necessary to maintain the dignity, safety and welfare of the British Empire," and the House of Commons in similar vein.[18] The reply in the Lords was carried 63 to 13, in the Commons, 264 to 73.[19]

However, though now assured of the new Parliament's backing for vigorous measures against the rebellious colonists, the administration had not yet received word of the action of the Continental Congress, without which, it had been decided, "no particular measure would be determined."[20]

Through "a private correspondence," supposedly communicating "every step" taken by the Congress, the administration had learned various details concerning its proceedings, including the dispute over the articles to be excepted from the proposed non-importation agreement and the decision to present a Petition to the King.[21] But authentic word of the proceedings other than the contents of the Petition to the King was not received until December 13, and the latter not until eight days later.[22]

By that time, most members of Parliament had left or were about to leave London for the Christmas holidays,[23] and there is no evidence of any Cabinet meeting to consider the problems presented by the actions of the Congress before January 13, 1775.[24] In the meanwhile, additional letters from Gage concerning developments in New England up to December 15, 1774 had been received.[25]

At the meeting on January 13, the Cabinet[26] voted favorably on the following measures:

To reinforce Gage as soon as practicable with two regiments of infantry, one of light cavalry, and 600 marines.

To approve the proposal of Timothy Ruggles, colonel of a Massachusetts regiment in the Seven Years' War and now a leading Tory, to raise "a corps of irregulars";[27]

To propose in Parliament that "the associated Colonies should be prohibited for a limited time from trading to any other ports than those of Great Britain, Ireland & the Islands in the West Indies, and also restrained from carrying on the fishery."[28]

This plan to put commercial pressure on the recalcitrant colonies to submit, and at the same time prepare to compel submission by force if commercial pressure proved insufficient, was carried out during the next few months.

The additional troops, together with three general officers—William Howe, John Burgoyne, and Henry Clinton—were sent to America,[29] and Gage was instructed to encourage Ruggles to raise his proposed corps of Tories.[30]

A bill was promptly (February 10) introduced and passed prohibiting shipment by water of any New England products to any place but Great Britain, Ireland, or the British West Indies; prohibiting vessels owned in New England to fish anywhere on the Newfoundland banks or the coast of North America; and prohibiting importation by water into the New England colonies of any goods whatever except articles from Great Britain, Ireland, or the British West Indies. The first provision was to take effect July 1; the second, July 21; the third, September 1, 1775.[31] (An act was soon afterwards passed imposing similar restraints on the commerce of New Jersey, Pennsylvania, Maryland, Virginia and South Carolina.)[32]

The Cabinet's plan was, however, not limited to the application of commercial pressure and preparation for war. At the Cabinet meeting on January 13, some member, probably Dartmouth, proposed that commissioners be sent to America to try to work out "a nearer Union with the Colonies for the mutual Interest of both parts of the Empire. . . ."[33] This proposal was not adopted. But on January 28, the King informed Dartmouth that he planned to offer Sir Jeffery Amherst the command of the British troops in North America in place of Gage, not only for military reasons but also "the political one" of "having some one in America unattached to any particular Province, ready to transmit the sentiments of those who wish well to English Government. . . ."

This plan, the King pointed out, would "be a good succedanium to your original idea of a Commission; for, as he [Amherst] is respected by the Colonies, they will give more credit to his assertions than those of any other person" and hopefully might bring the "deluded people to due obedience without putting the dagger to their throats."[34]

The plan fell through when Amherst declined the offer.[35] But on January 21, the Cabinet adopted a plan apparently designed to secure a peaceful settlement, namely to ask both Houses of Parliament "to declare that if the Colonies shall make sufficient and permanent provision for the support of the civil government and administration of justice and for the defence and protection of the said Colonies, and in time of war contribute extraordinary supplies, in a reasonable proportion to what is raised by Great Britain, we will in that case desist from the exercize of the power of taxation, except for commercial purposes only. . . ."[36]

Pursuant to this plan, North, on February 20, moved in the House of Commons for a resolution that Parliament would forbear taxing any colony which contributed its proportion to the common defense and for the support of its own civil government in such amounts as the King and Parliament approved. Any duties imposed by Parliament for the regulation of commerce collected in such a colony were to be credited to the account of the colony. However, there was no indication of what amounts would be acceptable, nor was there any proposal for suspension, amendment, or repeal of the Intolerable Acts of 1774[37] or amelioration of the acts restricting colonial trade.

Benjamin Franklin wrote that North's proposal, coupled with the sending of reinforcements of troops to the colonies, was like that of "a Highwayman, who presents his Pistol and Hat at a Coach Window, demanding no specific Sum, but if you will give . . . what he is pleas'd to think sufficient, he will civilly omit putting his own Hands into your Pockets; if not, there is his Pistol."[38]

Chatham denounced it as "mere verbiage, a most puerile mockery," and Richard Champion, a moderate English Whig, described it as "falsely termed conciliatory," declaring that North "knew it could not be adopted, and had no other hope than that it would delude and divide, if not the Colonies, at least the few friends the Americans had at home."[39] Edmund Burke, a prominent member of the Rockingham party and London Agent for New York, wrote, "Last Night my Lord North produced his resolution for forcing the Colonies, by a continuance of Penal Statutes and the sending of Troops, to offer such a revenue as . . . shall be agreeable to our fancy . . . Yet this was held out to us as a plan of conciliation; though at the same time, Lord North plainly told us that he was convinced the Colonies would not accept it."[40]

North's motion was carried 274 to 88.[41] No list of voters has come to light, but of those known to have spoken, nine, including John Dunning, Isaac Barré, and Edmund Burke, members of the opposition, opposed the motion because it offered too little toward conciliation, the other five because it offered any concession at all.[42]

Speaking in support of his motion, North declared that his plan was presented in the hope of laying the basis for a peaceful settlement of the dispute with the colonies.[43] But a letter from him to the King, written the day before, stating, "Lord North hopes for great utility (if not in America at least on this side of the water) to arise to the publick from this motion. He is confident it gives up no right, . . . [and] will greatly facilitate the passing the Bill now in the House for restraining the trade of New England . . . ,"[44] lends color to the suspicion of Burke and others recently quoted.

Without waiting to hear from the Ministry, Lord Chatham had made a dramatic move in the House of Lords for reconciliation. On January 20, the day after Parliament reconvened following the Christmas recess,[45] he spoke at length in favor of repeal of all British acts levying taxes for revenue on the colonies, concluding with a motion for an address to the King "to advise and beseech" him that, "in order to open the way for a happy settlement of the dangerous troubles in America, . . . orders may be despatched to General Gage for removing his Majesty's Forces from the Town of Boston. . . ."[46] The motion was defeated by a vote of 68 to 18.[47]

Three days later, a plea for "healing remedies" was made to the House of Commons in a petition presented on behalf of "the Merchants, Traders, and others of the City of London, concerned in the Commerce of North America,"[48] by George Hayley, one of the members for the City of London. This petition was in effect shelved by the defeat, 197 to 81, of a motion for consideration of the petition by a select committee instead of by the House sitting in Committee of the Whole.[49]

Undeterred by the defeat of his motion for removal of the troops from Boston, Chatham, on February 1, presented to the Lords, an elaborate plan for conciliation.

Its outstanding features were for Parliament to:

Declare its authority "to bind the people of the British Colonies in America, in all matters touching the general weal of the whole Dominion of the Imperial Crown of Great Britain, and beyond the competency of the local representatives of a distinct Colony, most especially . . . to make and Ordain laws for regulating navigation and trade";

Declare that no tax would be levied in the colonies without the consent of the Assembly of the colony on which the tax was to be imposed;

Pass acts confining the jurisdiction of colonial admiralty courts to matters generally recognized as within the jurisdiction of admiralty courts and forbidding trials for capital offenses to be held other than in the colony in which the alleged offense was committed;

Temporarily suspend all other acts objected to by the First Continental Congress in its Petition to the King, and repeal them "from the day that the due recognition of the Supreme Legislative authority and superintending power of Parliament over the Colonies shall have been made on the part of the said Colonies."

On their part, the colonies represented at the forthcoming Second

Continental Congress were to "take into consideration . . . the making a free grant . . . of a certain perpetual revenue . . . to the alleviation of the National debt" and fix the proportion to be borne by each of the colonies of any revenue so granted.[50]

Chatham's plan, if adopted, might have achieved conciliation,[51] but the plan was rejected by a vote of 61 to 32.[52]

Various projects for conciliation discussed by Benjamin Franklin with two leading English Quakers, encouraged by Dartmouth, and with Admiral Lord Howe, which are described in an appendix to this chapter, also came to nothing.

Final efforts for peace were made by Burke and David Hartley in the House of Commons in March, 1775.

On March 22, Burke proposed that Parliament go on record as waiving the right to tax the colonies for revenue and relying on a favorable response by the several colonial Legislatures to requisitions (appeals) by the Crown for funds for imperial purposes. He supported his proposal by a speech justly famed for its eloquence.[53] But he spoke in vain; in a test vote, his proposal was rejected 270 to 78.[54]

On March 27, Hartley moved to suspend, for a period of three years, operation of the Boston Port Act and Massachusetts Regulating Act. But his proposal was defeated without even a division.[55]

The measures of the administration pursuant to the Cabinet decisions of January 13 and 21, described earlier, were supplemented by two other measures, taken, so far as is known, without formal action by the Cabinet.

One was a motion, supported by an opinion of the Attorney- and Solicitor-Generals,[56] for an Address to the King declaring that "a rebellion at this time actually exists" in Massachusetts, and asking him to "take the most effectual measures to enforce due obedience to the laws and authority of the supreme Legislature. . . ." This motion, presented by North to the Commons on February 2, was promptly adopted by large majorities in both Houses.[57]

The other was a letter from Dartmouth to Gage of January 27, 1775 (quoted in Chapter 30),[58] which, as we shall see, led directly to the British march to Concord and the outbreak of war.

CHAPTER 28

THE COLONIAL RESPONSE
TO THE CONGRESS

THE resolution of the Continental Congress for the general adoption of a uniform non-importation, non-exportation, and non-consumption Association was accompanied (it will be recalled from Chapter 24) by a resolution for establishment of local committees to enforce the Association.

Such committees were promptly established throughout the colonies represented at the Congress.

On November 12, 1774, a meeting called by the Philadelphia committee described in Chapter 20, chose a committee of sixty-six to enforce the Association in the city and suburbs of Philadelphia.[1] A few weeks later, the new committee published notice directing consignees of banned goods imported after December 1 to notify the committee whether they chose to send back such goods, to store them, or to deliver them to the committee to be sold, and describing the procedure that would be followed in selling goods so delivered. The notice also reminded consignees of the provision in the Association for publication of the names of any who violated its terms.[2]

On November 20, a meeting engineered by the New York Committee of Fifty-One, described in Chapter 20, in collaboration with a local committee of mechanics,[3] chose an enforcement committee of sixty members.[4]

On December 7, a Boston town meeting elected a similar committee of sixty-two members "to carry the Resolutions of the Continental Congress into Execution."[5]

At Charleston, fourth of the leading colonial ports, some group, presumably members of the committee elected in July, 1774, described in Chapter 20, assumed responsibility for enforcing the Association there.[6]

The establishment of enforcement committees was, however, not limited to the four leading port cities.

According to Governor Lord Dunmore of Virginia, by the end of December, 1774, "A Committee has been chosen in every County [of Virginia] whose business it is to carry the Association of the Congress into execution, which Committee assumes an authority . . . to watch the conduct of every inhabitant, without distinction, and . . . to stigmatize, as they term it, such as they find transgressing what they are now hardy enough to call the Laws of the Congress . . . [by] inviting the vengeance of an outrageous and lawless mob to be exercized upon the unhappy victims."[7] There also is evidence of the establishment and effective activity of enforcement committees in the other colonies represented at the Congress.[8]

The outbreak of war a few months after the committees were formed defeated the original purpose of securing redress of colonial grievances by a commercial boycott. But, as observed in earlier chapters, they proved to be of immense value as a network of local units ready and able promptly to help execute the war measures adopted by the Second Continental Congress.

The response to the Congress' proposal for a Second Continental Congress also was generally favorable. By April 5, 1775, the regular Assembly or a special convention in eleven of the twelve colonies represented at the First Congress had approved its proceedings and elected delegates to the Second Continental Congress.[9]

Only New York held back. In February, 1775, the New York Assembly refused to approve the proceedings of the First Continental Congress or elect delegates to the proposed second.[10] A New York provincial convention eventually elected delegates to the Second Congress, but not until after the outbreak of war.[11]

Except for Nathaniel Folsom of New Hampshire (replaced by John Langdon), Isaac Low and John Haring of New York, and Joseph Galloway and Samuel Rhoads of Pennsylvania, the delegates who had served at the First Congress were reelected to and served in the Second.[12] In addition, John Hancock of Massachusetts, John Hall and Thomas Stone of Maryland, and Philip Schuyler, George Clinton, Lewis Morris, Francis Lewis, and Robert R. Livingston of New York were chosen delegates from their respective colonies.[13]

Seven of the colonial Assemblies or conventions also responded favorably to the Congress' recommendation "to be in all respects prepared for every contingency,"[14] i.e., for war.

As early as October 20, a Massachusetts convention began the warlike preparations described in the next chapter, and at its October session, the Connecticut General Assembly passed an act that "the several towns in this Colony . . . provide as soon as may be double the quantity of powder, ball and flints that they were heretofore by law obliged to provide. . . ."[15]

The Rhode Island General Assembly, meeting in December, 1774, adopted a number of warlike measures summarized in a letter of December 14 from Samuel Ward, one of the Rhode Island delegates to the recent Congress, to John Dickinson. The Assembly, he wrote, had "ordered the Cannon at our Fort . . . [near Newport] to be sent to Providence where it will be safe and ready for Service; 200 blls of Powder and a proportionate Quantity of Lead and Flints and several pieces of brass Cannon for the Artillery Company were ordered to be purchased; a Major General was appointed, several Companies of Light Infantry, Fusileers and etc. were established, the Militia was ordered to be disciplined and the Commanding Officers impowered to march our Troops to the Assistance of any Sister Colony. . . .

"The Idea," Ward added, "of taking up Arms against the parent State is shocking to Us who still feel the strongest Attachment to our Sovereign and warmest affection for our Brethren in Britain . . . but if We must either become Slaves or fly to Arms I shall not (and hope no American will) hesitate one Moment which to choose. . . ."[16]

A New Hampshire convention, meeting in January, 1775, approved a circular letter to the officers of the colony's militia urging them to learn "the manual exercise . . . best calculated to qualify persons for real action" and "to improve themselves in those evolutions which are necessary for infantry in time of engagement."[17] (Several hundred New Hampshire men had previously taken steps to secure arms and ammunition by descending on Fort William and Mary at the entrance to Portsmouth harbor and carrying off over a hundred barrels of powder, sixteen cannon, and a large number of muskets.)[18]

In December, a Maryland convention resolved that "if the late Acts of Parliament relative to the Massachusetts Bay shall be attempted to be carried into force in that Colony; or if the assumed power of Parliament to tax the Colonies shall be attempted to be carried into execution by force in that or any other Colony, . . . this Province will support such Colony to the utmost of their power." This resolution was accompanied by another advising the immediate formation of military companies throughout the province and the raising of £10,000 by the counties of the province, according to quotas stated in the resolution, to purchase arms and ammunition.[19]

In January, 1775, a South Carolina convention passed a resolution recommending "to all the Inhabitants of this Colony that they be diligently attentive in learning the use of Arms, and that their officers be requested to train and exercize them at least once a fortnight."[20]

The Virginia convention, third and last of those outside New England to prepare for war, did not meet until March 20, 1775, because of the expectation, until well into the new year, of a meeting of the House of Burgesses at which action would be taken.[21]

However, long before March 20, the people in many counties of Virginia had begun to prepare for war by organizing so-called "independent" companies, i.e., independent of the provincial militia commanded by officers appointed by, and subject to, the orders of the Crown-appointed Governor of the colony.

On January 6, George Washington wrote an unidentified correspondent, "In this County [Fairfax], Prince William, Loudoun, Fauquier, Berkley and many others round about, . . . Men are forming themselves into independent companies, chusing their officers, arming, equipping and training for the worst Event."[22] Washington's correspondence and diary from mid-October to March of 1774–1775 are full of references to his own activities in forming, equipping, and inspecting the Fairfax and Prince William Counties independent companies.[23]

Meeting March 20–27, the Virginia convention gave its stamp of approval to these military preparations by recommending that every county in the colony "form one or more companies of Infantry and Troops of Horse . . . to be in constant training and readiness to act on any emergency" and that county committees raise funds "sufficient to purchase half a pound of Gunpowder, one pound of Lead, necessary Flints and Cartridge Papers for every tithable person in their County." The convention also chose a central committee to act as purchasing agent for such counties as "may not be apprized of the most certain and speedy method of procuring the articles before-mentioned. . . ."[24]

According to James Parker of Norfolk, Virginia, Patrick Henry tried to have the convention take over the reins of government and levy taxes to raise and equip a provincial army, but was defeated.[25]

"The convention at Richmond," wrote Parker, "is over now. . . . There was a motion made by P. Henry supported by T. Jefferson, G. Washington and Richard Henry Lee for referring to a committee the raising eighty-six men out of each county, and equipping them with arms, ammunition etc.[26] This was carried by a majority of 65 to 60, but the Committee could not agree upon the ways and means for their support. What flattened them all down was a Plea presented by P. Henry,[27] no less than taking of Government into their hands, appointing magistrates and levying money. The Treasurer [Robert Carter Nicholas], Coll. B. Harrison, Bland and Coll. Ruddick [Riddick] saw into this and formed an opposition which overset the scheme. . . ."[28]

However, even if the convention would not go as far as Henry wished, it encouraged and offered to facilitate the preparations for war already under way in the colony.

New York, New Jersey, Pennsylvania,[29] Delaware, and North Carolina took no measures to make or encourage preparations for war, and New York and Delaware even gave their delegates to the Second Continental Congress instructions apparently designed to deter them from supporting any warlike resolutions that might be proposed there.[30] But when the Second Congress met, following the outbreak of war in Massachusetts, the delegations from these colonies joined with those from the others in voting for war measures. Presumably they shared the feeling of James Duane, one of the New York delegates, who, in justifying his support of war measures at the Second Congress, said, "It is sufficient ground for my conduct that the sword of ministerial vengeance has been drawn against our Brethren in the Massachusetts Bay and their innocent blood been shed . . . in our common cause. . . ."[31] Instructions given before the day of Lexington and Concord had become obsolete.

CHAPTER 29

MASSACHUSETTS PREPARES FOR WAR: OCTOBER, 1774–APRIL, 1775

DURING the summer of 1774, Massachusetts Whigs, as we saw in Chapter 26, successfully opposed the execution of the Massachusetts Regulating Act of 1774. Town meetings were held without permission from Governor General Gage; all the newly appointed mandamus councilors living outside Boston who accepted and retained their appointments were compelled to seek safety in Boston; and judges throughout the province, while suffered to retain office, were prevented from holding court under the Regulating Act. Furthermore, assuming that Gage, when reinforced, would attempt to execute the act by military force, Whig leaders throughout Massachusetts took steps to prepare for war.

As early as August 10, a convention of delegates from most of the towns of Worcester County in central Massachusetts proposed a provincial convention to adopt measures to prevent execution of the Regulating Act. Several other Massachusetts county conventions repeated the proposal and the project was brought to a head by a resolution of Middlesex County, supported by the Suffolk County Resolves (described in Chapter 22), calling for the assembling of a provincial convention at Concord on October 11.[1]

Delegates from most towns of the province assembled at Concord on the appointed day.[2] John Hancock was elected President and Benjamin Lincoln of Hingham, Secretary of the Congress, and a steering committee of fifteen was chosen. This committee, called the Committee on the State of the Province, consisted of Hancock, Joseph Warren, and Benjamin Church of Boston and twelve leading Whigs from other parts of the province, including Joseph Hawley of Northampton, Artemas Ward of Shrewsbury, James Warren of Plymouth, William Heath of Roxbury, and Elbridge Gerry of Marblehead. On their return from Philadelphia, the Massachusetts delegates to the First Continental Congress, Samuel and John Adams, Thomas Cushing, and Robert Treat Paine, were added to this important committee.[3]

Though dealing with a variety of other matters, the Congress, which sat (with an adjournment of a few weeks) until December 10,[4] was occupied chiefly in preparing for defense.

The first step was to secure funds to finance a projected army by calling up all officials responsible for the collection of provincial taxes to turn over their collections to a Receiver-General, elected by the Congress, instead of to the provincial treasurer, a Tory.[5]

The second was to call for the election of officers of the provincial militia to replace existing officers, many of whom, appointed by successive royal Governors, were Tories. The new system was to be democratic. The company officers were to be elected by the men of the company, and the field (battalion) officers by the company officers. Only the general officers, Jedediah Preble of Falmouth, Ward, Seth Pomeroy of Northampton, John Thomas of Kingston, and Heath (in this order of rank), were appointed by the Congress.[6]

The third was to provide for a special body of "minute men," enlisted to the number of "one quarter at least," of each company of militia, who were "to equip and hold themselves in readiness on the shortest notice . . . to march to the place of rendezvous." They were to be organized into companies of fifty privates each and battalions of nine companies each, the officers to be elected in the same way as those of the ordinary militia. The minute men were to be drilled "three times a week and oftener as opportunity may offer." The Congress made no provision for their pay, but recommended that the several towns from which they come pay the men "a reasonable consideration" for their services and furnish each with "an effective fire arm, bayonet, pouch, knapsack, thirty rounds of cartridges and balls."[7]

The fourth step was to elect a Committee of Safety of nine members "to continue in office until the further order of this or some other Congress or house of representatives of the province," with authority to call out as many men as they thought best "whenever they shall judge it necessary for the safety and defence of the inhabitants of this province." Presumably because this important committee would have to meet frequently and, in an emergency, very quickly, its membership was limited to residents of Boston and near-by towns. The Boston members were the same as those on the Committee on the State of the Province, Hancock, Warren, and Church; the others were Richard Devens of Charlestown, Benjamin White of Brookline, Joseph Palmer and Norton Quincy of Braintree, Abraham Watson of Cambridge, Azor Orne of Marblehead, John Pigeon of Newton, and General Heath.[8]

Various other provisions for an army of defense were adopted, including the establishment of a Committee of Supplies. The committee was to provide for "the reception and support" of men in the field when called into service by the Committee of Safety and to procure immediately, at a cost not to exceed £20,887, 20 pieces of field artillery, carriages for 12 battering cannon, 4 mortars, 20 tons of grape and round shot, 10 tons of bombshells, 5 tons of lead balls, 1,000 barrels of powder, 5,000 arms and bayonets, and 75,000 flints.[9]

The Congress also protested to Gage against the fortification of Boston Neck, elected delegates to the forthcoming Second Continental Congress, and, before rising on December 10, called for the election of a second provincial congress to meet at Cambridge on February 1, 1775.[10]

One other proceeding of this Congress must be noted. This was a motion for the appointment of a committee to consider a letter submitted to the Congress proposing that "while we are attempting to . . . preserve ourselves from slavery, that we also take into consideration the state and circumstances of the negro slaves in this province."[11] The irony of colonial Whigs clamoring against Great Britain's attempted "enslavement" of British North America, while they themselves took no steps even to mitigate the actual slavery of the blacks held by so many of them, is discussed in an appendix to this chapter. Suffice to say here that the journals of the Massachusetts Congress record, "After some debate thereon, the question was put whether the matter now subside, and it passed the affirmative."[12]

The Second Massachusetts Congress called for by the First Congress met at the scheduled time and place. Gage wrote Lord Dartmouth that many of the delegates were "Sent by their Towns to oppose the violent Party."[13] But the journals of this Congress record measures no less spirited than those of the First, with one exception, discussed later in this chapter.

These measures included an appeal to the people of the province to prevent anyone from furnishing Gage with lumber, wagons, horses, or other articles of military use; election of a committee to prepare rules necessary for the good order of "the constitutional army which may be raised in this province"; and a resolution to continue the Committee of Safety, with authority to call into the field "so many of the militia of this province as they shall judge necessary" to oppose any attempt by Gage to execute the Regulating Act "by force."[14]

On February 16, the Congress adjourned until March 22, to reconvene at Concord instead of Cambridge.[15] The journals give no hint as to why Concord, which had fewer facilities than Cambridge for housing the delegates, was chosen as the place of meeting. But a letter of January 15, 1775, from James Warren to John Adams suggests that the danger of the delegates being seized while attending the Congress in a town so near Boston as Cambridge, was the reason for the change.[16]

The existence of such danger is clear from letters of January 18 from Gage to Dartmouth suggesting that the Ministry order "the most obnoxious of the Leaders seized," and February 14 from Major John Pitcairn to Lord Sandwich, First Lord of the Admiralty, stating, "I often wish to have orders to march to Cambridge and seize those impudent rascals [in the Massachusetts Congress] . . . and send them to England."[17]

On receipt, soon after the Congress adjourned, of a report that more troops were being sent to Gage,[18] the Committee of Safety and the Committee of Supplies became very active. At joint sessions held daily February 21–24, they voted to purchase medicines, canteens, and "all kinds of warlike stores, sufficient for an army of fifteen thousand men to take the field," move all the colony's arms at Boston and Roxbury to Worcester, and send two pieces of field artillery to Colonels Ward of Shrewsbury,

Heath of Roxbury, Thomas Gardner of Cambridge, Edward Mitchell of Bridgewater, James Warren of Plymouth, Jedediah Foster of Brookfield, and Lemuel Robinson of Dorchester.[19]

The great and dangerous power conferred by the Congress on the Committee of Safety evidently troubled Joseph Hawley, a leading delegate from western Massachusetts to both the First and Second provincial Congresses and a member of the important Committee on the State of the Province.

On returning to his home in Northampton during the recess of the Congress, Hawley wrote Cushing, a fellow member of this committee, pointing out, "If we, by order of our Committee of Safety, should begin the attack and so bring on hostilities before the general consent of the Colonies that hostilities were altogether unavoidable . . . , there will be infinite hazard that the other governments will say that we have unnecessarily and madly plunged into war, and therefore must get out of the scrape as we can. . . ."[20]

The impact of Hawley's letter is reflected in a resolution adopted by the Congress, soon after it reassembled on March 25, virtually ordering the Committee of Safety not to call out the militia unless "the Army under command of General Gage, or any part thereof to the Number of Five Hundred, shall march out of the Town of Boston, with Artillery and Baggage. . . ."[21]

Having passed this resolution and several others of less importance, nearly half the members of the Congress favored another adjournment; but the majority voted (April 1) to remain sitting for a few days longer in the expectation of receiving news from England.[22]

The very next day, two vessels sailed into Marblehead from Falmouth, England, with news from London up to February 11, which, as James Warren wrote his wife, left the people of Massachusetts "no longer at a loss what is intended for us by our dear Mother: We have ask'd for Bread and she gives us a Stone, and a serpent for a Fish."[23]

The news included the text of the Address of both Houses of Parliament to the King, quoted in Chapter 27, declaring Massachusetts to be in rebellion and asking him to take effectual measures to suppress the rebellion, and the King's answer that he would take the most speedy means of doing so. There was also a report under a London dateline of January 31 that the Cabinet had just decided to send six more regiments to Gage immediately and another report that the government was planning to send at some unstated time 10,000 additional troops to Boston and 2,000 additional sailors to man the ships stationed there.[24]

The news galvanized the Congress into intense activity, evidenced by its journals of April 3–15.

Appeals were published for all towns that had not elected delegates to the Congress to do so and for absent delegates from Hampshire, Berkshire, Worcester, and Bristol Counties to attend immediately.

Preparations were made to embody Indian volunteers at Stockbridge, Massachusetts, into a company of rangers, and a message was sent to the Mohawks and other tribes of the Six Nations in the province of New York promising to supply them with powder and guns and inviting them to "whet your hatchet and be prepared with us to defend our liberties and lives."[25]

Rules for the regulation of the proposed Massachusetts army and a resolution to enlist and pay six companies of artillerymen to be "constantly in exercize" were adopted. Also a resolution, offered by the Committee on the State of the Province, to establish a New England army and send committees to Connecticut, Rhode Island, and New Hampshire to secure their cooperation was adopted (April 8) by a vote of 96 to 7.[26]

One of the most interesting of the resolutions of this period indicates that the plan for a corps of minute men to enlist on their own initiative and elect their officers had been disappointing.[27] This resolution (April 4) provided for a reversion to the method of recruiting employed in earlier wars in which officers were appointed and made responsible for drumming up recruits to the units they were to command.[28]

It is notable that even in the intense excitement of this period, the Congress evidently was determined to adhere to its recent resolution to avoid precipitating hostilities. In a circular letter to all the towns in Bristol County, they were advised to get into "the best posture of defence," but to "act on the defensive only, until the further direction of this Congress."[29]

On April 15, the Congress adjourned until May 10, but with the precaution of authorizing the members of the Congress from Charlestown, Cambridge, Brookline, Roxbury, and Dorchester, to order an earlier meeting of the Congress at Concord in case of emergency.[30]

In writing Dartmouth concerning the consternation of "the Faction" in Boston over the news received on April 2, Gage reported that "the most active left Town before the Night," and James Warren wrote his wife on April 7, that "H and A [Hancock and Samuel Adams] go no more into that Garrison."[31] Thus, when Dartmouth's fateful letter of January 27, quoted in Chapter 31, finally reached Gage on April 14, the two foremost rebel leaders in Massachusetts[32] were beyond easy reach.

CHAPTER 30

GAGE'S MILITARY ACTIVITIES WHILE AWAITING ORDERS FROM ENGLAND

WHEN Governor General Gage arrived at Boston in May, 1774, he had only one regiment under his immediate command, the Sixty-fourth Regiment of infantry stationed at Castle William near the entrance of Boston harbor. In June and July, the administration sent him four more regiments—the Fourth, Fifth, Thirty-eighth, and Forty-third—from England and Ireland.[1] But Gage's greatest accession of strength came from dipping into the mass of British troops sent to North America during the Seven Years' War and in large part, kept there ever since.[2]

Exercising his authority as Commander-in-Chief of the British Army in North America, Gage, from August to November, moved regiment after regiment of these troops from various posts in the east to Boston. He drew the Twenty-third from New York City, the Fifty-ninth from Halifax, Nova Scotia, the Forty-seventh from New Jersey, the Tenth and Fifty-second from Quebec, several companies of the Eighteenth from Philadelphia, and three companies of the Sixty-fifth from Newfoundland.[3] He also collected a sizable park of artillery[4] and men to serve it.

On November 2, Gage wrote Secretary of State Lord Dartmouth that on the accession of the Tenth and Fifty-second Regiments, which were just coming into Boston harbor from Quebec, he would have "a Force of near Three Thousand Men exclusive of a regiment [the Sixty-fourth] for the Defence of Castle William."[5] In December he was further strengthened by the addition of nearly 400 marines.[6] Thus, by the end of the year Gage must have had over 3,500 men in or near Boston.

A considerable squadron of warships under the command of Admiral Samuel Graves had also by this time assembled there.[7]

This combined force had been able to enforce rigorously the Boston Port Act. But Gage, while awaiting further instructions from the administration, made no effort to enforce the Massachusetts Regulating Act outside Boston.[8]

He explained his policy in a letter to Lord Dartmouth, dated September 2, stating, "I mean, my Lord to . . . avoid any bloody Crisis as long as possible, unless forced into it by [the rebels] themselves. . . . His Majesty will in the mean Time Judge what is best to be done, but your Lordship will permit me to mention that . . . if it will be resolved to stem the Torrent . . . We shou'd . . . be strong and proceed on a good Foundation before any thing decisive is tried. . . ."

He wrote again in similar vein on October 30, "Affairs are at such a

Pitch thro' a general union of the whole, that I am obliged to use more caution than would otherwise be necessary, least all the Continent should unite in hostile Proceedings against us, which I apprehend His Majesty would by all Means wish to avoid unless driven to it by their own Conduct."[9]

Gage, however, was not idle while awaiting his expected instructions from London.

On September 1, with the cooperation of Admiral Graves, he shipped a detachment of 260 men from the regiment at Castle William to a point on the Mystic River a short march from the provincial powderhouse at Quarry Hill in Charlestown. Striking quickly, the detachment carried away from there a large store of powder before the rebel forces could gather to prevent the seizure or attack the detachment on its return.[10]

Gage's next step was to ensure himself against attack by strongly fortifying Boston neck,[11] the only entrance to Boston by land—a measure prompted by the gathering at Cambridge of several thousand men aroused by word of the seizure of the powder at nearby Charlestown.[12]

Having completed the fortification of Boston in December,[13] Gage, with Graves' cooperation, carried out several further operations designed to seize rebel military supplies or to support groups of Tories outside Boston in places that could easily be reached by water.

On January 23, he shipped a detachment of 100 men of the King's Own (Fourth) Regiment to Marshfield, Massachusetts, to protect a group of Tories there. The detachment landed without resistance, and remained in Marshfield until shortly after the day of Lexington and Concord, when it was shipped back to Boston.[14]

On February 25, Gage shipped a detachment of 200 men to Marblehead, Massachusetts, by night to seize some cannon reported to be at nearby Salem.[15] The report was false or the cannon had been hidden, and the detachment returned empty-handed.[16] But a detachment sent secretly by water on April 8 to Fort Pownall, a Massachusetts outpost on the Penobscot River, proved to be highly successful. It secured, without fighting, 16 cannon, nearly 500 cannon balls, and much other military matériel.[17]

In March, responding to an appeal for arms and ammunition from Thomas Gilbert of Freetown, Massachusetts, a Tory colonel of militia, Gage shipped to Freetown a quantity of both. Gilbert armed a considerable band of Tory followers, but they scattered on the approach of a much larger rebel force.[18]

Gage also took various other steps to strengthen his position if and when war broke out. He secured assurance from Governor General Guy Carleton of Quebec that he could count on the aid of a large force of Canadians and Indians,[19] built up a rather impressive espionage service,[20] sent out a couple of officers who succeeded in mapping roads for military operations as far west as Worcester,[21] and sent out party after party on marches in the vicinity of Boston,[22] thus familiarizing his officers and men with the neighboring terrain.

As noted in the Introduction it was widely believed in Great Britain that the colonists were a cowardly people—a belief probably attributable chiefly to letters from British officers serving in America during the French and Indian War depicting the colonial troops as, in general, egregiously lacking not only discipline but courage.[23]

The belief in the cowardice of colonial troops, at least those of Massachusetts, evidently prevailed among Gage's officers, whose letters home repeatedly expressed contempt for the Massachusetts rebels and an itch for orders from home to have a go at them.

On July 6, three weeks after his arrival at Boston, Captain William Glanville Evelyn, writing his father of the expected arrival of additional British troops, remarked, "With this force we have no apprehensions from the very great numbers in this province . . . , for, though upon paper they are the bravest fellows in the world, yet in reality I believe there does not exist so great a set of rascals and poltroons."[24]

In December he wrote his cousin Mrs. John Leveson-Gower (married to a first cousin of the Lord Gower who was a member of the Cabinet), "We are all in high spirits at the speedy return of the [warship] 'Scarbro' and of this re-inforcement of men-of-war. We hope they are in earnest of the spirited resolutions of the people at home no longer to suffer the treason and rebellion of these villains to go unpunished. Never were any set of men more anxious to be employed on so laudable a work. We only fear they will avail themselves of the clemency and generosity of the English, and by some abject submission evade the chastisement due to unexampled villainy, and which we are so impatiently waiting to inflict."[25]

A couple of months later Captain Evelyn had become, if anything, even more contemptuous and impatient. "The hour is now very nigh," he wrote his father on February 18, "in which this affair will be brought to a crisis. . . . We have great confidence in the spirit and pride of our countrymen that they will not tamely suffer such insolence and disobedience from a set of upstart vagabonds, the dregs and scorn of the human species, and that we shall shortly receive such orders as will authorize us to scourge the rebellion with rods of iron."[26]

Colonel Lord Percy, eldest son of the Duke of Northumberland and a son-in-law of Lord Bute, wrote in similar vein. A letter from him to his father in July, 1774, scoffing at the "cowards" who "whenever we appear . . . are frightened out of their wits," was quoted in the Introduction. Several days later he wrote a cousin, Henry Reveley, "The people here are a set of sly, artful hypocritical rascals, cruel and cowards. I must own I cannot but despise them compleately."[27]

Before many months Percy, too, grew impatient for action against the despised rebels. On November 25, describing "the People here" as "the most designing Artfull Villains in the World . . . [without] the least Idea of either Religion or Morality," he wrote to the Reverend Thomas Percy (editor of the celebrated "Reliques of Ancient English Poetry") that they "have now got to such lengths that nothing can secure the Colonies to the Mother Country, but the conquest of them"; and on February 9, 1775, to General Edward Harvey, Adjutant-General of the army, "We are waiting with impatience the determinations and orders from your side of the water. Whatever they are I hope they will be pointed and effectual. . . ."[28]

Major John Pitcairn, commanding officer of the marines stationed under Gage in Boston, wrote in similar vein to Lord Sandwich, First Lord of the Admiralty, on February 14. "The deluded people," he said, "are made believe that they are invincible. . . . When this army is ordered to act against them, they will soon be convinced that they are very insignificant when opposed to regular troops. I have sent your Lordships enclosed with this the newspaper with the recent resolves of the Provincial Congress. . . . I often wish to have orders to march to Cambridge and seize those impudent rascals that have the assurance to make such resolves . . . but we have no orders to do what I wish to do, and what I think may easily be done, I mean to seize them all and send them to England."[29]

Three weeks later Major Pitcairn wrote Sandwich, "Orders are anxiously expected from England to chastise these very bad people. I am satisfied that one active campaign, a smart action and burning one or two of their towns will set everything to rights. . . . The people behaved [in the recent expedition to Salem, mentioned earlier in this chapter] as I suppose they will ever do, make a great noise when there is nobody to oppose them, but the moment they see us in arms they will talk very differently."[30]

Gage's letters disclose no such contempt for the New Englanders as those of Evelyn, Percy, and Pitcairn; however, a letter from him to Lord Barrington dated February 10 indicates that he, too, was now impatient for orders to take the offensive though at the risk of counterattack and war.[31]

This letter crossed the letter from Dartmouth to Gage of January 27, referred to in Chapter 27, which finally reached him on April 14.[32]

CHAPTER 31

DARTMOUTH'S LETTER GALVANIZES
GAGE INTO ACTION

ARTMOUTH'S letter to Gage of January 27, 1775, stated
that the King and Ministry considered "the first & essential
step to be taken towards re-establishing Government, would be
to arrest and imprison the principal actors & abettors in the
Provincial Congress (whose proceedings appear in every light to be acts
of treason & rebellion) if regardless of your Proclamation[1] & in defiance
of it they should presume again to assemble for such rebellious purposes
. . . ," even though this be "a Signal for Hostilities."[2] However, said
Dartmouth, "there are other Cases that must occur, in which the affording
the Assistance of the Military will probably become unavoidable," and
"would become a Test of the People's resolution to resist. . . ."[3]

Thus, though Dartmouth's letter did not explicitly order Gage to take
the offensive, it strongly hinted that the King and Ministry expected
him to do so.

If Gage had been able to carry out Dartmouth's proposal that the
people's "resolution to resist" be tested by seizing the principal actors in
the provincial Congress, the Revolution might perhaps have been averted.
Such action would almost certainly have been retaliated (as the Continental Congress had advised)[4] by the seizure of Crown officials stationed
throughout North America, many of whom had influential British family
and other connections. These hostages would have given colonial Whigs
a bargaining power for redress of colonial grievances more immediate and
compelling than the threat of economic boycott.

But Dartmouth's proposal, earlier suggested by Gage himself,[5] was no
longer practicable after the provincial Congress moved from Cambridge,
only a few miles from Boston, to Concord, nearly twenty miles away. By
the time an expedition from there reached Concord, the members of the
Congress would almost certainly be warned in time to disperse. Furthermore, arrangements for an expedition to Concord would take some days to
prepare, and Gage knew that the Congress was about to rise and its
members disperse.[6]

He evidently decided, however, that some incisive action must be taken,[7]
and, knowing from his informers of a large quantity of rebel military
supplies at Concord,[8] he decided to send out a strong force to destroy them.

Marching a force to a point so distant from Boston would, of course,
invite attack, but Dartmouth's letter clearly implied that, far from this
being a deterrent, the administration would welcome an immediate test
of the rebels' resolution to resist.

On April 15, Gage issued an order that the grenadier and light infantry companies of all ten regiments in Boston were to be excused from ordinary duty, ostensibly "in order to learn Grenadiers Exercize and new evolutions,"[9] but in fact, as soon developed, to form an expedition to Concord.

Gage chose Lieutenant-Colonel Francis Smith of the Tenth Regiment to lead the expedition consisting probably of around 700 officers and men.[10] Major John Pitcairn, whose letters to Lord Sandwich were quoted in Chapter 30, was second in command.[11] Gage's orders to Smith, issued April 18, stated:

"Having received Intelligence, that a Quantity of Ammunition, Provision, Artillery, Tents and small Arms, having been collected at Concord, for the Avowed Purpose of raising and supporting a Rebellion against His Majesty, you will March with the Corps of Grenadiers and light Infantry, put under your Command, with the utmost expedition and Secrecy to Concord, where you will seize and destroy . . . [these]. But you will take care that the Soldiers do not plunder the Inhabitants, or hurt private property.

"You have a Draught of Concord, on which is marked the Houses, Barns, etc. which contain the above Military Stores. . . . You will observe by the Draught that it will be necessary to secure the two Bridges as soon as possible; you will therefore Order a party of the best Marchers, to go on with expedition for that purpose. A small party on Horseback is ordered out to stop all advice of your March getting to Concord before you, and a small number of Artillery[12] go out in Chaises to wait for you on the Road, with Sledge Hammers, Spikes etc.

"You will open your business, and return with the Troops, as soon as possible, which I must leave to your own Judgment and Discretion."[13]

The orders, it will be observed, gave Smith no direction as to what he should do if rebel troops should try to block his march or fire on him from cover.

The normal route for the expedition from Boston to Concord, which lay north of the Charles River, would be to march by way of Boston neck, Roxbury, and Brookline, which lay south of the river, to the bridge over the Charles at Cambridge (where the familiar Larz Anderson Memorial Bridge now stands), cross there, and proceed through Cambridge to Concord. But marching through the populous village of Roxbury would inevitably give early notice of the expedition to the rebels, who, knowing or suspecting that it was headed for Concord, certainly would alarm the towns through which the expedition must pass and might remove or destroy the bridge at Cambridge. Gage therefore arranged with Admiral Samuel Graves to ferry Smith's troops to a sparsely inhabited spot on the north shore of the Charles just across from Boston in present Somerville.[14]

There is little contemporary evidence of what the rebel leaders were doing at this critical juncture.

A letter of John Hancock, dated Lexington, April 18, discloses that he had heard of some British officers on their way to Concord and said he would send word of this to Concord, and minutes of a meeting of the Committees of Safety and Supplies on the same day at Menotomy (now Arlington), near the village of Cambridge, record various resolutions concerning the disposition of military supplies.[15]

But the most important activity was the dispatch by someone in Boston, said to have been Dr. Joseph Warren,[16] of messengers to Lexington to give warning of the impending expedition. Though the colorful story of the hanging of the lanterns to signal whether the British were leaving Boston by land or by sea is drawn from statements made many years later by Paul Revere,[17] most famous of the messengers, there is ample contemporary evidence that messengers were sent,[18] that they gave timely notice of the expedition and that Revere was one of them.[19]

Since the British detachment was marching out without baggage or artillery, attack by the Massachusetts militia would be in conflict with the resolution adopted by the Second Massachusetts Congress on March 30, quoted in Chapter 29, authorizing attack only if Gage's army "or any part thereof to the Number of Five Hundred shall march out of the Town of Boston with Artillery and Baggage." But if the detachment reached Concord before the provincials had time to remove all or part of their military stores collected there, would they have timidly stood by while these precious stores were destroyed?

If so, they would have gone far toward convincing the British that they were, indeed, the poltroons whom Evelyn, Percy, and Pitcairn held them to be. But they were not put to the test. Before the detachment reached Concord, the shedding of American blood at Lexington had destroyed whatever force the Congress' cautious injunction might otherwise have had.

CHAPTER 32

THE DAY OF LEXINGTON AND CONCORD:
APRIL 19, 1775

O N April 19, 1775, the Massachusetts Committee of Safety dispatched the following message, which, forwarded by express rider from one town committee to another as far south as Williamsburg, Virginia,[1] electrified the colonies:

"Watertown Wednesday Morning near 10 oClock

"To all the Friends of American Liberty. Be it known that this Morning before Break of Day a Brigade consistg of about 1000 or 1200 Men Landed at Phips' Farm at Cambridge & marched to Lexington, where they found a Company of our Colony Militia in Arms, upon which they fir'd without any Provocation & killed 6 Men & wounded 4 others; by an Express from Boston this Moment we find another Brigade are now upon the March from Boston, supposed to be about 1000; the Bearer Mr. Israel Bissel is charged to alarm the Country quite to Connecticut & all Persons are Desired to furnish him fresh Horses as they may be needed. I have spoken with several persons who have seen the Dead & wounded. . . .

"Jos. Palmer, one of the Committee."[2]

Six days later the *Essex Gazette* of Salem gave a fuller report of the provincial (Whig) version of the events of the fateful Day:

"Last Wednesday, the 19th of April, the Troops of His Britannick Majesty commenced Hostilities upon the People of this Province, attended with Circumstances of Cruelty, not less brutal than what our venerable Ancestors received from the vilest Savages of the Wilderness. The Particulars relative to this interesting Event, by which we are involved in all the Horrors of a civil War, we have endeavoured to collect as well as the present confused State of Affairs will admit.

"On Tuesday Evening a Detachment from the Army, consisting, it is said, of 8 or 900 men,[3] commanded by Lieut. Col. Smith, embarked at the Bottom of the Common in Boston, on board a Number of Boats, and landed at Phipps's Farm, a little way up Charles River [in present-day Somerville], from whence they proceeded with Silence and Expedition on their way to Concord, about 18 Miles from Boston. The People were soon alarmed, and began to assemble in several Towns, before Day-Light, in order to watch the Motion of the Troops.

"At Lexington, 6 Miles below Concord, a Company of Militia, of about 100 men,[4] mustered near the Meeting-House; the Troops came in Sight of them just before Sun-rise; and running within a few Rods of them, the Commanding Officer accosted the Militia in Words to this effect:—
'*Disperse, you Rebels—Damn you, throw down your Arms and disperse*':

Upon which the Troops huzza'd, and immediately one or two Officers discharged their Pistols, which were instantaneously followed by the Firing of 4 or 5 of the Soldiers, and then there seemed to be a general Discharge from the whole Body: Eight of our Men were killed, and nine wounded.

"In a few Minutes after this Action the Enemy renewed their March for Concord; at which Place they destroyed several Carriages, Carriage Wheels, and about 20 Barrels of Flour,[5] all belonging to the Province. Here about 150 Men going towards a Bridge, of which the Enemy were in Possession, the latter fired, and killed 2 of our Men, who then returned the Fire, and obliged the Enemy to retreat back to Lexington, where they met Lord Percy, with a large Reinforcement, with two Pieces of Cannon.

"The Enemy now having a Body of about 1800 Men,[6] made a Halt, picked up many of their Dead, and took Care of their wounded. . . . [They then] continued their Retreat from Lexington to Charlestown with great Precipitation; and notwithstanding their Field Pieces, our People continued the Pursuit, firing at them till they got to Charlestown Neck, (which they reached a little after Sunset,) over which the Enemy passed, proceeded up Bunker's Hill, and soon afterwards went into the Town, under the Protection of the *Somerset* Man of War of 64 Guns.

"In Lexington the Enemy set Fire to Deacon Joseph Loring's House and Barn, Mrs. Mulliken's House and Shop, and Mr. Joshua Bond's House and Shop, which were all consumed. They also set Fire to several other Houses, but our People extinguished the Flames. They pillaged almost every House they passed by, breaking and destroying Doors, Windows, Glasses, etc and carrying off Cloathing and other valuable Effects. It appeared to be their Design to burn and destroy all before them; and nothing but our vigorous Pursuit prevented their infernal Purposes from being put in Execution. But the savage Barbarity exercised upon the Bodies of our unfortunate Brethren who fell, is almost incredible: Not contented with shooting down the unarmed, aged and infirm, they disregarded the Cries of the wounded, killing them without Mercy, and mangling their Bodies in the most shocking Manner.

"We have the Pleasure to say, that, notwithstanding the highest Provocations given by the Enemy, not one instance of Cruelty, that we have heard of, was committed by our victorious Militia; but, listening to the merciful Dictates of the Christian Religion, they 'breathed higher sentiments of humanity.' . . .

"The following is a list of the Provincials who were killed or wounded:

[Here follows a list of forty-nine killed and thirty-nine wounded[7] by towns from which they came: Lexington,[8] Concord, Cambridge, Charlestown, Watertown, Sudbury, Acton, Bedford, Needham, Medford, Newton, Woburn, Billerica, Chelmsford, Framingham, Stow, Dedham, Brookline, Salem, Danvers, Beverly, and Lynn.]

"We have seen an account of the loss of the enemy . . . by which it appears that sixty-three of the Regulars and forty-nine of the Marines were killed, and one hundred and three of both wounded . . . and about twelve soldiers are prisoners. . . .[9]

"The public most sincerely sympathize with the friends and relations of our deceased brethren, who gloriously sacrificed their lives in fighting for the liberties of their Country. By their noble and intrepid conduct, in helping to defeat the forces of an ungrateful tyrant, they have endeared their memories to the present generation, who will transmit their names to posterity with the highest honour. . . ."[10]

The *Gazette's* account is supported and amplified by depositions quoted and discussed in the appendix to this chapter.

Gage's account of the expedition is given in a statement enclosed by him in a letter of April 29, to Governor Jonathan Trumbull of Connecticut.[11] Gage wrote:

"On Tuesday the 19th of April, about half-past ten at night, Lieutenant Colonel Smith, of the Tenth Regiment, embarked from the Common, at Boston, with the Grenadiers and Light-Infantry of the Troops there, and landed on the opposite side; from whence he began his march towards Concord, where he was ordered to destroy a magazine of military stores, deposited there for the use of an Army to be assembled in order to act against His Majesty and his Government.

"The Colonel called his officers together, and gave orders that the Troops should not fire unless fired upon; and after marching a few miles, detached six Companies of Light-Infantry, under the command of Major Pitcairn, to take possession of two bridges on the other side of Concord. Soon after, they heard many signal guns, and the ringing of alarmbells repeatedly, which convinced them that the country was rising to oppose them, and that it was a preconcerted scheme to oppose the King's Troops, whenever there should be a favourable opportunity for it.

"About three o'clock the next morning, the Troops being advanced within two miles of Lexington, intelligence was received that about five hundred men in arms were assembled, and determined to oppose the King's Troops; and on Major Pitcairn's galloping up to the head of the advanced Companies, two officers informed him that a man (advanced from those that were assembled) had presented his musket, and attempted to shoot them, but the piece flashed in the pan. On this the Major gave directions to the Troops to move forward, but on no account to fire, nor even to attempt it without orders.[12]

"When they arrived at the end of the village, they observed about two hundred armed men[13] drawn up on a green, and when the Troops came within one hundred yards of them, they began to file off towards some stone walls on their right flank; the Light-Infantry observing this, ran after them. The Major instantly called to the soldiers not to fire, but to surround and disarm them. Some of them who had jumped over a wall, then fired four or five shot at the Troops, wounded a man of the Tenth Regiment, and the Major's horse in two places, and at the same time several shots were fired from a meeting-house on the left. Upon this, without any order or regularity, the Light-Infantry began a scattered fire, and killed several of the country people, but were silenced as soon as the authority of their officers could make them.

"After this, Colonel Smith marched up with the remainder of the detachment, and the whole body proceeded to Concord, where they arrived about nine o'clock, without any thing further happening; but vast numbers of armed people were seen assembling on all the heights.

"While Colonel Smith, with the Grenadiers and part of the Light-Infantry, remained at Concord to search for cannon, etc., there, he detached Captain Parsons, with six light companies, to secure a bridge at some distance from Concord, and to proceed from thence to certain houses, where it was supposed there was cannon and ammunition. Captain Parsons, in pursuance of these orders, posted three companies at the bridge, and on some heights near it, under the command of Captain Laurie, of the Forty-Third Regiment, and with the remainder went and destroyed some cannon-wheels, powder, and ball.

"The people still continued increasing on the heights, and in about an hour after, a large body of them began to move towards the bridge. The light companies of the Fourth and Tenth then descended and joined Captain Laurie. The people continued to advance in great numbers, and fired upon the King's Troops; killed three men, wounded four officers, one sergeant, and four privates; upon which (after returning the fire) Captain Laurie and his officers thought it prudent to retreat towards the main body at Concord, and were soon joined by two companies of Grenadiers.[14]

"When Captain Parsons returned with the three Companies over the bridge,[15] they observed three soldiers on the ground, one of them scalped, his head much mangled, and his ears cut off, though not quite dead—a sight which struck the soldiers with horrour. Captain Parsons marched on and joined the main body, who were only waiting for his coming up to march back to Boston.

"Colonel Smith had executed his orders, without opposition, by destroying all the military stores he could find. Both the Colonel and Major Pitcairn having taken all possible pains to convince the inhabitants that no injury was intended them, and that if they opened their doors when required to search for said stores, not the slightest mischief should be done. Neither had any of the people the least occasion to complain; but they were sulky, and one of them even struck Major Pitcairn.

"Except upon Captain Laurie at the bridge, no hostilities happened from the affair at Lexington, until the Troops began their march back. As soon as the Troops had got out of the Town of Concord, they received a heavy fire on them from all sides—from walls, fences, houses, trees, barns, etc., which continued, without intermission, till they met the First Brigade, with two field-pieces, near Lexington, ordered out under the command of Lord Percy to support them. Upon the firing of the field-pieces, the people's fire was for a while silenced; but as they still continued to increase greatly in numbers, they fired again, as before, from all places where they could find cover, upon the whole body, and continued so doing for the space of fifteen miles.

"Notwithstanding their numbers,[16] they did not attack openly during the whole day, but kept under cover on all occasions. The Troops were very much fatigued; the greater part of them having been under arms all night, and made a march of upwards of forty miles before they arrived at Charlestown, from whence they ferried over to Boston.[17]

"The Troops had above fifty killed, and many more wounded; reports are various about the loss sustained by the country people; some make it very considerable, others not so much."[18]

Gage's account is supported by contemporary statements of Major Pitcairn and other British officers, which are quoted and discussed in the appendix to this chapter.

So far as is known, Gage made no comment on the provincials' morale beyond writing to the Secretary at War, Lord Barrington, that "The whole Country was Assembled in Arms with Surprising expedition."[19] But Lord Percy, whose previous contempt for the fighting quality of the rebels was described in letters quoted in Chapter 30, now wrote:

"During the whole affair the Rebels attacked us in a very scattered irregular manner, but with perseverance & resolution, nor did they ever dare to form into any regular body. Indeed, they knew too well what was proper, to do so. Whosoever looks upon them as an irregular mob, will find himself much mistaken. They have men amongst them who know very well what they are about, having been employed as Rangers against the Indians & Canadians, & this country being much covered with wood, and hilly, is very advantageous for their method of fighting.

"Nor are several of their men void of a spirit of enthusiasm, as we experienced yesterday, for many of them concealed themselves in houses, & advanced within 10 yards to fire at me & other officers, tho' they were morally certain of being put to death themselves in an instant.

"You may depend upon it, that, as the Rebels have now had time to prepare, they are determined to go thro' with it, nor will the insurrection here turn out so despicable as it is perhaps imagined at home. For my part, I never believed, I confess, that they would have attacked the King's troops, or have had the perseverance I found in them yesterday."[20]

As will be seen, the British and provincial versions of which side fired first at Lexington and at Concord and of alleged atrocities are utterly irreconcilable. The evidence bearing on the principal points in dispute is analyzed in the appendix to this chapter. Suffice to say here, that the provincials (as they called themselves) apparently believed and certainly were able to convince the majority of their fellow Americans that the British fired first both at Lexington and Concord and were guilty of hideous atrocities throughout the course of the day.

Many in the colonies tried to stem the tide of rebellion against British rule that swept through the colonies following the day of Lexington and Concord. But appeals to self-interest and to ties of a common English heritage were unavailing to prevail against the force of passion aroused by the shedding of American blood on the nineteenth of April. When the Second Continental Congress assembled in Philadelphia a few weeks later, the delegations from all twelve of the colonies at the Congress (Georgia was not yet represented) united in preparations for war.

FIRST APPENDIX TO THE INTRODUCTION
IRRITANTS BEFORE 1765

IN my *Origin of the American Revolution,* I described the following irritants contributing to the violent colonial opposition to the Stamp Act in 1765–1766.

First: In 1759 the Privy Council disallowed Virginia's so-called Twopenny Act of 1758 on the ground, among others, that a provincial law amending an existing provincial law which had been allowed by the Crown must contain a clause suspending operation of the amending law until it was passed upon by the Crown. Later, the British Board of Trade advised the London Agents of Massachusetts and South Carolina of its having recommended disallowance of recent amending acts of these colonies on this same ground.

Since the laws of all the royal colonies (including Virginia, Massachusetts, New York, New Hampshire, New Jersey, the Carolinas, and Georgia) were subject to review and disallowance by the Crown, this action implied that in the royal colonies no law which had been allowed by the Crown could be amended without a clause in the amending law suspending its operation until it was approved, perhaps after a delay of several years, by the Privy Council in England.

Second: Encouraged by the Bishop of London, several members of the established Church of England in Virginia brought suit for the difference between the salary payable under an earlier act and the salary payable under the Twopenny Act on the ground that the latter was void from its inception because the Governor of Virginia, in approving it, had violated his instructions from the Crown.

If successful, these suits would not only immediately be costly to Virginia taxpayers, but (far more alarming) would establish the general principle that all colonial laws, past or future, in conflict with Crown instructions previously issued to the Governor of the colony were void.

Third: In 1760, on application by British customs officers, the Superior (Supreme) Court of Massachusetts granted them general writs of assistance. These writs authorized the officers under certain conditions, to enter and, if necessary, break into warehouses, stores, and homes to search for smuggled goods, without their having presented to the court ground for suspecting presence of such goods in the place subjected to search.

Fourth: In 1761, the Crown instructed the Governors of all the royal colonies that commissions thereafter issued to judges must be revocable at the pleasure of the Crown, thus providing for continued Crown control and influence over the judges in these colonies.

Fifth: From 1761 to 1763, Thomas Secker, Archbishop of Canterbury, member of the Privy Council, and President of the London-based Church of England Society for the Propagation of the Gospel in Foreign Parts, took steps alarming to New England Congregationalists. He secured or encouraged establishment of an Anglican Mission Church within a stone's throw of Harvard College, a center of education for New England's Congregational ministry; participated in securing disallowance by the Privy Council of a Massachusetts act sponsored by Massachusetts Congregationalists that incorporated a society for mission work among the North American Indians; and encouraged the revival of a project for the establishment of an Anglican bishopric in the colonies.

Sixth: In 1763, the Surveyor- General of the King's Woods began vigorous enforcement of hitherto laxly enforced British acts of 1722 and 1729 severely restricting the cutting of white pine trees in the colonies.

Seventh: In 1763, the British government began vigorous enforcement of the wide range of British restrictions on colonial trade by stationing a fleet of British warships and armed sloops along the North American coast to assist the regular customs officers in the enforcement of these restrictions.

Eighth: In 1763, the King issued a proclamation forbidding settlement on any land west of the Alleghenies.

Ninth: In 1764, Parliament passed the American Act of 1764, imposing additional restrictions on colonial trade and levying duties for revenue on several colonial imports. The act also gave jurisdiction to Crown-appointed admiralty judges, sitting without jury, over all cases involving alleged violations of this and earlier British acts levying duties in the colonies or restricting colonial trade.

Tenth: In 1764 the Board of Trade instructed the Acting Governor of New York to try to secure the annulment of title to an ancient Crown grant of land in New York known as the Kayaderosseras patent, on grounds that would jeopardize title to a large part of the privately owned land in the colony.

Several of these irritants ceased or were minimized after 1765.

The demand for a suspending clause in laws of the royal colonies amending an existing law allowed by the Crown was not pursued.[1]

The threat to give Crown instructions to Governors of the royal colonies the force of law was removed by a decision of the Privy Council in 1766, in effect sustaining the validity of the Virginia Twopenny Act.[2]

The Society for the Propagation of the Gospel in Foreign Parts took no further steps to establish mission churches in colonial communities already served by other churches, and, so far as is known, Frederick Cornwallis, who succeeded Secker as Archbishop and President of the Society, in 1768, held aloof from the efforts of some colonial Anglican clergymen to revive the movement for establishing a Church of England bishopric in the colonies.[3]

General writs of assistance issued to customs officers in Massachusetts continued to be an irritant in that colony; but friction over these was minimized by the refusal of courts in colonies other than Massachusetts and New Hampshire to grant general writs.[4]

The threat to annul the Kayaderosseras land grant was removed in 1768 by a compromise effected in that year.[5]

The ban on settlement of land west of the Alleghenies was favorably modified in 1768 and 1770, after treaties with the Indians, by permission from the Crown to settle large areas beyond the Alleghenies south of the Ohio River.[6]

Nevertheless, several of the irritants continued in full force. The instruction to Governors of the royal colonies to issue commissions to judges revocable at the pleasure of the Crown was retained and observed.[7] Enforcement of the White Pine Acts was not abated.[8] And, most important, the American Act of 1764 continued to be a major source of colonial discontent.[9]

SECOND APPENDIX TO THE INTRODUCTION

COLONIAL TORIES AND WHIGS

I HAVE not found any perfectly satisfactory definition of the terms *Whig* and *Tory* as applied to the colonists in the period covered by this book. The least unsatisfactory seems to be the one given in the Introduction, namely *Whig* to describe a colonist who favored stronger action than petitioning when petitioning had failed to procure redress of colonial grievances, and *Tory* to describe a colonist who favored no protest or protest limited to petitioning.[1] Before the outbreak of the war, many, perhaps most of the colonists, from indifference or because they could not decide which side to take, were neither Whigs nor Tories.

I use the term *Tory* rather than *loyalist,* now much in vogue, not only because *Tory* was the word commonly used by colonial writers in the period of this book,[2] but because calling the Tories *loyalists* tends to imply that the Whigs were disloyal, whereas they, too, were loyal, though to a different concept.

Judging from the evidence of contemporary correspondence and diaries, newspapers, pamphlets, almanacs, sermons,[3] and records of the colonial Assemblies[4] before the war, the Whigs far outnumbered the Tories in all thirteen colonies except possibly Georgia, Delaware, and New York.

But fear of British invincibility aroused by the easy British victories at Brooklyn and New York City in August and September, 1776, drew into the Tory ranks many former Whigs and neutrals.[5]

This was noted in an important letter of October, 1776, from Benjamin Franklin and Robert Morris, members of the Secret Committee of the Second Continental Congress, to Silas Deane, the Committee's agent in France. They wrote: "The Only Source of uneasiness amongst us arises from the Number of Tories we find in every State; they are More Numerous than formerly & speak more openly; . . . some are so from real attachment to Britain; some from interested Views; many, very many, from fear of British Force; some because they are dissatisfied with the General Measures of Congress, more because they disapprove of the Men in power & the measures in their respective States; . . . if America falls it will be owing to such division more than the force of our Enemies."[6]

Fortunately, those interested in the story of the Tories are no longer limited to Eardley-Wilmot's *Historical View* (1815); Sabine's pioneer study, *The American Loyalists,* published in 1847, his later, superior, and better-known *Biographical Sketches of Loyalists of the American Revolution* (1864), and other books and articles concerning the Tories published before 1950.[7] Since then the admirable studies of Wright, Commager and Morris, Nelson, Paul H. Smith, Wallace Brown, Callahan, and Benton[8] have thrown much additional light on the subject, and valuable studies of loyalism are currently appearing or reported in progress.[9]

In general my findings as to what made men Tories in the period dealt with in this book, that is, before the war, are the same as those of previous students.

One of the most important forces was sentimental attachment to the motherland. This force was, of course, likely to be particularly strong in the case of the many British-born residents of the colonies (notably Scottish merchants in Virginia, Maryland, and the Carolinas) who were in America only temporarily on business and the thousands of other native Britons who, though intending to remain in the colonies, had close ties with parents, brothers, and sisters, or other near relatives still living in England or Scotland. But the tie of sentiment for the motherland, the Crown, or both, of many natives of the colonies also must be taken into account.

Crown officers in the colonies, colonists having British government contracts,[10] and those seeking Crown appointment or British government contracts naturally were particularly prone to take a stand that would be acceptable to the British government. Anglican missionaries in the colonies who were dependent for their livelihood on the London-based Society for the Propagation of the Gospel in Foreign Parts, also naturally took a stand that would meet the approval of the Society.

The violence in Boston, New York, and other cities accompanying colonial opposition to the Stamp Act and other British measures made many colonists, particularly city residents of large property, fear that any opposition beyond petitioning would lead to renewed domestic violence. Merchants who had suffered economically during the period of the non-importation agreements of 1768 to 1770 were reluctant to participate in another commercial boycott, the more so when it became evident in 1774 that many of the Whig leaders favored agreements for non-exportation, as well as for non-importation. Quakers and other pacifists were, of course, averse to any form of colonial opposition likely to precipitate war.

Others, who were not city residents, merchants, or pacifists and were as greatly concerned as anyone over the danger of recent British measures to colonial liberty, were fearful that the British would almost certainly win the war, or even if unsuccessful would devastate the regions overrun by their armed forces. The latter fear was particularly keen among those living on the seacoast or navigable rivers open to easy attack by British warships and expeditionary forces based on them, or living on frontiers vulnerable to attack by Indians under British influence.

Still others were fearful that separation from Great Britain threatened dangers more serious than the danger of continued British rule on British terms—danger that the colonies would fight among themselves, danger of attack by the French. Others feared that elimination of the veto power of the Crown would subject them to unfavorable legislation by their own provincial Legislatures. This fear is particularly understandable in the case of members of minority religious bodies, including Anglicans in New England, where Congregationalists were decidedly in the majority, and of members of the Quaker and other pacifist sects in Pennsylvania where non-pacifists greatly outnumbered them.

In pointing out the fears influencing the colonists toward Toryism, I do not mean to imply that all of those subject to these fears were Tories; many of them, despite their fears, were staunch Whigs.

Some of those I classify as Tories because they opposed going beyond petitioning for repeal of existing British taxes for revenue on the colonies were as convinced as the Whigs of the unconstitutionality of British taxation of the colonies. But they believed that there was some chance of securing relief from a petition for redress by the Continental Congress and were opposed to jeopardizing this supposed chance by antagonizing the British people, the Ministry, and members of Parliament by a boycott of trade with Great Britain.[11]

Though, as previously stated, my findings are in general the same as those already published, I would lay greater stress on two points than most writers on the colonial Tories have done: on local political factionalism, particularly (as brought out later in this appendix and in the appendix to Chapter 28) in Massachusetts and New York, and on the influence of family connection upon persons not themselves holding Crown office or supported by the Society for the Propagation of the Gospel in Foreign Parts.

The foregoing discussion relates solely to Toryism during the period before the war. As previously noted, many who had been Whigs, neutral, or indifferent had been drawn into the Tory ranks early in the war through fear of British invincibility aroused by the easy victories of the British at Brooklyn and New York City during the summer of 1776. Later, more became Tories or classified as Tories when, during the British occupation of the whole of lower New York and much of New Jersey, eastern Pennsylvania, South Carolina, and Georgia, a large part of the residents of the occupied territory submitted to restored British rule.

It was "Tories" such as these latter whom the American Colonel William Stephens Smith evidently had in mind in writing George Washington in 1783, of the "fifteen thousand inhabitants" about to "be driven from this Country [New York state]" who are "not conscious of any other Crime than of residing in the British Lines. . . ."[12]

Estimates have been made from time to time as to the numbers or percentages of loyalists in particular colonies or in the thirteen colonies as a whole.

John Adams, writing as "Novanglus" in February, 1775, stated that in Massachusetts Whigs outnumbered Tories nineteen to one.[13] Many years later (1815) Adams wrote that the colonists had been almost unanimous in resisting the Stamp Act, but that, by 1775, the British had "formed and drilled and disciplined a party in favor of Great Britain and . . . seduced nearly one third of the people of the colonies,"[14] meaning apparently those of the thirteen colonies.

A statement in 1789 by Phineas Bond, British consul in Philadelphia, that the loss of inhabitants of the thirteen colonies "occasioned by the war" was "perhaps little short of 100,000 men," has sometimes been interpreted to mean that almost 100,000 loyalist families left the colonies. But this interpretation of Bond's letter is open to doubt.[15]

Three notable studies of colonial loyalism, Nelson's *The American Tory;* Smith's "The American Loyalists; Notes on Their Organization and Numerical Strength"; and Brown's *The King's Friends,* have tackled the perplexing question of how large a percentage of the residents of the thirteen colonies were loyalists.

On various grounds Nelson estimates the following: "Only in New York is it reasonably certain that the Loyalists numbered half the population. Throughout the Middle Colonies, including New York, the Loyalists may have been almost as numerous as their opponents. In the South, however, they could hardly have amounted to more than a fourth or a third of the population, and in New England to scarcely a tenth." His overall estimate is that the Loyalists were roughly "a third, and the revolutionists two-thirds of the politically active population of the colonies."[16]

Smith's estimate, based on evidence of the colonists who, at one time or another during the Revolution, "formally took up arms in support of the Crown to suppress the American rebellion," is about "19.8% of the white Americans."[17]

Brown's estimate, based chiefly on the remaining records of the claims allowed at least in part by the "Claims commission set up by the British government to indemnify American Loyalists for losses caused by the Revolution," is "between 7.6 and 18.0 per cent of the white population of 2,100,000." But he adds that "if equivocal and quietist Loyalists were considered, the figures would go up again."[18]

I, too, have tried some figuring as to the percentage of Tories both before and during the war. But I have not found sufficient evidence to make even a guess, beyond saying I think John Adams' estimate that in 1775 nearly one-third of the people of the thirteen colonies were loyalists is much too high.

One of the most interesting features of Brown's study is the evidence, confirming earlier studies, of the small number of American-born Tories in Virginia compared with Massachusetts, whose white population was approximately the same as Virginia's.

Of the 2,908 persons part or all of whose claims were allowed by the commissioners, only 130 were from Virginia, and, of these, only 24 are identified as American born.[19] Massachusetts furnished 313 claimants of whom nearly two-thirds (203) are identified as American born.[20]

In the earliest detailed study of Virginia Tories, Harrell's *Loyalism in Virginia,* the author suggested that the weakness of loyalism among native Virginians was perhaps due chiefly to economic factors, particularly the very heavy indebtedness of Virginia planters to British creditors. The planters were, wrote Harrell, "hopelessly in debt to the British merchants," with the result that "current [political] theories in the colonies and the economic interests of the planters were in harmony."[21] This explanation is also advanced by Gipson in his *British Empire* and his "Virginia Planter Debts."[22]

There is ample evidence that before and at the outbreak of the Revolutionary War, many Virginia planters were very heavily in debt to British creditors.[23] But, if Harrell and Gipson's explanation is sound, one would expect to find evidence that, in general, the planters heavily in debt were Whigs and those less heavily in debt, or not in debt at all, were Tories. Harrell and Gipson give no evidence of this, and I have found none.

Brown's *The King's Friends* suggests another possible explanation: "The weakness of Loyalism in Virginia," he wrote, "may not be a paradox at all. Virginia was a homogeneous society in the sense of being free from serious internal divisions. There was no equivalent of the Hutchinson and Oliver–Adams and Otis split in Massachusetts."[24]

Brown's statement that Virginia was free from serious internal divisions likewise is open to question.

Votes in the Virginia House of Burgesses were very rarely recorded, so that it is difficult to detect divisions, serious or otherwise, in the House. But the journals of the Virginia Council record many instances of the Council's refusal to concur in bills or resolutions adopted by a majority of the House,[25] some relating to matters apparently of serious import.[26] The active members of the Council in Virginia, unlike those in some of the other colonies, were nearly all natives of the colony.[27]

Furthermore, though there is evidence of a split along party lines in Massachusetts in 1762,[28] I have found no evidence of this in connection with the later controversy over British taxation of the colonies.[29]

A striking difference in the position taken in 1764 by the Lower Houses of Virginia and Massachusetts respectively, and the known influence of Lieutenant Governor Thomas Hutchinson of Massachusetts on the position taken by the Massachusetts House, suggest a third possible explanation.

In the fall of 1764, the House of Burgesses in Virginia and the House of Representatives in Massachusetts adopted protests against British taxation of the colonies. The Virginia protest was based on the ground that British taxation of the colonies infringed upon a constitutional "right" of the people of Virginia to be taxed exclusively by a body in which they were represented.[30] The Massachusetts protest was based on the weak, Tory-oriented ground that British taxation of the colonies infringed upon merely a long-enjoyed "privilege" of the people of Massachusetts to be taxed exclusively by a body in which they were represented.[31]

The adoption by the Massachusetts House of this protest was apparently due chiefly to the influence of the most distinguished citizen and influential political leader of the colony, Thomas Hutchinson.[32]

In 1764, Hutchinson, scion of an old, important Massachusetts family, was the Lieutenant Governor of the colony by appointment of the Crown, judge of probate for Suffolk County, and Chief Justice of the Massachusetts Superior (Supreme) Court by appointment of successive royal Governors of the colony, and a senior member of the provincial Council by annual election for every year since 1749 by joint vote of members of the outgoing Council and incoming House of Representatives.[33]

Though Hutchinson was dropped from the Council in 1766, he at all times held posts of great political influence in the colony until he left for England in 1774,[34] and continued openly to support the right of Parliament to tax the colonies.

The leading political figure in Virginia in 1764 was John Robinson, Speaker of the House of Burgesses and Treasurer of the colony, who died in 1766.[35] I have found no direct evidence of the stand taken by Robinson on the Virginia protest, but the fact that the protest committee was probably chosen by him as Speaker suggests that he himself favored the stand taken by the committee.[36] At any rate, there is no evidence that he or any other politically influential leader in Virginia openly espoused the stand taken by Hutchinson.

Possibly there were not many latent Tories among native Virginians,[37] but, if there were, they had no such encouragement as had those in Massachusetts to declare themselves.

APPENDIX TO CHAPTER 1

GEORGE III AND ESTABLISHMENT OF THE ROCKINGHAM MINISTRY

DURING his long reign (1760–1820), George III on several occasions exercised the great political power of the King still existing at this period (largely through retention of almost unlimited authority of appointment to, and dismissal from, public office) to overturn a Ministry which he had come to dislike. One of his most striking actions was the dismissal of the powerful Grenville Ministry and the establishment of the relatively weak Rockingham Ministry, in office at the opening of our period.

In March, 1765, George Grenville, head of the Treasury and First Minister, importuned the King to appoint as Governor of Cork in Ireland the Ministry's candidate for this office, instead of a candidate favored by Lord Northumberland, whose son was married to a daughter of the King's dear friend, Lord Bute.[1] Grenville also plagued the King to appoint as Registrar to the Scottish Order of the Thistle the Ministry's candidate favored by Bute's brother, James Stuart Mackenzie. According to his own account, Grenville, on learning from the King that "he had determined to give that office to Sir Henry Erskine . . . , argued and pressed strongly for Mr. Duff, but in vain."[2]

Soon after this controversy with Grenville over appointment to Crown offices, the King encouraged Northumberland to have a talk with the King's long-estranged uncle, the Duke of Cumberland, one of the leaders of the principal opposition parties, the Newcastle–Rockingham Whigs, in the course of which Cumberland indicated a readiness for reconciliation with the King.[3] But, so far as is known, the King made no further advance to Cumberland at this time.

However, a few weeks later the King was again provoked by the Ministry. At his request a bill was introduced into Parliament by the Ministry, providing for a regency in case the King died before his oldest surviving son reached the age of eighteen. Yet the King's mother was omitted from the list of those eligible to serve as regent[4]—an omission seeming to countenance gossip that she and Bute were lovers.[5] Though the bill was later amended to include the queen mother,[6] Northumberland, presumably at the King's request, now had another talk with Cumberland in which Northumberland said that "the King was determined to part" with his chief Ministers and authorized Cumberland to negotiate with William Pitt; his brother-in-law, Lord Temple; the Duke of Newcastle; and Lord Rockingham to form a new Ministry.[7]

The following day, George III confirmed this at a conference with Cumberland, in the course of which the King said that "his present Ministers . . . treated him personally ill . . . forced him to do every thing they would," that "reversions, pensions, etc. to support themselves, were all they had in view; that they promised . . . to do great things for the publick," but that he "found nothing done; North America greatly discontented and . . . the same discontent at home also."[8]

Cumberland tried to form a Ministry along the lines indicated by the King, but Pitt and Temple declined for various reasons[9] to take office, and the project failed.[10]

On learning of the unsuccessful effort to displace them, Grenville and three other members of the Cabinet (the President of the Council, the Duke of Bedford, and the Secretaries of State, Lords Halifax and Sandwich) threatened to resign unless the King agreed to the following conditions: Bute to "have nothing to do in His Majesty's Councils or Government, in any manner or shape whatever"; Mackenzie to "be removed from his office of Lord Privy Seal of Scotland, and from the authority and influence which has been given to him in that Kingdom"; Lord Holland to be dismissed as Paymaster-General and that office disposed of as had been usual in the House of Commons; Lord Granby to be appointed Commander-in-Chief of the Army; and the Government of Ireland to be settled, not by the King independently, but "with his Ministers."[11]

Though much distressed, particularly over "the article relating to Mr. Mackenzie,"[12] the King yielded.[13]

On June 12, Bedford again offended the King by complaining of his marked coldness to members of the Ministry and of his continuing to consult with Bute, and threatening to resign if the members of the Ministry "did not meet with a kind reception, & those they thought their Enemys were not frown'd upon."[14]

Bursting with "indignation . . . at so very offensive a declaration,"[15] the King now moved decisively to form a new Ministry.[16] He first tried to persuade Pitt and Temple to take office;[17] but, though Pitt was willing to come in,[18] Temple was not,[19] and Pitt declined to take office without him. Whereupon Cumberland persuaded Newcastle, Rockingham, and Henry S. Conway to form a Ministry without Pitt and Temple.[20]

The new Ministry, with Rockingham as head of the Treasury and First Minister, was launched July 10, 1765.

APPENDIX TO CHAPTER 2

THE ACT OF 1696 AND THE
DECLARATORY ACT OF 1766

IN Volume XIII of *The British Empire before the American Revolution*, Gipson, one of the most respected, and justly respected, of our colonial historians, seems to maintain that the Declaratory Act of 1766 merely reaffirmed a claim of authority to legislate for the colonies made as early as 1696.[1]

The legislative background[2] and the title, preamble, and context of the pertinent section (section 9) of the Act of 1696[3] indicate that this act was intended solely to declare that acts of Parliament regulating colonial trade were binding on the colonies irrespective (quoting section 9 of the act) of "all laws, by-laws, usages or customs . . . in any of the said plantations [colonies] which are in any wise repugnant to the before mentioned laws." There is no evidence or reason to believe that Parliament intended to declare in this act that it had unlimited authority, i.e., authority unbounded by constitutional limitations, to legislate for the colonies.

The Declaratory Act of 1766 was of a different character. In stating that "the King's majesty, by and with the advice and consent of the lords spiritual and temporal, and commons of *Great Britain,* in Parliament assembled, had, hath, and of right ought to have, full power and authority to make laws and statutes of sufficient force and validity to bind the colonies and people of *America,* subjects of the crown of *Great Britain,* in all cases whatsoever," this act apparently was intended to establish that Parliament was not bound by constitutional limitations in dealing with the colonies.

The colonists, as Gipson points out,[4] had generally accepted the proposition enunciated in the Act of 1696 that Parliament had authority to pass acts regulating colonial trade.[5] But such acceptance by no means implied that the colonists had accepted or were prepared to accept the doctrine that Parliament had unlimited authority to pass any kind of laws it pleased in dealing with them.

As brought out in my *Origin of the Revolution,* after the publication in 1756 of Blackstone's influential *An Analysis of the Laws of England,* the doctrine of the unlimited legislative authority of the King in Parliament seems to have become generally, though by no means universally,[6] accepted in Great Britain, but not in the colonies.[7]

There is ample evidence that the following statement in a letter of February 15, 1768, from Thomas Cushing, Speaker of the Massachusetts House of Representatives, to Lord Shelburne, Secretary of State for the Southern Department, expressed general colonial opinion.

"There are, my Lord," wrote Cushing, "fundamental rules of the constitution, which it is humbly presumed, neither the supreme legislative [i.e., the King in Parliament] nor the supreme executive [i.e., the Crown acting alone] can alter . . . [and] it is humbly referred to your Lordship's judgment, whether the supreme legislature of the empire may rightly leap the bounds of it [the constitution] in the exercize of power over the subjects in America any more than those of Great Britain."[8]

Indeed, there was more reason to believe and maintain that there were constitutional limitations on the authority of Parliament in dealing with the colonies than in dealing with Great Britain itself. The people of Great Britain were to some extent, however inadequately, represented in Parliament. Furthermore, legislation for Great Britain affected the members of Parliament themselves. Consequently, there was some safeguard for the people of Great Britain against oppressive legislation by Parliament, even without constitutional limitations. But in the case of Parliamentary legislation affecting the colonies exclusively, there were not even these safeguards against oppressive laws.

The danger to the colonists was peculiarly great in the field of taxation, since, as Governor Stephen Hopkins of Rhode Island observed, "if the people of America are to be taxed by the representatives of the people in Britain, their malady . . . must always grow greater by time. Whatever burdens are laid upon the Americans will be so much taken off the Britons' and doing it will soon be [so] extremely popular . . . that members of the House of Commons must obtain the votes of the people by promising to take more and more of the taxes off them by putting it on the Americans."[9]

In 1778 the Declaratory Act of 1766 was modified by an act, 18 Geo. III ch. 12, stating that thereafter Parliament would levy no taxes or duties on the colonies "except only such duties as it may be expedient to impose for the Regulation of Commerce: the net produce of such duties to be always paid and applied to and for the use of the Colony . . . in which the same shall be respectively levied . . . ,"[10] but this protection was not afforded the colonies until three years after war had begun.

Gipson's further statement, "So long as a subject recognized his obligation to obey the law in question until it was changed, he was free to protest that it was unconstitutional,"[11] also is questionable. After 1766, the House of Commons consistently refused to receive petitions or remonstrances from colonial Assemblies challenging the constitutionality of acts of Parliament taxing the colonies, on the ground that the Declaratory Act foreclosed denial of the right of Parliament to tax the colonies.[12]

THE ACT OF 1663 AND COLONIAL
ADMIRALTY COURTS

IN 1663, the English Parliament passed the famous act of 15 Chas. II ch. 7 forbidding importation into the colonies of any products of continental Europe, other than salt, except from English ports[1] and providing for suit for forfeiture of ship or cargo alleged to have been involved in a breach of the act.[2] The act uniting England and Scotland passed in 1707 put the latter on the same favored footing as England.[3]

Enforcement of the Act of 1663 in the ordinary colonial courts, the courts of common law, was difficult because the owner was entitled to trial by jury in these courts and juries were reluctant to bring in a verdict against the owner.[4]

In 1702 the principal law officers of the Crown in England held that section 7 of the so-called Statute of Frauds of 1696 had overcome this difficulty[5] by giving colonial admiralty courts, in which the judge sat without jury, jurisdiction over suits for penalties and forfeitures alleged to have been incurred. However, their opinion took no notice of an act of 15 Richard II ch. 3 (1391) narrowly limiting the jurisdiction of admiralty courts.

In 1720, Richard West, standing counsel to the Board of Trade, gave an opinion to the Board holding that this early act applied to colonial admiralty courts, as well as to admiralty courts in England and must be taken into account in determining the jurisdiction of colonial admiralty courts over suits for forfeiture for alleged violation of acts of trade applying to the colonies. He also held that the Superior Court of Massachusetts, the highest court of common law in the province, had properly issued writs of prohibition to the admiralty judge at Boston forbidding him to proceed with a case over which he had no jurisdiction.[6]

Whether or not West's opinion was known in the colonies does not appear. But in any case, the Massachusetts courts of common law acted in harmony with it, as appears from the following letter written in 1743 by William Bollan, Advocate General for the Crown in Massachusetts, to the Board of Trade:

"There has lately been Carried on here a large illicit Trade (Destructive to the Interest of Great Britain in her Trade to her own Plantations, and Contrary to the main intent of all her Laws made to regulate that Trade) by importing into this province large Quantities of European Goods of Almost all Sorts from diverse parts of Europe . . . .[7] I shall now recount to your Lordships the Difficulties which attend the Suppression of this Mischief; The First and one of the Principal is that Breach of the Statute of the 15th Chs. 2d Chap. 7 [the Act of 1663] . . . are not Cognizible in the Court of Admiralty . . . [and] a Tryall by Jury [in courts of common law] is only trying one Illicite Trader by his Fellows, or at least his well wishers . . . [who] defeat all Seizure & prosecutions for the Crown. . . .

"The Statute made in the 7th & 8th of Wm. the 3rd 'for preventing Frauds and regulating Abuses in the Plantation Trade' is so Obscurely penn'd in the point of the Admiralty's Jurisdiction that it has received different Constructions and that Court has been frequently prohibited in this Province to take Cognizance of some of the Main Offences against that Statute, and of late I hear that like prohibitions have been granted in the province of New York. . . ."

Bollan proposed that Parliament pass an act clearly giving colonial admiralty courts jurisdiction over all offenses committed in the colonies against British acts restricting colonial trade.[8]

One of the prohibitions in New York referred to by Bollan presumably was that issued in the case of *Archibald Kennedy Esq. qui tam*[9] *etc. against the Sloop Mary & Margaret, Thomas Fowles Reclaimant,* arising out of the seizure of the *Mary & Margaret* in 1739 by Kennedy, Collector of the Port of New York.

Kennedy brought suit in the admiralty court at New York for forfeiture of the vessel for alleged violation of the Act of 1663 by importing into the port of New York from the Dutch colony of St. Eustatia gunpowder manufactured on the continent of Europe.

Fowles, owner of the sloop and powder, plead that the court of admiralty had no jurisdiction over the suit, on the following reasoning. It was well established that, legally speaking, "importation" did not take place until a vessel entered port;[10] the port of New York was within the body of the County of New York;[11] and an English act of 1391 excluding admiralty courts from taking jurisdiction over suits arising within the body of a county was applicable to the colonies, as well as to England.

The presiding admiralty judge, Lewis Morris, rejected this plea. Thereupon Fowles secured from the New York Supreme Court a writ prohibiting Judge Morris from proceeding with the suit.[12] Morris at first declined to obey the writ, but, after much legal skirmishing,[13] he gave way to the Governor and Council of New York sitting as a court of error, which, on April 17, 1741, affirmed the Supreme Court's decision.[14]

Kennedy then appealed to the Privy Council in England, the court of last resort for appeals from colonial courts of common law.[15] Pursuant to established practice, the Privy Council referred the appeal to its Committee of Council for hearing Appeals from the Plantations.[16] The Committee advised affirmance, and on March 23, 1743, the Privy Council issued an order in accord with the Committee's advice.[17]

Since ports throughout the colonies generally were within the body of some county, this decision of the Privy Council in effect established that colonial admiralty courts had no jurisdiction over suits for forfeiture under the Act of 1663.

The decision in the *Kennedy* case directly involved only the Act of 1663, but the principle of the decision applied with equal force to the Act of 1721, (7 Geo. I, first session, ch. 21, sec. 9) prohibiting importation into the colonies of any products of the East Indies except from Great Britain.[18]

While the appeal in the *Kennedy* case was pending in the Privy Council, the British Admiralty Board submitted to the Treasury Board a proposed bill for an act giving colonial admiralty courts jurdisdiction over suits in all cases involving British acts of trade and revenue affecting the colonies.[19] But no such act was passed until 1764.

Section 15 of the Act of 1764 explicitly granted colonial admiralty courts jurisdiction over suits for "all the forfeitures and penalties inflicted by this or any other act or acts of parliament relating to the trade and revenues of the said British colonies or plantations in America." This plainly gave colonial admiralty courts jurisdiction over suits under the acts of 1663 and 1721,[20] whether the alleged offense was committed without or within the body of a county.

THE NEW ADMIRALTY COURT AT HALIFAX

In a memorandum of March 14, 1764, the Admiralty Board suggested to the Treasury Board the appointment of a person learned in civil law as a "judge of the Admiralty for all North America . . . who may have a Concurrency of Powers with the several judges of the Vice Admiralty Court already appointed in each Province." He called attention to an opinion of the Attorney-General and Solicitor-General that, though the Admiralty had authority to appoint a judge having jurisdiction throughout the colonies, he could not "entertain jurisdiction in Cases where particular Acts of Parliament have confined the Recovery of Penalties and Forfeitures to Local Jurdisdictions."[21]

Presumably in response to this memorandum, Parliament, in section 41 of the Act of 1764, authorized the establishment of a new admiralty court having jurisdiction "over all America," concurrently with existing admiralty courts, over suits for "the forfeitures and penalties inflicted by this or any other act or acts of parliament relating to the trade and revenues of the said British colonies or plantations in America, which shall be incurred there."

Soon after passage of this act, the Privy Council approved establishment of a new court along the lines thus set forth in the act.[22]

On June 15, 1764, the Admiralty Board issued a commission to William Spry, a lawyer learned in the civil law, as "Commissary Deputy and Surrogate in and throughout all and every of the Provinces of America and Maritime Ports thereof and thereto adjacent whatsoever, with a Concurrency of Powers with the General Judges of the Vice-Admiralty Courts already appointed or to be appointed in each Province, but without power of hearing appeals from those Courts."[23]

Early in October, Spry opened the new court at Halifax, Nova Scotia,[24] which, though the headquarters of the British fleet in North America, was hardly more than a village[25] and was far removed from the centers of colonial trade.

The choice of this out-of-the-way site for the new court had been suggested months earlier in a letter from Admiral Lord Colville, in command of the British fleet in North American waters, to Philip Stephens, Secretary of the Navy Board, recommending the establishment of an admiralty court having jurdisdiction throughout the colonies, with Halifax as its seat. He stated that the admiralty judges in New York and New England were reputedly "too much interested in the welfare of their Neighbours" or might be "intimidated from giving an impartial Verdict by the threats and well known mobbish Disposition of the Inhabitants . . . ," whereas a judge sitting at Halifax would be free from such influences.[26]

Establishment of the new court at Halifax, of course, alarmed colonial merchants and shipowners, who feared they might be compelled to defend their vessels and cargoes from forfeiture in a court hundreds of miles from their homes and places of business.[27] But, for some unexplained reason or reasons,[28] apparently only one suit for forfeiture of property seized outside Nova Scotia had been brought in the new court[29] by the time it was abolished four years after its establishment.[30]

SECOND APPENDIX TO CHAPTER 3
THE FREE PORT ACT OF 1766

THE island of Dominica lying midway between, and close to, the rich French West Indian colonies of Guadeloupe and Martinique was, in 1766, a British colony and subject as such to the British Navigation Act of 1660, forbidding foreign vessels to import anything but silver and gold into the British colonies.[1] If this act were amended to permit foreign vessels to bring produce of foreign colonies into Dominica, the French islanders might well be tempted to smuggle out sugar and other local produce in small vessels to Dominica in defiance of French laws giving a monopoly or near monopoly of the trade of these islands to France.[2]

In 1766, the Rockingham administration sponsored passage of an act,[3] the Free Port Act of 1766, 6 Geo. III ch. 49, to hold out this temptation by amending the Navigation Act of 1660 to permit foreign vessels having not more than one deck to import all produce except tobacco of the foreign colonies in America into two Dominican ports: Prince Ruperts Bay in northern Dominica, only about fifty miles from Guadeloupe, and Roseau in southern Dominica, less than fifty miles from Martinique.[4]

British North American merchant shipowners, who had long carried on a flourishing but risky trade[5] with Guadeloupe and Martinque would have had reason to be grateful to Parliament for attracting sugar and other products of these islands to Dominica, where British subjects could pick them up without risk, provided they could be freely reexported from Dominica. But the Free Port Act did not permit this.

Section 7 of the act prohibited reexportation from Dominica of foreign colonial "wool, cotton wool [cotton], indigo, cochineal, fustic and all manner of dying, drugs or woods, drugs used in medicine, hair, furrs, hides and skins, pot and pearl ashes, whale fins [whalebone] and raw silk" to any place but Great Britain, thereby forbidding export of these products to the British colonies. Also section 9, though permitting carriage of the most important product of the French islands, sugar, to European ports south of Cape Finisterre, limited this permission to vessels built or owned in Great Britain, thereby excluding colonial-built ships owned by colonial merchants from this carrying trade.[6]

Thus, the Free Port Act, as well as the Act of 1766 (described in Chapter 3), made a mockery, so far as the northern British colonies were concerned, of Secretary of State Conway's assurance (quoted in Chapter 3) that in view of the "kind, indulgent Disposition prevailing both in His Majesty & his Parliament," the colonists could count on the mother country's giving "to the Trade & interests of America every Relief which the true State of their Circumstances . . . admits."

APPENDIX TO CHAPTER 5

GENERAL WRITS OF ASSISTANCE

IN 1662, Parliament passed the act of 13 and 14 Chas. II ch. 11 "for preventing frauds and regulating abuses in his Majesty's customs."

Section 4 of this act gave customs officers the right at any time to board vessels, to search for, and to seize supposedly smuggled goods.

Section 5 clause 2 of the act gave "any person or persons," including, of course, customs officers, the right when "authorized by writ of assistance under the seal of his majesty's court of exchequer, to take a constable, headborough or other publick officer, inhabiting near unto the place, and in the day time to enter, and go into any house, shop, cellar, warehouse or room or other place, and in case of resistance to break open doors, chests, trunks and other package, there to seize, and from there to bring any kind of goods or merchandizes whatsoever prohibited and uncustomed, and to put and secure the same in his majesty's storehouse, in the port next to the place where such seizure shall be made."

This section, it will be observed, did not indicate whether the writ of assistance to be issued by the Court of Exchequer was to be a special writ issued for a particular search upon statement by the applicant under oath of the particular premises to be entered and the particular smuggled goods supposed to be lodged there, or a general writ issued without statement as to any particular premises to be entered or suspected goods to be searched for and running for an indefinite time.[1] Customs officers naturally preferred general writs since such writs spared them the bother of making repeated application for writs, permitted them to act immediately on tips as to where smuggled goods were thought to be concealed, and enabled them to make "fishing" raids at will.

The English Court of Exchequer had long granted such writs[2] when Parliament in 1696 passed the act of 7 and 8 Wm. III ch. 22, to tighten enforcement of acts of Parliament dealing with colonial trade, section 6 of which provided that "the officers for collecting and managing his Majesty's revenue, and inspecting the plantation trade, in any of the said plantations [colonies] shall have the same powers and authorities as are provided for the officers of the customs in England by the said last mentioned act [the Act of 1662 quoted above] . . . to enter houses or warehouses, to search for and seize such [prohibited or uncustomed] goods. . . ."

This section of the Act of 1696, it will be noted, provided that customs officers should have the "same powers" as customs officers in England, which included search of premises on land under writs of assistance issued by the English Court of Exchequer, but by this court alone. No provision was made in the Act of 1696 for issuance of writs of assistance by colonial courts, and, so far as is known, no colonial court assumed the power to issue writs of assistance under this act[3] until 1756, when the Superior Court of Massachusetts issued general writs to British customs officers in the colony,[4] apparently on the assumption that under a Massachusetts act of 1699 giving the Massachusetts Court jurisdiction to act as a court of exchequer, it had authority to issue such writs under section 6 of the English Act of 1696 quoted above.[5]

Five years later, when the death of George II, during whose reign the existing writs in Massachusetts had been issued made it necessary for the customs officers to apply for new writs,[6] the authority of the Massachusetts Court to issue general writs was challenged (February, 1761) by James Otis and Oxenbridge Thacher as counsel for a group of Massachusetts merchants. Thacher argued that the English Court of Exchequer did not issue general writs and that if the Massachusetts Court assumed authority to act as a court of exchequer it should follow the practice of the English Court in this respect and also that an earlier decision of the Massachusetts Court renouncing the equity jurisdiction of the English Court of Exchequer indicated doubt whether the Massachusetts Court had authority to act as a court of exchequer in any case. Otis explicitly admitted the authority of the Massachusetts Court (whether as a court of exchequer or otherwise) to issue special writs of assistance, but denied its authority to issue general writs on the ground that if the English Acts of 1662 and 1696 had expressly authorized the issuance of general writs (which they did not), the acts must be held unconstitutional and void as being "against natural Equity."[7]

The Massachusetts Court, presided over by Chief Justice Thomas Hutchinson, reserved judgment pending inquiry into the practice of the English Court of Exchequer and, when informed that, contrary to Thacher's assertion, the English Court issued general writs, decided (November, 1761) in favor of issuing general writs, and thereupon issued several general writs similar to those issued by the English Court.[8]

Presumably encouraged by the action of the Massachusetts Court, the Collector of Customs at New London, Connecticut, in 1766 approached the Superior Court of Connecticut for a writ of assistance, presumably a general writ, but the court indicated that it had no authority to issue the requested writ.[9]

The Connecticut Court's position was sustained by William De Grey, the Crown's Attorney-General in England, who gave an opinion dated October 17, 1766, that the Acts of 1662 and 1696 granted authority only to the English Court of Exchequer to issue general writs of assistance, from which it followed that these acts did not authorize any colonial courts to issue such writs.[10]

Section 10 of the Townshend Act, 7 Geo. III ch. 46 (1767), referred to in Chapter 5, was thereupon passed to give colonial superior courts the authority which De Grey held they did not have under existing law.[11] Section 10 stated that "whereas by an act of parliament made in the fourteenth year of the reign of King Charles the Second . . . it is lawful for any officer of his Majesty's customs, authorized by writ of assistance under the seal of his Majesty's court of exchequer, to go into any house . . . or other place . . . and whereas by an act made in the seventh and eighth years of the reign of King William the Third . . . it is . . . enacted, that the officers . . . in America, shall have the same powers and authorities to enter houses or warehouses . . . but no authority . . . [was] given . . . by the said [latter] act, to any particular court to grant such writs of assistance . . . be it enacted . . . That . . . [beginning November 20, 1767] such writs . . . shall and may be granted by the . . . superior or supreme court of justice having jurisdiction within such colony or plantation respectively."

Pursuant to this act, the American Customs Board at Boston (discussed in Chapter 8) sent orders to customs officers throughout the colonies to secure general writs.[12] However, despite the new act, the Connecticut Superior Court still refused (1768) to issue the requested writs, the Chief Justice, Jonathan Trumbull, calling them "unconstitutional,"[13] and the Chief Justice of the Supreme Court of Pennsylvania also flatly refused, stating, "I am not Warranted by Law to issue any such Warrant."[14] The Supreme Courts of Rhode Island, Maryland, and South Carolina reached the same result simply by taking no action at all.[15]

The New York Supreme Court did, indeed, now issue writs to customs officers in New York, but even these differed materially from the general writs granted by the English Court of Exchequer and the Massachusetts Superior Court, in that the New York writs omitted the words "from time to time" and "suspected to be concealed,"[16] thus leaving open the question whether the writ was good only for a particular search.

Again called upon for an opinion, De Grey held (August 20, 1768): "There can be no doubt, but that the Superior Courts of Justice in America are bound by the 7th Geo. 3d to issue such Writs of Assistance as the Court of Exchequer in England issues in similar Cases, to the Officers of the Customs," and recommended sending over to the several colonies "the Form of Writ issued by the Court of Exchequer in England," showing that these were general writs, i.e., writs "not granted upon a previous Information, nor to any particular Person, nor on a special Occasion."[17]

On the strength of this opinion and after consultation with Chief Justice Hutchinson,[18] the American Customs Board sent a circular letter in March, 1769, signed by the Board's solicitor, to customs officers throughout the colonies, enclosing "the Form of a Writ of Assistance to the Officers of the Customs, as issued by the superior Court here [in Massachusetts]; likewise blank Forms of the Writ, and a copy of the Opinion of the Attorney General in England in relation thereto," and requesting them to obtain similar writs from the superior courts of their several provinces.[19]

But apparently none of the colonial courts acted favorably on the letter. In 1769 the Connecticut Superior Court referred the matter to the Legislature,[20] after which apparently nothing further was done.[21] The New York Supreme Court repeatedly deferred consideration of the matter to a later date and then apparently dropped it.[22] The Rhode Island Superior Court took the matter under consideration, but apparently took no further action, and the South Carolina and Maryland Courts also continued to do nothing.[23]

Furthermore, the Supreme Court of Pennsylvania again flatly refused to grant a general writ, stating that it would grant "particular writs whenever they are applied for upon oath" by the petitioning officer that he "either has an information or his reasons to believe that prohibited or uncustomed goods are lodged in any particular place," and no other.[24]

The Virginia Superior Court, consisting of the Governor (Lord Botetourt) and the provincial Council, approved a form of special writ prepared, at its request, by John Randolph, Attorney-General of Virginia; but the court refused to grant the form of writ called for by the American Customs Board, because such a writ "was too general; . . . the Writ ought not to be a standing one, but granted from time to time, as the information of the Officer to the Supreme Court, on oath, may render necessary."[25]

The grounds for this decision are indicated in a letter of January 4, 1774, from John Randolph's brother, Peyton Randolph, and other members of the Virginia Committee of Correspondence to a similar Committee in Connecticut. Pointing out that the Townshend Act conferred on colonial supreme courts the same, but only the same, authority to issue writs of assistance in the colonies as the English Court of Exchequer had in England, the Committee asserted that the only kind of writ the English Court had authority to issue was the form of writ prescribed by an act of 12 Chas. II ch. 19 (1660), which provided that writs were to be issued only on information under oath furnished the court by the person requesting the writ as to particular goods to be searched for, i.e., particular, not general writs.[26]

Two of the most learned students of the controversy over writs of assistance, Horace Gray and Joseph R. Frese, have ably maintained the soundness of this view.[27] But I agree with the opinion of Edward Thurlow, De Grey's successor as Attorney General, given in August, 1771, that, since the Act of 1662 made no mention of the Act of 1660, the English Court of Exchequer was given discretion by the later act to issue such writs of assistance as it chose; that it had seen fit to issue general writs; and that, therefore, under the Townshend Act of 1767, the colonial superior and supreme courts were authorized and required to issue similar writs.[28]

After Thurlow had given his opinion, the American Customs Board made a final effort to secure general writs throughout the colonies,[29] and this time (April, 1773) it was successful in South Carolina, the native members of whose supreme court had recently been replaced by judges sent out from Great Britain.[30] But South Carolina stood alone. Elsewhere the courts that had previously declined to issue general writs, stood by their guns,[31] and, as Thurlow stated in his opinion, there seemed to be no way to compel them to issue the writs.[32]

As might be expected, the attempted use by British customs officers in Massachusetts of general writs of assistance that the merchants in the colony considered illegal led to clashes between them and the customs officers making or attempting to make searches and seizures under authority of the writs.[33]

The earliest of these, at Falmouth, Massachusetts, seems to have been little noticed, but one at Boston, involving Daniel Malcom (among the merchants who retained Otis and Thacher to oppose renewal of general writs of assistance in 1761) created a great stir.

On September 24, 1766, William Sheaffe, Deputy Collector, and Benjamin Hallowell, Comptroller of Customs at Boston, armed with a general writ of assistance issued by the Massachusetts Superior Court to Hallowell,[34] in daylight hours and accompanied by a local enforcement officer as required by the Act of 1662, demanded of Malcom that he let them into a locked inner cellar of his home to search for alleged contraband stored there.

Malcom refused and, arming himself with a couple of pistols and a cutlass, swore "if any Man attempted it he would blow his brains out. . . ." This threat, coupled with threats by members of a large crowd gathered near Malcom's house that they would forcibly prevent anyone from entering the house unless "the Customs House Officers would go before a Justice and make Oath who their Informer was . . . ," which, of course, they would not do, deterred them from breaking into the cellar and getting possession of the contraband, if any, stored there.[35]

On submission of a report of the affair to De Grey, he held, consistently with his opinion in the Connecticut case referred to above, that "no Civil or Criminal Prosecution can be brought against any of the Parties complained of, for obstructing the Affairs of the Customs . . . inasmuch as the Writ of Assistance by Virtue of which they entered the House and Cellar, was not in this case a legal Authority."[36] But the highly colored report of the clash sent by officials at Boston to officials in London[37] presumably contributed to Boston's reputation in British ruling circles of being particularly unruly.

No evidence has been found of any later attempted use of general writs of assistance in Massachusetts. But after the arrival from England in 1771 of judges sent from England to sit on the South Carolina Supreme Court, general writs were issued by that court,[38] and the power given to "officers of the customs . . . to break open and enter houses without the authority of any civil magistrate founded on legal information" is among the grievances recited in the First Continental Congress' Address to the King in 1774.[39]

PROJECT FOR ANGLICAN BISHOPS
IN THE COLONIES

IN 1750, an unsuccessful movement to settle one or more Church of England bishops in America had aroused much opposition in the colonies.[1]

It was argued by those in favor of the project that because, under canon law, only a bishop had authority to confirm members and ordain candidates for the ministry of the Church of England, at least one bishop should be settled in America to enable colonial Anglicans to be confirmed and colonial candidates for ordination to be ordained without making a long, expensive, and hazardous trip abroad.[2]

The calm acceptance in the United States of bishops of the American Protestant Episcopal Church after the Revolution[3] indicates that there probably would have been no great opposition to the settlement of Church of England bishops in the colonies if the colonists had been convinced that confirmation and ordination were all that those favoring the project had in mind. But many colonists feared that once bishops were established in the colonies, they would seek and obtain the temporal powers of English bishops, such as jurisdiction over the probate of estates and some form of taxation to support them.[4]

The position of those opposing the project was stated in a letter of December 12, 1750, from Josiah Willard, Secretary of Massachusetts, a Congregationalist, to the Acting Governor, Spencer Phipps, an Anglican. "The universal dissatisfaction to that Scheme among Persons of our Communion," wrote Willard, "is . . . [from] expecting that if once Bishops should be settled in America it would be judged for some Reason or other necessary to extend their Jurisdiction equally to what that Order of Men are possessed of in Great Britain."[5] Since confirmation and ordination could have been handled by occasional visits to the colonies from one of the more than forty bishops of the established church in England, Ireland, and the Isle of Man, and yet none ever came,[6] there was some justification for the fear that a colonial bishop having more than ecclesiastical powers was contemplated.

After passage of the American Act of 1764 and the Stamp Act, there was a more acute fear that Parliament might saddle the colonists with taxes for the support of bishops established in the colonies.[7] Various suggestions were made for their support by the Crown,[8] but I have found no evidence that any of these was acceptable to the British government.

The movement for colonial bishops was revived in 1758, when Thomas Secker,[9] who as Bishop of Oxford had been a leader in the earlier movement for colonial bishops, became Archbishop of Canterbury and President of the Society for the Propagation of the Gospel in Foreign Parts, hereinafter referred to as "the Society."

Learning of Secker's elevation of these offices, a convention of eleven Anglican clergymen of New York and New Jersey, meeting in New York City, addressed a letter to him, dated June 22, 1758, stating, "As we are well assured that nothing would give You Greater satisfaction than to see us under the immediate Inspection of a Bishop, we heartily pray that this may be one of the Blessings of Your Grace's Archepiscopate."[10] The letter was signed by all the members of the convention, headed by the Reverend Samuel Johnson, President of King's College (now Columbia University.)[11]

Secker replied on September 22 to Johnson outlining plans for mission work in the colonies, and continuing,

"All these things will contribute, directly or indirectly, to facilitate what we must ever pray and labor for, till we obtain it, the establishment of bishops of our church in America. This I have long had at heart; and not only said but written a great deal in favor of it. . . . Nor, unsuccessful as the attempts have been, shall I ever abandon the scheme as long as I live, but pushing it openly at present would certainly prove both fruitless and detrimental. They alone are judges of opportunities who know the dispositions of persons and parties; which cannot always be explained to others."[12]

During the next few years, Secker and Johnson corresponded concerning various affairs of the Anglican Church in the colonies, including particularly the project for colonial bishops.[13]

Secker wrote in May, 1764, "Lord Willoughby of Parham, the only English Dissenting Peer, and Dr. Chandler [the Reverend Samuel Chandler, one of the most distinguished non-Anglican ministers in England] have declared, after our scheme was fully laid before them, that they saw no objection against it. The Duke of Bedford, Lord President [of the Privy Council], hath given a calm and favorable hearing to it. . . . Indeed, I see not how Protestant Bishops can be decently refused us, as in all probability a Popish one will be allowed, by connivance at least, in Canada. . . . The Archbishop of York is very active in our business [business of the Society]. . . . But these, and particularly what relates to Bishops, must be managed in a quiet, private manner."[14]

When a year passed without further word, a convention of New York and New Jersey clergy, headed by the Reverend Myles Cooper, who had succeeded Johnson as President of King's College, undertook to spur Anglican leaders in England.[15] In October, 1765, a committee chosen for this purpose adopted an address to be presented by Secker to the King asking that "one or more Bishops may be speedily sent us." The Archbishop of York, the Bishop of London, and the Secretary of the Society were to be solicited to support the request.[16]

As we have seen, Secker had given assurance of the Archbishop of York's interest in the project. As to the Society, since it helped support a large number of Anglican missionaries in the colonies,[17] its members could be expected to support a movement designed to strengthen the Church of England's position there. The Bishop of London, formerly under a commission from the King,[18] now informally by custom, supervised all Anglican churches and ministers in the colonies,[19] so that he, too, could be expected to take a particular interest.

Those pleading for colonial bishops were very shortly fortified by the shipwreck and death of two young men returning to the colonies from ordination in England.[20] Johnson immediately (May 2, 1766) wrote Secker of the tragedy, pleading for colonial bishops to relieve colonial candidates for the Anglican ministry from the danger of a trip to England for ordination.

"I have the great mortification and grief," he wrote, "to inform your Grace that . . . two hopeful young gentlemen who were ordained last had the misfortune to be lost on their arrival on the coast. . . . Those two make up ten valuable lives that have now been lost for want of ordaining power[21] here . . . in litle more than 40 years. . . .

"If such a thing as sending us one or two bishops can at all be done for us, . . . now that all America are over-flowing with joy for the repeal of the Stamp Act, would be the happiest juncture for it that could be, for I believe they would rather have 20 bishops were sent than that Act enforced."[22]

The Archbishop replied,

"Earnest and continued endeavors [for colonial bishops] have been used with our successive ministers [of state], but without obtaining more than promises to consider and confer about the matter; which promises have never been fulfilled. The king hath expressed himself repeatedly in favor of the scheme and hath proposed that if objections are imagined to lie against other places, a Protestant bishop should be sent to Quebec, where there is a popish one, and where there are few Dissenters to take offence. . . .[23] Of late indeed it hath not been prudent to do anything unless at Quebec. And therefore the address from the clergy of Connecticut . . . and that from the clergy of New York and New Jersey, which arrived in January, have not been presented to the King. But he hath been acquainted with the purport of them, and directed them to be postponed to a fitter time."[24]

The King's idea of sending an Anglican bishop to Quebec apparently had little appeal to Johnson. In replying to the Archbishop, he proposed that instead of sending a bishop to Canada, three bishops be "provided for in America, . . . one should be for all the Islands, one at Virginia, for all the southern provinces, and one I think would be best placed at Albany, where there are few Dissenters and where he would be best situated to take what care is needful at Canada, and to ordain and govern the affairs of the Church in the provinces of New England, New York and Pennsylvania."[25]

The Reverend Thomas Bradbury Chandler of New Jersey was even cooler to the King's idea. "As to Canada," he wrote Johnson, "I must confess I had rather see no bishop come to America than to see him smuggled into and concealed in that country."[26]

Convinced by the Archbishop's letter that there was little hope of securing a Church of England bishop or bishops for the colonies, except possibly in Quebec, without widespread appeals from America, Johnson wrote in April, 1767, to the Reverend John Camm, rector of York-Hampton parish, Virginia,

"The kind manner in which you speak of me in your letter to my friend Mr. Holt,[27] in answer to his inquiry, at my desire, about the disposition of the Virginians towards episcopacy, emboldens me to take the liberty of writing to you on that important subject. . . .

"Our most excellent Archbishop, who has been much engaged in this great affair, . . . has lately informed me that he has not been able to gain the attention of the ministry to it, though his Majesty is very kindly disposed to favour and promote it. I am therefore very apprehensive that our solicitations will fail of gaining the point, unless we could bring it to a general cry, and prevail with the southern provinces to join us in a zealous application to the government at home. . . .

"Reverend Sir, I beg leave to intercede with you to influence as far as possible both the clergy and the laity of your province, and if possible of all your southern provinces, to join in the cry, when the honor and interest of the Church and true religion so much lies at stake."[28]

Johnson also sought to promote the desired "general cry" by encouraging

Chandler to write and publish a pamphlet in support of the establishment of an American episcopate.[29]

This pamphlet, *An appeal to the Public in Behalf of the Church of England in America. By Thomas Bradbury Chandler, D.D., Rector of St. John's Church, in Elizabeth-Town New-Jersey, and Missionary from the Society for the Propagation of the Gospel,* was published in New York City in October, 1767.[30]

Together with a recently published sermon of the Bishop of Llandaff (John Ewer) in support of bishops for the colonies,[31] Chandler's pamphlet touched off a paper war of pamphlets and newspaper articles over an American episcopate, which continued for several years.[32] Chandler was the chief spokesman for those in favor of the project, the Reverend Charles Chauncy, pastor of the First Church of Boston (Congregational), and William Livingston, a lawyer and leading member of the Presbyterian Church in New York City, of those against.[33] The latter, incensed over the recent successful opposition by Anglicans in New York and England to a petition for a charter by the Presbyterian Church of New York City,[34] was particularly bitter in his attacks on the proposed episcopate.

In 1770, supporters of the project sought support for it by the Anglican clergy of Maryland and Virginia in which the Church of England was the established church.

In September 1770, following a visit to Maryland by President Cooper,[35] a convention of nine out of forty-odd members of the Maryland Anglican clergy adopted a proposed Address from "the Clergy of Maryland of the Communion of the Church of England" to the King for "the Admission of an American Bishop." The convention also adopted addresses for an American bishop to the Archbishop of Canterbury, the Bishop of London, and Lord Baltimore, Proprietor of Maryland, asking them to support the address to the King.[36]

In response to the objection of Robert Eden, Governor of the province, that the whole Anglican clergy of the province ought to be canvassed on so important a matter,[37] a committee of the convention sent a circular letter to the Anglican clergy of the province reporting the convention's plan and asking them to write the Reverend Jonathan Boucher whether they were for or against it.[38]

Ten members were reported to have opposed the Address,[39] but presumably a majority voted favorably, since English newspapers of the following November carried word of the presentation of an Address to the King from the Maryland clergy "asking a Bishop for that province."[40]

In December, 1770, members of the Anglican clergy in New York, New Jersey, and Connecticut sent a circular letter to "the principal Clergymen in Virginia & the two Carolinas" asking their support for the "Plan of our Episcopate."[41]

They received a reply from the Reverend James Horrocks, President of the College of William and Mary and the Bishop of London's commissary for Virginia, that he would "use his influence with all his Brethren in Virginia at their general Meeting this Spring, to transmit Petitions to England for that Purpose,"[42] and in May, 1771, he published notice of a convention of the Virginia clergy to be held in Williamsburg, on June 4, to consider "the Expediency of an Application to proper Authority for an American Episcopate."[43]

The convention voted "that a Committee be appointed to draw up an Address to the King for an American Episcopate; and that the Committee shall apply for the hands of the majority of the [Anglican] Clergy of this Colony; in which, if they succeed, the Bishop of London is to be humbly addressed for his concurrence, and requested to present their Address to his Majesty. . . .[44]

Four of the twelve ministers attending the convention[45] voted against the resolution, and two of the opponents, Samuel Henley and Thomas Gwatkin, published a protest in the June 6 issue of the *Virginia Gazette* (Purdie) stating the grounds of their protest.[46] Furthermore, the Virginia House of Burgesses at its next (July, 1771) session passed a resolution, "Nemine Contradicente," thanking the four opponents "for the wise and well timed Opposition they made to the pernicious Project of a few mistaken Clergymen for introducing an American Bishop; a Measure by which much Disturbance, great Anxiety and Apprehension would certainly take Place among his Majesty's faithful American Subjects. . . ."[47]

I have found no evidence concerning the outcome of the application, if made, to the clergy of the colony for their support of the project;[48] but it was reported in June, 1772, that Horrocks had presented a Petition to the King for a colonial bishop.[49]

The petitions from the southern colonies were no more successful than those from the north; no Anglican bishop was established in the colonies until after the Revolution, when (1787) Charles Inglis, former assistant minister of Trinity Church, New York City, was consecrated Bishop of Nova Scotia.[50]

In 1768 an Anglican clergyman recently returned from England reported that Secker had told him "the Ministry were intirely aversed to sending Bishops to America," for the reason, among others, "that as America seemed on the point of Rebellion & Independency, the Ministry were determined to retain every hold on America: that by necessitating the American Episcopalians to have recourse to England for Ordination they would be held in part. This hold would be lost if a Bishop should be sent, & the whole Hierarchy be erected complete in America."[51]

But probably the decisive reason was the unwillingness of successive British Ministries to intensify colonial unrest by approving a measure for which they had little or no enthusiasm,[52] and which would assuredly antagonize a large number of the colonists.[53]

APPENDIX TO CHAPTER 9

THE ADMIRALTY COURT AT HALIFAX
AND ITS SUCCESSORS

THE admiralty court referred to in Chapter 3, having jurisdiction throughout the colonies, established at Halifax, Nova Scotia, in 1764,[1] was initially a court of first instance (trial court) only. But sect. 68 of the Stamp Act of 1765, 5 Geo. III ch. 12, gave the court jurisdiction over appeals from all colonial admiralty courts in cases involving penalties inflicted by the Stamp Act or "by any other act of parliament relating to the trade or revenue of the said colonies or plantations. . . ."

The act of 6 Geo. III ch. 12 (1766) repealing the Stamp Act included repeal of the provision giving appellate jurisdiction of the admiralty court at Halifax, which again became a court of first instance only.

Colonial fears[2] that customs officers would compel the owners of seized property to defend it from condemnation in a court sitting perhaps more than a thousand miles from the place of seizure and the owner's home or place of business proved to be unfounded. So far as is known, the only suit brought in the new court at Halifax for an alleged offense against a British act of trade or revenue committed outside Nova Scotia, was brought (successfully) in 1765 for forfeiture of the sloop *Polly,* seized by customs officers at Dighton, Massachusetts, in April, 1765, for nonpayment of the three pence per gallon import duty on foreign colonial molasses levied by the Act of 1764.[3] And the basis for removing whatever fear on this score may have remained was laid by the passage in 1768 of the act of 8 Geo. III 23, authorizing the Crown to replace the single court at Halifax by several new courts.

Pursuant to this act, the Crown abolished the Halifax court and replaced it with four district admiralty courts for North America, sitting at Halifax, Boston, Philadelphia, and Charleston, South Carolina,[4] each having jurisdiction over ordinary admiralty cases and cases involving offenses against the British acts of trade and revenue arising within its particular district.[5] The new courts were also given jurisdiction over appeals from all colonial admiralty courts within their respective districts.[6]

Unfortunately this favorable change was marred by the extravagantly high (according to colonial standards) salaries of £600 sterling a year granted all four of the judges[7] and the offensive background of Jared Ingersoll of Connecticut, judge of the Philadelphia district, and Augustus Johnston of Rhode Island, judge of the Charleston district, whose only discernible claim to preference over equally well-qualified local lawyers was their having been stamp distributors for their respective colonies until compelled by irate fellow citizens to resign.[8]

These irritants and other minor ones in connection with the establishment of the new courts were dilated upon by various colonial writers,[9] but even with its drawbacks, the change was favorable to the colonies in assuring colonial merchants and shipowners that they could not be compelled to appear in a distant court in order to defend their property.

APPENDIX TO CHAPTER 10

UNEVEN OBSERVANCE OF THE NON-IMPORTATION AGREEMENTS

OBSERVANCE of the non-importation agreements was very uneven in the several colonies in which such agreements were adopted.

In Virginia, most important of the southern colonies, the agreement was little observed. In July, 1770, George Mason, one of the leaders of the movement in Virginia, wrote Richard Henry Lee of "experience having fully proved that when goods are here, many of our people [fellow planters] will purchase, even some who effect to be called gentlemen,"[1] and, a month later, Lee wrote his brother William in London of the shameful neglect of the agreement among the merchants in the colony.[2] These statements are confirmed by other evidence.

Though no figures as to Virginia alone are available, those covering exports from England to Virginia and Maryland combined disclose that they actually rose from £475,954 in 1768,[3] the year before the Virginia agreement, to £488,362 in 1769, during the most of which it was operative, and to £717,782 in 1770,[4] during nearly the whole of which it was nominally in force.[5]

The figures of exports to South and North Carolina, Pennsylvania, and New England, which included the three major ports of Charleston, Philadelphia, and Boston, respectively, show a varied record.

The Charleston agreement did not become operative until well into 1769 and terminated at the end of 1770; the relevant years for comparison are, therefore, 1769 and 1770. In these years the exports from England to the Carolinas fell from £306,600 in 1769, to £146,273 in 1770.[6]

The Philadelphia agreement did not become operative until well into 1769 and terminated some months before the end of 1770. The exports from England to Pennsylvania in this period fell from £432,107 in 1768, to £199,909 in 1769, and £134,881 in 1770.[7]

The record of New England, including Boston, was roughly the same as for the Carolinas. The exports from England to New England fell from £419,797 in 1768 to £207,993 in 1769,[8] the only year in which the Boston agreement was operative for the entire year.

New York had much the best record. The figures for New York including New York City, show that exports from England to New York fell from £482,530 in 1768, to £74,918 in 1769,[9] the only year in which the New York City agreement was operative for the entire year. Other evidence supports the conclusion that the agreement of the New York City merchants was faithfully kept.[10]

The relatively poor showing of New England was due largely to developments at ports other than Boston. As noted in Chapter 7, Portsmouth, New Hampshire, a fairly busy port, never joined the importation movement. Furthermore, Newport, Rhode Island, an important port at that period, did not join the movement until late (October, 1769); left large loopholes in the agreement then adopted; and terminated even this loose agreement as early as the following May.[11]

But the record of Boston itself was far poorer than that of Philadelphia and New York City.

A number of Boston merchants, emboldened by the presence of the British troops,[12] long refused to sign or observe the local agreement.[13] Besides, as widely publicized by John Mein and William Fleeming, Tory printers in Boston,[14] bills of lading on file in the Boston Customs House showed that several Boston signers had violated the agreement[15] and that John Hancock, one of the leaders in the Boston movement, had violated the spirit, though not the letter of the agreement, by permitting the captains of his vessels to carry articles banned by the agreement.[16]

FIRST APPENDIX TO CHAPTER 11
IMPRESSMENT AND THE CASE OF MICHAEL CORBET

O N April 22, 1769, the brig *Pitt Packet,* owned by Richard Hooper of Marblehead, Massachusetts, manned with a crew of six men, was approaching her home port with a load of salt from Spain when she was boarded by a press gang[1] under Lieutenant Henry Panton of H.M. Frigate *Rose.*

Two of the men, who were residents of Massachusetts and exempt from impressment under the agreement between Captain John Corner and the Massachusetts Council (described in Chapter 8) stood their ground. The other four, who were Irish, hid in the forepeak and, as Panton approached their hideaway, warned him not to lay hands on them. When he gave orders to break down a bulkhead protecting the men, their leader, Michael Corbet, stuck a harpoon into Panton's throat, fatally wounding him. All six members of the crew were seized and taken aboard the *Rose,* but the Massachusetts men were promptly released.[2]

A few weeks later, Corbet and his three companions were brought to trial for murder before a special court convened in Boston under a British act of 11 and 12 Wm. III ch. 7 (1700) providing for the trial of piracy or other felonies committed on the high seas or elsewhere within admiralty jurisdiction in colonial waters.[3]

The members of the court consisted of twelve officers of the Crown: the Governor, Chief Justice of the Superior Court, and Secretary of Massachusetts; the judge of the admiralty court for Massachusetts and New Hampshire; Commodore Samuel Hood; the Governor and two members of the Council of New Hampshire; the judge of the Rhode Island court of admiralty; the Collectors of Customs for the Ports of Boston and Salem, Massachusetts, and the Comptroller of Customs for the Port of Portsmouth, New Hampshire.[4]

The defendants, represented by John Adams and James Otis,[5] pleaded that, under acts of 1536 and 1717, they were entitled to trial by a jury chosen from inhabitants of the shire or county in which the trial was held, namely Suffolk County, Massachusetts.[6] But the plea was denied, and the special court proceeded to try the case without a jury.[7]

No one can say what might have happened if the court, in which trial by jury was denied, had found the men guilty. The feeling against impressment and the denial of trial by jury ran so high in the colonies that there might well have been an attempt forcibly to rescue the convicted men from jail and a resulting clash between Bostonians and the British armed forces at Boston even more bloody than the Boston "Massacre" ten months later.[8] But after examining the witnesses, the court (June 17) acquitted Corbet and his companions on a verdict of "justifiable homicide."[9]

The court did not state the ground for its verdict. Presumably it was based on one or both of the following grounds:[10] that section 9 of the wartime act of 6 Anne ch. 37 (1708), forbidding impressment in the colonies except of deserters from the royal navy, was still in force;[11] or that impressment was legal only if authorized by a warrant to impress from the British Admiralty Board, and that no such warrant had been issued to Panton or his commanding officer.

Governor William Shirley of Massachusetts wrote in 1747 of the view held throughout the colonies that impressment there was "illegal by virtue of a Clause in a statute of Queen Anne,"[12] and in June, 1768, a Boston town meeting adopted an instruction to the town's representatives in the Massachusetts House of Representatives, maintaining that the act of 6 Anne ch. 37 sec. 9 was still in force and prohibited impressment, except of deserters, in the colonies.[13]

But, apparently, the court's decision was based solely on the second ground. Thomas Hutchinson, who was a member of the court, stated in the third volume of his *The History of the Colony and Province of Massachusetts-Bay*, that the decision had been based on the lack of the required admiralty warrant for impressment. He wrote that "neither the lieutenant nor any of his superior officers were authorized to impress, by any warrant or special authority from the lords of the admiralty; and the court (the commanding officer of the King's ships being one of the commissioners) was [therefore] unanimously of opinion that the prisoners had a good right to defend themselves . . . and ought to be acquitted. . . ."[14]

This explanation, though suspect because written long after the event,[15] is credible. As Crown officers, the members of the court presumably would choose to hold Panton's action illegal on the narrow ground of his lacking the required warrant for the particular impressment at issue, rather than on the broad ground that the act of 6 Anne ch. 37 prohibited any impressment in the colonies.

SECOND APPENDIX TO CHAPTER 11
CLASHES BETWEEN CIVILIANS AND BRITISH TROOPS IN NEW YORK

EVER since 1765 there had been occasional clashes between British soldiers in New York City, headquarters of the British army in North America, and local civilians,[1] due chiefly, it seems, to the soldiers' working in their free time on civilian jobs at cut-rate wages.[2]

Clashes described in the Boston newspapers, referred to in Chapter 11, had begun on January 13, 1770, when a group of soldiers tried unsuccessfully to destroy a Liberty Pole, first erected on the city commons in 1766 to celebrate repeal of the Stamp Act. Jeered at by some bystanders for their failure, the soldiers attacked and broke the windows of a neighboring popular tavern, before being driven away by a crowd of civilians.[3]

Soon afterward, a handbill signed "Brutus" was circulated in the city, denouncing the conduct of the soldiers and of local employers for hiring them for work that ought to be given to civilians. In a rhetorical question addressed to these employers, the writer insulted the soldiers by exclaiming "is it not enough that you pay Money to support the Soldiers [by contributing to the funds appropriated by the Legislature as required by the Quartering Act] and a Poor Tax to maintain many of their Whores and Bastards in the Work House, without giving them the Employment" that ought to be given to the city's poor workmen.[4]

On the night of January 16–17, the Liberty Pole was again attacked, and this time was torn down.[5] The attack aparently was attributed to soldiers of the Sixteenth Regiment. Two days later, a handbill signed "16th Regiment of Foot" was issued, declaring that the pole had been destroyed "without the assistance of the army" and denouncing the "pretended S——s of L——[Sons of Liberty]" as "enemies to society" for trying "to stir up the minds of his Majesty's good subjects to sedition."[6]

Two soldiers who were posting up one of the handbills were seized and haled before the Mayor of the city. A crowd of their fellows gathered to support them, leading to a battle royal between soldiers and civilians, the so-called Battle of Golden Hill,[7] in which, after several persons on each side were injured, the soldiers were defeated and driven away.[8]

APPENDIX TO CHAPTER 13
THE REFUND OF DUTY ON TEA

T HE statement in Chapter 13 that the refund of the British tea duty requested by the East India Company would be about 3d. a pound is based on the following calculation:

1. The value per pound of the different varieties of tea in 1773, as stated in a table in (Oxford University Press') Labaree *Tea Party* 335, was:

Bohea	2 shillings
Congou	2 shillings 3 pence
Singlo	2 shillings 8 pence
Suchong	3 shillings
Hyson	5 shillings

2. The sale in the colonies of Bohea tea exceeded that of all other varieties combined, as indicated by the Company's shipment in 1773 of 1,826 chests of Bohea tea and 565 chests of all other varieties combined, *same* 335.

3. The British import duty on tea was about 24% ad valorem, Farrand "Taxation of Tea" 266.

4. The additional refund requested by the Company was three-fifths, or 40%, of the British import duty, i.e., 40% of about 24%, or about 9.6%.

5. The refund of the British tea duty on Bohea tea valued at 2s. (24d.) a pound would be about 9.6% of 24d., or about 2.3d. a pound (Two shillings = 2s.; pence is represented by d.)

6. The requested additional refund on the most expensive varieties of tea would run to more than 3d. a pound—in the case of Hyson to 5.76d. a pound.

7. The requested refund applied to all varieties of tea would come to around 2.5d. a pound in 1773.

8. The prices of tea in 1773 were very much depressed, as shown by the table of prices of tea from 1763 to 1773 in the table of prices in Labaree *Tea Party* 332–333.

9. When, as might be expected, the price of tea returned to the higher level of most earlier years, the refund would average out to around 3d. a pound.

APPENDIX TO CHAPTER 14

WAS THE *DARTMOUTH* ORDERED
TO ENTER PORT?

I N a "Narrative" written long after the event, Thomas Hutchinson stated: "The Governor [i.e., he himself] forseeing the difficulty that must attend this affair, advised the consignees to order the vessels when they arrived, to anchor below the Castle [i.e., outside port], that if it should appear unsafe to land the tea, they might go to sea again; and when the first ship [the *Dartmouth*] arrived, she anchored accordingly; but when the master came up to town Mr. [Samuel] Adams and others, a committe of the town, ordered him at his peril, to bring the ship up to land the other goods, but to suffer no tea to be taken out."[1]

As stated in Chapter 14, this statement (and a similar one in Hutchinson's *History of Massachusetts-Bay,* also written long after the event)[2] has been adopted by reputable biographers and historians.

John C. Miller's (1936) *Sam Adams Pioneer in Propaganda* states:

"If the tea ships anchored below Castle William [at the mouth of Boston harbor] instead of entering the port of Boston, they could return to England without out a pass from the governor, payment of duty, or observance of any of the formalities required by Parliamentary law. But if the ships came beyond Castle William they could not again put to sea until the tea had been landed or the duty paid. Hutchinson planned to avert the crisis he saw gathering in Boston by ordering the tea ships to anchor below the Castle so that, if it appeared the tea could not be landed, they could set sail for the mother country.

"But Sam Adams had very different plans for the 'plagued' East India tea. . . . Adams seldom let slip an opportunity to plunge the colonies deeper into controversy with Great Britain; and he soon showed that he had no intention of allowing the crisis brought on by the East India Tea Act to pass quietly. When the first tea ship anchored below Castle William, its captain was summoned before the Boston committee of correspondence, where he was ordered by Adams and other committeemen to bring his ship up to the Boston wharves and land all the cargo except the tea on pain of being tarred and feathered by the Liberty Boys. . . . In Philadelphia, where there was no Sam Adams to evolve a desperate scheme to destroy the tea, the ships were ordered by the Sons of Liberty to anchor below the port in order that the cargo might not become liable to port duties."[3]

More recently (1958) Clifford K. Shipton has written, "When he [Hutchinson] heard the wind begin to rise he decided to keep the ships below the Castle so that they could be sent back to England without clearance. Adams, however, saw to it that the ships were brought up to the town so that duty would have to be paid, or the Governor would himself have to override the law."[4]

No contemporary evidence has been adduced to support these statements, and there is strong contemporary evidence that they are untrue.

In the first place, if the alleged order by the consignees to the master of the *Dartmouth* to enter and the Committee's countermanding order had in fact been given, would not these probably be mentioned in the *Dartmouth's* log for November 28 or 29? But the log mentions no such orders; the only non-routine matter mentioned is that "at 10 at night [November 28] two Customs-House officers were boarded upon us by the Castle, we being the first ship ever boarded in this manner. . . ."5

Also, when the master of the *Dartmouth,* James Hall, some weeks later (February, 1774) testified before the Privy Council concerning the whole tea affair, would he not have mentioned so interesting and material a circumstance as these orders?6 Yet no such orders are mentioned.

Furthermore, if these alleged orders had been given, would they not have been at least mentioned, if not stressed, by Hutchinson in a letter of December 1, 1773, from him to Governor William Tryon of New York, concerning the recent arrival of the *Dartmouth* and in other surviving letters written by him soon after the destruction of the tea?7 But there is not a word concerning them in any of these letters.

The conduct of the Boston radicals after the *Dartmouth's* arrival also has some bearing on their probable action before she entered port. According to Hutchinson himself, writing in January, 1774, Boston radicals "tried every method they could think of to force the tea back to England."8

There is contemporary evidence that when the *Dartmouth* came into port, a Boston committee ordered it to tie up at a designated dock;9 but this was after the tea on board had become subject to duty by entering the port.10

While questioning the statements of others, I take occasion to correct one of my own. In my "Samuel Adams," *Proceedings of the American Antiquarian Society* Vol. 70 Part 2 (1961) p. 9, I stated that "Hutchinson was pleased that the consignees did not send back the tea to England before it became liable to duty." This statement was based on a letter of Hutchinson as published in Richard Frothingham's "Tea Party," in *Proceedings of the Massachusetts Historical Society* for 1873–1875, reading:

"The day before [a meeting of the provincial Council] one of the ships arrived with 114 chests of tea, and *is* [italics added] below the castle. . . . They [those opposing the landing of the tea] resolved that the tea should be sent back to England. . . . The friends of old Mr. [Richard] Clarke . . . pressed his sons and the other consignees to a full compliance; but they could obtain no more than an offer to suspend the sale of the tea until the East India Company could be made acquainted with the state of affairs. . . . I hope the gentlemen will continue firm, and should not have the least doubt of it, if it was not for the solicitation of the friends of Mr. Clarke [p. 18]."11

I later discovered, upon reading the letter in manuscript, that Hutchinson had not said the vessel "is" below the Castle,12 i.e., had not yet entered the Port of Boston at the time his letter was written. He had, in fact, written that the vessel "anchored" below the Castle, i.e., had anchored there when she first approached Boston, not that she was still there at the time he was writing. Hence, Hutchinson's letter does not justify my statement that even while the *Dartmouth* was still outside the port, he preferred to have her enter port, thus subjecting the tea on board to liability for duty, rather than have her return, with the tea intact, to England.

FIRST APPENDIX TO CHAPTER 20

ELECTION OF DELEGATES FROM PENNSYLVANIA

THE Pennsylvania Assembly's vote to send delegates to the Continental Congress was the culmination of proceedings extending over a period of more than two months.

The committe of nineteen chosen at the mass meeting in Philadelphia on May 20, referred to in Chapter 20, was instructed to ask Governor John Penn to call a special meeting of the Pennsylvania Assembly, which would not otherwise meet until after the date proposed for the assembling of the projected congress.[1]

It is not clear what action, if any, the committee had taken on this instruction when, on June 7, Governor Penn was handed a petition signed by "near nine hundred respectable Freeholders in and near the City of Philadelphia." The petition denounced the Boston Port Act and asked the Governor to call a special session of the Assembly "to devise measures to compose and relieve the anxieties of the people" over this act.[2] On the advice of his Council, the Governor replied that calling the Assembly to meet at this time was neither expedient nor consistent with his duty.[3]

On June 18 a mass meeting in Philadelphia, presided over by Thomas Willing and John Dickinson, passed a resolution denouncing the act closing the Port of Boston as "unconstitutional, oppressive to the inhabitants of that town [and] dangerous to the liberties of the British Colonies." The meeting further resolved that "a Congress of Deputies from the several Colonies in North America is the most probable and proper mode of procuring relief"; and chose a committee consisting of sixteen of the original committee and twenty-eight additional members to take measures "for procuring this Province to be represented at the said Congress. . . ."[4]

Before this enlarged committee had taken action, the Governor, on June 27, referring to reports of an Indian outbreak on the Pennsylvania frontiers, summoned the Assembly to meet in Philadelphia on July 18.[5] Nevertheless, the committee decided to call a convention, and on June 28, issued a circular letter proposing the election of delegates to a convention to meet in Philadelphia on July 15, three days before the Assembly was to meet.[6]

This decision probably was prompted by fear that, because of the grossly disproportionate influence of Quakers over the Assembly,[7] it would either choose delegates to the congress who could be counted on to oppose any measures that might lead to British retaliation and eventually to war,[8] or give the delegates instructions to this same purpose.

The call for a convention was highly successful: seventy-five delegates from all eleven counties of the province and the City of Philadelphia assembled at the Carpenters' Hall in Philadelphia on the appointed day[9] and immediately resolved that "there is an absolute necessity that a Congress of Deputies from the several Colonies be immediately assembled . . . to form a general plan . . . [for] obtaining redress of our grievances. . . ." The convention further resolved that "it is our earnest desire that the Congress should first try the gentler mode of stating our grievances, and making a firm and decent claim of redress . . . , yet, notwithstanding, as an unanimity of counsels and measures is indispensably necessary for the common welfare, if the Congress shall judge agreements of non-importation and non-exportation expedient, the people of this Province will join . . . in such an Association of non-importation from, and non-exportation to, Great Britain, as shall be agreed on at the Congress."[10]

On July 21, the members of the convention approved, and in a body presented to the Assembly, a document requesting it to "appoint a proper number of persons to attend a Congress of Deputies from the several Colonies," with instructions "to agree to any measures that shall be approved by the Congress."[11]

Two days later, the Assembly elected its Speaker, Joseph Galloway,[12] and six other of its members—Samuel Rhoads, Thomas Mifflin,[13] Charles Humphreys, John Morton, George Ross, and Edward Biddle—as delegates to the proposed congress, with instructions to join with those from the other colonies in endeavoring "to form and adopt a plan which shall afford the best prospect of obtaining a redress of American grievances, ascertaining American rights, and establishing that union and harmony which is most essential to the welfare and happiness of both countries," but "to avoid every thing indecent or disrespectful to the mother state."[14]

NEW YORK POLITICS AND THE NEW YORK
DELEGATION TO THE CONGRESS

T HE New York Assembly did not sit from March 19, 1774, to January 10, 1775, and, so far as is known, neither its Speaker, John Cruger, nor any other member of the Assembly made any effort to call a convention to elect delegates to the proposed Continental Congress.

The initiative for the election of a New York delegation was taken by the New York City Committee of Fifty-One, referred to in Chapter 20, which, on July 4, 1774, nominated Philip Livingston, John Alsop, Isaac Lowe, James Duane, and John Jay to represent the City and County of New York,[1] (hereafter referred to as the City) at the proposed Congress. This slate, supported by a "Committee of Mechanics,"[2] was elected on July 28.[3]

The Committee of Fifty-One then sent a circular letter to correspondents in the other thirteen counties of the colony giving the names of the City's delegates and inviting the respective counties to elect delegates of their own or authorize the City's delegates to represent them.[4]

In response to this letter, four of the counties authorized the City's delegation to represent them, and three others elected delegates of their own—Simon Boerum of Kings County, William Floyd of Suffolk County, and Henry Wisner and John Haring of Orange County. But six of New York's fourteen counties failed to elect any delegate or to authorize the City delegation to represent them.[5] Furthermore, not one of the City's large delegation was a member of the Assembly and only one of the other delegations (Boerum) was.[6]

This peculiarity in the inception and composition of the New York delegation stemmed from a train of events reaching back to the dissolution of the New York Assembly on January 2, 1769, and the ensuing general election of a new Assembly —the Assembly still in office in 1774.

The dissolution of the Assembly in 1769 was occasioned by its adoption on December 31, 1768, of resolutions virtually denying the authority of Parliament to pass the New York Suspending Act of 1767 (described in Chapter 4) and instructing the Speaker of the Assembly to make a favorable reply to the Massachusetts circular letter of February, 1768 (described in Chapter 7).[7]

Two days later, the colony's Crown-appointed Governor, Sir Henry Moore, dissolved the Assembly, stating, "The extraordinary nature of certain resolves lately entered on your journals, some flatly repugnant to the laws of Great Britain and others, with an apparent tendency to give offence . . . have put it out of my power to continue this Assembly any longer."[8]

It was suggested (by whom is not clear) that all the old members for New York City—Philip Livingston, James De Lancey, Jacob Walton, and James Jauncey[9]— having lost office for supporting colonial liberty, should be reelected without opposition. But this proposal was not acceptable to a group of Dissenters, who, on January 3 (the day after the dissolution of the old Assembly), held a meeting described in the following letter from William Smith, a leading Presbyterian of the City, to Robert R. Livingston:

"Tuesday evening [January 3] upon a talk that the four old members were to be Set up, there was a Meeting of Delegates of all the Dissenting Churches—a Card was Sent to the other Party consenting that they may Set up two Churchmen & we two dissenters. They answered yesterday at Eleven that they could not comply. . . ."[10]

I have found no evidence as to who attended this meeting or who were the "two dissenters" whom the attendants at the meeting had in mind. One probably was John Morin Scott, a prominent lawyer who had polled a large vote, but was defeated in the election of 1768.[11] Be that as it may, two rival tickets were put forward.

One consisted of the old members, De Lancey, Walton, and Jauncey, and a fourth, John Cruger,[12] connected by marriage with De Lancey and Walton,[13] the other of Livingston, Scott, Livingston's brother, Peter Van Brugh Livingston, and Theodorus Van Wyck. De Lancey and Walton were members of the Church of England, Jauncey was a Presbyterian, and Cruger a member of the Dutch Reformed Church.[14] All four of the "Livingston" ticket were Dissenters. Philip Livingston was a member of the Dutch Reformed· Church,[15] and so was Van Wyck.[16] Scott and Peter Van Brugh Livingston[17] were leading Presbyterians.

All four members of the so-called "Church" or "De Lancey" ticket were elected. De Lancey, who headed it, polled 936 votes to 666 for Philip Livingston, who polled the largest vote of those on his ticket. Even Jauncey, who ran last on the Church ticket, defeated Livingston by over 200 votes.[18]

The victory of this ticket was attributed largely to the disgust of many voters over the attempt of the other ticket to make political capital out of the current furor over a projected Anglican episcopate,[19] described in the appendix to Chapter 7. But, apparently, an important factor in the victory of the De Lancey ticket was the support given it by what Governor Moore described as "a licentious set of Men who call themselves the Sons of Liberty."[20]

So far as is known, the organized body of Sons of Liberty formed at the time of the Stamp Act controversy in 1765–1766[21] no longer existed in New York City at the time of the election in January, 1769.[22] But Isaac Sears,[23] who had been a leader of the Sons of Liberty at the earlier time[24] and publicly supported the De Lancey ticket in the recent election,[25] presumably was among those referred to by Moore. Who else were the Sons he had in mind is obscure. Probably he used the term in a general way to describe those whom he considered overzealous in their opposition to unpopular British measures.

Such zealots would naturally be drawn to the De Lancey ticket on the strength of the voting record of De Lancey, Walton, and Jauncey, compared with that of Philip Livingston and his co-candidates on the only two divisions in the Assembly in 1768 related to the controversy between Great Britain and the colonies.

The first of these divisions stemmed from a demonstration in New York City in November, 1768, against Governor Francis Bernard of Massachusetts and Stephen Greenleaf, sheriff of Suffolk County, Massachusetts, for having tried to evict tenants of a building in Boston to provide quarters for British troops sent there under the circumstances described in Chapter 11.[26] Governor Moore offered a reward for information leading to the arrest and conviction of the ringleaders of the demonstration, and asked the Assembly for a grant of funds to pay the reward.[27] A motion in favor of the grant was carried by a vote of 17 to 5.[28]

The five members voting against the grant included De Lancey, Walton, and

Jauncey. (The other two were John Thomas of Westchester County and Daniel Kissam of Queens County.)

The second vote was on a motion by De Lancey to sharpen the resolution against the New York Suspending Act of 1767, mentioned above, by denouncing this act as "a high infringment of the freedom of the inhabitants of this colony."[29]

The motion was defeated 17 to 6.[30] The six members voting for the motion again included De Lancey, Walton, and Jauncey. (The other three were Thomas, John De Lancey of Westchester Borough, and Eleazor Miller of Suffolk County.)

On the first of these divisions, Philip Livingston, who was presiding as Speaker of the House, did not vote. (When presiding as Speaker, he could vote only to break a tie.) But his nephew, Peter R. Livingston of Livingston Manor,[31] and two of Philip's connections by marriage, Abraham Ten Broeck of Rensselaerwyck Manor and Pierre Van Cortlandt of Cortlandt Manor,[32] voted with the majority.

On the second, these three again voted with the majority and were joined by Philip Livingston, who could now vote because the Assembly was sitting in Committee of the Whole, chaired by another member.

Thus, in the only two divisions in the 1768 Assembly bearing on the controversy with Great Britain, James De Lancey, Walton, and Jauncey had, in each instance, supported the pro-colonial side, while the Livingston partisans had supported the other.

In the first (April) session of the Assembly elected in 1769 there were no votes bearing on the controversy with Great Britain. But one of the votes was interesting in foreshadowing the line-up in the second (October) session of a Livingston group on one side and a group headed by the four New York City members—James De Lancey, Walton, Jauncey, and Cruger—on the other.

Though Philip Livingston was defeated for reelection as a member for New York City, he appeared in the new Assembly as the member for Livingston Manor, Peter R. Livingston having stepped aside for reelection as member for the Manor in the hope that Philip would be reelected Speaker of the Assembly.[33] This hope proved to be ill-founded (Cruger got the plum),[34] and an even greater blow to the Livingstons soon followed.

A few weeks after the April session opened, a motion was made to oust Philip Livingston from the Assembly as ineligible to sit for the Manor under a New York act providing that a member must be a resident of the constituency for which he is elected. This motion was carried 17 to 6.[35]

The six members voting in favor of seating Livingston were Ten Broeck, Van Cortlandt, Philip Schuyler, Jacob Ten Eyck, Jacobus Myndertse (or Mynderse), and Charles De Witt. James De Lancey did not vote on this motion, but the other three members for New York City were among those voting in favor of the ouster.

Even before Philip's ouster, Peter R. Livingston, as evidenced by a letter from him to Schuyler, was contemplating the possiblity of forcing a new election in which the Livingston partisans might regain their ascendancy in the Assembly. Philip's cousin, Judge Robert R. Livingston, had been defeated for reelection as a member of Dutchess County,[36] and the letter referred only to the Judge. But now that Philip, too, had been unseated, there was all the more reason to try to force the new election contemplated by Peter in the hope of all three Livingstons, Philip, Robert R., and Peter, securing election to the Assembly.

"I am extreamly sorry," said Peter, "the Judge[37] did not suceed owing to all the Tenants of Beeckman [Henry Beekman] & R G Livingston's voting against him not withstanding all the pains was taking with them that could be thought necessary.[38] He is determined to try again when ever an oppertunity offers which may be soon if properly managed as no doubt given [giving] the Money so often to the Soldiers will beat up a brise soon, as I am informed some folks say they will not be for given any more, which properly improved may answer the End of another Dissolution. The Money we granted [at the 1768 session of the Assembly][39] has been expended these two months past, and £200 in advance."[40]

Peter evidently had in mind that if the Assembly refused to vote any more funds for furnishing the British troops quartered in New York with the supplies required by the British Quartering Act (described in Chapters 3 and 4), the Governor would be practically forced to dissolve the recently elected Assembly and call for the election of a new one. This would, of course, give the Livingstons another opportunity for possible election.

In November, 1769, Cadwallader Colden, who had recently become Acting Governor of New York upon the death of Moore, requested the Assembly to provide funds for additional supplies required by the Quartering Act.[41] For the past two years, without dissent, the Assembly had voted funds in the treasury for these supplies.[42] But it now voted to grant the supplies[43] exclusively out of currency to be issued under a pending bill for the issuance of paper currency,[44] which Colden could sign only by violating the Currency Act of 1764 (described in Chapter 3). The proposal to grant the required supplies only as thus conditioned was, therefore, in effect a refusal to grant them, a refusal that would virtually make it necessary for Colden to dissolve the Assembly and call for the election of a new.

Before final action on the proposed grant of supplies as thus conditioned, Assemblyman William Nicoll of Suffolk County moved (December 15) for a substitute bill providing for a grant of £2,000, half to be paid in the proposed new currency, but the other half out of funds already in the provincial treasury.[45] This motion to grant £1,000 from funds available in the treasury was carried by 12 votes to 11, as follows:

For the supplies (12)

Jacob Walton	N.Y. City and County
James Jauncey	N.Y. City and County
Captain [James] De Lancey	N.Y. City and County
Mr. Speaker [John Cruger]	N.Y. City and County
Simon Boerum	Kings County
John Rapalje	Kings County
Frederick Philipse	Westchester County
John Thomas	Westchester County
Col. [Benjamin] Seaman	Richmond County
Christopher Billop	Richmond County
William Nicoll	Suffolk County
Leonard Van Kleeck	Dutchess County

Against the supplies (11)

Abraham Ten Broeck	Rensselaerwyk Manor
Pierre Van Cortlandt	Cortlandt Manor
Jacobus Myndertse	Schenectady District
John De Lancey	Westchester Borough[46]
Nathaniel Woodhull	Suffolk County
John De Noyelles	Orange County
Samuel Gale	Orange County
Jacob Ten Eyck	Albany County
Capt. [Zebulon] Seaman	Queens County
Charles De Witt	Ulster County
George Clinton	Ulster County[47]

Schuyler did not vote on Nicoll's motion to grant the £2,000 for supplying the troops. But the other five members who had voted to seat Philip Livingston, namely, Ten Broeck, Van Cortlandt, Myndertse, Ten Eyck, and De Witt, voted against the motion, and, on a later proceeding on the bill, Schuyler voted with them.[48] On the other hand, James De Lancey and the other New York City members, including Cruger, voted solidly in favor of the motion.

The line-up on Nicoll's motion remained almost the same on the final vote on the supply bill, which was carried (December 30) by a vote of 12 to 10.[49] The only changes on the final vote were that John De Lancey switched sides; Daniel Kissam of Queens County, who had not voted on Nicoll's motion, now voted in favor of the appropriation; Thomas now did not vote; and Cruger, sitting as Speaker on the final division, also now did not vote.

By voting solidly in favor of supplying the troops, the New York City members escaped the danger of dissolution and possible defeat at the election of a new Assembly, but at the cost of losing the support of Sears and other ardent Whigs commonly referred to as the Sons of Liberty or Liberty Boys.[50]

Two days after the vote in favor of Nicoll's motion, a handbill, signed "A Son of Liberty," was circulated in New York City, denouncing the New York City members for thus "betraying the common cause of liberty" and asserting that there was a coalition of "the De Lancey family . . . with Mr. [Acting Governor] Colden . . . to secure to them the sovereign lordship of this colony."[51]

At the same time, though the members of the Livingston group failed to secure a majority that would force dissolution of the Assembly, they, instead of the De Lancey group, were now in the position of championing colonial liberty.

During the next few months, Peter R. Livingston, Philip Livingston, Alexander McDougall, an outstanding supporter of the Livingston ticket in the New York City election of 1769,[52] and John Morin Scott, one of the candidates on the Livingston ticket in that election, strengthened this position.

Soon after the clashes between the soldiers and civilians in January, 1770, over destruction of the Liberty Pole (described in the second appendix to Chapter 11), several New Yorkers petitioned the Mayor of the City for permission to erect a new liberty pole on the site of the old or on another suitable piece of city property.[53] The Common Council of the city rejected this petition. Whereupon

Peter R. Livingston came to the fore, offering a strip of land owned by him near the site of the old pole as the site for the new.[54]

Next came the turn of McDougall, Philip Livingston, and Scott to demonstrate their championship of colonial liberty.

Following publication of the Sons of Liberty handbill in December, 1769, the New York Assembly voted this to be "a false, seditious and infamous Libel," and, at the Assembly's request, Colden offered a reward of £100 to anyone who identified the author or authors of the handbill "so that they may be brought to condign Punishment."[55] On February 7, James Parker, printer of the handbill, identified McDougall as the person who had hired him to print it.[56] For some months, McDougall refused to secure release from imprisonment by giving bail, thereby becoming the American John Wilkes.[57] When he finally consented to give bail, one of his two bondsmen was Philip Livingston,[58] and Scott acted as his attorney at the trial.[59]

Peter R. Livingston, too, apparently was active in supporting McDougall, judging from his letter to a Boston correspondent stating that he was "indeavoring to make Capt. McDougall's Cause as popular as possible that in case he should be convicted the fine may be light. . . ."[60]

Members of the Livingston family in the City continued to advance their standing as champions of colonial liberty. They abstained from the movement in 1770 for dilution of the New York merchants' non-importation agreement (described in Chapter 10),[61] and in 1773 Philip acted with Sears and McDougall to try to persuade Governor William Tryon of New York not to protect the landing of the East India Company's tea consigned to New York (described in Chapter 14).[62]

On the other hand, De Lancey and the other New York City members of the Assembly further alienated the supporters of colonial liberty by favoring dilution of the non-importation agreement[63] and by not opposing, openly at least, the landing of the tea.[64]

It is, therefore, understandable that when residents of New York City responded in 1774 to the appeal for an intercolonial congress, they chose Philip Livingston, defeated candidate for the Assembly, as one of their delegates,[65] and did not include a single one of the City's representatives in the Assembly.

MEMBERS OF THE FIRST CONTINENTAL CONGRESS

T HE fifty-six members of the First Continental Congress are listed below
by colonies from north to south and, except in the case of New York, in
order of precedence as stated in the credentials submitted by them to the
Congress.

The few marked with asterisks had not been elected to any colonial Assembly;
the others had served or were serving in the Assembly of their respective colonies
at the time of their election to the Congress. Nine of them—Caswell, Cushing,
Galloway, Hopkins, Philip Livingston, Middleton, Randolph, Rodney, and Tilghman—were currently or had been Speakers.

I point out and emphasize that my statements concerning occupations are
based in some cases on biographical sketches in *Biographical Directory of the
American Congress, Appleton's Cyclopaedia,* or local histories which do not give
the source or sources on which the sketches are based. But though the list may be
inaccurate in detail, it is safe to say that about half of the members were practic-
ing lawyers and the other half a miscellany of businessmen, planters, and farmers.
A number of them also were in part-time public office.

The businesses of those listed as engaged in business were of wide range. Most
of them, including Cushing, Philip Livingston, Alsop, Low, and Mifflin, were
merchants, but Rhoads, for example, was a builder, Humphreys a miller, and
Gadsden a wharfinger. The employment listed is the member's apparent chief
current employment.

Massachusetts
Thomas Cushing, businessman
Samuel Adams, Clerk of Mass. House of Representatives
John Adams, lawyer
Robert Treat Paine, lawyer

New Hampshire
John Folsom, businessman
John Sullivan, lawyer*

Connecticut
Eliphalet Dyer, lawyer
Silas Deane, businessman
Roger Sherman, lawyer

Rhode Island
Stephen Hopkins, businessman
Samuel Ward, businessman

New York (listed in the order of election notice in 4 *Force* I 308, 322n.)
New York City and County
Philip Livingston, businessman

John Alsop, businessman*
Isaac Low, businessman*
James Duane, lawyer*
John Jay, lawyer*
Orange County
  Henry Wisner, businessman
  John Haring, lawyer*
Suffolk County
  William Floyd, farmer*
Kings County
  Simon Boerum, farmer

New Jersey
  James Kinsey, lawyer
  William Livingston, lawyer
  John Dehart, farmer
  Stephen Crane, farmer
  Richard Smith, lawyer

Pennsylvania
  Joseph Galloway, lawyer
  Samuel Rhoads, businessman
  Thomas Mifflin, businessman
  Charles Humphreys, businessman
  John Morton, farmer
  George Ross, lawyer
  Edward Biddle, lawyer
  John Dickinson (added to the Pennsylvania delegation near the close
  of the Congress), lawyer

Delaware
  Caesar Rodney, planter
  Thomas McKean, lawyer
  George Read, lawyer

Maryland
  Matthew Tilghman, planter
  Thomas Johnson, lawyer
  Robert Goldsborough, lawyer
  William Paca, lawyer
  Samuel Chase, lawyer

Virginia
  Peyton Randolph, lawyer
  Richard Henry Lee, planter
  George Washington, planter
  Patrick Henry, lawyer
  Richard Bland, lawyer
  Benjamin Harrison, planter
  Edmund Pendleton, lawyer

North Carolina
   William Hooper, lawyer
   Joseph Hewes, businessman
   Richard Caswell, lawyer

South Carolina
   Henry Middleton, planter
   John Rutledge, lawyer
   Thomas Lynch, planter
   Christopher Gadsden, businessman
   Edward Rutledge, lawyer

FOURTH APPENDIX TO CHAPTER 20

SAMUEL ADAMS' CONDUCT AS COLLECTOR OF TAXES

IN 1773, Thomas Hutchinson, Governor of Massachusetts, wrote of Samuel Adams to Lord Dartmouth, "From large defalcations, as collector of taxes for the town of Boston, . . . his influence was small until within these [past] seven years. . . ."[1] Peter Oliver, former Chief Justice of Massachusetts, wrote in his *Origin and Progress of the American Rebellion,* that Adams "had embezzled the publick Monies of Boston." The Reverend William Gordon, pastor for many years of the Third Congregational Church at Roxbury, Massachusetts, wrote in his *History of the Independence of the United States,* "His [Adams'] necessities probably . . . urged him to supply himself, time after time, from the cash in hand [as Collector of taxes], without attending to the accumulation of the balance against him till called upon to settle."[2]

The evidence bearing on these charges follows.

In May, 1763, a committee of twelve leading citizens of Boston appointed at a recent Boston town meeting "to examine the state of the Town Treasury . . ." made the following report:

"There appear'd to be due the Town from the respective Collectors of Taxes to the 25 of April last, Six thousand eight hundred and four Pounds, but as the said Collectors had not then been paid their Premium [fees] for the Year 1761, which with what will be due to them as Premiums for 1762, amounts to one Thousand and eighty five Pounds four Shillings and six Pence, and as they are to be allowed for the abatements made and to be made in that Year,[3] which the Assessors estimate at about £1,000, the sum really due from them will be four thousand seven hundred and eighteen pounds fifteen shillings and six pence for the taxes of the year 1762. . . .

"Your committee [further] find by certificate from the province treasurer that there is now due to the province for the year 1761, four thousand and thirty two pounds five shillings and seven pence vizt.—

From John Ruddock Esq.	£ 883:10: 4
Mr. Samuel Adams	2179: 1:10
Mr. Jonathan Payson	696:
	4032: 5: 7
And the whole tax for the year 1762	8570:13: 7
	12602:19: 2
which, with the aforesaid sum due [for 1762] to the town treasurer of	4718:15: 6
makes	17321: 4: 8."[4]

In explanation of the above statement, it should be pointed out that the taxes payable by residents of Boston to the Collectors elected by the town were to be apportioned among the town, the province, and the County of Suffolk, of which Boston was the county seat.[5]

So far as appears, no action was taken at this time to enforce payment of the amounts found by the committee to be overdue.

In March, 1765, the town again chose a committee to examine the state of the town treasury. This committee reported the following May that, as of March 21, 1765, the Collectors owed the town £9,878 and the province, £18,126. Most of this was for the year 1764; but Adams owed the town £1,111 for 1763 and the province £3,067 for 1762 and 1763. The committee expressed the opinion that "it would be to the Interest of the Town to take some effectual Measures to have the Taxes collected and paid into the Treasury by the Time fixed by the Town for the payment of the same. . . ."[6] But, again, apparently no action was taken.

Two years later (March 16, 1767), a committee elected to report "respecting the Moneys due to the Town from the present and late Collectors of Taxes," reported debts due from several current or past Collectors and recommended that bonds of office given by the delinquent Collectors "be put in suit" at the July term of court. The chief delinquent was Adams, who owed £1,633 to the town for 1764 and £2,301 to the province for 1763 and 1764.[7]

On June 26, David Jeffries, treasurer of the town of Boston, brought suit against Adams, returnable at the July term of the Court of Common Pleas of Suffolk County on a bond for £5,000 given by him covering his 1764–1765 term of office. The county court gave judgment for Adams, but on appeal, the Massachusetts Superior Court gave judgment against him on March 8, 1768, for £1,463 plus costs of about £5.[8]

Soon afterward (March 14) a Boston town meeting granted petitions from Adams that "Six months be allowed him for Collecting his Taxes, and that the [Town] Treasurer be directed to stay Execution untill that time."[9] On March 22, the town further voted that Harrison Gray, treasurer of the province, be requested to suspend for six months an execution against Adams for 1764 taxes due the province, which had been levied at Gray's order by the sheriff of Suffolk County.[10]

Gray replied to the town's request, "I can appeal to Mr. Adams that I have treated him with great tenderness and delicacy. But as I have delivered to Mr. Sheriff [Stephen Greenleaf] an execution against him . . . I do not think it prudent or safe for me to give Mr. Greenleaf any particular directions concerning it. He no doubt knows his duty; if he fails in the execution of it he alone is recountable."[11]

So far as is known, Greenleaf took no proceedings against Adams.

On March 13, 1769, Adams presented a petition to a Boston town meeting, reciting that from various mishaps to persons owing him taxes, it was "very difficult" for them to pay him, with the result that he "was obliged finally, contrary to his Judgment in ordinary Cases, to make use of the first Money he could collect in a new year to make good the Deficiencys of the year preceding"; that "having satisfyed the Demands of the several [province, county, and town] Treasurers for all the said Years except the last, viz. 1764, the Treasurer of the Province issued Execution against him for said year And afterwards the Town Treasurer, by order of the Town put his bond in suit, & recovered Judgment for the Sum due, but thro' the Indulgence of the Town Execution was stayed."

Adams further stated that he had "lodged with the Selectmen a List of his outstanding Debts, which . . . he verily thinks a true List of Debts"; had "exhibited a State of his Account, by which it appears that the Sum of £1,106.11, together with the said List of Debts, will fully compleat the Sum in which he still remains indebted to the several Treasurers;" and therefore prayed "That the Town would order him final Discharge, upon Condition of his paying the aforesaid sum of £1,106.11 into the Province Treasury, and would also make Choice of some suitable Person to receive said List, upon the Condition aforesaid, & collect the outstanding Taxes therein mentioned."[12]

Adams' petition did not mention the source of the £1,106 offered by him toward settlement of his debt; but probably it came chiefly from a subscription of £1,072 "towards Mr. Adams's debt," made by a number of Boston citizens, including John Hancock, who subscribed one-fourth of the amount.[13]

The town voted in favor of the proposed settlement, and chose Robert Pierpont, one of the sureties on Adams' bond as Collector for 1764, to collect the outstanding tax debts shown on the list submitted by Adams.[14]

Three years later (March 9, 1772), a committee chosen at a Boston town meeting "to make a full enquiry into the state of the Town Treasury and the Debts & Credits of the Town," reported that "from the Information given us by Mr. Robert Pierpont it appears that there is no probability of any part of the sum of £1,149 remaining unpaid of Mr. Adams Debt to the Town will ever be received and paid into the Treasury."[15]

The next and final record on this matter is a vote of a town meeting in March, 1774, directing the town treasurer to write off his books "what Samuel Adams, a late Collector, erroneously stands Debtor for on Town Treasury Books."[16]

Hutchinson's charge that Adams "made defalcation," using "defalcation" in the sense of failing to collect money that he was responsible for collecting,[17] is clearly sustained. But whether Adams' applying money collected for a later year against an earlier year's deficiency in collection constitutes "embezzlement" involves a fine point of law on which opinions probably would differ.[18]

As to the charge that Adams used public funds "to supply himself, time after time, from cash on hand," Gordon gives no evidence to support this, and I have found none. The other is described in the well-known letter of August 11, 1774, from John Andrews, a moderate Whig and Boston merchant, to his brother-in-law, William Barrell of Philadelphia, concerning the outfitting and financing of Adams shortly before he left for Philadelphia as a delegate to the First Continental Congress.

"However some may despise him," wrote Andrews, "he has certainly *very* many friends.[19] For not long since some persons (their names unknown) sent and ask'd his permission to build him a new barn, the old one being decay'd, which was executed in a few days. A second sent to ask leave to repair his house, which was thoroughly effected soon. A third sent to beg the favor of him to call at a taylor's shop and be measur'd for a suit of cloaths. . . . A fourth presented him with a new wig, a fifth with a new Hatt, a sixth with six pair of the best silk hose, a seventh with six pair of fine thread ditto, a eighth with six pair shoes, and a ninth . . . oblig'd him to accept a purse containing 15 or 20 Johannes."[20]

I have not found evidence as to what occasioned Adams' financial difficulties, but judging from an entry in John Adams' diary of December 30, 1772, his cousin's penchant for entertaining friends handsomely and keeping up an elegant appearance may have been his financial undoing.

The diary entry states, "Spent this Evening with Mr. Samuel Adams at his House. . . . He affects to despize Riches, and not to dread Poverty. But no Man is more ambitious of entertaining his Friends handsomely, or of making a decent, elegant Appearance than he. He has lately new covered and glased his House and painted it very neatly, and has new papered, painted and furnished his Rooms. So that You visit at a very genteel House and are very politely received and entertained."[21]

APPENDIX TO CHAPTER 22

GALLOWAY'S PLAN OF UNION

ON September 28, 1774, Joseph Galloway moved and James Duane, John Jay, and Edward Rutledge supported, a resolution envisaging two measures:[1] approval of a Plan of Union[2] between Great Britain and the colonies and adoption of a petition to the King for redress of colonial grievances.

The plan provided for a "grand council" of the thirteen old continental colonies to be elected every three years by the Assemblies of the several colonies, in "proportions" left blank by Galloway, to meet "once in every year, if they shall think it necessary and oftener if occasion should require . . .," and the apointment of a "President General" by the King to "hold his office during the pleasure of the King . . ."

Each of the participating colonies was to "retain its present constitution and powers of regulating and governing its own internal police in all cases whatever"; but the power to legislate in all matters concerning "the general police and affairs of the colonies, in which Great-Britain and the colonies or any of them, the colonies in general, or more than one colony, are in any manner concerned," was to be lodged jointly in Parliament and the Grand Council. Either of these bodies could initiate such legislation, but it would not be valid without the assent of the other.[3]

In his pamphlet, *A Candid Examination of the Mutual Claims of Great Britain and the Colonies,* published a few months after the close of the Congress,[4] Galloway stated that three objections were made to his plan: (1) "The delegates did not come with authority to consent to a political union between the two countries"; (2) "the members of the grand council would be corrupted, and betray the interest of the colonies"; and (3) the plan "deprived the colonial legislatures of a part of their rights."[5]

Probably other reasons contributed to the rejection of the plan, the most obvious of which is the provision in the plan that the several colonial Assemblies should "choose members for the Grand Council in the following proportions."[6] Galloway left the "proportions" blank, but they would have to be filled in to complete the plan, thus reopening the extremely ticklish and potentially disruptive question of whether each colony should have but a single vote, and, if not, how many votes each colony was to have. Furthermore, statements in the *Candid Examination* indicate that Galloway envisaged deferment of other action to secure redress until his plan was considered and acted upon by the King or Parliament or both,[7] a course utterly unacceptable to most members of the Congress.[8]

In the *Candid Examination,* Galloway wrote with particular bitterness of the Congress' having expunged from its minutes all record of his "resolve, Plan, and rule [resolution], referring them to further consideration," which, he believed, was part of a "malevolent" effort to smear him as a tool of Lord North.[9]

There was, however, nothing exceptional in the Congress' expunging the plan and proceedings concerning it from its minutes. All of the rejected motions known from diaries and notes of debates are missing from the journals of the Congress, having probably been expunged by the committee chosen shortly before the Congress rose "to revise the minutes of the Congress."[10]

GRIEVANCES AGAINST THE CROWN

AS brought out in Chapter 23, the Congress' Statement of Rights and Grievances included three grievances against the Crown: (1) abridging the right of the colonists "to assemble, consider of their grievances and petition the King"; (2) "keeping a Standing army in these colonies, in time of peace, without the consent of the legislature in which such army is kept"; and (3) exercising "legislative power in several colonies by a council appointed during pleasure by the crown."

Grounds for the first two complaints are described in Chapters 7 and 9 of this book. The explanation of the third is apparently as follows.

All of the royal colonies had a Council acting both as an advisory body to the Governor and as an Upper House of the Legislature. In all of these, except Massachusetts before 1774, the Council, usually of around twelve members, was appointed by the King or the Crown-appointed Governor pursuant to an order (mandamus) from the King.[1]

The commission from the King appointing the Governor to office authorized him to suspend councilors for 'just cause." It also directed him, in case the Council were reduced to fewer than seven by "suspension . . . or otherwise," to appoint "as many Persons out of the Principal Freeholders, Inhabitants thereof as will make up the full Number of Our said Council to be seven . . . untill either they shall be confirmed by Us, or that by Nomination of Others by Us . . . Our said Council shall have seven or more Persons in it."[2] Instructions from the King added the further direction that councilors were to be persons of "good life, well affected to our government, of good estates and of abilities suitable to their employments."[3]

Labaree *Royal Government* (p. 135) states that councilors "normally served for life," and I have found no evidence to the contrary. But the royal mandamus for the appointment of councilors said nothing as to tenure,[4] and the King himself, as distinguished from the Governor, could, if he so willed, dismiss a councilor with or without "just cause," i.e., at the pleasure of the Crown.[5]

There were occasional conflicts over various bills in all the royal colonies between the Crown-appointed Council and the elected Assembly. But, on the whole, relations between the two Houses had been tolerably amicable except in the Carolinas and Georgia, where they had, from time to time, fought bitterly over various issues.[6]

The most protracted of these conflicts stemmed from resolutions of the South Carolina Assembly (Commons House) at the close of the November–December, 1769, session of the Legislature "That the Public Treasurer do advance the sum of ten thousand five hundred Pounds Currency out of any money in the Treasury to be paid into the Hands of Mr. Speaker . . . [and six other named members of the Assembly] who are to remit the same to Great Britain, for the support of the just and Constitutional Rights and Liberties of the People of Great Britain and America" and "That this House will make provision to reimburse the Public Treasurer the said sum."[7]

The money to be paid pursuant to this resolution was to be sent by the recipients to the Society of the Supporters of the Bill of Rights in England toward payment of the debts of the popular John Wilkes, who was battling to be seated as a member of the British House of Commons to which he had been repeatedly elected for Middlesex County.[8]

The treasurer having obeyed the order, the Assembly included in its next appropriation bill an item to repay him. The Council rejected the bill on the ground that a bill to indemnify the treasurer was in effect a bill for the appropriation of public funds and that it was the right and duty of the Council to refuse to pass a bill including so improper an item as financing Wilkes.[9] Bills repeating this item were passed by the Assembly at every session from 1770 through 1773, and consistently rejected by the Council.[10]

The conflict over this issue was intensified by the character of membership of the Council in South Carolina.

The instructions to Governors of the royal colonies, quoted earlier in this appendix, stated that councilors of the colony were to be chosen from the "Principal Freeholders, Inhabitants thereof."

In most of the colonies, the Council was of this character; but in South Carolina (for reasons not clear) most of those appointed to the Council were persons who were in the colony only because of holding some Crown office there other than their councilorship,[11] and recently a number of Crown officers who were not resident freeholders had been appointed councilors in North Carolina and Georgia.[12]

The seeming intention to have the Crown dominate the Council in the royal colonies was further indicated by a clause of the Massachusetts Regulating Act of 1774. This provided explicitly that members of the Massachusetts Council (previously elected, but thereafter to be appointed by the Crown) were to hold office only "for and during the pleasure of his Majesty . . . ,"[13] thus disabling the King, even if he wished, from granting them commissions on "good behavior" tenure.

In light of these developments, it is understandable that members of the Continental Congress feared that in all the royal colonies, the Council, instead of being a legislative body representing the principal resident landowners of the colony, comparable to the British House of Lords, was to be made a mere creature of the Crown.[14]

THE SUFFOLK COUNTY RESOLVES

THE first of the resolutions adopted by the convention of Suffolk County, Massachusetts, in September, 1774, acknowledges George III to be "our rightful sovereign" and as such "justly entitled to the allegiance . . . of the English colonies in America."

The second states the duty, "by all lawful ways" to "preserve these civil and religious rights and liberties for which, many of our fathers fought, bled and died; and to hand them down entire to future generations."

The third and fourth denounce the recent Boston Port Act and Massachusetts Regulating Act as "gross infractions of those rights to which we are justly entitled by the laws of nature, the British constitution and the charter of this province," and declare that these acts should "be rejected as the attempts of a wicked administration to enslave America."

The fifth and sixth declare that "no regard" be paid to the courts of the province as established under the Massachusetts Regulating Act and that the county "will support and hold harmless" all sheriffs and other officers who refused to execute orders of these "unconstitutional" courts.

The seventh recommends that Collectors of taxes retain all taxes collected by them pending orders from "the proposed provincial Congress," and the sixteenth calls for the assembling of the proposed congress on October 11.

The eighth declares that persons who refused to resign their commissions as members of the Crown-appointed Council under the recent Massachusetts Regulating Act be considered as "incorrigible enemies to the country."

The eleventh advises that militia officers appointed by the royal Governor be supplanted by officers elected by the towns from among persons "who have evidenced themselves the inflexible friends to the liberties of the people" and that all persons qualified for military service "use their utmost diligence to acquaint themselves with the art of war as soon as possible, and do, for that purpose, appear under arms at least once a week."

The twelfth declares that "we are determined to act merely upon the defensive so long as such conduct may be vindicated by reason and the principles of self-preservation, but no longer," and the nineteenth provides for securing help from all parts of the province "should our enemies by any sudden manoeuvres render it necessary to ask the aid and assistance of our brethren. . . ."

The thirteenth recommends that if any person "conspicuous in contending for the violated rights and liberties of their countrymen" were seized, the people should "seize and keep in safe custody every servant of the present tyrannical and unconstitutional government throughout the . . . province until the persons so apprehended be . . . restored safe and uninjured to their respective friends and families."

THE SOLEMN LEAGUE AND COVENANT

ON May 13, 1774, a Boston town meeting chose a committee, headed by Samuel Adams, to take into consideration the Boston Port Act. At a subsequent meeting May 30, the town instructed this committee "to prepare a Paper, to be carried to each Family in the Town . . . [agreeing] not to purchase any Articles of British Manufactures that can be obtained amoung ourselves & that they will purchase Nothing of, but totally desert those who shall Counter-work the Salutary Measures of the Town." Futhermore, the meeting instructed the Boston standing Committee of Correspondence, also headed by Adams, "to communicate the Non Consumption Agreement aforesaid to other Towns in the province."[1]

These resolutions of May 30 obviously were intended to encourage home industry but not to ban the consumption of all articles of British manufacture. The Boston Committee of Correspondence nevertheless sent a circular letter, dated June 8, to towns throughout the province, enclosing a form of agreement, with a covering letter proposing "a solemn league" to be formed by securing the signatures of "all adult persons of both sexes" to the enclosed "form of covenant."

The proposed covenant bound the subscribers "to suspend all commercial intercourse with . . . Great Britain until the said act for blocking up the said harbor [of Boston] be repealed and a full restoration of our charter rights be obtained"; not "to buy, purchase or consume . . . any goods, wares or merchandizes which shall arrive in America from Great Britain aforesaid, from and after the last day of August next ensuing"; and, "after this covenant has been offered to any person and they refuse to sign it," to "withdraw all commercial connexions with them forever, and publish their names to the world."[2]

The proposed covenant, known as the Solemn League and Covenant,[3] was objectionable to the merchants of the province, Whig and Tory alike, because it called for stoppage of all imports from Great Britain, rather than only those competing with home industry and because of the early cut-off date, August 31, specified in the covenant.[4] Even if a merchant immediately wrote his suppliers in Great Britain canceling all orders for goods, much, if not most, of the goods reaching Massachusetts after August 31 would have been shipped before notice of cancellation could reach Great Britain. Consequently, even the most cooperative merchants would be severely penalized by having goods arrive after the deadline, which the covenant would forbid them to sell. Yet it was approved by several Massachusetts county conventions[5] and adopted by many inland towns of the province.[6]

However, the important Boston town meeting of June 27 and 28, discussed in Chapter 26, though expressing confidence in the "upright Intentions" of the Boston Committee of Correspondence and approval of its "honest Zeal," passed no resolution approving the covenant which the Committee had circulated throughout the province.[7]

Following this meeting the Committee of Correspondence of Salem, next to Boston the most important commercial town in the province, wrote a committee at Falmouth (now Portland, Maine) on July 12, recommending suspension of all "measures for a cessation of commerce with Great Britain, till we know the result of the deliberations of the grand american congress . . . because we do not find any of the southern colonies or even Boston itself intend to pursue active measures till then. . . ."[8] At least seven other Massachusetts towns took similar action.[9]

Thus, in large measure, Massachusetts rejected the covenant and fell in line with the other colonies in deferring adoption of a general non-importation and non-consumption agreement pending action by the Continental Congress scheduled to meet in September.

FIRST APPENDIX TO CHAPTER 27

WHO FURNISHED THE INFORMATION ABOUT PROCEEDINGS OF THE CONGRESS?

THE question of who furnished the British Ministry with the information concerning the proceedings in the First Continental Congress mentioned by John Pownall to Thomas Hutchinson, referred to in Chapter 27, has not been and perhaps never will be answered. There is some evidence pointing to John Jay; but for reasons discussed later in this appendix, I believe he was not the source of the Ministry's information.

On February 27, 1775, Franklin wrote from London to his friend Joseph Galloway in Pennsylvania that "it is whisper'd here by ministerial People that yourself and Mr. Jay of New York are Friends of their Measures, and give them private Intelligence of the Views of the Popular or Country Party in America. I do not believe this; but I thought it a Duty of Friendship to acquaint you with the Report."[1]

The same day William Lee, a London merchant, formerly of Virginia, wrote his brother Francis Lightfoot Lee in Virginia, "Jay, one of the delegates from New York to the last Congress, has by letter betrayed its secrets to administration here."[2] But he gave no evidence to support this accusation.

Many years later (1783) the Reverend John Vardill, in a statement to the "Commissioners . . . for enquiring into the losses and services of the American Loyalists," stated that he had "furnished Government with much and valuable information by an exterior correspondence with Congress leaders" named by him,[3] two of whom, Jay and James Duane, were members of the First Congress.

Vardill, formerly of New York, wrote Duane from London on September 15, 1774, while Duane was attending the Congress, "Might I venture to sollicit Mr. Duane's sentiments, digested in his regular, convincing and elegant method, as *communication* of them to Persons in power here might [give me] an Opportunity of being happy by *promoting his interest*."[4] But I have found no evidence that Duane replied to Vardill or in any other way divulged proceedings of the Congress.

Somewhat earlier, Vardill had also written to Jay along somewhat the same lines in a letter delivered to Jay by William Laight, a common friend of his and Vardill. The letter is missing, but the general nature of its contents appears from Jay's reply of September 24, 1775, stating,

"I am obliged to be very reserved on this Subject by the Injunction of Secrecy laid on all the Members of the Congress tho I am aware of the Confidence I might repose in your Prudence. I must nevertheless submit to the Controul of Honor, perhaps on this occasion too delicate. By the next opportunity I hope I shall be able to be more explicit. You may then expect my sentiments at large."[5]

It seems evident that Jay's hope of later being able to be more explicit was based on the expectation that the Congress might lift the ban on secrecy. But, whatever he may have meant, I have found no evidence that he wrote any further letter or letters to Vardill.

In his letter to Vardill of September 24, Jay enclosed a letter to his brother, Sir James Jay, who was in England, with the request that Vardill forward the letter to him.[6] In this letter, which also is missing, Jay, trusting to his brother's discretion, may conceivably have given information concerning proceedings in the Congress, which was passed on to the Ministry by Vardill, Sir James, or someone else. But unless this letter turns up and is found to contain incriminating evidence, it would be unfair to condemn Jay on the strength of William Lee's unsubstantiated charge against him.

Who then, if not Jay, was the person whose "private correspondence" furnished the Ministry with word of "every step" taken by the Congress? Pownall did not say that this person was a member of the Congress,[7] and may have referred to someone outside the Congress who gathered or pretended to gather information as to the proceedings of the Congress and sent it to England.

SECOND APPENDIX TO CHAPTER 27
PEACE NEGOTIATIONS OF
BENJAMIN FRANKLIN

ON December 1, 1774, David Barclay, merchant and banker and a leading English Quaker, called on Benjamin Franklin to discuss a forthcoming meeting of London merchants trading to North America to petition the House of Commons for conciliatory measures.[1] Franklin had remained in London after the hearing before the Privy Council Committee described in Chapter 17, as Agent for the Pennsylvania Assembly, the Massachusetts House of Representatives, and the colonies of New Jersey and Georgia.[2]

In the course of their conversation, Barclay told Franklin he was convinced that most members of the North Ministry wished to avoid a "Civil War" and would be happy "to get out of their present Embarassment on any Terms, only saving the Honour and Dignity of Government." He suggested that Franklin think of some plan of accommodation and then have another meeting with him to discuss the matter.[3] Soon afterward, Franklin received letters from Barclay and another leading English Quaker, the distinguished London physician, Dr. John Fothergill, inviting him to meet them at Fothergill's home on December 4.[4]

At this meeting Fothergill assured Franklin that however violent some of the Ministry might be, others, "he had *good reason* to believe, . . . were differently dispos'd." He asked Franklin to draw up a plan which, if judged reasonable by Barclay and himself, could be "communicated to some of the most moderate among the Ministers, who would consider it with attention."[5]

At a meeting two days later, Franklin presented them with a paper which he called "Hints for Conversation upon the Subject of Terms that might probably produce a durable Union between Britain and the Colonies," the cardinal points of which follow.

1. The destroyed tea was to be paid for; the duty on tea was to be repealed.

2. No money was to be raised in the colonies in time of peace except by the colonies' own Legislatures for the support of their own governments; the colonies to contribute to war expenses according to a suggested formula based on the additional British land tax levied by Parliament for war purposes.

3. The Boston Port Act and Massachusetts Regulating Act were to be repealed.

4. Extension of the Treason Act of Henry VIII to the colonies was to be disclaimed.

5. Admiralty courts in the colonies were to have no wider powers than those exercised by such courts in England,[6] where they had no jurisdiction over alleged violation of acts of Parliament regulating trade.

The would-be peacemakers asked for copies of Franklin's "Hints"; Fothergill said he intended to show his to Lord Dartmouth, whom he had "an Opportunity of seeing daily" and of "whose good Disposition he had a high Opinion," and Barclay asked if he might show his copy to Lord Hyde. Barclay said that, though Hyde was "not in the Ministry properly speaking," he was "a good deal attended to by them," and Franklin, who "knew Lord Hyde a little, and had an Esteem for him," approved Barclay's proposed use of the "Hints."[7]

A few days later, Franklin sent Barclay a revised copy of the "Hints," incorporating changes suggested by Barclay and Fothergill.[8]

On December 22, Barclay informed Franklin that Hyde thought his propositions "too hard,"[9] and Fothergill told Frankin that Dartmouth found "some of them appear'd reasonable, but others were inadmissable or impracticable."[10]

There the matter rested until February 4, 1775, when Barclay and Fothergill resumed negotiations by presenting Franklin with a paper of "Observations" which, they intimated, was approved by the administration. The "Observations" itemized the points in Franklin's "Hints" that were approved outright or conditionally and those disapproved or found inadmissible. Since one of those disapproved was the proposed repeal of the Massachusetts Regulating Act, Franklin told them there could be no agreement, because this act rendered the colonists "unsafe in every Privilege we had a Right to. . . ."[11]

Despite this seeming impasse, Barclay, after talking with Hyde, asked for another conference, at which (February 16) he and Fothergill presented Franklin with a counterplan. This, too, contained no proposal for repeal of the Massachusetts Regulating Act. However, they assured Franklin that the Ministry still "only wanted some . . . Ground on which to found the commencement of conciliatory Measures," and that a petition from the colonial Agents in London engaging the destroyed tea would be paid for if the Boston Port Act were suspended, would furnish the required ground. Franklin replied that it would be impractical to have the Agents jointly make such an engagement, but that he himself would do so "if there were, as they suppos'd, a clear Probability of Good to be done by it. . . ."[12]

Barclay and Fothergill, apparently hopeful that Franklin's offer might lead to something useful, asked to meet him again the following day. But the meeting proved to be fruitless, since there still was no assent to repeal of the Massachusetts Regulating Act.[13]

So far as is known, Franklin heard nothing further from either Barclay or Fothergill until the evening before he left London for America late in March, 1775. He then received a letter from Fothergill asking him to assemble some of the latter's friends and others in Philadelphia and "inform them that, whatever specious Pretences are offered [by the administration] they are all hollow; and that to get a larger Field on which to fatten a Herd of worthless Parasites, is all that is regarded. . . ."[14]

A month earlier, Franklin had written in similar vein to Joseph Galloway concerning the latter's Plan of Union with Great Britain (described in Chapter 22).

"I cannot but apprehend," wrote Franklin, "more Mischief than Benefit from a closer Union; . . . their [the British ruling class'] wide-wasting Prodigity and Profusion is a Gulph that will swallow up every Aid we may distress ourselves to afford them.

"Here Numberless and needless Places, enormous Salaries, Pensions, Perquisites, Bribes . . . false Accounts or no Accounts, and Jobbs, devour all Revenue and

produce continual Necessity in the Midst of natural Plenty. I apprehend, therefore, that to unite us intimately will only be to corrupt and poison us also. It
seems like Mezentius's coupling and binding together the dead and the living.

'Tormenti genus, et sanie taboque fluentes,

Complexu in misero, longâ sic morte necabat.'

However, I would try any thing, and bear any thing that can be borne with
Safety to our just Liberties, rather than engage in a War with such near relations. . . ."[15]

During the progress of the negotiations with Barclay and Fothergill, another
negotiation was opened with Franklin through the good offices of the Honorable
Mrs. Caroline Howe, widow of John Howe, with whom Franklin had recently been
playing chess.[16]

Mrs. Howe (a Howe by birth as well as by marriage) had three brothers notable
in American history. The eldest, Colonel George Augustus Howe, third Viscount
Howe in the Irish peerage, a popular officer in the French and Indian War, was
killed near Fort Ticonderoga during that war. His successor in the peerage was
Admiral Richard Howe, a distinguished member of the House of Commons and
Treasurer of the Navy during part of Rockingham's administration and the whole
of Chatham's. He and his younger brother, General William Howe, are, of course,
well-known figures in the War of the American Revolution.[17]

Mrs. Howe arranged for a meeting between Franklin and Admiral Howe on
Christmas night, at which Howe made an approach similar to Barclay's. He
assured Franklin that "some of the Ministry were extremely well dispos'd to any
reasonable Accomodation, preserving only the Dignity of Government," and asked
for a paper "containing the Terms on which I [Franklin] conceived a good Understanding might be obtained. . . ."[18]

Howe arranged for another meeting three days later, at which he said that
"there was a Communication between him and the Ministry," and he could now
assure Franklin "of a Certainty that there was a sincere Disposition in Lord
North and Lord Dartmouth to accommodate the Differences with America, and to
listen favourably to any Proposition that might have a probable tendency to
answer that salutary Purpose." He added however, that, having seen a copy of the
"Hints" submitted by Franklin to Barclay and Fothergill, he had "reason to think
there was no likelyhood of the Admission of those Propositions."

Howe, therefore, asked Franklin, who had not yet drawn up the requested
paper, to "form some Plan that might be acceptable here." He also threw in
the suggestion that it might be well for the administration to send "a Person
of Rank and Dignity, who had a Character of recognized Candour, Integrity and
Wisdom" to America to try to find "some Means of composing our Differences."[19]

A day or two later, Franklin delivered a paper to Mrs. Howe differing little
in substance from his revised "Hints," but adding the suggestion that the forthcoming Second Continental Congress "be authoriz'd by Government (as was that
held at Albany in 1754) and a Person of Weight and Dignity of Character be
appointed to preside at it on Behalf of the Crown."[20]

On January 2, 1775, Howe reported to Franklin through Mrs. Howe that, having
read this paper, he feared "the desired accommodation threatens to be attended
with much greater difficulty" than he had apprehended, but would, nevertheless,
"forward the propositions as intended."[21]

There the negotiation with Howe rested until February 17, the day after

Franklin had the talk with Barclay and Fothergill at which he made the conditional offer to pay for the destroyed tea, as described earlier. Howe now proposed that Franklin see Hyde, with whom Franklin had not yet talked.[22]

At the ensuing conference on March 1, Franklin found that Hyde had nothing to offer concerning colonial taxation than had been offered in Lord North's motion of February 20, 1775, described in Chapter 27, which was utterly unacceptable.

Franklin also pointed out to Hyde, as he had to Barclay and Fothergill, that the administration had not made any offer at all to settle the "new Dispute . . . rais'd by the Parliament's pretending in the Massachusetts Regulating Act to a power of altering our Charters and establish'd Laws; which was of still more importance to us than their Claim of Taxation, as it set us all adrift, and left us without a privilege we could depend on, but at their Pleasure. . . ."

Hyde replied that, while the administration had "a sincere desire of restoring Harmony with America," they would "never obtain better terms than were now offer'd by Lord North,"[23] thus ending the negotiations.

APPENDIX TO CHAPTER 28

NEW YORK AND THE CONTINENTAL
CONGRESS: 1775

I N January, 1775, Abraham Ten Broeck, member for Rensselaerwyck Manor
in the New York Assembly,[1] moved that the Assembly "take into consideration
the Proceedings of the Continental Congress." This motion was defeated,[2]
as were two subsequent motions relating to the Congress: a motion to thank
the New York delegates to the Congress for "their faithful and judicious discharge
of the trust reposed in them by the good people of this colony"; and a motion to
thank the merchants and other inhabitants of the colony for their firm adherence
to the Association for non-importation, non-exportation, and non-consumption
recommended by the Congress.

A fourth motion relating to the Congress, a motion on February 23 by John
Thomas, a member for Westchester County, to consider "the necessity of appointing Delegates for the Colony to meet with Delegates for other colonies on this
Continent in general Congress," also was defeated. The vote on this motion was
as follows:

For (9)

Philip Schuyler	Albany County
George Clinton	Ulster County
Charles De Witt	Ulster County
Abraham Ten Broeck	Rensselaerwyck Manor
Peter R. Livingston	Livingston Manor
Zebulon Seaman	Queens County ·
John Thomas	Westchester County
Nathaniel Woodhull	Suffolk County
Simon Boerum	Kings County

Against (17)

James De Lancey	New York City and County (Manhattan Island)
Jacob Walton	New York City and County
James Jauncey	New York City and County
Benjamin Seaman	Richmond County (Staten Island)
Christopher Billop	Richmond County
Daniel Kissam	Queens County (Long Island)
John Rapalje	Kings County (Long Island)

William Nicoll	Suffolk County (Long Island)
Crean Brush	Cumberland County (upper New York)
Samuel Wells	Cumberland County
Frederick Philipse (Philips)	Westchester County (lower Hudson Valley)
Isaac Wilkins	Westchester Borough (lower Hudson Valley)
Jacob H. Ten Eyck	Albany County (upper Hudson Valley)
Leonard Van Kleeck	Dutchess County (upper Hudson Valley)
Dirk Brinckerhoff	Dutchess County
Samuel Gale	Orange County (lower Hudson Valley)
John Coe	Orange County[3]

As shown in the second appendix to Chapter 20, describing the election of the New York delegation to the First Continental Congress in 1774, members of the New York Assembly had long been divided into two rather well-defined parties.

The division along party lines now apparently affected the Assembly's vote on Thomas' motion to consider the election of delegates from New York to the Second Continental Congress.

Seventeen of the members who in 1769 had voted on the motion to grant supplies for British troops, as required by the British Quartering Act, now voted on Thomas' motion. Of these, James De Lancey, Walton, Jauncey, Benjamin Seaman, Billop, Rapalje, Nicoll, Philipse, and Van Kleeck had voted for the supplies. Clinton, De Witt, Ten Broeck, Zebulon Seaman, Thomas, Woodhull, and Boerum had voted against furnishing them. Only three now switched from the group with which they had voted on the motion for the supplies. Thomas and Boerum, who had voted for the supplies, now voted in favor of Thomas' motion; Ten Eyck, who voted against the supplies, now voted against Thomas' motion.[4]

Apart from party solidarity or Tory leaning, however, there were weighty reasons for members to vote against approving in their entirety the proceedings of the First Continental Congress and against electing delegates to the Second.

Many moderate Whigs, as well as Tories, in New York thought that the New York delegation to the Congress had gone too far in acquiescing in two measures adopted by the Congress.

The first was the Congress' adoption of the provision in the Association calling for non-exportation as well as non-importation. So far as is known, the New York delegates other than those from New York City and County had made no commitment as to what their stand would be on putting commercial pressure on Great Britain; but four of the five delegates from New York City had clearly implied that they would at most support a ban on importation.[5]

The second was the Congress' resolution virtually approving the fiery Suffolk Resolves,[6] quoted in Chapter 23, which went far toward committing the colonies to support the people of Massachusetts if they resisted British troops trying to enforce the British Acts denounced in these Resolves.

In case of war, New York was likely to be particularly hard hit because so much of the thickly settled part of the colony—Manhattan Island (New York City and County), Staten Island (Richmond county), Long Island (Kings, Queens, and Suffolk Counties),[7] and the Hudson River Valley south of the Highlands—was vulnerable to attack by British warships and British troops operating from, and covered by, them.

By voting not to approve the proceedings of the First Congress and not to send delegates to the Second, New York might possibly escape this danger.

These considerations had just been forcefully brought home to the people of New York in a series of pamphlets[8] published in New York City by the Reverend Samuel Seabury.[9]

In view of the circumstances just described, a member of the New York Assembly who voted against approving the proceedings of the First Congress and electing delegates to the Second did not necessarily identify himself as a Tory. But subsequent proceedings in the New York Assembly brought to light a considerable number of members clearly identifiable as Tories.

On March 3, a committee appointed some weeks earlier "to prepare a statement of the Grievances of this Colony" against Great Britain presented its report.[10] This included a resolution that "it is the opinion of the Committee that his Majesty, and the Parliament have a right to regulate the Trade of the Colonies, and to levy Duties on articles that are imported directly into this Colony from any foreign country or plantation, which may interfere with the Products or Manufactures of Great Britain, or any other parts of his Majesty's Dominions."

As thus phrased, the resolution might be construed to recognize the right of Parliament to levy certain duties for the purpose of raising a revenue, as well as for the regulation of trade. Schuyler therefore moved to amend the resolution by adding, "Excluding every idea of Taxation, internal or external, for the purpose of raising a Revenue on the subjects in America, without their consent." This motion was carried by a vote of 14 to 11.[11]

The vote against it was, in effect, a vote in favor of recognizing the right of Parliament to levy certain import duties for revenue on the colonies and clearly stamped the eleven so voting—Jauncey, Brush, Wilkins, Rapalje, Kissam, Cruger, De Lancey, Billop, Philipse, Wells, and Nicoll—as Tories.

In the end, New York colony sent a delegation to the Second Continental Congress. Soon after the defeat of Thomas' motion, the New York City Committee of Fifty-One (described in Chapter 20) tooks steps to convene a colonywide convention,[12] and on April 22, this convention elected a strong delegation to the Second Congress.[13]

COLONIAL WHIGS AND NEGRO SLAVERY:
1765–1775

DOCTOR Samuel Johnson's familiar quip, "how is it that we hear the loudest yelps for liberty among the drivers of negroes?"[1] was but one of many remarks of the period which pointed to the incongruity between the colonists' outcry against British encroachment on colonial liberty and their continuing to hold tens of thousands of blacks in abject slavery.[2]

Replying in 1765 to the argument of Richard Bland, a leading Virginia Whig, that Parliament had no right to "impose laws upon us . . . relative to our INTERNAL Government," because "Under an English government all men are born free," the Reverend John Camm pointed out the condition of Bland's "own domestics," who were slaves from birth.[3]

In 1767, the Philadelphia Quaker,[4] Anthony Benezet wrote, "At a time when . . . the preservation of those valuable privileges transmitted to us from our ancestors are become so much the subjects of consideration, can it be an inquiry indifferent to any, how many of those who distinguish themselves as the Advocates of Liberty, remain insensible and inattentive to the treatment of thousands of our fellow men, who, from motives of avarice, and the inexorable decree of tyrant custom, are at this very time kept in the deplorable state of slavery. . . ."[5]

In 1773, some Massachusetts slaves wrote a circular letter to members of the Massachusetts House of Representatives, stating, "The efforts made by the Legislature of this province in their last sessions to free themselves from *Slavery*,[6] . . . [we] cannot but expect your House will . . . take our deplorable case into serious consideration, and give us that ample relief, which, *as men,* we have a natural right to."[7]

In this same year, the unidentified author of *Brief Considerations on Slavery,* published in New Jersey, observed, "In the present contest with Great Britain . . . it seems particularly necessary on our parts to convince her that our opposition to her is not merely from selfish motives . . . but from a disinterested generous love to liberty . . . and a conviction that it is the inalienable right of man. But how can she believe this when, so loudly complaining of her attacks on our political liberties, all the colonies tolerate and many of them greatly encourage . . . subjecting the Africans not only to the deprivation of all property, but even to the most abject state of perpetual slavery."[8]

The following year, the Reverend John Allen[9] in his *Watchman's Alarm,* exclaimed, "Blush ye pretended votaries for freedom! ye trifling patriots! who are making . . . a mockery of your profession by trampling on the sacred natural rights and privileges of Africans; for while you are fasting, praying, non-importing, non-exporting, remonstrating, resolving and pleading for a restoration of your charter rights, you at the same time are continuing this lawless, cruel, inhuman and abominable practice of enslaving your fellow creatures. . . ."[10]

Granville Sharp, later the great English anti-slavery leader, wrote (1774) in similar vein of colonial Whigs, "Let them put away *the accursed thing* (that horrid Oppression) from among them, before they presume to implore the interposition of *divine* Justice" for their relief.[11]

About the same time, Abigail Adams was writing to her husband, John, at the First Continental Congress, "I wish most sincerely there was not a Slave in the province. It always appear'd a most iniquitous scheme to me—fight ourselfs for what we are daily robbing and plundering from those who have as good a right to freedom as we have. You know my mind upon this subject."[12]

But John Adams, though he replied to other passages in Abigail's letter, made no mention of her remarks on slavery,[13] and the Congress took no action toward even the gradual abolition of slavery in the colonies.[14]

Probably most of the slaveholders in the Congress shared the sentiments of Patrick Henry, expressed by him in a letter of January 18, 1773, to Robert Pleasants, a Virginia Quaker.

"I take this opportunity [wrote Henry] to acknowledge the receipt of A. Benezets Book against the Slave Trade. I thank you for it. . . . Is it not amazing that, at a time when the Rights of Humanity are defined and understood with precision, in a Country above all others fond of Liberty, . . . we find Men . . . adopting a Principle as repugnant to humanity as it is inconsistent with the Bible and destructive to Liberty.

"Every thinking honest Man rejects it in Speculation, how few in Practise from conscienscious Motives? . . . Would any one believe that I am Master of Slaves of my own purchase! I am drawn along by the general inconvenience of living without them; I will not, I cannot justify it. However culpable my Conduct, I will so far pay my devoir to Virtue as to own the excellence & rectitude of her Precepts, & to lament my want of conforming to them. . . . I know not where to stop; I could say many things on this Subject, a serious review of which gives a gloomy perspective to future times. . . ."[15]

So far as I have found, George Washington was the only slaveowner at the First Continental Congress to make provision to free his slaves.[16] His will, signed in July, 1799, five months before his death, provided for their manumission and support.[17]

What John Adams and other non-slaveholders in the Congress thought about the matter does not appear. Some may have been indifferent; those who were not probably reasoned that it was not a time to raise so potentially divisive a question when unity was of the essence.

The Rhode Island General Assembly apparently was the only colonial legislative body that took any steps at this time to deal with negro slavery, and even its action was feeble.

In May, 1774, a Providence town meeting passed a resolution that "Whereas, the inhabitants of America are engaged in the preservation of their rights and liberties, and, as personal liberty is an essential part of the natural rights of mankind, the Deputies of the town are directed to obtain an act of the General Assembly . . . that all negroes born in the Colony should be free at obtaining to a certain age."[18]

Presumably in response to pressure from the members for Providence, headed by Stephen Hopkins,[19] the Rhode Island Assembly, in June, 1774, passed an act dealing with slavery. But after a high-sounding recital, "Whereas the inhabitants of America are generally engaged in the preservation of their own rights and liberties . . . [and] as those who are desirous of enjoying all the advantages of liberty themselves, should be willing to extend personal liberty to others," the act made no provision whatever toward freeing the slaves already held in the colony.[20]

The act provided only that "for the future, no negro or mulatto slave shall be brought into this colony," and even this ban on future importation was qualified. It was followed by the proviso that "nothing in this act shall extend . . . to any negro or mulatto slave, belonging to any inhabitant of either of the British colonies . . . who shall come into this colony with intention to reside or settle for a number of years, therein . . . ," or "to any negro or mulatto slave brought from the coast of Africa into the West Indies, on board any vessel belonging to this colony, and which negro or mulatto slave could not be disposed of in the West Indies but shall be brought into this colony."[21]

Massachusetts legislators did not go even this far. The slaves' circular letter of 1773 to members of the Massachusetts House of Representatives, quoted earlier in this appendix, apparently was ignored by the House, and, as brought out in Chapter 29, the Massachusetts Congress of 1774 rejected the request to "take into consideration the state and circumstances of the negro slaves in this province."

No wonder that Whig leaders in the colonies had no good answer to Johnson's quip!

APRIL 19th: THE CONFLICT OF EVIDENCE

THE Massachusetts Committee of Safety's brief letter of April 19, quoted in Chapter 32, was supplemented by several other provincial accounts of the day of Lexington and Concord.

The first was a circular letter of the Massachusetts Committee of Safety, sent soon after April 19, to towns throughout the province, stating:

"Gentlemen:—The barbarous murders committed upon our innocent brethren, on Wednesday, the 19th instant, have made it absolutely necessary, that we immediately raise an army to defend our wives and children from the butchering hands of an inhuman soldiery, who, incensed at the obstacles they meet with in their bloody progress, and enraged at being repulsed from the field of slaughter, will, without the least doubt, take the first opportunity in their power, to ravage this devoted county with fire and sword.

"We conjure you, therefore, by all that is sacred, that you give assistance in forming an army. Our all is at stake. Death and devastation are the certain consequences of delay. Every moment is infinitely precious. An hour lost may deluge your country in blood, and entail perpetual slavery upon the few of our posterity who may survive the carnage."[1]

Later in the month, the Massachusetts Congress secured depositions from eyewitnesses of the events of April 19, which it sent (April 26) with an accompanying "true and authentic Account" to the London Agent of the Massachusetts House of Representatives "to be immediately printed and Dispersed thro' every Town in England."[2]

This account told of the killing of eight unresisting men of Lexington and stated, as to "the Ravages of the Troops as they retreated from Concord to Charlestown. . . , Let it suffice to say that a great Number of the Houses on the road were plundered and rendered unfit for Use; several were burnt; Women in child bed were driven by the Soldiery naked into the Streets; old Men peaceably in their Houses were shot dead; and such Scenes exhibited as would disgrace the annals of the most uncivilized Nation."[3]

The provincial version of the events of April 19th, as given in the above documents and in the *Essex Gazette* of April 25, quoted in Chapter 32, conflicts with that of General Gage, also quoted in Chapter 32, on four material points: who fired first at Lexington; who fired first at Concord; alleged American atrocities; and alleged British atrocities.

WHO FIRED FIRST AT LEXINGTON?

The most impressive evidence in support of the provincial version that the British fired first at Lexington are depositions dated April 25, 1775, of Captain John Parker and thirty-four members of the Lexington company of militia under his command. Parker states:

"I, John Parker, of lawful Age and Commander of the Militia in Lexington, do testify and declare, that on the 19th Instant in the Morning, about one of the Clock, being informed that there were a number of Regular Officers, riding up and down the Road, stopping and insulting People as they passed the Road, and also . . . informed that a Number of Regular Troops were on their march from Boston in order to take the Province Stores at Concord, ordered our Militia to meet on the Common in said Lexington to consult what to do, and concluded not to be discovered, nor meddle or make with said Regular Troops (if they should approach) unless they should insult or molest us; and, upon their sudden Approach, I immediately ordered our Militia to disperse and not to fire:[4]—Immediately said Troops made their appearance and rushed furiously, fired upon, and killed eight of our Party without receiving any Provocation from us."[5]

The deposition of the thirty-four members of Parker's company states:

"On the 19th of April instant about one or two o'Clock in the morning, . . . understanding that a body of Regulars were marching from Boston towards Concord, with intent (as it was supposed) to take the Stores, belonging to the Colony, in that town we were alarmed, and having met at the place of our Company's Parade, were dismissed by our Captain, John Parker, for the Present, with orders to be ready to attend at the beat of the drum. . . . About five o'Clock in the morning, hearing our drum beat,[6] we proceeded towards the Parade and soon found a Large body of troops were marching towards us.

"Some of our Company were coming up to the Parade and others had reached it, at which time the Company began to disperse. While our backs were Turned on the Troops, we were fired on by them, and a number of our men were Instantly killed or wounded. Not a Gun was fired by any Person in our Company on the Regulars, to our knowledge, before they fired on us, and they continued Firing until we had all made our Escape."[7]

On the British side, Major John Pitcairn, commander of the British advance party at Lexington, in response to a request from Gage for "the particulars" of the happenings there, wrote:

"When I arrived at the end of the Village, I observed drawn up upon a Green near 200 Rebels; when I came within about One Hundred Yards of them, they began to File off towards some stone Walls on our Right Flank. The Light Infantry observing this, ran after them. I instantly called to the Soldiers not to Fire, but to surround and disarm them, and after several repetitions of those positive Orders to the men, not to Fire etc., some of the Rebels who had jumped over the Wall, Fired Four or Five Shott at the Soldiers, which wounded a man of the Tenth, and my Horse was Wounded in two places, from some quarter or other, and at the same time several Shott were fired from a Meeting House on our Left—upon this, without any order or Regularity, the Light Infantry began a scattering Fire, and continued in that situation for some time, contrary to the repeated orders both of me and the [other] officers that were present."[8]

This version of the firing was corroborated by contemporary statements of two British officers, Lieutenants William Sutherland and John Barker, who apparently were with Pitcairn.

Sutherland said in a statement dated April 26 that "instantly some of the Villains [who] were got over the hedge, fired at us, & it was then & not before that the Soldiers fired. . . ."[9]

Barker's diary for April 19, states that "at about 5 oclock we arrived there [Lexington] and saw a number of People, I believe between 2 and 300, formed on a Common in the middle of the Town; . . . on our coming near them, they fired one or two shots, upon which our Men without any orders rushed in upon them, fired and put 'em to flight. . . ."[10]

At first glance it seems impossible to reconcile the American and British versions of who fired first. But the following statement, dated May 4, of George Leonard suggests that the two versions are in fact reconcilable:

"George Leonard of Boston[11] Deposes that he went from Boston on the nineteenth of april; with the Brigade commanded by Lord Percy upon their march to Lexington; that being on horse back and having no connexion with the army: he several times went forward of the Brigade; in one of which excursions he met with a Countryman who was wounded supported by two others who were arm'd; this was about a mile on this [Boston] side of Lexington meeting House; that the Deponent asked the wounded person what was the matter with him, he answered that the Regulars had shot him; the Deponent then asked what provoked them to do it—he said that Some of our pepol fired upon the Regulars; and they fell on us Like Bull Dogs and killed eight & wounded nineteen.

"He said further that it was not the Company he belonged to that fired but some of our Country pepol that were on the other side of the Road: the Deponent enquired of the other men if they were present; they answered, yes, and Related the affair much as the wounded man had Done: and all three Blamed the rashness of their own pepol for fireing first: and said they supposed now the Regulars would kill every Body they met with."[12]

The deposition of the members of the Lexington militia quoted above states, "Not a gun was fired *by any Person in our Company* [italics added] . . . before they fired on us," and Captain Parker declared, "said Troops . . . fired upon, and killed eight of *our Party*, without receiving any Provocation therefor *from us* [italics added]."

Both these affidavits, it will be observed, leave open the possibility, indeed, even tend to imply that some person or persons not in "our Company," not "of our Party" might have fired first.

WHO FIRED FIRST AT CONCORD?

Convincing the world that the British troops fired first at Concord obviously was of less importance than establishing that they had fired first at Lexington, since few, if any, whose support the Massachusetts patriots were seeking would doubt the rightness of firing on the British troops once they had begun hostilities. But even so, the Massachusetts Congress collected depositions of many eyewitnesses that the British had fired first at Concord, too. The most impressive of these, a deposition dated April 23 of sixteen officers and men of Concord engaged in the fighting there, states:

"We, Nathan Barrett, Captain; Jonathan Farrar, Joseph Butler, and Francis Wheeler, Lieutenants; [etc.] all of Concord, in the County of Middlesex, in the province of the Massachusetts Bay, of Lawfull Age, Testify and Declare, that on Wednesday, the Nineteenth Instant, about an Hour after sun rise, we Assembled on a Hill near the meeting House, in Concord aforesaid, in consequence of an information, that a number of regular Troops had killed six of our Countrymen, at Lexington, and were on their march to said Concord; and about an Hour afterwards, we saw them approaching, to the number, as we Imagine, of about Twelve

Hundred; on which we retreated to a Hill about Eighty rods back, and the aforesaid Troops then took possession of a Hill where we were first posted.

"Presently after this, we saw them moving towards the North Bridge, about one mile from the said meeting House; we then immediately went before them, and passed the bridge just before a party of them to the number of about Two Hundred, arrived. . . . We then seeing several fires in the Town, thought our houses were in Danger, and immediately march'd back towards said bridge, and the troops who were station'd there, observing our approach, march'd back over the bridge, and then took up some of the planks. We then hastened our Steps towards the bridge, and when we had got near the bridge, they fir'd on our men, first three guns, one after the other, and then a Considerable number more; upon which, and not before, (having orders from our Commanding Officer not to fire till we were fired upon) we fir'd upon the regulars, and they retreated."[13]

This deposition was supported by several other depositions of American participants and of a British officer and a British soldier in American hands.[14]

Two other British officers (not held by the Americans) who were present at the first fire at Concord made statements in conflict with each other. Captain Walter S. Laurie of the Forty-third Regiment wrote in a statement dated April 26, "By this time they ["the Country people"] were close upon us, and I imagine myself that a man of my Company (afterwards killed) did fire his piece, tho' Mr. Southerland has since assured me that the Country people first fired. A general popping from them ensued. The Company of the 4th Regt. gave a fire, as did a few of my own. . . ," while Lieutenant Sutherland wrote on April 26, "the Enemy [at Concord bridge] . . . fired a few shot which our men returned. . . ."[15]

The weight of evidence on this point obviously is in favor of the American version.

THE AMERICAN "ATROCITIES"

Smith's account of the events of April 19, sent by Gage to Lord Dartmouth, states: "It appears that . . . they scalped and otherwise ill-treated one or two of the men who were either killed or severely wounded. . . ." Colonel Lord Percy reported that "the Rebels . . . scalped & cut off the ears of some of the wounded men who fell into their hands." Anne Hulton, sister of one of the Customs Commissioners at Boston, wrote a friend in England, "The Troops . . . found two or three of their people Lying in the Agonies of Death, scalp'd & their Noses and ears cut off & Eyes bored out."[16]

The only known contemporary or near contemporary account by an American of the mangling of the British soldier or soldiers at Concord is that of Reverend William Gordon, pastor of the Congregational church of the third parish of Roxbury, who after a visit to Concord a few weeks after April 19, wrote an unidentified correspondent (May 17, 1775):

"The Reverend Mr. Emerson informed me how the matter was, with great concern for its having happened. A young fellow coming over the bridge in order to join the country people, and seeing the soldier wounded and attempting to get up, not being under the feelings of humanity, very barbarously broke his skull, and let out his brains with a small axe, (apprehended of the tomahawk kind) but as to his being scalped and having his ears cut off, there was nothing in it. The poor object lived an hour or two before he expired."[17]

THE BRITISH "ATROCITIES"

The shocking account of alleged British atrocities in the *Essex Gazette* of April 25, quoted in Chapter 32, was repeated word for word in a "Narrative" published by the Second Massachusetts Congress in May, 1775,[18] and in substance in the account sent to London by the Massachusetts Congress quoted above.

The British "atrocities" also were described in several letters published in British newspapers in June, 1775, and in a horrifying letter of April 23 from Wethersfield, Connecticut, which apparently did not reach the British press.

The *London Evening Post* of June 17 carried a Boston letter of April 22, reporting that of the more than forty Americans killed, "the greater part were murthered by the troops going into their houses to steal their effects. *The Gazetteer and New Daily Advertiser* (London) of June 16 carried a Boston letter of April 23 stating that "the troops broke into every house [along their line of march] and put all the males to the sword, and plundered the houses." *Lloyd's Evening Post* (London) of June 21 published a letter from a "Gentlemen of Rank in New England," dated April 25, declaring that having "gone over the whole of the ground of the late engagement," he had seen "some homes that had been set on fire, and some old men, women and children that had been killed." The Wethersfield letter reported, "In one house a woman and seven children were slaughtered" by a soldiery guilty of "cruelties and barbarity, never equalled by the Savages of America."[19]

The reports of extensive plundering were true.[20] And so were those concerning the burning of many houses.[21] But the Americans were using houses along the road as cover from which to fire on the passing British troops,[22] and the houses burned may well have been among those from which the provincials were firing or had fired.

As to the other alleged British atrocities, the depositions gathered by the Second Massachusetts Congress cited only the following: Two old, unarmed men were stabbed and clubbed to death[23] and one woman in bed with a very young infant was forced to leave the house with her infant for fear of being burned to death when the house was set on fire.[24] There is no evidence in the depositions of any children being killed, wounded, or molested. Moreover, even the adults mentioned—the two unarmed old men and the woman in child bed—may have been in houses from which the Americans had fired.[25]

The truth seems to be that, though guilty of much plundering, the British troops otherwise behaved with remarkable restraint.

NOTES

INTRODUCTION

1. The colonial uprising of 1765–1766 is described in many books, including Knollenberg *Origin* 221–237, 373–380, Morgan *Stamp Act* 88–252, and Maier *Resistance* 51–96.

2. This act was 5 Geo. III ch. 12, Pickering *Statutes* XXVII 20. (Unless otherwise stated, my source for all acts of Parliament cited or quoted is Pickering *Statutes.*) John Adams wrote in his diary for Dec. 18, 1765, that this act made "People, even to the lowest Ranks, . . . more attentive to their Liberties, more inquisitive about them and more determined to defend them than . . . ever before," *Adams Papers* I 263.

3. The subsequent history of the other disturbing measures is given in the first appendix to this chapter or will appear in later chapters of this book.

4. This act was 6 Geo. III ch. 12 (1766). It remained intact until amended in effect by the Renunciation Act of 1778, 18 Geo. III ch. 12, declaring that henceforth Parliament would not impose any tax or duty on the American colonies except for regulation of commerce.

5. The undocumented statements here and later in this chapter are documented in later chapters of this book.

6. My estimate of British voters is based on data in Namier and Brooke *Commons* I 2–461, and of British population on sources cited in Knollenberg *Origin* 298n.

7. Evidence of the King's support of British taxation of the colonies: George III's memorandum of March, 1763, *Bute* 201–202, and letters and memorandum of the King from 1766 to 1775 cited in later chapters.

8. Franklin to Charles Thomson March 18, 1770, Smyth *Franklin* V 253. (Thomson as addressee is identified in Crane *Franklin's Letters to Press* 209.)

9. I discuss colonial Whigs and Tories (Loyalists) before and during the Revolutionary War in the second appendix to this chapter. Suffice to say here that I classify as Whigs in the period before the war the colonists who denied the right of Parliament to pass acts taxing the colonies and, when colonial petitions for repeal of the tax acts failed, favored putting commercial pressure on Parliament to secure repeal.

10. *Conn. Colonial Records* XII 299, 653–671.

11. Gov. Thomas Fitch to Jackson Dec. 7, 1764, *Fitch* II 304–305.

12. The Petition or Address is published in *Bowdoin-Temple Papers* 32–36. The circumstances of its adoption Nov. 3, 1764, are described in Knollenberg *Origin* 200–201, 364.

13. Thomas Cushing, Speaker, to Jasper Mauduit, London Agent, Nov. 12, 1764, *Mauduit* 167.

14. Knollenberg *Origin* 204–206, 210, 213, 215–218, 229, 365, 369–372, 376; and Morgan *Stamp Act passim.*

15. *Franklin* XIII 129–162 at 139; 144–145.

16. Circular instruction of the Crown to colonial Governors, May 5, 1732, with subsequent modifications, Labaree *Instructions* I 146–147.

17. P. 756. The accuracy of these figures even as rough estimates has been questioned; but I have found no reason to doubt that they correctly reflect the relative population of the several colonies or that the total of around 2 million whites and blacks in 1770 given in the table is roughly correct.

18. The outline in this chapter deals exclusively with irritants affecting, directly or indirectly, all thirteen colonies; additional irritants affecting only one or a few colonies are discussed in subsequent chapters or appendixes.

19. Franklin to William Franklin March 22, 1775, quoting what he had recently said to Lord Hyde, Smyth *Franklin* VI 392–393.

20. Instruction from the Crown in 1732 and subsequent years, Labaree *Instructions* I 146–147.

21. Franklin to William Franklin March 22, 1775, quoting what he had recently said to Lord Hyde, Smyth *Franklin* VI 392.

22. Wolfe to Lord George Sackville (later, Germain) May 12 and Aug. 7, 1758, Willson *Wolfe* 364, 392.

23. Percy to Northumberland July 27, 1774, *Percy* 28–29.

24. Grant in the Commons Feb. 2, 1775, 4 *Force* I 1542. As to Grant and his important role in both the French and Indian War and the American Revolution, Grant *James Grant, passim.*

25. Sandwich in the Lords March 16, 1775, 4 *Force* I 1681. Though the Duke of Richmond and several other English friends of the colonists predicted they would put up a stiff fight, I have found no evidence that any member of the Cabinet thought so, until after word of the Battle of Bunker Hill reached London.

26. To Lord North Feb. 15, 1775, *Geo. III* III 175. Further evidence of British contempt of colonial troops and the probable explanation for this are given in Chapter 30.

27. Had war been averted at this time, might Great Britain and its North American colonies eventually have reached a settlement without war? I think not. I believe Parliament might at some point have relinquished colonial taxation for revenue, but not restriction of colonial trade, which would have become increasingly vexing as the colonists in North America increased in population, wealth, and a sense of self-reliance and destiny. But who can say?

CHAPTER 1

1. The Stamp Act, 5 Geo. III ch. 12 (1765), is published in full in Pickering *Statutes* XXVI 179–204 and, with important omissions, in Macdonald *Documentary Source Book* 123–132, Morgan *Prologue* 35–43, and other collections of documents relating to the American Revolution.

2. Evidence collected in Knollenberg *Origin* 275–281 indicates that George III's illness at the time of the passage of the Stamp Act was pleurisy or another respiratory illness, not as generally stated, insanity. (Macalpin and Hunter "The 'Insanity' of George III" conclude that the King's illness was porphyria.)

3. Passage of the Stamp Act and its nullification in the colonies, Knollenberg *Origin* 221–237 and Morgan *Stamp Act* 119–257.

4. The Stamp Act Congress of Oct. 7–24, 1765, Niles *Principles* 155–169; Morgan *Stamp Act* 103–111.

5. The colonial merchants' movement including non-importation agreements to put pressure on British commercial interests to secure repeal of the Stamp Act, Schlesinger *Col. Merchants* 77–91; Andrews "Boston Merchants" 198–201; Baxter *Hancock* 237. The N.Y. merchants' non-importation agreement, Oct. 31, 1765, is in Jensen *Eng. Hist. Doc.* 671–672.

6. George Grenville's statement on enforcement of the Stamp Act July 30, 1765, *Grenville* III 215–216. In a similar vein, Grenville moved in the House of Commons Dec. 17 to add to a proposed Address to the King words to express the House's indignation over the "Insurrections" in North America and "assure His Majesty that his faithful Commons . . . will firmly and effectively support . . . Measures . . . for enforcing . . . Obedience to the Laws. . . ."

7. Sketch of Lord Rockingham's career to 1765, Guttridge *Rockingham* 11–43.

8. Three years earlier, in a talk with Cumberland, Newcastle had mentioned his age as an objection to his heading a new Ministry, Newcastle's memorandum of Oct. 3, 1762, covering a recent talk with Cumberland, Namier *England* 407. He had also at that time told his friend the Duke of Devonshire that if he was to have office again he would prefer "the Privy Seal," Newcastle's memorandum of Aug. 2, 1762, covering a recent talk with Devonshire. The latter, rather than Rockingham, might well have been chosen head of the new Ministry if he had been living and in good health, but, after a long illness, he had died in October, 1764.

9. As to the new Ministry's hope of securing Pitt's support, Newcastle to White, June 29, 1765, *Newcastle* 32, Duke of Grafton to Pitt Aug. 20, 1765, *Grafton* 57.

10. Pitt had had a bitter political dispute with Newcastle in 1761 and was later offended with him on other grounds. As to the dispute in 1761, sources cited in Knollenberg *Origin* 288; as to later grounds of offense or supposed offense, Pitt to Newcastle Oct. 13, 1763, *Pitt* II 260; Newcastle to White June 19, 1764, Add. Mss 32960:17–19; and Pitt to Newcastle Oct. (no day) 1764, *Pitt* II 297.

11. Sketch of Henry S. Conway in *D.N.B.* A biography of him is much needed. As to his Leadership in the House of Commons, Conway to Lord Hertford Nov. 7, 1765, speaking as "Leader of the Commons," Lewis Coll.; correspondence between Conway and the King Dec. 17, 1765, to June 3, 1766, *Geo. III* I 201–353 *passim*. As to the responsibility of the Secretary of State for the Southern Department for colonial affairs, Knollenberg *Origin* 47.

12. Conway's opposition to the proposed stamp tax, speech of Feb. 15, 1765, Jared Ingersoll to Gov. Thomas Fitch of Conn. March 6, *Fitch* II 334; *Boston Gazette* June 5; *Maryland Gazette* June 13; *Georgia Gazette* Aug. 1.

13. I assume that the persons named were of the Cabinet because their offices customarily carried Cabinet rank, but a letter of Newcastle to White Dec. 3, 1765,

indicates that Winchilsea was not included in the Cabinet at that time, *Newcastle* 40. William Dowdeswell, Chancellor of the Exchequer, Charles Yorke, the Attorney-General, and Charles Townshend, Paymaster-General, were important members of the Ministry, Guttridge *Rockingham* 46–48, but I have found no evidence of their having been members of the Cabinet in the Rockingham Ministry.

14. Grafton later said that Cumberland "was present at all our Council's" *Grafton* 55. Contemporary evidence of his participation: Rockingham to Newcastle July 25, 1765, "R.R.H. [His Royal Highness] will come up for Monday's Conciliabulum," Add. Mss. 32968:241; Cabinet meetings to be held at his house, Aug. 13 and 30, *same* 32969:207 and 257; Rockingham to Cumberland Oct. 20, asking for his "directions," *Rockingham* I 242; and Augustus Hervey to Grenville Nov. 2, stating that Cumberland was to have attended a "Council . . . about American affairs" the night he died, *Grenville* III 105.

15. Conway's pacific letter of Oct. 24, 1765, to Gov. Francis Bernard of Mass. concerning calling for military aid, *Barrington–Bernard Corresp.* 241–242, and the similar circular letter to Governors other than Bernard, e.g., Conway to Gov. Fitch of Conn. Oct. 24, *Fitch* II 362–363. On the same day Conway wrote Gen. Thomas Gage and Admiral Lord Colville, commanding the British land and naval forces in North America, in a similarly pacific strain, *Gage* II 29; *Barrington–Bernard Corresp.* 242.

16. Decision at meeting of the Privy Council Committee on Plantation Affairs Oct. 22, 1765, foreshadowing the tenor of Conway's letter of Oct. 24, P.C. 2:111:386 (P.R.O.) digested in *Acts P.C.* IV 733. As to Grantham (Thomas Robinson) and his relations with Newcastle, *D.N.B.* Newcastle to Rockingham Oct. 12, regretting his, Newcastle's, inability to attend "our" meeting tomorrow night, the object of which he supposed was "upon the American Disputes," presumably refers to a Cabinet meeting. I have found no evidence of what occurred there.

17. George Cooke to Pitt Dec. 5, 1765, concerning Newcastle's statement as to the Ministry's disposition favorable to the colonists concerning the Stamp Act, *Pitt* II 338–340. The King, too, at this time favored a conciliatory policy toward the colonies, as appears from a letter of his to Conway, Dec. 5, 1765, stating that dealing with the colonial opposition to the stamp tax "requires more deliberation, candour [charity] and temper [good temper] than I fear it will meet with," *Rockingham* I 256–257.

18. Pitt to Cooke, Dec. 5, 1765, rejecting Newcastle's overture and refusing to disclose his position as to repeal of the Stamp Act, *Pitt* II 343.

19. As to the Ministry's perplexity caused by news of the outbreak at New York, Newcastle to Rockingham Dec. 10, 1765, George Onslow to Newcastle Dec. 11, and Rockingham to Newcastle Dec. 12, Add. Mss. 32973: 190, 202, and 214; William Bollan to Hutchinson Dec. 26, Mass. Arch. XXV 43–43a; Charles Garth to S.C. Comm. of Corresp. Dec. 25, Garth Papers, S.C. Hist. Soc.

20. Letters of Gen. Gage of Nov. 4 and 8, 1765, reporting the outbreak in New York City from Oct. 31 to Nov. 5, were received Dec. 10 and 11, *Gage* I 71, 73.

21. Lord Northington to the King Dec. 12, 1765, concerning the discussion of what to do about the Stamp Act at a meeting which he considered to be a Cabinet meeting the night before, *Geo. III* I 428–429. Northington was in favor of enforcement, the others "seemed to be" against, *same* 429.

22. The King's speech and the proposed noncommittal replies of the two Houses of Parliament, Dec. 17, 1765, *Journals H. of C.* XXX 437. (The King's speeches and the Houses' replies, were known to be prepared by, and reflective of, the policy of the Cabinet.)

23. Grenville's motion Dec. 17, 1765, to amend the proposed Commons' reply to the King's speech, *same* 437–438. The fact that Grenville proposed the amendment is stated in Conway to the King Dec. 17, *Geo. III* I 201–202.

24. Discussion and withdrawal of Grenville's motion, *same.*

25. Motion by Lord Suffolk in the House of Lords Dec. 17, 1765, and its support by the Duke of Bedford and his supporters, including Lords Gower and Sandwich, Hugh Hamersley to Gov. Horatio Sharpe of Md. Dec. 20, *Sharpe* III 244; Rockingham to the King Dec. 17 *Geo. III* I 203, with Namier *Additions* 42; and *Journals H. of L.* XXXI 227. Grafton, Lord Dartmouth, President of the Board of Trade, and Lord Shelburne, a follower of Pitt, spoke against the amendment, Hamersley to Sharpe Dec. 20, *Sharpe* III 248, Rockingham to the King Dec. 17, *George III* I 203, and Shelburne to Pitt, *Pitt* II 354—355.

26. Suffolk's motion defeated 80 to 24, Rockingham to the King Dec. 17, 1765, *Geo. III* I 203, with Namier *Additions* 42.

27. Northington's statement in the House of Lords Dec. 17, 1765, Hamersley to Sharpe *Sharpe* III 247, 249.

28. Charles Townshend's statement in the House of Commons on Dec. 17, 1765, Hamersley to Sharpe Dec. 20, *same* 249, and Cooke to Pitt Dec. 17, *Pitt* II 351.

29. Newcastle to Rockingham Jan. 1, 1766, concerning the meeting of Rockingham, Lord Egmont, and others on Dec. 27, Add. Mss. 32973: 3–4. Newcastle's words were "the last, or the Two last, I hear, were strongly objected to by Lord Egmont and Mr. Conway."

30. Rockingham to Newcastle Jan. 2, 1766, as to attendees and developments at a recent political dinner, *same* 11–13.

31. As to the Declaratory Act relating to Ireland, 6 Geo. I ch. 5 (1719), Knollenberg *Origin,* 160, 348, 380–381.

32. As to the proposed amendment, Benjamin Franklin stated in an undated memorandum that the proposal was to restrict the stamp tax "to a stamp on commissions for profitable offices and on cards and dice," Smyth *Franklin* X 231, but I have found no confirmation of this. As to suspension, Franklin had suggested to Dartmouth Nov. 6, 1765, "to suspend the execution of the act for a term of years . . . , then drop it on some decent pretence," Franklin to William Franklin Nov. 9, Niles *Principles* 475.

33. Rockingham to Newcastle Jan. 2, 1766, as to division in the Ministry and sending Thomas Townshend to talk with Pitt, Add. Mss. 32973: 11–13. Though Rockingham mentioned only Charles Yorke and Lord Northington as initially opposed to repeal, the Chancellor of the Exchequer, William Dowdeswell, was also reputed to have favored modification rather than repeal, Harris "Debates," quoted in Namier and Brooke *Commons* II 333.

34. Newcastle's reply to Rockingham Jan. 3, 1766, favoring repeal on commercial grounds and deprecating the proposed Declaratory Act, Add. Mss. 32973: 25. To same effect, Newcastle to John White June 28, *Newcastle* 75. Newcastle had written Rockingham in a somewhat similar vein in a letter of Oct. 12, 1765,

stating "I see . . . very little Effect by supporting the Execution of the last act of parliament for laying on the Stamp Duty, by force . . . ," Rockingham Papers.

35. Thomas Townshend's unsuccessful mission to Pitt, Pitt's terms, Newcastle's offer to resign, and the King's refusal to treat with Pitt on his terms, Newcastle to John Page, Jan. 7, 1766, Add. Mss. 32973:55; the King to Northington Jan. 9, *Geo. III* I 216–217; the King to Lord Bute [Jan. 10] *Bute* 243.

36. The King's Address and the proposed replies of Jan. 14, 1766, *Parl. Hist.* XVI 90–96.

37. Speech in House of Commons Jan. 14, 1766, of Robert Nugent (created Viscount Clare and Baron Nugent in 1767 and Earl Nugent in 1776), supporting colonial taxation by Parliament.

38. Pitt's reply Jan. 14, 1766, to Nugent, *Parl. Hist.* XVI 96–100. It is not entirely clear from this and other reports of Pitt's speeches on Jan. 14 precisely where he stood on the issue of British taxation of the colonies. Apparently he maintained that Parliament had no right to levy any kind of tax for revenue on the colonies, but that duties imposed for the regulation of trade were not taxes and that Parliament had the right to impose such duties on the colonies.

39. Grenville's speech of Jan. 14, 1766, in favor of the Stamp Act and Pitt's reply, *same* XVI 101–108. Other accounts of Pitt's speeches on Jan. 14, William *Pitt* II 346; Garth to S.C. Comm. of Corresp. Jan. 19, *So. Car. Hist. Mag.* XXVI (1925) 68–73; Lord George Sackville to Gen. John Irwin, Jan. 17, 1766, *Stopford* I 104; Franklin undated report, Smyth *Franklin* IV 405–408.

40. Rockingham to the King Jan. 15, 1766, as to Pitt's "amazing power and influence," *Rockingham* I 270.

41. Rockingham to Charles Yorke as to the decision to propose repeal of the Stamp Act and an accompanying Declaratory Act, Add. Mss. 35430:31. This letter is dated "Sunday night, near 1 o'clock, January 17th 1766," but, as pointed out in Namier & Brooke *Townshend* 139, "Sunday" was the 19th not the 17th and the letter presumably was written early in the morning of Jan. 20. The quotation from the letter in *same* 139–140 is inaccurate but substantially correct.

42. The proposed resolution (undated) for a Declaratory Act quoted in the text, *Rockingham* I 287.

43. Rockingham to Yorke Jan. 25, 1766, concerning Yorke's suggested change quoted in the text, *same* 287. Yorke's suggestion probably was intended to counteract Pitt's statement in the House of Commons Jan. 14, 1766, that "Taxation is no part of the governing or legislative power," *Parl. Hist.* XVI 99. A second postscript in Yorke's reply, Jan. 25, to Rockingham's letter indicates that he still thought his proposed change in wording on this point should be adopted, Rockingham Papers. (The partial quotation from this letter in *Rockingham* I 288 is garbled and misleading.)

44. Rockingham's objection to Yorke's proposed change in wording of the proposed Declaratory Act, Rockingham to Yorke, *same* 287. I suppose an important reason for Rockingham's objection was fear that the mention specifically of taxation would offend Pitt. This is unquestionably true of Rockingham's objection to a suggestion by Yorke that the word "undoubted" be inserted before the word "right" in another of the proposed resolutions, *same* 287.

45. The act as passed differed from the resolution only in dropping the word "a" before "right" and inserting "Subjects of the Crown of Great Britain" after "America."

46. The King's preference for modification, rather than repeal, of the Stamp Act is discussed in Chapter 2. I have found no evidence as to the kind and extent of modification he had in mind.

47. The King's intention to support the Ministry's plan is indicated in a letter from him to Rockingham, Jan. 21, 1766, stating "Talbot is as right as I can desire on the Stamp Act; strong for our declaring our right but willing to repeal . . . ," *Geo. III* I 244. "Talbot" was Lord Talbot (William Earl Talbot), Steward of the royal household. (Talbot later voted against the resolution for repeal, giving as his reason that "he must in conscience be against repeal," Newcastle to White in a letter begun Feb. 27, *Newcastle* 50.)

CHAPTER 2

1. Presentation to the House of Commons Jan. 27, 1766, by George Cooke, a follower of William Pitt, of the Stamp Act Congress' petition, *Journals H. of C.* XXX 499–500, with Lord George Sackville to Gen. John Irwin Jan. 31, *Stopford* I 105–106. A memorial of the Congress to the Lords was withheld because "nothing of that Sort can be presented to them but under the designation of an Humble Petition," Joseph Sherwood to Gov. Samuel Ward of R.I. March 13, Kimball *R.I.* II 383; Dennys De Berdt to Samuel White Feb. 15, 1766, Matthews "De Berdt" 312.

2. Pitt's speech in support of the petition and its rejection, Sackville to Irwin, Jan. 31, 1766, *Stopford* I 105–106; Henry S. Conway to the King Jan. 28, *Geo. III* I 246; Charles Garth to Md. Comm. of Corresp. Feb. 26 and March 5, *Md. Hist. Mag.* VI (1911) 283–289; Lord Hardwicke to Charles Yorke Jan. 28, *Rockingham* I 290; William Rouet to Baron Mure *Caldwell* Part 2, II 65.

3. The proposed declaratory resolution Feb. 3, 1766, *Rockingham* I 287. It is not in the journals of the Houses of this date because their proceedings when sitting in committee were not officially recorded. The Duke of Grafton introduced the proposed resolution in the Lords, Lord Rockingham to the King Feb. 3, *same* 253, and Conway in the Commons, Garth to S.C. Comm. of Corresp. Feb. 9, *So. Car. Hist. Mag.* XXVI (1925) 76. (Namier and Brooke *Commons* II 483–485 has a sketch of Charles Garth, who was a member of Parliament, as well as London Agent for the S.C. Commons House.)

4. Lord Camden's speech Feb. 3 (misdated Feb. 10), 1766, against the resolution for a Declaratory Act on the ground that the authority of Parliament was subject to constitutional limitations, *Parl. Hist.* XVI 168. However, Camden later said that since Parliament had declared its unlimited auhority to legislate for the colonies, "he did not think himself, or any man else, at liberty to call it in question," William S. Johnson to Roger Sherman Sept. 28, 1768, quoting Camden, Quincy *Reports* 516–517.

5. Lord Chancellor Northington's statement that "Every government can arbitrarily impose laws on all its subjects . . . ," *Parl. Hist.* XVI 170, put in a nutshell the view voiced by all those opposing Camden's position. This doctrine had been recently popularized by another distinguished member of Parliament in

1766, William Blackstone, whose *Commentaries* (I 162) asserted, "So long therefore as the English constitution lasts, we may venture to affirm that the power of parliament is absolute and without control."

6. Debate and vote in Lords Feb. 3, 1766, on the proposed declaratory resolution, Rockingham to the King Feb. 3, and Grafton to the King Feb. 4, *Geo. III* I 253, 254; report of the debate (misdated Feb. 10), *Parl. Hist.* XVI 167–177; Rouet to Mure Feb. 4, *Caldwell* Part 2 II 68–70; Hugh Hamersley to Gov. Horatio Sharpe of Md. Feb. 20, *Sharpe* III 262–272; Philip Francis to a "Mr. Allen" Feb. 4, *Francis Letters* I 73–75.

7. The names of the five lords voting against the resolution for the Declaratory Act, Rockingham to the King, Feb. 3, 1766, *Geo. III* I 253. All were attached directly, or through Shelburne, to Pitt. Cornwallis was the Cornwallis who surrendered at Yorktown in 1781. Shelburne, Earl of Shelburne in the Irish peerage, and Baron Wycombe in the English, was customarily referred to by his higher title, but in the journals of the British House of Lords was designated by his lower title, Wycombe.

8. Conway, in debates on the Stamp Act in 1765, had denied Parliament's authority to tax the colonies, Knollenberg *Origin* 225, 374. He now conceded this authority, but held it should be exercised "in the most extraordinary cases only," Garth to S.C. Comm. of Corresp. Feb. 9, 1767, *So. Car. Hist. Mag.* XXVI (1925) 77.

9. The debates in the Commons Feb. 3, 1766, on the proposed declaratory resolution, Conway to the King Feb. 4, 1766, *Geo. III* I 254–255; Rouet to Mure Feb. 4, *Caldwell* Part 2 II 70; Grey Cooper's notes, *A.H.R.* XVII (1912) 565–574; Nathaniel Ryder's notes for Feb. 3, Gipson "The Great Debate" 14–21; Garth to S.C. Comm. of Corresp. Feb. 9, *So. Car. Hist. Mag.* XXVI (1925) 76–86. Namier and Brooke *Commons* has sketches of Isaac Barré, William Beckford, and James Hewett. Edmund Burke apparently hedged, questioning the wisdom of the bill, but voting for it, *Burke* I 242–243, 242n.

10. Barré's motion seconded by Pitt Feb. 3, 1766, to amend the proposed declaratory resolution by striking out the words "in all cases whatsoever," Garth to S.C. Comm. of Corresp. Feb. 9, 1766, *So. Car. Hist. Mag.* XXV (1925) 77; Grey Cooper's notes for Feb. 3, *A.H.R.* XVII (1912) 571, 572–3; Conway to the King Feb. 4, *Geo. III* I 254.

11. Defeat of Barré's motion and adoption of the proposed declaratory resolution without a division, Rouet to Mure Feb. 4, 1766, *Caldwell* Part 2 II 70; Conway to the King Feb. 4, *Geo. III* I 254. Conway supposed there would not have been as many as four votes against the resolution if there had been a division. Garth wrote the S.C. Comm. of Corresp. Feb. 9, "I believe from the Sound there were not more than ten dissenting voices," *So. Car. Hist. Mag.* XXVI (1925) 84. To same effect, Garth to the Md. Comm. Corresp. March 5, *Md. Hist. Mag.* VI 291–302.

12. The collateral resolutions and the proceedings in the two Houses from February 4 to 7, 1766, referred to in the text, can be followed in the documents cited in the three immediately preceding notes, together with *Rockingham* I 286; *Geo. III* I 255–256, 261–264; *Grenville* III 357–358; *Stopford* I 106–107; *Newcastle* 47; Gipson *Brit. Empire* X 390–392; and, most fully, in Gipson "The Great Debate" 22–31.

13. Introduction and proceedings in the House of Commons on the bill for a Declaratory Act, Feb. 26–March 4, 1766, *Journals H. of C.* XXX 609, 612, 615, 621, 626–627.

14. Introduction in the House of Lords March 5, 1766, of bill for the Declaratory Act and proceedings on it March 5, 7, and 10, *Journals H. of L.* XXXI 291, 297, 300.

15. Camden's speech was made at some point in the proceedings on the bill March 5–10, 1766. Rockingham to the King March 10, mentions a debate on the preamble to the bill in the Lords but does not mention Camden, *Geo. III* I 278. Charlemont to Flood March 13, Rodd *Charlemont* 14; Hamersley to Sharpe March 22, *Sharpe* III 279; and *Parl. Hist.* XVI 178–182 at 178 give Camden's speech. Further details, letters of William Gerard Hamilton to John Calcraft March 5–13, all misdated by the editor three weeks too early, *Pitt* II 378–386.

16. The Lord's passage of the bill for the Declaratory Act March 11, 1766, *Journals H. of L.* XXXI 302.

17. Led by the merchants of New York City, two hundred of whom signed an agreement Oct. 31, 1765, not to buy any goods shipped from Great Britain after Jan. 1, 1766, until the Stamp Act was repealed, the merchants of Philadelphia and Boston, some weeks later, entered into similar agreements, Schlesinger *Col. Merchants* 78–80. The *London Chronicle* of Dec. 17 reported a threatened loss of £700,000 sterling from the countermanding of orders of goods from Great Britain.

18. As to debts of British North American colonies of "upwards of four millions," *Annual Register* for 1766, 32; "*five Millions* Sterling," Henry Cruger, Jr., to Henry Cruger, Sr., Feb. 14, *R.I. Commerce* I 140; "upwards of Four Millions Sterling," *St. James Chronicle* Feb. 15, 1766; over £4,450,000, undated memorandum, Bayse *Board of Trade* 152n; and Jensen *Hist. Doc.* 688; "Six Millions sterling," Dennys De Berdt to Lord Dartmouth, undated, *Col. Soc. Public.* XIII 441. Evidence as to the loss of trade and that only repeal would restore colonial good will is given in later footnotes.

19. London merchants' petition, undated, *Parl. Hist.* XVI 133–135, probably adopted at a meeting headed by Alderman Barlow Trecothick of London Dec. 4, 1765, *Gentleman's Mag.* for Dec. 1765 (Vol. 35) 588. As to Trecothick, who spent some years in Boston and married a Boston girl (Grizzel Apthorp), Jervey "Trecothick" and passages indexed under "Trecothick, Barlow" in Foote *King's Chapel* II 672 and Beavan *Aldermen* II cvii.

20. "General Letter from Comm. of North American Merchants to the outports & to the manufacturing Towns, December 6, 1765," Wentworth–Fitzwilliam Manuscripts. An undated note is appended stating: "N.B. This Letter concerted between the Marquess of R. & Mr. Trecothick [was] the principal Instrument in the happy repeal of the stamp act which without giving up the British authority quieted the Empire." The letter is published with unimportant differences in Morgan *Prologue* 129.

21. Henry Cruger, Jr., of Bristol, England to Aaron Lopez, March 1, 1766, concerning unauthorized delay in filling his order, so as to put pressure on British manufacturers, *R.I. Commerce* I 145. Cruger, American born, wrote his father Henry Cruger, Sr., of New York City, Feb. 14, "I was three Weeks in London, and every Day with some one Member of Parliament, talking [for repeal] as it were for

my own Life," *same* 139. The great importance of the colonial trade to Bristol, Minchinton *Bristol passim* and Minchinton "Stamp Act Crisis" 145–153, the latter of which (152–153) brings out the activities of Bristol merchants for repeal.

22. Many petitions from merchants and manufacturers throughout Great Britain, particularly one printed Jan. 17, 1766, from London merchants, as to loss of colonial trade, *Parl. Hist.* XVI 135–136. As to Edmund Burke's importance in this connection, Sutherland "Burke" 62–65.

23. The names of many, but not all, of the witnesses in the House of Commons, including Trecothick, Capel Hanbury, and George Hayley of London, William Reeve of Bristol, and John Glasford of Glasgow, are listed in *Journals H. of C.* XXX 513. The testimony of Trecothick, Reeve, and Glasford is in Jensen *Eng. Col. Doc.* 686–691. See also Gipson "The Great Debate" 31–33.

24. Benjamin Franklin's testimony before the House of Commons Feb. 13, 1766, that the colonists did not object in principle to external taxes, *Franklin* XIII 124–162 at 139, 144, 156. See also Gipson "The Great Debate" 34–35; Morgan "Colonial Ideas of Parl. Power"; and Van Doren *Franklin* 336–353. As to Franklin's testimony greatly contributing to the repeal of the Stamp Act, *Pa. Mag. Hist.* X (1886) 96–97; Sparks *Franklin* VII 312n; Crane *Franklin's Letters to Press* 73–74.

25. Richard Jackson wrote Gov. Francis Bernard March 15, 1766, "I endeavored to shew in the House of Commons, that in all ages and nations a difference has been made and felt . . . between external and internal taxes . . . ," Bradford *Mass. Papers* 73. As to Jackson's career in the House of Commons from 1762 to 1784, Namier and Brooke *Commons* II 669–672, and as to his colonial agencies, the dozens of references to him listed under "Jackson, Richard" in the indexes of Knollenberg *Origin;* Kammen *Agents;* and Sosin *Agents.*

26. Diary of Thomas Hollis Oct. 13, 1765, to Feb. 8, 1766, recording payments to Noah Thomas, manager of the *St. James Chronicle.* Hollis "gave him his Clue" and paid him "four Guineas more to keep him steady," Hollis' Diary, Institute, Williamsburg, Va. For pro-colonial articles in the *St. James Chronicle* from Oct. 26, 1765, to Feb. 13, 1766, Hinkhouse *Preliminaries* 62, 63, 65. As to Hollis, Robbins "Hollis" 406–453; Robbins *Commonwealthman* 260–360 *passim;* Knollenberg "Hollis and Mayhew" 102–193.

27. Cadwallader Colden to Grenville Oct. 22, 1768, reporting what Major Thomas James had told him, *Colden* 1877, 177. I believe Colden's statement was substantially true because it explains the otherwise puzzling conduct of James in having testified against himself in the House of Commons as reported in James to Colden, undated but evidently February or March, 1766, *same* 1923, 99.

28. The effort of Grenville, the Duke of Bedford, and Lord Bute, acting through the Duke of York, to enlist the King's support to block repeal, Bedford's undated memorandum covering proceedings from Jan. 31 to Feb. 19, 1766 (erroneously entitled "Minutes Made By H.R.H. The Duke of York"), *Bedford* III 326–329, with a Memorandum of York Feb. 18, and York's reply of Feb. 18, *Geo. III* I 272–273.

29. The King to York Feb. 18, 1766, declining to intervene as quoted in the text, *same* 273. The King's statement to York supports the following statement of Lord Hillsborough, a former member of the Cabinet, to Thomas Hutchinson, as recorded in Hutchinson's diary for Feb. 17, 1775: "The King . . . always will leave

his own sentiments, and conform to his Ministers, tho' he will argue with them, and very sensibly; but if they adhere to their own opinion, he will say—'Well . . . then let it be'," Hutchinson *Diary* I 378.

30. Resolution for a bill to repeal the Stamp Act, Feb. 21, 1766, Conway to the King, Feb. 22, *same* 273–274. Garth to S.C. Comm. of Corresp., Feb. 22, 1766, *So. Car. Hist. Mag.* XXVI 90. Garth says Conway introduced the resolution, *same;* Hamersley to Sharpe Feb. 25, *Sharpe* III 274 says it was Burke. Since Garth was a member of the House of Commons and active in the proceedings for repeal and Hamersley was not a member, I follow Garth's version.

31. Burke's impressive speech in favor of repeal, Rouet to Mure Feb. 22, *Caldwell* Part 2 II 73–74; Lord Charlemont to Henry Flood, date not given, *Pitt* II 390–391n; Richard Burke, Sr., to James Barry, Feb. 11, and John Rindge to Edmund and William Burke about March 1, *Burke* 238, 242–243. As to Burke and Rockingham, *same* xxi.

32. Debate on resolution for repeal in the House of Commons sitting in Committee of the Whole, Feb. 21, Conway to the King Feb. 22, *Geo. III* I 273–274; Hamersley to Sharpe Feb. 25, *Sharpe* III 274; Ryder's notes, Feb. 21 and 22, Gipson "The Great Debate" 35–39.

33. Conway to Lord Hertford Feb. 12, 1766, concerning the King's statements, quoted in the text, W. S. Lewis Collection, Farmington Conn. Other documents relating to this matter: the King to Rockingham Jan. 21, *Geo. III* I 244; Lord Harcourt's statement of Jan. 30, quoted in George Grenville's diary Jan. 31, *Grenville* III 353; John Offley to Rockingham Feb. 11 and undated memoranda by the King, *Rockingham* I 300–302; John Cruger, Jr., to John Cruger, Sr., Feb. 14, *R.I. Commerce* I 141; Duke of Newcastle to John White April 1, *Newcastle* 51–52.

34. Rouet to Mure Feb. 18, 1766, as to puzzlement of those desiring to know the King's "secret wishes" as to repeal, *Caldwell* Part 2, II 73. Rouet wrote Mure Feb. 22 that most of those who had just voted for repeal did so "because they clearly saw that no amendments at all would make the colonys accept the Act, and thereby we should only be exposed to new insults upon Government; but might expect to be better prepared to repell such audacious conduct upon any future occasion," *same* 74.

35. List of sixty-eight placemen in the House of Commons voting against repeal, Winstanley *Government* 304–305.

36. Of 558, 442, or about 80%, of the members of the House of Commons voted on the resolution of Feb. 21, 1766, for repeal, Namier *Structure* (1957) 154. Two hundred seven members of the House of Commons elected in 1761 held Crown places, Namier *Eng.* 262, and probably the number was substantially the same in 1766. If the proportion of placemen voting was the same as that of the House as a whole, 166 placemen voted. Deducting the 68 placemen known to have voted against repeal, leaves 98 voting for repeal.

37. The resolution for repeal adopted in Committee of the Whole by 275 to 167, "after Two this morning" on Feb. 22, 1766, Conway to the King Feb. 22, *Geo. III* I 273–274. The vote was on a motion by Charles Jenkinson, a follower of Grenville, to substitute "explain and Amend" for "repeal," William Baker to William Talbot Feb. 25, Watson "Baker" 261–262; Garth to S.C. Comm. of Corresp. Feb. 22, *So. Car. Hist. Mag.* XXVI 90. Namier *Structure* I 187 has an interesting analysis of the vote on the basis of English, Scottish, and Welsh constituencies.

38. A motion to recommit the resolution when introduced into the House in regular session was defeated Feb. 24, 1766, by 240 to 133, *Journals H. of C.* XXX 602. This motion, made by James Oswald, and two other dilatory motions by Lord Strange and Justice William Blackstone, are mentioned in Conway to the King Feb. 25, *Geo. III* I 276 and discussed in Baker to Talbot Feb. 25, Watson "Baker" 263–264.

39. The repeal bill was introduced Feb. 26, *Journals H. of C.* XXX 609. Rockingham tried again at this time to persuade Pitt to join him, but when Pitt demanded full power to form whatever Cabinet he pleased (Shelburne to Pitt and Pitt's reply, both on Feb. 24, 1766, *Shelburne* I 377–381; Thomas Nuthall to Pitt Feb. 26, reporting a conversation he had just had with Rockingham, Pitt's reply of Feb. 27 and Nuthall's letter of Feb. 28, repeating a further talk with Rockingham, *Chatham* II 397–400), efforts to form an alliance with Pitt apparently ceased.

40. Passage of the repeal bill by the House of Commons March 4, 1766, 250 to 122, Conway to the King March 5, *Geo. III* I 277. Of the fifty-two members who were merchants, only six voted against repeal, Namier *Eng.* 295.

41. Motion March 11, 1766, that the bill for repeal of the Stamp Act be committed, *Journals H. of L.* XXXI 303.

42. The only report I have seen of the debate March 11, 1766, on the bill for repeal is Lord Hardwicke's undated report in *A.H.R.* XVII (1912) 579–586, beginning "*Duke of Newcastle* moves." This report covers the debate on the proposed Declaratory Act (577–578), as well as the debate on the bill for repeal.

43. Hardwicke's undated report on Grafton's motion for commitment of the bill for repeal, including objection by Lord Coventry to the bill and Newcastle's reply in favor of it, *same* XVII (1912) 579–586. Rockingham to the King March 12, gives a list of the speakers, *Geo. III* I 280–281. Hardwicke voted for repeal only "from the necessity of the times," Hardwicke's undated narrative, *Rockingham* I 284–285, and Lord Chesterfield wrote his son, Philip Stanhope, March 17, that he voted for repeal because he "saw more inconveniences from enforcing, than from repealing it," *Chesterfield* I 447.

44. Northington's argument is given in Hardwicke's report, *same* 582–583 and in Edmund Burke to Charles O'Hara March 11, *Burke* I 244. Sackville wrote Irwin March 11, that "many will be influenced with the danger that would attend continuing this tax after the Commons had repealed it by so great a majority," *Stopford* 108.

45. Arguments of Lords Sandwich, Halifax, Suffolk, Lyttelton, and Mansfield March 11, 1766, against repeal of the Stamp Act, Hardwicke's report, *A.H.R.* XVII 580–585. For other references to this day's debate on repeal, William Gerard Hamilton to John Calcraft March 12 [misdated Feb. 19] *Pitt* II 384 and Newcastle to White, April 1, *Newcastle* 52. A more elaborate statement of Lyttelton's speech is in Phillimore *Lyttelton* I 692–703.

46. Statement signed by thirty-three Lords, giving their reasons for voting against repeal, *Parl. Hist.* XVI 181–187.

47. Newcastle wrote White April 1, 1766, that the King had informed the Archbishop of Canterbury (Thomas Secker) that he favored repeal, "of which the Archbishop had made very good use of with the bench [of bishops]," *Newcastle* 52. For other pertinent developments between March 5 and 11, Hamilton to Calcraft March 5–13 (all misdated by the editor three weeks too early) *Pitt* II 378–386.

48. The Lords vote on March 11, 1766, in favor of committing the bill for repeal, 105 to 71, counting proxies, Rockingham to the King March 12, *Geo. III* I 281. Passage without a division, March 17, *Journals H. of L.* XXXI 311.

49. The Repeal Act, 6 Geo. III ch. 11, and the Declaratory Act, 6 Geo. III ch. 12, were assented to by the King March 18, 1766, *same* XXXI 314. The Declaratory Act of 1766 followed the wording of a similar act relating to Ireland, 6 Geo. I ch. 5 (1720), with the addition in the Act of 1766 of the words "in all cases whatsoever." The difference in intent between the Declaratory Act and a superficially similar provision of the Statute of Frauds of 1696 (7 and 8 William III ch. 22 sec. 9) is discussed in the appendix to this chapter.

50. The indemnity act canceling penalties for violations of the Stamp Act was 6 Geo. III ch. 51 (1766). On Feb. 5, 1766, Grenville proposed a resolution for such an act, but with the added words "under proper restrictions," Ryder's notes for Feb. 5, Gipson "Great Debate" 25. Grenville had apparently intended this limitation to relieve only those who now paid the stamp taxes previously payable, and the bill for the act as introduced into the House sitting in the Committee of the Whole contained such a provision, but it was struck out, Thomas Whately to Grenville May 24, *Grenville* III 239.

51. The obsolescence of the Crown's prerogative of veto and its last exercise over legislation, Everett "Last Royal Veto" 156–163. The King's control over a large number of lucrative places for which members of Parliament or their adherents were eligible and over the conferring of highly prized honors, notably the creation of peers, gave him immense influence in Parliament, especially the House of Lords. But he exercised this kind of control over legislation as a political boss, not as a detached reviewer of legislation submitted to him for approval.

CHAPTER 3

1. The quotations from the English merchants' circular letter of Feb. 28, 1766, *M.H.S. Proc.* 55 (1922) 215–217. This was followed by a letter from fifty-five British merchants to John Hancock, dated March 18, reporting the repeal of the Stamp Act, *same* 217–220.

2. Benjamin Franklin wrote Joseph Galloway June 13, 1767, of complaints from English merchants that the circular letters sent by them "to the Merchants of the several Colonies, containing their best and most friendly Advice were either answered with unkind Reflections, or contemptuously left without answer," and that the captain of a vessel sent to the colonies to spread the good news of repeal of the Stamp Act was "every where treated with Neglect and Contempt instead of Civility and Hospitality . . . ," Labaree *Franklin* XIV (1970) 183.

3. Mason's forecast that Englishmen would later maintain that repeal of the stamp tax had encouraged the colonists' "impudence" in opposing subsequent British measures proved to be correct. This thesis was maintained repeatedly in later years.

4. George Mason's letter of June 6, 1766, signed "A Virginia Planter," quoted in the text, Rowland *Mason* I 381–389. The letter, published in the London Public Ledger of Sept. 4, 1766, probably is the one referred to in Thomas Whately to George Grenville Sept. 6, as a "very saucy paper from America," *Grenville* III 315. Another able reply, undated, signed "A British American," is in *Gentleman's Mag.* XXXVI (1766) 612–616.

5. Reports of colonial rejoicing over repeal of the Stamp Act are in all the colonial newspapers for May and June, 1766. See also Charles Thomson of Pa. to Benjamin Franklin May 20, *Thomson Papers* 15–16; Gov. William Bull of S.C. to Henry S. Conway June 9, *Prior Documents* 93; Diary of John Rowe of Mass. May 19 and 23, *Rowe* 95, 97; Joseph Galloway of Pa. to Franklin, May 23, Sparks *Franklin* VII 318; Gen. Thomas Gage at New York May 28, and Gov. Samuel Ward of R.I. July 19, to Conway, *Gage* I 92, and *Prior Documents* 102–103; William Nelson of Va. to John Norton, July 25, *Norton* 14; sermons in 1766, Love *Fast and Thanksgiving Days* 331–333; Gipson *Brit. Empire* XI 4–6.

6. Sec. 4 of 6 Geo. III ch. 52 (1766) levied colonial import duty of a penny a gallon on molasses, including molasses imported from the British West Indian colonies into the British North American colonies, which, from 1769 to 1774 yielded a gross revenue averaging over £14,000 a year, Channing *History* 90n.

7. The Quartering Acts of 1765 and 1766, 5 Geo. III ch. 33 and 6 Geo. III ch. 18, are described in Chapter 4.

8. The colonial currency act of 1764 was 4 Geo. III ch. 53. The history of this act and efforts to secure its amendment are described in Ferguson "Currency Finance" 177–180; Greene and Jellison "Currency Act" 485–518; *Quest For Power* 387–397; Sosin "Paper Money" 174–198; Ernst "Currency Act Repeal" 177–211. The act was amended in 1770 by 10 Geo. III ch. 35 permitting N.Y. to issue paper money tenderable in payment of taxes and other obligations owed to the colony itself and in 1773 by a similar act, 13 Geo. III ch. 57, applying to all but the New England colonies.

9. The act of 24 Geo. II ch. 53 (1751) prohibited the New England colonies from issuing paper currency tenderable in payment of private debts, but permitted the issue of paper currency redeemable in two years, tenderable in payment of taxes or other debts owed the issuing colony.

10. Sec. 1 of the Act of 1764 levied duties on colonial imports of sugar, indigo, coffee, wine, silk, calico, cambric, and French lawn. The rates of duty indicate that some of the duties were primarily for revenue, others primarily to restrict colonial trade. (The duties on silk, calico, cambric, and French lawn were repealed in 1766 by 6 Geo. III sec. 2; the others were retained.) Sec. 13 of the Act of 1764 also in effect levied a duty on many products of continental Europe or the East Indies, reexported from Great Britain to the colonies, by repealing a refund of British import duly previously allowed on most of such products.

11. British restriction of colonial trade before the American Act of 1764 has been dealt with in many books and articles including, among the more recent, Egnal and Ernst "Economic Interpretation of the Am. Revolution" *W.&M.Q.* XXIX (1972) 3–32; Barrow *Trade* 1–185, "Background to the Grenville Program" 93–104, and "English Point of View" 125–139; Knollenberg *Origin* 168–175, 263–268, 352–356, 389–392. Older works on the subject are cited in these books and articles.

12. The restrictions on colonial exports imposed by the Navigation Act of 1660 and subsequent acts before 1764 are described in Knollenberg *Origin* 168–171, 352–353.

13. Secs. 27 and 28 of the act of 4 Geo. III ch. 15 (1764), hereinafter called the American Act of 1764, imposed the additional restrictions on exports described in the text. (The act was amended by sec. 22 of the act of 5 Geo. III ch. 45 (1765)

to permit the exportation of iron and lumber to Ireland and lumber to Madeira, the Azores, and continental Europe south of Cape Finisterre.) The genesis of the American Act of 1764, Barrow "Background to the Grenville Program" 93–102; Barrow *Trade* 174–181, 314–315; Knollenberg *Origin* 358.

14. The restrictions on colonial imports imposed by the Navigation Act of 1663, with subsequent amendments, are described in *same* 168–169, 352.

15. Importance of colonial trade direct with Madeira, the Azores, and the Canaries, *same* 263–264, 389–390; Bezanson *Prices* 231–237; index to White *Beekman Papers* III under "Wines-Madeira" and "Wines-Fayal, Teneriffe and Vidonia"; and Huntley "Seaboard Trade of Va." 304–305.

16. Sec. 1 of the Act of 1764 levied a duty of £7 sterling a ton on direct importation into the colonies of "wine of the growth of the Madeira, or of any other island or place from whence such may be lawfully imported," whereas, if imported through Great Britain, the duty was £4—ten shillings payable in the colonies under sec. 1, plus three pounds ten shillings payable in Great Britain under sec. 12.

17. The extremely complicated "old subsidy" (import duties) and drawback (refund) of duties allowed on reexportation of the dutied imports are described in Saxby *The British Customs* 3–12.

18. Sec. 13 of the Act of 1764 provided that "no part of the rate or duty, commonly called *The old subsidy,* shall be repaid or drawn back for any . . . goods of the growth, production or manufacture of . . . the East Indies which shall be exported from this kingdom to any British colony or plantation in America. . . ."

19. Sec. 9 of the Hovering Act of 1763, 3 Geo. III ch. 22, authorized the seizure of vessels of fifty tons or less hovering off the coasts of the colonies. I have found little evidence of enforcement of this section of the act. The intimation in Syrett and Johnson's "The New York Affair" that the cargo condemned in that case was condemned under the "hovering statute" (p. 449) is, I think, erroneous if, as therein stated, the carrying vessel was "over fifty tons burden."

20. Sec. 4 of the Hovering Act of 1763 provided for use of the navy in colonial waters "for the more effectual prevention of the infamous practice of smuggling" and for the distribution of part of the proceeds from the sale of condemned seizures among "the officers and seamen employed in such service" for their "better encouragement . . . to do their duty therein." This section was amended by 4 Geo. III ch. 15 (1764) and 5 Geo. III ch. 45 (1765) to clear up ambiguities.

21. The names of the twenty British naval vessels assigned to North America, together with their stations, are listed in the *Providence Gazette* of Sept. 24, 1763. The ships' arrivals at their respective stations are noted from time to time in colonial newspapers and correspondence from Oct., 1763, to Jan., 1764, e.g., *Newport Mercury* from Nov. 21, 1763, to Jan. 2, 1764, *Providence Gazette* from Oct. 22 to Jan. 2, 1764, Gov. Cadwallader Colden of N.Y. to Admiral Lord Colville Nov. 12, 1763, *Colden* (1876) p. 251. Seventeen other vessels were assigned to the West Indies and seven to Newfoundland, *Providence Gazette* Sept. 24, 1763.

22. From 1723 to 1742 the British customs service was administered by a single British board subordinate to the British Treasury, but in 1742, the service was divided, one board for England and a smaller board for Scotland, with the

colonial branch of the service under the English board, Andrews *Guide to P.R.O.* II 111–112.

23. I have not found copies of the commissions as customs officers issued at this time (1763) to the naval commanders, but a circular letter from Secretary of State Lord Egremont July 9, 1763, indicates that they were to be issued promptly, *Fitch* II 257.

24. Sec 1 of the Navigation Act of 1660, 12 Chas. II ch. 18, prohibiting foreign and certain other ships to trade with the colonies, provided that "commanders at sea of any ships of war or other ships having commission from his Majesty or from his heirs or successors are hereby authorized and strictly required to seize and bring in as prize all such ships or vessels as shall have offended contrary hereunto. . . ."

25. The use of the navy to curb colonial trade with the enemy in time of war is described in Beer *Brit. Col. Policy* 86–113; Pares *War and Trade* 446–467; Pitman *West Indies* 313–317; Hedges *The Browns* 49–52; Barrow *Trade* 161–163; and other standard works.

26. Order in Council June 1, 1763, providing for payment to the seizing officer of a varying but, in all cases, large share of the proceeds from the sale of condemned ships and cargo seized by naval officers "duly authorized to make seizures," published in *Providence Gazette* Oct. 1, 1763, and, in part, in *Acts P.C.* IV 560–562. Sec. 42 of 4 Geo. III ch. 15 (1764) amended sec. 4 of 3 Geo. III ch. 22 (1763) requiring a new Order in Council, and a new order, similar to the order of June 1, 1763, was issued Oct. 12, 1764, *London Chronicle* Oct. 16, 1764.

27. Officers of the navy in colonial waters began promptly to exercise their new office, as is shown by seizures by the middle of 1764 by the commanders of the *Fortune,* the *Hawk,* the *Sardoine* [misspelled *Sardine* in the report], and the *St. John,* Quincy *Reports* 387–394; Hough *Reports* 215–219, 219–220; *R.I. Col. Rec. VI* 428.

28. Orders in July and Oct., 1763, to customs officers, colonial Governors, and General Jeffery Amherst, Commander in Chief of the British army in North America, as summarized in the text, Knollenberg *Origin* 143, 341.

29. As to the application of sec. 45 concerning the burden of proof, *Dawson v. The Jenny* (1773), *Adams Legal Papers* II 238, 240, 241.

30. 30 Geo. II ch. 9 secs. 1, 4, and 6 (1757) provided, as a war measure, that persons shipping any foodstuff in the colonies must take out a cocket from a customs officer belonging to the port from which the foodstuff was shipped specifying the nature and amount of it and giving bond not to ship it outside the colony except by river or "across harbours were clearances have not usually been taken"; but the requirements were to be in force only "during the continuance of the present war with France."

31. The Navigation Act of 1660, 12 Chas. II ch. 18, sec. 19, required the giving of bond to customs officers covering all shipments of sugar, tobacco, and other so-called "enumerated products," whether overseas or coastwise, but vessels carrying other colonial products were not required to clear with customs unless loaded with cargo to be "carried to the open sea," 13 and 14 Chas. II ch. 11 sec. 7 (1662) extended to the colonies by 7 and 8 Wm. III ch. 22 sec. 6 (1696). For details, Knollenberg *Origin* 177–178, 356.

32. Sec. 29 of the Act of 1764 requiring cockets covering shipments from one colony to another made no exception in favor of small vessels, but sec. 25 of the act of 5 Geo. III ch. 45 (1765) exempted "any boat, flat, shallop, or other vessel without a deck, not exceeding twenty tons burthen . . . not carried out to sea more than one league from the shore." It will be noted that even this exemption applied only in case the small vessel did not put out more than a league (three miles) from shore.

33. As to the vast importance to the colonies of coastwise and river traffic, Knollenberg *Origin* 178, 357.

34. Of previous British acts giving colonial admiralty courts jurisdiction over non-maritime cases, the Sugar Act of 1733, with later extensions, had expired in 1764, *same* 138–149, 338–344; the Stamp Act of 1765 was repealed in 1766, *same* 221–237, 373–380; and the White Pine Acts not only had a maritime connection but their object, preservation of trees needed for masting the British navy, was beneficial to the colonies, *same* 127–137, 333–338, with writings cited therein, and *Adams Legal Papers* II (1965) 247–274.

35. Colonial pamphlets protesting against the American Act of 1764 include Oxenbridge Thacher *Sentiments* (Boston, 1764); Stephen Hopkins *Rights of Colonies* (Providence, 1765); and John Dickinson *Late Regulations* (Philadelphia, 1765), reprinted in Bailyn *Pamphlets* 490–498, 507–522, 669–691.

36. Letters of protest include several from Mass. (Thomas Cushing to Jasper Mauduit Nov. 28, 1764, *Mauduit* 171–179, Andrew Oliver to Richard Jackson June, 1765, and Mass. Committee to Jackson Nov. 7, 1765, Wells *Adams* I 81); several from N.Y. in Harrington *N.Y. Merchant* 321–324; William Bull of S.C. to B. of T. Sept. 8, 1765, C.O.5:378:1:fols. 18–20; James Parker of N.J. to Cortland Skinner Nov., 1765, Kemmerer *N.J.* 282n.

37. Protests and instructions against the American Act were adopted by the Legislatures of Mass., N.Y., Pa., S.C., and R.I., Knollenberg *Origin* 354, 365, 368, 372.

38. Henry S. Conway's letter of March 31, 1766, to colonial Governors promising favorable revision of British restrictions on colonial trade, *Fitch* 397–399 and *N.Y. Col. Doc.* VII 823–824. A month earlier (Feb. 26) Henry Cruger, Jr., in Bristol, England, had written Henry Cruger, Sr., in N.Y. predicting that Parliament would "rescind all the restrictive clauses" of the Act of 1764 because "they seem convinc'd what vast Benefit will accrue to this Kingdom, by giving you almost an unlimited trade, so farr as doth not interfere with British Manufactures," *R.I. Commerce* I 143.

39. Sections 1 and 4 of the Act of 1766, 6 Geo. III ch. 52, reduced the rate of duty on foreign colonial molasses from three pence to a penny a gallon. As to the importance of foreign colonial molasses, Knollenberg *Origin* 138–147, 338–347. Sec. 1 of this act also repealed a small duty on British colonial sugar shipped from one British colony to another, levied by 25 Chas. II ch. 7 sec. 2 (1673). Background and passage of the Act of 1766, Jensen *Founding* 176–177.

40. Favorable readjustment of the colonial duties levied in 1764 on domestic colonial coffee and pimento and foreign sugar, coffee, and indigo are in sections 1, 4, 15, 16, and 17 of the Act of 1766. The duties on colonial imports of cambric, East Indian silk, and colored calico and French lawn levied in 1764 were re-

pealed by section 2 of the Act of 1766, but were replaced by substantially equivalent duties payable in Great Britain imposed by sections 5–11.

41. Secs. 4 and 5 of the Act of 1766 levied the reduced molasses duty of a penny a gallon on "all" molasses imported into the colonies except molasses re-exported from Dominica, on which a duty had already been paid.

42. Sec. 23 of the Act of 1766 provided that "all sugars which shall be imported into Great Britain from any part of the British colonies or plantations on the continent of America shall be deemed and taken to be French sugars," subject as such to a higher rate of British import duty than British colonial sugar. To prevent northern colonial merchants from sending to Great Britain foreign colonial sugar mislabeled British was, of course, reasonable; the grievance was adoption of so drastic a curb without at least trying out some less radical corrective.

43. My supposition that the Act of 1766 passed without a division—in either House of Parliament—is based on the absence of any record of a division on it in the *Journals* of either House or any mention of a division on it in the correspondence of the period.

44. The restrictions imposed before 1764 on the export of colonial "enumerated" products, Knollenberg *Origin* 168–171, 352–353. (As brought out in *same* 172–174, 183–184, 354–355, 359–360, 375–387, these earlier restrictions were sometimes accompanied by British tariff preferences, bounties, or other benefits in favor of the restricted products, which in a few cases compensated and, in the case of sugar, more than compensated for the restrictions.)

45. Sec. 30 of the Act of 1766 prohibited the export of any non-enumerated products, including those mentioned in the text, to any part of Europe north of Cape Finisterre (Spain). Sec. 31 excepted Spanish ports on the Bay of Biscay.

46. The importance of the legal direct trade between Ireland and the northern colonies, particularly with New York and Philadelphia, which would be affected by the restriction imposed in 1766 on exports from the colonies to Ireland, is brought out in James "Irish Colonial Trade" 574–584.

47. Sec. 30 of the Act of 1766 required the bonds described in the text; sec. 31 provided for the exception as to Spanish ports on the Bay of Biscay. The Navigation Act of 1660, 12 Chas. II ch. 18 sec. 19, had long required similar bonds from vessels loading tobacco and other so-called "enumerated" products.

48. Charles Garth to S.C. Comm. of Corresp. June 6, 1766, enclosed a clause to amend the bill for the Act of 1766, which he had asked to have incorporated in the bill, *S.C. Hist. Mag.* XXVIII (1927) 232, 234–235. Garth asked for the exemption only of "small decked Vessels or Schooners," apparently assuming that all undecked vessels were exempted from giving bond, but, as stated in the text, the Act of 1766 does not exempt them.

49. The practice in some colonies of exempting undecked and even small decked vessels from giving bonds is indicated by Samuel Adams to Richard Jackson Nov. 7, 1765, Wells *Adams* I 81–82 and by an order in 1766 of the Governor of S.C., Barrow *Trade* 204. Jonathan Sewall, Attorney-General of Mass., gave an opinion Feb. 13, 1769, that coasting vessels sailing from one port to another within the same colony were not required to give bond, T:1:474 (P.R.O.), but I have found no evidence that this view was adopted by the customs officers.

50. The officers harassing small vessels in coastwise trade could justify them-selves by the printed instructions and accompanying appendix issued in 1769 by the American Customs Board to customs officers in America, Mass. Hist. Soc. These give a digest of the Act of 1766, without any indication of an exception to be made in favor of small coasting vessels, decked or undecked, with respect to the bonds required by this act. (A copy of the instructions dated Feb. 28, 1769, but not of the important appendix, is in Morison *Sources* 74–83.)

51. Daniel Dulany's *Considerations,* published in Annapolis, Md. in Oct., 1765, was republished there and in New York, Boston, and London in 1765 and 1766, Adams *Bibliography* 8–11. As to Dulany, *D.A.B.* and Land *The Dulanys* 52, 116, 153–333 *passim*. The duties levied on importation of colonial tobacco into Great Britain were refundable on reexportation, 9 Geo. I ch. 21 sec. 6 (1732).

52. By 1764, around 90% of the more than one hundred million pounds of British colonial tobacco shipped to Great Britain each year was being reexported, Knollenberg *Origin* 174, 355, largely by way of Scotland, Price "Glasgow in Tobacco Trade" 480. Harper "Effect" 25–26 reasons that most of this would have gone directly to continental Europe but for the restrictive Act of 1660, and Knol-lenberg *Origin* 173–174, 355 brings out that the British tariff differential granted British colonial tobacco was by 1764 of little if any value to colonial tobacco planters.

53. Dulany's estimate of £270,000 (presumably sterling) a year as the loss on tobacco shipped from Va. and Md., which would include much of that grown in N.C., too, and his method of arriving at this figure are in *Considerations* 52 (reprinted in Bailyn *Pamphlets* 655). I question some of Dulany's reasoning but, judging from Harper's finding (Harper "Effect" 37) that the British restriction on the export of colonial tobacco cost the colonies over $2 million in 1773, Dulany's estimate is apparently not excessively high.

54. The record of the Grenville administration with respect to colonial trade was, if anything, better than that of the Rockingham because the former sponsored a number of temporary acts favorable to colonial trade, somewhat off-setting the unfavorable Act of 1764, namely 4 Geo. III ch. 11 (sec. 3), 19, 22, 26, 27, and 29.

55. The N.Y. and Mass. petitions in 1766 reciting colonial grievances, described in Chapter 4, included no mention of the Declaratory Act, and George Mason of Va., in his well-known bitter reply of June 6, 1766, to the English merchants' circular letter of February 28, calling for colonial gratitude for the impending repeal of the Stamp Act, barely mentions the Declaratory Act, *Mason* (Rowland) I 383. John Adams' diary for April 26 mentions his "Apprehensions" over the bill for the Declaratory Act, *Adams Papers* I 309; but there is no further mention of the act in his diary until 1774, *same* I 309, II 100.

56. Benjamin Franklin, joint London Agent for the Pa. Assembly, wrote its Speaker, Joseph Fox, March 1, 1766, "This [Declaratory Act] is merely to save Appearances, and to guard against the Effects of the Clamour made by the late Ministry as if the Rights of this Nation were sacrificed to America," *Franklin Papers* XIII 186. To similar effect, Richard Jackson, member of Parliament and joint London Agent for the Pa. Assembly, the colony of Conn. and the Mass. House of Representatives, to Gov. Francis Bernard of Mass., March 3, Bradford *Mass. Papers* 72.

57. The passage as to the Declaratory Act quoted in the text is from an article of Samuel Adams ("Alfred") in the *Boston Gazette* of Oct. 2, 1769, reviewing the controversy between the colonies and Great Britain since 1765, Wells *S. Adams* I 118.

CHAPTER 4

1. The Duke of Grafton's statement to the King Apr. 28, 1766, that he must resign and his reasons, the King to Lord Northington Apr. 28 and to Lord Bute May 3, *Geo. III* I 295 and *Bute* 246.

2. The understanding between the King and Lord Egmont as to what the latter should say at a Cabinet meeting May 1, 1766, the King to Egmont May 1, *Geo. III* I 297.

3. The King to Bute May 3, 1766, and Egmont to the King May 1, as to proposal to Lord Rockingham and Henry S. Conway that they consider a coalition with friends of Bute, and their refusal, *Bute* 248 and *Geo. III* I 298.

4. The King to Bute May 3, 1766, quoting Northington as saying that "he was alone attach'd to me, and would support whatever men I chose to entrust in Government," *Bute* 247.

5. Egmont to the King May 1, 1766, as to the refusal of Rockingham, Conway, Lord Winchilsea, and the Duke of Newcastle to form "a cordial union with the Friends of Lord Bute," and their reason, *Geo. III* I 298. To similar effect, the King to Bute May 3, *Bute* 247–248 and Newcastle to John White May 3, *Newcastle* 60–62.

6. The King wrote Bute May 3, 1766, as to forming a new ministry, based "on those who call themselves attached to you," together with others, excluding only Grenville and Lords Halifax and Sandwich, *Bute* 248.

7. The King wrote Bute July 12, 1766, "your letter in the spring [presumably a missing letter in reply to the King's of May 3, cited in note 6] made me give over all hopes of any formation without either Mr. Pitt or Mr. Greenville at the head of it," *same* 250.

8. The Duke of Richmond succeeded Grafton as Secretary of State May 23, 1766, Beatson *Pol. Index* I 277. At this same time Henry S. Conway, who had been Secretary for the Southern Department, switched to the Northern, and Richmond replaced him as Secretary for the Southern.

9. My statement as to the Ministry's carrying on without serious difficulty is based on the proceedings from May 5 to June 6, 1766, reported in *Journals H. of C.* XXX 792–846 and Lord George Sackville to John Irwin June 10, *Stopford* I 111–112. On the only issue to which there seems to have been serious controversy— a tax on windows—the Ministry was victorious in the Commons, May 12, by a vote of 104 to 51, *Journals H. of C.* XXX 817, and in the Lords, May 28, 57 to 16, *Geo. III* I 342. Parliament rose on June 6, *Journals H. of C.* XXX 846.

10. Horace Walpole, Conway's cousin and close friend, who was eagerly following political developments at this time, wrote Horace Mann June 9, 1766, "The session of Parliament has at last ended and the ministry have a lease of five or six months longer," Lewis *Walpole* XXII 424. (Parliament did not sit again until Nov. 11, 1766, *Journals H. of C.* XXXI 3.)

11. The King wrote Egmont May 28, 1766, that "Six Weeks ago" Rockingham had authorized him to tell his brothers, and he had done so, that a bill would be brought into the current session of Parliament to grant them £24,000 a year and had confirmed this on May 25, *Geo. III* I 347. The giving of this promise is corroborated by Newcastle to White June 28, *Newcastle* 71 and Walpole to Mann June 9, Lewis *Walpole* XXII 424–425.

12. Walpole to Mann June 9, 1766, concerning Conway's objection to carrying out Rockingham's promise concerning the proposed settlement on the King's brothers, *same.*

13. Rockingham to the King May 27, 1766, stating (without mentioning Conway) that "because of the lateness of the Session & the Thinness of Parl at this Juncture," the Ministry had decided to defer proposing the grant to the King's brothers until the next session of Parliament, *Geo. III* I 345.

14. The Ministry soothes the King's brothers by agreeing to introduce into Parliament at the next session a resolution for a grant to them, the King to Rockingham and Richmond, and Richmond to the King June 2, 1766, *same* 351–352. (This agreement was carried out June 3, *Journals H. of C.* XXX 842.)

15. The King to Bute July 12, 1766, giving the account quoted in the text of his decision, after "the strange scene concerning the money for my brothers" to have a new Ministry, *Bute* 251–252. To similar effect, the King to Egmont May 28, stating, "because a few Weak Boys are unwilling this Session to pass the provision for my Brothers my word is to be set at naught; *my prudence is now exhausted; I am enclin'd to take any Step that will preserve my honour,*" *Geo. III* I 347.

16. Pitt's speech in the House of Commons against exclusion of Bute's relations and friends, which "convinced everybody that Mr. Pitt wished to be in office," March 4, 1766, Sackville to Irwin March 11, 1766, *Stopford* I 109. To same effect, William Rouet to Baron Mure March 6, fixing the date of Pitt's speech as March 4, *Caldwell* 77–79. The King wrote Bute, July 12, that Pitt's speech in Parliament "has bound him not to change the language" favorable to Bute, previously used privately to the King, *Bute* 253.

17. The King's determination to secure his "independency," his "freedom" from domination by party groups ("factions" as he called them) is stated repeatedly in letters to Bute, Nov., 1762,–August, 1766, *same* 154–155, 156, 167, 187, 203, 217, 224, 227, 240, 257, and in letters to Pitt July 7 and Dec. 2, 1766, *Geo. III* I 368 and *Pitt* III 137.

18. Pitt's speech in the House of Commons denouncing faction, Apr. 24, 1766, quoted in the text, Richard Rigby to the Duke of Bedford Apr. 24, *Bedford* III 333.

19. In 1761–62 John Wilkes had skillfully exploited English anti-Scottism to whip up resentment against Bute as a Scot whose undue influence over the King was used to favor Scots over Englishmen, and as a person whose alleged adultery with the King's mother brought disgrace on the nation, Knollenberg *Origin* 31–32.

20. Northington's dissatisfaction with his colleagues appears from his letters to the King Jan. 8–June 5, 1766, *Geo. III* I 214–356 *passim* and from the King to Bute Jan. 10, May 3, and July 12, *Bute* 241–252. The King wrote Bute that he had "encouraged" both Northington and Egmont in their opinions as to the "purility" of their fellow Cabinet ministers, *same*, 252.

21. Northington's letters give the impression of his trying to curry favor with the King in the hope that when the King, as he evidently wished to do, displaced the Rockingham Ministry he would insist on Northington's being well taken care of by the new Ministry. (Northington was, in the event, extremely well taken care of; he was made President of the Council and given a fat pension to boot, Walpole to Mann Aug. 1, Lewis *Walpole* XXII 443, 443n.)

22. The King to Bute July 12, 1766, telling of Northington's request, described in the text, *Bute* 252. The date, July 6, is known from Richmond's journal of that day, *Rockingham* I 358. The King not only gave his permission, but "very much approved" of Northington's proposal, since this "would bring things to an issue very honourably to myself," *Bute* 252. Northington's picking a quarrel with his colleagues over the instructions to be given the Governor of Quebec is described in Richmond's journal of June 27, *Rockingham* I 351–355.

23. The King to Bute July 12, 1766, telling of his having Northington sound out Lord Camden as to "the best channel of getting at Mr. Pitt," and Camden's reply, *Bute* 252. Northington, at some earlier, unstated date, had informed the King that Camden had told him, "Mr. Pitt was ready to come in if called upon . . . to try and form an Administration of the best of all partys . . . ," *same* 251.

24. The King to Pitt July 7, 1766, asking Pitt, who was at his home at Hayes (Kent), to come to London to give the King his "thoughts how an able and dignified ministry may be formed," *Geo. III* I 368. The King's covering letter to Northington July 6 is in *same* 367, and a covering letter from Northington to Pitt, July 7, in *Pitt* II 434–435.

25. The "infirmity" was the gout, which had afflicted Pitt, on and off, for many years. It was this infirmity, making it foreseeably difficult for him to sustain the heavy load of debate he would have to carry in the House of Commons, that probably explains his otherwise puzzling acceptance of a peerage, which would weaken his popularity and power by removing him from the House of Commons to the House of Lords.

26. Pitt's reply to the King's letter July 8, 1766, *Geo. III* I 368. Pitt reached London at noon July 11, Richmond's journal of that date, *Rockingham* I 364, and had a long talk with Northington that night, Northington to the King July 11, *Geo. III* I 371. The King had told Rockingham, Conway, Richmond, and Newcastle the day before (July 10) that "he had sent for Mr. Pitt," adding to Conway alone that he hoped he would remain in "whatever administration he [the King] should have," Newcastle to White July 11, *Newcastle* 78–79.

27. Offer of the place of First Lord of the Treasury to Lord Temple, Northington to the King July 11 and 14, 1766, and the King to Pitt July 15, *Geo. III* I 371, 372, 374, and Temple's refusal, saying he would be a mere "cypher," King to Northington July 17, *same* 371 and Temple to Grenville July 18, *Grenville* III 267. Temple's reason for thinking he would be but a cipher was Pitt's refusal of his request that Lord Lyttelton be given "a Cabinet office" and Lord Gower appointed one of the Secretaries of State, Temple, to an unidentified correspondent, July 20, *same* 278.

28. Lord Chesterfield's comment in a letter of Aug. 1, 1766, to his son Philip Stanhope "To withdraw, in the fullness of his [Pitt's] power . . . from the House of Commons, (which procured him his power, and which alone can insure it to

him) and to go into that Hospital of Incurables, the House of Lords, is a measure so unaccountable that nothing but proof positive could have made me believe it; but true it is," Mahon *Chesterfield* IV 455–456, apparently expressed the general opinion. For example, Edmund Burke to Charles O'Hara July 29, *Burke* 263 and *Gentleman's Mag.* for Aug., 1766, XXXVI 352.

29. George III to Pitt July 29, 1766, as to his pleasure over conclusion of arrangements for the new Ministry, *Geo. III* I 385.

30. Newcastle to White July 11, 25, and 30, 1766, concerning the King's informing members of Rockingham Ministry of his decision to have Pitt form a new Ministry, and Pitt's takeover on July 30, *Newcastle* 80, 87–88, 94.

31. Pitt was created a peer with the title Earl of Chatham July 29, 1766, *Home Office Papers* 1766–69, p. 111.

32. The dates of accession to office of the other members of the Ministry noted in the text, Beatson *Pol. Index* I 246–277 *passim* and *Gentleman's Mag.* for Aug., 1766, XXXVI 391.

33. Conway's continuance as Leader in the House of Commons is evident from his correspondence with the King Nov. 11, 1766, to May 9, 1767, *Geo. III* I 441–473 *passim.*

34. Replacement of Egmont, who resigned in Sept., 1766, first by Sir Charles Saunders and in December by Sir Edward Hawke, Beatson *Pol. Index* I 271. (For Conway's explanation of Egmont's resignation—dislike of Pitt and some of his policies—Lady Mary Coke's journal for Aug. 22, quoting Conway, Lewis *Walpole* XXII 449n.)

35. Lord Granby's inclusion in the Cabinet is evidenced by minutes of a Cabinet meeting Aug. 5, 1766, probably the first of the new Ministry, at which Chatham, Grafton, Conway, Camden, Northington, Lord Shelburne, and Lord Granby were present, Chatham Pap. G.D.8:97 (P.R.O.). (Soon afterward [Aug. 13], Granby was given the highest command in the army, "Captain-General of the Land Forces," Lewis *Walpole* XXII 449n.)

36. Grafton later wrote that Townshend was included in the Cabinet as early as "the very night preceding Lord Chatham's first journey to Bath," *Grafton* 105. A letter of Lord Shelburne to Chatham Oct. 5, 1766, indicates this date was about Oct. 1, 1766, *Pitt* III 90. Chatham to Grafton, Oct. 19, indicates that Townshend was of the Cabinet then, *Grafton* 109.

37. Charles Townshend took office as Chancellor of the Exchequer Aug. 2, 1766, *Gentleman's Mag.* for Aug., 1766, XXXVI 391. The negotiations leading to his switch from the office of Paymaster-General in the Rockingham Ministry to Chancellor of the Exchequer in Chatham's are described in Namier and Brooke *Townshend* 147–154.

38. Restoration of James Stuart Mackenzie to the office of Lord Privy Seal for Scotland, *Gentleman's Mag.* for Sept., 1766, XXXVI 439.

39. Pitt's statement in his speech of Jan. 14, 1766, "It is my opinion, that this kingdom has no right to lay a tax upon the colonies," is in *Parl. Hist.* XVI 90.

40. Pitt's statement in his speech of Jan. 14, 1766, "let prudence and temper come first from this side. I will undertake for America, that she will follow the example," is in *same* 107.

41. As shown in the text of this chapter, Pitt yielded to no one in his expressions of humility when addressing the King. But in general his letters display such imperious pride as to give point to Edmund Burke's remark in a letter to his friend Henry Flood at the time of the ministerial crisis in the sprng of 1765, described in Chapter 1, Pitt's "Gout is worse than ever; but his Pride may disable him [as a statesman] more than his Gout," Burke to Henry Flood May 18, 1765, *Burke* I 194.

42. Pitt's numerous abrupt shifts were described in the Aug., 1766 *Gentleman's Mag.* XXXVI 347–351 in "An Enquiry into the Conduct of a late Right Honourable Commoner." It is notable that "A short View . . . ," containing "a full Refutation of . . . An Enquiry into the Conduct of a late Right Honourable Commoner" extolling Pitt, and justly so, for his great contributions to the nation, does not even attempt to discredit the account in the "Enquiry" of Pitt's abrupt shifts of policy, *same* 370–376.

43. Knollenberg *Origin* 161–163, 349–350, and Chapter 21 of this volume discusses the British doctrine of the absolute supremacy of Parliament.

44. Newcastle had served as Secretary of State for the Southern Department, responsible for colonial affairs, from 1724 to 1748, four years longer than the combined periods of service of his successors, the Duke of Bedford, Lord Holderness, Sir Thomas Robinson, Henry Fox, William Pitt, Lord Egremont, Lord Halifax, Henry S. Conway, the Duke of Richmond and Lord Shelburne. The sneers of Horace Walpole, parroted by many subsequent writers, as to Newcastle's ignorance of the colonies are discredited by his voluminous papers, mainly unpublished, in the British Public Record Office and the British Museum.

45. Newcastle's questioning of the proposed Declaratory Act is described in Chapter 1.

46. Granby's speaking and voting against repeal of the Stamp Act is described in Chapter 2.

47. Person after person, friends and political foes alike, spoke of Townshend in the same vein as George III, who wrote Bute Feb. 10, 1763, of Townshend's being "so fickle that no man can depend on him," *Bute* 189. To same effect, Namier and Brooke *Townshend* 9–16; letters from 1759 to 1767 of David Hume, Rae *Smith* 144; also Tom Ramsden, *Jenkinson* 104; Lord Chesterfield, *Chesterfield* IV 378, 431; Henry Fox, Ilchester *Fox* II 229; Horace Walpole, Toynbee *Walpole* V 439, VI 174, 263, 381, VII 31; Edmund Burke *Burke* I 209; Lord Chatham, *Grafton* 110; Lord Charlemont *Pitt* III 178n.; and Lady Mary Hervey, *Hervey* 325.

48. Townshend, a "meer Weather Cock," Dennys De Berdt to Stephen Sayre July 29, 1766, *Col. Soc. Publ.* XIII 318. Townshend's reputation for changeableness, Namier and Brooke *Commons* III 542–544.

49. Townshend to the Duke of Newcastle Sept. 13, 1754, recommending an act of Parliament to tax the colonies, Gipson *Brit. Empire* V 164.

50. Townshend's proposal in March, 1764, for lowering the foreign molasses duty "in order more effectually to secure the payment," Jasper Mauduit to the Mass. Council March 23, 1763, Bancroft Papers, N.Y.P.L., with the King to Bute, undated, *Bute* 203–204.

51. Jared Ingersoll to Gov. Thomas Fitch of Conn. Feb. 11, 1765, concerning Townshend's support of the bill for a colonial stamp tax, *Fitch* II 321–322.

52. Townshend's speech in the House of Commons supporting repeal Feb. 7, 1766, Lord Rockingham to the King Feb. 7, *Geo. III* I 268. (See also Nathaniel Ryder's notes of Townshend's speech, Namier and Brooke *Townshend* 24.) But, on Feb. 11, he declared his supporting repeal was "not on account of [any doubt as to] the right . . . but only if at all, on the impracticability, or inexpediency of it, or the inability of the colonies to pay the tax," James West to Newcastle, Feb. 11, reporting the debate in the House of Commons that day, *same* 25 (date of letter supplied from Add. Mss. 32973:413).

53. The distribution of British troops, Table of "General Distribution of Troops in North America" Feb. 22, 1767, by Gen. Thomas Gage, Commander in Chief of the British forces in North America, Alvord and Carter *New Regime* 512–513. Most of the troops were stationed outside the settlements of the old thirteen colonies, but of those stationed in the old colonies, New York, which was Gage's headquarters, had more than twice as many as any other colony.

54. The Quartering Act of 1765, 5 Geo. III ch. 33 secs. 6 and 7. An act of this kind was proposed in a letter and enclosed memorandum from Gage to Halifax Jan. 23, 1765, *Gage* I 49, II 263–266. Shy *Towards Lexington* 163–164, 184–188 and Labaree *Franklin* XII 106–107, 118–120 have a full account of the background of the act and the successful efforts to eliminate quartering in private houses, initially proposed.

55. Message of Gov. Sir Henry Moore of N.Y. Dec. 3, 1765, applying for supplies required by the Quartering Act of 1765, and the Assembly's noncompliance and evasive reply of Dec. 13, *N.Y. Assembly Journal* (1691–1765) II 788–789, 802–803; Gage to Conway Dec. 21, 1765, and Feb. 23, 1766, and to the Secretary at War, Lord Barrington, Dec. 2, 1765, and Feb. 21, 1766, *Gage* I 77, 84, II 328–329, 339.

56. The threatened change of judicial procedure in N.Y., which would have lessened the weight of juries, vigorously supported by Acting Gov. Cadwallader Colden of N.Y. in the case of *Forsey* v. *Cunningham* (1764–1766) is discussed in Smith *Appeals* 390–412; Klein "Prelude to Revolution in N.Y." 453–462; John Watts to Gen. Robert Monckton, former Gov. of N.Y., Oct. 12, 1765, *Aspinwall* II 579; William Smith to Monckton, Nov. 8, 1765, Sabine *William Smith* I 30–31.

57. The Stamp Act was repealed March 18, 1766. The proposed change in judicial procedure in N.Y. had been disapproved by an opinion of the chief law officers of the Crown Nov. 5, 1765, *N.Y. Col. Doc.* VII 815–816, but this was not known in N.Y. until Feb., 1766, Moore to B. of T. Feb. 22, 1766, *same* 814.

58. Moore to Conway June 20, 1766, reporting the failure of the N.Y. Assembly to provide all the supplies required by the Quartering Act, *same* VII 831, which had recently been extended for a year by 6 Geo. III ch. 18 (1766). The N.Y. act providing only part of the required supplies is an act of July 3, 1766, *N.Y. Laws* IV 901–903.

59. Shelburne's letter to Gov. Moore Aug. 9, 1766, quoted in the text concerning the Quartering Act. *N.Y. Col. Doc.* VII 847–848. Shelburne wrote in similar vein to Chatham Sept. 20, predicting that "the remains of the Storm" in the colonies over the Stamp Act would soon subside, Chatham Papers 30:8:56:60 (P.R.O.). Shelburne's letter had been approved in substance at a Cabinet meeting on Aug. 5, Ritcheson *Brit. Politics* 85.

60. N.Y. Assembly's address to Moore, Dec. 15, 1766, refusing to comply with the Quartering Act, *Prior Documents* 155–156. (British troops stationed in New York City had recently—Aug. 10—irritated the people by tearing down a Liberty Pole. As to this incident, involving the local radical leader, John Lamb, Leake *Lamb* 32–33, and Gage to the Duke of Richmond Aug. 26, *Gage* I 103–104.)

61. Moore to Shelburne Dec. 19, 1766, concerning the N.Y. Assembly's refusal to obey the Quartering Act, Dec. 19, 1766, *N.Y. Col. Doc.* VII 883–884.

62. Shelburne to Chatham Feb. 1, 1767, concerning the N.Y. Assembly's recent refusal to comply with the Quartering Act and also as to the New York merchants' petition, *Pitt* III 186–188. Shelburne wrote that letters from N.Y. said members of the Assembly refused to comply with the act for fear of establishing a dangerous precedent.

63. N.Y. merchants' petition, *Prior Documents* 163–167 and *Journals H. of C.* XXXI 158–160, enclosed in Moore to B. of T. Dec. 10, 1766, Shelburne Papers 51:649–653. Shelburne wrote Chatham Feb. 18, 1767, that the petition contained 240 signatures, *Pitt* III 186. (The Pa. Assembly voted Oct. 18, 1766, to have its London Agent, Richard Jackson, try to secure revision of the restrictive acts of 1764 and 1766, *Pa. Assembly* VII 5644–5647, but I have seen no evidence of action on this.)

64. Chatham's reply to Shelburne Feb. 3, 1767, *Pitt* III 188–189. Chatham's long and severe attack of gout is frequently mentioned in his correspondence from Aug. 26, 1766, to Feb. 7, 1767, *same* 55–194 *passim.*

65. I do not know why Chatham considered the timing of the N.Y. merchants' petition absurd. Conceivably he had in mind the recent appearance of a pamphlet attacking repeal of the Stamp Act, encouraging the colonists to shake off British restriction on colonial trade, in *Conduct of the Late Administration* written by one of Grenville's followers, Charles Lloyd, advertised in the *London Chronicle* for Dec. 20, 1766, as published "This Day." But the merchants could not have known of this pamphlet when they sent off their petition. (As to Lloyd's authorship, sketch of Lloyd in *D.N.B.* and also *H. & L. Dict.* I 403).

66. As pointed out in Parliament Feb. 3 or 4, 1766, by William Blackstone, author of the famous "Commentaries," Grey Cooper's Notes, *A.H.R.* XVII (1912) 569, and in the protest of the N.J. Assembly quoted in Gov. William Franklin of N.J. to Shelburne Dec. 18, 1766, *Prior Documents* 121, the Quartering Act obviously was a form of colonial taxation by act of Parliament.

67. 4 Geo. III ch. 15 sec. 28 (1764) prohibited export of iron and lumber from the colonies directly to Ireland. 5 Geo. III ch. 45 sec. 22 (1765) repealed this restriction; but 6 Geo. III ch. 52 sec. 30 (1766) prohibiting the export of all non-enumerated colonial products directly to continental Europe or Ireland had restored it.

68. 7 Geo. III ch. 2, passed Dec. 16, 1766, *Journals H. of C.* XXXI 15–46 *passim* again repealed the prohibition on exports of colonial iron and lumber directly to Ireland. (For the importance of the Irish–colonial trade to New York and Philadelphia, James "Colonial Irish Trade" 580–583.)

69. The N.Y. merchants' petition, *Prior Documents* 166, included a protest against a supposed provision in the Free Ports Act of 1766, 6 Geo. III ch. 49, prohibiting the export of sugar and other West Indian products except molasses from Dominica to New York; but there is no such prohibition in the act, and I

have found no evidence that customs officers tried to enforce such a restriction. The act (sec. 10) prohibited reexport of all West Indian products from Dominica to the other British West Indies, but not to the British colonies in North America.

70. Shelburne to Chatham Feb. 6, 1767, as to the unanimous opinion of those present at a Cabinet meeting attended by Northington, Shelburne himself, and others not named that no notice be taken of the N.Y. merchants' petition unless "Mr. Grenville moved for it," *Pitt* III 192–193.

71. Chatham's reply Feb. 7, 1767, advising against smothering the merchants' petition, *same* 193–194.

72. Lord Clare's presentation of the N.Y. merchants' petition to the House of Commons Feb. 16, 1767, and the House's order concerning it, *Journals H. of C.* XXXI 160; Charles Garth to S.C. Comm. of Corresp. March 12, *So. Car. Hist. Mag.* XXIX (1928) 216. Clare had succeeded Lord Hillsborough as President of the Board of Trade in Dec., 1766, Beatson *Pol. Index* I 446.

73. Shelburne to Chatham Feb. 16, 1767, as to coercing N.Y. to comply with the Quartering Act, Chatham Papers P.R.O. 30:8:207–215; published in part in *Pitt* III 206–211, but omitting the important statement of the Cabinet's indecision and what Shelburne himself thought should be done.

74. Grafton to Chatham March 13, 1767, *same* 231, that at a Cabinet meeting the night before, "the New York point was settled and that it should be by act of parliament." He did not say what the proposed act was to provide, adding merely that Conway "had his doubts, but would endeavour every thing he could to bring his mind to it."

75. Shelburne to Chatham Apr. 26, 1767, reporting discussion and decisions of a Cabinet meeting Apr. 24, Chatham Papers 30:8:56 Part I 86–90 (P.R.O.). Townshend proposed asking Parliament to address the King to refuse his assent to any law passed by the N.Y. Legislature until the Quartering Act was "fully obey'd." At Northington's insistence the plan was changed to propose an act of Parliament, instead of action by the King. Shelburne refers to reservation of a final decision until a meeting on May 1, of which I have found no record.

76. Shelburne to Chatham Apr. 26, 1767, describing the plan adopted at the Cabinet meeting of Apr. 24, *same*. Shelburne's letter is referred to in Tunstall *Pitt* 391 as "proposed" by him and in Ritcheson *British Politics* 90 as his "own plan"; but Shelburne's letter refers to it as one of several to be considered by Chatham, without indication that Shelburne proposed, or even favored, it.

77. Chatham's letters to Shelburne and Grafton of Feb. 7–Feb. 26, 1767, are in *Pitt* III 193–222, and there is an important letter early in May from Chatham to Grafton in *Grafton* 124, which the editor of the Grafton papers dates "probably March 11," but probably should be dated March 4, Brooke *Chatham* 111n. None of these letters indicates any opposition by Chatham toward the proposal to compel New York to obey the Quartering Act.

78. Resolutions for the New York Restraining Act, May 13 and 15, 1767, *Journals H. of C.* XXXI 358, 364, and letters cited in note 80 below.

79. Conway seems to have temporarily relinquished his Leadership of the House of Commons, perhaps because of his opposition to the proposed Restraining Act. His last known report to the King as Leader of the House during this session was on May 8, 1767, *Geo. III* I 472–473.

80. Debates on the resolutions for the restraining act May 13 and 15, 1767, and adoption of the resolutions May 15, Thomas Bradshaw to Grafton May 14 and 16, *Grafton* 176–180; W. S. Johnson to Gov. William Pitkin May 16, *Trumbull* 231–234; Garth to S.C. Comm. of Corresp. May 17, *So. Car. Hist. Mag.* XXIX (1928) 223–230; Thomas Pownall's speech of May 15, *Parl. Hist.* XVI 331–341.

81. Grenville's successful motion on May 15, 1767, for an address to the King asking him to bestow marks of favor on those in the colonies who had suffered through obedience to acts of Parliament, Johnson to Pitkin May 16, *Trumbull* 234; Bradshaw to Grafton May 16 *Grafton* 180.

82. The bill to suspend the N.Y. Legislature was introduced May 27, and passed the House of Commons on June 15, 1767. Its progress through this House and the House of Lords and the King's assent can be followed in *Journals H. of C.* XXXI 387–405 *passim,* 418, and in *Journals H. of L.* XXXI 543–665 *passim.* Also see Varga "N.Y. Restraining Act" 243–250.

83. The act, known as the New York Suspending, or Restraining, Act, 7 Geo. III ch. 59 (1767). The background, passage, and effects of this act are described in Varga "N.Y. Restraining Act" 233–258.

84. Shortly before the New York Restraining Act was passed, the Quartering Act (which was to expire in March, 1768) was again extended, apparently without any opposition in Parliament, to March 24, 1769, 7 Geo. III ch. 55 (1767). The bill for the extension can be followed in *Journals H. of C.* XXXI 387–405; *Journals H. of L.* XXXI 643–665 *passim.*

85. The act of 9 Geo. III ch. 18 (1769) amended earlier acts by exempting any colony which passed a provincial act providing quarters and supplies for British troops in the colony. But this amending act was of no substantial benefit to the colonies; it simply substituted one form of demand for another. Also, as General Gage wrote Barrington (*Gage* II 579), it was objectionable to the colonists because of its requirement of a so-called suspending clause, which had long been a sore point with them, Knollenberg *Origin* 54, 57, 63, 66, 69.

86. The Quartering Act of 1766, 6 Geo. III ch. 8, extended by 7 Geo. III ch. 55, was annually renewed from 1768 to 1774 by the following acts: 8 Geo. III ch. 19; 9 Geo. III ch. 18; 10 Geo. III ch. 15; 11 Geo. III ch. 11; 12 Geo. III ch. 12; 13 Geo. III ch. 24; 14 Geo. III ch. 6; and 15 Geo. III ch. 6.

87. The furnishing of British troops in barracks near Boston with supplies by the Governor and Council of Mass. and the House's complaint concerning this can be followed in Gov. Francis Bernard of Mass. to Shelburne Dec. 24, 1766, *Prior Documents* 126–127, and exchange of messages between Bernard and the Mass. House Jan. 30–Feb. 4, 1767, Bradford *Mass. Papers* 105–107.

88. Bernard to the Mass. House Feb. 17, 1767, pointing out that the supplies furnished the British troops "consisted of fuel and candles only, which . . . always have been allowed in these barracks . . . ," *same* 108.

89. The Boston merchants' petition was enclosed in a letter from their Committee to Dennys De Berdt, London Agent for the Mass. House of Representatives, Jan. 17, 1767, *Mass. Papers* 28–29. The petition has not been found, but part at least of its substance is known from the Committee's letter and undated memoranda from De Berdt to Shelburne, Matthews "De Berdt" 446–450, denouncing the granting of "unlimitted power of the Officer to carry the Vessel he

seizes into what port he pleases" and the provision that if the seizure were found wrongful, the officer would be "liable to no Cost."

90. Complaints against Capt. Hugh Palliser by New England fishermen, Cushing to De Berdt Jan. 17, 1767, "Cushing Letters" 347; Rothney "Case of Bayne" 268–270; Kerr "Newfoundland" 75–76; *Quebec Gazette* Oct. 31, 1765; minutes of the Privy Council March 27, 1766, *Acts P.C.* VI 426–427; William S. Johnson to Gov. William Pitkin of Conn. March 19, 1767, *Trumbull* 219–220; corresp. April and May, 1767, *Home Office Pap.* (for 1766–69) 170. Shelburne promised to have any just cause of complaint removed, De Berdt to Cushing and to Boston merchants Feb. 14 and March 14, 1767, Matthews "De Berdt" 450–452.

91. De Berdt to Boston merchants March 9 and 14, 1767, stating that he had handed their petition to Shelburne; that the latter had advised him not to "push it," since the House of Commons was offended by the conduct of New York; and that he was therefore withholding it awaiting a more favorable opportunity to present it to the House, Matthews "De Berdt" 451–452. I have found no evidence of its ever being presented.

92. The Opposition's unsuccessful proceedings in Parliament, led by the Duke of Bedford, concerning the Mass. Indemnity Act, Apr. 10 to May 26, 1767, described in letters and diary entries April 10 to July 6, *Geo. III* I 468, 475; *Grenville* IV 222–225; *Pitt* III 248; Lewis *Walpole* XXII 507–508, 520, 525; *Trumbull* 224–225, 236–237; Groce *Johnson* 73; *Bowdoin–Temple Papers* 81–83; Duke of Bedford's diary Apr., 1767, *Cavendish* I 601–603; *Newcastle* 101–102; Winstanley *Chatham* 133–137; and minutes of the House of Lords Apr. 10–May 26, *Journals H. of L.* XXXI 566–618 *passim*.

93. The Massachusetts Act of Indemnity, passed after long delay Dec. 6, 1766, contained the obnoxious pardon clause, *Mass. Acts.* IV 903–904, added apparently to secure the support of Joseph Hawley, a leading member from western Massachusetts, some of whose clients had been convicted of rioting to prevent execution of the Stamp Act, Hutchinson to an unidentified correspondent Nov. 7, 1766, Mass. Arch. XXVI 249; Brown *Hawley* 107–110; Brown "Hawley's Law Career" 502–504; Quincy *Reports* 248–250. Reasons for the long delay appear in Brennan *Mass. 1760–1780* 81–87 and *Mass. Acts* IV 939.

94. The Privy Council did, indeed, issue an order May 13, 1767, approving a recommendation of the Privy Council Committee on Plantation Affairs that the Mass. Indemnity Act be disallowed, *Mass. Acts* IV 944. But this disallowance made no practical difference since warrants for payment of indemnity to the sufferers from the riots had been issued in Dec., 1766, *same* 941, and, as Hutchinson wrote Richard Jackson Oct. 20, 1767, the rioters were safe since "nobody will prosecute them," Mass Arch. XXVI 205.

95. The N.Y. act appropriating up to £3,000 fully covering the cost of supplies required by the Quartering Act for the British troops stationed in N.Y., was signed by Gov. Moore June 6, 1767, *N.Y. Col. Laws* 947–948.

96. The principal law officers of the Crown advised, July 24, 1768, that the N.Y. appropriations act sufficiently complied with the N.Y. Restraining Act, Shelburne Papers 61:713–714, Clements Lib., and the Privy Council issued an order Aug. 12 giving effect to this opinion, *Acts. P.C.* V 137–139. See also B. of T. to the King May 7, 1768, *N.Y. Col. Doc.* VIII 63–64, concerning this matter.

97. The N.Y. Legislature continued to pass annual acts similar to the act of June 6, 1767, making appropriations for supplying British troops in the colony, *N.Y. Col. Laws* IV 950, 1022, 1078; V 23, 178, 271, 613, despite occasional denunciation by various New Yorkers of this compliance, Gipson *Brit. Empire* XI 68–69.

98. The fluctuating conduct of colonies other than N.Y. with respect to the Quartering Act appears from Gage's many letters on the subject cited under "Mutiny Act" and "Quartering of Troops" in *Gage* II 721, 726, especially Gage to Lord Hillsborough July 2, 1771, *same* I 302, and Shy *Toward Lexington* 250–258.

CHAPTER 5

1. Estimate of the cost, £405,607, of the British troops stationed in the colonies and elsewhere (e.g., Gibraltar) outside Great Britain and Ireland for the current year, submitted by Lord Barrington to the House of Commons Jan. 20, 1767, and considered by the House Jan. 26, *Journals H. of C.* XXXI 54, 70.

2. Barrington's estimate for the troops stationed in the colonies was under £300,000, but Charles Garth, London Agent for S.C., to the S.C. Comm. of Corresp., Jan. 31, 1767, brings out that George Grenville added the cost of "Contingencies," bringing the total to "upwards of £400,000," *S.C. Hist. Mag.* XXIX 132. William Beckford to Lord Chatham Jan. 27 *Pitt* III 178 and William Rouet to Baron Mure Jan. 27 *Caldwell* Part 2 II 100 also speak of Grenville's motion calling for over £400,000 to be required from the colonies.

3. Henry S. Conway to the King "Monday evening" [Jan. 26, 1767] quoting Grenville's motion to require the colonies to pay for the British troops stationed there, *Geo. III* I 451. Thomas Whately had written Grenville Oct. 20, 1766, of rumors of a project for "providing an American revenue" from "the quit-rents in the colonies" payable to the Crown "sufficient to support the military establishment there," *Grenville* III 334.

4. The defeat of Grenville's motion 106 to 35, Conway to the King [Jan. 26, 1767] *Geo. III* I 451. This motion probably contributed to Benjamin Franklin's comment, in a letter of Dec. 1, 1767 to Joseph Galloway that Grenville "behaves as if a little out of his head on the article of America," Smyth *Franklin* V 472.

5. Charles Townshend's speech in the Commons promising to introduce a bill to tax the colonies for at least part of the expense of providing for their "safety and preservation," Rouet to Mure Jan. 27, 1767, *Caldwell* Part 2 II 101; Lord Shelburne to Chatham Feb. 1 *Pitt* III 184–185; and other contemporary sources cited in Thomas "Townshend" 35n.

6. Townshend's statement as to planning "by degrees" for a revenue which eventually would "bear the whole" cost of colonial administration, Sir Roger Newdigate's diary for Jan. 26 Chaffin "Townshend Acts" 99.

7. Chatham at Bath Jan. 31, 1767, "my pains [from gout] are abated," *Pitt* III 181; Feb. 7, still at Bath, "My gout still hangs"; Chatham at Marlborough, en route to London Feb. 26, "gout is not so severe"; Lord Chesterfield in London to Philip Stanhope March 3, Chatham arrived "yesterday, full of gout," *same* 225n. Williams *Pitt* II 242, 243n, citing medical experts, says Pitt's ailment was "diffused gout probably complicated with Bright's disease."

8. Shelburne to Chatham Feb. 1, 1767, as to what he had heard "from general conversation" as to Townshend's plan, *Pitt* III 185. Shelburne himself had plans for raising a revenue from the colonies, Shelburne to Gen. Thomas Gage, Dec. 11, 1766, *Gage* II 48; Shelburne to Chatham Feb. 1, 1767, *Pitt* III 185; memorandum of March 30, Alvord and Carter *New Regime* 540.

9. The dispute within the Cabinet over whether to require the East India Company to share its territorial revenue with the British government, Brooke *Chatham Administration* 72–79, 99–102, 111n.; Sutherland *East India Co.* 138–176; William Beckford to Chatham Feb. 18, 1767; Chatham to Duke of Grafton "Wednesday" [probably March 4, 1767] *Grafton* 124; Brooke *Chatham Administration* 111n. North was offered the Chancellorship of the Exchequer in place of Townshend, but declined, Grafton to the King March 5; the King's reply the same day, *Geo. III* I 459–460; North to Grafton "Wednesday night," *Grafton* 123.

10. Chatham's reply to Shelburne, Feb. 3, 1767, making no comment on Shelburne's report of Townshend's statement concerning colonial taxation, *Pitt* III 188–190.

11. Lord Barrington, Secretary at War, had prepared a plan dated May 10, 1766, to draw most of the troops in North America to the Atlantic seabord (a large part of them to Nova Scotia) to save expense and to have "a good Corps of Troops always within readiness within a few days sail" to keep the colonists "to Duty & Obedience," Alvord and Carter *New Regime* 234–243. Comments of Shelburne and Gage on this plan, and Gage's distribution of the troops in North America, *Gage* I 124–128; *Gage* II 48; Alvord and Carter *New Regime* 312–313, 538, 551–552.

12. The highlights of the problem of "Indian charges" are brought out in the Board of Trade Plan of July, 1764, Alvord and Carter *Critical Period* 273–281, with the comments on it by Sir William Johnson, Northern Indian Superintendent, *same* 327–342; Richard Jackson, Alvord and Carter *New Regime* 422–426, and Benjamin Franklin, Smyth *Franklin* IV 467–471; and in Barrington's Plan of May, 1766, with comments on it by Gage and Jackson, Alvord and Carter *New Regime* 234–243, 243–245, 426–430. For further light, Alden *Stuart* 180–268 and Sosin *Whitehall and Wilderness* 53–148.

13. Grafton to Chatham March 13, 1767, reporting Townshend's statement as to colonial taxation at a Cabinet meeting the night before, *Pitt* III 232. To same effect, Shelburne to Chatham March 13, *same* 233.

14. The question of regulating the Indian trade, along with other matters relating to the Indians, was presented to the Board of Trade by a letter of Shelburne dated Oct. 5, 1767, Alvord and Carter *Trade and Politics* 77–81. The Board's report dated March 7, 1768, is in *same* 183–204.

15. On Sept. 11, 1767, the Cabinet voted to ask the Board of Trade to consider how best to reduce the expense of regulating the American Indian Trade, and on Oct. 5, Shelburne asked the Board for advice on this point, *same* 21 and 77–81. The Board replied March 7, 1768, advising that management of the Indian trade be entrusted to the colonies whose inhabitants were interested in it, *same* 183–204 at 192, and orders for this were given in letters of April 15, from Lord Hillsborough, Secretary of State for the Colonies, to the appropriate colonial officials, *same* 247–254 and *N.Y. Col. Doc.* VIII 57–58.

16. Chatham to Grafton "Friday [March 13, 1767] ½ past Eleven," replying to his letter of the same date, Grafton Mss. 572.

17. There is no evidence that Townshend secured Cabinet approval of his colonial tax plan. An undated letter from Townshend to Grafton, perhaps of May 5, 1767, published and discussed in Norris *Shelburne* 50–51, Clafflin "Townshend Acts" 112, Namier and Brooke *Townshend* 177–178, and Thomas "Townshend" 47–48, asserts that Shelburne had approved the plan at a recent Cabinet meeting, but not that the Cabinet had. I have not found Grafton's reply, if any.

18. Townshend's budget speech of Apr. 15, 1767, mentioning his proposed "American Tax," Thomas "Townshend" 43; Clafflin "Townshend Acts" 108–109.

19. When first mentioning his project for colonial taxation, in his speech of Jan. 26, 1767, Townshend treated "the distinction between external and internal taxes as ridiculous in every body's opinion except the Americans . . . ," Shelburne to Chatham Feb. 1, *Pitt* III 184. (In his speech of Jan. 14, 1766, favoring repeal of the Stamp Act, *Parl. Hist.* XVI 105, Chatham himself had drawn a line between "internal and external taxes," but his further remarks showed that the "external taxes" sanctioned by him were duties for the regulation of trade, not for revenue.)

20. Townshend's statement of May 13, 1767, as to external taxes and the acceptance of them by many Americans, Thomas "Townshend" 44 quoting Nathaniel Ryder's notes of debate for that date. Townshend added that anyhow the controversy over taxes "must soon come to an issue. The superiority of the Mother Country can at no time be better exerted than now," James West to the Duke of Newcastle May 13, Add. Mss. 32981:375–380 (B.M.).

21. Townshend's statement as to freeing Crown officials in the colonies from dependence "upon the pleasure of any Assembly," Garth to S.C. Comm. of Corresp. May 17, *So. Car. Hist. Mag.* XXIX (1928) 227. In 1753, while Townshend was a member of the Board of Trade, the Board had sponsored a very drastic instruction to the Governor of N.Y. designed to secure a permanent salary for himself and the colony's judges, freeing them from future dependence on the N.Y. Legislature, Labaree *Instructions* I 190–192.

22. Townshend's plan for colonial taxation outlined in the House of Commons May 13, 1767, Garth to S.C. Comm. of Corresp. May 17, *So. Car. Hist. Mag* XXIX (1928) 227–229; William Samuel Johnson, London Agent for Conn., to Gov. William Pitkin of Conn., May 16 (differing in some details from Garth's account), *Trumbull* 231; Clafflin "Townshend Acts" 114–116. A similar plan had been considered by the Rockingham Ministry in 1766, John Huske to Townshend Apr. 9, 1767, Namier and Brooke *Townshend* 187.

23. Townshend's estimate in his statement of May 13, 1767, that the proposed duties would yield £30,000 to £40,000 a year, Nathaniel Ryder's notes for May 13, Thomas "Townshend" 44.

24. Grenville's speech May 13, 1767, against Townshend's proposed relaxation of the restriction of colonial imports directly from southern Europe, Thomas Bradshaw to Grafton [May 14] *Grafton* 177, William Samuel Johnson, London Agent for Conn., to Gov. William Pitkin of Conn. May 16, *Trumbull* 231. (The meaty letters of Johnson during his Agency in London, Feb., 1767, to June, 1771, *same* 214–490, are wonderfully valuable because he was not only able and diligent but exceptionally judicious.)

25. Franklin and Johnson wrote that British merchants trading to Portugal and Spain had "made a clamour about the intention of suffering ships to go directly with wine, fruit and oil to America," and that others declared it was "dangerous to relax the Act of Navigation, the chief security of the Supremacy of this country, while the Colonies were disputing and denying that very sovereignty which this act was principally intended to establish," Franklin to Joseph Galloway, June 13, 1767, Smyth *Franklin* V 29; Johnson to Pitkin and to Jared Ingersoll June 9, *Trumbull* 236 and "Ingersoll Letters" 408.

26. Taxing colonial imports of tea was envisaged by Townshend in his initial promise to bring in a bill to tax the colonies, Shelburne to Chatham Feb. 1, 1767, *Pitt* III 185, and had again been mentioned by him in May, Thomas Bradshaw to Grafton May 14, *Grafton* 177. (On Feb. 11, 1764, Franklin had written a member of Parliament, Richard Jackson, that a duty on colonial imports of tea "might perhaps not be amiss" if "money *must* be raised from us . . . ," Van Doren *Franklin and Jackson* 140, but I have found no evidence that Townshend knew of Franklin's suggestion.)

27. Townshend's plan presented to the House of Commons in Committee June 1, 1767, and in regular session June 2, *Journals H. of C.* XXXI 392, 394–395; Garth to S.C. Comm. of Corresp. June 6, *So. Car. Hist. Mag.* XXIX (1928) 295–296. The details of the duties other than those on paper are in *Journals H. of C.* XXXI 394. The duties on paper are from the act as passed, 7 Geo. III ch. 46 sec. 1.

28. Townshend's estimates of the revenue from the proposed duties, *same* 295. (Thomas "Townshend" 48n. speaks of Townshend's estimate of £20,000, based on the assumption of duty-paid colonial imports of 1.6 million pounds of tea a year, as "wildly" optimistic, but in 1771 Gov. Thomas Hutchinson of Mass. estimated colonial consumption of tea to be 6 million pounds a year, *M.H.S. Proc.* XIX 136, and in 1773, Gilbert Barkly, a Philadelphia merchant, 5.7 million, Drake *Tea Leaves* 200.)

29. The provision in the Acts of 1764, 1765, and 1766 for application of the revenue from the acts toward "defending," etc., the colonies, 4 Geo. III ch. 15 sec. 1; 5 Geo. III ch. 12, preamble; 6 Geo. III ch. 52 sec. 12.

30. Proposed application of revenue from the Townshend Act primarily to salaries of judges and other civil officials in the colonies, resolutions presented to the House of Commons June 2, 1767, *Journals H. of C.* XXXI 394.

31. The efforts over many years of the British government to persuade or compel colonial Legislatures to provide for permanent, rather than year-to-year, salaries for Crown-appointed colonial Governors and judges have been described in various books and articles on American colonial history, notably Labaree *Royal Government* 271–311.

32. Adoption of the resolutions for Townshend's plan and passage of the bill embodying them can be followed in proceedings of the Commons June 2–20, *Journals H. of C.* XXXI 394–395, 398, 401, 407, 408, 412, and in proceedings of the Lords, June 20–29, *Journals H. of L.* XXXI 640–659 *passim.*

33. Garth wrote the S.C. Comm. of Corresp. July 5, 1767, that there had been "an intimation" in the House of Commons of dissatisfaction with the bill, but that "the friends of America are too few to have any share in a Struggle with a Chancellor of the Exchequer," *S.C. Hist. Mag.* XXIX (1928) 300. What the "inti-

mation" was or by whom is not stated. I have found no evidence of any out-right opposition.

34. The statements in Miller *Origins* 249–250 that the House of Commons voted 180 to 98 in favor of the duties and that "Grenville and Burke both cast their votes against the act" are supported by an editorial note to a letter from Bradshaw to Grafton of May 14, 1767, *Grafton* 176n. But the letter itself (*same* 176–178), read in the light of the minutes of Parliament for May 13 and 15 (*Journals H. of C.* XXXI 358 and 364), shows that the vote referred to was on the New York Restraining Act.

35. The act imposing colonial import duties, 7 Geo. III ch. 46 (1767), was assented to by a commission from the King June 29, 1767, *Journals H. of C.* XXXI 414.

36. Undocumented statement in Williams *Pitt* II 238 that Chatham was vexed with Townshend because of his "threats to tax America."

37. Lord George Sackville wrote John Irwin March 2, 1767, that the Lord Chancellor (Lord Camden), who was Chatham's particular friend in the Cabinet, had recently "held very stout language in the House of Lords" favoring vigorous action to control the colonies and that it was believed that Chatham, too, "has changed his ideas about America, and means to act with vigour," *Stopford H.M.C.* 120.

38. The difficulty of the Rockingham party's attacking the bill for the Townshend Act was recognized in a letter of Aug. 14, 1768, from William Dowdeswell to Rockingham concerning a suggestion that the Rockingham party sponsor an act to repeal the Townshend Act. Dowdeswell pointed out that the molasses duty levied by the Act of 1766, sponsored by the Rockingham Ministry, was "to say the truth for revenue not for [regulation of] commerce," Hoffman *Burke* 55.

39. Most of the British pamphlets of 1765, 1766, and early 1767 denouncing the colonists are listed in Dickerson *Navigation Acts* 309–316. Some of the articles in British newspapers and magazines are cited and discussed in Hinkhouse *Preliminaries* 52–125 *passim*. Among the most important of the pamphlets are *Good Humour or a Way with the Colonies;* [Josiah Tucker] *Letter from a Merchant in London;* and Charles Lloyd *Conduct of the Late Administration.*

40. Franklin's pieces of this period ably defending the colonists are in Crane *Franklin's Letters to Press* 38–99. Several other London imprints for 1766, listed in Dickerson *Navigation Acts* 311–316, were pro-colonial.

41. Letters concerning the tide having turned in Great Britain against America, Thomas Whately to John Temple Feb. 25, 1767, *Bowdoin–Temple Papers* 79–80; Lord George Sackville to Gen. John Irwin Feb. 13, *Stopford* I 119; Johnson to Gov. Pitkin May 16 and June 9, *Trumbull* 235–238, and to Samuel Johnson May 18, Beardsley *W. S. Johnson* 45; Franklin to Galloway June 13, Smyth *Franklin* V 25.

42. British merchants' resentment over failure of colonial merchants to reply to their circular letters as to repeal of the Stamp Act (discussed in Chapter 3), Franklin to Galloway June 13, 1767, Smyth *Franklin* V 28–29; Johnson to Pitkin Oct. 20, 1768, *Trumbull* 298.

43. Franklin's testimony in the House of Commons and his statement of the names of the members who questioned him and their respective questions are in *The Examination of Dr. Franklin* (London, 1767) reprinted in Smyth *Franklin*

IV 412–448; X 230–233. His testimony as to colonial acceptance of duties levied by Parliament "to regulate commerce," is in *same* IV 419–422, 446.

44. Franklin's statement that external taxes were not objected to in principle by the colonists, *same* 424, 431, 446; Nathaniel Ryder's notes of debates, Gipson "The Great Debate" 34–35. Franklin wrote Lord Kames April 11, 1767, that the published account of his testimony was "imperfect," *same* V 16, but I have found no evidence that he ever denied being correctly quoted on this point.

45. William Strahan to David Hall April 7 as to the powerful impression made by Franklin's testimony, *Pa. Mag. Hist.* X (1886) 96–97. To similar effect, contemporary letters in Sparks *Franklin* VII 312–313 and William Knox in *The Controversy* (London, 1769) 111.

46. The emptiness of the distinction between internal and external taxes had been pointed out in Parliament by both Grenville and Townshend. Grenville wrote Lord Buckinghamshire Jan. 27, 1767, that in the Commons, the day before, Townshend had treated the "distinction between *Internal* and *External* Taxes with the same contempt that I did, . . . calling it *absurd,* nonsensical and ridiculous . . . ," *Lothian* 274–275.

47. Franklin's letter signed "Benevolus" in the *London Chronicle* Apr. 11, 1767 (reprinted in the *Gazetteer* of London June 8), reiterating the colonists' acceptance of Parliament's authority to impose external, though not internal, taxes on them, Crane *Franklin's Letters to Press* 91.

48. There was little protest in the colonies against the duty on molasses levied by the act of Geo. III ch. 52 (1766); even the sweeping protest by New York merchants in December, 1766, against numerous objectionable British measures (described in Chapter 4), said nothing against the duty on molasses levied by this act. (Figures of colonial imports of molasses reported for customs 1768–1770 in Harper "Mercantilism" 11n. and for 1772 in Jensen *Hist. Doc.* 407 indicate that the molasses duty levied by the Act of 1766 yielded over £16,000 sterling a year.)

49. In outlining his colonial tax plan to the Commons, May 13, 1767, Townshend said he proposed "to lay taxes upon America but not internal taxes, because, though he did not acknowledge the distinction, it was accepted by many Americans and this was sufficient," Ryder's diary for May 13, Thomas "Townshend" 44.

50. None of the proposed duties could be considered immoderately high, and (as brought out in Chapter 13 of this book) the principal duty, the duty on tea, was more than offset by refund of British import duties on tea reexported to the colonies provided for by an act (7 Geo. III ch. 56) passed at the same session in which the Townshend Act was passed.

51. The background of the act authorizing establishment of the American Board of Customs Commissioners is discussed in Chaffin "Townshend Acts" 109–111. The establishment of such a Board was recommended in a report from the English Customs Board to the Treasury Apr. 30, 1767, approved by the Treasury the next day, Barrow *Trade* 219–220, 318.

52. The motion in the House of Commons June 2, 1767, for leave to bring in a bill for the act for an American Customs Board, the rapid progress of the bill through the Commons, apparently without a division at any stage, its approval by the House of Lords June 18, and assent by the King June 29 can be followed in *Journals H. of C.* XXXI 395–415. The act was 7 Geo. III ch. 4 (1767). The background of the act is given in Chaffin "Townshend Acts" 109–111.

CHAPTER 6

1. Examples of colonial complaints concerning the Townshend Act on or before the date (Nov. 20, 1767) it was to take effect, Charles Carroll of Carrollton to Henry Graves Aug. 27, 1767, *Carroll Letters* 148–149; John Rowe's diary for Nov. 20, *Rowe* 146; *Providence Gazette* Sept. 19, 1767; *New-York Journal* Nov. 19; *Boston Evening-Post* Sept. 14, Oct. 26; and the items in the *Boston Gazette* cited in note 2 below.

2. Items against the act were published in the *Boston Gazette* Aug. 17, 24, 31; Oct. 26, 1767.

3. Vote of Boston town meeting Oct. 28, 1767, approving a subscription paper not to purchase any of nearly forty articles listed in the paper, *Boston Records* (for 1758–1769) 221–224. There is a good discussion of the non-consumption movement of 1767–1768 in Schlesinger *Col. Merchants* 106–113, which is supplemented by Jensen *Founding* 245, 268–270.

4. Vote of Boston town meeting Nov. 20, 1767, denouncing threatening papers posted in the town and resolving to assist the magistrates in suppressing disorders, *Boston Records* (for 1758–1769) 225. I have not identified the "threatening Papers" referred to in the proceedings of the meeting, but James Otis' speech, quoted in the text, indicates that they were directed against the Townshend Act.

5. Governor Francis Bernard to Lord Shelburne Oct. 30 and Nov. 21, 1767, concerning James Otis, Bernard Papers VI 249–50, 255. To same effect, Thomas Hutchinson to Richard Jackson Nov. 19 (should be 20), 1767, Mass. Arch. XXV 226–227.

6. The uncontrolled mob violence accompanying the opposition to execution of the Stamp Act is described in Knollenberg *Origin* 229, 232, 234, 377–378; Morgan *Stamp Act* 124–127, 146–147, 195–196; Maier *Resistance* 54–60.

7. The tenants' uprising on the Hudson, encouraged by the anti-Stamp Acts riots, is described in Mark *Agrarian Conflicts* 135–151. Soon afterward, Gen. Thomas Gage wrote Henry S. Conway (June 24, 1766) that "the Rich and most Powerfull People of the Province," greatly alarmed, had got what they deserved, since their opposition to execution of the Stamp Act had taught the populace "to rise in Opposition to the Laws," *Gage* I 95.

8. Gage to Conway Sept. 23, 1765, and to the Duke of Richmond Aug. 26, 1766, as to the fear aroused, especially among "the better Sort," in the colonies by uncontrollable mob violence, *same* I 67–68, 104. Gov. Henry Moore of N.Y. wrote Lord Hillsborough July 7, 1768, that the reluctance of N.Y. merchants to join the non-importation agreement was partly attributable to the fact that "The Apprehensions which every Person of property was under during our late Commotions from the Licentiousness of the Populace are not yet forgotten," *N.Y. Col. Doc.* VIII 80.

9. Franklin's testimony in the House of Commons had been published in pamphlet form in Philadelphia (Sept., 1766), New York (Sept., 1766), Boston (Oct., 1766), and Williamsburg (Dec., 1766), Adams *Bibliography* 21–25, and had been applauded by friends of his in the colonies, Sparks *Franklin* VII 317–319. Furthermore, his current article signed "Benevolus," referred to in Chapter 5, had been republished in June, 1767, without indication of disapproval, in several colonial newspapers, Crane *Franklin's Letters to Press* 87.

10. The incongruity of colonial Whigs challenging the Townshend Act was brought out by "A True Patriot," who published a letter in the *Boston Evening-Post* of Oct. 19, 1767, stating "assuredly they cannot pretend to dispute the right of [Parliament to levy] an external one [tax] as that is a point that has been given up these many years by all the colonies in America, particularly during the disputes over the stamp act."

11. Franklin stated in his testimony to the House of Commons in Feb., 1766, that if Parliament should levy a duty on colonial exports so high "as to lessen the demand for it," the colonists, while not denying Parliament's right to levy it, "would complain of it as a burthen, and petition you to lighten it," Smyth *Franklin* IV 431.

12. Labaree *Franklin* XII 66n. states that, "In general, advertisements cost from 3s to 5s local currency, with substantial discounts for repeated insertions," giving an average of not more than 4s. per advertisement. Wright *Am. Negotiator* (London, 1765) lxii gives the ratio of Pa. currency to sterling as not less than 1.6 to 1, so that the cost per advertisement in sterling would be not more than 2.5 pence (4 divided by 1.6) per advertisement. Thus, the stamp tax of 2s. sterling per advertisement, would be, as stated in the text, about 80% of the price of the advertisement.

13. The *Pa. Gazette* was printed on a single sheet requiring a stamp of one penny sterling a copy. An advertisement of the prospective *Pa. Chronicle* published in the *Gazette* of Dec. 25, 1766, indicates that the subscription rate of each was 10s a year, or about 2.3 pence weekly per issue, doubtless in Pa. currency. In terms of sterling this would be less than 1.5 pence a copy. Thus, the stamp tax of one penny sterling a copy would be, as stated in the text, about 70% of the price of the newspaper.

14. The annual subscription price of the relatively low-priced weekly *Boston Chronicle,* printed on one whole sheet, is stated in its opening issue of Dec. 21, 1767, to be 6s 8d (80 pence) or 1.54 pence per issue "lawful." The ratio of "lawful" money to sterling was 1.33⅓ to 1, Wright *Am. Negotiator* lxi–lxii, so that the price in sterling would be about 1.15 pence per copy. Thus, the stamp tax of a penny sterling would be about 86% of the price of the *Boston Chronicle.*

15. The Stamp Act levied a duty of 4 pence sterling a copy on almanacs. The first page of the 1766 issue of the famous *Astronomical Diary,* or, *Almanack* of Nathaniel Ames, published in Boston, gives the price as "2s 8d per dozen," or 2.66 pence a copy, presumably lawful money. Converting the stamp tax of 4 pence sterling to lawful money would give 5.32 pence or exactly twice the cost of the *Almanack* itself.

16. David Hall to Franklin June 20 and Oct. 14, 1765, concerning the threat of the Stamp Act to colonial newspaper publishers, Labaree *Franklin* XII 189, 320.

17. James Parker to Franklin Apr. 25, 1765, concerning his thought of giving up his printing business because of his "Apprehensions" over the effect the "Cruel Stamp-Duty" will have on colonial printers, *same* 112. On Aug. 8, he wrote Franklin that he was planning, after all, to go on with his printing business "tho' to little purpose" since "the Stamp-Duty like a killing Frost, strikes a deadly blow at all that business . . . ," *same* 230.

18. The duties payable under the Stamp Act, 5 Geo. III ch. 12 (1765), covered so wide a range of transactions that it takes ten pages of Pickering *Statutes* to list them all.

19. The difference between the Stamp Act and the Townshend Act in impact on the merchants was noted by John Dickinson in *A Copy of a Letter from a Gentleman in Virginia, to a Merchant in Philadelphia* (1768), Ford *Dickinson* 441–442. Berating Philadelphia merchants for not joining those of Boston in a non-importation agreement, Dickinson pointed out that the Stamp Act obliged the merchants "to sacrifice a very considerable Interest," while the Townshend Act duties could be passed along by them to their customers.

20. Kaestle "Farmer's Letters" 35 describes twenty-three newspapers published in the thirteen colonies in December, 1767, and the first five months of 1768. Brigham *Am. Newspapers* I 39–40, 471–477; II 851–852, 962–63 adds four more published in this period: Daniel and Robert Fowle *The New-Hampshire Gazette, and Historical Chronicle* of Portsmouth; Christoper Sauer *Germantowner Zeitung;* Henrich Miller *Wochentliche Philadelphische Zeitung*; and Benjamin Mecom *Connecticut Gazette* of New Haven, which expired with the issue of Feb. 19, 1768.

21. Kaestle "Farmer's Letters" 351 lists nineteen newspapers that carried some or all of the letters. In addition, the *Connecticut Gazette* also carried the first three letters and the *New-Hampshire Gazette* most, if not all, of them. I have not seen files of the German-language papers published in Pa.; but Hildeburn *Printing in Pa.* II 75n. states they did not carry any of the letters. Kaestle's well-reasoned guess as to the three S.C. papers is correct. Crouch and Timothy published the letters; Wells did not.

22. Details as to publication in 1768 and influence of John Dickinson's letters of "A Farmer"—the pamphlet edition was entitled *Letters from a Farmer in Pennsylvania, to the Inhabitants of the British Colonies* —are in Kaestle "Farmer's Letters" 329–359; Ford *Dickinson* 282–284; and Tyler *History* 236–239. The Letters were later published in pamphlet form in Virginia in combination with Arthur Lee's "Monitor's Letters," and in England, Ireland, and in a French translation purportedly printed in Amsterdam, Ford *Dickinson* 284–285 and Adams *Bibliography* 37–41.

23. The vast influence of Thomas Paine's *Common Sense* is evidenced not only by the great number of editions of the pamphlet, twenty-five (Gimbel *Common Sense passim* and Adams *Bibliography* 164–177), but by many references to it in the correspondence of the time.

24. Dickinson's *The Late Regulations* . . . (Philadelphia, 1765) *same* 211–245. Other less well-known earlier pamphlets by Dickinson are reprinted in *same* 1–205.

25. Facts as to Dickinson's early life, Stillé *Dickinson, passim; D.A.B.;* Colbourn "Dickinson" and "Dickinson's London Letters" 241–286; Jacobson *Dickinson* 1–8, 129–130. A new, documented biography of Dickinson is much needed.

26. As to the political struggle in Pa. from 1759 to 1765, with Franklin and Dickinson on opposite sides, Knollenberg *Origin* 210–213; Jacobson *Dickinson* 9–26; Labaree *Franklin* XI, XII *passim*.

27. Dickinson's service in the Pa. Assembly as representative of the County of Philadelphia from 1762 to 1765, 8 *Pa. Arch.* VI 5367–5502, VII 5503–5788 *passim;* Knollenberg *Origin* 212, 369–370. As to Dickinson's service with the Stamp Act Congress of 1765, Niles *Principles* 159, 163–168 and Ford *Dickinson* 191.

28. Dickinson's defeat for the Pa. Assembly in 1765 and 1766, Stillé *Dickinson* 65; Labaree *Franklin* XII 290–291n., XIII 447–448n. See also 8 *Pa. Arch.* VII 5669, 5788. He was again elected in 1770, not this time for Philadelphia County, but as one of the two members for the city of Philadelphia, *same* 6582. He was not again elected until 1774—this time for the county, *same* VIII 7148.

29. First Farmer's Letter, denouncing the N.Y. Restraining Act of 1767, Ford *Dickinson* 307–312 at 308, 310–311. While disapproving of Parliament's right to compel the colonists to furnish the supplies specified in the Quartering Act, Dickinson approved of colonial Legislatures providing for troops stationed in their colonies in a way consistent with the denial of the right of Parliament to demand these supplies, *same* 308.

30. Evidence of the effect of Dickinson's Letters at Boston is found in a letter from the American Customs Board there to the Treasury Board Feb. 12, 1768, denouncing the letters as of "the most mischievous tendency" and in a letter of Joseph Harrison, Collector of Customs at Boston, to Lord Rockingham, June 17, stating that he believed the letters were "the principal means of spreading this almost general Disaffection among the People, which has at last broke out in open Acts of Violence . . . ," Wolkins "Liberty" 265 and Watson "Harrison" 588.

31. Dickinson recognized that there was a real difference in principle between taxes for revenue and taxes for the regulation of trade, and that it would be possible to draw a line between them in practice by Parliament's providing that any revenue arising incidentally from the application of acts designed to regulate colonial trade be paid over to the respective colonies in which it was collected. This was done in the Declaratory Act of 1778, 18 Geo. III ch. 12.

32. In 1732 and 1736 Parliament restricted colonial manufacture of felt hats and sailcloth (canvas) and in 1750 prohibited the construction in the colonies of any new mill for slitting, rolling, or plating iron with a tilt hammer or new furnace for making steel, Knollenberg *Origin* 170–171, 33–354.

33. Second Letter, Ford *Dickinson* 312–322.

34. Third Letter, *same* 322–328 at 322–324.

35. Third Letter, *same* 325, 327–328. Dickinson pointed out that colonial revolution would be far more sweeping in its effects than the deposition by a nation of its king or race of kings because "Torn from the body to which we are united by religion, liberty, laws, affection, relation, language and commerce, we must bleed at every vein," *same* 26. This and subsequent letters contain additional points not mentioned in the text. I have tried to cover only those which seem the most important.

36. Fourth Letter, *same* 328–335. Dickinson did not mention Franklin, with whom he had been at loggerheads over a proposed change of the form of government in Pennsylvania, Knollenberg *Origin* 210–213, but presumably Dickinson had him particularly in mind in repudiating those who drew a distinction between "internal" and "external" taxes.

37. Fifth Letter, Ford *Dickinson* 335–344 at 337, 339–40. Dickinson did not give any estimate of the cost to the colonies of the restrictions on their trade imposed for the benefit of the mother country; but Daniel Dulany of Md. in his *Considerations* (1765) had estimated this cost to be £767,000 a year and in a letter of Jan. 14, 1768, to De Berdt, the Mass. House of Representatives gave an estimate of

£400,000 a year, Bradford *Mass. Papers* 128. A recent estimate is $2,560,000 to $7,038,000 a year, Harper "Effect" 37.

38. Sixth Letter, Ford *Dickinson* 344–349 at 345–346.

39. Seventh and eighth Letters, *same* 349–364 at 355, 363. In the eighth letter, Dickinson brought out the additional point that, in recently defending the colonists from the French, Great Britain's motive was not so much concern for the colonists as the preservation of a valuable asset, and that she not only succeeded in this but gained a vast accession of land, which, far from benefiting the inhabitants of the old British colonies, injured them by lowering the value of land in those colonies, *same* 360–361.

40. Ninth *Letter, same* 364–374 at 372–373. This letter made the additional point that because of differences in the judicial system in England and the colonies, authority to issue general writs of assistance there was not as dangerous as it would be in the colonies, *same* 368.

41. Tenth *Letter, same* 374–386 at 375–380.

42. Tenth *Letter, same* 382.

43. Eleventh *Letter, same* 386–397 at 396–397.

44. Twelfth *Letter, same* 397–406.

45. Gov. Francis Bernard to Richard Jackson Feb. 28, 1768, concerning the Farmer's Letters, Bernard Papers VI 90–94 at 93–94, Harvard Lib. Further indication of Bernard's estimate of the importance of the letters is his sending two sets of them to Under Secretary of State John Pownall, *same*.

46. Jensen *Founding* 242–243 has a good sampling of the many surviving contemporary statements concerning the immense effect of the Farmer's Letters on colonial thought and action.

CHAPTER 7

1. John Dickinson to James Otis Dec. 5. 1767, enclosing copies of his Farmer's Letters and urging that Mass. take the lead in opposing the Townshend Act, *Warren–Adams* I 3–4. As to the internal political feud in Pa., which precluded hope of the Assembly there taking the initiative, Knollenberg *Origin* 210–213, 368–370. The word "there" is correctly printed from Dickinson's manuscript at M.H.S.

2. Otis' missing reply to Dickinson is known from the latter's acknowledgment to Otis Jan. 25, 1768, stating "I have just receiv'd your Favor of the first of this Month, and am extremely happy in finding myself so much esteemed by you," *Warren–Adams* I 4–5.

3. The first two of the Farmer's Letters were published in the *Boston Evening Post* and the *Boston Chronicle* of Dec. 21, 1767, and the first letter in the *Boston Gazette* of that date. Subsequent letters were published serially in all three of these papers.

4. Instructions of the Boston town meeting of Dec. 22, 1767, presided over by Otis, to the Boston members of the Mass. House to try to secure a petition to the King for repeal of the Townshend Act, *Boston Records* (for 1758–1769) 227–230. The Boston members were Otis himself, Thomas Cushing, Samuel Adams, and John Hancock, *same* 211.

5. Mass. House's Petition to the King Jan. 20, 1768, asserting the right of the colonists to be "taxed only by representatives of their own free election" and begging relief from taxes levied by Parliament on the colonies, together with supporting letters, *Prior Documents* 167–189. The Petition was delivered by the House's London Agent, Dennys De Berdt, to Secretary of State Lord Hillsborough for presentation to the King, De Berdt to Thomas Cushing June 27, 1768, Matthews "De Berdt" 332.

6. Mass. House's circular letter of Feb. 11, 1768, to the Speakers of the Assemblies of the other British colonies in North America, reporting its action and suggesting "united" applications for relief, *same* 191–193. The resolution for this (Feb. 11) and its background, *Mass. House Journals* (for 1767–1768) 129, 135, 148, 157.

7. The Mass. circular letter of Feb. 11, 1768, laid before the Va. House of Burgesses, March 31, by its Speaker Peyton Randolph, *Va. Journals* (for 1766–1769) 143.

8. Petition to the King, Memorial to the House of Lords, and Remonstrance to the House of Commons adopted, "nemine contradicente," by the Va. House Apr. 14, 1768, *same* 165–171. (Weight was added to these remonstrances by the concurrence on Apr. 15 of the Crown-appointed Va. Council, *same* 176). The Remonstrance to the House of Commons stated, "That the Parliament may make Laws for regulating the Trade of the Colonies has been granted" and that such regulation included the imposition of "Duties . . . to restrain the Commerce" of the colonies, as distinguished from duties "for the sole Purpose of raising a Revenue," *same* 170.

9. Va. House requests Acting Governor, "President" John Blair, to send copies of its petitions to the Secretary of State and directs its Speaker to report its proceedings to the Speakers of other colonial Assemblies, April 15, 1768, *same* 173–174. A copy of the Speaker's letter, May 9, is in *N.J. Col. Doc.* X 21–25. The House also directed its Committee of Correspondence to send copies of the documents to the House's London Agent, requesting him to join the Va. Council's London Agent in securing favorable action, *Va. Journals* (for 1766–1769) 174.

10. N.J. Assembly's Petition to the King, signed by the Speaker, Cortlandt Skinner, May 6, 1768, *N.J. Col. Doc.* X 18–21.

11. Petition of Conn. Legislature to the King against the Townshend Act, June 10, 1768, and letter from Gov. William Pitkin to Secretary of State Lord Hillsborough requesting presentation of the Petition to the King June 10, *Conn. Col. Rec.* XIII 76, 84–88.

12. Proposed transfer of colonial affairs from the Secretary of State for the Southern Department to a separate, new department, Shelburne's memorandum Dec. 11 and 12, 1767, *Geo. III* I 510–511; Shelburne to Lady Chatham Dec. 13, *Pitt* III 292–296. Earlier proposals for this were made in 1757, Basye *Board of Trade* 96; in 1765, Ritcheson "Pitt and an American Department" 376; and in July, 1767, *Geo. III* I 500. See also Brooke *Chatham* 309n.

13. Grafton urges Shelburne to take the new American Department because of distrust of the Bedfords' principles (presumably those concerning the colonies), Shelburne's memorandum of conference with Grafton Dec. 12, 1767, *Shelburne* II 73, and Shelburne to Lady Chatham Dec. 13, *Pitt* III 297.

14. Shelburne's choice of the Southern Department and reason for his choice, Shelburne to Grafton Dec. 13, 1767, *same* 298–299. Shelburne wrote Lady Chat-

ham Dec. 13, that he had refused the new department because "I think the general system affected by it," *same* 297, an explanation which seems to make no sense. The greater prestige attached to the older office (Basye "Secretary of State" 13–23) and its jurisdiction over Irish affairs in which Shelburne, as one of the great Irish landowners, had a special interest (*Shelburne* II 81–117) probably influenced his choice.

15. Lord Hillsborough (Earl of Hillsborough in the Irish peerage, Baron Harwich in the English) was appointed Secretary of State for the American Department, i.e., for the colonies, Jan. 20, 1768, Beatson *Pol. Index* II 362. (He resigned as joint Postmaster-General in favor of Sandwich on this same date, *same* I 446.) For the history of the department, which was abolished in 1782, Spector *American Department*.

16. Hillsborough was appointed President of the Board of Trade in July, 1768, Basye *Board of Trade* 171. (The statement in Beatson *Pol. Index* 373 that he was appointed to this office Jan. 20, 1768. is erroneous.)

17. As to the Board's important participation in colonial affairs, Basye *Board of Trade, passim* and Knollenberg *Origin* 456 citations in index under "Board of Trade."

18. As to Hillsborough's political career, sketch of him in *D.N.B.* and Alvord *Mississippi Valley* I 197–199, II 16–21. His first appointment to the Board of Trade was attributed to Lord Halifax, Secretary of State in the Grenville Ministry, Lord Holland to George Selwyn Aug. 16, 1765, Jesse *Selwyn* I 392. He was Chatham's personal choice for the second term as President of the Board, Chatham to Shelburne Aug. 18, 1766, *Pitt* III 116. Hillsborough wrote Grenville Aug. 6, 1766, that he also had been offered, but declined, a seat in the Cabinet, *Grenville* III 296.

19. Hillsborough attended all but 3 of the 279 meetings of the Board of Trade during his two earlier Presidencies, Basye *Board of Trade* 109, 224–225. Cecilius Calvert wrote Gov. Horatio Sharpe of Md. March 10, 1764, that Hillsborough was "very assiduous and by proficiency has turned out much business . . . ," *Sharpe* III 144.

20. As to Hillsborough's friendly relations with Grenville, Hillsborough to Grenville Aug. 6, 1766; William Knox to Grenville May 24, Aug. 20, and Sept. 15, 1768, *Grenville* III 296, IV 297, 344, 364. Their relations were of long standing. George Bubb Dodington wrote in his diary June 10, 1754, that Grenville was a "bosom friend" of Hillsborough, *Dodington* 304–305.

21. Lord Holland wrote George Selwyn Aug. 16, 1765, that, though Hillsborough was "very well," i.e., on good terms, with the late Grenville Ministry in which he served as President of the Board of Trade, he was "too wise to be of their opinion and they had been wiser had they consulted him," *Selwyn* I 392–393. Furthermore, the Grenvillites opposed repeal of the Stamp Act, whereas Hillsborough (so he said in 1769 without any known contradiction) that he had voted for a repeal, William S. Johnson to Gov. William Pitkin Jan. 3, 1769, *Trumbull* 306.

22. Grenville to Lord Trevor Dec. 31, 1767, wondering what stand Hillsborough was likely to take concerning the colonies, *Grenville* IV 206. Similar puzzlement was mentioned by Dennys De Berdt, Agent for the Mass. House, to

Thomas Cushing Dec. 24, 1767, Matthews "De Berdt" 330; and by Benjamin Franklin, Agent for the Pa. Assembly, to Joseph Galloway Jan. 9, 1768, Smyth *Franklin* V 91.

23. Hillsborough to Gen. Thomas Gage March 12, 1768, and Benjamin Franklin to William Franklin March 13, concerning Hillsborough's attitude toward colonial non-importation and the *Farmer's Letters,* quoted in the text, *Gage,* II 60 and Smyth *Franklin* V 114.

24. Presumably such important letters of April, 1768, quoted in the text were not written without Cabinet approval; but I have not found any Cabinet minute concerning them.

25. Hillsborough's circular letter of April 21, 1768, quoted in the text, *Eng. Hist. Documents* (Jensen) IX 716–717.

26. Hillsborough to Gov. Francis Bernard April 22, 1768, quoted in the text, ordering rescission of the Mass. circular letter, *Prior Documents* 203–205.

27. Bernard to Hillsborough June 25 and 28 and July 1, 1768, as to the vote on rescission quoted in the text; *Letters to Ministry* 39–46 at 43. (Bernard gives 91 as the number voting against rescission.) The names of the 92 voting for rescission and the 17 against, on June 30, are listed in the *Boston Chronicle* of July 11, 1768. A large number in the House was appointed to provincial offices by the Governor and thus subject to his influence, Brennan *Massachusetts* 72–73.

28. The twelve Rescinders holding office under Bernard or his predecessors were William Browne, Peter Frye, Jacob Fowle, and Richard Saltonstall of Essex County; John Chadwick and John Ashley of Berkshire; Jonathan Sayward of York; Matthew Mayhew of Dukes; Josiah Edson of Plymouth; Israel Williams of Hampshire; Timothy Ruggles of Worcester; and Chillingsworth Foster of Barnstable, Indexes to Whitmore *Civil List* 165–172. Four of the remaining five (John Calef of Essex; Jonathan Bliss, Jonathan Ashley, and Joseph Root of Hampshire) were subsequently appointed to office by Gov. Thomas Hutchinson, *same.*

29. Bernard to Hillsborough July 1, 1768, concerning his proclamation dissolving the Mass. Legislature, *Letters to Ministry* 46. The proclamation, dated July 1, is in the *Boston Chronicle* of July 11.

30. The names of the representatives in the new House in 1769 and the towns they represented are in *Mass. Acts* XVIII 372–374. The five Rescinders in the new House were Bliss, Williams, John Ashley, Ruggles, and Foster. All five Rescinders from Essex County, including the two representatives of Salem, next to Boston the most important commercial town of Massachusetts, were replaced by new men. Three of the towns represented in the old House by Rescinders sent no representative to the new.

31. Bernard to Hillsborough June 1, 1769, concerning the defeat of several "Tories" for reelection to the Mass. Council in May, 1769, quoted in the text, Brown *Democracy in Mass.* 259. Those called "Tories," Bernard wrote, were "those who are disposed to support the King's government, to acknowledge the authority of Parliament, and to preserve the people from a democratical despotism . . . ," *same.*

32. Petitions to the King complaining of the Townshend Act as unconstitutional and asking relief: Md., June 21, 1768, *Md. Arch.* LXI 406–409; R.I., Sept. 12, *R.I. Col. Rec.* VI 556, 559–564; Pa., Sept. 22, *Pa. Assembly* VII 6271–6273; Del.,

Oct., 27, *Gentleman's Mag.* XXXIX (Jan., 1769) 28–29; N.H., Oct. 29, *N.H. Papers* VII 187–188, 248–249; S.C., Nov. 19, *S.C. Gazette, Extraordinary* Nov. 24 and Smith *S.C.* 362–363; N.C., Dec. 5, *N.C. Col. Rec.* VII 980–982; Ga., Dec. 24, *Ga. Col. Rec.* XIV 643–645. Pa. and N.Y. also appealed to both Houses of Parliament, *Pa. Assembly* VII 5274–5277; Gipson *Brit. Empire* XI 173.

33. New York Assembly convened Oct. 27, 1768, *N.Y. Journals 1766–76* Oct., 1768, session, 1.

34. The maneuvering in the N.Y. Assembly over action on the Mass. circular letter can be followed in *same* 16, 30, 34, 46, 48, 53; Smith *Memoirs* I 46–50; Champagne "Family Politics" 68–71; Friedman "New York Assembly" 11–14.

35. Adoption, without dissent, Dec. 12, 1768, of a Petition to the King, Memorial to the House of Lords, and Representation to the House of Commons for repeal of the Townshend Act, *N.Y. Journals 1766–76* Oct., 1768, to Jan., 1769, session, 11–17.

36. Vote December 31, 1768, for an instruction to the Speaker of the Assembly, Philip Livingston, to make a favorable reply to the Mass. circular letter, *same* Oct., 1768, to Jan., 1769, session, 72. On the same day, the Assembly passed resolutions asserting its right to petition the King, correspond with other colonies, and, with a fling at the Restraining Act of 1767 (discussed in Chapter 4), asserting the right not to be dissolved by any authority other than the Crown, *same* 70. The Governor, Sir Henry Moore, dissolved the Assembly two days later, *same* 75–76.

37. Resolutions of the Va. House of Burgesses defying Hillsborough's circular letter, adopted *"Nemine Contradicente,"* May 16, 1769, *Va. Journals* (for 1766–1769) 213–215.

38. An earlier unsuccessful effort (March–June, 1768) to launch a concerted movement for non-importation is described in Schlesinger *Col. Merchants* 114–119; Jensen *Founding* 270–273; *Mass. Papers* 58–60; *Rowe;* 152–155.

39. In a list published in Boston in 1774, *Adams Family Corresp.* I following p. 80, twenty-seven persons were listed as "Merchants," meaning presumably persons engaged in business chiefly as importers and wholesalers (though some of them probably sold goods at retail, too). Thirty-six others, classified collectively as "Traders," were listed as shopkeeper, factor, iron dealer, dealer in small wares, retailing factor of crockery ware, toy-seller, apothecary, jeweler, or wine-seller.

40. Agreement of Boston merchants and traders Aug. 1, 1768, Andrews "Boston Merchants" 205, with Rowe's diary for Aug. 1, *Rowe* 171. The exempted items presumably were those deemed essential and not otherwise available. (On Nov. 7, 1769, the agreement was revised by enlarging the list of exempted items and by providing that non-importation of all except the exempted articles should continue until the Townshend Act duties were repealed, Andrews "Boston Merchants" 231.)

41. Additional subscriptions obtained the next day, Rowe's diary for Aug. 2, 1768, *Rowe* 172. The statement in the text as to the subscriptions by Aug. 10 is based on a letter of Thomas Hutchinson to an unidentified correspondent Aug. 10, Mass Arch. XXVI 322.

42. The Salem non-importation agreement adopted Sept. 6, 1768, followed that of Boston, Andrews "Boston Merchants" 206.

43. N.Y. merchants' agreement Aug. 27, 1768, same 207; *New York Journal* Sept. 8. The N.Y. agreement did not exempt hemp, duck, shot, or fish hooks and lines, exempted in Boston, but exempted grindstones, chalk, tin, sheet copper, and German steel, not on the Boston list of exemptions. The N.Y. merchants agreed also not to import anything from Hamburg and Holland except tiles and bricks.

44. N.Y. tradesmen's agreement of Sept. 5, 1768, *Annual Register* (for 1768) 236–237. "Tradesmen" might, if not otherwise explained, mean either a shop-keeper or one who followed a trade, i.e., a mechanic, artisan, or craftsman. The statement in the N.Y. tradesmen's agreement of 1768 that "we will not . . . buy any kind of goods from any merchant, store-keeper or retailer . . . who shall re-fuse . . . in signing the said agreement" shows that "tradesmen" was used here in the latter sense.

45. John Dickinson's broadside *A Copy of a Letter from a Gentleman in Virginia, to a Merchant in Philadelphia,* is in Ford *Dickinson* 439–445; the quotation is at 444. The broadside, undated, was written apparently soon after the Philadelphia merchants had refused in Sept., 1768, to join with those of Boston and N.Y.

46. Initial refusal of Philadelphia merchants pending British action on the Pa. Assembly's petitions for repeal, to take action, including failure of most of the dry goods merchants to attend a meeting held Sept. 22, 1768, Schlesinger *Col. Merchants* 126–127. The Assembly's petitions were dated Sept. 22, the merchants' own memorial, Nov. 1, *same* 126–128. The memorial gave notice that the merchants would join in the non-importation movement if their appeal were not successful, *same* 128. There is a good account of the attitude and actions of the Philadelphia merchants in a letter of Apr. 8, 1769, signed by eighteen of them to their London mercantile correspondents, *London Chronicle* June 10, 1769, and *Pa. Mag. Hist.* XXVII (1903) 84–87.

47. Philadelphia merchants' agreement of Feb. 6, 1769, suspending further orders until March 10, Hamilton *Letters to Washington* III 350–351. As to the background of this action, Schlesinger *Col. Merchants* 128–219; Jensen *Philadelphia* 172–179; Brunhouse *"Townshend Acts"* 355–360.

48. Philadelphia agreement of March 10, 1769, Hamilton *Letters to Washington* III 351–352. A copy of the agreement was sent by a committee of Philadelphia merchants, headed by John Reynell and William West, with a covering letter of March 15, to Charles Wallace and other merchants in Annapolis, Md., *same* 349–350, who forwarded the papers to George Washington, Washington to George Mason Apr. 5, 1769, Fitzpatrick *Washington* II 500. The Boston agreement covered only imports from "Great Britain," the Philadelphia agreement from "any . . . part of Europe (except Linens & Provisions from Ireland . . .)."

49. New Haven and New London, Conn., and Newcastle County, Delaware, adopt non-importation agreements in July and Aug., 1769, Schlesinger *Col. Merchants* 149–150.

50. As to the tardy and initially defective agreement of the merchants of Newport, R.I., Oct. 30, 1769, which was not revised in a manner satisfactory to the merchants of other colonies until Jan., 1770, *same* 154–155. As to an earlier agreement in Providence, R.I., *same* 153.

51. Though no evidence has been found of any non-importation agreement among N.J. merchants, they apparently abstained from importing, since the N.J. House voted Oct. 18, 1769, to thank the merchants of the colony, as well as those of N.Y. and Pa., for not importing British merchandise, *N.J. Col. Doc.* XXVI 546. The failure of the N.H. merchants to act is discussed in Upton *N.H.* 8–9 and Schlesinger *Col. Merchants* 155.

52. Substantial duties were being collected on colonial imports of sugar, wine, and molasses under the acts of Geo. III ch. 13 (1733), 4 Geo. III ch. 15 (1764), and 6 Geo. III ch. 52 (1766). In 1768 the duty collected on molasses amounted to nearly £12,000, on sugar to over £4,000, and on wine to over £7,000, Dickerson *Navigation Acts* 185.

53. Boston merchants' resolution of Oct. 17, 1769, to maintain the boycott until all duties for revenue were repealed, refusal of New York and Philadelphia merchants to concur, and Boston merchants' recession on Dec. 4, Schlesinger *Col. Merchants* 131–133; Broadside of Dec. 6, *Am. Bibliography* IV 167. Cushing and other Boston merchants to De Berdt Dec. 29, 1769, *Mass. Papers* 128–129. See also Jonathan and John Amory's letters Aug. and Sept., 1769, as to background of the Boston revision of Oct., 1769, Meredith *Amory* 157–161.

54. Washington to Mason Apr. 5, 1769, warmly advocating the adoption of a non-importation agreement in Va., but pointing out the particular difficulty of carrying out such an agreement in Va. and the other tobacco colonies, Fitzpatrick *Washington* II 500–501; Knollenberg *Washington: The Virginia Period* 104–105, 187–188.

55. Mason to Washington Apr. 5, 1769, replying to his letter of the same date and heartily agreeing with him as to a non-importation agreement for Va., Hamilton *Washington* III 342–344.

56. On Apr. 23, 1769, Mason wrote Washington, enclosing some amendments to a draft of a proposed agreement ("Association") previously sent him, *same* 345–346. I have not found just when Mason's original draft was sent. It is in *same* 346–349, erroneously headed "1767 & 1774."

57. Washington's diary records that he "Set of [off] for Williamsburg" on Apr. 30, 1769, arriving there three days later, *Washington Diaries* I 322, 324.

58. Gov. Lord Botetourt's dissolution of the Va. House of Burgesses for its resolutions of the day before, denying the right of Parliament to tax the colonies and denouncing its action in addressing the King to bring persons accused of treason in the colonies to England for trial, *Va. Journals* (for 1766–1769) 214–218.

59. Members, or more accurately the ex-members of the Va. House of Burgesses assemble at the Raleigh Tavern ("the House of Mr. Anthony Hay"), where a committee was appointed to prepare a non-importation agreement, which was adopted the next day, *same* xxxix, xl. Washington was a member of this committee, *Washington Diaries* I 325.

60. The Va. non-importation agreement of May 18, 1769, is in *Va. Journals* (for 1766–1769) xl–xlii.

61. The Va. non-importation agreement was initially signed by 88 former members of the recently dissolved Va. House, including Peyton Randolph, Speaker, George Washington, Richard Henry Lee, Thomas Jefferson, and Patrick Henry, and by Richard Clarke "Clerk to the Association." The names of twenty

later signers are in *same* xliii, and presumably there were many more, *same* xliii. However, most of the importing merchants refrained from signing, Jensen *Founding* 356.

62 The articles other than those imported from Great Britain or the European continent, taxed for revenue by acts of Parliament included such important items as wine from Madeira and the Azores and molasses from the West Indies, taxable under Acts of 1764 and 1766.

63. The provision for non-purchase after Sept. 1, 1769, in the Va. agreement was similar to agreements in other colonies not to drink tea, described in Schlesinger *Col. Merchants* 109, 185–186; Labaree *Tea Party* 26–36, 273–274, and *Patriots* 24–25.

64. The Va. agreement of May 18, 1769, *Va. Journals* xl–xlii. The agreement excepted from the class of goods banned "Paper, not exceeding Eight Shillings Sterling per reem" and "such Articles of the Produce or [misprinted "of"] Manufacture of Ireland as may be immediately brought from thence . . . ," *same* xli.

65. The Md. agreement, dated June 22, 1769, effective immediately except as to goods already ordered, is in *Md. Arch.* LXII 458–462. Though similar to the Va. agreement, its list of banned goods is somewhat more extensive than the Va. list, and contains an enforcement provision not in the Va. agreement. Barker *Md.* 320–326 describes the implementation of the agreement in Md.

66. The non-importation movement in S.C., culminating in the meetings of July 20 and 22, 1769, is described at length in Schlesinger *Col. Merchants* 141–145; McCrady *South Carolina* 645–651; Sellers *Charleston* 204–210, which quotes the list of articles excepted from the ban on importation.

67. The S.C. non-importation agreement of July 30, 1769, published in the *South Carolina Gazette* of July 27, 1769, is reprinted in Andrews "Boston Merchants" 217–219.

68. The Ga. non-importation agreement of Sept. 19, 1769, is discussed in Coleman *Ga.* 29–32; Andrews "Boston Merchants" 220–221; and Schlesinger *Col. Merchants* 147–148. The background of the N.C. agreement of Nov. 7, 1769, and its provisions, similar to those of the Va. agreement of May 18, are described in *same* 148–149.

69. The project for an American episcopate of the Church of England; the war of pamphlets, and articles in the colonial press precipitated by the pamphlets referred to in the text; and the refusal of successive British Ministries to support the project are discussed in an appendix to this chapter.

70. Gov. Bernard's messages of July 6 and 12, 1769, to the Mass. House of Representatives demanding payment for supplies for the British troops barracked in the colony, required by the colonial Quartering Act, and the House's flat refusal to comply, Bradford *Mass. Papers* 183–187.

CHAPTER 8

1. Assault on the Collector of Customs at Pocomoke, Md., early in 1765, Barrow *Trade* 191, 316.

2. The *Polly* affair at Dighton, Mass., in April, 1765, Morgan *Stamp Act* 44–46.

3. Rescue of goods seized by customs officers at Newbury, Mass., in March, 1766, Barrow *Trade* 191, 316.

4. The rescue of goods seized by customs officers at the storehouse of Enoch Illfley at Falmouth, Mass. (now Portland, Maine), Gipson *Brit. Empire* XI 34–35. As pointed out in the second appendix to Chapter 5, this incident also involved opposition to use of general writs of assistance.

5. The controversies at Charleston, S.C., in 1766–1768, and Henry Laurens leading part in some of them, Barrow *Trade* 204–209, 234–235, 317–318, 320; Gipson *Brit. Empire* XI 552–559; Wallace *Laurens* 137–149; Sellers *Charleston* 192–202 (marred by some misdating).

6. There are sketches of the members of the Board in Clark "American Customs Board" 781–782 and Channing "Commissioners" 479–481. Further details as to John Temple, son-in-law of James Bowdoin of Boston, are in *Bowdoin–Temple Papers* xv–xvii and as to Charles Paxton, in Wolkins "Paxton" 343–347. Little is known of Burch, who was described in Thomas Hollis to Andrew Eliot May 25, 1768, as of little fortune, but "a learned, ingenious, virtuous good man, a Lover of Truth & Liberty," Hollis Papers, Mass. Hist. Soc.

7. The Commission establishing the American Customs Board Sept. 8, 1767, is in *American Gazette* (London, 1768) 112–120. Details concerning the Board's personnel and operations are in Clark "American Customs Board" 777–806; Channing "Commissioners" 477–490; Dickerson "British Control of American Newspapers"; and Dickerson "Use Made of the Revenue." The initial plan was to establish the American Board in Philadelphia, Customs Board report of Jan. 6, 1767, cited in Chaffin "Townshend Acts" 110n.

8. The Board held its first meeting Nov. 17, 1767, Paxton to Lord Townshend Feb. 24, 1768, Wolkins "Paxton" 348. The Townshend Act, 7 Geo. III ch. 46 (1767), provided that the duties levied by the act were to take effect Nov. 20, 1767.

9. William S. Johnson to Jared Ingersoll Nov. 12, 1767, as to Paxton's influence with Charles Townshend having led to the choice of Boston as headquarters, "Ingersoll Letters" 416–417. As to Paxton's connection with Townshend, Wolkins "Paxton" 349–350. Conjectures as to possible other reasons for choosing Boston are given in Gipson *Brit. Empire* XI 118–119 and Dickerson *Navigation Acts* 198–199. Philadelphia initially had been proposed, Claffin "Townshend Acts" 110.

10. Bernard to Shelburne Sept. 21, 1767, as to threats against the Commissioners, particularly Paxton, Barrow *Trade* 227, 319. Paxton had shown particular zeal in enforcing the obnoxious British acts of trade and revenue as Surveyor of Customs at Boston, *same* 170, and had apparently diverted to himself funds which should have been paid into the Massachusetts Treasury, *Mass. Journals* XXXVII Part 1, 1760–1761, 107, 122; XXXVIII Part 2, 1761, 180–181, 231–248; and report of cases of *Gray* v. *Paxton* (1761, 1762) in Quincy *Reports* 541–552.

11. Ann Hulton, sister of Commissioner Henry Hulton, to Mrs. Adam Lightbody Dec. 17, 1767, and Lord George Germain to Gen. John Irwin Dec. 29, concerning the reception at Boston on Nov. 5, of Commissioners Paxton, Henry Hulton, and William Burch, *Hulton Letters* 8 and *Stopford* I 126. Temple was

probably already there and the fifth, John Robinson, arrived Nov. 28, American Customs Board to the Treasury Board Feb. 12, 1768, Wolkins "Paxton" 263.

12. Paxton wrote Lord Townshend Feb. 24, 1768, "I have since my arrival Suffered the Indignitie of being burnt in Effigie," *same* 270. To same effect, Commissioners to Treasury Feb. 12, Wolkins "Liberty" 265. I have seen no evidence as to when and under what circumstances this incident occurred.

13. The hanging of Paxton and Inspector-General John Williams in effigy on March 18, 1768, Commissioners to Treasury March 28, *same* 269–270; Bernard to Lord Shelburne March 19, *Letters to Ministry* 17–19. The Commissioners explained to the Treasury in their letter of March 28, that Williams was considered obnoxious "by being our immediate Instrument in regulating this Port. . . ."

14. Boston town meeting votes May 4, 1768, not to permit use of Faneuil Hall for the Election Day dinner if the Commissioners were invited, *Boston Records* (for 1758–1769) 250.

15. Joseph Harrison to Lord Rockingham concerning Hancock's wealth and popularity with "the Mob," and his "generous, benevolent Disposition," and his being "very charitable to the Poor," June 17, 1768, Watson "Harrison" 589, 592. Thomas Hutchinson to Thomas Whately, June 18, also refers to Hancock's wealth and "great influence over the populace," Mauduit *Franklin* 17, and Commodore Samuel Hood wrote George Grenville July 11 that he was "by far the richest man in the province," *Grenville* IV 307. As to his extensive business activities, Baxter *Hancock* 146–278 and Brown *Hancock* 14–152.

16. John Hancock had the unique distinction at this time of being both a selectman of Boston and one of its four representatives in the Mass. House of Representatives, *Boston Records* (for 1758–1769) 232, 245.

17. Commissioners' statement to the Treasury May 12, 1768, concerning Hancock's and others' opposition to them, enclosed in letter of the same date from Samuel Venner, Secretary to the American Customs Boards, to Thomas Bradshaw, Secretary to the Treasury Board, T:1:348, 358, P.R.O.

18. One of the complaints against the Commissioners, published in the *New York Journal* of March 2, 1769, was the affectation by these "mushroom gentry" of "high life, not only in their dress, attendants and in rolling from house to house in their chariots the best of weather"; but in dining at the *"courtly hour"* of four, when the "hours for dining in this town, time out of mind" was one or two o'clock, *Journal of Times* 57. Hutchinson [to Whately] Aug. 8 and 10, 1768, explained that in allegedly "taking too much state upon them," the Commissioners were merely following the practice of the English Customs Board, Mass. Arch. XXVI 320–322.

19. John Palfrey to William Holt June 13, 1768, Palfrey *New Eng.* V 387 and Gov. John Wentworth of N.H. to Paul Wentworth Nov. 15, Mayo *Langdon* 35n. and to "Dr. Belham" Aug. 9, Mayo *Wentworth* 120, concerning the Commissioners' arrogance. The attitude of Hulton may be gathered from his letter to an unidentified correspondent June 20, 1775, deploring the death of so many British officers at Bunker Hill, particularly because they were killed by enemies not one of whom "has the least pretension to be called a gentleman," *Hulton Letters* 99.

20. Similar comments by others: Thomas Cushing to Dennys De Berdt Sept. 27, 1768, Cushing *S. Adams* I 245; John Rowe's diary for Dec. 15 as to the "very Insolent" behavior of "their High Mightinesses," *Rowe* 181; Hutchinson's nephew, Nathaniel Rogers, to W.S. Johnson Nov. 23, spoke of the Commissioner's carrying "their Ideas of Superiority" too high as "one great cause of their ill usage," Shipton *Harvard Graduates* XIII 634.

21. Joshua Loring to John Swift, Collector of Customs at Philadelphia, Aug. 4, 1771, attributed Swift's difficulties with the Board to his letters not having "Flummery eno' in them alias not big eno' with respect," Custom House Papers XI 1405, Hist. Soc. of Pa., and Hutchinson wrote Whately in Aug., 1768, "There is too much hauteur, some of their officers say, in the treatment they receive," Mauduit *Franklin* 20.

22. The American Customs Board, as its name implies, also was responsible for enforcement of British duties levied in the colonies, and Hutchinson wrote Whately in Aug., 1768, that one of the reasons for the Board's extreme unpopularity was that because the Townshend Act duties happened to take place just about the time the Commissioners arrived, people "have absurdly connected [imposition] of the duties and the Board . . . ," *same.*

23. The Commissioners wrote the Treasury Feb. 12, 1768, that for two years and a half before their arrival only six seizures for violations of the British acts of trade and customs had been made in New England, Barrow "Customs Service" 464. Hutchinson wrote Lord Hillsborough Feb. 3, 1769, of the Commissioners' exertions "to restore the Acts of Trade which for two or three years together no officer dared to carry into execution," *same* 481, and Bernard wrote in similar vein to Barrington Feb. 20, 1769, *Barrington–Bernard* 190.

24. Hutchinson wrote Whately Aug. [no day], 1768, that he was satisfied the root of the complaints against the Commissioners was their "vigilance . . . in carrying the acts of trade into execution . . . especially in this port where the Board is constantly held," Mauduit *Franklin* 21. (The staff of customs officers at Boston and additional officers recommended for better enforcement are given in a letter from the Collector and Comptroller at Boston to the American Customs Board April 30, 1768, Wolkins "Boston Customs District" 418–443.)

25. Copy of the merchants' protest, Document 0215:31 in the Price Papers, Mass. Hist. Soc. Additional evidence of the Commissioners' activities at Boston and the baneful effects on trade there will be found in Dickerson *Boston* 10, 49, 59–60, 84 and Dickerson *Navigation Acts* 213–218, 220–221, 227–229, 257–260. Wroth "Mass. Vice-Admiralty Court" 56 points out that suits for violations of British Acts of Trade and Revenue in the Mass. Admiralty Court rose from three or four a year in 1765–1767 to twenty-four in 1768 and twenty-eight in 1769.

26. Temple (son-in-law of James Bowdoin, a leading Boston Whig), who disassociated himself as far as practicable from the other Commissioners, Wolkins "Liberty" 261n., 267n., *Barrington–Bernard Corresp.* 190 and Hulton *Letters* 15, complained to Grenville Nov. 7, 1768, of his fellow Commissioners' undue severity, *Grenville* IV 397, but in writing the Duke of Grafton Oct. 25, 1769, of the injury to trade at Boston from the Board's "unnecessary severities" he blamed these on instructions (now missing) received from England, Barrow "Colonial Customs" 481.

27. The *Fortune* (stationed at Boston in 1763 under the new enforcement program, described in Chapter 3) left Boston in July, 1766, John Rowe's diary for July 27, *Rowe* 105. Apparently she was not replaced until the *Romney* arrived at Boston in May, 1768. According to a letter of July 5, 1766, from Bernard to the British Admiralty, the *Fortune's* commander, Captain Thomas Bishop, had "so discouraged the practice of illegal trade" at Boston that there was now "less of it in this port than in other places," Quincy *Reports* 432n., which may explain the delay in replacing the *Fortune*.

28. American Customs Board to Treasury Board Feb. 12, 1768, intimating the necessity for troops and ships of war at Boston to assist the Board in its enforcement measures, Wolkins "Liberty" 207, and to Commodore Samuel Hood March 4, 1768, for naval support at Boston, Channing *History* III 93.

29. Gov. Bernard wrote Lord Shelburne March 12 and 19, 1768, as to the need for troops at Boston, *Letters to Ministry* 13–22, and on May 18, Paxton wrote Lord Townshend "Tis the Opinion of the wisest Men here that unless we have immediately three or four men of war and at least one Regiment [at Boston] every thing will be in the greatest confusion and disorder," Wolkins "Paxton" 348. Paxton had written in similar vein to Lord Townshend on Feb. 24, same 348.

30. Instructions dated May 2, 1768, from Samuel Hood as "Commander in Chief of His Majesty's Ships and Vessels employed . . . in the River St. Lawrence Along the Coast of Nova Scotia . . . to New York" to Captain John Corner, commander of the *Romney,* to "proceed without loss of time . . . to Boston," Wolkins "Liberty" 271–272.

31. John Rowe's diary for May 18, 1768, records the arrival of the *Romney* "this day in Kingsroad [Boston]," *Rowe* 162.

32. By June 16, 1768, Corner had impressed eighteen men, Report of Committee of Mass. Council to the Council June 16, *same* 250n. Hutchinson wrote Jackson June 16 that, although Corner had refrained from pressing men "belonging to the Prov. [Massachusetts] who have families," his seizure of "Seamen out of all inward bound Vessels" had aroused so much fear that "it prevents Coasters as well as other Vessels coming in freely, and it adds more fewel to the great stock among us before," *same* 283.

33. Gov. Edward Trelawney of Jamaica to Duke of Newcastle July 29, 1742, Knollenberg *Origin* 193, 362 n.19.

34. Section 9 of 6 Anne ch. 37 (1708) exempted from impressment all persons in the colonies except deserters from the British navy. The grounds for the view that this act prohibiting impressment in the colonies was still in force in 1768 are set forth in Knollenberg *Origin* 194, 362 and John Adams' proposed argument in *Rex.* v. *Corbet* (1769) *Adams Legal Papers* II 323–325. See also the appendix to Chapter 11 of this volume relating to the *Corbet* case.

35. The Commissioners wrote the Treasury Board March 28, 1768, that persons who had applied for "the usual indulgences" with respect to imports of wine had been told that "full Duties would be required," Wolkins "Liberty" 268. Hutchinson had earlier (Oct. 20, 1767) written Richard Jackson that the custom officers at Boston must be winking at the illegal importation of "Wines from the Islands," since they "are sold so Cheap that there is no need of other Evidence that they pay no duty," Mass. Arch. XXV 205–208.

36. The "indulgence" allowed with respect to wine perhaps was similar to that with respect to the duty on foreign colonial molasses, described in Knollenberg *Origin* 138–139, 338–339, namely to permit the importer to declare for duty only a small fraction of the molasses.

37. Commissioners to Treasury Board March 28, 1768, reporting the refusal to grant Daniel Malcom, among others, "the usual indulgence" with respect to a cargo of expected wine, Wolkins "Liberty" 268. As to the subsequent landing of this "Fayal" (Azores) wine without payment of duty and the refusal of witnesses to testify against Malcom, *same* and Bernard to Shelburne March 21, *Letters to Ministry* 23. (An earlier—1766—clash between Malcom and Boston customs officers is described in the appendix to Chapter 5).

38. The affidavit of the informer, Thomas Kirk, as to the alleged violation on May 9, dated June 10, 1768, is in *Letters to Ministry* 121–122. Kirk explained his long delay in lodging the information by stating he had been fearful of reprisals if he failed to keep silent, *Adams Legal Papers* II 175 n.6.

39. The Commissioner's proceedings, including the order to the Collector and the seeking of legal advice before ordering seizure of the *Liberty,* are described in the sources cited in *same* n.7.

40. Harrison, Collector of the Port of Boston, to Rockingham June 17, 1768, as to arranging for assistance from the *Romney* and seizure of the *Liberty,* Watson "Harrison" 590. The cutting or affixing of a broad arrow was the customary method of formally seizing a ship or cargo as the basis for condemnation proceedings for alleged violation of British laws of trade or customs. Hutchinson to Jackson June 16 mentions that the "broad arrow" was cut on the mast of the *Liberty,* Wolkins "Liberty" 281.

41. The seizure of the *Liberty* for alleged false entry was clearly legal and justified. But the attempt to secure condemnation, on a technicality, of some tar and oil in the *Liberty;* another suit, inspired by the Commissioners, for extremely heavy penalties against Hancock and associates for smuggling wine from the *Liberty;* and the harassment of Hancock over another of his vessels, the *Lydia,* have led respected scholars to charge the Commissioners with "racketeering." I agree with the editors of the *Adams Legal Papers,* that the Commissioners' actions probably were not improper, *same* 174, 178, 188, 181–210.

42. The absence of opposition to the customs officers' formal seizure of the *Liberty* is clearly implied in Hutchinson to Jackson June 16, 1768, Wolkins "Liberty" 281 and Harrison to Rockingham June 17, Watson "Harrison" 590. Hutchinson to Jackson June 16, 1768, stated that "the Comptroller [Benjamin Hallowell] . . . made a signal for the man of war boats to come ashoar," Wolkins "Liberty" 281.

43. Hutchinson to Jackson June 16, 1768, as to the *Liberty* incident, *same* 281–284.

44. Hutchinson wrote Thomas Whately June 18 that "it is pretended that the removal and not the seizure incensed the people. It seems not very material which it was," Mauduit *Franklin* 17. It was, of course, highly material toward establishing that there was no effort to prevent the customs officers from doing their duty in formally seizing the *Liberty* and that they were attacked only after, and because, the landing party, coming ashore at Hallowell's signal, conducted itself as described in Hutchinson's letter to Jackson cited in note 43 above.

45. The affidavits of numerous eyewitnesses that the customs officers were not attacked until the move was made to remove the *Liberty* from her berth are published in *American Gazette* No. 2 97–110. According to these affidavits, the landing party's conduct was particularly provocative because the master of the landing party used abusive language and gave orders, luckily not obeyed, for his men to fire. See also Boston committee's statement of June 17, 1768, in *Boston Records* (for 1758–1769) 278. (The words *fasts* is misprinted *forts* there.)

46. Report of the *Liberty* incident in the Commissioners' Minutes of June 13, 1768, enclosed in a memorial to the Treasury dated June 16 is in *Letters to Ministry* 114–116.

47. The report of Bernard to Secretary of State Lord Hillsborough June 11 and 13 is in *same* 26–28. The misimpression given by this letter and the Commissioners' report or both is reflected in the statement concerning the incident in the opinion of Attorney General William De Grey July 25, Wolkins "Liberty" 274–275.

48. A report dated June 17, 1768, of a committee including two of the town's leading lawyers, John Adams and Richard Dana, appointed to investigate the *Liberty* riot, denounced the cutting of the vessel from her moorings and removing her from her berth as illegal, *Boston Records* (for 1758–1769) 257–258. This view seems to be sound in view of the fact that the *Liberty* had not even been libeled, much less condemned, when the seizure was made. She was not libeled until June 22, and not condemned until Aug. 17, 1768, *Adams Legal Papers* II 177, 178.

49. Report of a committee of the Mass. Council June 16, 1768, as to Captain Corner's asurance not to impress certain categories of seamen, Wolkins "Liberty" 252n. and statement in the *Boston Chronicle* of June 20.

50. Proceedings against the *Liberty* in the Admiralty Court at Boston and her condemnation Aug. 17, 1768, on the ground that wine had been unloaded from her before the ship had been entered for customs as required by 15 Cha. II ch. 7 sec. 8 (1663), *Adams Legal Papers* II 177–179 and sources therein cited. Suits filed on Oct. 29 against Hancock and four others for treble the value of the wine illegally imported by the *Liberty,* for having allegedly connived in the illegal importation, were dismissed on motion of the Crown March 25, 1769, *same* 180, 183.

CHAPTER 9

1. Rumors of Lord Chatham's mental illness were current as early as April and May, 1767, Walpole to Mann Apr. 5 and May 12, Lewis *Walpole* XXII 505–513; Lord George Sackville to John Irwin Apr. 7, *Stopford* I 121; Lady Chatham to Lord Temple April 18, *Grenville* IV 9; Edmund Burke to Lady Rockingham Apr. 28, *Burke* I 310; Franklin to Cadwallader Evans May 5, Smyth *Franklin* V 24; William Samuel Johnson to William Pitkin May 16, *Trumbull* 234. Details of Chatham's mental collapse are given in Williams *Pitt* II 240–246, 253.

2. On July 2, 1767, Chatham wrote the King, in Lady Chatham's hand, reporting his "utter disability" to suggest a plan requested by the King, *Geo. III* I 494, 495, with comment in Namier *Additions* 78–79, and on July 30, Thomas Whately wrote George Grenville that Chatham was reported to be "most of the day leaning his head upon his hands . . . [and] is so averse to speaking, that he commonly intimates his desire to be let alone, by some signal rather than by any expression," *Grenville* IV 123–124.

3. The quoted characterization of the Duke of Grafton is from John Brooke's sketch of him in Namier and Brooke *Commons* II 435. Grafton, thirty-one-years old when he became head of the Ministry, had served in the House of Commons for a few months in 1757 and since then in the House of Lords; but had held important offices for less than two years.

4. Negotiations of the Ministry with Lord Rockingham were opened through Henry Seymour Conway on the evening of July 3, 1767, Rockingham to the Duke of Newcastle July 4, with Newcastle to John White, July 6, *Newcastle* 104–106.

5. The negotiations for a "broad-bottom" Ministry including followers of Rockingham, the Duke of Bedford, and Grenville, described in Brooke *Chatham* 170–210, failed July 21, 1767, when Bedford refused Rockingham's demand that Conway remain Leader in the House of Commons, *same* 209–210; Newcastle's memorandum of July 21, *Newcastle* 146; Whately to Grenville July 24, Phillimore *Lyttelton* II 727–728. I do not know why Bedford took this stand. Perhaps he thought that with Conway as Leader in the Commons, the Rockingham party would be overpowering or considered Conway too pro-colonial to be acceptable.

6. Negotiations between Grafton and Rockingham independently of the Bedfords broke down on July 23, 1767, when Rockingham refused to "undertake Administration but upon full power given him by the King himself," Rockingham's undated memorandum written apparently soon after July 24, Rockingham Papers R 1:537; and Rockingham to Newcastle July 24, *Newcastle* 154–155.

7. The negotiations and arrangement as to offices for Lords Gower and Weymouth and two other Bedfordites, are described in Horace Walpole to Horace Mann Dec. 14 and 25, 1767, Lewis *Walpole* XXII 569, 571–572, Whately to Grenville Dec. 14, *Grenville* IV 195–196. Grafton to the King Dec. 11–22, *Geo. III* I 509–511 and memoranda and letters of Lord Shelburne Dec. 11–13, *Shelburne* II 68–73 and *Pitt* III 292–299 give further details. Gower was appointed President of the Council Dec. 23, 1767, and Weymouth Secretary of State Jan. 20, 1768.

8. Since Leadership of the House of Commons was not a formal office, the date of accession can sometimes be ascertained, as in the instant case, only by reference to the time when the old Leader ceases and the new begins to report the proceedings of the House to the King. Conway's last known report is dated Feb. 16, 1768; Lord North's first, Feb. 28, *Ellis* 3rd Ser. IV 385 and *Geo. III* II 12. Conway apparently remained in the Council until well into 1770. Walpole's "Journal of Events," under date of Nov. 13, 1770, mentions Conway's having "left the Cabinet Council." See also Namier and Brooke *Commons* I 246.

9. Charles Townshend's unexpected death Sept. 4, 1767, was reported in *Gentleman's Mag.* for Sept., 1767, XXXVII 479. North was appointed Chancellor of the Exchequer Oct. 7, 1767, *same* for Oct., 1767, XXXVII 521, and North wrote his father, Lord Guilford, Oct. 12, 1767, that he was to be called to the Cabinet, North "North" 787. According to letters from Newcastle to Lord Mansfield Sept. 22 and Walpole to Mann Sept. 27, Lewis *Walpole* XXII 552n., 552, the King promised North that after his father's death he should have the continuance of a pension enjoyed by his father.

10. The general election of March, 1768, is discussed in Winstanley *Chatham* 212–218; Brooke *Chatham Administration* 337–353; Namier and Brooke *Commons*

67–80. The election seems to have been even more corrupt than usual, Winstanley *Chatham* 213–215; Franklin's letters May 13 and 14, 1768, Smyth *Franklin* V 112, 117, 133; Johnson to Pitkin Apr. 29, *Trumbull* 270–272. (The new, Thirteenth, Parliament sat briefly in May, 1768, but passed only one act—an act extending the life of several acts about to expire.)

11. The dissension between Shelburne and other members of the Cabinet, Jacques Bataille de Francés, French Charge d'Affaires in London, to the Duc de Choiseul July 22, 1768, Bancroft Papers Vol. 71; Knox to Grenville Sept. 15, *Grenville* IV 364; the King to Grafton Sept. 15 and Oct. 5, 1768, *Geo. III* II 42–43, 49; Shelburne and Grafton correspondence June and Sept., *Shelburne* II 128, 140–141; William Gerard Hamilton to John Calcraft July 20, *Pitt* III 333–335n.

12. Shelburne resigned Oct. 19, 1768, *London Chronicle* Oct. 20, thus forestalling the projected dismissal of him, discussed in the King to Grafton Oct. 5, *Geo. III* II 49. Shelburne's procedure in resigning is described in Whately to Grenville Oct. 27, *Grenville* IV 390.

13. Lord Rochford succeeded Shelburne Oct. 21, 1768, Beatson *Pol. Index* I 277. As to Rochford's career, *D.N.B.* His political tie if any was apparently with Lord Albemarle (who was in turn affiliated with Newcastle and Rockingham), Newcastle to Albemarle Sept. 11, 1768, Winstanley *Chatham* 236n. He had been talked of as Shelburne's successor some months earlier, William Gerard Hamilton to John Calcraft Aug. 15, 1768, *Pitt* III 335n.

14. Chatham wrote Grafton Oct. 12, 1768, stating his wish to resign because of ill health and on Oct. 14, to the King, declining to reconsider, *Geo. III* II 54, 57–58. Though Chatham's letter to the King assigned only ill health as the ground for resignation, his letter to Grafton and a memorandum of Lady Chatham of Oct. 9 indicate that the report (confirmed to him by Grafton, *Grafton* 222) of the proposed dismissal of Shelburne was an important factor. Chatham also was offended by the removal of his friend Gen. Sir Jeffery Amherst from the sinecure Governorship of Va., *Geo. III* II 54.

15. Lord Bristol succeeded Chatham as Lord Privy Seal on Nov. 2, Beatson *Pol. Index* I 251, but without a seat in the Cabinet, *Grafton* 226, 232. Weymouth switched at this time to the more important Southern Department following Shelburne's resignation, and Rochford took the Northern, *same* 226n.

16. Hillsborough, North, and Rochford may be classified as so-called "King's Friends" in the sense that, not being "friends," i.e., followers of the leader of any political bloc, they depended exclusively on the King for their political fortunes.

17. King's speech and replies of both Houses Nov. 8, 1768, *Parl. Hist.* XVI 466–474. (The King in making his opening speech was regarded as speaking for the Ministry, Johnson to Pitkin Nov. 18, *Trumbull* 301.)

18. Resolutions by Hillsborough denouncing the conduct of Mass. and Boston were introduced into the House of Lords Dec. 15, 1768, and promptly adopted, *Parl. Hist.* XVI 476–480; *Journals H. of L.* XXXII 209–210.

19. Bedford's proposed Address to the King asking him to obtain information as to treason in Mass., same citations as in note 18 above. The act for punishing treason or misprision of treason committed outside the realm, referred to in the Address, was 35 Henry VIII ch. 2 (1543), which the Solicitor General, John

Dunning, stated in the House of Commons was still in force and applied to the colonies, Johnson to Pitkin Feb. 9, 1769, *Trumbull* 316.

20. North's leadership in the debate in the Commons Jan. 26, 1769, Cavendish *Debates* I 194–217. North stated that "The meeting of the 12th September [in Boston], the voting a standing army to be contrary to the bill of rights, the calling upon the inhabitants to arm on the report of a French war, and the intention to seize Castle William were all acts . . . approaching treason. . . ." As to the apparently unfounded rumor of a plan to seize Castle William at the entrance to Boston harbor, Miller *Sam Adams* 148. The other acts referred to by North are described in Chapter 11 of this volume.

21. Resolutions and address of the House of Lords concerning Mass. debated and adopted by the Commons Jan. 26 and reaffirmed Feb. 8, 1769, by rejection, 169 to 65, of a motion to recommit, Charles Garth to S.C. Comm. of Corresp. Feb. 9, *S.C. Hist. Mag.* XXXI (1930) 46–49; *Parl. Hist.* XVI 485–510. The resolutions were based on letters submitted to both Houses from Francis Bernard, Governor of Mass., the American Board of Customs Commissioners, and others, listed in *Journals H. of L.* XXXII 182–184, painting in lurid colors the opposition in Mass. to British measures, particularly the Townshend Act.

22. The King's reply to the Address Feb. 14, 1769, *same* 251. Lord Barrington, Secretary at War, to Gov. Bernard Feb. 12, 1769, *Barrington–Bernard Corresp.* 184, referred to James Otis, chairman of the Boston town meeting of Sept. 13, 1768, and the Boston selectmen, including John Hancock, as particular culprits who should be punished.

23. Hillsborough to Bernard Feb. 20, 1769, directing him to gather and transmit such evidence of treason or misprision of treason as would support a prosecution in England under the Treason Act of 35 Henry VIII, Instructions to the Governors, Mass. Hist. Soc. This letter from a member of the Cabinet militates against the credibility of a statement by a non-Cabinet minister (joint Secretary of the Treasury), Grey Cooper, in the Commons Feb. 8 that the administration did not mean "to put the [treason] act in execution, but only to shew to America what government could do if pushed to it," *Parl. Hist.* XVI 507.

24. Hillsborough's undated memorandum proposing an act of Parliament concerning Mass., enclosed in Hillsborough to the King Feb. 15, 1769, *Geo. III* II 81–83. Hillsborough also made several less important suggestions concerning Mass. and also N.Y., *same* 83–84.

25. Hillsborough wrote the King Feb. 15, 1769, that "The Lords of the Cabinet, except Lord Chancellor [Camden] & General Conway, I rather think approved the measures [set forth in Hillsborough's memorandum], but none expressed themselves explicitly," *same* 82.

26. The King's undated memorandum unfavorably commenting on Hillsborough's proposals concerning Mass., described in the text, *same* 84–85. The King made a suggestion (*same* 85) to provide for "dissolving the Commissions of the Peace in the Province of Massachusetts," presumably by an act of Parliament giving the Crown or the Governor of Mass. authority to do this without the approval of the Mass. Council as probably required by the charter of Mass.

27. The Cabinet not only rejected Hillsborough's provocative proposals but sponsored an act (9 Geo. III ch. 18) modifying the colonial Quartering Act to

make it less unpalatable to the colonists, and acts (9 Geo. III ch. 27, 38, and 39 sec. 1) liberalizing the British restriction on the export of colonial rice, granting a bounty on colonial raw silk imported into the Port of London, and exempting colonial raw hides and skins from British tariff duties for a period of five years.

28. Thomas Pownall's motion of April 19, 1769, in the House of Commons for repeal of the Townshend Act, and the proceedings on this proposal, Garth to S.C. Comm. of Corresp., *S.C. Hist. Mag.* XXXI (1930) 58–59; *Parl. Hist.* XVI 610–622; Johnson to Pitkin Apr. 26, *Trumbull* 334; Cavandish *Debates* I 399–401; Franklin, not wholly accurate, to Samuel Cooper Apr. 27, Smyth *Franklin* V 205.

29. Cabinet resolution of May 1, 1769, for future repeal of the duties on paper, glass, and paint, *Grafton* 232. The King favored retention of the duty on tea, *Geo. III* II 85, but the statement in Bancroft *History* VI 277–278 that he persuaded North, contrary to the latter's wish, to vote against total repeal, is not supported by the source, Cavendish *Debates* I 485, cited by Bancroft. (Hillsborough had earlier proposed to exempt from the Townshend Act all colonies that made provision for such support of their civil officers as the Crown approved, Hillsborough's memorandum to the King about Feb. 15, *Geo. III* II 83–84.)

30. Grafton's statement in his autobiography that he, Lord Camden, Lord Granby, and Conway had voted in favor of total repeal of the Townshend Act duties, *Grafton* 229–230. These four, together with Sir Edward Hawke, who was not present at the meeting (*same* 232) were the Chathamite members of the Cabinet. The other members present were North and Lords Gower, Weymouth, Rochford, and Hillsborough, *same* 232. (Grafton's autobiography was not written until 1804 and later, *same* viii.)

31. An undated letter from Camden to Hillsborough, written apparently about June 10, 1769, *same* 231–232 objected to a statement in the minutes of the Cabinet meeting of May 1, as recorded by Hillsborough (*same* 232), that "It is the unanimous opinion," etc., furnishes contemporary evidence that there was division in the Cabinet at the meeting of May 1. See also Grafton's comment on Hillsborough's minutes of this meeting, *same* 234.

32. Statements of Grafton and Weymouth in the Lords, March 5, 1776, quoted in the text, 4 *Force* VI 312. Grafton thought that if Sir Edward Hawke, who was absent, had been present, he would have voted in favor of total repeal, *Grafton* 230. (Weymouth recollected that the proposal for total repeal had been defeated by a tie vote, 4 *Force* VI 312. Since the minutes of the meeting reveal nine members present, *Grafton* 232, Weymouth's recollection of a tie vote must be mistaken, unless one of the members present abstained from voting.)

33. Johnson to Pitkin May 25, 1769, reporting that the Ministry had spread word of its intention to propose partial repeal among "the merchants here, to be by them transmitted to their correspondents abroad," *Trumbull* 346. He thought the object was "to create division among the colonies," and wreck the non-importation movement, and that, in any case, the colonists should take the announcement with a grain of salt since the Ministry "may not continue in power" and anyway "can never want pretences and plausible excuses" for not carrying the resolution into effect, *same* 347.

34. Hillsborough's circular letter of May 13, 1769, announcing the proposed partial repeal of the Townshend Act at the next session of Parliament, *N.Y. Col.*

Doc. VIII 164–165 and *Grafton* 233. Camden wrote Hillsborough on or about June 11 objecting to the second sentence of Hillsborough's circular letter, *same* 232, presumably because of the provocative phrase, "men with factious and seditious views," which was not in the minutes of the meeting, *same* 233.

35. The Va. resolutions of May 16, 1769, given in the text also asserted the right to petition the King for redress of grievances and to procure the concurrence of the other citizens in this, *Va. Journals* (for 1766–1769) 214–215.

36. A copy of the circular letter from Peyton Randolph, Speaker of the House, to other Speakers dated May 19, is in *R.I. Col. Rec.* VI 586–587.

37. The sources for the statement in the text concerning resolutions in 1769 of the Assemblies of N.J., Del., S.C., N.C., and N.Y., are in Jensen *Founding* 303, 305, 312; the R.I. Assembly's resolution Oct. 25, 1769, is in *R.I. Col. Rec.* VI 604. The Md. resolutions and an accompanying order to the Speaker of the Md. Lower House of Assembly to send copies of the resolutions to Speakers of the Assemblies of other colonies, are in *Md. Archives* LXII 110–111. For additional details, Jensen *Founding* 303, 304, and sources cited therein.

38. Peter Gilman, Speaker of the N.H. Assembly, wrote Randolph Apr. 11, 1770, expressing the thanks of the Assembly for the Va. resolutions and stating that their "sentiments" were similar to those expressed in the Va. resolutions, *N.H. Papers* VII 225, but I have found no record of any notice of Randolph's letter by the Assemblies of Pa. or Ga. Joseph Galloway, Speaker of the Pa. Assembly, laid the resolutions of the Md. Lower House and its Speaker's accompanying letter before the Assembly May 15, *Pa. Assembly* VII 6525, but the Assembly apparently took no action on the matter.

39. The Mass. resolutions of June 29, 1769, similar to those of Va., Bradford *Mass. Papers* 180.

40. No evidence has been found that Gov. Bernard of Mass. tried to carry out Hillsborough's instruction of Feb., 1769, to secure information of treason or misprision of treason on which to arrest and send the alleged offenders to Great Britain for trial. But, as brought out in the discussion of the *Gaspee* affair in R.I. in 1772, efforts were then made to secure evidence on which persons could be indicted and sent from R.I. to Great Britain to be tried for treason.

CHAPTER 10

1. As to George III's determination to keep Wilkes from being seated in the House of Commons, the King to Lord North Apr. 25, 1768, and to Lord Hertford Jan. 27, 1769, *Geo. III* II 21, 75. The King's enmity to Wilkes probably was chiefly because of slurs on the King's mother and himself in *The North Briton* published by Wilkes in 1763, discussed in Bleackley *Wilkes* 71–143 and Knollenberg *Origin* 31–33, 35–41, 294–296.

2. John Wilkes' repeated elections in 1768 and 1769 to the House of Commons by the voters of populous Middlesex County (including a large part of London), his exclusion from his seat on the ground of his conviction for criminal libel, and the House's seating of his chief opponent, Col. Henry Luttrell, whom he had last defeated by a vote of 1143 to 296, are described in Bleackley *Wilkes* 189–232; Rudé "Wilkes and Liberty" 41–107; Macoby *English Radicalism* 88–115. Wilkes'

earlier conviction of criminal libel and flight to France are described in Knollenberg *Origin* 36–40.

3. Lord Chatham's and William Dowdeswell's motions in the Lords and Commons respectively, Jan. 9, 1770, to amend the proposed address of thanks to the King, and their speeches in support of the motions, *Parl. Hist.* XVI 647–653, 656–665, 679–680.

4. Defeat of both motions for amendment, 203 to 36 in the Lords and 254 to 138 in the Commons, *same* 665, 727.

5. Lord Camden spoke and voted in favor of Chatham's motion Jan. 9, 1770, *same* 644–645, 666. Camden was dismissed Jan. 16, 1770, and his place as Lord Chancellor was given the next day to Charles Yorke, *London Mag.* for Jan., 1770 XXXIX 53. Yorke died a few days later, *same,* and no one was appointed to succeed him for over a year, Beatson *Pol. Index* I 235.

6. Lord Granby voted in favor of Dowdeswell's motion in the House of Commons, *Parl. Hist.* XVI 727, and had collaborated with Chatham and Camden in preparing the attack, Chatham's correspondence Jan. 7–15, 1770, *Pitt* III 384–393. Granby resigned as Master General of the Ordnance on Jan. 17, 1770, *Gentleman's Mag.* for Jan., 1770 XL 44. No successor was appointed until 1772, Beatson *Pol. Index* I 393. "Lord Granby" was a courtesy title accorded John Manners, a commoner, as eldest son of the Duke of Rutland.

7. As to the vitriolic attacks on the Duke of Grafton by "Junius" in letters to the London *Public Advertiser* from Jan. 21 to Dec. 12, 1769, Wade *Junius* I 103–254. At least forty-seven people have been suggested as the author of the famous letter of Junius, Pargellis *Bibliography* 22. See also Cordasco *Junius Bibliography.* The evidence marshaled and examined in Leslie Stephens' biography of Philip Francis in *D.N.B.* points to Francis as the probable author.

8. Grafton resigned Jan. 28, 1770, *Gentleman's Mag.* for Feb., 1770 XL 93. For various contemporary surmises as to the reason or reasons for his resignation, *same* 93; Horace Walpole to Sir Horace Mann Jan. 30, Toynbee *Walpole* VII 361–362; and William S. Johnson to Gov. Jonathan Trumbull of Conn. Feb. 3, *Trumbull* 408.

9. Lord North succeeded Grafton as First Lord of the Treasury Jan. 28, 1770, *Gentleman's Mag.* for Feb., 1770 XL 93.

10. My description of North's political career before 1770 is drawn from Valentine *North* I 27–186 and Lucas *Lord North* I 25–198, the sketch of his life in *D.N.B.,* and the sketch in Namier and Brooke *Commons* II 206–207.

11. William S. Johnson to Gov. William Pitkin concerning North, Nov. 13, 1767, *Trumbull* 246.

12. North is listed among those voting in 1766 against repeal of the Stamp Act, *List of Voters in Commons against Repeal* 308.

13. Johnson to Trumbull Feb. 3, 1770, reporting that North, "now at the head of all affairs," said the Ministry would move for repeal of the duties on paper, glass, and paint, *Trumbull* 405–406. To same effect, Thomas Pownall to Samuel Cooper Jan. 29, 1769, Griffin *Junius* 256–257. North stated in the House of Commons May 9 that he was "the only man" in the re-formed Cabinet who was "decidedly for the repeal," i.e., partial repeal of the Townshend Act, as promised in 1769, Cavendish *Debates* II 32.

14. North's presentation to the House of Commons March 5, 1770, of the petition from London merchants and traders described in the text, *Journals H. of C.* XXXII 664–665. Benjamin Franklin wrote Charles Thomson March 18, "The merchants here [London] were at length prevailed on to present a petition," but "The manufacturing towns absolutely refused to move at all . . . ," Smyth *Franklin* V 253. (The addressee is identified in Crane *Franklin's Letters to Press* 209.)

15. North's motion March 5, 1770, for leave to bring in a bill for partial repeal of the Townshend Act, *Parl. Hist.* XV 852–853. The present plan for partial repeal differed from the one adopted by the Cabinet in 1768 only in that the earlier plan contemplated repeal of the duties on foreign, as well as British-made, paper, glass, and paint.

16. British policy of encouraging the export of British manufactures was manifested not only by refraining from levying export taxes on articles of British manufacture, but by offering bounties or the refund of British excise duties on a number of such articles including sailcloth, spirits, silk, gunpowder, linen, candles, starch, hides, boots, shoes, and gloves, Saxby *The British Customs* (1757) 363–381, with subsequent acts extending the bounties listed in Saxby as soon to expire.

17. Franklin wrote Samuel Cooper on June 8, 1770, and Joseph Galloway on June 11 that he had "reason to believe" Lord North favored total repeal, Smyth *Franklin* V 259 and Van Doren *Franklin's Writings* 193. But he gave no indication of what reason he had for this belief, and I have found no evidence supporting Franklin's supposition.

18. North's speech in support of his motion for partial repeal March 5, 1770, *same* I 484–489; *Parl. Hist.* XVI 853–855, Johnson to Trumbull March 6, *Trumbull* 421–422. The quotation is from Johnson's letter (p. 421). The statements in Schlesinger *Col. Merchants* 213 and Van Tyne *Causes* 269 that the duty on tea was retained "because the king believed that 'there must always be one tax to keep up the right' " is based on a letter from the King written over four years later (Sept. 11, 1774), *Geo. III* III 131. I have found no evidence of the King's having influenced the Ministry's decision on the question of repeal in 1770.

19. Thomas Pownall, popular Governor of Massachusetts from 1757 to 1760 and member of the House of Commons from 1767 to 1780, Schutz *Pownall;* Pownall *Pownall; D.A.B.;* Namier and Brooke *Commons* III 316–318; letters to and from him in Griffin *Junius* 204–299, *A.H.R.,* VIII 301–329, *Bowdoin–Temple Letters* 173–273 *passim,* and *M.H.S. Proc.* (1860–1862) 237–241. His long interest in colonial affairs can be followed in Knollenberg *Origin* index entry "Pownall, Thomas," and in the many editions of his *Administration of the Colonies,* discussed in Guttridge "Pownall's *Administration of the Colonies*" and Shy "Pownall."

20. As to the East India Company's curious and apparently vacillating conduct at this time concerning repeal of the Townshend Act duty on tea, Johnson to Trumbull Jan. 2, Feb. 3, March 6, and March 28, 1770, *Trumbull* 394–395, 423, 427, 406–407, and Labaree *Tea Party* 45–46, 277.

21. Lord Barrington, member of the House of Commons from 1740 to 1778 and Secretary at War from 1765 to 1778, was an important member of the Ministry, but was not in the Cabinet. He was an Irish peer and hence, unlike an English or Scotch peer, was eligible for election to the Commons.

22. Pownall's motion March 5, 1770, for total repeal of the Townshend Act; his, Conway's, and Isaac Barré's speeches in support of the motion; and the counter-suggestions of Welbore Ellis and Lord Barrington, Cavendish *Debates* I 489–491, 497–500; *Parl. Hist.* XVI 852–874; Johnson to Trumbull March 6, *Trumbull* 421–425; Edward Montague to Va. Comm. of Corresp. March 6, *Va. Mag.* XII (1905) 168–169; Charles Garth to S.C. Comm. of Corresp. March 6, *So. Car. Hist. Mag.* XXXI (1930) 228–233.

23. Pownall's motion for total repeal defeated March 5, 1770, 204 to 142, Cavendish *Debates* I 500; *Parl. Hist.* XVI 874; Garth to S.C. Comm. of Corresp. March 6, *So. Car. Hist. Mag.* XXXI (1930) 233. (The statement in Johnson to Trumbull March 6, *Trumbull* 423, that the vote was 244 to 142 was erroneous or is a misprint.) The large vote for total repeal was probably attributable chiefly to the combination of Lord Rockingham and Chatham's followers as to which see Benjamin Franklin to Charles Thomson March 18, Smyth *Franklin* V 252, with Crane *Franklin's Letters to Press* 209.

24. Proceedings in the House of Commons on the bill for partial repeal of the Townshend Act March 9–Apr. 6, 1770, including passage of the bill on April 6, *Journals H. of C.* XXXII 798–870 *passim*.

25. The bill was presented to the Lords Apr. 6, passed the Lords Apr. 11, and was approved by the King the next day, *Journals H. of L.* XXXII 540, 548, 550. The act, 10 Geo. III ch. 17 (1770), not only repealed the colonial duties on paper, glass, and paint manufactured in Great Britain, but restored the drawback (refund) of British import duties on china exported to the colonies which had been repealed by the Townshend Act.

26. N.Y. committee's circular letter of June 2, 1770, proposing a meeting at Norwalk, Conn., to discuss possible revision of the non-importation agreements to apply only to imports subject to duty under the Townshend Act, *New-London Gazette* of June 15.

27. Refusal of Philadelphia merchants June 5, 1770, to consider modification of their non-importation agreement, *Pa. Gazette* June 7; Jensen *Philadelphia* 189, 283. Similar action by Boston merchants June 7, *Boston Gazette* June 11; Andrews "Boston Merchants" 243. Conn., R.I., and N.J. merchants also voted not to send delegates to the proposed meeting at Norwalk to consider modification, Gipson *Brit. Empire* XI 268; Schlesinger *Col. Merchants* 221–222.

28. New York merchants' decision July 10, 1770, "to import for the future all kinds of goods that pays no Duties," James Beekman to Fludyer, March, and Hudson, July 10, White *Beekman Papers* II 727. Becker *New York* 88 states that news of passage of a British act permitting the N.Y. Legislature to issue paper currency reached N.Y. "probably late in June" and influenced the decision, citing "*New York Col. Doc.* VIII 215." The letter printed there does not support this statement. The earliest colonial notice I have found of this news is in the *New-York Gazette* of July 30, 1770. As shown in Mason "Becker" and Klein "Democracy," many statements in Becker *New York* are open to question.

29. Gen. Thomas Gage to Lord Barrington July 6, *Gage* II 546; Cadwallader Colden to Lord Hillsborough July 10, *N.Y. Col. Doc.* VIII 218; and Alexander Colden to Anthony Todd July 11, *same* 218–220, give the background of the N.Y. merchants' decision.

30. Bitter condemnation of N.Y. decision in Albany and in other colonies on receipt of notification of the decision promptly circulated by the N.Y. merchants, Schlesinger *Col. Merchants* 227–229; Andrews "Boston Merchants" 245–249; and items in the *Pa. Gazette, Boston Gazette, South-Carolina Gazette,* and *Md. Gazette* July–Oct., 1770, excoriating the N.Y. merchants.

31. Isaac Low, chairman of committee of inspection of N.Y. merchants, to Boston committee of merchants, headed by Thomas Cushing, Aug. 18, 1770, justifying the New Yorkers' decision, *New-York Journal* Aug. 30, reprinted in Stevens *Col. Records* Part 2 76–77. I have not found the Boston letter of protest of July 24, which is referred to in *same* 76.

32. Philadelphia merchants vote Sept. 20, 1774, for modification the same as in N.Y., Schleslinger *Col. Merchants* 231. Boston merchants follow suit Oct. 12, *same* 233. Seventy-two were present at the decisive meeting on Oct. 12, John Rowe's diary for Oct. 12, *Rowe* 208, but Rowe does not state how many, if any, voted against the decision, and I have found no evidence elsewhere on this point. Rowe's diary Sept. 5–Oct. 12 has several entries recording his attendance at meetings of Boston merchants, but does not state what action was taken, *same* 206–208.

33. Baltimore merchants decide early in Oct., 1770, to modify their agreement along the lines of the revised agreements of N.Y. and Phil. and reaffirm this on Oct. 25, Schlesinger *Col. Merchants* 233–234.

34. Modification of S.C. agreement conforming to modification elsewhere Dec. 13, 1770, Gov. William Bull of S.C. to Lord Hillsborough Dec. 13, McCrady *South Carolina* 682–683. (The statement in Sellers *Charleston* 220 that "non-importation was given up except for tea" is inaccurate.)

35. Though efforts were made to enforce the N.C. non-importation agreement, Schlesinger *Col. Merchants* 208–209 and Ashe *N.C.* I 354, the agreement was apparently not well observed there. Gov. William Tryon of N.C. wrote Hillsborough Feb. 1, 1771, "the several ports of this province have been open ever since the repeal of the Stamp Act for every kind of British manufactures to the full extent of the credit of the country," *N.C. Col. Rec.* VIII 496. The little observance of the agreement in Ga., Coleman *Ga.* 31–32, 292–293; *Historical Statistics* 757.

36. Modification of the Va. agreement in July, 1771, *Va. Gazette* (Rind) July 18, 1771; Jensen *Founding* 370. The modified agreement conformed to those elsewhere. (Washington's letter to William Carey & Co., July 20, stating that "our Association in Virginia for the Non-importation of Goods is now at an end except against Tea, paper, glass and painters' Colours of Foreign Manufacture," *Washington* III 60, is inaccurate: dutied wine imported from Great Britain was still banned.)

37. The modified Va. agreement of June 22, 1770, was designed to secure better observance by, on the one hand liberalizing the range of articles that could be imported, and on the other hand providing for the establishment of a committee of five in every county to inspect invoices of imported goods and publish the names of any persons found to have violated the agreement, *Jefferson* I 43–47.

38. Figures of exports from England to Va. and Md. for 1770 indicating continuing failure of Va. agreement, *Historical Statistics* 757. George Mason of Va. wrote an unidentified correspondent Dec. 6, 1770, of the "very languishing" of the "non-importation agreements here," Rowland *Mason* 148, and Nathaniel Savage wrote John Norton to the same effect Jan. 9, 1771, Jensen *Founding* 370.

39. John Temple to James Bowdoin Dec. 4, 1771, as quoted in the text, *Bowdoin–Temple Papers* 283–284. Temple believed that Parliament would have repealed the Townshend Act if the colonists had shown a "little more sincerity & manly firmness," *same* 284. Franklin had written in similar vein March 18, 1770, predicting that Parliament would yield if the non-importation agreements were continued and faithfully observed for "another year," Smyth *Franklin* V 254, identified in Crane *Franklin* 209 as having been written to Charles Thomson of Philadelphia.

40. Ralph Izard to Edward Rutledge Nov. 15, 1774, as to the breakdown of the non-importation agreement in 1770 having "given wonderful confidence to our enemies" in Great Britain, *Izard* 31.

41. The words *tradesmen, mechanics, artisans, artificers, manufacturers, craftsmen* all are found in the colonial press to designate skilled manual laborers, but what selective meaning, if any, each term had is obscure. Bridenbaugh's classic *The Colonial Craftsman,* particularly 1–2, 64–147, 155–180, throws light on the problem. Perhaps *craftsman,* the word selected by him, is the best generic term; but *tradesman* or *mechanic* seems to have been the more commonly used in the colonial press in 1766–1775.

42. Charleston mechanics and the local non-importation agreement, Walsh *Charleston's Sons of Liberty* 47–53.

43. Attendance of tradesmen at the meeting in Boston referred to in the text, *Boston Gazette* Sept. 17, 1770.

44. Opposition of Philadelphia tradesmen (mechanics) in May and June, 1770, to relaxation of the local merchants' non-importation agreement described in the text, Olton "Philadelphia's Mechanics" 321–323.

45. The qualification in the text as to availability of domestic material is necessary because many of the tradesmen must have suffered from the non-importation agreements through the lack of materials—for example, silk, thread, and fine woolen cloth—not produced in the colonies.

CHAPTER 11

1. Lord Hillsborough, Shelburne's successor in charge of colonial matters, to Gen. Thomas Gage June 8, 1768, enclosing copies of the American Customs Commissioners' and Governor Francis Bernard's letters to officials in England as to the need of troops at Boston and ordering Gage immediately to send forces to Boston, *Gage* II 68–69. Statements or implication in Miller *Origins* 293 and Fisher *Struggle for Independence* I 127–128 that the *Liberty* riot of June 10, 1768, led to the initial sending of troops to Boston are erroneous. This led only to strengthening the garrison there, Lord Hillsborough to Gage, July 30, *Gage* II 72–73.

2. Gage to Hillsborough Sept. 10, 1768, reporting the decision to send two regiments from Halifax to Boston under the command of Lieutenant-Colonel William Dalrymple, *Gage* I 195, one to be stationed in Boston, the other at Castle William, Gage to Bernard Sept. 12, *Bowdoin–Temple Papers* 100–101. Hillsborough's letter was not received by Gage until Sept. 7, *Gage* II 69; but a duplicate, referred to in *same* I 191, had evidently been received by Aug. 31, when he ordered his aide-de-camp to confer with Bernard concerning the troops for Boston, Gage Mss. Clements Lib.

3. Bernard to Hillsborough Sept. 16, 1768, reporting that on Sept. 8 he had let it be known locally that British troops were ordered to Boston, *Letters to Ministry* 70–71. Hillsborough wrote Bernard June 11 that at least one regiment would be sent to Boston, transcripts of instructions to Provincial Governors VII:2407–2408 Mass. Hist. Soc., but this letter apparently did not reach Bernard until Sept. 3, Bernard to Hillsborough Sept. 9, *Letters to Ministry* 68.

4. Talk at Boston of preventing landing of the troops, Bernard to Hillsborough Sept. 16, 1768, *same* 71; and evidence cited in Miller "Mass. Convention" 457–460.

5. Fiery resolves of Boston town meeting. Minutes of meetings Sept. 13, 1768, *Boston Records* (for 1758–1769) 262–264. The town had asked Bernard Sept. 12, 1768, to call a special session of the Mass. Legislature, but Bernard refused to do so, Minutes of Boston town meetings Sept. 12 and 13, *same* 260–261. Bernard thought that a letter from Hillsborough to him of Apr. 22, 1768, implied that unless the Mass. circular letter (referred to in Chapter 7) was rescinded, he was not again to convene the Legislature until instructed to do so, Bernard to Hillsborough Aug. 6, *Letters to Ministry* 62–63.

6. Statement by James Otis, chairman of the town meeting of Sept. 13, 1768, as to delivery of arms, Bernard to Hillsborough Sept. 16, *same* 72–73.

7. Vote of Boston town meeting Sept. 13, 1768, as to standing army, *Boston Records* (for 1758–1769) 263.

8. Vote by Boston town meeting of Sept. 13, 1768, for its selectmen to call a provincial convention, and choice of Boston's representatives James Otis, Thomas Cushing, Samuel Adams, and John Hancock for the convention, *same* 263–264. A copy of the selectmen's circular letter of Sept. 14 to the other towns in the province inviting them to the proposed convention is in *Boston Chronicle* Sept. 19 (362–363) and *M.H.S. Proc.* (for 1858–1860) 385–387.

9. The *Boston Chronicle* of Oct. 3, 1768, reported that committees from 96 towns and 6 districts attended the convention; the *Boston Gazette* of Oct. 10, 1768, said 98 towns and 8 districts. (Districts were communities not yet having representatives in the Mass. House of Representatives). There were about 150 towns represented at the exceptionally full House of 1769–1770, *Mass. Acts* XVIII 372–374.

10. The convention opened as scheduled on Sept. 22, 1768, and "sat exactly a week," Bernard to Hillsborough Sept. 27 and Oct. 3, *Letters to Ministry* 88, 92. The convention and its activities, Miller "Mass. Convention 1768"; Brown *Democracy in Mass.* 252–254 and, most important, Brown "Mass. Convention of 1768" 94–104.

11. The convention's statements, apparently made near the beginning and end of its sittings, are in the *Boston Chronicle* of Sept. 26 and Oct. 3, 1768 (366, 382–383). The convention also addressed a rather plaintive letter to Bernard on Sept. 24, and Thomas Cushing, chairman of the convention, wrote a mild letter, dated Sept. 27, to Dennys De Berdt, London Agent for the Mass. House of Representatives, enclosing a petition to the King, Cushing *S. Adams* I 241–243.

12. The 700 troops from Halifax landed at Boston Oct. 1, 1768, consisted of most of the Fourteenth and Twenty-ninth regiments under Dalrymple and Lieut. Col. Maurice Carr, a detachment from the Fifty-ninth and a company of artillery, *Boston Chronicle* Oct. 3 and Dec. 5, 1758, and Gage to Hillsborough May 13, 1769,

Gage I 225. The nominal strength of the Fourteenth and Twenty-ninth was 500 men each, *Journals H. of C.* XXXI 441, but they were evidently much below full strength as was characteristic of regiments stationed in America, Shy *Toward Lexington* 269.

13. Bernard to Hillsborough Oct. 1, 1768, reporting the landing of the troops "not only without opposition, but with tolerable good humor," *Letters to Ministry* 92. To same effect, Rev. Andrew Eliot to Thomas Hollis Oct. 17, 1768, "Eliot Letters" 432.

14. Part of the Sixty-fourth and Sixty-fifth Regiments from Ireland reached Boston on or shortly before Nov. 10, 1768, Dickerson *Boston* 21. The rest of the Sixty-fourth under Col. John Pomeroy arrived Nov. 13, *Boston Chronicle* Nov. 14, but the transport carrying three companies of the Sixty-fifth, with its commander, Major General Alexander Mackay, did not arrive until Apr. 30, 1769, *Gage* I 225. The full quota of troops occupying Boston was very formidable considering that its population was only about 20,000, Drake *Boston* 772.

15. Gage wrote Bernard June 5, 1769, that he had ordered the company of artillery and the Sixty-fourth and Sixty-fifth Regiments to be sent from Boston to Halifax, Bernard Papers X 103, Harv. Coll. Lib. The Sixty-fifth sailed on June 24, the Sixty-fourth on July 25, "Boyle's Journal" 259. The detachment from the Fifty-ninth from Halifax which arrived in Oct., 1768, had been sent back to Halifax in May, 1769, *Gage* I 105.

16. American Customs Commissioners' return to Boston without opposition Nov. 8, 1768, Dickerson *Boston* 20. As to their subsequent administration and difficulties, Clark "American Customs Board" 788–806; Clark *British Treasury* 183–188; Dickerson *Navigation Acts* 245–255; and Dickerson "Commissioners of Customs" 322–325.

17. Bernard's request to the Mass. Council Sept. 19, 1768, to prepare quarters in Boston for the expected British troops and the Council's refusal Sept. 29 to do so on the ground that adequate quarters were available at Castle William on Castle Island, *Bowdoin–Temple Papers* 101–111 and Bernard to Hillsborough Sept. 23 and 24, *Letters to Ministry* 75–83. As to eventual quartering of the troops, Bernard to Gage Oct. 24, Gage Papers Clements Lib. and Gage to Hillsborough *Gage* I 203, 208–209.

18. Though within the township (town) of Boston, Castle Island was three miles by water and, when accessible at low tide, seven by land from the city of Boston, Dr. Robert Honeyman's diary for March 30, 1775, describing his visit to the island (now a peninsula), *Honeyman's Journal* 56–57, and Gage to Hillsborough Oct. 19, 1768, *Gage* I 201. For the history of fort Castle William on Castle Island, Shurtleff *Boston,* index under "Castle Island" and "Fort William."

19. Bernard's messages to the Mass. House July 5 and 12, 1769, requesting funds for the supplies required by the British Quartering Act, and the House's adverse reply July 15, Bradford *Mass. Papers* 183–187.

20. The reports in the *New-York Journal* of clashes between British troops and civilians in Boston from Oct., 1768, through July, 1769, referred to in the text are collected and reprinted in Dickerson *Boston* 7–119 *passim.*

21. The unreliability of the reports from Boston published in the *New-York Journal* and the attribution of these reports to William Cooper, Samuel Adams,

and others in Boston are discussed in Schlesinger *Prelude* 100–102, 312–313. The absolute falsity or gross exaggeration of the reports of early clashes between the troops and civilians is evidenced by Andrew Eliot to Thomas Hollis, Jan. 29, 1769, "Eliot Letters" 437–438, and Richard Cary to an unidentified correspondent, Feb. 7, that all was "quiet," *Mass. Papers* 113–114.

22. Michael Corbet, in resisting impressment, harpooned and killed Lieutenant Henry Panton of H.M. Frigate *Rose,* April 19, 1769, *Adams Legal Papers* 276–277.

23. The account of John Riley's knocking down Jonathan Winship, a Cambridge butcher, in Boston July 13, 1769, is based on affidavits of Justice of the Peace Edmund Quincy and Peter Barbour, dated July 24, and an account in the *Boston Evening-Post* of Oct. 2, reprinted in Dickerson *Boston* 119–120.

24. Dr. John Loring, a Boston physician, gave an affidavit dated July 24, 1769, that, on Winship's complaining of Riley to Col. Dalrymple, the latter had said, in front of several soldiers, "You was saucy, they served you right, and I don't care if they knock you down again," Dickerson *Boston* 121. To similar effect, affidavit of Edward Jackson July 24, *same* 122. (This is not characteristic; in general, the higher officers apparently did their best to prevent collisions.) Further details: *Adams Legal Papers* II 431–435; Zobel *Boston Massacre* 137–139, 338–339.

25. The arrest and fining of Riley and his attack on the constable, Peter Barbour, who tried (July 14, 1769) to take him into custody for refusal to pay the fine are described in affidavits of Quincy, Barbour, Jeremiah Belknap, Loring, and Jackson, dated July 24, and an undated statement of Stephen Greenleaf, all published in the *Boston Evening-Post* of October 2, and reprinted in Dickerson *Boston* 119–123. The soldiers' side of the affair was presented over a year later in depositions digested in Shy *Toward Lexington* 314–315.

26. Zobel *Boston Massacre* 146–149, 340–341 has a full, well-documented account of James Otis' clash with John Robinson Sept. 5, 1769. Several British officers were present but, so far as is known, did not join in the affray.

27. Claim by Robert Pierpont, as lessee from the town of Boston of land on Boston Neck on which the British had built a guard house and stationed a guard of soldiers, newspaper report of Nov. 9, 1768, in Dickerson *Boston* 21; resolution adopted at a Boston town meeting, *Boston Records* (for 1758–1769) 273; and Dalrymple to Gage Sept. 27, 1769, Gage Papers Clements Lib.

28. Attack on British detachment under Ensign John Ness Oct. 24, 1769, including part played by Captain Ponsonby Molesworth, who took over the command of the detachment while it was being pelted, and his and Ness' later legal difficulties, Zobel *Boston Massacre* 139–143, 339. (Some of Zobel's passages are based on statements of dubious probative value because made long after the event, but his more important ones are based on contemporary evidence.)

29. The accounts of the Boston Massacre in the *Boston Gazette* of March 12, 1770, reprinted in Jensen *Hist. Doc.* 746; the "Case of Thomas Preston," March 13, *same* 751; and soldiers' depositions of Aug. and Sept. digested in Shy *Toward Lexington* 316–317 and mentioned in Gage to Dalrymple Nov. 19, Adams *New Light* 91, refer to many squabbles, in the months before the massacre, between the soldiers and townspeople—attributed by Preston to the greater boldness of the latter after withdrawal of the Sixty-fourth and Sixty-fifth Regiments in the summer of 1769.

30. Revised Boston non-importation agreement of Dec. 4, 1769, described in the text, Schlesinger *Col. Merchants* 133 and letters of Thomas Hutchinson to Francis Bernard and to Thomas Pownall Dec. 6, cited therein. (On Oct. 15, a majority of Boston merchants had provisionally agreed to extend the ban until *all* British acts levying duties for revenue on the colonies were repealed, but, on N.Y. and Philadelphia refusing to go this far, Boston receded, *same* 131-133.)

31. The pressure in Dec., 1769, and Jan., 1770, on the Boston holdouts which had brought some of them, including Gov. Hutchinson's sons, into line is described in *same* 175-176; *Boston Gazette* and *Boston Evening-Post* of Jan. 22 and *Mass. Gazette* of Jan. 25; Rowe's diary for Jan. 17, 18, and 23, 1770, *Rowe* 196-197; Samuel Cooper to Thomas Pownall Jan. 30, Tuckerman "Cooper Letters" 314-316; Cushing et al. to Dennys De Berdt Jan. 30, *Mass. Papers* 131-135; and *Mass. Broadsides* 208.

32. The final holdouts were four firms of non-natives of the colonies, John Bernard, James & Patrick McMasters & Co., Anne and Elizabeth Cummins, and John Mein, and four native Bostonians, Nathaniel Rogers, William Jackson, Theophilus Lillie, and John Taylor, Drake *Boston* 767n.; Greenough *New Eng. Almanacs* 17-18.

33. John Rowe's diary for Jan. 23, states, "the Lieut. Governor . . . sent the Sheriff [Stephen Greenleaf] & ordered them to disperse which they took no notice of," Rowe *Diary* 196. Lieutenant-Governor Thomas Hutchinson had been Acting Governor since the departure of Gov. Bernard for England Aug. 1, 1769, becoming Governor March 14, 1771, Rowe's diary for these dates, *Rowe* 191, 212.

34. Denunciation of holdouts at meeting of Jan. 23, 1770, Greenough *New Eng. Almanacs* 17-18 and Evans *Am. Bibliography* IV 216.

35. The *Massachusetts Gazette* of January 11, 1770, published a letter of Lillie, saying: "it always seemed strange to me that People who contend so much for civil and religious Liberty should be so ready to deprive others of their natural liberty—That Men who are guarding against being subject to Laws which they never gave their consent [to] . . . , should at the same time make Laws, and in the most effectual manner execute them upon me and others, to which laws I am sure I never gave my consent. . . . I own I had rather be a slave under one Master . . . than a slave to a hundred or more. . . ."

36. The boys' harassment of Lillie, Thursday, Feb. 22, 1770, *Adams Legal Papers* 398. Thursday was a customary school holiday, *same* 397. Hutchinson wrote Gage Feb. 25 that the boys had been "set on by Men" to harass Lillie, Mass. Arch. XXVI 445, but he does not give the source of this information or suspicion. Lillie's store was located "near Mr. Pemberton's Meeting-house [New Brick Church on present Hanover street] North End," Drake *Boston* 767n. William Jackson, another holdout, also was much harassed, Zobel *Boston Massacre* 172-173.

37. Ebenezer Richardson's being a notorious informer, Hutchinson to Bernard Feb. 28, 1770, referring to Richardson, as a person "whose name you must remember as an informer," Mass. Arch. XXVI 450-451; also Dickerson "Commissioners of Customs" 310-313; *Boston Gazette,* Supplement Feb. 26, *Boston Gazette* March 5; William Palfrey to John Wilkes March 5, Elsey "Wilkes and Palfrey" 416; Richardson's petition Jan. 19, 1775, stating he had given "informa-

tion of several breeches of the Acts of Trade," T:1:517:258 (P.R.O.) cited in Zobel *Boston Massacre* 344 n.23.

38. The attack on Richardson's house and his shooting and fatally wounding Christopher Snider and injuring John Gore, *Boston Evening Post* Feb. 26, 1770; *Adams Legal Papers* II 398–399. The name of the slain boy is spelled variously Snider, Seider, and Syder, as, for example, in the contemporary documents quoted in *same* 410n., 418, 424, but Snider is the most usual.

39. Hutchinson to Commodore Samuel Hood Feb. 23, 1770, as to the crowd's threat to hang Richardson, and his commitment to jail, Mass. Arch. XXVI 444–445. To similar effect, Hutchinson to Gage Feb. 25, *same* XXVI 448. Death of Snider eight hours after he was shot, Zobel *Boston Massacre* 345 n.29. Richardson was convicted of murder in April, 1770, but the court, which thought he was guilty at most of manslaughter, deferred sentencing him until March 10, 1772, by which time a pardon from the King had arrived, and he was discharged and fled, *Adams Legal Papers* II 405–406, 410.

40. John Adams' diary entry on or about Feb. 26, 1770, concerning Snider's funeral, *Adams Papers* I 349–350. John Rowe estimated that 2,000 people were in the funeral procession, Rowe's diary for Feb. 26, *Rowe* 197.

41. John Adams' statement Dec. 4, 1770, concerning the effect on civilians and British soldiers in Boston of the report of recent clashes between British soldiers and civilians in New York City, *Adams Legal Papers* III 254–265. These clashes are described in the second appendix to this chapter.

42. The incident on March 2, 1770, at Gray's rope-walk, affidavits dated March 17–21, *Short Narrative* 39–41, 48. "Wouldring sticks" or "wolder" sticks are made of hard wood, generally about $3\frac{1}{2}$ to 4 feet in length with a diameter of about 2 inches in the middle, tapering to about an inch at each rounded end, letter to the author, July 26, 1963, from Ralph Weaver, Vice President in Charge of Manufacturing of Plymouth Cordage Company, Plymouth, Mass.

43. Rumors of preparation for renewal of the fight at the rope-walk, depositions of John Fisher and three others March 17–22, 1770, *Short Narrative* 40–44. Capt. Thomas Preston's account, March 13, 1770, Jensen *Hist. Doc.* 750. Gage to Hillsborough Apr. 10 attributes the incident of March 5 directly to the fight at Gray's rope-walk, *Gage* I 249.

44. Clashes on night of March 5, 1770, before the affray at the Customs House, testimony at the trial of soldiers, Kidder *Boston Massacre* 154–157, 182–211; *Boston Gazette* March 12, 1770, reprinted in Jensen *Hist. Doc.* 746–747; unpublished depositions of officers and soldiers, Gay Transcripts of "State Papers" XII 40–145 at the Mass. Hist. Soc.; *Fair Account*, Appendix 3–12; and *Adams Legal Papers* III 50–276 *passim*. References to the moonlight, Kidder *Boston Massacre* 28, 47, 49, 72. The classic account of the "Massacre" and ensuing trials, Zobel *Boston Massacre* 184–294, 346–356.

45. As to Edward Garrick, a barber's apprentice, having taunted a British officer, Captain John Goldfinch, and as to the sentry Hugh White, stationed at the Customs House, hitting Garrick with the butt of a gun, on the night of March 5, 1770, depositions before, and testimony at, the trial of the British soldiers, *same* 64, 105. An editorial note in *Adams Legal Papers* III 94 says that the boy's name was Gerrish.

46. The testimony at the trial of the soldiers varied greatly as to the size, 20–100, of the crowd at the Customs House and as to whether or not of boys and youths, Kidder *Boston Massacre* 71, 83, 104–105, 129, 135, 137, 146, 190, 200, 208, 211, 215. One witness testified that some were "in the habits of sailors" *Adams Legal Papers* III 105; and two others that they had seen a band of twenty or thirty all or most of whom were "drest in sailors cloaths" or "appeared to be sailors," a few blocks from the customs house before the firing, *same* 117, 121.

47. Garrick denounces White, and the crowd's threats and throwing things at White, testimony at the trial of the soldiers, *same* 138, 200–202.

48. Gage wrote Hillsborough April 10, 1770, that Capt. Preston "detached a Sergent and twelve Men" and "soon afterwards" followed them, *Gage* I 250. But there is conclusive evidence from various sources that the relief party consisted of seven men, including a non-commissioned officer, William Wemms, that Wemms was a corporal, not a sergeant, and that Preston accompanied the party.

49. Preston's men marched with fixed bayonets, depositions before trial and testimony at the trial of the soldiers, Kidder *Boston Massacre* 72, 83, 85, 140. Their guns not loaded until after the soldiers arrived at the Customs House, "Case of Thomas Preston," Matthews "Preston" 8, and depositions of Peter Cunningham and William Wyat March 7, 1770, *Short Narrative* 65, 72. Cunningham and Wyat swore they heard the officer in charge of Preston's party order the men to load, *same* 65, 72; Preston said the men loaded without orders from him, Matthews "Preston" 8.

50. Various witnesses estimated the crowd after the arrival of Preston and his party at about 40–200, Kidder *Boston Massacre* 131, 133, 139, 146, 157, 199, 201, 211, 215. Witnesses testified at the trial of the soldiers that the crowd attacking the soldiers was led by "the mulatto"—a "stout man" carrying "a large cord-wood stick" and "Dressed Sailor like"—whom they later saw dead, *same* 139–140, 205, and *Adams Legal Papers* III 191–192. This was Crispus Attucks, supposedly of Natick Indian and Negro blood, *same* 29, 29n. and Quarles *The Negro in the American Revolution* 4–8.

51. Testimony as to pelting of the soldiers with snow balls, ice, oyster shells, and sticks, Kidder *Boston Massacre* 131, 132, 141, 142, 147, 152, 190, 201, 202, 204, 208, 215, 216. Gage to Hillsborough Apr. 10, 1770, and to Barrington Apr. 24, *Gage* I 250, II 537, state that the crowd threw bricks and stones, too, but this is not corroborated by the depositions before, or testimony at, the trial of the soldiers.

52. Peter Cunningham deposed March 20, 1770, that he heard Preston order his men to load their guns soon after reaching the Customs House, *Short Narrative* 65. In his "Case of Capt. Thomas Preston," March 13, 1770, Preston says "I suffered the Troops to go to the Spot where the unhappy Affair took place, without any Loading in their Pieces, nor did I ever give Orders for loading them," Matthews "Preston" 8 and Jensen *Hist. Doc.* 751.

53. Members of the crowd striking at the soldiers with clubs and a cutlass, Kidder *Boston Massacre* 138, 152, 203, 205, and calling them "bloody backs" and daring them to fire, "Case of Thomas Preston," March 13, 1770, Jensen *Hist. Doc.* 751.

54. Hutchinson wrote Gen. Gage Apr. 1, 1770, that "There are several Witnesses who are very positive they heard Capt. Preston give orders to fire, others, who were as near, swear that the men fired without orders . . . ," Adams *New Light* 42. The testimony at Preston's trial was similarly conflicting.

55. Attucks, Samuel Gray, and James Caldwell were shot and killed on the spot; Samuel Maverick, a youth of seventeen, and Patrick Carr died of their wounds soon afterward, Boston Committee's report March 19, 1770, Kidder *Boston Massacre* 29–30. William Palfrey wrote John Wilkes March 13 that six others had been wounded, *M.H.S. Proc.* VI 480.

56. Preston and the soldiers were arrested a few hours after the shooting, Boston Committee's report March 19, 1770, and they and Edward Manwaring and three other men accused of having fired from the Customs House were indicted March 13, Kidder *Boston Massacre* 42, 123. All pleaded "Not Guilty" when arraigned on Sept. 7, Matthews "Preston" 18n.

57. As to postponement of the trial in order to give the people of Boston time to cool, Hutchinson to Gage Apr. 1, 1770, Apr. 13, May 9, and June 1, Adams "New Light" 298, 303, 309, 309–10. The postponement also gave time for the King to grant reprieves for Preston and the men in case they were convicted of murder, and by June 22, Hutchinson had received orders for a reprieve, "until His Majesty's pleasure should be known," Hutchinson to Gage June 22, *same* 312.

58. Affidavits of March 7, 15, 20, 1770, of William Wyat, Joseph Hooten, Jr., and Charles Hobby that, being near the soldiers and their officer before the Customs House, they heard the officer order the men to fire, *Brief Narrative* 70, 72, 63.

59. Hutchinson to Bernard March 30, 1770, reporting Robert Auchmuty's statement as to strong evidence of Preston's order to fire, Mass. Arch. XXXVI 467. Hutchinson, still Chief Justice of the Mass. Superior Court, as well as Lieutenant- and Acting Governor, did not sit at the trials of Preston and the soldiers.

60. Auchmuty, John Adams, and Josiah Quincy, Jr., were counsel for Preston. As to Adams and Auchmuty, Robert Treat Paine's Minutes of Arguments, *Adams Legal Papers* III 86–89 and other sources. As to Quincy, Josiah Quincy, Sr., to his son, Josiah Quincy, Jr., March 22, 1770, and the latter's reply of March 26, *same* 6–7. In his autobiography written years later, Adams, in characteristic self-praise, wrote that Quincy agreed to act only after he himself had the grit to do so, *same* 6, but Quincy's letter to his father indicates the contrary.

61. The King's Attorney (Prosecuting Attorney) for Suffolk County, Samuel Quincy, and Paine as counsel for the Crown in prosecuting Preston, Paine's Minutes of Arguments, *same* 61, 90, and Paine's diary (manuscript) for Oct. 24, 1770, in Mass. Hist. Soc. Paine was retained as special attorney to aid "the King's Attorney . . . in the tryal of the Murtherers" at a Boston town meeting March 13, 1770, *Boston Records* (for 1770–1777) 14.

62. Wigmore *Evidence* III 685–686 as to testimony in trials for felony. An interesting illustration of the advantage the accused might derive from the right to examine witnesses was the following question put by Preston to Capt. James Gifford, an officer who was a witness at his trial, "Did you ever know an Officer order Men to fire with their Bayonets charged," to which Gifford answered, "No." This answer, linked with previous testimony that the men had their bayonets

charged (i.e., fixed) when the alleged call to "fire" was given, strongly implied that Preston had not given the order.

63. Judges John Cushing and Benjamin Lynde in charging the jury in Preston's trial, said "The principal Q[uestion] whether Prisoner gave Order [to fire]," *Adams Legal Papers* III 79.

64. Petition of three of the accused soldiers, Hugh White, James Hartigan, and Matthew Kilroy, Oct. 24, 1770, that they be tried at the same time as Preston, Noble "Fifth of March Papers" 66; *Adams Legal Papers* III 17n.

65. The fullest and best accounts of all aspects of the trial are in *same* III 1–31, 46–98 and Zobel *Boston Massacre* 267–294.

66. Verdict of Not Guilty in Preston's case, Oct. 30, 1770, Matthews "Preston" 18n.

67. Preston to Gage Oct. 31, 1770, concerning the contrasting merits of counsel for and against him, Adams "New Light" 338–339. Paine, counsel for the prosecution, was so "unfit" (ill) that a postponement was granted for his closing speech, Justice Peter Oliver to Hutchinson Oct. 27, Kidder *Boston Massacre* 20. Palfrey wrote Wilkes Oct. 24 that the trial was a "farce" because the sheriff had packed the jury with so many of Preston's "friends and most intimate acquaintances," Elsey "Wilkes and Palfrey" 423–424.

68. As to Preston's excellent reputation in Boston, diary entries and letters from March 5 to June 28, 1770, of John Rowe, Andrew Oliver, Jr., William Palfrey, and Rev. Andrew Eliot, quoted and cited in Matthews "Preston" 3, and testimony of Capt. James Gifford and Hutchinson at Preston's trial, *Adams Legal Papers* III 79n., 81.

69. The testimony in the Preston trial is given in *same* 50–80. William Palfrey wrote John Wilkes Oct. 30, 1770, "the witnesses both for the Crown & the prisoners differed materially in some parts of their testimony, and even in my own mind there still remains a doubt whether Capt. Preston gave the order to fire, as the two Witnesses who swore to that point, declared also that Capt. Preston had on a Surtout Coat, which he proved was not the case," Elsey "Wilkes and Palfrey" 425. To similar effect, Samuel Adams to Stephen Sayre Nov. 16, Cushing *S. Adams* II 59.

70. Trial of the soldiers Nov. 27 to Dec. 5, 1770, including names of counsel, *same* III 98–314 and Kidder *Boston Massacre* 125, 127, 219–259, 285, with Hutchinson to Gage Dec. 6, Adams "New Light" 351. Sampson S. Blowers presumably was the lawyer referred to in Hutchinson to Gage Nov. 26, stating, "I advised Captain Preston to engage one of the Bar over and above the Counsel to conduct the Cause in Court, . . . who should make a very diligent inquiry into the characters and principles of all who are returned for jury service," *same* 348.

71. The testimony in the trial of the soldiers, William Wemms, James Hartigan, William McCauley, Hugh White, Matthew Kilroy, William Warren, John Carrol, and Hugh Montgomery, *Rex v. Wemms et al.,* is in *Adams Legal Papers* III 102–226; and Kidder *Boston Massacre* 128–158, 182–219.

72. At least three other of the soldiers besides Montgomery and Kilroy fired, but there was no clear evidence that the shots fired by any except the latter two had struck any of the persons killed, judges' charges to the jury, *Adams Legal Papers* III 282–312.

73. There was voluminous testimony and but little contradiction of the throwing of missles at the soldiers which would naturally induce them to fire to protect themselves from serious injury.

74. The lengthy charges to the jury by the two junior judges, Edmund Trowbridge and Peter Oliver, and the briefer charges of the senior judges, John Cushing and Benjamin Lynde, are in *Adams Legal Papers* III 282–312.

75. Verdicts in the trial of the accused soldiers, *same* 312–314. (Zobel "Boston Massacre" 123–127 publishes undated statements by Hutchinson charging John Adams with having suppressed evidence favorable to his clients, the soldiers, lest it put Boston in a bad light. I give no weight to these statements because they may have been written long after the event. Incidentally, they contradict each other on another point; one gives Kilroy, the other Montgomery, as the first to fire.)

76. Montgomery and Kilroy "prayed the Benefit of Clergy, which was allowed them, and thereupon they were each of them burnt in the hand, in open Court, and discharged," *same* 314. Burning the hand (specifically "the Crown of the left thumb") with a hot iron, Blackstone *Commentaries* IV 366, served the double purpose of inflicting immediate punishment and leaving an indelible mark that the branded man had had the benefit of clergy once and was not entitled to it again. As to the Mass. background of this plea, Cross "Benefit of Clergy" 154–161.

77. Trial and acquittal on Dec. 12, 1770, of Edward Manwaring and his three companions in the Customs House, *Trial of William Wemms* 211–217; Kidder *Boston Massacre* 285. As brought out in Dickerson "Commissioners of Customs" 315–319 evidence collected before the trial, especially a deposition of Charlotte Bourgatte, a boy apprenticed to Manwaring, in *Short Narrative* 75–76, looked black for Manwaring; but at the trial, the prosecution's case collapsed, *Trial of William Wemms* 211–217.

78. As to the curious and sometimes mad conduct of James Otis, Jr., over many years, the adjudication of him as insane in Dec., 1771, and his temporary recoveries and final collapse, biography of Otis in *D.A.B.;* Shipton *Harvard Graduates* 254–286; Brennan "Otis" 690–725; Hutchinson to John Pownall Sept. 20, 1771, Mass. Arch. XXVII 231; Rowe's dairy (1770) *Rowe* 199, 201; John Adams' diary 1762–1772 *Adams Papers* I 225–226, 236–237, 275, 343, 348, 349, II 14, 49, 50, 64–66; Waters *Otis Family* 177–179. As to Otis' earlier leadership of the Boston Whigs, *same passim* and Knollenberg *Origin* 67–69, 145, 163–164, 196–200.

79. Samuel Adams, writing under the pen name "Vindex," denounces the conduct and outcome of the trials in the *Boston Gazette* Dec. 10, 1770, to Jan. 28, 1771, Cushing *S. Adams* II 77–162 *passim*.

80. Period of calm in Boston following the "Massacre" trials, Hutchinson to Bernard Dec. 10 and 16, 1770, Mass. Arch. XXVII 72–74, 77; to John Pownall Jan. 7, 1771, and to Thomas Whately Jan. 25, *same* 90–91, 106–107; Anne Hulton to Mrs. Adam Lightbody Dec. 21, 1770, *Hulton Letters* 28–29; Gage to Barrington Jan. 1771, *Gage* II 567; Rev. Andrew Eliot to Thomas Hollis Jan. 26, Apr. 25 and June 19, 1771, "Eliot Letters" 458–460; John Adams' diary for May 1, *Adams Papers* II 10.

81. The flight of the Customs Commissioners to Castle William after the Boston Massacre, Gage to Barrington July 6, 1770, *Gage* II 547, and their return to Boston

after the trials, Anne Hulton to Mrs. Adam Lightbody Dec. 21, *Hulton Letters* 28.

82. The Commissioners again fled to Castle William late in 1773, at the time of the commotions in Boston over the British East India Company's sending of tea there, Anne Hulton to Mrs. Adam Lightbody Jan. 31, 1774, *same* 69.

83. At a Boston town meeting the morning after the massacre, the town chose a committee to inform Acting Governor Hutchinson that the town could be quieted only by "the immediate removal of the Troops," *Boston Records* (for 1770–1777) 2. Upon receiving word from Hutchinson that the commanding officer consented to remove only the Twenty-ninth Regiment, another committee was chosen to inform Hutchinson that the town would be satisfied with "nothing less . . . than a total and immediate removal of the troops," *same* 2–3.

84. Lieut. Col. William Dalrymple was the commanding officer at Boston from Aug., 1769, to March, 1770, and at Castle William from then until July, 1772, when he was sent with his regiment (the Fourteenth) to the island of St. Vincent to help quell a Carib rebellion, *Gage* I 327, II 614, leaving no British troops in or near Boston.

85. Dalrymple wrote Gage March 7, 1770, that Hutchinson, by the advice of his Council, had "desired and required" him to remove the troops, Adams *New Light* 22. Hutchinson wrote Gage March 18 that he had not made "a Requisition," i.e., had not required (ordered) Dalrymple to remove the troops, Gage Papers Clements Lib., printed, with an unimportant omission, in *same* 36–37. Since the minutes of the Mass. Council May 6, 1770, state that the Council advised Hutchinson "to pray," i.e., ask, Dalrymple to remove the troops, *same* 19, and I have found no other relevant evidence, I suppose Hutchinson's version is correct.

86. Dalrymple wrote Gage March 12, 1770, that removal of the Twenty-ninth Regiment to Castle William would be completed "this night," *same* 25, and the Fourteenth Regiment followed on March 16, Rowe's diary, *Rowe* 199.

87. The Twenty-ninth Regiment was transferred by way of Providence, R.I., to New Jersey, May 17, 1770, Zobel *Boston Massacre* 228, 352n. 46 and Gage to Lord Barrington June 1, 1770, *Gage* II 542. The Fourteenth Regiment remained at Castle William until 1772, when it was replaced by the Sixty-fourth, *same* I 330.

88. The orations by James Lovell in 1771, Dr. Joseph Warren in 1772, Dr. Benjamin Church in 1773, John Hancock in 1774, and Warren again in 1775 are collected in *Orations at Boston* 3–70.

89. In his oration in 1772 Joseph Warren "reminded" his hearers of "The horrors of that dreadful night . . . when our streets were stained with the BLOOD OF OUR BRETHREN, when our ears were wounded by the groans of the dying, and our eyes were tormented by the sight of the mangled bodies of the dead. When our alarmed imagination presented to our view our houses wrapped in flames . . . our beauteous virgins exposed to the influence of unbridled passion; our virtuous wives . . . falling a sacrifice to worse than brutal violence" etc., *same* 20.

90. In 1774 John Hancock recalled "that dismal night . . . when Satan with his chosen band opened the sluices of New England's blood, and sacrilegiously polluted our land with the dead bodies of her guiltless sons." "Let not," he pleaded, "the heaving bosom cease to burn with a manly indignation at the barbarous story . . . and all America join in one common prayer to Heaven,

that the inhuman, unprovoked murders of March 1770 . . . may ever stand on history without parallel," *same* 43.

CHAPTER 12

1. The official figures of exports of tea from England to America in Labaree *Tea Party* 331 show that the volume of tea shipped to New England and the southern colonies was about as large as before the non-importation movement was launched. There was a heavy falling off of shipments from England only to N.Y. and Pa., where, as brought out in *same* 52–55, there was extensive smuggling of tea.

2. The controversy from June, 1769, to June, 1772, between the Mass. House of Representatives and successive Governors of Mass. (Francis Bernard and Thomas Hutchinson) over the Governors assembling the Legislature (general court) at Cambridge instead of Boston, where it customarily met, is well covered and documented in Lord and Calhoon "Removal of the Mass. General Court" 735–755 and Wells *Adams I* 256–258, 344–345, 403–404, 467–468, 472, 476–479. Other less bitter and protracted controversies over constitutional issues in Mass. (in 1770 and 1771) are described in Gipson *Brit. Empire* XII 43–45.

3. The so-called Wilkes Fund controversy from Feb., 1769, to March, 1774, between the S.C. Commons House and successive Governors of S.C. (Lord Charles Montague and William Bull) over the House's claim of right to appropriate public funds without the concurrence of the Governor and Council is well covered and documented in Greene "Bridge to Revolution" 19–52; Greene *Quest For Power* 402–416; and Smith *S.C.* 369–386, 388–389, 393–394. Changes in the judicial system of S.C. also gave rise to controversy in S.C. from 1768 to 1772, Greene *Quest For Power* 400–402; Smith *S.C.* 134–140.

4. There are particularly good accounts of the Regulator Insurrection in N.C. from 1768 to 1771, culminating (May, 1771) in the Battle of the Alamance, in Gipson *Brit. Empire* XI 510–537; Basset "Regulators" 141–212.

5. The controversies in Md. over officials and fees of the established (Church of England) clergy from 1770 to 1773 is well covered and documented in Barker *Md.* 345–358, 360–364.

6. Clashes from 1770 to 1772 with customs officers near Salem, N.J., Philadelphia, Boston, Falmouth, Mass., are described in Jensen *Founding* 424, Jensen *Philadelphia* 150–151; Barrow *Trade* 245–246; Martin "King's Customs" 214–215. (Martin, on 202–216, has a valuable account of the operation and difficulties of many kinds experienced in the administration of the customs in the Philadelphia customs district from 1763 to 1774.)

7. Several of the clashes with customs officers from 1766 to 1769 have been described in previous chapters; others at Charleston, S.C., are described in Barrow *Trade* 203–209, 234–235, 317–318, 320; and at Newport, R.I., in note 9 below. Three of those at Charleston were particularly notable in antagonizing the conservative merchant-planter, Henry Laurens, *same* 206–209, 234–235; Jensen *Tracts* 185–206.

8. Firing on the British armed schooner *St. John* at Newport in 1764 and burning of a boat of the warship *Maidstone* there in 1765, Lovejoy *R.I. Politics* 36–37; Knollenberg *Samuel Ward* 15–16 and *Origin* 194–195. Burning of the armed

sloop *Liberty* at Newport in 1769, *R.I. Col. Rec.* VI 593–596; *Newport Mercury* May 14 and 22, July 24 and 31, and Aug. 7, 1769, T.1:147:200–225, 289–292, 371–385; and Joseph Chew to Sir William Johnson July 26, 1769, *Johnson* VII 71–72. In each case misconduct of officers or men of the vessels involved apparently had given provocation for the attack.

9. Lieutenant William Dudingston, commander of the *Gaspee,* to Admiral John Montagu March 24, 1773, indicates that he took up his station at Newport, R.I., on or shortly before Feb. 22, *R.I. Hist. Soc. Proc.* (for 1890–1891) 80. Montagu to Gov. Joseph Wanton Apr. 8 states that he had instructed Dudingston, among other things, "to prevent (if possible), the illicit trade that is carrying on in Rhode Island," *R.I. Col. Rec.* VII 62.

10. Dudingston had a reputation for brutal and insolent conduct while stationed in Pa. three years earlier, *Pa. Journal* June 26, 1769; *Newport Mercury* July 17; Clement Biddle to Thomas Richardson Oct. 22, 1770, Jensen *Commerce* 138, 270.

11. Wanton to Lord Hillsborough May 20, 1772, complaining of Dudingston's illegally carrying rum he had seized in R.I. to Boston, and Dudingston to Montagu May 22, saying he knew he was acting illegally, but that there was no other practical way to deal with the seized rum, *R.I. Col. Rec.* VII 64–65, 67. (The rum seems to have been that involved in a suit against Dudingston described in Bryant "R.I. Justice" 70–71.)

12. Commission of Inquiry to the King June 22, 1773, "There is also too much reason to believe that in some instances Lieutenant Dudingston from an intemperate, if not a reprehensible zeal to aid the revenue service exceeded the bounds of his duty," *R.I. Col. Rec.* VII 180. As those who suffered from Dudingston's conduct well knew, there was a further temptation to exceed the bounds of duty in that if vessel or cargo or both seized by him were tried and condemned, he would, as brought out in Chapter 3, be entitled to a large share of the proceeds from the sale of the condemned property.

13. Lieut. Gov. Darius Sessions of R.I. to Wanton March 21, 1772, reporting complaints that the *Gaspee,* cruising on Narragansett Bay, "Suffers no vessels to pass, not even packet boats, or others of an inferior kind, without a strict examination; and where any sort of unwillingness is discovered, they are compelled to submit by an armed force," *same* 60. Further details of Dudingston's provocative conduct are in Wanton to Hillsborough May 20, *same* 67; the *Providence Gazette* of March 21 and 28; and Henry Marchant to Benjamin Franklin Nov. 21, Lovejoy *R.I. Politics* 158, 215.

14. Wanton to Dudingston March 22 and 23, 1772, requesting that he "produce me your commission," and Wanton to Hillsborough May 20 stating that Dudingston, instead of complying, had sent one of his junior officers with merely a letter from the British Admiralty Board to the American Customs Board requesting a deputation in the customs for Dudingston, *R.I. Col. Rec.* VII 61–62, 67. Dudingston wrote Montagu March 24 that he had shown Wanton "a" deputation, *R.I. Hist. Soc. Proc.* (for 1890–1891) 8, but, unless Wanton lied, this must have been the Admiralty Board's request for a deputation or a deputation to someone other than Dudingston.

15. John Adams wrote in his diary for Dec. 29, 1772, that the "brutal, hoggish Manners" of Montagu, who was stationed at Boston, "are a Disgrace to the Royal

Navy and to the King's Service," but, judging from the sketch of him in *D.N.B.*, he was a successful officer, becoming Admiral of the White in 1787.

16. Hillsborough to Wanton Aug. 7, 1772, Dartmouth Papers, identifies the two letters here referred to by Montagu as Wanton's letters to him of March 22 and 23, described in *R.I. Col. Rec.* VII 61–62, cited in note 14 of this chapter.

17. Montagu to Wanton Apr. 8, 1772, denouncing him for his "insolent" letters to Dudingston, *same* 62–63. The letters in fact were not insolent; the first, after telling of the complaints made against Dudingston, said "I . . . expect that you do, without delay, produce me your commission and instructions, if any, you have, which was your duty to have done, when you first came within the jurisdiction of this colony," the second, after pointing out the failure to furnish the information called for said, "I expect you do, without delay, comply with my request of yesterday," *same* 61–62.

18. Wanton to Montagu May 8, 1772, replying to his letter of Apr. 8, *same* 63–64. Wanton secured the approval of this proposed reply by the R.I. General Assembly before sending it to Montagu, Proceedings of the Assembly, undated, *same* 47 and Dudingston to Montagu May 22, *same* 66.

19. Wanton to Hillsborough May 20, 1772, enclosing copies of Montagu's letter of Apr. 8 and his reply of May 8, and pointing out the misstatements in Montagu's letters, *same* 66–68. In replying under date of Aug. 7, Hillsborough did not mention the ill conduct of Dudingston and Montagu complained of by Wanton, but instead attacked Wanton himself by stating that "the Tone of Menace & Insult" of his "letters to Lieutenant Dudingston of the 22d & 23d of March last is considered by the King as highly disrespectful to His Majesty," Dartmouth Papers.

20. A deposition of Midshipman William Dickinson of the *Gaspee* June 11, 1772, *R.L. Col. Rec.* VII 82–84 stated that the *Gaspee* "came to anchor" near Pawtuxet; but others who gave evidence, cited in note 21 below, said she had run aground.

21. The time and place of the *Gaspee's* running aground is fixed by the affidavits dated June 10, 1772, of three sailors of the *Gaspee, same* 78–79. They stated that the vessel was bound for Providence to take on "some of His Majesty's seamen that were expected from Boston," *same.* The *Providence Gazette* of June 13, 1772, stated that when she ran aground the *Gaspee* was chasing the *Hannah,* a packet boat running between Newport and Providence. Perhaps both statements are true.

22. Sessions to Wanton June 11, 1772, concerning the attack on the *Gaspee,* enclosing the affidavits cited in note 21, and advising issuance of a proclamation offering a large reward for the apprehension and conviction of the attackers, *R.I. Col. Rec.* VII 77–79. (I have omitted the oft-repeated details of the attack and the names of its alleged leaders given by Ephraim Bowen and Dr. John Mawney, *same* 68–76, because their statements were not made until many years later, Bowen's in 1839 and Mawney's in 1826.)

23. Wanton's proclamation of June 11, 1772, concerning the *Gaspee, same* 81.

24. Undated statement of Aaron Briggs to Capt. John Linzee of the *Beaver* concerning the attack on the *Gaspee, same* 93–94. Samuel Tompkins, Briggs' master, in a deposition of July 11, 1772, described him as "a mulatto lad of about sixteen," *same* 96. The Reverend Ezra Stiles described him as a "Negro Indian," *Stiles Diary* I 335.

25. Montagu to Wanton July 8, 1772, enclosing Briggs' statement, *R.I. Col. Rec.* VII 93.

26. Report of the royal Commission of Inquiry June 22, 1773, as to Linzee's misbehavior and its finding that "here the civil magistrates ceased their endeavors to discover the offenders," *same* 179–180. As to issuance of the warrant dated July 16, 1772, and Linzee's refusal to permit it to be served, *same* 98–101. (It seems likely that Linzee refused to turn over Briggs because of fear that the means, brought out later in this chapter, by which he had secured Briggs' statement, would be exposed.)

27. Montagu wrote Philip Stephens, Secretary to the Admiralty, and Hillsborough June 12, 1772, bitter and extremely biased letters concerning the attack on the *Gaspee*, denouncing the people of Rhode Island, praising Dudingston, and expressing hope he would be favored if he lived, of which Montagu said he had little hopes, *R.I. Hist. Soc. Proc.* (for 1890–1891) 81–82 and *R.I. Col. Rec.* VII 89.

28. Cabinet meetings of July 30 and Aug. 20, 1772, concerning the *Gaspee* affair and Hillsborough to Wanton Aug. 7, Dartmouth Papers, digested in *Dartmouth* (1895) 85, 86. The proceedings and decision of the King in Council (the Privy Council) and those present at its meeting on Aug. 21, 1772, concerning the *Gaspee* affair, and the Council's approval on Aug. 26 of the documents implementing the decision, P.C. 2:116:421 and *Acts P.C.* V 356–357.

29. The King's proclamation of Aug. 26, 1772, offering rewards for information leading to the arrest and conviction of participants in the attack on the *Gaspee* and pardon for informers who were in the attack, other than the two supposed leaders, *R.I. Col. Rec.* VII 107–108. The King probably had the *Gaspee* affair primarily in mind in writing Lord North Aug. 1, advising conciliation in a pending dispute with France, since "we must get the Colonies into order before we engage with our neighbors," *Geo. III* II 372.

30. The Royal Commission to Wanton, Chief Justices Daniel Horsmanden of N.Y., Frederick Smythe of N.J., and Peter Oliver of Mass., and Admiralty Judge Robert Auchmuty, dated Sept. 2, 1772, together with their instructions of Sept. 4, are in *R.I. Col. Rec.* VII 108–112. Wanton was the only member of the Commission who was not a Crown official, and even he was no flaming Whig and when the Revolution broke out, became a loyalist, sketch of him in *D.A.B.*

31. The Dockyards Act of 12 Geo. III ch. 24 was assented to by the King Apr. 16, 1772, *Journals H. of C.* XXXIII 701. I have found no evidence in the proceedings of Parliament or elsewhere for its extraordinary provision authorizing trial in Great Britain of offenses against the act committed in places outside the realm, including the colonies. The act would almost certainly have alarmed the colonists even had it not been highlighted by the *Gaspee* incident.

32. Hillsborough wrote the Governor and Company of R.I. Aug. 7, 1772, enclosing a copy of the Dockyards Act and stating that the attackers of the *Gaspee* were to be proceeded against under it, Dartmouth Papers, digested in *Dartmouth* (1895) 86. This letter was recalled and canceled Aug. 22, *same*. To same effect Hillsborough and Lord Dartmouth to Gage Aug. 7 and Sept. 4, *Gage* II 146, 149.

33. Opinion of the Attorney-General and Solicitor-General, Edward Thurlow and Alexander C. Wedderburn, Aug. 10, 1772, that the burning of the *Gaspee*

was not punishable under the act of 12 Geo. III ch. 24, but was punishable as high treason, C.O. 5:159:26–27; "Gaspee Papers" 239–240; *Acts P.C.* VI 525; *Home Office Pap.* III 531. Parliament had resolved in 1769 that the ancient act of 35 Henry VIII ch. 2 (1543) providing for trial in England of treason or misprision of treason committed outside the realm applied to the colonies, *Parl. Hist.* XVI 479–511.

34. Decision of the Privy Council Aug. 21 and 26, 1772, to send those accused of burning the *Gaspee* to England for trial for high treason, *Acts P.C.* V 356–357.

35. For Lord Dartmouth, stepbrother of Lord North, and his political career, *D.N.B.* and Bargar *Dartmouth* 15–159.

36. Dartmouth to Wanton Sept. 4, 1772, ordering him to turn over persons accused of burning the *Gaspee* to Montagu to be "sent here" to be tried for "high treason," *R.I. Col. Rec.* VII 103–104, quoting the *Massachusetts Spy* of Dec. 31, 1772. The letter is published in full in Leslie "Gaspee Affair" 243.

37. Forfeiture of the convicted traitor's entire estate, real and personal, Blackstone *Commentaries* IV 381.

38. Punishment of the offender himself for treason, *same* 92–93. Blackstone points out that, at first by connivance, but "at length ripened by humanity into law," the offender was now preserved from the torment of being drawn on the ground to the place of execution by being drawn on a sledge or hurdle.

39. The Commisssioners sat at Newport Jan. 5–22, and May 26–June 24, 1773, *R.I. Col. Rec.* VII 120, 163, and entries in the diary of Ezra Stiles of Newport, *Stiles Diary* I 330, 338, 375, 391. Henry Marchant, Attorney-General of R.I., wrote former Gov. Samuel Ward of R.I. Jan. 28 that "The Commissioners have adjourned themselves to the 26th of next May in order I presume to report Home how Things appear to them . . . [and] have more explicit Instructions," Knollenberg *Samuel Ward* 22.

40. Peter May, of the crew of the *Gaspee,* testified Jan. 19, 1773, that one of the attackers, "a tall, slender man, wearing his own hair [i.e. without a wig] of a brown color" was "named Greene," but he apparently did not state how he knew the name, *R.I. Col. Rec.* VII 152.

41. Twenty-three Greenes are listed in the index to the volume just cited, (note 40) beating the runner-up, Brown, by two.

42. The Commissioners' report to the King June 22, 1773, discrediting Briggs' testimony, *same* 182. Captain Linzee's threats to Briggs to whip and then hang him if he did not "confess" are brought out in Chief Justice Horsmander of N.Y. to Dartmouth July 23, *same* 187. To similar effect, Chief Justice William Smythe of N.J. to Dartmouth Feb. 9, *N.J. Col. Arch.* X 396.

43. Chief Justice Stephen Hopkins and Justices of the R.I. Superior Court to the Commissioners concerning the Court's findings, June 11, 1773, *same* 175–176.

44. Commissioners to justices of the R.I. Superior Court June 12, 1773, declining to give "any sentiment or opinion" in response to the justices' invitation to comment on their findings, *same* 176.

45. Commissioners' report to the King June 22, 1773, *R.I. Col. Rec.* VII 178–182.

46. Though there are published letters as late as 1775 and 1777 dealing with the efforts of members of the Commission of Inquiry to secure money for services

and expenses in attending the meetings of the Commission (e.g., Thomas Hutchinson on behalf of Oliver and Horsmander on behalf of himself, *Home Office Pap.* (1773–1775) 320; *R.I. Col. Rec.* VII 188) I have found no evidence after July, 1773, of further efforts by the British government to secure punishment of the attackers of the *Gaspee.*

47. Admiral Augustus Keppel wrote Lord Rockingham Sept. [day not given], 1772, that he had heard Dartmouth "was resolved not to allow of any orders to issue for his office for bringing home for trial [a single] one of the prisoners accused of the riot in Rhode Island; that he considers it legal for the person to take his trial [only] in the country where the offence was committed . . . ," *Keppel* I 409.

48. Wanton laid Dartmouth's letter before the R.I. Assembly at its session beginning Dec. 9, 1772, *R.I. Col. Rec.* VII 199. The Assembly chose a committee, headed by Deputy Governor Sessions, to draft a letter in answer to Dartmouth's letter, *same* 202, but I have not found a copy of this letter nor any record of such a letter having been sent or even prepared.

49. Report in the *Providence Gazette* of Dec. 19, 1772, confirmed by a quotation from Dartmouth's letter of Sept. 4 in the *Massachusetts Spy* Dec. 31, quoted in *R.I. Col. Rec.* VII 114n., 103–104. (The statement in the *Gazette* that Montagu was to direct who was to be apprehended was inaccurate; who, if anyone, was to be sent to England for trial, was to be decided by the civil authorities of R.I.)

50. Colonial newspaper accounts of the threat of sending colonists to be tried for treason in England, Leslie "Gaspee Affair" 243–245; Jensen *Founding* 428–432. The excitement was fanned by John Allen's very popular pamphlet *An Oration, upon the Beauties of Liberty.* . . . Details of the *Oration,* published in seven editions in Boston, New London, Conn., Hartford, Conn., and Wilmington, N.C., from Jan., 1773–1775, and of its author, John Allen, Adams *Bibliography* 68–70; Bumstead and Clark "John Allen" 561–570.

51. Richard Henry Lee wrote Samuel Adams Feb. 4, 1773, for verification of the reported proposal "of removing Americans beyond the water to be tried for supposed offences committed here," Ballagh *Lee* I 82–83. Adams' reply of Apr. 10, 1773, confirmed the report, Cushing *S. Adams* III 25–28. Lee's letter referred to a reported "military parade" to assist in carrying out this measure. Dartmouth to Gage Sept. 4, 1772, had, indeed, ordered him to send troops if the Commissioners of Inquiry requested them, *Gage* II 149, but no request was made, and no troops were sent.

52. Resolution of the Va. House of Burgesses March 12, 1773, denouncing the proposal to send accused colonists overseas for trial and appointing a Committee of Correspondence to verify the report of this proposal and to maintain a correspondence with other colonies. *Va. House Journals* (for 1773–1776) 38. The report that the "Court of inquiry" had power to send persons beyond the seas for trial was erroneous; as brought out in an earlier note, the Commission of Inquiry did not have this power.

53. The instruction of the House of Burgesses to Speaker Peyton Randolph, March 12, 1773, *same* 38. A copy of his circular letter of March 19 is in *R.I. Col. Rec.* VII 225–227.

54. The favorable responses, May, 1773, to March, 1774, from the twelve other colonies to the Va. proposal for intercolonial Committees of Correspondence, sum-

marized in Collins "Committees" 251–271, are in *Va. Journals* (for 1773–1776) 48–64, 143–145; and 8 *Pa. Assembly* VIII 7037.

55. The act of 13 Wm. III ch. 2 (1701) provided that judges of the English courts should hold office during good behavior ("quam se bene gesserint") and be dismissible only on an address to the King by both Houses of Parliament, and that their salaries should not be diminished while in office. Until 1761 their commissions, like those of Crown officials in general, were terminated by the death of the sovereign; the act of 1 Geo. III ch. 23 (1761) provided that the commissions of judges should not be terminated even by the sovereign's death.

56. Commissions issued to the Governors of the royal colonies except Massachusetts authorized them "to constitute and appoint judges," without limitation as to the kind of tenure to be granted. Examples are the commission to Gov. George Clinton of N.Y. in 1741, *N.Y. Col. Doc.* VI 192 and to Gov. Francis Bernard of N.J. (later Governor of Mass.) in 1758, Greene *Provincial Governor* 230. The Governor's authority under this provision to issue "good behavior" commissions was upheld by the chief law officers of the Crown in an opinion dated July 25, 1753, *N.Y. Col. Doc.* VI 792.

57. Prior to 1753 instructions to the Governors of the royal colonies contained nothing to inhibit them from granting judges "good behavior" tenure. From 1753 onward, the Crown issued instructions to Governors of all the royal colonies except Massachusetts to issue "during pleasure only" commissions to judges, and in 1761 issued a peremptory circular letter reenforcing this institution, Labaree *Instructions* 367, 368.

58. A Crown letter of Dec. 12, 1761, referred to "the ancient [i.e., established] practice and usage" in the colonies to grant judicial commissions "during pleasure only," Labaree *Instructions* I 368; also Labaree *Royal Government* 390.

59. Governors of New York granted good behavior commissions to James De Lancey (1703–1760), Chief Justice of the New York Supreme Court in 1744 and to associate justices John Chambers, Daniel Horsmander, and David Jones in 1751, 1753, and 1758, *same* 792; Acting Governor Cadwallader Colden of N.Y. to Secretary of State William Pitt Aug. 11, 1761, *Colden* (1876) 104; O'Callaghan *N.Y. Commissions* 26, 36, 41, 51. Also, 1733–1761, Governors of New Jersey issued "good behavior" commissions to several judges of the New Jersey Supreme Court, Kemmerer *N.J.* 267, 269, 271, 360.

60. The controversy in several royal colonies from 1760 to 1762 is discussed in Labaree *Royal Government* 395–400; Greene *Quest for Power* 339–343; Knollenberg *Origin* 71–74, 309–310. (The discussion in the latter should have been clarified on 71 by inserting the words "as empowered by their commissions and" before the words "apparently authorized by this instruction.") Also, there was controversy in 1760 over judicial tenure in Pa., a proprietory colony, Bailyn *Pamphlets* 249–272.

61. The provision in the Mass. charter of 1691 empowered the Governor "with the advice and consent of the Council . . . to nominate and appoint Judges . . . ," without any statement as to tenure, *Mass. Acts* I 12.

62. A typical commission and set of instructions to the Governors of Mass., issued to Gov. William Shirley of Mass. in 1741 are in Lincoln *Shirley* I 28–76.

63. The custom in Massachusetts was to issue judicial commissions stating nothing as to tenure, letters between John Adams and William Brattle in the Mass. *Gazette* from Jan. 4 to Feb. 22, 1773, Adams *Works* III 516–574 at 559. The only Mass. judicial commissions before 1775 which I have found (those to Judges Sylvanus Bourne and John Cushing in 1744 and 1748, Cushing Papers, M.H.S.) are silent as to tenure.

64. Adams argued, and I think successfully, that commissions which were silent as to tenure were revocable at the pleasure of the Crown, Adams *Works* III 520–530, 536–574.

65. A typical vote of judicial salaries for one year only by the Mass. Legislature, April 15, 1772, is in *Mass. Acts* XVIII 578.

66. Order from Lord Hillsborough to the Treasury Board July 27, 1772, to pay £400 a year (sterling) to Chief Judge Peter Oliver and £200 each to the four associate judges of the Mass. Superior Court, *Calendar H.O. Papers* (for 1770–1772) 527. In line with the Crown policy of paying officers in the colonies put on the Crown payroll far more than the salary previously paid by the colony, the chief justice's salary from the Crown was over twice that—£160–200 Mass. money, worth less than sterling—previously paid by the province, *Mass. Acts* XVIII 86, 181, 283, 388, 441, 497, 503, 578.

67. A copy of the Treasury warrant, Aug. 6, 1772, for Oliver's salary, commencing the preceding July 5, is in Dickerson "Revenue" 239. The salaries were payable from "the Duties on Tea, imported into America," Treasury Minute July 28, T.29:42:215, 228.

68. Lieut. Gov. Andrew Oliver wrote Francis Bernard as early as Aug. 31, 1772, of a report concerning the Crown's proposed payment of the judges' salaries circulating in Boston, Brown *Democracy* 294. Samuel Adams wrote Elbridge Gerry Oct. 27 that Gov. Thomas Hutchinson was reputed to have recently received official word of this, Cushing *S. Adams* II 340.

69. Boston town meeting Oct. 28, 1772, chooses a committee headed by Samuel Adams to request Gov. Hutchinson for information as to the report of the Crown's paying the salaries of justices of the Mass. Superior Court, *Boston Records* (for 1770–1777) 89–90. Some months earlier, the Mass. House of Representatives had protested against Hutchinson's being paid his salary as Governor by the Crown instead of, as heretofore, by the province, messages exchanged by the House and the Governor, June 6–July 10, 1772, Bradford *Mass. Papers* 324–330.

70. Hutchinson's evasive answer (undated) as to the judges' salaries quoted in the text, and election at a Boston town meeting, Nov. 2, 1772, of a Committee of Correspondence headed by James Otis, Samuel Adams, and Joseph Warren, to prepare and circulate a statement of the rights of the colonies, etc., *Boston Records* (for 1770–1777) 92–93.

71. The Boston Committee's statement and proposed circular letter Nov. 20, 1772, *same* 95–108.

72. Boston town meeting Nov. 20, 1772, adopts the Committee's statement and proposed letter and orders their distribution by the town clerk, William Cooper, *same* 94. (A biographical sketch of Cooper is in Hassam "Suffolk Registers of Probate" 83–104).

73. Letters from over one hundred towns (out of about 240 in Mass.) in Boston Comm. of Corresp. papers, N.Y. Pub. Lib., and photocopies of pertinent town records at the Mass. Hist. Soc. are analyzed in Brown "Mass. Towns Reply" 25–38. Hutchinson's worried letters concerning the movement are cited and described in Brown "Democracy in Mass." 299.

74. Hutchinson's speech at the opening of the winter session of the Mass. Legislature Jan. 6, 1773, Bradford *Mass. Papers* 336–342. See also Hutchinson's speech of Feb. 16, *same* 368–383.

75. Mass. Council's reply to Hutchinson's speech, Jan. 25, 1773, *same* 342–351. The members of the Legislature had earlier been exasperated not only by Hutchinson's acceptance of a salary from the Crown, *same* 324–330, but also by a protracted controversy over removal of the place of meeting of the Legislature from Boston to Cambridge and Hutchinson's refusal for some time to reestablish Boston as the place of meeting, Lord and Calhoun "Removal" 735–755.

76. Mass. House of Representatives' reply Jan. 26, 1773, to Hutchinson's speech, Bradford *Mass. Papers* 351–365. The committee of eight members of the House chosen to prepare this reply was headed by Samuel Adams, John Hancock, and Joseph Hawley of Northampton.

77. Benjamin Franklin wrote Thomas Cushing May 6, 1773, that Dartmouth had recently told him he thought it necessary to lay before Parliament the "Declaration of the [Massachusetts] General Assembly, asserting its Independency . . . however unwilling he was to do it . . . ," Smyth *Franklin* VI 50. But there is no evidence that he did so until 1774, perhaps because the Ministry was reluctant to "widen the breach with the colonies . . . at this Time when the disturbed State of Europe gives some Apprehensions of a general War," *same* 48.

78. The Ministry laid before the House of Commons on April 21, 1774, copies of the whole series of Hutchinson's messages and the spirited replies of the Mass. House in 1772 and 1773, 4 *Force* I 74.

CHAPTER 13

1. 9 and 10 Wm. III ch. 44 secs. 61 and 69 (1698), with extensions listed in Pickering *Statutes* X 194, gave the United Company of Merchants Trading to the East Indies a monopoly of trade between Great Britain and the East Indies, with a proviso that the Company sell its imports at auction ("inch of candle") in England.

2. The Act of 1721 forbidding importation into the colonies of East Indian products, including tea, from any place but Great Britain was 7 Geo. I ch. 21 sec. 9.

3. The act of 18 Geo. II ch. 26 sec. 11 (1745) authorized the British Treasury Board to permit importation of tea into Great Britain by others than the British East India Company if the latter neglected to keep the British market supplied with tea at reasonable prices, but I have found no evidence that the Board ever granted such permission.

4. Smuggling of tea into the colonies from Holland and other non-British ports had long been common before passage of the Townshend Act, Labaree *Tea Party* 7–12. (The lower price of tea in Holland and other foreign countries as

compared with England is brought out in 192, 193. Competing foreign companies ope to be able to undersell the British Company pay heavy import duties on tea such as were *man's Mag.* for Dec., 1772, XLII 548.)

5. Labaree *Tea Party* 7 suggests as a safe gu of "1,200,000 pounds a year . . . three-quarters current estimates of colonial consumption of tea year, *Tea Leaves* 197, 200; *M.H.S. Proc.* XIX (188

6. Average annual exports of tea from England 1768 as given in the text, Labaree *Tea Party* 33. Si of tea into England, Mui "Smuggling" 44–73, some gland to the colonies may have been tea from for smuggled into England, but probably most, if not all, was tea imported into England by the Company. (I have seen no figures as to exports of tea from Scotland to the colonies.)

7. Exportation of tea from England to the thirteen colonies 1769–1772, Labaree *Tea Party* 33.

8. The Company's financial distress, Franklin to Cushing Jan. 5, 1773, Smyth *Franklin* VI 3–4. Franklin implies that the colonial boycott was the chief cause of the distress, but other, no less important, causes are brought out in Sutherland *East India Co.* 223–228; *Annual Register* (for 1773) 64–66; Macpherson *Hist. of Commerce with India* 196–198. Correspondence between the Ministry and the Company from Nov., 1772, to May, 1773, refers to the latter's desperate financial situation and the Ministry's readiness to assist, Miscellanies 20, India Office Lib.

9. Resolution quoted in the text adopted at stockholders' meeting Jan. 7, 1773, East India Company Court Minutes vol. 81 fol. 384, India Office Lib. (Repealing the Townshend Act duty on tea to help the Company regain its colonial market was suggested in an article in *Gentleman's Mag.* for Jan., 1773, XLIII 20, and Franklin wrote Cushing Jan. 5, that he had proposed this "in all Companies" Smyth *Franklin* VI 3.)

10. Petition voted by the stockholders of the Company Feb. 25, 1773, as quoted in the text, Labaree *Tea Party* 70, 282.

11. Petition of the Company to the House of Commons March 2, 1773, asking that "Leave may be given to export Teas, Duty-free, to America . . .," *Journals H. of C.* XXXIV 165. The petition also requested leave to export "Tea to Foreign Parts, free of all Duty, the Company being obliged to keep in their Warehouses a Quantity of Tea equal to Eighteen Months national Consumption."

12. The act of 12 Geo. III ch. 60 sec. 1 (1772) provided for the refund of three-fifths of the British import duty, amending an act of 7 Geo. III ch. 56, for refund of the entire British import duty on tea reexported to the colonies. These acts, including provisions collateral to the refunds, are discussed in Farrand "Taxation of Tea" 266–267.

13. The British import duty on tea was approximately 24% ad valorem, same 266.

14. Lord North's statement as to the tea duty quoted in the text is from a speech to the House of Commons April 26, 1773, Labaree *Tea Party* 71, 282.

15. The resoluti
to tea exporte
XXXIV 286
sitting i
An a

ns in the House of Commons April 27, 1773, for the bill as
to the colonies, described in the text, are in *Journals H. of C.*
They had been discussed and approved the day before in the House
Committee of the Whole, *same* 284 and Labaree *Tea Party* 70–73, 282.
t of 21 Geo. II ch. 14 (1748) had exempted from British inland duties tea
exported to the colonies. The provision as to inland duties in the resolution
quoted in the text would extend this exemption to tea reexported to foreign
parts.

16. There are good biographical sketches of William Dowdeswell, Barlow
Trecothick, George Johnstone, William Pulteney, and Charles Wolfram Cornwall
in Namier and Brooke *Commons* II, III *passim*. My statements in the text concerning them, unless otherwise noted, are from these sketches.

17. Dowdeswell's statement in the debate of April 26, 1773, quoted in the text,
Labaree *Tea Act* 71.

18. Charles Garth to S.C. Comm. of Corresp. May 4, 1773, quoting Trecothick's
remarks of April 26, 1773, Garth Papers, S.C. Archives Department, Columbia,
S.C. Trecothick, who had been brought up in the colonies and married a Boston
girl, was London Agent for N.H., 1766–1774, Kammen *Agents* 326. There are
many references to him cited in the index of *same* 348 and in Sosin *Agents* 266.
So far as is known, Garth, though a member of the House of Commons, did not
support Dowdeswell.

19. Remarks of Johnstone, Pulteney, and Cornwall on April 26, 1773, along
the same lines as those of Dowdeswell and Trecothick, Labaree *Tea Party* 72.

20. Garth to S.C. Comm. of Corresp. May 4, 1773, as to North declining "any
political argument touching the Right of Parliament to impose Taxes on the
Americans," Garth Papers, S.C. Archives Department, Columbia, S.C.

21. Dowdeswell's statement on April 26, 1773, digested in the text, was "It is
the peppercorn that was so much contended [for]; for this you risk the export of
two million [pounds of tea] to America," Labaree *Tea Act* 71. The allusion to
"peppercorn" was to earlier statements in Parliament that even if taxes imposed
by Parliament on the colonies yielded only a peppercorn, they should be retained in support of Parliament's assertion of right to tax the colonies.

22. I have found no evidence that Edmund Burke, though he was London Agent
for the N.Y. Assembly, spoke at any stage of the proceedings on the Tea Act. In
letters to the N.Y. Comm. of Corresp. April 16 and July 2, 1773, he did not mention the East India Company's petition, the proceedings on the Tea Act, or even
the Act itself, *Burke* II 428–430, 439–442. In the latter he wrote simply (p. 442),
"The Session is ended. The East India Companys Political and Financial affairs
are put into the hands of the Crown, but I am much afraid, with little Benefit
either to the Crown or the Publick."

23. The passage of the Tea Act of 1773, 13 Geo. III ch. 44, through the House
of Commons can be followed in the minutes of the Commons from Apr. 26 to
May 5, 1773, *Journals H. of C.* XXXIV 286–301 *passim*.

24. The bill for the Tea Act from the Commons passed the House of Lords
May 7, 1773, and was assented to by the King May 10, *Journals H. of L.* XXXIII
634, 638.

25. Arthur Lee in London to Samuel Adams Dec. 22, 1773, quoted in the text, charging the Ministry with deliberate provocation of the colonies, Samuel Adams Papers, N.Y.P.L.

26. John Almon's charge against George III quoted in the text, Almon *Pitt* II 242. My citation is to the seventh (1810) edition of the book, which was first published in or about 1793. Benjamin Franklin wrote William Franklin July 4, 1773, "the late Measures have been, I suspect, very much the King's own," but he did not charge the King with the design to bring the issue of colonial taxation to a head, Smyth *Franklin* VI 98.

27. I have not found any Cabinet minutes or any correspondence of any one in the North Ministry or of the King bearing on the question of deliberate provocation of the colonists. But the fact that at this same session of Parliament, the Ministry successfully sponsored an act, 13 Geo. III ch. 58 (1772), long sought for by the colonists, relaxing the restriction imposed by the Colonial Currency Act on the issue of currency, indicates that the Ministry had no desire to provoke the colonists. The protracted colonial efforts to secure such an act are described in Sosin "Paper Money" 186–198.

28. Assurances had been given by letters dated April, 1771, to May, 1773, from Boston and Philadelphia merchants to correspondents in England that the Company's tea would capture the colonial market if the Company tea could be offered for a lower price than smuggled tea, Drake *Tea Leaves* 191–201, and Charles Garth, London Agent for S.C., to the S.C. Comm. of Corresp. May 4, 1773, S.C. Transcripts, Garth Letter Book 1766–1775; Smyth *Franklin* VI 67 states that the Ministry believed this would be the case.

29. North observed in the Commons Apr. 26, 1773, "If the East India Company will export tea to America they will very much increase that [Townshend Act] duty," Labaree *Tea Party* 71; and John Norton wrote from London to correspondents in Va. July 6, of the government's making "a cat's paw of the Company . . . to establish the 3d per lb. American duty," *Norton* 337. To similar effect, Franklin to Cushing June 4, Franklin Letter Book, L.C. (copied, with the misprint of "confine" for "continue," in Smyth *Franklin* VI 57) and William Bollan to the Mass. Council Sept. 1, *Bowdoin–Temple Papers* 310.

30. William Palmer, one of the leading London tea merchants, wrote on May 19, 1773, that the Company's "present stock of tea is not only near seventeen million, but the quantity expected to arrive this season does also considerably exceed the demand of twelve months . . .," *Tea Leaves* 190.

31. A letter dated July 17, 1773, from an unidentified London correspondent, published in the *Pa. Gazette* of Oct. 6, states that "a few days ago," the Company had determined, over the protest of the Duke of Richmond, "that tea should be sent to America," Labaree *Tea Party* 75, 283.

32. The Company's petition to the Treasury Board Aug. [misprinted April] 19, 1773, for a license to export up to 600,000 pounds of tea to the colonies, *Tea Leaves* 246–247. The Treasury granted the Company a license, dated Aug. 20, to export to the colonies "a quantity of teas, equal in weight to one thousand seven hundred large chests of Bohea tea, which quantity will not exceed six hundred thousand pounds weight," *same* 248–249. The license was signed by

North, Charles James Fox, and Charles Townshend ("Spanish Charles"), a cousin of the sponsor of the Townshend Act.

33. The pounds of tea shipped and the names, destinations, and dates of sailing of the ships carrying the tea, Labaree *Tea Party* 78–79, 284, 335.

34. A list of all the tea consignees is given in Court of Directors of the Company to the Philadelphia consignees Oct. 1, 1773, "Papers relating to the Shipment of the Tea," Hist. Soc. of Pa. See also *Tea Leaves* 277, 351, 359, 363; Taylor "Philadelphia Tea Party" III 29. Most, if not all, of the chosen firms had been dealers in tea, and, though political considerations may well have influenced some of the appointments, I have not found persuasive evidence of this.

35. The Company's initial shipments of tea to the colonies in 1773 consisted of 1,586 chests of Bohea to 465 of all other varieties combined, Labaree *Tea Party* 335. The Company's suggested selling prices were: Bohea, 2s. per pound; Congou, 2s. 3d.; Singlo, 2s. 8d.; Suchong, 3s.; and Hyson, 5s., *same.*

36. William Kelly to the Company's Committee of Warehouses July 5, 1773, as to commissions payable to the Company's agents, *Tea Leaves* 224–225; see also Labaree *Tea Party* 76, 283–284. The sponsors in London were to give bond for the performance of the agreements, and for this and other services were, of course, to share in the net commissions. An agreement between Abraham Dupuis & Co., sponsors of Richard Clarke & Sons, provided that the former was to receive one-third of the net commissions, "Clarke Papers" 81–82.

37. The method and terms of sale of tea in the colonies prescribed by the Company, East India Co. Directors to Thomas & Isaac Wharton Oct. 1, 1773, "Papers relating to the Shipment of the Tea," Hist. Soc. of Pa.

38. The Company to the Boston consignees Sept. 15, 1773, as to mode of paying the Townshend Act duty on the tea shipped to them, East India Co. Misc. XXI fol. 2, India Office Library, London.

39. William Bollan to James Bowdoin of the Mass. Council, Sept. 11, 1773, *Bowdoin–Temple* 320. As to Bollan, *D.A.B.* and pages cited under "Bollan" in the index of Kammen *Agents* 342.

40. The Townshend Act duty of three pence a pound on 598,659 pounds of tea, the amount of the Company's initial shipment to the colonies, would be 1,795,977 pence, or over £7,483 sterling.

CHAPTER 14

1. Initial misunderstanding as to the meaning of the Tea Act, Labaree *Tea Party* 88–89, 286; *Conn. Journal* Sept. 3, 1773; *New-York Gazette* Sept. 6; *Boston Newsletter* Oct. 28; Rivington's *New-York Gazetteer* Oct. 28; Ben Booth to James & Drinker Oct. 28, Taylor "Philadelphia Tea Party" II 107; Gov. William Tryon of N.Y. to Dartmouth Nov. 3, *N.Y. Col. Doc.* VIII 400–401; John Dickinson's public letter of Oct. 30, correcting the misunderstanding, Ford *Dickinson* 457–458.

2. The passages quoted in the text from the *N.Y. Journal* and the *Pa. Journal*, Labaree *Tea Party* 90.

3. Denunciation of the Tea Act and the Company's plan by "Scaevola" (Thomas Mifflin) in the *Pa. Chronicle* Oct. 11, 1773; also by "Hamden" (Ben-

jamin Rush) in the *Pa. Journal* Oct. 20. Identification of "Scaevola" and "Hamden," Rush to William Gordon Oct. 10, *Rush* I 81–82.

4. Examples of the newspaper outcry against the act in other colonies: *Mass. Spy* Oct. 14 and Nov. 4, 1773, *New-York Journal* Oct. 24, and *S.C. Gazette* (Supplement) Nov. 15.

5. Resolutions of the Philadelphia mass meeting of Oct. 16, 1773, are in the *Pennsylvania Gazette* of Oct. 20 reprinted in Jensen *Hist. Doc.* 773–774. The circular letter from the Mass. Committee of Corresp. to similar Committees in other colonies Oct. 21, denouncing the British Ministry for "allowing the East India Company—to ship their Teas to America," a plan tending "both to destroy the Trade of the Colonies & increase the revenue" and calling for opposition by all the colonies, Cushing *S. Adams* III 67.

6. There was in fact no immediate threat of the Company's establishing a monopoly of the sale of tea at retail in the colonies; the Company's agents there were instructed to sell the tea at auction to all comers, but I have found no evidence that this was generally known in the colonies at the time of the outcry against the threatened monopoly. Moreover, nothing in the Tea Act forbade the Company to sell its tea at retail in the colonies if it later chose to do so.

7. The monopoly argument, Schlesinger *Col. Merchants* 264–276. The extension of the Company's privilege of direct sale in the colonies to other East Indian products was suggested (Oct. 5, 1773) by at least one of the Company's American agents, Thomas Wharton of Philadelphia, *Tea Leaves* 274–275. These products included pepper, other spices, silks, shellac, saltpeter, drugs, and china, Saxby *British Customs* 346, 351. Joseph Reed of Philadelphia wrote Lord Dartmouth Dec. 22 that "India goods compose one-third of our importations from England," Reed *Reed* I 53.

8. Schlesinger's statement quoted in the text as to the monopoly point, Schlesinger *Col. Merchants* 270.

9. Evidence that the tax point was at least as important as the threat of monopoly in arousing colonial opposition, Thomas Wharton in Philadelphia to Thomas Walpole Oct. 30, 1773, *Tea Leaves* 277; James & Drinker and Thomas and Isaac Wharton et al. in Philadelphia to various correspondents Nov. 6, Nov. 19, and Dec. 28, Taylor "Philadelphia Tea Party" III 22, 26, X 68–70; Abraham Lott in N.Y. to William Kelly Nov. 5, *Tea Leaves* 270; town meeting and Mass. Council Nov. 5 and 29, *Boston Records* (for 1770–1777) 143, *Tea Leaves* 316–317; also Labaree *Tea Party* 96–97, 287.

10. Nullification of the Stamp Act of 1765 by securing resignation of the colonial Stamp Distributors, Knollenberg *Origin* 229–234.

11. The Boston consignees included the firm of Thomas and Elisha Hutchinson, sons of Gov. Hutchinson. Gov. Hutchinson to William Palmer, prominent London tea merchant, Aug. 7, 1773, stating, "I wish you may succeed on behalf of my Sons to whom I have given a hint," Mass. Arch. XXVII 523, apparently refers to efforts by Palmer to secure the Company's tea agency at Boston for the Governor's sons.

12. Gov. Thomas Hutchinson's encouragement of the consignees to hold out, Hutchinson to Gov. William Tryon of N.Y. Nov. 21 and Dec. 1, 1773, and to an unidentified correspondent Nov. 24, Mass. Arch. 572–576; James Bowdoin to John

Temple Dec. 16, *Bowdoin–Temple* 328; Samuel Cooper to Benjamin Franklin Dec. 14, 4 *M.H.S. Coll.* IV 374.

13. Refusal of the Hutchinsons and other Boston consignees to resign, Schlesinger *Col. Merchants* 283–287 and Labaree *Tea Party* 109–123. (The statements in Schlesinger *Col. Merchants* 282 that Richard Clarke, member of one of the consignee firms at Boston that refused to resign, was Gov. Hutchinson's nephew, and in Labaree *Tea Party* 104 that the Governor's son Thomas married Clarke's daughter are apparently erroneous; I have found no such close tie of blood or marriage between the Governor and the Clarkes.)

14. Resolution of the North End Caucus Oct. 23, 1773, to prevent vending of tea in the colonies sent by the East India Company, Goff *Revere* II 641. Paul Revere, Abiel Ruddock, and John Lowell were chosen at this meeting to be a committee "to correspond with any Committee chosen in any part of town, on this occasion; and call this body together at any time they think necessary," *same*.

15. Hutchinson to Francis Bernard Aug. 28, 1770, refers to William Molineux (sometimes spelled Mollineux or Mollineaux) as "the infamous Molineux," Mass. Arch. XXVI 540–543; and John Rowe wrote in his diary Oct. 24, 1773, that Molineux was believed to be "first Leader in Dirty Matters," *Rowe* 286. Numerous entries concerning Molineux in Rowe's diary, *same* 76–224 *passim*, 286, indicate that though hot-tempered, he was respected by many substantial merchants of the town. Molineux is also referred to in Andrews "Boston Merchants" 163n, 164, 246, 247 and 2 *M.H.S. Proc.* X 38–86.

16. The efforts on Nov. 5, 1773, to frighten the Boston agents to resign are described in Richard Clarke & Sons to Abraham Dupuis Nov. [no day], 1773, *Tea Leaves* 279–286. Clarke states that William Dennie, Dr. Joseph Warren, Dr. Benjamin Church, Major [Nathaniel] Barber, [Benjamin] Henderson, Gabriel Johonnot, [Edward] Proctor, and Ezekiel Cheever accompanied Molineux, *same* 284. John Rowe's diary for Nov. 3 gives a somewhat different list, including Samuel Adams, *Rowe* 253. The night before, Johonnot and Proctor were chosen members of a committee "to wait upon the Committee of Correspondence of this town . . . ," presumably in connection with the tea matter, Goff *Revere* II 642–643.

17. Resolutions of Boston town meeting concerning the tea consignees Nov. 5, 1773, *Boston Records* (for 1770–1777) 142–143.

18. Consignees' replies Nov. 5 and 6, 1773, *same* 145–146. James Bowdoin wrote John Temple Dec. 16, crediting Hutchinson with "dictating all their [the consignees'] measures," *Bowdoin–Temple* 328, and Samuel Cooper wrote Benjamin Franklin Dec. 17 to similar effect, 4 *M.H.S. Proc.* IV 374. While, so far as is known, Hutchinson was not a partner in his sons' importing business, he had long taken an active part in their dealings in tea, as clearly appears from his correspondence with William Palmer, a leading tea exporter, from Nov. 23, 1768, to Aug. 7, 1773, Mass. Arch. XXVI 330–XXVII 523.

19. Jonathan Clarke's arrival at Boston from London Nov. 17, 1773, undated petition of the Boston tea consignees to the Governor and Council of Mass. considered by the Council Nov. 19, *Col. Soc. Public.* VIII 82–87 at 84.

20. Resolutions at Boston town meeting Nov. 18, 1773, calling for a definite answer from the consignees as to resigning, committee chosen to deliver the message, and the consignees' answer, *Boston Records* (for 1770–1777) 146–148.

21. Jonathan Clarke's promise to the selectmen of Boston at a meeting on Nov. 27, 1773, *Boston Selectmen's Minutes* (for 1769–1775) 202–203; John Scollay to Arthur Lee Dec. 23, 4 *M.H.S. Coll.* IV 381–382. Clarke probably was frightened, as well he might be, his father having recently had the windows of his home broken by a threatening mob, mentioned in Cooper to Franklin Dec. 17, *same* 374.

22. Log of the *Dartmouth* concerning her movements on Nov. 27 and 28, 1773, *Traits of the Tea Party* 259–260.

23. Log of the *Dartmouth* as to docking at Griffin's wharf Dec. 1, 1773, *same* 260. She had initially "turned up to" Rowe's wharf, *same,* but was apparently ordered by a committee of local Whigs to proceed to Griffin's, John Rowe's diary for Dec. 3, *Rowe* 256–257. She was formally entered at the Customs House on Nov. 30, "Tea Minutes" 16. Francis Rotch, her owner, had been asked by the Boston Committee of Correspondence to defer entry until that date, Rotch's statement to the Privy Council Feb. 19, 1774, *P.C.* 1:156.

24. Statements referred to in the text are quoted in the appendix to this chapter.

25. Boston selectmen's unsuccessful effort Nov. 28, 1773, to get in touch with Clarke, *Boston Selectmen's Minutes* (for 1769–1775) 203; Scollay to Lee Dec. 21, *M.H.S. Coll.* IV 382.

26. Lieut.-Col. Alexander Leslie at Castle William to Gen. Frederick Haldimand, Dec. 16, 1773, "the 4 Commissioners of Customs & the 5 Tea Agents took refuge with me the 29th ult. & are still here," *Montresor* 532. To same effect, Hutchinson to the Company Dec. 19, 1773, Mass. Arch. XXVII 597–599. (Hutchinson's advance arrangements for the consignees' reception there, Hutchinson to Gov. William Tryon Dec. 1, 1773, *same* 576, published in part in Frothingham "Tea Party" 186.)

27. The Commissioners of Customs, finding themselves again the special "object of the People's rage," fled to Castle William, Am. Customs Board to British Treasury Jan. 4, 1774, Barrow *Customs* 250, 322. They went there Nov. 29, 1773, Leslie to Haldimand, *Montresor* 532.

28. Meeting of the Boston Committee of Correspondence on arrival of the *Dartmouth* Nov. 28, 1773, Boston Comm. of Corresp. Minutes, (N.Y.P.L.); *Tea Leaves* xiii; Labaree *Tea Party* 120, 291. The Committee, consisting of twenty-one members, included James Otis, Samuel Adams, Dr. Joseph Warren, Dr. Benjamin Church, Dr. Thomas Young, and William Molineux, *Boston Records* (for 1770–1777) 93.

29. Handbills distributed in the early morning of Nov. 29, 1773, inviting the people to meet at Faneuil Hall at 9 A.M. that same day, John Scollay to Arthur Lee Dec. 23, 4 *M.H.S. Coll.* IV 381. A copy of the handbill is in *Tea Leaves* xliii. The Committee had previously (Oct. 21) sent a circular letter to Committees of Correspondence in other Mass. towns pointing out the dangers of allowing importation of the tea and the necessity of opposing it, Labaree *Tea Party* 107, 289.

30. Minutes of Boston mass meeting Nov. 29, 1773, resolving that the Company's tea be returned without payment of duty and that "there be a watch kept for the security of . . . vessel and cargo," with a list of the twenty-five men chosen for the initial watch, *M.H.S. Proc.* XX 10–11; Scollay to Lee Dec. 21, 1773, 4 *M.H.S. Coll.* IV 383. Rotch told the Privy Council Feb. 19, 1774, that the "most

active" persons at the meeting, presided over by Jonathan Williams, a nephew by marriage of Benjamin Franklin, were Samuel Adams, John Hancock, Dr. Young, Molineux, and Dr. Warren, P.C. 1:56.

31. Rotch's promise to return the tea without landing it, minutes of Boston mass meeting of Nov. 30, 1773, *M.H.S. Proc.* XX 10–15; Minute Book of Boston Comm. of Corresp. No. 6 457–459, Bancroft Papers N.Y. Pub. Lib.; testimony of Rotch and others before the Privy Council Feb. 19, 1774, *Acts P.C.* VI 551–554. As to Rotch's part ownership of the *Dartmouth, same* 551. His father, Joseph Rotch, apparently was the principal owner, Labaree *Tea Party* 120, 291.

32. Consignees' offer to store the tea, and rejection of the offer at the mass meeting of Nov. 30, 1773, John Singleton Copley to Isaac Winslow Clarke, Dec. 1, *Copley Letters* 211–213; Minutes of the Tea Meetings *M.H.S. Proc.* XX 12–13. A similar offer to the Governor and Council of Mass. Nov. 19 was rejected by the Council Nov. 29, *Tea Leaves* 310–312, 315–320. Thomas Hutchinson, Jr., wrote Dec. 14 that, being at the Castle, "surrounded with cannon, we [the consignees] have [given] them such answers as we shou'd not have dared to do in any other situation," Hutchinson *Diary and Letters* I 96.

33. The *Eleanor,* James Bruce master, reached Boston Dec. 1, 1773, *Tea Leaves* 355. The *Beaver,* Hezekiah Coffin master, reached Boston Dec. 7, but did not dock until Dec. 13, selectmen's minutes Dec. 7 and 13, *Boston Selectmen's Minutes* (for 1769–1775) 204, 206. The committee requiring the vessels to dock at Griffin's wharf, Rowe's diary for Dec. 2, *Rowe* 256–257 and Hutchinson to Dartmouth on or about Jan. 4, 1774, Mass. Arch. XXVI 166. The committee's members, mentioned by Rowe, indicate that it was the one, headed by Samuel Adams, chosen at a Boston mass meeting Nov. 30, 1773, *M.H.S. Proc.* XX 14.

34. The *William,* fourth of the Boston tea ships, was wrecked on Cape Cod Dec. 10, 1773, and, a few weeks later, the tea salvaged from her was reshipped and stored at Castle William, *Rowe* 257; Hutchinson to Dartmouth on or about Jan. 4, 1774, Mass. Arch. XXVI 166; Samuel Adams to James Warren Jan. 10, Frothingham "Tea Party" 205. I have not found what eventually became of this tea.

35. 13 and 14 Chas. II ch. 2 sec. 4 (1662), extended to the colonies by 7 and 8 Wm. III ch. 22 sec. 6 (1696), empowered customs officers, within twenty days after "first entry," to seize dutiable goods on which duty had not been paid; and 12 Geo. I ch. 28 sec. 19 (1725) authorized customs officers to auction off goods thus seized six months after they were impounded. "Entry" was construed to mean entering port with intent of the master to land the ship's cargo, opinion of Attorney-General Philip Yorke, Nov. 2, 1726, Chalmers *Opinions* 576.

36. As brought out in note 23 above, the *Dartmouth*'s master did not formally enter her until Nov. 30, 1773, but the tea became liable for duty on her actually entering the port of Boston Nov. 28.

37. Failure of Rotch, part owner of the *Dartmouth,* to prepare her for leaving, Scollay to Lee Dec. 23, 1773, 4 *M.H.S. Coll.* 384; Hutchinson to Israel Mauduit Dec. [about Dec. 27] Mass. Arch. XXVII 604–607. (The approximate date of this letter is indicated by a statement in the letter that the consignees had been at Castle William "four weeks.")

38. The mass meeting of Dec. 14, 1773, and developments there are reported in minutes of the Tea Meetings, *M.H.S. Proc.* XX 15.

39. Refusal of the Collector to grant clearance for the *Dartmouth* to return to England with the Company's tea on board, without payment of the duty incurred, report to mass meeting held in morning of Dec. 16, 1773, *same* 15–16.

40. Report that the tea on all the tea ships was about to be taken under protection of the British warships at Boston and carried to Castle Island, Cooper to Franklin Dec. 17, 1773, and Scollay to Lee Dec. 23, 4 *M.H.S. Coll.* IV 374–375, 384; diary of William Smith Dec. 20, Sabine *William Smith* I 163. I have found no evidence substantiating this report, but it seems worth noting that at the request of customs officers at Boston the tea salvaged from the *William,* wrecked on Cape Cod, was shipped to and stored at Castle Island, Hutchinson to Dartmouth Jan. 4, 1774, Boston Tea Party Papers, Havard College Lib.

41. Boston Whigs' fear that if the tea were lodged at Castle William, the consignees would be able to market it surreptitiously, Cooper to Franklin Dec. 17, 1773, 4 *M.H.S. Coll.* IV 374. Gov. Hutchinson wrote the directors of the Company Dec. 19 that his own sons alone had imported over 200 chests in some recent years, Mass. Arch. XXVII 597, which they sold "by stealth like smugglers," Hutchinson to Bernard Aug. 26, 1769, *same* XXVI 368–369.

42. As noted in Chapter 11, the Fourteenth Regiment, commanded by Lieut.-Col. William Dalrymple, was removed from Boston to Castle William, near the mouth of Boston Harbor, following the Boston "Massacre." It was replaced in Aug., 1772, by the Sixty-Fourth Regiment from Halifax, under Lieut.-Col. Alexander Leslie, *Gage* I 330, II 656.

43. Hutchinson to Israel Mauduit Dec. [no day], 1773, concerning his messages to Lieut.-Col. Leslie and Admiral John Montagu, Frothingham "Tea Party" 171. I have not found the dates of these messages, but a letter from Hutchinson to Gov. Tryon Dec. 1, 1773, expressing the hope that the consigness would remain firm, *same* 161, indicates that he was planning by then to take a firm stand.

44. Rotch ordered at mass meeting of Dec. 16, 1773, to apply to Hutchinson for a pass and his report that the pass was refused, minutes of the meeting, *M.H.S. Proc.* XX 16.

45. Hutchinson to Mauduit Dec., 1773, concerning the Tea Party, Mass. Arch. XXVII 604–607, published in part in Frothingham "Tea Party" 170–171. To much the same effect, Hutchinson to Dartmouth Dec. 17, 1773, *same* 172–173; accounts in the Boston newspapers of the time; Samuel Cooper to Franklin Dec. 17, Cushing and others to Arthur Lee Dec. 21, Scollay to Lee Dec. 21, 4 *M.H.S. Coll.* IV 373–386; and John Andrews to William Barrell Dec. 18, *M.H.S. Proc.* (for 1764–1765) 325–326.

46. The "men of property," John Hancock, William Phillips, John Rowe, and William Dennie, named by Hutchinson, were leading Boston merchants. The Boston selectmen (councilmen) were Hancock, John Scollay, Timothy Newell, Thomas Marshall, Samuel Austin, Oliver Wendell, and John Pitts, and the town clerk was William Cooper, *Boston Records* (for 1770–1777) 110.

47. It seems highly unlikely that the people "wished" to have the *Dartmouth* "stopped at the Castle," though many may well have feared this would happen if she sailed without a customs clearance or pass from Hutchinson.

48. Dr. Young was one of the most fiery of the Whig leaders in Boston at this time and until he left for Newport shortly before the outbreak of the Revolutionary War, Edes "Young" 4–54. James Hall testified before the Privy Council

Feb. 19, 1774, that Young had said at the great mass meeting of Nov. 29, 1773, "the only way to get rid of the tea was to throw it over board," but "the people declared against Dr. Young's proposal that the tea be destroyed," *Acts P.C.* VI 553.

49. Hutchinson evidently believed that a pass issued by him would be honored by the military and naval commanders, as appears from his letter of Jan. 1, 1774, to Bernard, stating: "It would have given me . . . painful reflection if I had saved it [the tea] by any concession to a lawless and highly criminal Assembly . . . ," Frothingham "Tea Party" 174. Granting the pass would, however, have involved a breach of his oath as Governor to enforce the British acts of trade and customs, Hutchinson to Samuel Swift Jan. 4, 1774, *same* 175.

50. Admiral Montagu, referred to by Hutchinson, was John Montagu, commander of the British fleet in North America, a key figure in the *Gaspee* affair. Captain James Hall was master of the *Dartmouth*.

51. Criticism of Hutchinson for not calling on Montagu to protect the tea ships, Labaree *Tea Party* 295–296 n.37, and sources cited therein. To similar effect, Samuel Adams to Arthur Lee Jan., or June, 1774, stating that Hutchinson, "by delaying to call on the naval power to protect the Tea . . . led them [the Boston Whigs] to determine their Choice of Difficulties," i.e., to destroy the tea as a last resort, Cushing *S. Adams* III 79. (The letter as published is dated Jan. 25; but internal evidence indicates that the correct date is probably June 25, 1774).

52. Hutchinson to Mauduit Dec. 17, 1773, and to Bernard Jan. 1, 1774, Frothingham "Tea Party" 170, 174, as to the assumption the tea would be safe since "so many men of property had made part of the meetings, and were in danger of being liable for the value of it."

53. Montagu wrote Philip Stephens, Secretary to the Admiralty Board, Dec. 8, 1773, that on application from the Governor or Commissioners of the Customs for protection, "I shall give the utmost assistance . . . agreeable to my instructions," and on Dec. 17, he wrote Stephens that had they called for assistance "I could easily have prevented the execution of this Plan [destruction of the tea] but must have endangered the Lives of many innocent people by firing on the town," Boston Tea Party Papers, Harv. Coll. Lib.

54. Leslie wrote Lord Barrington, Secretary at War Dec. 6, 1773, that he was ready to send his regiment (stationed at Castle William) to Boston any time Gov. Hutchinson so requested; on Dec. 17, in writing Barrington of the destruction of the tea, he said, "I am informed the [Mass.] Council would not agree to the Troops going to Town . . . ," *same*. A request for this to the Council seems to have been implied by Gov. Hutchinson in meetings with the Council Nov. 19–29, reported in *Tea Leaves* 310–320.

55. *Dartmouth* log entry of Dec. 16, 1773, as to the number assembled on the wharf and the boarding party being dressed and whooping like Indians, appendix to *Traits of the Tea Party* 261. The Indian dress and whooping of the members of the boarding party are referred to also in Samuel Cooper to Franklin Dec. 17, 4 *M.H.S. Coll.* IV 375.

56. Andrews to Barrell Dec. 18, 1773, as to the Tea Party, "Andrews Letters" 326. (Andrews had written Barrell Dec. 1, " 'twould puzzle any person to purchase a pair of p——ls in town, as they are all bought up, with a full determination to

repell force by force,' " *same* 325.) The log of the *Dartmouth* for Dec. 16 records that it was after six when "Indians" boarded the tea ships, *Traits of the Tea Party* 260. Having been completed, according to Andrews, before nine, the party evidently was over in less than three hours.

57. The item as to the boarding party's whoop and the answer is in the *Massachusetts Gazette* of Dec. 23, 1774, reprinted in Frothingham "Tea Party" 171.

58. John Dean Whitworth, one of the principal witnesses before the Privy Council concerning the Tea Party, probably was the "Dr. Whitworth," who (Hutchinson wrote to an unidentified correspondent Oct. 1, 1773) had "lost all his practice here by his attachment to Government," Mass. Arch. XXVII 548.

59. Whitworth testified before the Privy Council Feb. 19, 1774, that there were forty or fifty in the party which boarded the tea ships, *Acts. P.C.* VI 553, and this roughly tallies with the statement in the First Continental Congress' "Address to the People of Great Britain" Oct. 21, 1774, that the boarding party consisted of thirty or forty, *Journals Cont. Congress* I 87. However, Andrews wrote Barrell Dec. 18, 1773, that the party was said to muster about 200, "Andrews Letters" 326, and Samuel Cooper wrote Franklin Dec. 17, that it numbered 200 or 300, 4 *M.H.S. Coll.* IV 375.

60. Rotch's testimony before the Privy Council Feb. 19, 1774, as to Samuel Adams' statement at the meeting that "he did not see what more they could do to save their Country," P.C. 1:56. Dr. William Tyler testified that both Adams and Dr. Young spoke at the meeting "in support of a resolution that the tea be sent back to England without being landed," *same* 551. I have found no contemporary evidence for the statements in Bancroft *History* VI 485 and Quincy *Memoir* 124–125 as to Josiah Quincy, Jr., having made an eloquent speech at this meeting.

61. P. Michell, Secretary to the Court of Directors of the East India Company, to John Pownall, Feb. 16, 1774, "praying indemnity for the loss of their teas at Boston, amounting in value to £9,659/6s/4d," *Calendar H.O. Papers* (for 1773–1775) 184.

62. Cooper wrote Franklin Dec. 17, 1773, that there was no injury to "any other property or to any man's person" except one "interloper . . . who had found means to fill his pockets with tea [and] upon being discovered, was stripped of his booty and his clothes together and sent home naked," 4 *M.H.S. Coll.* IV 375. Andrews to Barrell Dec. 18 identified the offender as "one Captain Conner, . . . not many years remov'd from *dear Ireland*," who had been stripped of his clothes and given "a coat of mud, with a severe bruising in the bargain . . . ," "Andrews Letters" 326.

63. Descriptions of the "mobs" referred to in the text include those in *Hulton Letters* 12–72; Peters *History passim;* Oliver *Origin* 93–112 and sources cited in the editor's notes; Egerton *Loyalists passim;* Brown *King's Friends passim.*

64. Though Colonial tarring and featherings were much played up both at the time and later, I have found evidence of fewer than a dozen of these throughout the colonies from 1766 to April, 1775.

65. Anne Hulton, sister of a member of the American Customs Board, wrote on January 31, 1774, that the doctors said "it is impossible" that John Malcom,

a customs officer recently tarred and feathered in Boston, "can live," *Hulton Letters* 71. But he lived until 1788, Hersey "Malcom" 450, 470. Miss Hulton's report in June, 1768, that the Collector of Customs at Boston [Joseph Harrison], recently attacked by the "Sons of Violence," was "mortally" injured (*Hulton Letters* 11) also was untrue; he was still living in England as late as 1777, Sabine *Loyalists* I 520.

66. There is a good description of the wanton destruction of property in Boston, Newport, and New York in 1765 incident to the opposition to the Stamp Act, and the subsequent efforts of Whig leaders in the colonies to prevent a recurrence of this, in Maier *Resistance* 54–76 and sources cited therein. See also Wood "Mobs in the American Revolution" 635–642 and Maier "Popular Uprisings in America" 3–35.

67. The list of fifty-eight alleged participants in the party was furnished apparently in 1835 or shortly before by George R.T. Hewes to Benjamin Thatcher and published in *Traits of the Tea Party* (1835) 261–262. The later list, accompanying a reprint of the earlier list, is in *Tea Leaves* xclll–xciv. According to one of the yarns in Watson *Tea Party* 19–20, some of the party came from as far away as Lebanon, Maine.

68. The *Mass. Spy* (Worcester) of Sept. 13, 1775, reported a statement said to have been made by Abiel Wood of Pownallborough Mass. that John Hancock "was the first man that went on board the vessel, to destroy the tea." But it is hardly conceivable that a person so rich and generally known as Hancock would have risked detection and suit for damages, not to mention imprisonment, by actively participating in the Tea Party.

69. Hutchinson wrote in his diary Dec. 12, 1778, that "Will More" was reputed to have been "Captain of the men who destroyed the tea," Hutchinson *Diary and Letters* II 228, and a barber named Eckley was arrested at the time for alleged participation, but was acquitted for lack of evidence, Labaree *Tea Party* 150, 296.

70. John Adams to Hezekiah Niles May 10, 1819, as to not knowing the names of any of the participants, Adams *Works* II 334n.

71. Drake's statement in *Tea Leaves* lxvii as to who, he supposes, organized the Boston Tea Party.

72. The North End Caucus resolved Nov. 2, 1773, "this body are determined that the Tea shipped or to be shipped [to Boston] shall not be landed," Goff *Revere* II 642. The initial watch over the *Dartmouth* was composed chiefly of members of the North End Caucus, as appears from comparing the list of the watch in *M.H.S. Proc.* XX 10–11, with those mentioned as members of the Caucus in its minutes for 1772–1774, Goff *Revere* II 636–644. These minutes indicate that Nathaniel Barber, Thomas Hitchborn, John Lowell, Paul Revere, and Abiel Ruddock were particularly active in the Caucus at this period.

73. Resignation of the Charleston consignees before arrival of the tea ship *London,* and arrival of the ship at Charleston Dec. 2, Gov. William Bull to Dartmouth Dec. 24, *Tea Leaves* 339–341; also Labaree *Tea Party* 153.

74. Seizure and storage of the Company's tea after twenty days by local customs officers, John Morris to Corbyn Morris Dec. 22 and Bull to Dartmouth Dec. 24, 1773, *same* 339–342. See also Wallace "Chapter of S.C. History" 3–4, Labaree *Tea Party* 153–154, 297–298, and Sellers *Charleston* 223–224.

75. Seizure and sale of the tea by the S.C. Revolutionary government in 1776, Wallace "Chapter of S.C. History" 5, and S.C. Delegates at the Second Continental Congress to the President of S.C., John Rutledge, July 25, 1776, 5 Force *Am. Archives* III 16.

76. Resignation of the Philadelphia consignees before arrival of the tea ship *Polly* at Gloucester Point Dec. 26, Labaree *Tea Party* 98–102, 288–289; and newspaper account Dec. 27, 1773, *Tea Leaves* 361–362.

77. Proceedings at Philadelphia and return of the *Polly* from Gloucester Point to England without unloading her cargo, Reed to Dartmouth Dec. 27, 1773, Reed *Reed* I 54; Stone "Philadelphia" 385–393; Taylor "Philadelphia Tea Party" III 42–43, 49; "Wharton Letters" 321, 324; and newspaper account Dec. 27, *Tea Leaves* 363–366. News of the Boston Tea Party had reached Philadelphia Dec. 24, 1773, *Pennsylvania Journal* of Dec. 29.

78. Gloucester Point was within the limits of the Philadelphia customs house district established by the customs authorities, Labaree *Tea Party* 159–299.

79. Return of the *Polly* to England on Dec. 27, 1773, with the tea on board, after being provisioned, Reed to Dartmouth Dec. 27, Reed *Reed* I 54. Importation of tea into Great Britain except from "the place of its growth" was forbidden, under penalty of confiscation by 11 Geo. 1 ch. 30 sec. 8 (1725) and 21 Geo. II ch. 14 sec. 3 (1749). Orders were given by the Company in Jan., 1774, too late to affect proceedings at Philadelphia, to send rejected tea to Halifax, Nova Scotia, but the tea rejected at Philadelphia was evidently not confiscated when the *Polly* reached England, Labaree *Tea Party* 172–173, 301–302.

80. The "instrument of association" of the "Sons of Liberty of New York" concerning tea, Nov. 29, 1773, quoted in the text, broadside quoted in Barker *New York* 105–106; Leake *Lamb* 76–77; and letter of "Brutus" dated May 12, 1774, in 4 *Force* I 252–258n. at 253–254.

81. "Vast number" of signers of the instrument of association, New York newspapers of Dec. 16, 1773, quoted in *same* 254n. For additional details, William Smith's Journal for Dec. 11–25, 1773, Smith *Memoirs* I 157–164.

82. Tea consignees' letter of Dec. 27, 1773, to the tea ship headed for New York, quoted in the text, *Tea Leaves* 358–359.

83. Arrival of the tea ship *Nancy* Benjamin Lockyer, master April 19, 1774, on the night of April 18, Cadwallader Colden to Lord Dartmouth May 4, 1774, and account dated Apr. 28, 4 *Force* I 248–249. (The ship had first been driven by adverse winds to Antigua and on her resumed voyage to New York had lost a mast in a severe gale, *Mass. Spy* Apr. 7, 1774, quoted in Schlesinger *Col. Merchants* 293 and 4 *Force* I 249.)

84. Lockyer keeps the *Nancy* off Sandy Hook and comes to New York City in the pilot boat, account of April 28, 1774, *same* 249.

85. Lockyer to the consignees concerning the tea dated April 20, 1774, quoted in the text, and the consignees' reply of the same date, *Tea Leaves* 359–360.

86. Lockyer's promise to leave, quoted in the text, and the *Nancy's* leaving on Apr. 24, 1774, account of April 28, quoted in the text, 4 *Force* I 249, 251.

87. Tea shipped to the colonies by parties other than the East India Company was destroyed in several ports, Labaree *Tea Party* 164–168, 300–301. The most

notable of these incidents were at New York City in April, 1774, 4 *Force* I 250; and at Annapolis in Oct., 1774, Schlesinger *Col. Merchants* 389–392.

CHAPTER 15

1. The *London Chronicle* of Jan. 22, 1774, published a long account of the Boston Tea Party.

2. The Cabinet at this time (all members of the House of Lords except North, who was eldest son of an English peer) consisted of North, First Lord of the Treasury and Chancellor of the Exchequer; Apsley, Lord Chancellor; Gower, President of the Council; Sandwich, First Lord of the Admiralty; and three Secretaries of State—Rochford, Suffolk, and Dartmouth. Only North, Gower, and Rochford had been in the Cabinet when the decision was made in 1770 to retain the Townshend Act duty on tea.

3. Cabinet minutes Jan. 29, 1774, as to taking "effectual steps to secure the Dependance of the Colonies," Dartmouth Pap. II 799; inadequately summarized in *Dartmouth* (1895) 192. The Cabinet also resolved at this meeting to assent to a proposed motion by Lord Buckinghamshire for submission to the House of Lords of all papers bearing on the colonial opposition to landing the Company's tea, reported in *Journals H. of L.* XXXIV 58–61 and Lord Shelburne to Lord Chatham Feb. 3, *Pitt* IV 323–324. Summaries of this and later Cabinet meetings Jan.–March, Sosin "Mass. Acts of 1774" 238–242.

4. Sketches of all seven of the members of the Cabinet in 1774, named in the text, in *D.N.B.*

5. Minutes of Cabinet meeting Feb. 4, 1774, Dartmouth Pap. II 817, inadequately summarized in *Dartmouth* (1895) 195, and North to the King Feb. 5 (misdated Jan. as printed) as to the resolution for "punishing the Town of Boston" by removing the customs officials and the place of meeting of the Mass. Legislature from Boston, *Geo. III* III 55. In June, 1774, the Legislature and the American Customs Board were moved to Salem and the Boston customs officers to Plymouth, Mass., *Gage* II 357, 370 and Warren "Colonial Customs Service" 471. See also *H.O. Papers* (for 1773–1775) 182, 201; *Gage* II 160; Donoughue *British Politics* 63–64.

6. Cabinet minutes of Feb. 4, 1774, concerning possible prosecutions for treason, *Dartmouth* (1895) 195 and Dartmouth Pap. II 817. Minutes of a Cabinet meeting held the next day make clear that it was the Cabinet's intention to bring the accused to England for trial, *same* 819.

7. Dartmouth to Attorney-General Edward Thurlow, Feb. 5, 1774, asking the opinion of himself and Solicitor-General Alexander Wedderburn on questions of treason submitted in an accompanying document entitled "State of the Case," *H.O. Papers* (for 1773–1775) 178–179. This document (erroneously dated "1774, January") is listed and inadequately summarized in *Dartmouth* (1895) 193–194. There is a copy of it in C.O. 5:7:25 (P.R.O.).

8. The committee referred to in the law officers' reply is the one described in Chapter 14 as having threatened Richard Clarke and others if they refused to resign as Boston agents for the East India Company. The full names, as usually spelled, of the men named in the reply are William Molineux, William Dennie, Joseph Warren, Benjamin Church, and Gabriel Johonnot.

9. The involvement of Jonathan Williams, Samuel Adams, John Hancock, and Edward Proctor mentioned in the law officers' reply is indicated in Chapter 14.

10. "Mr. Scott" referred to in the law officers' reply was James Scott, master of John Hancock's ship *Hayley,* which brought the earliest news of the Tea Party to England. Scott (who twenty-odd years later married Hancock's widow) wrote Hancock Feb. 21, 1774, "I had a tolerable passage from Boston and . . . was immediately summoned up to Lord Dartmouth and asked a few questions but very trifling. . . . They have never sent for me since," *Old-Time New England* XXV (1934) 35–36. Part of this letter is published in Baxter *Hancock* 277–278, which (277n.) gives an account of the *Hayley.*

11. The law officers' statement that Scott was "the only Person in England who can give evidence" seems to imply that they had not yet heard of the persons from Boston, mentioned in note 15 below, but the officers may have meant that Scott was the only available eyewitness of the supposed treasonable conduct and hence the only person legally qualified to testify.

12. Judging from a statement of Wedderburn on Feb. 28, 1774, referred to in note 15, the meaning spoken of by Scott was the mass meeting in Boston on Nov. 29, 1773, described in Chapter 14.

13. Opinion of Thurlow and Wedderburn Feb. 11, 1774, Gage Pap., Clements Lib. (A copy enclosed in Dartmouth to Gen. Thomas Gage Apr. 19, 1774, same.) It is difficult to believe that these officers really considered the proceedings at Boston as amounting to making war on the King.

14. Dartmouth's rounding up twelve men lately arrived from Boston and interviewing them Feb. 16, 1774, Donoughue *British Politics* 57–58. The testimony of these men at a meeting of the Privy Council Feb. 19, 1774, in P.C. 1:56 (P.R.O.) is well summarized in *Acts P.C.* VI 551–553 and less well in *same* V 391–392.

15. Statement to the Cabinet by Thurlow and Wedderburn concerning trial for treason, Cabinet minutes Feb. 28, Dartmouth Pap. II:839, inadequately summarized in *Dartmouth* (1895) 199. "Minutes of Conversation with Lord Dartmouth," dated March 2, 1774, probably by Buckinghamshire, discloses that Wedderburn thought there was sufficient evidence to prosecute Williams, Hancock, and Molineux for treason, but that Thurlow disagreed, *Lothian* 290–291.

16. The plans and tentative proceedings of the Cabinet Feb. 4–16, 1774, to punish Boston and the Whig leaders there by executive action are described in Donoughue *British Politics* 50–65.

17. Minutes of Cabinet meeting of Feb. 19, 1774, quoted in the text, Dartmouth Pap. II 833–834, summarized inadequately in *Dartmouth* (1895) 198. William Lee wrote his brother Richard Henry Lee March 17 that the coercive measures adopted by the Cabinet had been opposed by Dartmouth and North (Dartmouth's stepbrother and close friend), Ford *William Lee* I 83, but no evidence of disagreement is recorded in any of the known Cabinet minutes. All members of the Cabinet but Suffolk attended the meeting on Feb. 19.

18. Cabinet meeting of Feb. 28, 1774, decided upon procedures to be initiated March 7, Dartmouth Pap. II 839, inadequately summarized in *Dartmouth* (1895) 199.

19. The message from the King to both Houses of Parliament with accompanying documents, May 7, 1774, 4 *Force* I 5–9, 32. On March 11, the administration submitted two important additional papers to both Houses, a letter from

Hutchinson to Dartmouth of Jan. 28, 1774, and a clipping from the *Massachusetts Gazette* of Jan. 27, both concerning the recent tarring and feathering in Boston of a customs officer, John Malcom, *same* 10, 35. The letter and clipping are published in Hersey "Malcom" 448–50.

20. Address of thanks to the King for his message and accompanying papers and assurance of action in accordance with his request adopted by both Houses March 7, 1774, 4 *Force* I 9–10, 32. Speeches in the House of Commons of North in favor of the address and of Rockingham's followers William Dowdeswell and Edmund Burke, warning against hasty action and the use of force are given and discussed in *same* 222–224, 32; *London Chronicle* for March 8; and Donoughue *British Politics* 73–75. The address was adopted in the Lords apparently without any discussion.

21. North's motion in the Commons March 14, 1774, for leave to bring in a bill to prohibit the landing or shipping of goods at Boston, 4 *Force* IV 38–39. Closing the Port of Boston would, of course, be a much more severe measure than that envisaged in Dartmouth's earlier proposal for removal of the customs officers from Boston, which, while burdensome to those using the Port of Boston by requiring them to go or send to some other town for clearance, would not ban the use of Boston as a port—as was recognized in Thurlow and Wedderburn to Dartmouth Feb. 11, Donoughue *British Politics* 63–64.

22. North's reference to two other times besides the tea affair when officers of the customs had been prevented from doing their duty at Boston presumably relates to the flight of the British Customs Commissioners from Boston at the time of the *Liberty* riot in 1768 and at the time of the Boston "Massacre" in 1770, described in Chapters 8 and 11.

23. Of the precedents cited by North for fining Boston because of the Boston Tea Party, the fine levied on Edinburgh in connection with the Captain John Porteous incident in 1736, Mahon *Hist. of Eng.* II 285–299, was the most closely in point.

24. North's speech in the Commons in support of his motion of March 14, 1774, 4 *Force* IV 37–38; *Parl. Hist.* XVII 1163–1167.

25. Adoption of North's motion, March 14, 1774, without division, *Geo. III* III 80, and speeches by William Dowdeswell and others opposing or questioning it, 4 *Force* IV 39–40. (Unpublished notes for 1772–1774 of debates in the House of Commons by Henry Cavendish, M.P. for Lostwithiel and for 1770–1774 by Matthew Breckdale, M.P. for Bristol, are used in Namier and Brooke *Commons* and the former in Donoughue *Brit. Politics*. However, they round out but do not essentially change the picture presented by the published reports of the Parliamentary debates in 1774 relating to the colonies.)

26. The bill defined the Port of Boston to include all of Boston Bay from Nahant Point on the north to Point Allerton on the south, embracing not only Boston, but the towns of Chelsea, Charlestown, Dorchester, Quincy, Weymouth, Hingham, and Hull.

27. The provision requiring "reasonable satisfaction" to "officers of his Majesty's revenue, and others" unquestionably included John Malcom, a British customs officer, tarred and feathered at Boston on Jan. 25, 1774, whose case is discussed in "Malcom (Hersey)" 442–454 and was referred to by Rose Fuller in

the House of Commons on March 23, 4 *Force* I 41. But, apparently, no other particular persons were identified, thus creating ambiguity as to just what was required.

28. The quotations in the text are from the bill as passed, 14 Geo. III ch. 19, which did not differ significantly from the bill as introduced.

29. East India Company to John Pownall, Under Secretary of State, Feb. 16, 1774, asking indemnity for the loss of its tea at Boston, valued at £9,659, *H.O. Papers* (for 1773–1775) 184.

30. The dangerous implications of authorizing the Crown to select particular wharfs as the exclusive places for legal landing of goods are brought out in Davidson *Propaganda* 120–121.

31. The Boston Port bill was read in the Commons on March 18, 1774, apparently without comment, 4 *Force* IV 41. At the second reading of the bill on March 21, George Byng, a staunch member of the Rockingham group, said "No," to it, Donoughue *British Politics* 80. But his seems to have been the only opposition voiced, and the reading passed without a division, the King to North March 21, *Geo. III* III 81.

32. Rose Fuller's speech March 23, 1774, not to punish Boston unless and until a specific indemnity had been demanded and refused, 4 *Force* I 41. According to an unsigned, undated statement in the Chatham Papers (P.R.O.) quoted in Sosin "Mass. Acts of 1774" 245, some London merchants offered to guarantee payment of over £16,000 to the East India Company if North would drop the proposed Boston Port bill, but that North insisted on their being "answerable for the future peaceable conduct & entire acquiescence" of the Bostonians, which, of course, they could not promise.

33. Byng, George Dempster, and others besides Fuller who spoke against the Boston Port bill March 23 and 25, 1774, 4 *Force* I 44–45, 48–56. For the constituencies represented by Byng, Dempster, and Fuller and brief biographical sketches of them, Namier and Brooke *Commons* II, III *passim*.

34. Charles Van's speech on March 23, 1774, declaring that Boston ought to be destroyed for its "flagitiousness," 4 *Force* IV 45–46. Speeches in the Commons by other supporters of the Boston Port bill are in *same* 41–45, 49–53.

35. Remarks of Henry S. Conway and Isaac Barré March 23, 1774, supporting the bill, *same* I 45, 46. (North's listing of Barré as speaking against the bill, *Geo. III* III 83, was evidently an error, Lewis *Walpole* XXVIII 142, with Walpole *Last Journals* I 332 and Barré's statement May 2, 4 *Force* I 86.)

36. There was no division on the bill on March 23 or 25, North to the King March 23 and 25, *Geo. III* III 82, 85.

37. Edmund Burke wrote the N.Y. Comm. of Corresp. Apr. 6, 1774, that the arguments made in the Commons by opponents of the bill "made so little impression that it was not thought advisable to divide the House," *Burke* II 528.

38. Motion March 25, 1774, to receive William Bollan's petition on behalf of Mass. against the bill defeated 170 to 40, 4 *Force* I 46; North to the King March 25, *Geo. III* III 85. See also Burke to N.Y. Comm. of Corresp. Apr. 6, *Burke* II 529, and Bollan to Committee of Mass. Council March 11, 15, 17 and 30, *Bowdoin–Temple* 353–357, 360–365.

39. The Boston Port bill was submitted to the House of Lords March 26, 1774, 4 *Force* I 57–58. Those speaking in favor of the bill in the Lords March 29, *same* 60; Lord Rochford to the King March 28 [should be 29], *Geo. III* III 86. As to Mansfield, Shelburne to Chatham Apr. 4, *Pitt* IV 339.

40. Speeches in opposition to the bill in the House of Lords by Lord Camden, the Duke of Richmond, Shelburne, and others March 29, 1774, 4 *Force* I 60; Burke to N.Y. Comm. of Corresp. Apr. 6, *Burke* II 529; and Shelburne to Chatham Apr. 4, *Pitt* IV 339–341.

41. Passage of the bill by the Lords without a division on March 30, and the King's assent the next day, 4 *Force* I 60. On March 31, thirty-one "Natives of America, then in London" headed by William Lee, vainly presented a petition to the King to suspend his assent to the bill, *same* 60–61.

42. Shelburne wrote Chatham March 15, 1774, that Dartmouth had "yesterday" told him of "his determination to cover America from the present storm, . . . even to repealing the act [the Townshend Act duty on tea], which I urged to him as the most expedient step the first moment he could bring his colleagues to listen to such a measure," *Pitt* IV 335. Dartmouth wrote John Thornton Feb. 12, that "he would be thought as mad as they [the Bostonians] if he were to say a word of repealing the tea duty," *Dartmouth* (1895) 197, and I have found no evidence that he proposed this.

43. Dartmouth to Joseph Reed of Philadelphia July 11, 1774, concerning the Intolerable Acts of 1774 indicates no disapproval of any of them, Reed *Reed* I 72–74; and the only evidence I have found of his even attempting to soften ministerial measure against the colonies is in the King to North March 14, 1774, mentioning Dartmouth's aversion to a proposed bill "for trying future Offenders [in Mass.] in Britain," and of "wanting in lieu of that, that Offenders of that particular province should be amenable to the Courts of Justice of Nova Scotia," *Geo. III* III 80–81.

44. Franklin to William Franklin July 13, 1773, and March 22, 1775, concerning Dartmouth, Smyth *Franklin* VI 98, 369. Arthur Lee advised Reed in a letter of Feb. 18, 1773, not to expect much good from Dartmouth's displacement of Hillsborough as Secretary of State for the colonies, since he was unlikely to "attempt any thing in our favour that will hazard his place," Reed *Reed* I 47. To similar effect, William Bollan to James Bowdoin Feb. 24, 1774, *Bowdoin–Temple Papers* 341.

45. Burke wrote the N.Y. Comm. of Corresp. May 4, 1774, "many Gentlemen who at first supported the Bill against that Town [Boston] asserted that they had been some way led to imagine that Ministry would propose the repeal of the Tea Duty; and they gave way in that Instance in hopes that a Measure of Lenity would be adopted, to qualify the Harshness of the Interdict under which the Act laid the unhappy Town of Boston," *Burke* II 533.

46. Fuller's motion in the House of Commons Apr. 19, 1774, for repeal of the Townshend Act duty on tea, North's opposition; Burke's speech, and proceedings on this motion, 4 *Force* I 132–166; North to the King Apr. 19, with enclosed list of speakers, *Geo. III* III 95; *London Chronicle* Apr. 26. (Burke's speech in favor of the motion is reprinted in Burke *Speeches* 1–63.) Dartmouth's statement on March 14 to Shelburne indicating his favoring repeal of the Townshend Act

(*Pitt* IV 385), quoted in note 42 above, may have led to the misunderstanding as to the Ministry's position.

47. Gage's statement to the King Feb. 4, 1774, that four regiments would suffice to deal with "any disturbance," the King to Lord North, Feb. 4, reporting a talk he had just had with Gage.

48. Dartmouth to the Admiralty Apr. 2, 1774, ordering transportation of the Fourth, Fifth, Thirty-eighth, and Forty-third Regiments to Boston, Donoughue *British Politics* 85n. and sources cited therein.

49. Gen. Gage's commission as Governor Apr. 7, 1774, *Col. Soc. Public.* II 174–183. The decision to send Gage to Boston as Governor of Mass. in place of Hutchinson was made as early as March 10, Dartmouth Pap. II 853, inadequately summarized in *Dartmouth* (1895) 202. Letters from Under Secretary of State Pownall to Dartmouth Aug. 5, 12 and 14, 1773, disclose that consideration had then been given for Hutchinson to come to England, but apparently for consultation rather than replacement, *Dartmouth* (1887) 338.

50. Gage's initial commission as Governor was substantially the same as those issued to his immediate predecessors, *same* 128–173 *passim,* but on or about Apr. 11, his commission was amended by a special commission giving him power to pardon persons convicted of murder or treason, instead of the usual power merely to suspend sentence with final action reserved to the King, Dartmouth to Gage Apr. 11, *Gage* II 162–163.

51. The customary instruction as to requirement of concurrence of the Council for declaration of martial law in any colony, Labaree *Instructions* I 397. The authority given to Gage singly to declare martial law is in his instructions dated Apr. 5, 1774, C.O.5:205:427–461. However, Dartmouth to Gage Apr. 9 qualifies this by stating, "I do not mean that any Constitutional power or authority vested in them should be set aside by these instructions," *Gage* II 161.

52. Attorney-General Edward Thurlow and Solicitor-General Alexander Wedderburn advised the Cabinet at a meeting on Apr. 7, 1774, attended by Gage, that the Governor of a colony in his capacity as first civil magistrate could call on the military for assistance in quelling disturbances, Dartmouth Pap. II 883, inadequately summarized in *Dartmouth* (1895) 208. Dartmouth wrote Gage June 3 confirming this opinion, *Gage* II 168. For further details, Donoughue *British Politics* 92–93.

53. Dartmouth to Gage Apr. 9, 1774, enclosing a copy of the law officers' opinion of Feb. 11 concerning treason at Boston and instructing him to try to secure evidence for indictments against "the principal actors," the trials to be in Mass. and not in England, *Gage* II 160–161.

54. Dartmouth to Gage Apr. 9, 1774, enclosing Gage's commission and instruction in a covering letter for his further guidance, *same* II 158–162.

55. Cabinet resolutions of March 1, 1774, for a bill to alter the constitution of Mass., Dartmouth Pap. II 842, inadequately summarized in *Dartmouth* (1895) 200.

CHAPTER 16

1. Pertinent letters and other papers from Feb., 1768, to Jan., 1774, by the American Customs Board as to the need for changes to secure British control of

Massachusetts are published in Wolkins "Liberty" 263–271, 278; others, unpublished, are cited and described in Barrow *Trade* 319–322.

2. Gen. Thomas Gage, who succeeded Sir Jeffery Amherst as acting Commander-in-Chief of the British army in North America in Nov., 1763, and titular comander a year later, retained this post until October, 1775, Alden *Gage* 22–283 *passim*. Gage's older brother, William, Lord Gage, was a viscount in the Irish peerage and a member of the British House of Commons 1754–1780; Gen. Gage's wife, Margaret Kemble, was the daughter of Peter Kemble and Gertrude Bayard of New Jersey, *same* 9–11, 44n. The jurisdiction of his command is described in *same* 75–88; Labaree *Royal Government* 108–109; Carter "Commander in Chief" 175–213.

3. Lord Barrington, a viscount in the Irish peerage and a member of the British House of Commons 1740–1778, wrote his friend Andrew Mitchell in March, 1761, of his "invariable rule to ask nothing, to refuse nothing . . . and do my best wherever I am placed," Namier *Eng.* 440. He was Secretary at War, 1755–1761; Chancellor of the Exchequer, 1761–1762; Treasurer of the Navy, 1762–1765; and Secretary at War again, July, 1765, to Dec., 1778.

4. Initially a protege of the Duke of Newcastle, after Newcastle's fall from power in 1762, Barrington allied himself with no political party. His political career from then on was one of the "King's Friends." He assured the King in 1765 that he would not accept any office "which did not come directly from his Majesty and was not held solely under him," Namier and Brooke *Commons* 55–57, and his conduct from 1762 to 1778 was consistent with this statement.

5. Gage to Barrington June 28, 1768, as to acting resolutely to "Quash . . . at a Blow" the threatened revolt of Boston and Mass. as a whole, *Gage* II 480.

6. Gage to Barrington June 28, 1768, as to the importance of vigorous measures against Mass. to "damp the spirit of Insurrection" elsewhere in the colonies. Earlier letters (Jan. 17, 1767, and March 10, 1768) from Gage to Barrington had spoken in similar vein of the necessity of "spirited conduct" to keep the colonists dependent on Great Britain and recommended the prevention of emigration to the colonies, thus ensuring that "our new Settlements should be peopled from the old ones, which would be a means to thin them and put it less in their power to do Mischief," *same* II 406, 450.

7. Blackstone *Commentaries* IV 259 defines impeachment, in the case of commoners, as a proceeding for alleged "high misdeameanors" brought by "articles of impeachment, . . . a kind of bill of indictment found by the house of commons and afterwards tried by the lords." The punishment to be inflicted if the accused were found guilty seems to have been at the discretion of Parliament.

8. Those "who signed the Letters of Convention," mentioned in the text—the Mass. Convention of 1768—were five selectmen of Boston: Joseph Jackson, John Ruddock, John Hancock, John Rowe, and Samuel Pemberton, Gov. Francis Bernard to an unidentified correspondent Dec. 23, 1768, *Barrington–Bernard Corresp.* 225.

9. All Mass. towns, including Boston, were governed by selectmen elected by popular vote at town meetings. In recommending a corporation form of government, Gage apparently contemplated a Mayor with considerable powers, appointed by the Crown-appointed Governor of the colony, as, for example, in New York.

10. Gage to Barrington May 14, 1769, recommending impeachment of a number of persons in Mass. and changes in the form of government of the province and of Boston, *Gage* II 509–510.

11. Appointment by the Crown of members of the provincial Council in all the royal colonies except Mass., Labaree *Royal Government* 134–138.

12. The Mass. Charter of 1691 named the members of the first Council and provided for the annual election of the Council thereafter "by the Generall Court . . . newly chosen," *Mass. Acts* I 10, 12. The "Generall Court" consisted of two bodies, the House of Representatives and the Council, both annually elected. Since the only existing Council at the time of choosing a new Council was the outgoing Council, the practice was to elect the new Council by joint ballot of the incoming House and the outgoing Council.

13. The Mass. Charter of 1691 gave the Crown-appointed Governor "the Negative voice" in "all Elections" by the general court, *same* 17. This power had been used with great restraint (with one exception) before 1766, but in that year, Gov. Bernard negatived six; in 1767, five; in 1768, six; and in 1769, eleven of those named to the Council; Whitmore *Mass. Civil List* 65.

14. Gage to Barrington Sept. 8, 1770, suggesting changes in the form of government in Mass., *Gage* II 557. A few months earlier (July 6) referring to a recent attack on the home of one of the members of the American Customs Board, which had driven the Board to take refuge again at Castle William, Gage had written Barrington that "a very considerable Force, and that Force empower'd to act" was required to preserve Mass. from "Anarchy," *same* II 547. The details of this attack are given in Ann Hulton to Mrs. Adam Lightbody July 25, *Hulton Letters* 22–24.

15. Gage to Barrington Nov. 20, 1770, as to the colonists in general being mere bullies, *Gage* II 564.

16. The extensive unrest in England from 1768 to 1771 mentioned in the text is described in detail in Rudé *Wilkes and Liberty* 66–168, the Falkland Island controversy of 1770–1771 in Gipson *Brit. Empire* XI 1–11. The letters of Horace Walpole to Sir Horace Mann from Dec., 1768, to Dec., 1771, and accompanying footnotes contain useful information on both matters, Lewis *Walpole* XXIII 77–359 *passim*.

17. Gage to Barrington Apr. 13, 1772, and Feb. 8, 1773, pointing out that the time was now ripe for Great Britain to establish its supremacy over the colonies and the unwisdom of yielding to any colonial demands, *Gage* II 603, 636–637.

18. Barrington to Gage Apr. 16, 1768, saying he had shown Hillsborough his recent letter (Gage to Barrington March 10, 1768, quoted in note 6 above, *same* II 450) recommending that the colonies be kept as weak as possible, Gage Papers, Clements Lib. Hillsborough wrote Gage Oct. 3, 1770, in a letter marked "Private & secret," "I seldom trouble you with private Letters because I have all the benefit of your Correspondence with our Common Friend Lord Barrington," *Gage* II 118–119.

19. Barrington to Gage Sept. 28, 1772, stating that he had shown extracts of Gage's recent letter opposing establishment of a new colony on the Ohio to Lords North and Dartmouth and the President of the Council, Gage Papers, Clements Lib. The letter thus shown was Gage to Barrington Aug. 5, 1772,

Gage II 615–161, dealing with the much discussed Vandalia project, in which Benjamin Franklin was involved. The account of this in Sosin *Whitehall and the Wilderness,* 184–210 is particularly full and good.

20. Barrington to Gage Sept. 20, 1769, stating that the King "sees most of your private Letters to me," Gage Papers, Clements Lib. The King also probably was among those referred to by Barrington in writing Gage Nov. 28, 1769, that he communicated "the intelligence which comes to me in your private letters . . . where it will do good," *same.* Unlike his private letters, Gage's official letters (*Gage* I 79–341, II 331–627) deal almost exclusively with Indian and non-political affairs.

21. Bernard's wife was a first cousin of Barrington. The latter wrote Bernard Feb. 23, 1764, that he had informed Hillsborough, "the most intimate friend I have in the world," of his "connexions with and good opinion of" Bernard, *Barrington–Bernard Corresp.* 73.

22. The controversy between Bernard and the Mass. Legislature over its refusal to reelect a number of Mass. officials, appointed by the Crown or the Governor, to the Mass. Council and Bernard's refusal to approve those elected in their stead can be followed in his messages to, and replies from, the Mass. House of Representatives and Council in 1766 and 1767, Bradford, *Mass. Papers* 75–109 *passim* and in Bernard's letters from 1766 to 1769 to various officials in the Harvard College Lib.

23. Bernard's complaints of the failure of the Mass. Council to support him on various occasions from 1766 to 1769 are in his letter books referred to in note 22 above (many of which are printed in *Select Letters . . . by Governor Bernard* (Boston, 1774), *Letters to Hillsborough* (Boston, 1769), *Letters to Ministry* (Boston, 1774), *Barrington–Bernard Corresp.,* and elsewhere). He was particularly incensed over the Council's refusal, referred to in Chapter 11, to provide barracks for the British troops sent to Boston in 1768.

24. Bernard to Hillsborough Sept. 26, 1768, *Letters to Ministry* 86, to Barrington Oct. 20, 1768, and March 18, May 30, and June 1, 1769, and to an unidentified correspondent Dec. 23, 1768, *Barrington–Bernard Corresp.* 179, 184, 203–204, 256–257, advocated amendment of the Mass. charter to provide for appointment by the King of the members of the Mass. Council.

25. Bernard to an unidentified correspondent Dec. 23, 1768, recommending revocation of the commissions of all justices of the peace in Suffolk County, Mass., of which Boston was the county seat, and appointment of a new set of justices by the Governor or the King, *same* 255–256.

26. Bernard to Hillsborough Sept. 9, 1768, suggesting that grand juries, then popularly elected, be impaneled hereafter by county sheriffs who were appointed by the Governor, *Letters to Hillsborough* 12–13. Bernard made a similar recommendation to the Committee on Plantation Affairs of the Privy Council at a hearing in London June 26 and 27, 1770, *Acts P.C.* V 248–261.

27. For Thomas Hutchinson's life and political career in Mass. to 1775, Freiberg Prelude to Purgatory: Thomas Hutchinson 1760–1770 (Ph.D. dissertation Brown U. Lib.), "Hutchinson . . . 1711–1761," "Hutchinson and the Currency," and "Governor Hutchinson"; Hosmer *Hutchinson;* the sketch of Hutchinson in Shipton *Harvard Graduates* VIII 149–217; typed copies of his letters in the Mass.

Archives at the Mass. Hist. Soc.; and Hutchinson *Hist. of Mass.* vol. III and *Diary and Letters* I.

28. Hutchinson to Richard Jackson Apr. 21, 1766, as to the necessity of requiring the colonists to "explicitly acknowledge a general subjection" to Parliament, Mass. Arch. XXVI 228.

29. Hutchinson to John Pownall Apr. 19, 1770, and to Hillsborough April 27, as to the necessity that the colonies be "kept in awe by a power superior to them" and receive a "check from the Supreme Authority," *same* XXVI 473, XXV 391–394. Hutchinson wrote again in similar vein to Hillsborough Oct. 9 concerning the necessity of action by Parliament to suppress the non-importation "confederacies" Oct. 9, 1770, *same* XXV 443, printed in part in Hosmer *Hutchinson* 167–168.

30. Hutchinson to Pownall July 27, 1770, hoping Parliament would make "thorough work" at its next session in punishing the ringleaders of the colonial non-importation agreements, Mass. Arch. XXVI 524, and Hutchinson to Hillsborough Jan. 22, 1771, urging determined action by Parliament to secure the colonists' recognition of its supreme authority, *Remembrancer* for 1771 Part I 160–162.

31. Hutchinson to Pownall Apr. 18, 1771, suggesting that Parliament pass an act making it high treason to deny, in writing or print, the validity of acts of Parliament, Mass. Arch. XXVII 149–150.

32. Hutchinson to Pownall Oct. 3, 1769, Apr. 3 and 6, 1771, and May 24, 1771, *same* XXVI 394, XXVII 143–144, XXVII 171–173, and to Hillsborough Oct. 9, 1770, *same* XXV 441–447, as to Boston town meetings.

33. Hutchinson to Hillsborough Oct. 9, 1770, as to juries in Mass., *same* XXV 441–447.

34. Hutchinson to Hillsborough concerning the Mass. Council, Oct. [no day], 1770, *same* XXVII 22–23 and Jan. 22, 1771, *Remembrancer* for 1776 Part I 158–160. Many other letters from Hutchinson to persons in public life in England urging exertion of increased authority are cited in Bancroft *History* VI 305–307.

CHAPTER 17

1. Benjamin Franklin, who had been in London as Agent for the Pennsylvania Assembly since 1764, was now (1772) also London Agent for Georgia, New Jersey, and the Massachusetts Assembly, Kammen *Agents* 324.

2. Franklin to Thomas Cushing Dec. 2, 1772, enclosing letters of Thomas Hutchinson, Andrew Oliver, and others to Thomas Whately, Smyth *Franklin* VI 265–268. The date is from *same* V 448.

3. Hutchinson's letters from June 18, 1768, to Oct. 26, 1769, Oliver's from May 6, 1767, to Aug. 12, 1769, and Charles Paxton's of June 20, 1768, are in Mauduit *Franklin* 17–48. The fact that they were written to, or were in the possession of, Thomas Whately is known from a speech of Alexander Wedderburn Jan. 29, 1774, *same* 81–83. As to Whately, who had died in May, 1772, and his political career and connection with George Grenville, sketch of Whately in *D.N.B.*

4. The mystery of how Franklin got the letters is discussed in Knollenberg "Franklin and the Hutchinson Letters" 1–9.

5. The damaging letters of Hutchinson quoted in Chapter 16 did not come to light until 1775, *Warren–Adams* 49, 49n.; French *First Year* 730–731. Hutchinson's injunctions to English correspondents in several of the letters quoted in Chapter 16, and others cited in Bancroft *History* VI 307, to keep his reports secret, evidently had been faithfully observed.

6. Hutchinson's letters quoted in the text, Mauduit *Franklin* 18–31 *passim*. In his letter of Oct. 26, 1769, Hutchinson enjoined Whately to "keep secret everything I write, until we are in a more settled state . . . ," *same* 30.

7. Hutchinson's letter of Jan. 20, 1769, as to impracticability of distant colonies enjoying "all the liberty of the parent state . . . ," *same* 29. (Freiberg "Letter" 189 points out differences between the published copy of this letter and the copy in Hutchinson's letter book; but the two do not differ in substance.)

8. As brought out in Chapter 3, Parliament had prohibited the colonists to import manufactures of continental Europe except by way of Great Britain, had restricted the manufacture of felt, hats, and steel in the colonies, and presumably would impose such further restrictions on colonial manufacturing as might be needed to discourage the development of other colonial manufactures.

9. Oliver to Whately May 7, 1767, quoted in the text, Mauduit *Franklin* 35–36. Another suggestion in Oliver's letters was for the King to create "an order of Patricians or Esquires" in the colony, because at present there was no way "to put a man of fortune above the common level and exempt him from being chosen by the people into the lower offices, but his being appointed a Justice of the Peace" which "is frequently done when there is no expectation of his undertaking the Trust, and has its inconveniences," *same* 43.

10. Charles Paxton to Whately June 20, 1768, recommending the sending of two or three British regiments to Boston, immediately, *same* 48. As noted in Chapter 8, Paxton was the most unpopular member of the unpopular American Customs Board even before this letter of his was made public.

11. Franklin to Cushing Dec. 2, 1772, imposing the restriction quoted in the text on the use of the enclosed letters. Smyth *Franklin* VI 266–267.

12. Petition of the Mass. House to the King for the removal of Hutchinson and Lieut. Governor Oliver, June 23, 1773, Mauduit *Franklin* 69–71. The date is from Cushing *S. Adams* III 45–48. The petition was preceded by a resolution of the House, June 16, denouncing Hutchinson, Oliver, and Paxton, Bradford *Mass. Papers* 405–409. Also the House and the Mass. Council jointly adopted a letter to Lord Dartmouth June 29, denouncing generally all those who had frustrated efforts to restore harmony between Great Britain and the colonies, *same* 398–400.

13. Cushing to Franklin June 25, 1773, enclosing the petition and other papers. Sparks *Franklin* VIII 52–53. In this letter Cushing also instructed Franklin to present earlier petitions from the House to the King concerning payment by the Crown of the Governor's and judges salaries, which Franklin had withheld. As to these earlier petitions and Franklin's reasons for withholding them, Franklin to Cushing Sept. 3 and Dec. 2, 1772, and June 2 and July 7, 1773, Smyth *Franklin* V 435, 448–451, VI 55–56, 74.

14. Cushing's instruction to employ Arthur Lee as counsel, quoted in the text, *same* 53. Lee, a Virginian, younger brother of Richard Henry Lee, had

studied law in England, but was not admitted to the English bar until 1775, sketch of Lee in *D.A.B.*

15. Franklin to Cushing Aug. 24, 1773, acknowledging receipt of the Petition for the removal of Hutchinson and Oliver and saying he had sent it to Dartmouth, Smyth *Franklin* VI 172. Franklin's letter of Aug. 21 to Dartmouth enclosing the Petition is in Mauduit *Franklin* 67.

16. John Pownall to the Clerk of the Privy Council Dec. 3, 1773, transmitting the Petition and stating it was to "be laid before his Majesty in his Privy Council," *same* 68.

17. Franklin to Cushing Jan. 5, 1774, as to a probable hearing on the Petition by "a committee of the Privy Council, and that I should have notice to be heard in support of it," Smyth *Franklin* VI 172.

18. The Privy Council's Committee for Plantation [colonial] Affairs and the invariable acceptance by the Privy Council (King in Council) of its recommendations, Knollenberg *Origin* 47–48, 300. (The Committee is sometimes referred to as the Committee "on" or "of" Plantation Affairs.)

19. The *O.E.D.* describes the "Cockpit" as "the part of the Treasury buildings which fronts Whitehall," so-called because located on a former cockpit built by Henry VIII.

20. Franklin to Cushing Feb. 15, 1774, stating "on Saturday the 8th of January . . . I received notice . . . that the Lords of the Committee for Plantation Affairs, would, on the Tuesday following at twelve, meet at the Cockpit to take into consideration the petition referred to them by his Majesty," and that, having then appeared, he secured a postponement until Jan. 29, Smyth *Franklin* VI 182–186.

21. Franklin to Cushing Feb. 15, 1774, stating that Arthur Lee was ineligible to act as counsel, "not yet being called to the bar," *same* 182.

22. Franklin to Cushing Feb. 15, 1774, stating, "I employed a solicitor" who "retained Mr. [John] Dunning and Mr. John Lee," *same* 187. Thomas Life is identified as the solicitor by Franklin's statement of the expenses of the hearing, *M.H.S. Proc.* 56 (1923) 96, 97, 108, 117. Life was an experienced solicitor, Kammen *Agents,* under "Life" in the index, 346; Sosin *Agents* 8, 9n., 79, 177, 194–195, 222–223. As to the distinguished careers of Dunning (later Lord Ashburton), who had been Solicitor-General in the Grafton administration, and John Lee, biographical sketches of them in *D.N.B.*

23. Franklin's initial plan for supporting the Petition at the hearing and, with the assistance of Arthur Lee, preparing a brief for this, Franklin to Cushing Feb. 15, 1774, Smyth *Franklin* VI 187–188. (William Bollan, London Agent for the Mass. Council, who had earlier collaborated with Franklin in connection with the Petition, did not, so far as is known, collaborate in preparing the brief. As to Bollan's earlier collaboration, Franklin to Cushing Feb. 15, *same* 182–183, 187, and Bollan to James Bowdoin Feb. 2, *Bowdoin–Temple Papers* 336–337.)

24. The decision of Dunning and John Lee as to method of supporting the Petition, quoted in the text, Smyth *Franklin* VI 188.

25. Franklin to Cushing Feb. 15, 1774, as to the attendance at the hearing on Jan. 29, *same* 188–189. Franklin thought there had been a "preconcerted" effort to ensure a large unfriendly gathering "for all the courtiers were invited," *same* 188.

26. Edmund Burke, London Agent for the N.Y. Assembly, wrote the Assembly's Committee of Correspondence, Feb. 2, "The Council was the fullest I have ever known. It did not seem absolutely necessary from the Nature of the Case that there should be any public Trial whatsoever. But it was obviously intended to give all possible weight and solemnity to the decision." The members of the Privy Council present at the hearing are listed in Mauduit *Franklin* 118. They include Dartmouth and most of the other members of the Cabinet, but not Lord North.

27. The quotation in the text of the argument for the Petition is from Burke to the N.Y. Committee of Correspondence, Feb. 2, 1774, *Burke* II 521. Burke was not a member of the Privy Council, but as London Agent for the N.Y. Assembly he presumably made it a point to attend a hearing of great interest to all the colonies.

28. The hearing before the Privy Council's Committee for Plantation Affairs, including Alexander Wedderburn's speech at the hearing, is reported in Burke to the N.Y. Committee of Correspondence Feb. 2, 1774, *same* 521–522; Mauduit *Franklin* 75–104; Franklin to Cushing Feb. 15, Smyth *Franklin* VI 189–190.

29. Mauduit *Franklin* 76–77 quotes Wedderburn as saying, "the whole foundation of this Address rests upon events of five and six years standing and this makes it necessary to take up the history of them from their original. In the beginning of the year 1764 ****. My Lords, after having gone through the history of this people for the last ten years I now come to consider the argument upon that footing my learned friends [Dunning and Lee] have chosen to place it." But, as indicated by the asterisks, the "history" as related by Wedderburn is omitted.

30. Franklin to Cushing Feb. 15, 1774, describing Wedderburn's speech as quoted in the text, Smyth *Franklin* VI 189.

31. The recommendation Jan. 29, 1774, of the Committee for Plantation Affairs, quoted in the text, that the Petition be dismissed, Mauduit *Franklin* 120.

32. The Privy Council, with the King present, met Feb. 7, 1774, and dismissed the Petition, *same* 116, 120–121.

33. Wedderburn's attack on Franklin at the hearing on the Massachusetts Petition, Jan. 29, 1774, *same* 87–103. Franklin's dismissal Jan. 30 from his office of Joint Deputy of Postmaster for the British colonies in North America north of North Carolina, Smyth *Franklin* VI 191. A copy of Franklin's commission dated Sept. 25, 1765, is in *Franklin* XII 281–282.

CHAPTER 18

1. Cabinet resolution of March 1, 1774, as to bill to alter the constitution of Mass. immediately, Dartmouth Pap. II 842, inadequately summarized in *Dartmouth* (1895) 200.

2. Cabinet resolution of Feb. 19, 1774, that "Leave to bring in a Bill to alter the Constitution of the province of Massachusetts Bay, . . . be, according to what shall be judged most advisable hereafter, either put forward in the present Session or suspended till the next, in order to give an Opportunity to the General Court [Mass. Legislature] to shew cause . . . why such an alteration should not be made," Dartmouth Pap. II 833–834, inadequately summarized in *Dartmouth* (1895) 198.

3. Thomas Hutchinson to an unidentified correspondent July 8, 1774, quoting Lord North's explanation to him of the Cabinet's decision as to the Mass. Regulating bill, Hutchinson *Diary* I 181–182. Hutchinson had suggested the advisability of giving Mass. the opportunity to be heard on the bill because "perhaps the apprehensions of such an Act might produce such a change of conduct as to render it unnecessary," and because even if the act were later passed, the opportunity to be heard might make the act "less grievous," *same* 181.

4. North's outline of the proposed Mass. Regulating bill to the House of Commons March 28, 1773, and vote for leave to bring in the proposed bill, 4 *Force* I 65–67. North was strongly supported by Lord George Germain, *same* I 67–68. From now on Germain was a leading proponent of coercive measures against the colonies. For the background of his appointment to succeed Lord Dartmouth as Secretary of State in 1775 and his conduct of the war until 1778, Brown *The American Secretary . . . Germain* 24–173.

5. North's introduction of the Mass. Regulating bill Apr. 15, 1774, 4 *Force* I 68–69. For convenience, I base my summary on the act as passed, rather than on the bill. The act fills in dates and other blanks (e.g., number of councilors) in the bill as introduced, and is arranged differently, but does not differ substantially, from the bill, a printed copy of which is among the papers in the Record Office, House of Lords. Unless otherwise noted, my later references to provisions of the bills for the Intolerable Acts of 1774 are to the acts, rather than the bills.

6. Provision in the Mass. Charter of Oct. 7, 1691, for election of members of the Mass. Council, Mass. *Acts* I 12. Sec. 1 of Mass. Regulating Act provided that beginning Aug. 1, 1774, all members of the Council were to be appointed by the King. They might be either inhabitants or proprietors of land within Mass.

7. Provision in the Mass. Charter of 1691 for appointment of judges, justices of the peace, sheriffs etc., by the Governor "with the advice and consent of the Council," Mass. *Acts* I 12. Secs. 3, 5, and 6 of Mass. Regulating Act gave the Governor power to appoint judges, justices of the peace, sheriffs, etc., without the advice and consent of the Council.

8. John Adams had clashed with William Brattle in a newspaper controversy in the *Boston Gazette* in 1772–1773, Adams *Works* III 513–574, over whether judges in Mass. had tenure during good behavior and, if not, whether they might be removed without consent of the Mass. Council. The Mass. Regulating Act left unclear the tenure of judges already in office, but provided in secs. 3 and 6 that judges thereafter appointed were removable at pleasure without consent of the Council—those of the inferior courts by the Governor, those of the superior court by the King.

9. Chap. 29 of Mass. Acts of 1692 as to calling and the powers of town meetings, *Mass. Acts* I 64–68. Sec. 7 of Mass. Regulating Act contained the restrictions as to town meetings described in the text.

10. Chap. 24 of Mass. Acts of 1694–1695, *same* I 193, as to choosing members of grand juries and Chap. 29 of Mass. Acts of 1759–1760 extended by Chap. 20 of Mass. Acts of 1766–1767, *same* IV 318–319, 920, as to choosing members of petty juries. Secs. 8–23 of Mass. Regulating Act provided for new method of selecting jurors.

11. As to Thomas Pownall, Gov. of Mass. 1757–1759, M.P. 1767–1780, and, until 1775, a supporter of conciliatory measures, sketch in *D.A.B.* and Namier and

Brooke *Commons* II 316–318; Pownall *Pownall;* Schutz *Pownall.* Shy "Pownall" 161–185 gives an admirable analysis of the first five editions (1764–1774) of Pownall's most important work, *The Administration of the Colonies.*

12. Speakers in the House of Commons opposing the Mass. Regulating bill Apr. 22 and May 2, 1774, 4 *Force* I 74–77, 83–94; North to the King Apr. 22 and May 2, *Geo. III* III 96, 102; Edmund Burke to N.Y. Comm. of Corresp. May 4, *Burke* II 532–533.

13. Division on the bill May 2, 1774, on motion for its third and final reading in the Commons, resulting in a vote of 239 to 64 in favor of the bill, and passage of the bill on May 11, 4 *Force* I 91; *Geo. III* III 102. For the progress of the bill through the House March 28 to May 2, 4 *Force* I 66–94.

14. The Duke of Richmond and Lords Camden and Shelburne spoke against the bill March 29, 1774, Shelburne to Lord Chatham Apr. 4, *Pitt* IV 339–340, with Walpole *Last Journal* I 364. Furthermore, Lord Rockingham and nine other peers, not recorded as having spoken against the bill, signed a protest against its passage, 4 *Force* I 93–95; and one of the Lord Bishops, Jonathan Shipley, Bishop of St. Asaph, published a tract, *A Speech Intended to Have Been Spoken,* condemning the bill, *same* 97–104.

15. William Bollan to Mass. Council May 12, 1774, *Bowdoin–Temple Papers* 369, gives the vote on the Regulating bill May 11, 1774, as 57 in favor of the bill to 21 against. Walpole *Last Journal* I 364 gives the vote of members present as about 57 to 20, with additional proxies in favor of the bill. (The statement in the *Annual Register* for 1774 72, that the vote was 92 to 20 in favor of the bill, is probably erroneous.) There is no record in the published journals of the House of Lords of any vote on the bill; it apparently passed that House without even a division.

16. Progress of the Regulating bill through the House of Lords May 3–11, 1774, 4 *Force* I 92–96; *Geo. III* III 96–103 *passim.* The House of Commons voted May 16 to accept the Lords' amendments, *same* 96. The King assented to the act May 20, *same* 96.

17. The firmly established rule that a colonial act approved by the Crown could not thereafter be repealed or amended by the Crown, Knollenberg *Origin* 46, 299.

18. Rose Fuller's motion for repeal of the tea duty, April 19, 1774, 4 *Force* I 131–133.

19. Edmund Burke's speech April 19, 1774, in support of Fuller's motion, *same* 135–168. Burke's speech has often been reprinted, as in Burke *Speeches* 1–63. Burke reviewed the history of the controversy with the colonies since 1764 and defended the conduct of the colonists. He maintained that, assuming Parliament had the right to tax the colonies, it should as a matter of expediency and justice refrain from doing so; that the benefit to Great Britain from the British acts regulating colonial trade was ample compensation for her protection of the colonies.

20. Vote April 19, 1774, of 182 against, and only 49 for, repeal of the Townshend Act duty on tea, 4 *Force* I 166.

21. North's speech April 19, 1774, as quoted in the text, *same* 166.

22. The King to North Feb. 4, 1774, reporting the talk he had just had with Gage, *Geo. III* III 59. The King was much impressed by Gage, whose language, the King said, "was very consonant to his Character of an honest, determined Man . . . ," *same*. The King enjoined North to see Gage "and hear his ideas as to the mode of compelling Boston to submit to whatever may be thought necessary," *same*—an injunction which North doubtless obeyed, though no record of the suggested conference between him and Gage has been found.

23. The Administration of Justice Act was 14 Geo. III ch. 39 (1774). The act apparently was prompted by statements of Gage and his predecessor as Commander-in-Chief, Gen. Jeffery Amherst, at a Cabinet meeting March 30, 1774, that British soldiers would not have a fair trial for their lives if arrested for killing anyone at Boston in the suppression of a riot, Ritcheson *British Politics* 161, citing Hinchingbrooke (Lord Sandwich) Papers. The act provided also for the compulsory attendance at the trial of witnesses whose expenses were to be paid by the Crown.

24. The introduction and progress of the Administration of Justice bill through both Houses from Apr. 15 to May 18, 1774, including a vote of 127 to 24 in favor of the bill in the Commons on May 6, and 43 to 12 in the Lords on May 18, can be followed in 4 *Force* I 112–219. Additional details are in the correspondence of the King with North Apr. 15 to May 6, *Geo. III* III 93–104; Burke to N.Y. Comm. of Corresp. May 4, *Burke* II 530–34; and Donoughue *British Politics* 91–95, 99–101.

25. The formal protest against passage of the Administration of Justice bill filed by eight peers, Richmond, Rockingham, Leinster, Fitzwilliam, Portland, Manchester, Ponsonby, and Craven, May 18, 1774, is in 4 *Force* I 128–129. The King assented to the bill May 20, *same* 129.

26. The new Quartering Act of 1774 was 14 Geo. III ch. 54. The old quartering acts could be construed to require that if barracks supplied by the colony were available they must be used no matter how inconveniently located. The new act gave the Commander-in-Chief of the British forces in North America unlimited authority to provide for housing the troops in such buildings other than inhabited houses as he chose to requisition and pay for. The new act also directed Governors to cooperate in providing quarters independently of the provincial Council.

27. Proceedings in the House of Commons on the Quartering bill from Apr. 29, 1774, when leave for the bill was voted, to its passage by that House May 9, 4 *Force* I 165–167. There is no record of any division on the bill there.

28. Chatham had last spoken in the House of Lords May 19, 1772—for a bill favorable to dissenters, Williams *Pitt* II 350.

29. Chatham's speech in the House of Lords May 26, 1774, opposing the Quartering bill and deploring other measures taken or proposed concerning Boston and Mass., 4 *Force* I 167–169, Rockingham to William Dowdeswell, Kirtland *Letters* 18. (I have found no contemporary evidence confirming the ludicrous description of Chatham's appearance on this occasion in Horace Walpole's *Last Journal* I 369, much if not all of which was written long after the events described in it.)

30. The bill passed the House of Lords on its third reading May 26, 1774, 57 to 16, 4 *Force* I 169, and was assented to by the King on June 2, *same* 170.

CHAPTER 19

1. The government of the province of Quebec by British military Governors, 1763–1774, Coffin *Quebec* 326–389; S & D *Doc.* I 163–483.

2. The Royal Proclamation of Oct. 7, 1763, reserved "for the use of the . . . Indians, . . . all the Lands and Territories lying to the Westward of the Sources of the Rivers which fall into the Sea from the West and Northwest . . . ," i.e., most of the valley of the Mississippi and its tributaries east of the great river. The region was under the police of General Thomas Gage as Commander in Chief of the British army in North America assisted by Indian superintendents as described in Carter "Commander in Chief," 176–195; Alden *Gage* 83–88; Knollenberg *Origin* 103, 323.

3. Bill for the Quebec Act introduced in the House of Lords by Lord Dartmouth May 2, 1774, and its passage by that House, with no record of any division, May 17, 4 *Force* I 169–171. A motion to limit the proposed act to seven years was rejected, apparently by voice vote, *same* 171.

4. Attack on the Quebec bill in the House of Commons May 26 to June 13, 1774, when submitted there for concurrence, *same* 179–211; Cavendish *Quebec Bill* 1–296.

5. Amendments of the bill by the House of Commons and its passage, as amended, June 13, 1774, 56 to 20, 4 *Force* I 211, Cavendish *Quebec Bill* 296. As to the amendments, *Journals H. of C.* XXXIV 810–812 and S. & D. *Doc.* I 554–560. The very thin attendance is explained by the following fact: "The session was drawing near to the usual time of recess; and the greatest number of the members, fatigued with a long attendance on the American bills, were retired into the country," *Annual Register* (for 1774) 74.

6. Lord Chatham's speech in the House of Lords June 17, 1774, denouncing the Quebec bill for abolishing trial by jury in civil cases; failing to guarantee the writ of *habeas corpus;* perpetuating Quebec's "despotic" system of government; restoring the Roman Catholic clergy's right to tithes from the Roman Catholic inhabitants of Quebec; and annexation to the province of the "vast, fertile region . . . capable of containing (if fully peopled) 30 million souls," *Parl. Hist.* XVII 1402–1406.

7. The Quebec bill passed the House of Lords June 17, 1774, by a majority of 26 to 7, with only the Duke of Gloucester and Lords Coventry, Effingham, Spencer, Sandys, and King joining Chatham in voting against it, *same* 1407 and 4 *Force* I 211–214 (the latter misdated June 18).

8. The petition of the Lord Mayor and Aldermen of London June 22, 1774, to the King not to assent to the Quebec bill, and the King's reply, *same* 214–216. As to the King's attitude toward the petition, which he had heard was to be presented, the King to North June 18, *Geo. III* III 112.

9. The King assented to the act June 22, 1774, 4 *Force* I 216. The act was 14 Geo. III ch. 83.

10. Lord Apsley to Lord Dartmouth Aug. 4, 1773, concerning a plan for the government of Quebec, S & D *Doc.* I.534n.

11. Francis Maseres to Dartmouth Aug. 26, 1773, as to Lord North's plan for Quebec, *same* 534n., and Under Secretary of State John Pownall to Under Secretary of State William Knox Dec. 3, as to North's pressing him for "a precis of the affairs of Quebec," *Knox* 111.

12. Dartmouth to Hector Cramahé Dec. 1, 1773, concerning the "Arrangements" for Quebec, C.O. 42:32 (P.R.O.). The settlements, chiefly French Canadian, referred to in Dartmouth's letter were at Detroit and several places in the Mississippi Valley, such as Vincennes.

13. Solicitor-General Alexander Wedderburn reported to the Privy Council Dec. 6, 1772, that the dues payable to the Catholic clergy had been "one thirteenth part of the fruits of the earth in the name of tythe," enforceable in "the Spiritual Court," *Can. Doc.* I 428; but Diamond "Experiment in Feudalism" 29 gives the dues as only one twenty-sixth of the produce, excluding fish, eggs, timber, and livestock; and Munro *Seignioral System* 183–184 as merely one twenty-sixth of the grain raised. (Sec. 6 added an ambiguous statement as to ecclesiastical dues payable by non-Catholic inhabitants of Quebec.)

14. Roman Catholics had practically been barred from office in Quebec by an oath required by the act of 1 Elizabeth ch. 1 (1558) to which, as Catholics, they could not swear. Furthermore, a Crown instruction to Carleton in 1768 required members of the Council in Quebec to take oaths repugnant to Catholics, *Can. Doc.* I 302. This instruction was dropped in a new set of instructions issued by the Crown Jan. 3, 1775, *same* 595–714.

15. Guy Carleton, Governor of Quebec, had written Secretary of State Lord Shelburne Dec. 24, 1767, (*same* 288–289) that a Quebec ordinance of Sept. 17, 1764, (*same* 205–210) and other provincial laws passed under British rule had unjustly "overturned" Canadian property rights existing at the time of the British conquest of Canada; sec. 8 was designed to restore or confirm all such rights, except those of "religious orders and communities."

16. North, in discussing the bill, told the House of Commons that it was intended "the majority [of the Council] shall be Protestants," Cavendish *Quebec Bill* 241. Twenty-two members were named by the King in instructions to Carleton Jan. 3, 1775 (S & D *Doc.* II 595), of whom "seven were Catholic Canadians, all chosen from the minor nobility and the seignioral class," Lanctot *Canada* 41. To same effect, Burt *Quebec* 191.

17. Royal instructions to Carleton of Jan. 3, directed him to grant the Council members tenure only "during Our Will and Pleasure," S & D *Doc.* II 595.

18. The provision for legislation in sections 12, 13, and 14 was supplemented by a provision of sec. 15 that "no ordinance touching religion, or by which any punishment may be inflicted greater than fine or imprisonment for three months shall be of any force or effect, until the same shall have received his Majesty's approbation."

19. No Assembly for Quebec was established until passage of the Constitutional Act of 1791 (31 Geo. III ch. 31) dividing Quebec into Upper Canada and Lower Canada, each of which was to have an assembly, S & D *Doc.* II 1031. Carleton wrote Lord Shelburne Jan. 20, 1768, that "the better Sort of Canadians fear

nothing more than popular Assemblies, which, they conceive tend only to render the People refractory and insolent," and he himself doubted the wisdom of granting "a popular Assembly . . . in a Country where all Men appear nearly upon a Level," *same* I 296.

20. Munro *Seignioral System* 52–144, 159–166, Munro *Documents, passim;* Diamond "Experiment in Feudalism" 14–29 *passim;* and Parkman *The Old Regime* 307–313 discuss the semi-feudal system of land tenure in Canada, but do not make clear what obligations of tenure in seigneurie survived at the time of the British conquest and were reestablished in 1771. However, an account of the rendering of homage to Gov. James Murray by a Canadian seignior on his inheritance of land (*same* 308–309) indicates that at least this feature of tenure in seigneurie was retained.

21. The percentage of the purchase price nominally payable as the "fine" under tenure in fief, or seigneurie, was the "quint," i.e., one-fifth; but Parkman states, *same* 312, that in practice "the greater part was deducted [i.e., remitted] for immediate payment." (Refugee loyalists from the old British colonies, granted land in Quebec after the American Revolution, petitioned the King Apr. 11, 1785, to be freed from tenure "so different from the mild Tenure to which they have ever been accustomed . . . ," *Can. Doc.* II 773–777 at 774, 777.)

22. The instructions of Dec. 7, 1763, from the Crown to Murray, Carleton's predecessor, directed him to grant Crown land in Quebec on the following terms: ten shillings (standard of currency not stated) purchase price and two shillings sterling per year quit rent for every hundred acres, S & D *Doc.* I 196, and cultivation and improvement of the land within specified years after the grant was received. (As to the terms of grants of Crown land in other colonies, Labaree *Instructions* II 458–568.)

23. Carleton to Shelburne Apr. 12, 1768, as to the old form of tenure securing "a proper subordination of the Province to Great Britain," *same* I 300. He had previously (Dec. 24, 1767) written Shelburne in similar vein, extolling the old form because "it established Subordination from the first to the lowest," *same* 281. (However, the supposition that the seigniors could dominate their tenants proved to be erroneous, Chief Justice Hey to Apsley Aug. 28, 1775, and Carleton to Lord George Germain Sept. 28, 1776, and May 9, 1777, *same* II 668–671, 675–677.)

24. Royal instruction to Carleton July 2, 1771, as to granting Crown land "in Fief and Seigneurie," *same* I 423. This instruction was confirmed by the instructions to Carleton of Jan. 3, 1775, implementing the Quebec Act, *same* II 608. The instructions contained no stipulation as to purchase price or quit rent, but made grants of Crown land in Quebec, unlike in other colonies, subject to ratification by the King, *same* I 423, II 608.

25. The Royal Proclamation of Oct. 7, 1763, established as the western boundary of Quebec a line running from the St. Lawrence at the point where the 45th degree of north latitude intersects the river (near present Cornwall, Ontario) northwestward to the south end of Lake Nipissing, reserving "for the present" the rest of former Canada for "the use of the . . . Indians," *Can. Doc.* I 164, 167.

26. The proviso in sec. 2 of the Quebec Act was designed primarily to avoid curtailing the boundaries of Pa. and N.Y., Cavendish *Quebec Bill* 188–197;

Edmund Burke to N.Y. Comm. of Corresp. May 30, 1774, *Burke* II 538–539; petition of William Baker May 31, 4 *Force* I 185; Baker to Charles Lee Sept. 3, *Lee Papers* I 32.

27. The proviso could be construed to preserve the "sea to sea" charter claims of Conn. and Mass. and the vast territory north of the Ohio claimed by Va. under its early charters, the last of which had been annulled in 1624. As to the Va. charters, the territory claimed under them and annulment of the last (third) charter, Thorpe *Charters* VII 3783–3810; Hinsdale *Old Northwest* 72–78; *Dinwiddie* I 380–381; Andrews *Col. Period* I 173–178.

28. The attacks in colonial newspapers and Sullivan's letter quoted in the text evidence the understanding in the colonies that the Quebec Act was intended to include the vast territory described in the text.

29. A similar view seems to have prevailed in Great Britain: the Solicitor-General, Alexander Wedderburn, supporting the bill for the act, said in the House of Commons, May 26, 1774, "one great advantage of the extension of territory [of Quebec]" is that this will say to inhabitants of the old British colonies "this is the border, beyond which for the advantage of the whole empire, you shall not extend yourself," Cavendish *Quebec Bill* 58.

30. Dartmouth wrote Hillsborough May 1, 1774, that "nothing can more effectually discourage" settlement in the territory to be annexed to Quebec, than such annexation, *Can. Doc.* I 554.

31. The Quebec Act's vast expansion of the territory of a province inhabited chiefly by Roman Catholics was particularly stressed in attacks on the act in colonial newspapers, Metzger *Quebec Act, passim;* Schlesinger Prelude 199; Miller *Origins* 190–191, 374–375. Though much of the clamor in the colonial newspapers against this feature of the act may have been propaganda, the owners and readers of the papers probably needed no incitement for alarm over this.

32. John Sullivan to John Langdon Sept. [actually Oct.] 5, 1774, expressing fear as to the Quebec Act, *Sullivan* I 38. Sullivan's fear was well-founded; on Sept. 4, Gage had asked Carleton "whether a Body of Canadians and Indians might be collected and confided in, for the Service of this Country should matters come to extremities," to which Carleton (who had just arrived from England) replied on Sept. 20, proposing the immediate raising of a battalion of Canadians which, he thought, would "go far to influence" the Indians, *Can. Doc.* II 583–584.

33. Richard Henry Lee's denunciation of the act on the floor of Congress, Oct. 17, 1774, James Duane's notes of debates, Burnett *Letters* I 78. Patrick Henry also assailed the act (Oct. 14) as one of "the capital" colonial grievances, *same* 75.

34. Reed to Dartmouth Sept. 25, 1774, as to the effect of the Quebec Act in preparing the people to support "any plan the Congress advise, should it be war itself," Reed *Reed* I 78.

35. Carleton, who was in England in 1773 and 1774 when the bill was being drafted (sketch of Carleton in *D.N.B.*), was in touch with Dartmouth through Knox, if not directly, concerning the bill (Knox to Dartmouth Apr. 30, 1774, *Can. Doc.* I 553); and spoke strongly in its favor in hearings in the House of Commons, June 2 and 3, Cavendish *Quebec Bill* 100–120 and *Parl. Hist.* XVII 1367–70.

36. Carleton to Gage Feb. 15, 1767, and to Hillsborough Nov. 20, 1768, as to the Canadians quoted in the text, S & D *Doc.* I 280. Carleton wrote Lord George Germain, Dartmouth's successor, after the outbreak of the American war (Sept. 28, 1776), "I have given my opinion so amply on . . . how much the Canadians may be depended upon, and under what circumstances they may be usefull, in former letters . . . that I must beg leave to refer you to them . . . [as showing] I had a war of this sort constantly in view . . .," *Can. Doc.* II 675–676.

37. Knox's collaboration with Dartmouth on the Quebec bill is indicated by a letter from him to Dartmouth Apr. 30, 1774, giving Carleton's objections to the initial draft of the bill; and by Dartmouth to Hillsborough May 1, 1774, as to a talk by him, Dartmouth, with Knox concerning Hillsborough's objections to the bill, *same* I 553, 554.

38. Statements as to possible use of Canadians against the old colonies in pamphlets of Knox, Martin *Empire* 109–110. Other pamphlets published in England in 1774, cited and quoted by Martin (109–110), contain similar statements.

39. Lord Lyttelton's statement in the House of Lords June 17, 1774, concerning the Quebec bill, quoted in the text, *Parl. Hist.* XVII 1406.

40. The bill for the Quebec Revenue Act, 14 Geo. III ch. 88, was introduced in the House of Commons June 1, 1774, after preliminary consideration of raising a revenue in Quebec. It passed the Commons June 10; was concurred in by the House of Lords June 14; and was assented to by the King June 22, *Journals H. of C.* XXXIV 785, 791–792, 807, 810, 817, 820.

41. Sec. 1 of the Quebec Revenue Act levied the discriminatory import duties on brandy, rum, spirits, molasses, and other syrups described in the text. (In addition, sec. 5 levied a license tax on innkeepers and retailers of liquor and wine; and sec. 6 continued the "territorial or casual revenues, fines, rents or profits" payable to the King of France before the conquest.)

42. The provision as to entry for customs is in sec. 3 of the Quebec Revenue Act. As to the threat to the Indian trade of the old colonies by this section, Ebenezer Hazard to Silas Deane Feb. 25, 1775, *N.Y. Hist. Soc. Coll.* (1890) 538; protest of N.Y. Assembly March 3, 1775, 4 *Force* I 1300.

43. The act was amended May 26, 1775 (*Journals H. of L.* XXXIV 481) by 15 Geo. III ch. 40, exempting the part of Quebec added to the province by the Quebec Act from the duty on rum, brandy, and other spirits.

CHAPTER 20

1. News of the Boston Port Act reached Boston May 10, 1774, diary of John Rowe, May 10, *Rowe* 269.

2. Resolution as to non-importation and non-exportation adopted at a Boston town meeting May 13, 1774, to be sent by the moderator of the meeting, Samuel Adams, with a covering letter, to other colonies and to towns throughout Mass., *Boston Records* (for 1770–1777) 174. The town also passed a resolution requesting its Committee of Correspondence to send the other colonies "the Letters etc. they have wrote relative to shutting up this Harbour etc.," *same*. The letters dated May 13 sent in accordance with these resolutions, are in Cushing *S. Adams* III 107–111.

3. Adams reported to a Boston town meeting May 18, 1774, that "agreeable to the Order of the Town, he had enclosed an attested Copy of Town Votes in Letters to the several Provinces by Mr. Reviere who set out last Saturday [May 14]," *Boston Town Records* (for 1770–1777) 175. As to Paul Revere's activities in the North End Caucus and as messenger for Boston and Mass. from May, 1774, to his famous ride to Lexington on the night of April 18, 1775, Goss *Revere* I 115–199, II 637–641.

4. Resolution of the town of Providence, R.I., May 17, 1774, requesting its representatives in the R.I. General Assembly to promote "a Congress . . . of the several Colonies and Provinces in North America," 4 *Force* I 333.

5. An intercolonial congress similar to the Stamp Act Congress of 1765 had been frequently proposed during the past year, Frothingham *Rise of the Republic* 314, 329, 331–333n.; Benjamin Franklin to Thomas Cushing July 7, 1773, Smyth *Franklin* VI 82–83; "Observations" in *Boston Gazette* Sept. 27, 1773; Wells *Adams* II 90; "Union" in *Boston Gazette* Dec. 27, 1773; John Hancock's oration March 5, 1774, *Orations on the Boston Massacre* 51; Arthur Lee to Francis L. Lee Apr. 2, 1774, Lee *Arthur Lee* I 39.

6. Descriptions of the Philadelphia mass meeting of May 20, Thomas Mifflin to Samuel Adams May 21, 1774, S. Adams Papers, N.Y. Pub. Lib., and Edward Tilghman, Jr., to Edward Tilghman, Sr., May 26, Stillé *Dickinson* 106–107. (Description based on much later accounts, Jacobson *Dickinson* 72–74.) The resolutions of the mass meeting, directing the committee chosen there to ask the Governor of Pa. to summon a meeting of the Pa. Assembly, and authorizing the committee to call another "meeting of the Inhabitants when necessary," Smith *Smith* I 492.

7. Philadelphia Committee to Boston Committee May 21, 1774, quoted in the text, 4 *Force* I 341–342.

8. Nomination and election of the N.Y. Committee of Fifty-One, May 16 and 19, 1774, *same* 293–295. A letter (date not given) from Jonathan Blake, signed as chairman of "the body of Mechanics," a body discussed in the second appendix to this chapter, reported that it concurred in this choice of members for the Committee, *same* 295. The meeting of May 19 is described in an oft-quoted letter of Gouverneur Morris to Mr. [John] Penn, May 20, *same* 342–343; Jensen *Hist. Doc.* 860–863.

9. Letter of New York Committee of Correspondence signed by its Chairman, Isaac Low, to Boston Committee May 23, 1774, quoted in the text, rejecting the Boston proposal for an immediate non-importation and non-exportation agreement, 4 *Force* I 297–298.

10. Resolution of the Va. House of Burgesses May 24, 1774, for "a day of Fasting, Humiliation and Prayer," *Va. Journals* (for 1773–1776) 124. George Mason wrote Martin Cockburn May 26 that resolves of the House "intended for the preservation of our rights and liberties" were "proposed with a great deal of privacy, and by very few members, of whom Patrick Henry is the principal," Rowland *Mason* I 169, and, years later, Thomas Jefferson wrote that he, Patrick Henry, Richard Henry Lee, and a few other members had "cooked up" the resolution of May 24, Boyd *Jefferson* I 106n.

11. Gov. Lord Dunmore of Va. dissolved the House May 26, 1774, because its resolutions "reflect highly upon his Majesty and the Parliament of Great Britain," *Va. Journals* (for 1773–1776) 132.

12. I suppose saltpeter was exempted from the proposed ban on importation because it was an essential ingredient of gunpowder, and spices because they were considered so important (in days before refrigeration) in preserving food-stuffs or at least in making high meats palatable. (An order of Washington to England in 1772 included four pounds each of white ginger, mace, nutmegs, cinammon, and cloves, *Washington* III 91.)

13. Resolutions of meeting of May 27, quoted in the text, *Va. Journals* (1773–1776) xiii–xiv. Washington wrote George William Fairfax June 10, 1774, that the day after Dunmore dissolved the House, "the Members convened themselves at the Raleigh Tavern and entered into the Inclosed Association [resolutions]," *same* III 223. The Va. Comm. of Corresp. promptly sent out the circular letter to other colonial Committees as resolved upon at the meeting. There is a copy of it, dated May 28, in *Pa. Assembly* VIII 7091.

14. The facts as to arrival of the letter from Boston, the names of the twenty-five members of the Va. House present at the emergency meeting, and their resolutions are in a circular letter of May 31, 1774, from these members to their fellow members, Hamilton *Letters of Washington* III 354–356.

15. The names of the sixty-one Va. counties, each having two representatives (plus three boroughs and the College of William and Mary, each having one) and of the members of the House in 1774 are in *Va. Journals* (for 1773–1776) 67–68. The names of the 108 delegates to the Va. convention are in Niles *Principles* 274–275. Washington wrote Thomas Johnson of Md. Aug. 5, 1774, "We never had so full a Meeting of delegates at any one Time, as upon the present Occasion," i.e., so many members of the House of Burgesses attending at any one time, *Washington* III 236.

16. Resolutions of thirty Va. county conventions (June and July, 1774) are in 4 *Force* IV 388–643 *passim,* and those of one other (Isle of Wight) are in *Va. Gazette* (Rind) of July 28. These are analyzed in Schlesinger *Col. Merchants* 365–367 and Freeman *Washington* III 360–361. (Freeman's statement that Dinwiddie, as well as Middlesex County, opposed "any stern action" is not borne out by the *Dinwiddie* resolutions, 4 *Force* I 552–553.)

17. Fairfax County resolutions of July 18, 1774, quoted in the text, 4 *Force* I 597–602. These resolutions have been attributed to George Mason on the strength of evidence discussed in Rowland *Mason* I 172, 427, and *Mason* (Rutland) I 199–200, 209–210. However, two weeks earlier, in a letter of July 4 to Bryan Fairfax, Washington had expressed sentiments similar to those of the Fairfax resolutions, *Washington* III 228–229.

18. Westmoreland County's spirited resolutions of June 22, 1774, quoted in the text, 4 *Force* I 437–438. Richard Henry Lee was one of the county's two delegates to the Va. convention of Aug. 1–6, *same* 438. Similarly spirited resolutions of Albemarle County, probably drafted by Thomas Jefferson, are in Boyd *Jefferson* I 117–118, 118–119n.

19. Resolution of Conn. House of Representatives June 3, 1774, authorizing the Conn. Committee of Correspondence to appoint delegates to a proposed inter-colonial congress, *Journals Cont. Cong.* I 17–18.

20. R.I. General Assembly's resolution of June 15, 1774, appointing delegates to a proposed intercolonial congress, 4 *Force* I 416–417.

21. A letter of May 31, 1774, from Samuel Adams to Silas Deane discloses that Adams had hoped to secure earlier action by the Mass. House. His letter states, "Our Assembly was unexpectedly adjourned on Saturday last [May 28] . . . by which means I am prevented mentioning a Congress to the Members . . .," Cushing *S. Adams* III 126.

22. Resolution of Mass. House June 17, 1774, proposing an intercolonial conference at Philadelphia Sept. 1, and electing delegates to it, 4 *Force* I 421. The New York City Committee of Fifty-One had written to the Boston Comm. of Corresp. June 7, 1774, inviting the latter to designate a time and place for the proposed intercolonial congress, *same* I 303–304.

23. Copies of the Mass. circular letter of June 17, 1774, sent out by Thomas Cushing as Speaker of the Mass. House, to Speakers of the Assemblies of N.H., R.I., Conn., N.Y., N.J., Pa., Del., Md., Va., N.C., S.C., and Ga. Nova Scotia and West Fla. had Assemblies, but I have found no evidence that copies of the letter were sent to their Speakers. Quebec and East Fla. had no Assemblies. Copies of the letter are in *Va. Journals* (for 1773–1776) 156 and *Pa. Assembly* VIII 7088–7089.

24. Cushing had represented Boston in the House continuously since 1761, and had been its Speaker continuously since 1766, when Gov. Francis Bernard had accepted him as Speaker after rejecting James Otis, Jr. Cushing was then and, with occasional fluctuations, continued to be one of the more moderate of the Boston Whig leaders. No biography of him has been published; but there is a brief sketch of him in *D.A.B.* and a better, more detailed, one in Shipton *Harvard Graduates* XI 377–395.

25. John Adams' principal law office was in Boston, and he was one of the Boston representatives in the House in 1770–1771. But he resided most of the time in Braintree, a town in Suffolk County (of which Boston was the county seat), about twelve miles south of Boston. Thanks to exceptional ability and hard work he was by this time, at the age of thirty-eight, one of the outstanding lawyers of New England.

26. James Bowdoin, former member of the Mass. Council (Wallett "Bowdoin" 320–328 and "Mass. Council" 609–622), declined to serve as a delegate because of the serious illness of his wife, Bowdoin to Benjamin Franklin Sept. 6, 1774, Frothingham "Tea Party" 153–154.

27. Samuel Adams was graduated from Harvard in 1740, Cushing in 1744, Bowdoin in 1745, Robert Treat Paine in 1749, and John Adams in 1755, *Harvard Quinquennial Catalogue* 1214, 1235, 1264, 1380. There are interesting biographical sketches of all of them in Shipton *Harvard Graduates* XI, XII, XIII. All but John Adams, as sons of locally distinguished fathers, stood high in the class listings; John Adams was listed fourteenth in a class of twenty-five.

28. The fact that a body composed chiefly of representatives of farming communities in central and western Mass. chose a group consisting exclusively of non-farmers from the seacoast is interesting as indicating great solidarity of sentiment throughout the colony on issues likely to come before the projected congress; otherwise, representatives from outside the Boston area presumably would have demanded and secured a representative or representatives of their own.

29. Action of the Md. convention held at Annapolis, June 22–25, 1774, 4 *Force* I 438–440; Schlesinger *Col. Merchants* 361–362. The convention had been initiated by resolutions of a county mass meeting at Baltimore, May 31, 4 *Force* I 367.

30. Proceedings of the Va. convention of Aug. 1–6, 1774, *same* I 686–690. The names of the delegates from Va. and those from other colonies mentioned later in this chapter are in *Journals Cont. Cong.* I 13–14, 19, 21, 22, 30, 31, 53. The apparent consensus in Virginia for spirited measures and possible reasons for this are discussed in the second appendix to the Introduction.

31. Methods of electing delegates from the several colonies, *same* 15–24, 30.

32. Election of the Conn. delegates, *same* 17–19; Zeichner *Conn.* 165–166, 322.

33. Choice of delegates for S.C. at a mass meeting in Charleston July 6 and 8, 1774, and confirmation by the S.C. Commons House (Assembly) Aug. 2, 4 *Force* I 525–527, 671. The committee chosen at the mass meeting was composed of thirty members representing Charleston and sixty-nine representing the parishes of the colony outside Charleston.

34. The movement in Ga. from July 14 to Sept. 2, 1774, to cooperate with the other colonies and the failure to send delegates to the Continental Congress are described in *same* I 549, 633–634, 638–639, 766–767; Coleman *Ga.* 40–44, 293–294; and Schlesinger *Col. Merchants* 379–386.

35. The estimate of expense for 1773–1774 for the civil officers of Ga., submitted to the House of Commons Feb. 25, 1774, was £3.086, *Journals H. of C.* IV 501.

36. Georgia, youngest of the thirteen colonies that rebelled, had been founded only in 1732, and had a white population, widely scattered, of probably under 40,000 in 1774. War with the Creek Indians broke out in Dec., 1773, and was not finally ended until Oct. 20, 1774, Alden *Stuart* 306–311. Coleman *Ga.* 1–38 and Abbott *Governors of Ga.* 3–165 outline developments in Ga. 1754–1774.

37. The best-known of the delegates listed in the paragraph of the text to which this footnote relates was William Livingston (later the first Governor of the state of New Jersey), who, before moving from New York had been well known there and elsewhere for his political writings; see Klein *Independent Reflector*, Dillon *New York Triumverate;* the biographical sketch of him in *D.A.B.* and *Livingston* (Sedgwick) *passim.*

38. John Hancock was unique in being both a representative of Boston in the Mass. House and one of the town's selectmen, in which latter capacity, at this critical juncture in the town's affairs, he was vitally needed at home. His recent reelection as selectman and representative, with the largest vote of any of the four chosen, and his election in Oct., 1774, as President of the Mass. Provincial Congress attest his outstanding popularity.

39. John Dickinson was elected a member for Philadelphia County to the Pa. Assembly which convened Oct. 14, 1774, *Pa. Assembly* VIII 7148. The next day the Assembly added him to the Pa. delegation, *same* 7152.

40. John Adams' diary entry for Aug. 31, 1774, describing Dickinson as frail but apparently with strong "Springs of Life," is an *Adams Papers* II 117. Dickin-

son lived until Feb. 14, 1808, Stillé *Dickinson* 336. Dickinson took his seat in the Congress Oct. 17, 1774, *Journals Cont. Cong.* I 74.

41. Cushing of Mass., Galloway of Pa., Tilghman of Md., Rodney of Del., Randolph of Va., and Caswell of N.C. were currently Speaker of their respective colonial Assemblies; Hopkins of R.I., Philip Livingston of N.Y., and Middleton of S.C. of earlier Assemblies.

42. My statement concerning the delegates' membership in the provincial assemblies is based on biographical sketches of them in *D.A.B.* and published records of the Assemblies of the several colonies represented at the Congress.

43. All three of the N.C. delegates were natives of other colonies, Richard Caswell of Md., Joseph Hewes of N.J., and William Hooper of Mass., and William Livingston, a N.J. delegate, as mentioned earlier, was a native and long a resident of N.Y.

44. John Adams to Abigail Adams Sept. 16, 1774, speaks of Episcopalian (Church of England), Quaker, Anabaptist, Presbyterian, and Congregationalist delegates, Burnett *Letters* I 32, and Philip Livingston was a member of the Dutch Reformed Church. Though there were many members of the Lutheran and Catholic churches, particularly in the middle colonies, none of the delegates in 1774, so far as I know, was a member of either of these churches. Charles Carrollton of Md. (Catholic) and Frederick A. C. Muhlenberg (Lutheran) were members of the Second Continental Congress, but not of the First.

45. The delegates to the Albany and Stamp Act Congresses are listed respectively in Gipson *Brit. Empire* V 114n., VI 329–330.

46. The statement concerning the delegates is based on sketches of them in *D.A.B.* and references to them in a wide range of other sources, chiefly local histories of their home communities.

47. The collection in 1769 of a fund to enable Samuel Adams to make a settlement with the town of Boston of a claim against him as collector of taxes is described in the fourth appendix to this chapter. The gifts in 1774 of a new wig, suit, shoes, silk stockings, and a sum of money to enable him to make a proper appearance as a delegate from Massachusetts to the First Continental Congress is described in a well-known letter (August 11, 1774) from John Andrews of Boston to his brother-in-law, William Barrel of Philadelphia, "Andrews Letters" 340.

48. Samuel Adams' finances and the charge that he embezzled public funds are discussed in the fourth appendix to this chapter.

49. Adams' writings for newspapers from 1764 to 1774 and as head of the Boston Committee of Correspondence from 1772 to 1774 are in Cushing *Adams* I, II, III *passim* and the papers of the Committee at the N.Y. Pub. Lib. Carey *Warren* 60–145 brings out that Joseph Warren should be given chief credit for some of the writings generally attributed to Adams. Dickinson, William Livingston, John Adams, and Lee had often written against various measures of the British government or Crown-appointed colonial Governors, but, so far as is known, not so continuously as Adams.

50. Resolutions or instructions for the delegates, 4 *Force* I 315–317 (N.Y.); 355–357 (Conn.); 416–417 (R.I.); 421–422 (Mass.); 439–440 (Md.); 525–527, 671 (S.C.); 608–609 (Pa.); 624–625 (N.J.); 667–668 (Del.); 686–690 (Va.); and 733–737 (N.C.).

The N.H. resolutions are in *Journals Cont. Cong.* I 15. (Passage of the Quebec Act was not yet known in the colonies when the instructions to demand repeal of the acts described in the text were given.)

CHAPTER 21

1. Bryan Fairfax to George Washington July 3 and 17 and Aug. 5, 1774, urging that the forthcoming Continental Congress confine itself to petitioning for redress of grievances, Hamilton *Letters to Washington* V 19–24, 34–44.

2. Washington to Fairfax July 20 and Aug. 24, 1774, quoted in the text, giving his reasons for favoring more drastic action by the Congress than mere petitioning, *Washington* III 231–232, 242.

3. Stephen Hopkins' statement concerning the grave danger to the colonies of Parliament's claim of right to tax the colonies, quoted in the text, is in *Rights of Colonies* (1764) 16–17; Bailyn *Pamphlets* I 517.

4. Evidence of the profligacy of the British government in the allowance of extravagant salaries and fees to British officials and in granting costly sinecures and pensions is given in Knollenberg *Origin* 269–274, 392–395. Probably few, if any, of the colonists had a full conception of the enormity of the waste; but, as shown in the statements in the text and in the documents cited in note 5 below, they had at least an inkling.

5. James Otis in *Considerations* (1765) 115 and Charles Carroll of Carrollton (the younger) to Henry Graves Sept. 15, 1765, *Carroll Letters* 90, concerning British wastage of public revenue, quoted in the text. Other similar statements by eminent colonists are quoted in Knollenberg *Origin* 191–192, 249. The passage quoted in *same* 249 from a letter of Benjamin Franklin to Joseph Galloway, Feb. 5, 1775 (Smyth *Franklin* VI 311–312) is particularly striking.

6. Charles Townshend's statements to the House of Commons Jan. 26 and 28, 1767, quoted in the text, Charles Garth, London Agent for S.C. and a member of Parliament, to the S.C. Committee of Correspondence, Jan. 31, *So. Car. Hist. Mag.* XIX (1928) 132 and entry in diary of Sir Roger Newdigate, member of Parliament, Jan. 26, quoted in Chaffin "Townshend Acts" 99.

7. The act of 7 Geo. III ch. 14 reduced the land tax from four shillings in the pound (20%) levied for many years, most recently by 6 Geo. III ch. 9 (1766), to three shillings in the pound (15%).

8. Citations for the Acts of 1660 and 1663 and the other restrictive acts described in later paragraphs of this chapter are given in Knollenberg *Origin* 352–354. Even salt could be legally imported directly from continental Europe under the Act of 1663 and amendments, only into colonies north of Maryland, *same* 169, 183, 216, 352, 371.

9. The Act of 1696 restricting colonial exports to Ireland, referred to in the text, prohibited the export of any colonial products to Ireland. This act was amended in 1731 and later to prohibit only the export of colonial enumerated products to Ireland, Harper *Navigation Laws* 397 n.35.

10. Parliament's restrictions on the export of colonial raw products were partly compensated by British tariff preferences and bounties on a number of British

colonial products imported into Great Britain, Dickerson *Navigation Acts* 12–15, 25–28; and pages cited in index under "Bounties," in Knollenberg *Origin* 457.

11. The Act of 1766, 6 Geo. III ch. 52 secs. 30 and 31 (1766) prohibited the export of all colonial non-enumerated products to any part of Europe north of "the ports of Spain within the bay of Biscay"; but this act was amended in 1767 to permit the exportation of non-enumerated products to Ireland, 7 Geo. III ch. 2. Earlier acts had, as previously noted, restricted the exportation of colonial *enumerated* products.

12. The repeated election of John Wilkes as member for Middlesex County, his expulsion from the House of Commons, and the movement in England for political reform, Rudé *Wilkes and Liberty* 59–72, 105–148 and sources cited therein. As brought out in *same* 21–35 and Knollenberg *Origin* 31–41, 293–296, Wilkes had earlier greatly offended the King, who now vigorously supported his expulsion, evidenced by his correspondence with Lord Hertford in Jan., 1769, *Geo. III* II 73–75.

13. The widespread knowledge in the colonies of the Wilkes affairs and the movement in England for political reform, Maier *Resistance* 163–169 and sources cited therein.

14. Lord North's support of Wilkes' expulsion from the House of Commons, the King to North Jan. 28, 1769, expressing his pleasure over the large majority in the House of Commons voting to expel Wilkes and attributing this "principaly to the ability shewn by You in planning the Measure & in the Execution of it . . .," *Geo. III* II 76.

15. North's speech in the House of Commons Jan. 28, 1770, in support of retaining the duty on tea to maintain "that just right, which I shall ever wish the mother country to possess, the right of taxing the Americans," *Parl. Hist.* XVI 854.

16. The ideological background: Rossiter *Seedtime;* Robbins *Eighteenth-Century Commonwealthman;* Colbourn *Lamp of Experience;* and articles by them cited in Gipson *Guide* under "Rossiter," "Robbins," and "Colbourn"; and, most extensively, Bailyn "Political Experience," *Pamphlets* I *passim, Ideological Origins,* and *Origins of American Politics.* There is an admirable synthesis of all these writings and those cited in note 17 below, in Shalhope "Toward a Republican Synthesis" 51–72.

17. The other writings referred to in the text include Cook *Literary Influences;* Mullett "Classical Influences" 92–104; Green "Flight from Determinism"; Buel "Democracy" 165–190; Saville *Seeds of Liberty* 282–427; Handlin "Burgh" 38–57; Pocock *The Ancient Constitution;* and articles cited in Gipson *Guide* under "Pocock"; and Wood *Creation of the American Republic* 3–45 and "Rhetoric" 3–32.

18. Adams *Bibliography* 1–115 describes over a hundred political pamphlets published from 1764 to Sept., 1774, of which eleven (published in 1764 and 1765) are reprinted with valuable comments in Bailyn *Pamphlets* I 292–691, 760–748. Dulany *Considerations* (1765), Dickinson *Farmer's Letters* (1768), Allen *Beauties of Liberty* (1773), and Hancock *Oration* (1774) were printed in several colonies. Also, Shipley *Sermon* (1773) and *Speech* (1774) and Robinson-Morris *Considerations* (1774), pro-colonial pamphlets by Englishmen and first published in London, were reprinted in several of the colonies.

19. *Newspapers:* Schlesinger *Prelude* 51–296; "Col. Newspapers" 63–83; "Politics" 309–322; and "Propaganda" 396–416; Davidson *Propaganda* 225–245; Rossiter *Seedtime* 329–330, 433–455, 520. *Sermons:* Baldwin *New England Clergy, passim* and Rossiter *Seedtime* 140, 328–329, 491, 519–520 and sources cited by him. *Almanacs: same* 129, 300, 488 n.57.

20. The influence of Addison's *Cato* is discussed in Litto "Addison's *Cato* in the Colonies" 442–447.

21. The influence of patriotic songs is discussed in Schlesinger "Songs" 77–88. The words of the most widely popular of these, John Dickinson's "The Liberty Song," are given in Ford *Dickinson* 425.

22. Washington, for example, wrote Fairfax July 20, 1774, "The stopping our exports would, no doubt be a shorter cut than the other [non-importation] to effect this purpose [putting commercial pressure on Great Britain]; but if we owe money to Great Britain, nothing but the last necessity can justify the non-payment of it; and . . ., therefore, I . . . wish to see the other method tried first . . .," *Washington* III 234.

23. The petitions of the colonial Assemblies or both the Assembly and provincial Council in 1764–1765 referred to in the text as recognizing the authority of Parliament to regulate colonial trade are discussed and cited in Knollenberg *Origin* 199–220, 364–373.

24. The members of the Va. House of Burgesses in 1764 are listed in *Va. Journals* (for 1761–1765) 201–202. The names of the members of the committee to draw the "memorial" (later termed "remonstrance") to the House of Commons are in *same* 257; the document, adopted Dec. 18, 1764, is in *same* 303–304. Peyton Randolph is the "Mr. Attorney" referred to in the list of members of the drafting committee.

25. Stephen Hopkins in his *Rights of Colonies* (1764) 22, wrote, "The Parliament, it is confessed, have power to regulate the trade of the whole empire," Bailyn *Pamphlets* I 506–530 at 521. Thomas Cushing wrote Dennys De Berdt Oct. 15, 1767, that "they [the colonists] . . . Acknowledge the Right of the British Parliament to regulate their Trade . . .," Arthur Lee Papers (Harv. Lib.).

26. Samuel Adams, writing as "Valerius Poplicola" in the *Boston Gazette* of Oct. 28, 1771, denied the authority of Parliament to legislate in any way concerning Mass., Wells *Adams* I 430.

27. The Fairfax County Resolves quoted in the text were adopted at a meeting on July 18, 1774. The resolves and the record of Washington's chairmanship of the meeting, 4 *Force* I 597. Washington's friend, Bryan Fairfax, saw a draft of the proposed resolutions, based on the ground that "The Parliament from Prescription have a Right to make Laws binding on the Colonies, except those imposing Taxes," Fairfax to Washington, July 17, 1774, Hamilton *Letters to Washington* V 29.

28. John Adams' diary for Aug. 17, 1774, records that Roger Sherman had told him he "thought the Reverse of the declaratory Act was true, vizt. that the Parliament of G.B. had Authority to make Laws for America in no Case whatever," *Adams Papers* II 100. To same effect, Sherman to Cushing Apr. 20, 1772, Boardman *Sherman* 17. Adams did not record his own view; but later, in his "Novanglus Letters" published early in 1775, he stated that "all the Colonies" conceded

the authority of Parliament "to regulate their trade, *Novanglus* 26, 33, 39, 78, 79, 89, 90, 101, 102, 124.

CHAPTER 22

1. John Andrews of Boston wrote William Barrell of Philadelphia Aug. 10, 1774, of the delegates setting out in "coach and four, preceded by two white servants well mounted and armed, with four blacks between in livery, two on horseback and two footmen," "Andrews Letters" 339. How far this retinue accompanied the delegates is unknown.

2. The itinerary from Boston to New Haven, Conn., is known from Paine's diary from Aug. 10–15, 1774, in M.H.S., quoted in part in *Adams Papers* II 97–98n. and Adams' (meaning John Adams') diary for Aug. 10, 15, and 16, *same* 97–100. The delegates stopped over for the night at Framingham, Spencer, and Springfield in Mass., and Hartford (two nights) and Middletown in Conn.

3. The statements concerning Deane's entertainment and John Adams' impression of Sherman, and the quotations and statements in this and the next two paragraphs are from, or based on, Adams' diary for Aug. 15–29, 1774, *same* 99–114, 115n.

4. The diary of Ward of R.I. for Aug. 30 to Sept. 1, 1774, records his arrival on Aug. 30 and the arrival of Hopkins of R.I. and the Conn. delegates on Aug. 31, Burnett *Letters* I 5. The *Pa. Gazette* of Aug. 17 and 24 reported the arrival of vessels from Charleston, S.C., the first carrying Middleton and Edward Rutledge, the second, Lynch, John Rutledge, and Gadsden. The journey of the Conn. delegates is described in letters of Aug. 29 and Sept. 6 from Deane to his wife, *Deane Papers* I 5–11.

5. The arrival of the N.J. delegates and two from N.Y. Sept. 1, 1774, is noted in Ward's diary of that date, Burnett *Letters* I 5.

6. The Mass. House of Representatives, as mentioned in Chapter 20, proposed Sept. 1, 1774, as the date for the Congress to open, and this date proved acceptable to several of the colonies. But S.C., Del., and Va. named the first Monday in Sept. (Sept. 5) and Md. and N.C., Sept. 20, as the date for their delegates to assemble in Philadelphia, 4 *Force* I 440, 525, 667, 689, 735. Washington wrote Johnson of Md. on Aug. 5 of the decision of S.C. and Va., *Washington* III 235, and most of the Md. delegates were on hand by Sept. 5, Burnett *Letters* I xlv–xlvii.

7. Randolph, Lee, Harrison, and Bland arrived Sept. 2, 1774, Adams' and Samuel Ward's diaries for Sept. 2, *same* 2, 5; also Chitwood *Lee* 61, 254.

8. Description of Lee's supping with the Mass. delegates, Adams diary for Sept. 2 and 3, 1774, Burnett *Letters* I 2–3.

9. Journey of Washington, Henry, and Pendleton, Washington's diary entries, Aug. 31 to Sept. 4, 1774, Washington *Diaries* II 162. Chitwood *Lee* 60 says they traveled "on horseback," and I think this statement probably is true, but I have found no evidence to support it.

10. All or most of the delegates from every colony represented at the Congress had arrived by September 4, 1774, Burnett *Letters* xli–lxvi. Hooper and Hewes of N.C. took their seats in the Congress on Sept. 14, Caswell, the third delegate

from N.C., on Sept. 17, *Journals Cont. Cong.* I 30–31. They could hardly have arrived much sooner, since they had been elected as late as Aug. 27, 4 *Force* I 735.

11. Opening entry in the records of the First Continental Congress Sept. 5, 1774, *Journals Cont. Cong.* I 13.

12. Deane to his wife Sept. 5 and 10, Burnett *Letters* I 2, 11, 28–29. As to "Col. Fitch" and the probable meaning of "hard" as used by Deane, Knollenberg *Washington* 190.

13. Description of Lee in Adams' diary for Sept. 2 and 3, 1774, Burnett *Letters* I 2.

14. Caesar Rodney to Thomas Rodney Sept. 9, 1774, describing "the Bostonians" as "moderate" compared with those of Va., S.C., and R.I., *same* 27. Gov. Cadwallader Colden of N.Y. to Lord Dartmouth Dec. 7, states (quoting Galloway and Duane) that "the Delegates from Virginia were the most violent of any— Those of Maryland and some of the Carolinians were little less so," *Colden* 1877 374. Lee and Henry of Va., Gadsden and Lynch of S.C., and Ward of R.I. were outstandingly radical, but not, I think, the other delegates from those colonies or any of the Md. delegates.

15. Deane to his wife Sept. 7, 1774, stating that Gadsden "leaves all New England Sons of Liberty far behind, for he is for taking up his firelock and marching direct to Boston," Burnett *Letters* I 18.

16. The only reference to Washington's speaking in Congress is in a letter from Deane to his wife Sept. 10, 1774, stating, "Col. Washington . . . speaks very modestly and in cool but determined style and accent," *same* 28. But even this may refer to reports as to Washington speaking in the Va. House of Burgesses as to which Deane had referred earlier in his letter.

17. Washington's speech in the Va. convention as to raising, equipping, and leading to Boston an army of a thousand men, Adams' diary for Aug. 31, 1774, *same* 2. Deane gives a similar report to his wife in the letter of Sept. 10, referred to in note 16 above, but, according to Deane's version, the speech was made in the Va. House of Burgesses, *same* 28.

18. Deane to his wife Aug. 10, 1774, as to Washington's having saved the remnant of Braddock's army, *same* 28.

19. I have found no evidence other than the reports of Deane and Adams of Washington's supposed speech or of his having saved Braddock's army, though he certainly played a gallant part in the disaster to that army, Knollenberg *Washington* 33–34, 154.

20. The descriptions of members are from Adams' diary Aug. 31 to Sept. 3, and Oct. 24, 1774, and Deane to his wife Sept. 7, Burnett *Letters* I 1, 2, 4, 18, 81.

21. In 1817, John Adams described himself as looking, when taking notes of a speech of Otis in 1761, "like a short, thick, fat archbishop of Canterbury, seated at the table with a pen in his hand . . . now and then minuting . . . notes," Adams *Works* X 245–246, and Benjamin Blythe's portrait of him in 1766 and many portraits in later life, collected in Oliver *Portraits of John and Abigail Adams,* bear out this description. Also a letter of Abigail Adams to her sister, Mrs. Mary Smith Cranch, in 1766, speaks of him as "very fat," *Adams Family Corresp.* I 156.

22. The resolution for secrecy Sept. 6, 1774, *Journals Cont. Cong.* I 26. Such a resolution was, of course, essential, since otherwise the members would hardly dare speak freely for fear of prosecution for treason.

23. Galloway's offer of the Pa. Assembly room at the Pa. State House for the sessions of the Congress and the desire of "a very few . . . chiefly from Pennsylvania and New York" to accept the offer, Deane to his wife Sept. 1–3, 1774; Adams' diary for Sept. 5, Duane's Notes of Sept. 5, Galloway to Gov. William Franklin Sept. 5, Burnett *Letters* I 4–9. The Second Continental Congress sat in this room, now known as Independence Hall because the Declaration of Independence was adopted there.

24. Offer of the Carpenters' Hall which Deane says was made by the city of Philadelphia, and Duane says by the carpenters themselves, Deane to his wife Sept. 1–3, 1774, Duane's notes of Sept. 5, *same* 4, 8. As to Lynch making the proposal to accept the offer, *same* 8.

25. Choice of the Carpenters' Hall by a large majority, Adams' diary for Sept. 5, 1774, *same* 6–7.

26. The "excellent library" referred to by Adams belonged to the Library Company of Philadelphia, *Journals Cont. Cong.* I 27. In 1774 the meeting room was less than half the size of the chamber now shown as the place of meeting; the room has been enlarged since 1774 by tearing out partitions, Plan on exhibition at Carpenters' Hall, Philadelphia, of the room as it was in 1774 and description in Peterson "Historic Philadelphia" 98–128.

27. "This Charles Thompson [Thomson] is the Sam. Adams of Phyladelphia— the Life of the Cause of Liberty, they say," Adams' diary Aug. 30, 1774, *Adams Papers* II 115. As to Thomson, Philadelphia merchant and former school teacher, Zimmerman "Thomson" 467–480. In Oct., 1774, he was elected one of Philadelphia City's representatives in the Pa. Assembly, John Adams to his wife Oct. 7, Adams *Family Corresp.* I 165.

28. Deane to his wife Sept. 3 and 5, 1774, as to rejecting offer of the State House and Galloway's having prevented inclusion of Thomson in the Pa. delegation, Burnett *Letters* I 4–5, 11. Galloway wrote William Franklin Sept. 5 that the choice of the Carpenters' Hall had been "privately settled" in advance by Mass., Va., and S.C. delegates, *same* 9, and an entry in Adams' diary as early as Aug. 30 stating, with apparent assurance, that the Congress was to sit in the Carpenters' Hall tends to support Galloway's suspicion, *Adams Papers* II 115.

29. Duane's "Notes" of Sept. 5, 1774, state, "A Question was then put what Title the Convention shall assume & it was agreed that it should be called *the Congress;* another Question was put what should be the Stile of Mr. Randolph, & it was agreed that he should be called the [without italics] *President,*" Duane Papers, N.Y. Hist. Soc.

30. Duane's "Notes" quoted in note 29 above; Caesar to Thomas Rodney Sept. 9, 1774, Burnett *Letters* I 27; and an entry in the Congress journals of Oct. 22, *Journals Cont. Cong.* I 102 indicate that the official title was "President," not "the President." But the journals of the Congress repeatedly refer to Randolph as "the President," e.g., *same* 29, 30, 40, 60. (The journal entry for Sept. 5, "The Congress proceeded to the choice of a President," *same* 14, is noncommittal.)

31. Randolph elected President and Thomson Secretary of the Congress Sept. 5, 1774, *Journals Cont. Cong.* I 14. As to Lynch's proposal of them, Duane "Notes of Proceedings" Sept. 5, Burnett *Letters* I 8. Galloway and some or all of the N.Y. delegates were unhappy over the election of Thomson, Adams' diary for Sept. 5; Galloway to William Franklin Sept. 5; and Deane to his wife Sept. 5 and 6, *same* I 7, 9, 11. Galloway thought that this, too, had been "privately settled" beforehand by the Bostonians, Virginians, and Carolinians, one of the Rutledges excepted, *same* 9.

32. On Sept. 5, 1774, Duane raised a question as to the status of the N.Y. delegates, whereupon it was decided unanimously that these delegates should be on the same footing as those from the other colonies, Duane's notes, *same* 9.

33. Resolutions of Sept. 6, 1774, that "no person shall speak more than twice and on the same point, without the leave of the Congress" and that "no question shall be determined the day on which it was agitated," if any colony asked for postponement to a later day, *Journals Cont. Cong.* I 26.

34. Resolution adopted Sept. 7, 1774, that the vote be by colonies, *same* 25. Isaac Low, Chairman of the N.Y. Comm. of Corresp. wrote the Supervisors of Albany County, July 29, that it was immaterial how many delegates the county might elect to the Continental Congress "since those of each Province, whether more or less, will conjointly have only one vote at the Congress," Jay Papers, Columbia U. Library. But there seems to have been no general advance agreement to this effect, since the point was raised in the Congress on Sept. 5, John Adams' diary for Sept. 5, Burnett *Letters* 7.

35. Ezra Stiles, a keen student of statistics, estimated the white population of the thirteen colonies (except Ga.) in 1774 to be 2,070,000, *Stiles Diary* I 488. Jensen in his *Hist. Doc.* 480 gives an estimate for all thirteen colonies in "1774–1775" of 2,145,000 whites as follows: N.H., 80,000; Mass. (including present-day Maine), 355,000; R.I. 54,500; Conn., 191,500; N.Y. (including present-day Vermont), 161,000; N.J., 117,000; Pa. and Del., 298,000; Md., 190,000; Va. (including present-day West Va. and Kentucky), 300,000; N.C., 260,000; S.C., 120,000; Ga., 18,000. The population of Del. in 1770 has been estimated at 35,496, *Hist. Statistics* 756. Assuming it was 40,000 by 1774, the estimated white population of Pa. would be 258,000 in 1774. Stiles' estimates differ widely from Jensen's only as to N.C. and S.C., which Stiles gives as 200,000 and 70,000, respectively.

36. Henry's statements as to voting, Duane's and Adams' notes of Sept. 6, 1774, Burnett *Letters* I 12, 14. Adams' diary for Sept. 5 also records Henry as pointing out the "great injustice if a little Colony should have the same weight in the councils of America as a great one . . . ," *same* 7. Though conceding that slaves were not to be counted in computing population, Henry presumably had in mind their inclusion in determing the factor of "opulence" mentioned in the text.

37. Jensen *Hist. Doc.* 480 estimates the blacks, mostly slaves, of course, in the thirteen colonies in 1774–1775 to be 409,500, as follows: N.H., 500; Mass., 5,000; R.I., 5,000; Conn., 8,000; N.Y., 21,000; N.J., 3,000; Pa. and Del., 2,000; Md., 60,000; Va., 200,000; N.C., 10,000; S.C., 80,000; and Ga., 15,000. The estimates for 1770 in *Hist. Statistics* 756 and for 1774 in Stiles *Diary* I 488 indicate that Jensen's estimates for N.C. are much too low.

38. Harrison of Va. argues for proportionate representation, Duane's notes of Sept. 6, Burnett *Letters* I 13.

39. Lynch of S.C. favors proportionate representation on the basis of "a compound of numbers and property," John Adams' notes for Sept. 6, 1774, *same* 14. The date of these notes and of several other documents cited in this and the next two chapters are supplied by Burnett as editor. Unless otherwise noted, I agree with and have followed his dating.

40. Statements of Sullivan of N.H., Ward of R.I. and Gadsden of S.C. in favor of each colony having but one vote, Adams' diary Sept. 5, 1774, Duane's notes Sept. 6 and John Adams' notes Sept. 6, *same* 7, 12, 14–15.

41. There is no record in the notes of debates on the question of proportionate vote, Adams' notes for Sept. 6, 1774, Burnett *Letters* 15. Adams had queried in his diary of Sept. 5, "whether it is possible to ascertain, at this time, the numbers of our people or the value of our trade," which ought to be ascertained, he added, not by taking "each others words," but "by authentic evidence from the records," *same* 8.

42. John to Abigail Adams Sept. 18, 1774, as to the "delicate course" the Mass. "embassy" had to steer, *same* 35.

43. John Adams to William Tudor Sept. 29, 1774, as to the necessity for the Mass. delegation to "keep . . . out of sight" and "to insinuate" their designs through delegates from other colonies, *same* 60. Caesar Rodney, a member of the Del. delegation, and Gov. Cadwallader Colden of N.Y., who had talked with Galloway, commented (Sept. 9 and Dec. 7, respectively) on the relative moderation of the Mass. delegates compared with those of Va. and S.C., *same* 27 and *Colden* 1877 374.

44. Remarks of Lee and Bland as to lack of data on which to base proportionate vote, Adams' notes for Sept. 6, 1774, Burnett *Letters* I 15. Adams had queried in his diary of Sept. 5, "whether it is possible to ascertain, at this time, the numbers of our people or the value of our trade," which ought to be ascertained, he added, not by taking "each others words," but "by authentic evidence from the records," *same* 8.

45. The *O.E.D.* under "Province" states that the term is "chiefly applied to those [British] colonies which were denominated provinces in their charters. . . . Generally . . . colonies having a royal governor and some having proprietary governors were 'provinces'." The differentiation is illustrated in the Charter of 1691 transforming Mass. into a royal province, which speaks of "the . . . Colony of the Massachusetts Bay" becoming a "reall [royal] Province by the Name of Our Province of the Massachusetts Bay in New England . . . ," *Mass. Acts* I 8.

46. The minutes of Congress for Sept. 6, 1774, as to method of voting, *Journals Cont. Cong.* I 25. The fact that this resolution is not recorded as carried unanimously indicates that one or more colonies voted against it; but I have found no evidence of the line-up. If the delegates of a colony were equally divided on a question, the colony lost its vote, Burnett *Letters* I 74, 89.

47. Statement that the words as to Congress' not having proper materials "at present" were added to prevent the vote in favor of one vote for each colony from being made a precedent, Conn. delegates to the Governor of Conn. (Jonathan Trumbull) Oct. 10, 1774, Burnett *Letters* I 69.

48. Retention of the rule of a single vote for each state in the proposed Articles of Confederation Aug. 20, 1776, and those adopted Nov. 15, 1777, *Journals Cont. Cong.* V 681, IX 910 and Jensen *Articles of Confederation* 140–145. The U.S. Constitution in effect perpetuates this rule by providing in Article 7 that no bill shall pass without concurrence of the Senate and in Article 3 that each state shall have two senators, the extreme unfairness of which is discussed in Knollenberg "Sagebrush Rule," *Atlantic Monthly* 149 (1932) 289–295; June, 1932, supplementary pp. 40, 42.

49. John Jay stated Sept. 6, 1774, "I am not clear that we ought not to be bound by a majority, though ever so small," John Adams' notes Sept. 6, Burnett *Letters* I 15; but I have found no debate on the question, and an important motion was, we know, carried by a bare majority, Deane's diary Oct. 5, 1774, "Deane Diary" 5–6, with *Journals Cont. Cong.* I 54–55. The Articles of Confederation agreed to by the Second Continental Congress Nov. 15, 1777, required the affirmative vote of nine states for important decisions, *same* IX 922.

50. A report reached Philadelphia Sept. 6, 1774, of the British cannonading of Boston and the killing of six of its inhabitants, diary entries and letters Sept. 6–8, Burnett *Letters* I 12, 13, 16, 18, 19. The chief source of the report apparently was a letter from Israel Putnam of Pomfret, Conn., to Aaron Cleveland Sept. 3, 4 *Force* I 325; Stiles *Diary* 476–485. As to the rapid progress of this report from town to town in Conn. by messenger from one Committee of Correspondence to another, and Putnam's labored explanation of his error, *same* 325, 942–944n.

51. The three known accounts of the incident concerning the proposal to open the Congress with prayer are in Duane's notes for Sept. 6, 1774, Samuel Adams to Joseph Warren Sept. 9, and John Adams to his wife Sept. 16, Burnett *Letters* I 13, 26–27, 32. The accounts of Duane and John Adams are somewhat conflicting; I follow Duane's because it is the closest in time to the event, and because Adams is inaccurate in stating that the motion was made "when Congress first met"—it was made the following day, *Journals Cont. Cong.* I 27. Samuel Adams' laconic statement is reconcilable with either.

52. Deane wrote his wife Sept. 7, 1774, that Duché [the Reverend Jacob Duché of Philadelphia] had "prayed with such fervency, purity and sublimity of style and sentiment, and with such an apparent sensibility of the scenes and business before us [a false rumor of the bombardment of Boston] that even Quakers shed tears," Burnett *Letters* I 18. John and Samuel Adams also highly praised Duché's prayer, John Adams' diary for Sept. 7, and Samuel Adams to Warren, Sept. 9, *same* 19, 27.

53. The journals of the Congress do not state how the members of this and other committees were chosen; but Duane's notes for Sept. 7, 1774, remark that the committee on the statement of rights to be "appointed" should be "composed of two members from each Colony to be recommended by their associates," *Journals Cont. Cong.* I 16. Hence, I infer that this committee was appointed by the President on recommendation from the several delegations, and I suppose this method was followed with respect to at least the more important committees later chosen.

54. The members, two from each colony, chosen Sept. 7, 1774, to draft the important Statement of Rights are named in *Journals Cont. Cong.* I 28. On the

arrival of two of the N.C. delegation on Sept. 14, they were immediately added to the committee, and on Sept. 19, there was a further addition of three important members (Cushing, Henry, and Mifflin) who had been members of the committee referred to in 54 below *same* 31, 41.

55. The resolution of Sept. 6, 1774, concerning a Statement of Rights, *same* 26. On this same day, the Congress resolved "That a Committee be appointed to examine & report the several Statutes which affect the trade and Manufactures of the colonies," and on Sept. 7, this committee, composed of one member from each colony, was chosen, *same* 26, 29. This committee made its report (which has not been found) on Sept. 17, *same* 40–41, and thereafter nothing further is known of it.

56. The Suffolk Resolves of Sept. 6, 1774, *same* I 31–38.

57. Resolution requesting merchants to stop ordering goods from Great Britain, passed unanimously Sept. 22, 1774, *same* I 43.

58. Adams' notes of debates Sept. 26 and 27, 1774, state, "Mr. Lee made a motion for a non-importation," Burnett *Letters* I 48. Lee's motion probably called for non-importation to begin Nov. 1, 1774, in accordance with the instructions of the Va. convention to the Va. delegates, 4 *Force* I 689. As later brought out, the motion finally adopted provided for non-importation to begin at a later date, and this probably explains why Lee's motion does not appear in the journals of the Congress, which contain only motions that were adopted.

59. Galloway wrote in a pamphlet published a few months after the Congress rose, that he had "uniformly opposed" a non-importation agreement at this time, *Candid Examination* 390. The opposition also is reported in the letter from his intimate friend, Governor William Franklin of N.J., quoted in note 60 below.

60. William Franklin wrote Lord Dartmouth Sept. 6, 1774, that Galloway "was in hopes to have formed a party among the Delegates sufficient to have prevented a non-importation agreement for the present, but he now seems to despair of Success," since even those delegates from New York, New Jersey and Pennsylvania" who are of different sentiments begin to think it will answer no good End to make any opposition," *Aspinwall* II 709. Franklin does not indicate which or how many of the delegates from the three colonies mentioned were thought to share Galloway's sentiments.

61. News of the King's assent to the Quebec Act reached the colonies in the latter part of August. See, for example, Ezra Stiles' bitter reaction to the news, recorded in his diary for Aug. 23, 1774, *Stiles Diary* I 455.

62. Joseph Reed to Dartmouth Sept. 25, 1774, and to Dennys De Berdt Sept. 26 concerning the effect of the Quebec Act, as quoted in the text, Reed *Reed* I 78, 81.

63. James Allen to Ralph Izard Oct. 29, 1774, concerning the effect of the Quebec Act, as quoted in the text, *Izard* 28.

64. Bland's proposal of date of shipment as basis for effective date of non-importation and Gadsden's and Lee's counterproposal that date of arrival be the basis, Adams' notes of debates Sept. 26 and 27, 1774, Burnett *Letters* I 48–49. The date of importation chosen, non-importation resolution Sept. 27, *Journals Cont. Cong.* I 43.

65. Mifflin's proposal of the date of arrival on or after Nov. 1, 1774, as the effective date for non-importation and Cushing and Edward Rutledge's counter-proposal that non-importation take place immediately, Adams' notes of debates, Sept. 26 and 27, Burnett *Letters* I 48, 50.

66. Debate concerning the date for non-importation to become effective, Adams' notes of debates Sept. 26 and 27, 1774, Burnett *Letters* I 48–50. The acceptance of Henry's view as to the effective date is evidenced by the resolution adopted Sept. 27, *Journals Cont. Cong.* I 43.

67. Mifflin's proposal for inclusion of "duted articles," no matter where from, in the non-importation resolution, Adams' notes Sept. 26 and 27, Burnett *Letters* I 49. Ward's diary for Sept. 29, *same* 59, records, "The Congress . . . considered a non-importation of all dutiable goods," but gives no indication of who supported the proposal. As brought out in Chapter 24, this proposal was later reviewed and adopted in large part.

68. Resolution as to non-importation adopted unanimously Sept. 27, 1774, *Journals Cont. Cong.* I 43.

69. Though none of the resolutions or instructions to delegates of the colonial Assemblies or conventions mentioned the inclusion of Ireland in the ban on non-importation, this had been included in the resolutions of Fairfax County, Va., described in Chapter 20, 4 *Force* I 600.

70. The N.J. resolutions (quoted in Chapter 20) called for a non-consumption, as well as a non-importation, agreement, and the Va. resolutions of Aug., 1774, included resolutions not to purchase, as well as not to import, East Indian products and slaves. Schlesinger *Col. Merchants* 63–64, 76–77, 106–114 *passim*, 146, 181–186 *passim*, 194, 196, 319–320, 369 describes other colonial non-consumption measures dating back to the Stamp Act crisis of 1765–1766.

71. Galloway's resolution for a Plan of Union, Sept. 28, 1774, *Journals Cont. Congress* I 49; Adams' notes of debates Sept. 28, 1774, Burnett *Letters* I 51–52; Cadwallader Colden to Dartmouth Dec. 7, *Colden* 1877 374. There are sketches of Galloway in *D.A.B.* and Baldwin "Galloway."

72. The quoted words concerning the actions of Congress on Galloway's plan are from Ward's diary for Sept. 28 and Oct. 22, 1774, Burnett *Letters* I 51, 80. These actions are discussed in the appendix to this chapter.

73. John Adams' notes of debates Sept. 28, 1774, quote Galloway as stating, "A general non-exportation I have ever looked on as an undigested proposition. . . . We, in this Province [of Pa.] should have tens of thousands of people thrown upon the cold hand of charity. Our ships would lie by the walls, our seamen would be thrown out of bread, our shipwrights, etc. out of employ, and it would affect the landed interests," Burnett *Letters* I 51.

74. Non-exportation resolution of Sept. 30, 1774, *Journals Cont. Cong.* I 51–52. A resolution Aug. 1, 1775, of the Second Continental Congress defines the "West Indies" as comprehending "all the West India islands, British and foreign . . . and also the Summer islands [Bermudas] Bahama Islands, Berbicia and Surinam on the Main [Dutch colonies on the South American mainland] and every other island within the latitude of the southern line of Georgia and the Equator," *same* II 239.

75. Remarks of Gadsden, Edward Rutledge, and Cushing opposing long defer-ment of date for non-exportation to take effect, Burnett *Letters* I 49–50. Chase seems to have blown hot and cold on the question, *same.*

76. As brought out in Chapter 20, the Va. delegates' instructions forbade them to assent to a date earlier than "after the 10th day of August, 1775," 4 *Force* I 689. The long deferment probably was proposed by Lee, who is the only member known to have spoken in favor of this, Adams' notes of debates Sept. 26–27, 1774, Burnett *Letters* I 49–50.

77. The resolution for non-exportation was not passed unanimously, *Journals Cont. Cong.* I 51.

78. Another question relating to the non-exportation agreement as to which I have found no evidence is why the Congress adopted Sept. 10, 1775, rather than the earlier date of Aug. 10, 1775, which (as brought out in Chapter 20) was the date specified by the Va. convention, for non-exportation to begin. Perhaps Sept. 10 was arrived at as a compromise between the Va. delegates and the N.C. dele-gates, who (as brought out in Chapter 20) were instructed in favor of Oct. 1, 1775, as the date for non-exportation to begin.

79. Deane's diary for Oct. 5 and 6, 1774, concerning Gadsden's motion to withhold payment to British creditors, "Deane Diary" 7.

CHAPTER 23

1. Draft of Statement of Rights submitted by the Committee on Rights Sept. 22, 1774, and adopted, after amendment, Oct. 14, *Journals Cont. Cong.* I 42, 63–73.

2. John Adams' comment on the waste of time in the Congress, Adams' diary for Oct. 10, 1774, *Adams Papers* II 150. Adams' diary for Oct. 24 has a similar complaint, *same* 156, and he wrote his wife (Oct. 9), "I believe if it was moved and seconded that We should come to a Resolution that Three and two make five. We should be entertained with Logick and Rhetorick, Law, History, Politics and Mathematicks concerning the Subject for two whole Days, and then We should pass the Resolution unanimously in the Affirmative," *Adams Family Corresp.* I 166.

3. John Adams' comment on Dyer and Sherman's tedious speaking, Adams diary for Oct. 10, 1774, *Adams Papers* II 150. Sherman apparently embarrassed his fellow New Englanders, judging not only from Adams' comment, but also from Deane's comment to his wife (Aug. 25), shortly after the Conn. delegates had had drinks with some of New York's elite, that his "odd questions" and "very odd and countrified cadence" made him "as badly calculated to appear in such a Company as a chestnut burr is for an eye-stone . . . ," *Deane Papers* I 6.

4. The Congress sat every day but Sunday, *Journals Cont. Cong.* I 13–75 *passim,* from nine A.M. to 3 P.M., John Adams to his wife Oct. 7, 1774, *Adams Family Corresp.* I 164.

5. Washington's diary Sept. 5–24, 1774, records that he dined at private houses every night but three and on one of these (Sept. 16) "Dined at the State House at an Entertainment given by the City to the Members of the Congress," *Washington*

Diaries II 163–165. Paine's description of the grand dinner given by the City of Philadelphia is in *Adams Papers* II 134n.

6. Washington's diary records the names of his hosts, and entries as to winnings and losses at cards appear in his book of accounts—he won £7 net. But what card game or games were played is not stated, Washington's Pocket Day Book, Huntington Lib., and Ledger B fol. 125, L.C., summarized in Freeman *Washington* III 377n.

7. The *O.E.D.* quotes an English recipe of 1688 for fool as a "Custard . . . made of Cream, Yolks of Eggs, Cinamon, Mace boiled: and served on Sippets [small pieces of toast or fried bread] with sliced Dates, Sugar and white and red Comfits [candied fruit] strawed [sprinkled] thereon."

8. Bullock *Williamsburg Art of Cookery* 221 quotes an English recipe of 1770 as stating that to make a trifle "Cover the Bottom of your Dish with Naples Biscuits broke in Pieces, Mackeroons, and Ratafia cakes [cakes tinctured with peach or apricot brandy], just wet them all with Sack [any strong, dry wine from southern Europe], pour on a good boiled Custard when cold, then a whipt Syllabub over that."

9. *Same* 232 quotes a Virginia recipe of 1742 stating that to make syllabubs (a favorite colonial dish) "Take a Quart of Cream, not too thick, and a Pint of Sack, and the Juice of two Lemons; sweeten it to your Palate, and put into a broad earthen Pan, and with a Whisk [egg-beater] whip it, and lay it in your Syllabub Glasses; but first you must sweeten some Claret or Sack or white-wine and strain it, and put seven or eight Spoonfuls of the Wine into your Glasses, and then gently lay in your Froth."

10. John Adams' descriptions of the dinners he attended and what was served, *Adams Papers* II 126–140.

11. John Adams to his wife Sept. 29, 1774, as to the continuing round of eating and drinking, *Adams Family Corresp.* I 164. Adams attributed his holding out "surprizingly" to his sticking to "Phyladelphia Beer and Porter" which agreed with him "infinitely better than . . . Spirituous Liquor," *same.* Adams complained again to his wife on Oct. 9 of "the perpetual Round of feasting . . . we are obliged to submit to . . . ," *same* 166. Also Deane wrote his wife Sept. 18 that after 3:00 P.M., the members did nothing but "eat and drink" and that he was "engaged to dine out every day this week," Burnett *Letters* I 34.

12. Connecticut delegates to Gov. Jonathan Trumbull of Conn. Oct. 10, 1774, explaining why the Congress was sitting so long, *same* 70.

13. A draft, undated, by Sullivan of a statement perhaps prepared for a subcommittee of the Committee on the Statement of Rights, is published in *Journals Cont. Cong.* I 63–71, but there is no evidence that the draft submitted by the committee to the Congress followed Sullivan's paper.

14. Statement of grounds for claim of colonial rights in the Statement of Rights as adopted, *same* 67. It will be noted that the statement refers to the "English" colonies, "English" liberty, and the "English" constitution, not to the "British" colonies, liberty, and constitution, serving to bring out that the rights claimed were long-established rights antedating the Act of 1707 uniting England and Scotland as Great Britain.

15. The Statement of Rights declared that the colonists were entitled to an "exclusive power . . . in all cases of taxation," *same* 69.

16. The act of 7 Geo. III ch. 46 (the Townshend Act of 1767) recited as a grievance in the statement, *same* 71, not only imposed colonial duties for revenue but provided (sec. 10) for issuing general writs of assistance in the colonies.

17. The acts before 1774 cited as grievances are referred to by year and section, *same* 71–72; the Intolerable Acts of 1774 are described, *same* 72–73.

18. The grievances recited against the Crown are in *same* 73. The complaints against the Crown are discussed in an appendix to this chapter. Evidently none of them was regarded as sufficiently serious to be included among the demands for redress in the Association later adopted by the Congress.

19. The resolution of the Delaware convention, Aug. 2, 1774, as to British restriction on colonial manufactures, quoted in the text, 4 *Force* I 667. The British acts restricting colonial manufactures are described in Knollenberg *Origin* 170–172, 353–354.

20. Proposal in the Statement of Rights of the means to be pursued for securing redress of the colonial grievances recited in the statement, *same*. Unlike the Stamp Act Congress of 1765, the First Continental Congress did not petition the Houses of Parliament, apparently having given up hope of relief from Parliament except under pressure from the King.

21. Debate in the Committee on the Statement of Rights by Lee, Duane, Jay, John Rutledge, and other members of the committee Sept. 8, 1774, as to ground or grounds on which to base the claim of colonial rights, Adams' notes for Sept. 8, Burnett *Letters* I 20–22.

22. Duane's leadership in securing some acknowledgment by the Congress of Parliament's authority to regulate colonial trade, Duane's "Propositions" Sept. 7–22, 1774, and his "Notes of Debates" of about Oct. 13, *same* 38–42, 72–74 and Adams' "Notes of Debates" of about Sept. 28, and his diary for Oct. 13, *same* 53, 74. (Duane's undated papers, *same* 39, 43, also suggest a proposal that the colonies offer to contribute an annual sum toward support of the British navy if the restrictions on colonial trade were removed. Undated notes of John Adams also mention this suggestion, *Adams Papers* II 145.)

23. Duane's motion (for an amendment) concerning recognition by the Congress of Parliament's limited authority to regulate colonial trade, Duane's "Notes of Debates" Oct. 12 and "Notes of Debates" of about Oct. 13, 1774, Burnett *Letters* I 72, 72–74; Adams' diary for Oct. 13, *same* 74. (Adams' diary entry suggests that Duane's motion was defeated only because it based the limited recognition of Parliament's authority to regulate colonial trade on "compact, acquiescence, necessity, protection," rather than "merely on our consent," *same* 74.)

24. Duane's motion defeated by 5 to 5 vote, Adams' diary for Oct. 13, 1774, *same* 74.

25. The division in R.I. was between Hopkins supporting, and Ward opposing, Duane's proposal, Ward diary for Oct. 13, 1774, Burnett *Letters* I 74. John Adams supported Duane's motion, Duane's "Notes of Debates" Oct. 12, *same* 72, but which one of the other three Mass. delegates stood with Adams is unknown to

me. (John Adams, in his *Novanglus* letters published a few months later, repeatedly acknowledged Parliament's authority "to regulate their [the colonies'] trade," *Novanglus* 26, 31, 33, 37–39, 41, 83, 89–91, 102–103, 124.)

26. Duane to Chase Dec. 29, 1774, tends to imply that the N.Y. and Md. delegations supported him, Burnett *Letters* I 87–88, and Paine's undated notes of debates, Paine Papers (M.H.S.), indicate that Chase, Paca, and Johnson of Md., a majority of the Md. delegates, favored Duane's proposal. Chase's support also is indicated by a note of Adams in Burnett *Letters* I 63 and a letter from Chase to Duane Feb. 5, 1775, stating, "The right bona fide to regulate our Commerciel I would recognize in the most clear and express terms," *Southern Hist. Assoc. Public.* X (1906) 303.

27. Passage quoted in the text as to Parliament's regulation of colonial commerce, Oct. 14, 1774, *Journals Cont. Cong.* I 68. In his autobiography, John Adams says he drafted this passage, Burnett *Letters* I 46n. I have found no contemporary evidence of this, except possibly a letter of Dec. 12, 1774, from him to an unidentified correspondent, stating he "had more anxiety" about this passage in the Statement of Rights "than all the rest," *same* 87.

28. Benjamin Franklin's statement to Lord Chatham March 22, 1775, that "excluding foreign Ships from our Ports . . . was as acceptable to us as it could be to Britain," Smyth *Franklin* VI 323, apparently was well founded. (Section 18 of 6 Geo. III ch. 15 (1764) prohibiting importation into the British colonies of foreign rum also was little protested, probably because it protected rum distillers in British North America, as well as those in the British West Indies.)

29. Galloway's statement quoted in the text denouncing the Congress for its double-talk concerning regulation of colonial trade in the Statement of Rights, *Mutual Claims* 372.

30. The journals of the Congress dated Sept. 17, 1774, state merely that the Suffolk County resolutions "were laid before the congress," *Journals Cont. Cong.* I 31–32. My statement that the Mass. delegation presented them is from a letter of Samuel Adams to Charles Chauncey Sept. 19, reporting that "Last Friday [Sept. 16] Mr. [Paul] Revere brought us the spirited and patriotick Resolves of Your County of Suffolk. We laid them before the Congress," Burnett *Letters* I 37.

31. Resolution of the Congress, quoted in the text, approving the conduct of Mass., *Journals Cont. Cong.* I 39. (This resolution is dated in the journals "Saturday September 18, 1774." Saturday was the 17th. It is highly improbable that the Congress sat on Sunday, and I therefore date the resolution Sept. 17.) The Suffolk Resolutions are in *same* 32–37.

32. The order for publication of the Suffolk County Resolutions, Sept. 17, 1774, *same* 40. The Congress also voted to send to Boston a copy of its own resolution of Sept. 17, and that this resolution, too, be published, *same* 40.

33. Referring to the action of the Congress on the Resolves, John Adams wrote in his diary for Sept. 17, 1774, "This day convinced me that America will support the Massachusetts or perish with her," and two days later Samuel Adams wrote Charles Chauncy, "I think I may assure you that America will make a point of supporting Boston to the utmost," Burnett *Letters* I 34, 37.

34. A letter from the Suffolk County convention to Gage, Sept. 9, 1774, protesting against his military activities in and around Boston, also was presented to the Congress, *Journals Cont. Cong.* I 37–38, and was implicitly approved, *same* 39.

35. Boston Comm. of Corresp. to the Congress Sept. 29, 1774, telling of Gage's menacing activities at Boston and requesting advice how to deal with them, *same* 55–56.

36. Resolution Oct. 8, 1774, as to supporting Mass., *same* 58. The Congress adopted supplementary resolutions on Oct. 10 and 11 advising the people of Boston to submit to a temporary "suspension of the administration of Justice" and to continue "to conduct themselves peaceably" toward the troops in Boston "as far as can possibly be consistent with their immediate safety," and a letter of Oct. 10 to Gen. Gage begging him to quiet the minds of the people of Boston by discontinuing fortifications in and about the town, *same* 59–62.

37. My supposition that someone in the Va. delegation moved the important resolution of Oct. 8, 1774, is based on the fact that the resolutions of the Va. convention of Aug., 1774, 4 *Force* I 690, discussed in Chapter 20, called for "resistance and reprisal" if Gage tried to enforce a proclamation of June 29, threatening punishment to anyone signing the so-called Solemn League and Covenant promoted by the Boston Comm. of Corresp., *same* 491–492.

38. The resolution of Oct. 8, 1774, concerning Mass. was not adopted unanimously, *Journals Cont. Cong.* I 58.

39. Gov. Cadwallader Colden of N.Y., shortly after talking with Galloway and Duane, wrote Dartmouth Dec. 4, 1774, that they had told him "they Dissented from the Proceedings of the Congress," *Colden* 1877 374, and, though Colden did not specify which of the proceedings they dissented from, later statements by them indicate that they protested against the resolution of Oct. 8, Burnett *Letters* I 66 and Alexander *Duane* 103, 121.

40. Adams' diary of Oct. 11, 1774, records Henry's denunciation of Galloway, Jay, and the Rutledges, Burnett *Letters* I 71.

41. John Adams to William Tudor Oct. 7, 1774, quoted in the text, Burnett *Letters* I 65. Also Adams to Joseph Palmer Sept. 26, *same* 48. Adams himself apparently wished the Congress to prepare for defense. He wrote James Warren July 17, "It may well be expected that many Men of Sound Judgment will be of the Assembly. But what avails Prudence, Wisdom . . . without Legions. When Demosthenes went Ambassador from Athens to . . . excite a Confederacy against Phillip, he did not go to propose a Non-Importation or Non-Consumption Agreement!!!" *Warren–Adams* I 29.

CHAPTER 24

1. Resolution for a committee to bring in a plan for carrying into effect the non-importation, non-consumption, and non-exportation resolved on, and names of the members chosen, Sept. 30, 1774, *Journals Cont. Cong.* I 53. I have not discovered how this and other committees of Congress were chosen. Three of the committee, Cushing, Low, and Mifflin, had been members of an earlier committee "to examine & report the several Statutes, which affect the trade and Manu-

factures of the colonies," which had brought in its report on Sept. 17, *same* 26, 29, 41.

2. The Association was submitted Oct. 12, 1774, and adopted Oct. 18, *same* 62–63.

3. The duties described in the text were imposed by the Acts of 1764 and 1766 (described in Chapter 3) and the Townshend Act of 1767. The repeal of these duties would leave only small duties levied by 25 Chas. II ch. 7 (1673) on several colonial products exported from one colony to another, which, as brought out in Knollenberg *Origin* 138, 159, 338, 348, had been levied primarily for commercial purposes, rather than for revenue.

4. The extension of the jurisdiction of the colonial admiralty courts, indemnification of the prosecutor on the judges's certificate, and the requirement of oppressive security from claimants, referred to in the text, which were provided for by several sections of the Act of 1764, were discussed in Chapter 3.

5. The "act for the better administration of justice" was the act of 14 Geo. III ch. 39, described in Chapter 18, authorizing trial in Great Britain or other colonies of soldiers or others charged with murder for acts committed in Mass. in alleged execution of duties of their office.

6. Article 7 of the Association stated, "We will use our utmost endeavours to improve the breed of sheep . . . ," *Journals Cont. Cong.* I 78. The provision doubtless was intended to increase the supply of wool available for manufacture and mending of woolen and linsey-woolsey cloth and clothing.

7. Article 1 of the Association states, "That from and after the first day of December next, we will not import," etc., *same* 76. Other articles of the Association (e.g., Articles 3 and 10) connected with Article 1 refer to importations "after" December first, and I therefore construe "from and after" in Article 1 to mean "after" this date. This interpretation was adopted by the Philadelphia committee responsible for enforcement of the Association there, 4 *Force* I 1026.

8. "Great Britain and Ireland" were defined in a resolution passed by the Second Continental Congress Aug. 1, 1775, as including "Jersey . . . and every [other] European island and settlement within the British dominions . . . ," *Journals Cont. Cong.* II 239.

9. I have found no evidence explaining the provision (*same* I 77) banning importation of tea even though not imported from Great Britain or Ireland or having any connection with the British East India Company. If this sweeping ban was an aspect of the program of "frugality" advocated in Article 8 of the Association (*same* 78), why was the importation of coffee not also totally banned? Perhaps the fear of the British Company tea being palmed off as Dutch tea was responsible for the ban on all tea.

10. The banning of imports of "paneles" (raw sugar) from the British West Indies and not other sugar is puzzling. A conceivable explanation is that the British Customs Board did not classify paneles as "sugar," within the meaning of 6 Geo. III ch. 52 sec. 1 (1766) repealing the duty on "sugar" levied by 25 Chas. II ch. 7 sec. 2 (1672). If so, shipments of paneles from one British colony to another would still be taxable and a proper article to be included in the ban.

11. The language of the Association, *Journals Cont. Cong.* 77, is "from the British Plantations or from Dominica." Perhaps Dominica was named separately

because, though now British, unlike the other British colonies in the West Indies it had been undisputably British only since the Treaty of Paris in 1763.

12. Article 1 of the Association banning imports from Great Britain, Ireland, and the British West Indies. This article left open imports from elsewhere. But, as noted in Chapter 3, importation of many commodities into the colonies except from Great Britain was already forbidden by British acts, and an act of 15 Geo. III ch. 18, passed in 1775, prohibited, on and after Sept. 1, 1775, *all* imports into most of the British continental colonies except from Great Britain, Ireland, or the British West Indies.

13. Article 2 of the Association banned importation of slaves and the engagement in the slave trade, *same* 77. This ban is discussed later in this chapter.

14. The agreement not to purchase or use (the so-called non-consumption agreement) quoted in the text is in Article 3 of the Association, *same* 77. An earlier passage in this article stated that, "from this day [presumably meaning the day the Association was signed] we will not purchase or use any tea, imported on account of the East-India company, or any on which a duty hath been or shall be paid . . . ."

15. The non-exportation provision of the Association, *same* 77, followed the non-exportation resolution of Sept. 30, 1774, quoted in Chapter 22, except for the exemption of rice.

16. Article 10 of the Association authorized the committee of inspection of the place where banned goods were imported "after the first day of December, and before the first day of February next" to permit the importer to store or sell the goods subject to the conditions stated in the text, *same* 78–79. Presumably, "on or after," rather than "after," December 1, was intended.

17. Statement in the Association of the proposed means of securing redress of colonial grievances, *same* 76–80.

18. Statement in the Association as to collateral matters described in the text, *same* 78–79. These follow rather closely the text of the Association adopted by the Va. convention of Aug., 1774 (described in Chapter 20), 4 *Force* IV 686–688.

19. Statement in the Association as to ban on imports, *Journals Cont. Cong.* I 76–77.

20. My supposition that Lee made the motion for banning importation of all duties articles is based on Adams' diary for Sept. 3, 1774, stating, "Lee is for making the repeal of every revenue law, the Boston Port Bill, the bill for altering the Massachusetts constitution and the Quebec Bill and the removal of all the troops, the end of the Congress, and an abstinence from all duties articles, the means . . . ," Burnett *Letters* I 2–3, combined with Deane's notes for Oct. 6, stating, "moved by Col. Lee to take the Duties Articles into Consideration," "Deane Notes" 8.

21. I have found no copy of the motion to ban importation and consumption of foreign, as well as British West Indian, molasses and sugar; but the fact that such a motion was made is deducible from Adams' notes of debates [Oct. 6, 1774], Burnett *Letters* I 63–64. Mifflin, who, as brought out in Chapter 22, had earlier made a similar motion, spoke on the present motion, *same* 64, but, whether for or against it, is not clear.

22. Opposition of Pendleton and Chase to the motion, and Low's remarks quoted in the text, Adams' notes of debates [Oct. 6, 1774], *same* 64.

23. The Va. convention of Aug. 1–6, 1774, adopted a resolution "We will neither ourselves import, nor purchase any slave or slaves imported by any other person, after the first day of November, next, either from Africa, the West Indies, or any other place," 4 *Force* I 687.

24. Motion made on Oct. 1, 1774, by an unidentified member and supported by Ward and Lynch that the export of flaxseed and lumber from the colonies be banned effective immediately, Deane's notes for Oct. 1 and 3, "Deane Notes" 3, 7–8. (Deane refers to the discussion of the motion on Oct. 3, as "the motion for Nonimportation of flaxseed," but this is obviously a slip of the pen for "non-exportation.")

25. Ross' objection as to singling out flaxseed; Sullivan's objection as to singling out lumber; and Galloway's, Dyer's, Johnson's, and Harrison's objections to singling out any article or articles, Deane's notes for Oct. 3 and 5, 1774, *same* 3, 7–8. As to export of flaxseed from Md., Conn., and Pa., statements of Mifflin, Johnson, and Dyer, *same* 7. A number of other members spoke on this motion, *same* 7–8, but Deane's notes are too confusing to enable one to say what stand they took.

26. The motion as to flaxseed and lumber "Negatived Nem. Con.," i.e., without a call for a vote, Deane's notes for Oct. 3, 1774, *same* 8.

27. The Association's exemption of rice, *Journals Cont. Cong.* I 77. Drayton *Memoirs of the Revolution* (1821) I 167, reprinted in Burnett *Letters* I 85–87, says Gadsden told the S.C. provincial congress in Jan. 1775, that the S.C. delegates other than himself had refused to sign the Association unless rice were excepted, thereby forcing the Congress to yield "for the sake of preserving the union of America." Henry to John Laurens Jan. 18, 1775, confirms Drayton as to Gadsden's stand, Clark *Naval Doc.* I 64.

28. The difference between the export market for colonial rice and for other colonial farm products was that most of the latter ordinarily was exported chiefly to foreign markets that were not banned by the Association, whereas two-thirds of the rice exported ordinarily went "to the ports of the mother country," which were banned by the Association, statement of John Rutledge, Drayton *Memoirs of the Revolution* I 167, quoted in Burnett *Letters* I 86–87.

29. A supplement to the Dec. 8, 1774, issue of the *New-York Journal* published the reasons given by the S.C. delegates for exempting rice.

30. Edward Rutledge wrote Ralph Izard Dec. 29, 1774, that he had been "totally against yielding as to indigo," *Izard* 23. See also an undated letter of around Oct., 1774, from Rutledge to Thomas Bee apparently concerning his stand on this, Burnett *Letters* I 84. The statement cited in note 29 above gave the reason for not exempting indigo. The S.C. provincial Congress voted Jan. 11, 1775, that part of the proceeds from exports of rice after Sept. 10, 1775, be shared with producers of indigo and several other S.C. products, 4 *Force* I 1114–1115.

31. Gadsden's proposal to stop remittances to Great Britain "after the 20th Sep[tr] 1774" and support for this by Ward and Ross, Deane's notes for Oct. 5 and 6, 1774, "Deane Notes" 7 which correctly prints the entry in the manuscript at the Conn. Hist. Society. But since Sept. 20, 1774, already was past, I think "Sep[tr]" probably was a slip of the pen for some later month.

32. Edward Rutledge and Galloway oppose Gadsden's proposal, same.

33. Duane's proposal of Oct. 14 or 17, 1774, as to excluding the Quebec Act, Duane's notes of debates, Burnett *Letters* I 77–78. He gave other reasons in addition to those quoted in the text, including, "Is it not a disputable point with respect to religion whether more is granted to the Canadians than was solemnly promised by the capitulation [of Montreal in 1760]." The dating is based on entries in the journals of the Congress recording debates over the Association on those days, *Journals Cont. Cong.* I 74–75.

34. Duane supported as to Quebec Act by Jay and opposed by Lee and McKean, Duane's notes of debates, Burnett *Letters* I 78. John Adams and Paine of Mass. and Henry also joined the debate apparently against Duane, but the notes of their remarks are obscure.

35. Duane's notes of debates contain the entry "Monday, 17th October 1774. Resolved that Quebec Bill be an article of the Grievances to be stood upon. I *dissented,* but entered unanimously," *same* 79. He had earlier objected to including the Quebec Act among the grievances recited in the petition to the King, Deane's diary for Oct. 5, "Deane Diary" 6, but then gave way, Burnett *Letters* I 77.

36. The Quebec Act is included in the Association as one of the grievances that must be redressed, *Journals Cont. Cong.* I 76.

37. Randolph "was taken with the gout, & besides, being Speaker [of the Va. House], was called home to attend the Assembly of Virginia," and, though he "left a Power of Attorney empowering Col. Washington to sign in his Name," it was decided not to add his signature, Ezra Stiles' diary Nov. 8, 1774, Stiles *Diary* I 473, 475. Rodney's signature was added pursuant to instructions given by him and several other absentees signed later, but Goldsborough, Rhoads, and Haring, who also were absent, evidently did not, *Journals Cont. Cong.* I 81n.

38. The Association signed, and the order that 120 copies of it be printed, Oct. 20, 1774, *same* I 80–81. I have not found evidence as to how the printing of this and other documents that the Congress had printed was paid for. So far as is known, the Congress had no source of revenue, and, unlike the Second Congress, issued no paper money.

39. The journals of the Congress for Oct. 11, 1774, record resolutions that "a Memorial be prepared to the people of British America etc. and that Mr. Lee, Mr. [William] Livingston and Mr. Jay . . . [be] a committee to prepare a draught of the Memorial . . . ," *same* 62. In the absence of evidence to the contrary, I assume that Lee, as head of the committee, was chiefly responsible for preparation of the memorial. (A letter from Jay to Lee's grandson, Richard H. Lee, Feb. 12, 1823, states that the Memorial "was written by Mr. Lee," Lee *Richard Henry Lee* I 270–271.)

40. Congress adopts the Memorial and orders not more than 120 copies of it to be printed, *Journals Cont. Cong.* I 101.

41. The Memorial to the Inhabitants of Great Britain, *same* 90–101.

42. The Address to the People of Great Britain, *same* 81–101. Lee, William Livingston, and Jay were also the committee to prepare this document, entry of Oct. 11, 1774, *same* 62.

CHAPTER 25

1. Resolution of thanks to British supporters, *Journals Cont. Cong.* I 104.

2. Committee chosen Oct. 1, 1774, to prepare an address to the King, *same* 53. The Stamp Act Congress of 1765 addressed each House of Parliament as well as the King. But in 1769, there was so much objection in the House of Commons to the receipt of a petition from the Pa. Assembly because it denied the right of Parliament to tax the colonies, Benjamin Franklin to Galloway, Van Doren *Franklin's Writings* 186–187, that, as Franklin to Cushing Dec. 2, 1772, pointed out, all petitions from the colonies now go "to the King only," Smyth *Franklin* V 449–450.

3. Gadsden to Samuel Adams June 28, 1774, as to not paying "for an ounce of the damn'd tea" destroyed at Boston, *Gadsden* 99.

4. Jay's motion of Oct. 1, 1774, to include in the Address to the King a proposal to pay for the tea destroyed at Boston, opposition by S.C. and other members and defeat of the motion "unanimously," Deane's notes for Oct. 1, "Deane Notes" 2–3. The defeat of Jay's motion is confirmed by the instructions to the committee, Oct. 3 and 5, and the Address itself, which say nothing as to paying for the tea, *Journals Cont. Cong.* I 53–55, 115–121.

5. Duane's motion Oct. 1, 1774, to include in the Address the statement as to colonial cooperation quoted in the text, Duane's "Proposed Resolve," Burnett *Letters* I 61. Burnett tentatively dates Duane's "Proposed Resolve" Oct. 3, but Deane's notes for Oct. 1 shows that the correct date is Oct. 1, "Deane Notes" 3. (The manuscript of the Duane resolution at the N.Y. Hist. Soc. seems to read "Councils Aid and Thought," but since Burnett's reading of the last word as "Strength" is possible and makes better sense, I follow his reading.)

6. Lee's motion concerning the militia, undated but probably Oct. 1, 1774, *Journals Cont. Cong.* I 54n.

7. Debate on Lee's militia motion, including Henry's spirited statement, Oct. 1 and 3, 1774, "Deane Notes" 5.

8. The instruction to the committee as to what should be said in the Address to the King concerning colonial militia, Oct. 3, 1774, *Journals Cont. Cong.* I 53–54.

9. I have not found a copy of the motion for an instruction to the committee to limit the statement of grievances to those arising since the close of the late war; but the substance of the motion is deducible from the statement in Deane's notes for Oct. 5, 1774, "the Motion of Yesterday [undescribed by Deane because he was at home unwell] taken up," "Deane's Notes" 5, coupled with his notes of the debates on the motion, *same* 5–6, and the instruction as finally adopted Oct. 5, *Journals Cont. Cong.* I 55.

10. Deane's notes for Oct. 5, 1774, state, "the Motion of Yesterday taken up; Mr. Read in favor of the Motion," and then record what Read said as quoted in the text, "Deane Notes" 5.

11. The rice, hat, and land acts referred to by Lynch, were 3 and 4 Anne sec. 12 (1704) forbidding exportation of rice to any place but England, later ameliorated but not repealed; 5 Geo. II ch. 7 (1732), making real estate in America subject to execution and sale for debts of all kind; and 5 Geo. II ch. 22 (1732),

forbidding the export of colonial-made hats or felt and restricting their manufacture.

12. The acts referred to by Lynch extending the jurisdiction of colonial courts of admiralty are discussed in Chapter 3 and the first appendix to that chapter. "Invidiously" implied that Lynch did not object to colonial admiralty courts exercising jurisdiction over cases involving maritime contracts and other matters traditionally dealt with by admiralty courts both in England and the colonies. As brought out in Chapter 21, the judge and officers of the admiralty court in Lynch's colony, S.C., had been particularly offensive.

13. The controversy in S.C. over Crown-appointed members of the provincial Council acting as a branch of the Legislature also was discussed in Chapter 21.

14. Lynch's objection to including only British acts passed since 1763 in the statement of grievances in the Address, Deane's notes for Oct. 5, 1774, "Deane Notes" 5.

15. John Rutledge ("Mr. Rutledge senior") supports Lynch's objection to limiting the recital of grievances to acts passed since 1763, *same* 6.

16. Biddle's opposition to the proposed limitation to post-1763 measures, *same*. Edward Rutledge's opposition, Edward Rutledge to Ralph Izard Oct. 29, *Izard* 22–23.

17. John Adams supports the original motion for the reason stated in the text, Deane's notes for Oct. 5, 1774, "Deane Notes" 5.

18. Low's objection to the motion as "not sufficiently explicit," putting the Congress "in a suspicious point of Light," *same*.

19. Amendments to the proposed instruction were offered by Dyer of Conn., Sullivan of N.H., Samuel Adams ["Mr. Adams senior"], and Lee, *same* 5–6.

20. Deane's notes for Oct. 5, 1774, state, "the Amendment Carried 6 to 5," *same* 6. This probably was Lee's amendment (no copy found), which was the last amendment recorded as having been proposed and was seconded by an unidentified member, *same*.

21. The amended instruction quoted in the text, adopted by the Congress Oct. 5, 1774, *Journals Cont. Cong.* I 54–55.

22. The six to five vote carrying the resolution, Deane's notes for Oct. 5, 1774, "Deane Notes" 6. Delaware is recorded by Deane as "3 Counties," Pennsylvania as "Phila."

23. My presumption as to the reason for S.C.'s dissent is based on the known opposition, as brought out in the text, of Lynch and the two Rutledges, being a majority of the S.C. delegates, to the limitation to postwar grievances.

24. The original draft of the Address was "read" in the Congress Oct. 21, 1774, *Journals Cont. Cong.* I 102. Whether Lee or Henry was its chief author is discussed in Wolfe "Authorship" 194–196, 203–209. Presumably, it represented the ideas of all five members, Lee, Henry, John Adams, Johnson, and John Rutledge. Adams' diary for Oct. 11 records, "Spent the evening with Mr. Henry at his lodgings, consulting about a petition to the King," Burnett *Letters* I 71.

25. John Dickinson, elected to the Pa. House early in Oct., 1774, had been added to the Pa. delegation to Congress on Oct. 15, the day after the House assembled, *Pa. Assembly* VIII 7148, 7152. At this same election, Thomson was

chosen to replace Benjamin Franklin, who was in England, and Mifflin was re-elected, *same* 7024, 7148. John Adams wrote his wife Oct. 7 that the election of these three "is considered here as a most compleat and decisive Victory in favour of the American Cause . . . ," *Adams Family Corresp.* I 165.

26. The Congress' recommitment of the committee's initial draft, and addition of Dickinson to the committee, Oct. 21, 1774, *Journals Cont. Cong.* I 102.

27. An undated draft of "a humble petition" to the King in Dickinson's hand and a letter from him to Charles Thomson, written apparently about Oct. 22, 1774, Wolfe "Authorship" 209–219, indicate that he prepared a revised draft which was at least the basis for the document adopted on Oct. 25. (Dickinson wrote George Logan Sept. 15, 1804, "The committee, on my being added to them, desired me to draw the address, which I did . . . ," Stillé *Dickinson* 146n.)

28. A revised draft of the Address was submitted to the Congress Oct. 24, 1774, and adopted, after "being debated paragraph by paragraph," on Oct. 25, *Journals Cont. Cong.* I 103–104. The document as adopted is in *same* 115–121.

29. Dickinson wrote George Logan Sept. 15, 1804, the statement quoted in the text, Stillé *Dickinson* 145–146n. Two or three harsh expressions in the undated drafts of the Address by Henry and Lee, Wolfe "Authorship" 206–209, were not in the Address adopted by the Congress, but these may already have been elimi-nated in the original draft of the Address submitted by the committee on the Address to the Congress and rejected on Oct. 21, 1774.

30. The proposed appeal to the King was uniformly referred to in the journals of the Congress up to and including Oct. 25, 1774, as "address," *Journals Cont. Cong.* I 53, 53–54, 55, 102, 103, 104.

31. The appeal to the King referred to as "humble petition" and "petition," *same* 116, 120. The discussion of this point probably evoked the comment in John Adams' diary for Oct. 24, 1774: "In Congress, nibbling and quibbling as usual. There is no greater mortification than to sit with half a dozen wits, deliberating upon a petition, address or memorial," Burnett *Letters* I 81. (This is the same entry in which Adams complained of Dickinson as "very . . . timid"—marking the change in his remarks on Dickinson from admiring to disparaging, discussed in Knollenberg "Dickinson" 139–141.)

32. The Petition to the King signed by, or for, all fifty-five members of the Congress except Randolph, Rhoads, Goldsborough, Haring, and Kinsey, *Journals Cont. Cong.* I 121. I have found no evidence that any of the five non-signers dis-favored the Petition. Randolph, Henry, Pendleton, Bland, and Harrison had left the Congress before the Petition was signed; Lee signed for Henry, and Washington for Pendleton, Bland, and Harrison, Burnett *Letters* I lxiv–lxvi.

33. Middleton to London Agents Oct. 26, 1774, stating, "We desire you will deliver the petition into the hands of his Majesty, & after it has been presented, we wish it may be made public thro' the press . . . ," *Journals Cont. Cong.* I 105. The Agents named were Benjamin Franklin, William Bollan, Arthur Lee, Thomas Life, Edmund Burke, and Charles Garth. As to the London Agents and their work, Kammen "Colonial Agents" 246n., and *Rope of Sand* and Sosin *Agents and Merchants.*

34. Middleton, who had recently succeeded Randolph as President of the Congress, in a letter of Oct. 26, 1774, refers to "the petition," and copies of the

document published in 1775 uniformly caption it "The Petition to the King," *Journals Cont. Cong.* I 105, 130, 131, 136. (Secretary Charles Thomson in letters to Benjamin Franklin of Oct. 26 and Nov. 1 referred to the document in one of them as "the petition," in the other as "the address," to the King, *same* 122.)

35. Statement in the Petition as to supporting the Crown's prerogative, quoted in the text, *same* 119. As shown by the passage quoted from the Statement of Rights in Chapter 23 concerning the regulation of colonial trade, the Congress had already explicitly recognized the most important of the elements of Crown authority in the colonies—the authority to "negative [acts of colonial Legislatures] in such manner as had heretofore been used and accustomed."

36. As late as Oct. 9, 1774, Washington wrote Robert Mackenzie that "no thinking man in North America" desired "independency," that "on the contrary, . . . it is the ardent wish of the warmest advocates for liberty that peace and tranquillity upon constitutional grounds, may be restored," *Washington* III 246–247. Prior to 1775, this sentiment was expressed by nearly every outstanding Whig leader in the colonies, and, I believe, in nearly if not quite all cases, truthfully.

37. The Privy Council's authority to hear and decide appeals from the highest court of every colony, Smith *Appeals passim;* Knollenberg *Origin* 46–47, 299. This authority was particularly important with respect to the colonies (R.I., Conn., and Md.) over whose laws the Crown otherwise had no control.

38. Veto power of the Crown-appointed Governors in the royal colonies, *same* 45–46, 299; Labaree *Royal Government* 99. Also the provincial Councils in all the royal colonies except Mass. were appointed by the Crown and in all the royal colonies except S.C. exercised without opposition the power of an Upper House of the Legislature. The opposition to exercise of this power in S.C., Smith *S.C.* 325–327, 387–393; McCrady *South Carolina* 717–723. The non-royal colonies were R.I., Conn., Pa., Del., and Md.

39. The Crown's prerogative of disallowance, Knollenberg *Origin* 45–46, 298–299. (As to the curious situation of Del., Andrews *Col. Period* II 292–297, 321–326; Thomas Penn to James Hamilton Feb. 12, 1749/1750, Wolff *Pa. Col. Agency* 118 n.11; Labaree *Franklin* XI 466–467, 474–475 and XII 207; Shepherd *Pa.* 345.) The Crown's prerogative to disallow was terminated once an act had been allowed by the King in Council, which, in the case of Mass. and Pa., was automatic if the act were not disallowed within the period specified in their charters, Knollenberg *Origin* 46, 299.

40. Instructions from the Crown protecting British shipping and goods from unfavorable colonial legislation, quoted in the text, especially the circular instruction of May 5, 1732, Labaree *Instructions* I 146–147; *Conn. Hist. Soc. Coll.* IV 254–255.

41. Little complaint in Great Britain of burdensome or discriminatory colonial legislation after 1732, Giesecke *Am. Col. Legis. before 1789* 17–99, indicating general colonial compliance with the instruction quoted in the text. A discriminatory act of Conn. of May, 1768, was repealed two years later after protest in England, *Trumbull* 387, 392, 419, 428–429; *Conn. Col. Rec.* XIII 72, 299. Even R.I., one of the least pliable of the colonies, observed the instruction by repealing an offending act in 1732, *R.I. Col. Rec.* IV 471; Kimball *R.I.* 173.

42. The only recognition I recall having seen of the advantage to Great Britain noted in the text is in a letter from the Duke of Newcastle to Lord Rockingham in 1766, quoted in another connection in Chapter 1, pointing out the advantages of Great Britain's trade with the colonies as compared with its foreign trade because the latter "depends so much on the Will & Caprice of the Powers with whom we trade," Add. Mss. 32973:25.

43. The circular letter to the inhabitants of St. John's, etc., adopted Oct. 22, 1774, *same* 102–103. The composition of the committee to prepare this letter and the date (Oct. 21) established, *same* 101.

44. The address to the inhabitants of the province of Quebec, adopted Oct. 26, 1774, *same* 105–113. The composition of the committee to prepare this address and the date (Oct. 21) established, *same* 101. I have found no evidence of who spoke concerning this address. Adams' diary for Oct. 4, stating "General Lee . . . showed me an Address from the C. to the people of Canada . . . ," Burnett *Letters* I 62, suggests that Gen. Charles Lee may have had a hand in preparing it.

45. Resolution for translation, printing, and distribution of the Quebec address, *Journals Cont. Cong.* I 113. The translation was by Eugène du Simitière, *same* 122, who later became famous as a painter of miniatures, including those of several members of the Congress.

46. Address to the inhabitants of Quebec, including the invitation (which was not accepted) to send representatives to the Continental Congress called for May 10, 1775, *same* 105–113. Metzger *Quebec Act* 158–159 points out the ludicrous contrast of a passage in this address, "We are too well acquainted with the liberality of sentiment distinguishing your [the French] nation to imagine that the differences of religion will prejudice you against a hearty amity with us," with the diatribes against the Catholic religion in the address to the people of Great Britain.

47. Congress' fear of seizure of members as quoted in the text, Hewes to James Iredell, Oct. 31, 1774, Burnett *Letters* I 83.

48. Resolution of Oct. 21, 1774, recommending retaliation for seizing or attempting to seize anyone to be transported overseas for trial, *Journals Cont. Cong.* I 102.

49. Samuel Adams wrote Thomas Young Oct. 17, 1774, acknowledging receipt of a letter from Young of Oct. 11, enclosing Samuel Dyer's affidavit, Cushing *S. Adams* III 162. Young's letter is in the Samuel Adams Papers at the N.Y. Public Library; the affidavit referred to in Young's letter is missing.

50. The quotation in the text as to releasing Dyer, Lord Dartmouth to Gen. Thomas Gage Aug. 23, 1774, *Gage* II 171. The history of the seizure, transportation, examination, and release of Dyer is brought out in Young's letter cited in note 49 above, Dartmouth's letter to Gage of Aug. 23, Gage's reply of Oct. 30, *Gage* I 380; Ebenezer Storer to Joseph Warren, Quincy *Memoirs* 401; John Andrews to William Barrell Oct. 17 and 18, "Andrews Letters" 377–378, the last of which describes Dyer's wild behavior on his return to Boston.

51. Appointment of a committee "to revise the minutes of the Congress" Oct. 21, 1774, *Journals Cont. Cong.* I 101.

52. As noted in Chapter 24, Kinsey, as well as Randolph, Rhoads, and Goldsborough, did not sign the Petition; but he signed the Association, which unlike the Petition would tend to incriminate him.

53. Gov. Cadwallader Colden wrote Dartmouth Dec. 7, 1774, "Mr. Galloway and Duane tell me that at the close of the Congress, they Dissented from the Proceedings, and insisted to have their Dissent entered on the Minutes, but could not by any Means get it allowed," *Colden* 1877 374, and Galloway and Duane themselves later wrote that they had exchanged certificates of having voted against the particularly seditious resolution of Oct. 8 (discussed in Chapter 22) encouraging the inhabitants of Mass. to oppose enforcement of the Intolerable Acts, Alexander *Duane* 103, 121; Burnett *Letters* I 66.

54. Resolution of Oct. 22, 1774, for another intercolonial congress, *Journals Cont. Cong.* I 102. On this same day, Henry Middleton of S.C. was chosen to preside over the closing sessions of the Congress in place of Randolph, who was "unable to attend on account of indisposition," *same.*

55. Resolutions of Oct. 26, 1774, thanking the Pa. House for its "politeness" to the Congress and to dissolve, *same* 113–114. ("A most elegant entertainment" was provided by the Pa. House on Oct. 20, at which "the whole House dined with the members of the Congress," John Adams' diary for Oct. 20, Burnett *Letters* I 79 and Washington diary for Oct. 20, Washington *Diaries* I 168. An appropriation voted by the House Oct. 21 refers to additional, undescribed expenses "attending the Sitting of the Congress," *Pa. Assembly* VIII 7158.)

56. Colden to Dartmouth Dec. 7, 1774, as to a combination of the Va., Md., and New England delegations and some of the South Carolina delegates against the other delegations, *Colden* 1877 374.

57. Unique record of vote by colonies, Oct. 5, 1774, referred to in the text, Deane's diary for Oct. 5, "Deane Diary" 6.

58. Delegates of Mass. and R.I. each equally divided in vote on Oct. 10, 1774, Adams' diary for Oct. 10, Burnett *Letters* I 74.

59. My statement as to Lee is based on Chitwood *Lee,* a valuable book, as to Johnson, on Delaplaine *Johnson* and the biographical sketch of him in *D.A.B.* A good biography of Johnson is much needed. Both men continued to play an important part in public life after 1774. Lee was an outstanding figure in the Second Continental Congress and was a Senator from Va. in the first United States Congress. Johnson became the first Governor of the state of Md. and an associate justice of the United States Supreme Court.

60. Lee's and Johnson's committee memberships described in the text, *Journals Cont. Cong.* I 28, 53, 62.

61. Most of the meager notes of debates in the First Continental Congress known to have survived are printed in Burnett *Letters* I 6–89. The only additional important evidence known to me is in "Deane Notes" 1–8. A few of the editorial notes in these "Notes" are incorrect, but only one reading as published is open to question; the word "dropping," in Sherman's statement on p. 6, I think, reads "damping."

62. Adams' diary for Oct. 10, 1774, as quoted in the text, Burnett *Letters* I 67. In this same diary entry Adams wrote disparagingly of John and Edward Rut-

ledge as speakers and also complained of Dyer and Sherman as speaking "often and long . . . very heavily and clumsily."

63. Assembling of eleven delegations to the Second Continental Congress by May 10, 1775, *Journals Cont. Cong.* II 11–12. The R.I. delegates, Ward and Hopkins, arrived May 15 and 18, respectively, and the parish of St. John's, Georgia, also sent a delegate, Lyman Hall, who apparently sat in the Congress but did not seek recognition as representing the colony as a whole, until he and other delegates elected by a Ga. provincial convention presented themselves several months later, *same* 44–45, 49–50, and Burnett *Letters* I xliii–xliv.

64. Conn. delegates to Gov. Jonathan Trumbull, as quoted in the text, Oct. 10, 1774, *same* 70.

65. The enlargement of the work of the committees to enforce the Association to include implementation of war measures is well exemplified by the developments in Va. described in Bowman "Va. Committees" 334–336. Modification of the Association by a resolution of the Second Continental Congress, April 6, 1776, *Journals Cont. Cong.* IV 257–259, somewhat changed the nature of the committee's activities.

CHAPTER 26

1. Gen̄. Thomas Gage wrote Lord Dartmouth from Boston May 19, 1774, "the Lively in which I Embarked at Plymouth on the 16th of April arrived here . . . on the 13th of this Month. . . . I went to Mr. [Thomas] Hutchinson and remained with him at Castle William till preparations were made for My Reception in Boston . . . ," *Gage* I 355. Rowe's dairy for May 17 records, "This morning Genl Gage Our New Governour . . . came to the Town House, had his commission read by the Secretary [Thomas Flucker, Secretary of Mass.] & took the Usual Oaths [of office]," *Rowe* 270.

2. The Boston Port Act, 14 Geo. III ch. 19 (1774), closed the Port of Boston to most private commerce, June 1, 1774. However, sec. 4 of the act permitted private vessels to enter the port with "fuel or victual brought coastwise . . . for the necessary use and sustenance of the inhabitants" of the town, provided they had cleared at Salem or Marblehead before proceeding to Boston and gave fourteen days' grace for outward-bound private vessels in port on or before June 1, to leave. News of the passage of the act had reached Boston May 10, 1774, John Rowe's diary for that date, *Rowe* 269.

3. The Mass. Regulating Act was 14 Geo. III ch. 45 (1774). The provision of the act for the Governor's appointment of the Council was to take effect Aug. 1, 1774; for his appointment and dismissal of sheriffs and judges without the consent of the Council, July 1; for limiting town meetings without the Governor's consent to one meeting a year, Aug. 1; and for the selection of jury panels by the sheriff, Oct. 1.

4. The "General Court" of Mass. consisted of the House of Representatives and the Council acting in its capacity as a branch of the Legislature. Legally speaking, the "legislature" included the Governor; but in line with modern usage I employ the term "legislature" to mean the Mass. House and Council alone. What we now speak of as courts were then referred to as the "'executive

courts," that is courts responsible for execution of the laws passed by the "General Court."

5. Dartmouth to Gage Apr. 9, 1774, giving him the instructions described in the text, *Gage* II 160–161. Also, the Treasury ordered the American Customs Board and its officers to establish themselves at Salem and the customs officers of the Port of Boston at any place "within the limits of the said port, as shall seem to them most proper . . . ," 4 *Force* I 246–247. The Board made arrangements on May 20 to move to Salem, *M.H.S. Proc.* Vol. 46 (1913) 470–471, and officers of the Boston Customs District moved to Plymouth June 1, *Boston Evening-Post* June 6.

6. Nine British war vessels stationed in or near Boston May 29, 1774, are listed in Rowe's diary for that date, *Rowe* 272–273. Arrival from June 1 to July 6, 1774, of the four British regiments sent from England and Ireland to Boston, Gage to Dartmouth June 26, July 5 and 6, *Gage* I 358–360.

7. The Mass. Legislature met at Boston May 25–28, 1774, during which period it passed a few unimportant bills, *Mass. Acts* XVIII 801–805; listened to a brief message from Gage, Bradford *Mass. Papers* 413–414; and, as the Regulating Act was not yet operative or even known, elected a Council of twenty-eight members, thirteen of whom were negatived by Gage, 4 *Force* I 357. (Gage to Dartmouth May 30 gives his reasons for negativing those rejected, *Gage* I 356.)

8. The general court obeyed Gage's summons to meet at Salem June 6, 1774, and sat there until dissolved by him as stated in the text, Gage to Dartmouth June 26, 1774, *same* 357; *Mass. Acts* V 409–410n.

9. Gage to Dartmouth June 26, 1774, reporting his deferment of action to prosecute traitors, guided by the opinion of "the Chief Justice of the Province [Peter Oliver] . . . that the times are not yet favorable for Prosecutions . . . ," *Gage* I 358. Under Gage's instructions of Apr. 9, the proposed prosecutions were to be "in the ordinary Courts of Justice within the Colony," *same* II 161.

10. John Andrews, Boston merchant and moderate Whig, to William Barrell May 18, 1774, concerning payment for the destroyed tea, quoted in the text, "Andrews Letters" 329. Andrews himself apparently was in favor of paying for the tea, Andrews to Barrell June 12, *same*, and so was the Boston moderate Whig merchant John Rowe, Rowe's diary for July 14, *Rowe* 278.

11. Hutchinson left Boston for England June 1, 1774, Hutchinson's "log" for that date, Hutchinson *Diary* I 152. He died in England June 3, 1780, without ever having returned to America, sketch of him in *D.A.B.*

12. Farewell address of 123 persons to Hutchinson May 28, 1774, including an assurance of their readiness to pay their proportion of the value of the destroyed tea, 4 *Force* I 362. The occupation of each of the signers is given in an undated paper in *M.H.S. Proc.* XI (1869–1870) 392–394. Joseph Warren wrote Samuel Adams June 13, of the "formidable" power of "the party who are for paying for the tea," Frothingham *Warren* 317.

13. Dr. Thomas Young of Boston wrote John Lamb of N.Y. June 19, 1774, that at a Boston town meeting on June 17, those who had "whispered in the conclave" in favor of payment for the tea had remained silent on this point at the town meeting, Leake *Lamb* 90. The minutes of the meeting are in *Boston Records* (for 1770–1777) 176–177.

14. Gage to Dartmouth July 5, 1774, of the plan "by the better sort," at the recent Boston town meeting, "to make a Push to pay for the Tea," *Gage* I 358. Gage said they were "outvoted," but the records of this meeting (June 27 and 28) and Rowe's diary entry concerning the meeting make no mention of a motion for payment, *Boston Records* (for 1770–1777) 177–178 and *Rowe* 276–277. Probably those favoring payment were deterred from making a motion for this by the overwhelming defeat of the motion to dismiss the Boston Committee of Corresp., referred to in note 15 below.

15. Motion to dismiss the Boston Comm. of Corresp. rejected at a Boston town meeting June 28, 1774, by a majority of four to one, Rowe's diary for June 28, *same* 277.

16. The progress and ultimate defeat of the movement for the Solemn League and Covenant is described in the appendix to this chapter.

17. Letters accompanying the gifts for the poor of Boston, usually describing the gifts, and the acknowledgments of the gifts from June 28, 1774, to Apr. 25, 1775, are published in *Donations* 4–272. Many of the gifts, of course, were from towns in Mass., e.g., Wrentham, Pepperell, and Charlemont, *same* 10–13. Those from other colonies are cited and described in subsequent notes.

18. Letters and gifts from Windham and Groton, Conn., June 28, Aug. 10, and Oct. 11, 1774, *same* 4–8, 48, 107–108. The large number of sheep sent from all parts of New England is particularly notable: raising sheep, probably chiefly for local use of flesh, wool, and hides, was apparently very extensive in New England.

19. Gifts by the end of Oct., 1774, from the other Conn. towns mentioned in the text, *same* 13–126 *passim*.

20. Samuel and Robert Purviance for the Comm. of Corresp. of Baltimore to the Boston Comm. of Corresp. Aug. 14, 1774, accompanying a gift of 3,000 bushels of corn, 20 barrels of rye flour, 2 barrels of port, and 20 barrels of bread; and assuring the Boston committee of further gifts from the people of Maryland "to maintain and support every sufferer in your and their common cause," *same* 39–40. This assurance was fulfilled; on Nov. 21, the Purviances sent Boston a bill of lading for 1,700 bushels of corn and rye from Talbot and Dorset Counties, Md., *same* 143–144.

21. Donations to Boston by the end of October, 1774, as stated in the text, *same* 22–129. These included gifts of a sloop-load of "provisions" from inhabitants of the Cape Fear region of N.C., accompanied by a letter of July 29, 1774, from James Moore (later a brigadier-general in the Continental army) to John Hancock and others assuring them of the sympathy and support; of over 2,000 bushels of corn from Northampton and Essex Counties, Va.; and of over 2,000 bushels of corn from the Edenton region of N.C., *same* 22–24, 63, 83, 85.

22. Outpouring of gifts, with accompanying letters of support, as stated in the text, from Nov., 1774, to April, 1775, *same* 129–273; *New Eng. Hist. and Gen. Reg.* XXX (1876) 374–380; and 2 *M.H.S. Coll.* IX (1822) 158–166. Friends (Quakers), who later contributed generously to relief, Cadbury "Quaker Relief" 46–179, held aloof at this time, lest, among other reasons (quoting a letter of Nov. 5, 1774, from leading Friends in Philadelphia to Friends in London), "our contributing to the relief of the distressed people of Boston should subject us to be considered as approvers of their conduct," *same* 45.

23. Emergency committee of eleven chosen by a Boston town meeting May 13, 1774, *Boston Records* (for 1770–1777) 173. The committee was usually referred to in the town minutes as "the Committee on Ways and Means," *same* 176–193 *passim;* but from Sept. onward the committee's letters acknowledging receipt of gifts were often signed "Committee of Donations," *Donations* 25–264 *passim.*

24. The emergency committee was increased to twenty-five July 19, 1774, and to thirty-five Oct. 25, *Boston Records* (for 1770–1777) 183, 193. On Aug. 9, the town of Boston directed the committee to apply 7% of the donations to the needy of the neighboring town of Charlestown, *same* 188, which was within the limits of the Port of Boston.

25. William Cooper, Boston town clerk, to an unidentified correspondent in N.Y. Sept. 12, 1774, concerning Boston employment quoted in the text, 4 *Force* I 783–784.

26. Boston town meetings of July 19 and Aug. 30, 1774, authorized the Committee on Ways and Means to build a town wharf and dig a town well, *Boston Records* (for 1770–1777) 181, 189. Also encouragement to home industry was given by the town's voting on May 30 to have the committee circulate a petition binding the subscribers "not to purchase any Articles of British Manufacture that can be obtained among Ourselves," *same* 176.

27. Replies of the committee July 5, 1774 to March 17, 1775, *Donations* 11–265 *passim.* The quotations in the text are from Samuel Adams to Fisher Gray of the committee in Farmington, stating, "The [Boston] Committee have a very grateful sense of the generosity of their friends in Farmington. . . . Boston is now suffering for the common liberties of America, and while they are aided and supported by their friends, I am persuaded they will struggle through the conflict, firm and steady," *same* 14–15.

28. Gage to Dartmouth May 19 to July 5, 1774, giving optimistic reports quoted in the text, *Gage* I 355–359.

29. Gage to Dartmouth July 20, 1774, telling of prospective opposition to the Mass. Regulating Act and observance of the "fast day" appointed by the "Faction," *same* I 361. The fast day of July 14, referred to by Gage, is discussed in Love *Fast Days* 335, and several of the sermons preached that day are listed in *same* 544–545. Date of receipt of this letter and the one of July 27, Dartmouth to Gage, Sept. 8, *Gage* II 172.

30. Gage to Dartmouth July 27, 1774, for the first time informing Dartmouth that the so-called "Faction" in Mass. was "numerous and powerful," *same* I 364. A letter from Dartmouth to Gage of June 3 indicates that Dartmouth was then still under the illusion that the opposition in Mass. consisted of but "a few desperate Men," *same* II 165–166.

31. Salem town meeting called by local Comm. of Corresp. held Aug. 22, 1774, Andrews to Barrell Aug. 23 and 25, "Andrews Letters" 345, 347; Gage to Dartmouth Aug. 27, *Gage* I 367. The two accounts differ somewhat as to Gage's efforts to stop the meeting, but both agree they were futile. By adjourning town meetings held before the act took effect, Boston was able to hold meetings without call by the selectmen, minutes of the adjourned meetings in Boston from Aug. 9, 1774, to March 27, 1775, *Boston Records* (for 1770–1777) 180–223 *passim.*

32. Gage to Dartmouth Sept. 2, 1774, saying nobody consulted by him could tell him "what to do" as to town meetings held throughout Mass. in defiance of the Mass. Regulating Act, *Gage* I 370.

33. Sec. 1 of the act provided for not fewer than twelve nor more than thirty-six Council members. The King appointed the full number, whose names were listed in an instruction to Gage accompanying the act. Only two of these, John Erving, Sr., of Boston and Samuel Danforth of Cambridge, were among the twenty-eight last elected councilors. Erving declined the King's nomination and Danforth, though initially accepting, soon resigned, Matthews "Royal Council" 465, 471, 472, 474.

34. Gage to Dartmouth Sept. 2 and 12, 1774, telling of the resignation of nine of the councilors who had accepted appointment, *Gage* I 370, 372, 374. None of those mentioned in Gage's original list as doubtful or unreachable later accepted; a list of the full membership of them as members, Matthews "Royal Council" 493.

35. The pressure on members of the new Council outside Boston is described in Matthews "Royal Council" 477–483 and Gage to Dartmouth Sept. 2 to Dec. 15, 1774, *Gage* I 370–387. They were Peter Oliver of Middleborough, William Brown of Salem, Timothy Ruggles of Hardwicke, Josiah Edson of Bridgewater, John Murray of Rutland, Nathaniel Roy Thomas of Marshfield, Daniel Leonard of Taunton, Thomas Oliver of Cambridge, and William Pepperell and Joshua Loring of Roxbury, *Rowe* 283 and various Mass. town histories.

36. There are biographical sketches of John Murray and his son Daniel in Jones *Loyalists of Mass.* 215–217 and Sabine *Loyalists* II 115–117.

37. Daniel Murray in Rutland, Mass., to his father, John Murray, Aug. 28, 1774, quoted in the text, Matthews "Royal Council" 478–479. John Murray retained his royal commission as councilor, and his son fought on the British side in the war, Jones *Loyalists of Mass.* 215–217. I have found no evidence that the threat to destroy buildings on the estate was carried out, but the estate was among the Tory estates confiscated by the Mass. government during the war, *same.*

38. I have seen several interesting letters and diaries written by ordinary farmers during the war; but none of much consequence bearing on the controversy with Great Britain in the pre-war (1765–1774) period. (I have seen more of such documents written by minors at college or by women not married to ordinary farmers than by such farmers.) Hopefully, the suggestion that the American Revolution Bicentennial Commission sponsor an intensive search for letters and diaries of the American rank and file during the period 1765–1783 will be adopted and prove fruitful.

39. A striking example of the lack of comment on the controversy with Great Britain appears in the well-known diary of Matthew Patten of the farming community of Bedford, New Hampshire, for the period of 1766 to April, 1775, *The Diary of Matthew Patten* (1903) 163–342. Diaries of the period, listed in Forbes *New England Diaries 1602–1800*, are similarly unenlightening as to the reaction of the diarists to the controversy with Great Britain in 1766–1774.

40. Gage to Dartmouth Aug. 27, 1744, stating that the Mass. courts "can and will be protected in many places," *same* 367. In a private letter of this same date

to Lord Barrington, Secretary at War, Gage stated he had "no doubt" that the New England colonies could be subdued "in a year or two" and that, though people in the southern colonies "talk very high," the "slaves in the bowells of their country and the Indians at their backs will always keep them quiet," Alden *Gage* 212.

41. Gage to Dartmouth Sept. 2, 1774, as to the impossibility of holding court after all, *same* 370. The *Massachusetts Gazette* of Feb. 23, 1775, gives a review of the methods used to prevent judges from sitting in various country courts, 4 *Force* I 1261. Additional details will be found in the sources cited in Newcomer *Embattled Farmers* 178 n.20, 21, 22.

42. Gage to Dartmouth Sept. 3, 1774, reporting Lieut. Gov. Thomas Oliver's enforced resignation of his commission as a mandamus councilor, *Gage* I 372–373. Oliver's estimate that the crowd compelling him to resign numbered 4,000 is in Oliver to Dartmouth Sept. 3, enclosed in Gage's letter. Oliver's letter is in Matthews "Royal Council" 485–487.

43. Gage to Dartmouth Sept. 1774, as to the resisters being "not a Boston Rabble, but the Freeholders and Farmers of the Country," *Gage* I 371.

44. Gage to Dartmouth Sept. 12, 1774, as to the uprising against the Mass. Regulating Act, *same* 373–375. Gage further warned Dartmouth on Sept. 26 that the Regulating Act could be enforced only by "first making a Conquest of the New-England Provinces," *same* 377.

CHAPTER 27

1. The statement in the text as to the initial optimism of those in power in Great Britain is based on Lord Dartmouth's letters to Governor General Thomas Gage July 6 and Aug. 3, 1774, *Gage* II 168, 170–171; the King to Lord North July 1, *Geo. III* III 116; and diary entries of ex-Governor Thomas Hutchinson, e.g., on July 9, Hutchinson *Diary* I 186.

2. Gage's alarming letters to Dartmouth of Aug. 27 and Sept. 2 and 3, 1774, *same* I 365–372, received Oct. 1, *Dartmouth* (1895) 228. Gage's reports to Dartmouth were confirmed by letters of Aug. 31 and Sept. 3, from Admiral Samuel Graves, commanding the British squadron at Boston, to the Admiralty Board, Aug. 31 and Sept. 3, *Calendar H.O. Papers* (1773–1775) 243–244; Gage to Lord Barrington, Secretary at War, Aug. 27, *Gage* II 652; and Lieut. Gov. Thomas Oliver to Dartmouth Sept 3, enclosed in one of Gage's letters, Matthews "Royal Council" 485–487.

3. Decision as to sending additional warships and marines to Boston at Cabinet meeting Oct. 3, 1774, quoted in the text, *Sandwich* I 56, digested in *Dartmouth* (1895) 228.

4. Lord Sandwich to Dartmouth Oct. 5, 1774, stating that the Cabinet's request for troops and marines could be met without "any material inconvenience," *Calendar H.O. Papers* (1773–1775) 247; Dartmouth to Gage Oct. 17, informing him of the ships and marines being sent to Boston, *Gage* II 174.

5. The King's proclamation Oct. 19, 1774, forbidding the export of arms or ammunition from Great Britain to the colonies for six months, *Acts P.C.* V 401; Clerk *Naval Doc.* I 9–10. The circular letter of Oct. 19, to colonial Governors

and naval commanders to prevent the importation of arms or ammunition into the colonies, *N.Y. Col. Doc.* VIII 509.

6. Gage to Dartmouth Sept. 12 and 25, 1774, describing the rebellion in most of New England, *Gage* I 373–377. The date of receipt, Nov. 18, Hutchinson's diary for that date, Hutchinson *Diary* I 296.

7. Corroborating letters of Admiral Graves to the Admiralty Board Sept. 23, 1774; *Calendar H.O. Papers* (1773–1775) 255; Gage to Barrington Sept. 25, *Gage* II 652; and Gage to Hutchinson Sept. 17, *Dartmouth* (1895) 226, and more fully in Donoughue *Brit. Politics* 210. In his letter to Hutchinson, Gage went so far as to suggest that "it would be policy to temporize a while by suspending the execution of the Acts for a time" until "Hanoverians [and] Hessians may be hired and other steps taken necessary to secure success," *same.*

8. The King to North Nov. 18, 1774, as to "Rebellion" and "blows must decide," *Geo. III* III 153. As early as Sept. 11 the King had written North, "the dye is now cast, the Colonies must either submit or triumph; I do not wish to come to severer measures but we must not retreat . . . . I have no objection . . . to their seeing that there is no inclination for the present to lay fresh taxes on them; but I am clear there must always be one tax to keep up the right, and as such I approve of the Tea Duty," *same* 131.

9. North's statement to Hutchinson as to "Rebellion," Hutchinson's diary for Nov. 19, 1774, Hutchinson *Diary* I 297. Both North and the King scoffed at Gage's suggestion that the acts provoking the rebellion be suspended, *same* I 297 and *Geo. III* III 154.

10. North told Hutchinson Nov. 12, 1774, that "until some further was known of what was doing in Philadelphia, no particular measures could be determined," Hutchinson's diary for that date, Hutchinson *Diary* I 293.

11. The Septennial Act of 1715, 1 Geo. I second session ch. 38, provided that "all parliaments . . . shall and may respectively have continuance for seven years and no longer. . . ." The Thirteenth Parliament had opened May 10, 1768, *Parl. Hist.* XVI 424.

12. The peace between Russia and Turkey was regarded by the King as threatening Great Britain presumably because this would free Russia for aggression against other nations. The unsettled state of the French Ministry was caused by the recent death of Louis XV and succession (May 10, 1774) of Louis XVI.

13. The King to North Aug. 24, 1774, suggesting acceleration of the elections for a new Parliament, *Geo. III* III 125–126. North later told Hutchinson that Parliament was dissolved to enable the Ministry to take such measures concerning the colonies "as we could depend upon a Parliament to prosecute to effect," Hutchinson's diary for Nov. 19, Hutchinson *Diary* I 298. But, as shown by the King's letter of Aug. 24, this was not the sole reason.

14. The King's proclamation Sept. 30, 1774, dissolving the existing Parliament and summoning a new, *Journals H. of C.* XXXV 3. The Cabinet had voted the day before "to submit their opinion to his Majesty that it would be advisable to dissolve the present Parliament and call for a new one," Donoughue *Brit. Politics* 179, inadequately summarized in *Dartmouth* (1895) 227.

15. The sang-froid with which political leaders bought borough seats in the Commons controlled by various "patrons" is illustrated by North to John

Robinson, Oct. 5 and Nov. 19, 1774, complaining of Lord Falmouth for demanding 2,500 guineas instead of pounds for each of three seats controlled by him and of Lord Edgecombe for demanding £3,000 each for five seats controlled by him—for which North thought he was to have £2,500 each, *H.M.C.* Appendix Part VI 67 and Laprade *Robinson* 26.

16. North to the King Nov. 14, 1774, enclosing a list showing that at the very least 321 members elected to the new House of Commons could be counted on to favor the administration, and the King's reply of the same date expressing his pleasure, *Geo. III* III 153–154. The total membership of the House was 558, Namier and Brooke *Commons* I 2. There are excellent accounts of the elections in *same* 73–80 and Donoughue *Brit. Politics* 181–200.

17. The analysis of the 1774 elections to the House of Commons, Namier and Brooke *Commons* I 75 states, "America was mentioned as an issue in not more than ten constituencies. . . ." The number of constituencies, 314, *same* I 513.

18. The King's speech Nov. 30, 1774, the day after the opening of Parliament and the answers of the two Houses, 4 *Force* I 1465–1466, 1474–1776.

19. The votes of Nov. 30 and Dec. 5, 1774, mentioned in the text, were on proposed amendments to proposed answers to the King's speech, *same* 1467, 1474; the answers proper were adopted apparently without a division. Edward Gibbon, the historian, to John Baker Holroyd, on or shortly after Dec. 6, 1774, gives an interesting account of the speeches in the Commons, Norton *Gibbon* II 45. The opposition in both Houses consisted of regular followers of Lord Rockingham and Chatham and a few unaligned members, notably Charles James Fox.

20. The quotation in the text as to the administration's decision to defer decision as to "particular" measures is from a diary entry, Dec. 12, 1774, of Hutchinson recording what North had just told him, Hutchinson *Diary* I 292–293.

21. John Pownall's statements to Hutchinson as to secret reports concerning the proceedings of the Congress, Hutchinson diary for Nov. 19, 1774, *same* 296–297. The question of the informer's identity is discussed in the first appendix to this chapter.

22. Arrival Dec. 13, 1774, of a copy of the proceedings of the Continental Congress other than the Petition to the King, *same* 323. Gov. Cadwallader Colden of N.Y. to Dartmouth Nov. 2, enclosed a copy of these proceedings, *N.Y. Col. Doc.* VIII 510. The Petition to the King was delivered on Dec. 21 by Benjamin Franklin and others to Dartmouth for presentation to the King, Franklin to Charles Thomson Feb. 5, 1775, Smyth *Franklin* VI 303–304, together with *Dartmouth* (1895) 241 and Hutchinson *Diary* I 330.

23. Parliament was adjourned on Dec. 23, 1774 (to reconvene Jan. 19, 1775), for the Christmas holidays, *Journals H. of C.* XXXV 62. Under Secretary of State William Knox told Hutchinson on Dec. 17 that "nothing will be done until after the holidays, the Members being all gone, and they the Ministry can hardly make a House . . . ," Hutchinson's diary for Dec. 15, Hutchinson *Diary* I 325.

24. Dartmouth wrote a circular letter dated Jan. 4, 1775, to colonial Governors directing them to "Use your utmost Endeavours" to prevent the election of delegates to attend the proposed Second Continental Congress and to "exhort all

Persons to desist from such an unjustifiable Proceeding . . . ," *Gage* II 179, but I have found no Cabinet order for this.

25. Gage to Dartmouth Oct. 3–Dec. 15, 1774, and Gage to Barrington Oct. 3, received Dec. 16, 1774, to Jan. 10, 1775, *same* I 377–388, II 656. A transport carrying Col. Richard Prescott bearing an important letter of Dec. 15, 1774, from Gage to Dartmouth, sailed from Boston on Dec. 16, *same* I 389; if the report that the letter was received Jan. 10, 1775, 4 *Force* I 1490, is correct, the vessel had an amazingly quick crossing.

26. The Cabinet, which had remained unchanged since 1771, consisted of North and Lords Gower, Sandwich, Suffolk, Dartmouth, Apsley, and Rochford, all of whom were members of the House of Lords except North, and he was the son and presumptive heir of an English peer, Lord Guilford. The Cabinet later (Jan. 21, 1775) decided to send three instead of two infantry regiments, *Dartmouth* (1887) 372–373.

27. The corps to be raised by Timothy Ruggles was proposed by him in a letter to Israel Mauduit Oct. 16, 1774, *Gage* II 180n. and Hutchinson *Diary* I 343, which probably was among the letters that Mauduit passed on to North, Jan. 9, 1775, *Dartmouth* (1895) 255. As to Ruggles, biographical sketch in *D.A.B.*

28. Cabinet minute Jan. 13, 1775, quoted or summarized in the text, Dartmouth Papers D1778:II 1102, Stafford County Lib., summarized in Donoughue *Brit. Politics* 220–221, and less adequately in *Dartmouth* (1895) 258.

29. Three warships with the additional marines aboard reached Boston May 23, 1775, the other troops several weeks later, Lieut. John Barker's diary. May 23 and June 15, Barker *Diary* 50, 59–60. The decision to send three major generals, William Howe, John Burgoyne, and Henry Clinton, Donoughue *Brit. Politics* 228–230.

30. Dartmouth to Gage Jan. 27, 1775, directed him to encourage Ruggles to raise a corps of loyalists, *Gage* II 180.

31. North's motion for an act restraining the New England fisheries and trade Feb. 10, 1775, 4 *Force* I 1622. The proposed act, 15 Geo. III ch. 10, passed in due course and was assented to March 30, *Journals H. of C.* XXXV 241.

32. The act restraining the trade of N.J., Pa., Md., Va., and S.C. was 15 Geo. III ch. 18, assented to April 13, 1775, *same* 308. N.Y., N.C., and Del. were omitted. The omission of N.Y. can be accounted for by the N.Y. Assembly's vote against supporting the measures of the Continental Congress which Acting Gov. Cadwallader Colden reported to Dartmouth Feb. 1 (*Colden* 1877 383), the omission of N.C. because the London Agents for N.C. watered down the N.C. protest, Lonn *Agents of the Southern Colonies* 210. I cannot account for the omission of Del.

33. The proposal at the Cabinet meeting of Jan. 13, 1775, quoted in the text, to send commissioners to America, *Dartmouth* (1887) 372–373. Hutchinson's diary for Jan. 25, Hutchinson *Diary* I 363 and the King to Dartmouth, Jan. 28, *Dartmouth* (1892) 501, indicate that the suggestion was made by Dartmouth.

34. The King to Dartmouth Jan. 28, 1775, as to sending Gen. Jeffery Amherst to America, *same* 501. The King had discouraged a plan for a commission, "much approv'd by Lord Mansfield," presented earlier by North because, said the King, "this looks so like the Mother Country being more affraid of the continuance

of the dispute than the Colonies, and I cannot think it likely to make them reasonable," North to the King "Tuesday Evening" [Dec. 13] and the King's reply Dec. 15, *Geo. III* III 158, 156.

35. The King to Dartmouth Jan. 31, 1775, as to Amherst's refusal, quoted in the text, *Dartmouth* (1892) 501. Amherst added "nothing but retreat would bring him to go again to America," *same* 501. Did Amherst mean a retreat by the administration from its recent colonial measures or a military retreat in case of war? I make no guess. Explanations of Amherst's refusal by Horace Walpole, Trevelyan, and Bancroft, none of them satisfying, are cited in Mayo *Amherst* 279.

36. Cabinet minute Jan. 21, 1775, quoted in the text, *Dartmouth* (1887) 372–373, and an additional undated minute probably of this meeting, Donoughue *Brit. Politics* 224. There was an intervening Cabinet meeting on Jan. 16, the King to North and North to the King Jan. 16, and Lord Rochford to the King Jan. 18, *Geo III* III 166, 167, but no minute of this meeting has been found.

37. North's "conciliatory" motion quoted in the text, presented to the House of Commons Feb. 20, 1775, as printed in the journals of the House for Feb. 27, *Journals H. of C.* XXV 161; also in 4 *Force* I 1598.

38. Benjamin Franklin to William Franklin March 22, 1775, quoted in the text, characterizing North's plan, *Letter to W. F.* 392.

39. Lord Chatham to Lord Mahon Feb. 20, 1775, and Richard Champion to Willing, Morris & Co. March 6, 1775, quoted in the text, as to North's motion, *Pitt* IV 403 and Guttridge *Champion* 51. To similar effect, Franklin to James Bowdoin Feb. 25, Smyth *Franklin* VI 309.

40. Edmund Burke to John Noble concerning North's motion, Feb. 21, 1775, *Burke* III 118. Further details of the motion and its reception, North to the King, *Geo. III* III 178, and Edward Gibbon, the historian, recently elected to the Commons, to John B. Holroyd, Feb. 25, *Gibbon* (Norton) II 61.

41. North's motion carried 274 to 88, Feb. 20, 1775, 4 *Force* I 1610.

42. The speakers for and against North's motion are listed in North to the King, *Geo. III* III 178–179. The speeches of several of those listed by North are in 4 *Force* I 1600–1608. The opposition speakers represented followers both of Chatham and of Lord Rockingham, leaders of the two principal opposition parties.

43. North's statement in the debate in the House on his motion, Feb. 20, 1775, as described in the text, *same* 1598–1599, 1599–1602n., 1608.

44. North to the King "Sunday morning" Feb. 19, 1775, as to North's proposed motion, *Geo. III* III 177.

45. Reconvening of Parliament Jan. 19, 1775, and presentation of over 100 documents to both Houses Jan. 19 and 20, bearing on colonial unrest, 4 *Force* I 1489–1493, 1513.

46. Chatham's speech and motion of Jan. 20, 1775, for withdrawal of the troops, *same* 1493–1504. Williams *Pitt* II 350 lists several reports of Chatham's speech in support of his motion, the best known of which is in 4 *Force* I 1493–1498. A good account not cited by Williams, by Josiah Quincy, dated Jan. 20, is in Quincy *Memoir* 264–276 and another, dated Jan. 21, in the hand of Benjamin Franklin's great-nephew Jonathan Williams, is in Knollenberg *Franklin* 11–18.

47. Defeat of Chatham's motion for removal of the troops and the names of those voting for the motion, Jan. 20, 1775, 4 *Force* I 1504. The eighteen peers voting for the motion were the Duke of Cumberland (brother of the King, with whom he was on bad terms), the Dukes of Richmond, Portland, and Manchester, the Bishop of Exeter (Frederick Keppel), and Lords Thanet, Abingdon, Fitzwilliam, Tankerville, Stanhope, Spencer, Chatham, Camden, Wycombe (Shelburne), Ponsonby, Sondes, and Grosvenor, most of whom were regular followers of Rockingham or Chatham.

48. Merchants' petition to House of Commons for "healing measures," *same* 1513–1518. The merchants' movements for conciliation are well covered in Sosin *Agents* 196–199, 218–221, and Kammen *Agents* 302–305 and sources cited therein. The merchants were spurred to action by Franklin and other London Agents of the colonies, but as brought out in Kammen *Agents passim,* the London Agents' influence had been greatly weakened from various causes by 1774. George Hayley, who presented the petition, was the brother-in-law of John Wilkes.

49. The motion for consideration of the London merchants' petition by a select committee, made by Sir William Meredith, member for Liverpool, is in 4 *Force* I 1516. The vote of 197 to 81 against the motion, a vote virtually shelving the petition, is in *same* 1518. I have found no list of those voting in favor of the amendment.

50. Chatham's plan for conciliation presented to the House of Lords Feb. 1, 1775, *same* 1503–1507. Expected contribution by the colonies as part of the plan did not include "the new provinces of East and West Florida, Georgia, Nova-Scotia, St. Johns [present-day Prince Edward Island] and Canada, the circumstances and abilities of the said Provinces being reserved for the wisdom of Parliament in their due time," *same* 1506. As to Benjamin Franklin's slight contribution to the plan, Franklin to William Franklin March 22, *Letter to W. F.* 368.

51. I recognize that not all colonial Whigs would have been satisfied by Chatham's plan had it passed, as illustrated by the contemporary criticism of it quoted in 4 *Force* I 1505–1506n. But I believe the dissatisfied would have been in the minority.

52. Rejection of Chatham's plan of conciliation Feb. 1, 1775, 61 to 32, *same* 1514.

53. Burke's motion and supporting speech for conciliation, March 22, 1775, described in the text, *same* 1745–1776. Burke's famous speech has been published many times, e.g., in Burke *Speeches* (1942) 76–141.

54. Rejection of Burke's plan, March 22, 1775, 4 *Force* I 1777.

55. David Hartley's plan of conciliation (March 27, 1775), which was defeated without a division, *same* 1781–1794. As to Hartley and his plan, Guttridge *Hartley passim,* Van Alstyne "Parliamentary Supremacy" 210–211, Namier and Brooke *Commons* II 592–593.

56. The motion declaring Mass. in rebellion was supported by the Attorney- and Solicitor-General's opinion Feb. 2, 1775, that some of the resolutions of the Mass. Provincial Congress "amount to high treason," *Calendar H. O. Papers* (for 1773–1775) 319. The law officers had previously (Dec. 13, 1774) given a similar

opinion as to the action on Aug. 26, 1774, of Joshua Bigelow, Edward Rawson, and others in compelling Timothy Paine of Worcester, Mass., to resign as a mandamus councilor, *same* 262, described in Paine to Gage, Aug. 27, Matthews "Mass. Royal Council" 476–478.

57. North's motion of Feb. 2, 1775, in the Commons for an address to the King as to a rebellion in Mass., quoted in the text, and its adoption Feb. 6, by a vote of 288 to 105; also the adoption of a similar motion in the Lords Feb. 7, by a vote of 104 to 29, 4 *Force* I 1542, 1548, 1564, 1570, 1585. Debates in both Houses on the proposed address, *same* 1542–1587. The vote in the Commons was on a motion to recommit the proposed address; the motion for the address itself was thereafter adopted without a division. The King's concurring reply Feb. 10 is in *same* 1590.

58. The letter of Dartmouth to Gage Jan. 27, 1775, referred to in the text, spurring Gage to action, *Gage* II 179–183. One of the quirks of historiography is that the great importance of this letter, part of which was quoted by Bancroft (Bancroft *History* VII 218–219), was not pointed out until the publication of John R. Alden's "Why the March to Concord?" in the *American Historical Review of* April, 1944.

CHAPTER 28

1. Notice dated Nov. 2, 1774, by the Philadelphia committee elected in June calling for a meeting on Nov. 12 at the State House to elect a committee to enforce the Association in Philadelphia, and election of a committee of sixty-six members for Philadelphia and suburbs, 4 *Force* I 956–957 and *Pa. Gazette* Nov. 16 and 23; Schlesinger *Col. Merchants* 456–459. (Opposition to this among local Quakers is described in *same* 496–498; Sharpless *Quakers in the Revolution* 106–110; 4 *Force* I 963–964, 1093–1094, 1176–1177, 1270.)

2. Notice issued by the Philadelphia enforcement committee, Dec. 6, 1774, concerning the disposal of banned goods arriving after Dec. 1, *same* 1026–1027.

3. Jonathan Blake, Daniel Dunscomb, and Christopher Duyckinck are named in May, 1774, Nov., 1774, and March, 1776, respectively, as "Chairman" of "the Body" or "the Committee" of Mechanics, 4 *Force* I 295, 987, V 439, but the composition of the group is obscure. Duyckinck, Abraham Brasher, Theophilus Anthony, Francis Van Dyck, and Jeremiah Platt signed an address in July, 1774, as "a Committee from a number of citizens," *same* 319, which Leake *Lamb* 94 speaks of as "A Committee from the Mechanics," but gives no evidence supporting this description of the committee.

4. Election of N.Y. City enforcement committee of sixty members Nov. 22, 1774, 4 *Force* I 330. The background of this election, initially called for Nov. 18, *same* 326–330; Becker *N.Y.* 162–167. Activity of the N.Y. City enforcement committee is indicated by its report April 17, 1775, of having netted £347 for the poor of Boston from the sale of imports from England, Ireland, Scotland, the British West Indies, and Madeira that had arrived after Dec. 1, 1774, 4 *Force* II 342–343.

5. Election of Boston enforcement committee of sixty-two members, any seven of whom were to constitute a quorum, at a Boston town meeting Dec. 7, 1774,

Boston Records (for 1770–1777) 205–207. (This meeting was a postponed meeting from several other meetings, the original one of which had legally been summoned before the Massachusetts Regulating Act, limiting town meetings without the Governor's consent, was in effect.)

6. Evidence of enforcement of the Association's ban on imports by some group at Charleston before the end of 1774, *S.C. Gazette* Dec. 19 and 26, 1774; Henry to John Laurens Jan. 4, 1775, Clark *Naval Doc.* I 5–52. Election by the S.C. Congress of Jan. 11–17, 1775, of enforcement committees except for St. Philip and St. Michael parishes in Charleston, 4 *Force* I 1113–1114, indicates that such a committee was already acting there. Henry to John Laurens Jan. 18, has interesting details of the meeting of this Congress, Clark *Naval Doc.* I 64.

7. Gov. Lord Dunmore of Va. to Lord Dartmouth Dec. 24, 1774, concerning the establishment and activities of committees throughout Va. to enforce the Association, 4 *Force* I 1061–1062. Details of the Va. committees and their activities are given in *same* I 964–1255, II 13–298 *passim;* Mays *Pendleton* I 299–304, 351–352; Edmund Pendleton and Walker Taliaferro to Peyton Randolph Dec. 29, 1770, Mays *Pendleton Letters* I 62; Bowman "Va. Committees" 322–324.

8. Formation and activities of committees throughout the colonies represented at the First Continental Congress, Schlesinger *Col. Merchants* 440–469, 478–529; Clark *Naval Doc.* I 5–235 *passim;* and sources cited, under the names of the several colonies, in 4 *Force* I, II. Exports from England to the twelve participating colonies dropped from £2,532,919 in 1774, and an average of £2,674,197 for the five years 1770–1774, to £82,385 in 1775, *Hist. Statistics* 757.

9. Delegates to the Second Continental Congress were elected from Nov. 3, 1774, to April 5, 1775, by the regular Assemblies of Conn., N.J., Pa., Del., S.C., and R.I. and by conventions in N.H., Mass., Md., Va., and N.C., *Journals Cont. Congress* II 15–20. Election by a convention rather than by the regular Assembly in the latter group of colonies resulted from the failure of the Governors of these colonies to call a meeting of the Assembly.

10. The refusal of a majority of members attending the Jan.–April, 1775, session of the N.Y. Assembly to approve the proceedings of the First Continental Congress or elect delegates to the proposed Second Congress, is described and discussed in an appendix to this chapter.

11. The proceedings of the N.Y. provincial convention, April 20–22, 1775, 4 *Force* II 351–358. Richmond and Cumberland counties, represented at the Jan.–April, 1775, session of the N.Y. Assembly, sent no delegates to the convention, and the delegates from Queens were so little representative of the county that they were not permitted to vote. (The N.Y. manors apparently were not granted representation in the convention; but Abraham Ten Broeck, member of the Assembly for Rensselaerwyck Manor, was among the convention delegates from Albany County.)

12. Reelection of delegates who served in the First Congress to the Second, and their service there, *Journals Cont. Cong.* II 13–21; Burnett *Letters* I xli–lxvi. Joseph Galloway of Pa. was reelected but declined to attend; Samuel Rhoads of Pa. was omitted because "being now the Mayor of the City of Philadelphia . . . he could not attend the service," *Pa. Assembly* VIII 7167, 7234. Isaac Low and John Haring of N.Y. asked to be omitted, 4 *Force* II 357. I have found no expla-

nation of the omission of Nathaniel Folsom of N.H., who continued to be a leading Whig in the province.

13. Addition of the persons named in the text to the Mass., N.Y., and Md. delegations and substitution in N.H., *Journals Cont. Cong.* II 13, 14, 15, 19. On May 6, 1775, Pa. Assembly added Benjamin Franklin, recently returned from England, Thomas Willing, and James Wilson to the Pa. delegation, *same* 18, and later there were many changes in the delegates to the Second Continental Congress. In July, 1775, Georgia held a convention which elected delegates to the Second Congress, Coleman *Ga.* 56–61.

14. Statement in the Memorial of the First Continental Congress adopted Oct. 21, 1774, which recommends preparedness for "every contingency," *Journals Cont. Cong.* I 101.

15. Measures in preparation for war in Conn. Oct., 1774, described in the text, *Conn. Col. Rec.* XIV 343. Furthermore, in Feb., 1775, the Conn. Council directed the provincial treasurer to buy for the use of the colony 300 barrels of powder, 15 tons of lead, and 60,000 flints, and in March the Conn. General Assembly provided for the establishment of additional military companies, *same* 386–387n., 402, 404.

16. Samuel Ward to John Dickinson, Dec. 14, 1774, describing the R.I. General Assembly's preparations for war, Knollenberg *Ward* 31. The warlike resolutions summarized by Ward are in *R.I. Col. Rec.* VII 262–264, 268–271. A possible implication in the instructions to the R.I. delegates to the Second Continental Congress, that they were not to vote for war measures in the Congress, *same* 267, is repelled by the Assembly's own war measures.

17. The resolution of the N.H. convention of Jan. 25, 1775, concerning the drilling of the colony's militia quoted in the text, 4 *Force* I 1182.

18. The seizure of powder, cannon, and muskets at Fort William and Mary near Portsmouth, N.H., on Dec. 14 and 15, 1774, Gov. John Wentworth of N.H. to Gen. Thomas Gage and Admiral Samuel Graves Dec. 16 and 20, Clark *Naval Doc.* I 27, 37.

19. Measures of the Md. convention Dec. 8–12, 1774, preparing for war, 4 *Force* I 1031–1033.

20. Resolution of the S.C. convention Jan. 17, 1775, recommending that all the inhabitants of the colony drill and otherwise train themselves in "the use of arms," *same* 1118.

21. Richard Henry Lee to Samuel Adams Feb. 4, 1775, explaining the delay in assembling a provincial convention in Va., Ballagh *Lee* I 127–128.

22. Washington to an unidentified correspondent Jan. 6, 1775, as to the widespread formation of "independent" companies, quoted in Samuel Chase to James Duane Feb. 5, 1775, *So. Hist. Assoc. Public.* XX (1906) 304. Dunmore wrote Lord Dartmouth Dec. 24, 1774, that "Every County . . . is now arming a Company of men, whom they call an Independent Company . . . to be employed against Government, if occasion require," 4 *Force* I 1062.

23. The references to the arming, equipping, and drill of independent companies in Washington's correspondence and diary from Oct., 1774, to March, 1775, Hamilton *Letters to Washington* V 57–109 *passim; Washington* III 256–276

passim; Washington *Diaries* II 170–188 *passim;* Knollenberg *Washington* 111, 190.

24. Va. convention's resolutions for preparedness for war, March 25, 1775, 4 *Force* II 169–170.

25. James Parker to Charles Steuart Apr. 6, 1775, quoted in the text, *Mag. Am. Hist.* III 151–161. Parker, a Tory, was not a member of the convention. I have found no similar account by any member of the convention, but the resolutions of the convention quoted in note 26 below are consistent with his account.

26. On March 23, the convention chose a committee, including Patrick Henry, Richard Henry Lee, Robert Carter Nicholas, Benjamin Harrison, Lemuel Riddick, George Washington, and Thomas Jefferson to prepare a plan for the army, and disciplining such a number of men as would put the colony immediately "into a posture of defence," 4 *Force* II 167–168.

27. The speech of Henry referred to by Parker probably was the one in which, according to a much later version, he exclaimed "as for me, give me liberty or give me death!" Parker's only comment on Henry's speech was "You never heard anything more infamously insolent than P. Henry's speech: he called the K——— a tyrant, a fool, a puppet and a tool to the ministry. Said there was no Englishmen, no Scots, no Britons, but a set of wretches sunk in Luxury; they had lost their native courage and unable to look the brave Americans in the face . . . ," *Mag. Am. Hist.* III 151–161.

28. Parker to Steuart, Apr. 6, 1775, *same* 151–161. The persons referred to in Parker's letter as defeating Henry's plan were Nicholas ("the Treasurer"), Harrison, Richard Bland, and Riddick. All except Bland were members of the military committee described in note 30 below.

29. In replying Jan. 29, 1775, to the letter from Ward to him, summarized earlier in the text of this chapter, Dickinson explained that in Pa., "a Party who have considerable weight in our Assembly" was so alarmed by the recent action of the Pa. convention of Jan. 23–28 (4 *Force* I 1169–72) in voting unqualified approval of the proceedings of the First Continental Congress, that "a good deal of delicacy" would be required to prevent the Pa. Assembly from giving "very restrictive instructions" to the delegates to the Second Congress, Knollenberg *Ward* 33.

30. The N.Y. delegates were instructed "to concert . . . such measures as shall be judged most effectual for the preservation of American rights and priviledges *and* [italics added] for the restoration of harmony between Great Britain and the colonies," *Journals Cont. Cong.* II 17; and the delegates "to concert . . . such further measures, as shall appear to them best calculated for the *accomodation* [italics added] of the unhappy differences between Great-Britain and the Colonies, on a constitutional foundation," *same* 17, 18.

31. Speech of James Duane of the N.Y. delegation in the Second Continental Congress May 25, 1775, quoted in the text, Burnett *Letters* I 99.

CHAPTER 29

1. Resolution of the Worcester County convention in the town of Worcester Aug. 10, 1774, referred to in the text, *Mass. Cong. Journals* 631. Similar resolu-

tions of Suffolk and other Mass. County conventions in Aug. and Sept., and recommendation of Middlesex County convention at Concord Aug. 31, for a provincial meeting to be held there Oct. 11, *same* 601–627 *passim*.

2. Assembling of the First Mass. Congress at Concord Oct. 11, 1774. Over 200 delegates from all thirteen counties of the province, except Nantucket and remote Lincoln in the present state of Maine, were elected, but I have not found how many attended, *same* 7–17, 49. There had been a preliminary meeting at Salem on Oct. 5–7, of ninety members of the House of Representatives, *same* 3–6, who had assembled there despite a proclamation of Gov. Thomas Gage Sept. 28, canceling the meeting of the House, 4 *Force* I 809–810.

3. Election of officers and Committee on the State of the Province described in the text, Oct. 11 and 12, 1774, *Mass. Cong. Journals* 16–17.

4. The Congress sat at Concord Oct. 7–14, 1774, and at Cambridge, Oct. 17–29 and Nov. 23–Dec. 10, *same* 1.

5. Congress' resolutions of Oct. 14, 28, and 29, 1774, calling upon constables and Collectors to withhold from the provincial treasurer taxes received by them and pay them instead to a Receiver-General, Henry Gardner of Stow, chosen by the Congress, *same* 19, 38, 45–46. Later resolutions indicate difficulties in securing compliance with this requisition, *same* 65–66, 98, 113. A report of April 25, 1775, states that only £5,000 of the £20,000 in taxes due for 1773 had been paid over to Gardner at that time, *same* 151.

6. Resolution of Oct. 26, 1774, as to replacement of officers of the militia, and the Congress' election (Oct. 27 and Dec. 8) as general officers of those named in the text, *same* 33–34, 36, 65. I have found no evidence that Jedediah Preble, the first-named general officer, accepted the appointment or ever served.

7. Resolution of Oct. 26 and Dec. 10, 1774, for recruiting and equipment of men to be ready to serve "on the shortest notice," *same* 33, 71. The journals of the Congress first referred to "minute men" in a resolution of Nov. 24, *same* 50; but the term was earlier used in resolutions on Sept. 20, of the Worcester County convention, *same* 643–644.

8. Establishment of a Committee of Safety Oct. 26 and 27, 1774, and its responsibilities and members, *same* 31–35. The first names and residences of the members are known from the list of members of the Congress and the towns they represented, *same* 7–9. Any five members were authorized to act for the whole, provided that not more than one of the five was from Boston.

9. Resolutions for defense other than those mentioned in previous paragraphs, *same* 27–74 *passim*.

10. Resolutions adopted by the Congress, as stated in the text, Oct. 13, Dec. 5, and Dec. 10, 1774, *same* 17–19, 57, 73. Delegates to the Mass. Congress were "to be chosen by such only as are qualified by law to vote for representatives in the general assembly," *same* 73.

11. Motion of Oct. 25, 1774, concerning slavery quoted in the text, *same* 29. The motion was in response to a letter from an unidentified writer to the Reverend Dr. Nathaniel Appleton, Congregational minister of Cambridge, "brought into Congress" by Joseph Wheeler, delegate from the town of Harvard, *same* 29.

12. Vote of the Congress, Oct. 25, 1774, that the proposal to "take into consideration the state and circumstances of the negro slaves in this province" should "now subside," *same* 29.

13. Gage to Lord Dartmouth Feb. 17, 1775, as to the election of many new, less "violent" delegates to the Second Mass. Congress, quoted in the text, *Gage* I 392. About a fourth of the delegates to this Congress had not been members of the First. Lists of members, *Mass. Cong. Journals* 7–15, 77–83. John Hancock and Benjamin Lincoln were reelected President and Secretary, *same* 83–84.

14. Various resolutions of Feb. 4–11, 1774, described in the text, *same* 85–97 *passim*. Resolutions of Feb. 8 and 9, 1774, concerning the Committee of Safety, *same* 88, 89. Jabez Fisher of Wrentham was elected to fill Norton Quincy's place on the Committee of Safety and, on Fisher's asking to be relieved, Thomas Gardner of Cambridge was chosen in his place, *same* 89, 143, 144. Again, any five members of the committee, provided not more than one was from Boston, were authorized to act for the whole, *same* 89–90.

15. Adjournment Feb. 16, 1775, to reconvene at Concord March 22, *same* 108.

16. James Warren wrote John Adams Jan. 15, 1775, "Is it consistent with prudence that we should hold our Sessions at Cambridge? . . . if we mean to do anything important, I think it too near the whole strength of our Enemies. If not, I shall repent leaving my friends at this severe Season," *Warren–Adams* I 46.

17. Gage to Dartmouth Jan. 18, 1775, and Major John Pitcairn to Lord Sandwich Feb. 14, quoted in the text, *Gage* I 390 and *Sandwich* I 57–58.

18. The *Essex Gazette* of Feb. 14, 1775, reported the impending embarkation in Ireland of four regiments to reinforce Gage. The Committee of Safety's minutes of Feb. 22 state, "on certain intelligence, or such as appears to the committee to be such, of the reenforcements coming to General Gage, that then the committee," etc., *Mass. Cong. Journals* 510.

19. Resolutions for war measures of the Committees of Safety and of Supplies Feb. 21–24, 1775, described in the text, *same* 509–512. Two more of the cannon mentioned in the text were assigned to the Boston artillery company, which apparently had not yet elected a new commander in place of Major Adino Paddock, a Tory.

20. Joseph Hawley's warning letter to Thomas Cushing Feb. 22, 1775, quoted in the text, *same* 748–750. Hawley pointed out that the Continental Congress' resolution of Oct. 8, 1774, "this Congress approve of the opposition by the Inhabitants of the Massachusetts-bay to the execution of the late acts of Parliament; and if the same shall be attempted to be carried into execution by force, in such case all America ought to support them in their opposition," *Journals Cont. Cong.* I 58, was "far too loose" to be considered a definite commitment.

21. Resolution of March 30, 1775, concerning what should be considered a hostile move by Gage justifying armed opposition, French *Day of Concord* 41, quoting the Heath Papers at M.H.S. The resolution was mentioned but not recorded in the journals of the Congress, *Mass. Cong. Journals* 112. The resolution further stated that on a hostile move by Gage, "the Military Force of the Province ought to be assembled, and an Army of Observation immediately formed, to act solely on the defensive so long as it can be justified on the Principles of Reason and Self Preservation and [no?] longer."

22. James Warren at Concord to his wife, Mercy Warren, Apr. 6, 1775, "Last Saturday [April 1] we came near to adjournment, were almost equally divided upon the question," but a majority decided to sit a little longer awaiting news from England, *Warren–Adams* I 44.

23. James to Mercy Warren Apr. 6, 1775, concerning the alarming news that arrived from England on Apr. 2, *Warren–Adams* 44. Gage wrote Dartmouth April 22, "Two vessels arrived from Falmouth at Marblehead on the 2nd Instant and brought Papers which . . . throw them ["the Faction"] into a Consternation . . . ," *Gage* I 396.

24. The reports from England described in the text were published in the *Essex Gazette* of April 4, 1775, which also gives other details of the reports and of the vessels bringing them.

25. A New York letter of Nov. 1, 1774, reported that Gen. Guy Carleton, Governor of Quebec, was prepared, if requested, to send a force of Indians, as well as 6,000 Canadians, to reinforce Gage, Willard *Letters* 19. As brought out in Chapter 30, Gage had recently sounded out Carleton as to the possibility of a reinforcement of Canadians and Indians and had received a favorable reply.

26. Resolutions of the Congress April 3–15, 1775, described in the text, *Mass. Cong. Journals* 117–147 *passim*. The vote on April 8, given in the text: "present 103, in favor 96," *same* 135. This is the only record in the *Journals* of the number of votes on any resolution. If the *Essex Gazette*'s report of March 28, that nearly 200 members were then attending, is correct, there evidently was a large exodus between then and April 8.

27. Evidence of the recruitment and officers of the minute men and some of the difficulties encountered, French *First Year* 40–43. James Warren wrote John Adams May 7, 1775, "We are embarrassed in officering our Army by the Establishment of Minute Men. I wish it had never taken place, and the necessity of having Field Officers *appointed* [italics added] is every day seen, and indeed in my Opinion that should have been the first thing done," *Warren–Adams* 47.

28. The Mass. Congress' resolution of April 14, 1775, states, "That a committee [the Committee of Safety] . . . apply to a suitable number of persons, to be in readiness . . . to act as field officers: such officers, in conjunction with the committee, to apply to proper persons as captains, and they do determine on such subaltern officers as may be necessary . . . , the committee and officers, *caeteris paribus,* to give the preference to persons who have been chosen officers in the regiments of minute men," *Mass. Cong. Journals* 143. Appointment of these officers, April 21–28, *same* 521, 523, 526.

29. Congress' advice of April 6, 1775, to all the towns of Bristol County to "exert yourselves that the militia and especially the minute men of your county be found in the best posture of defence"; but "whatever patience and forbearance it may require for the present, you would act on the defensive only, until the further direction of this Congress," *same* 130. Similar advice to a number of other towns was adopted the next day, *same* 134.

30. Resolution of April 15, 1775, adjourning the Congress until May 10, but with the provision for a call to reassemble sooner, described in the text, *same* 146.

31. Gage to Dartmouth April 22, 1774, and James to Mercy Warren April 7, as to flight from or non-return to Boston of Samuel Adams, John Hancock, and

other radical Whigs, *Gage* I 396 and *Warren–Adams* I 45. The question of whether or not Adams' chief lieutenant, Dr. Joseph Warren of Boston, was there on April 18, is discussed in the appendix to Chapter 31.

32. The reputation of Adams and Hancock as the outstanding rebel leaders is evidenced by Gage's proclamation of June 12, 1775, offering amnesty to all rebels who would "lay down their arms and return to their duties of peaceable subjects, except only . . . Samuel Adams and John Hancock," 4 *Force* II 969.

CHAPTER 30

1. The Sixty-Fourth Regiment drawn from Halifax in 1772 to replace the Fourteenth at Castle William, *Gage* I 326, was still stationed there as late as July 19, 1775, *same* II 690. Arrival at Boston of the Fourth, Fifth, Thirty-eighth, and Forty-third from England and Ireland in June and July, 1774, is recorded in Gage to Dartmouth June 26 and July 5 and 6, *same* I 357–360 and John Rowe's diary for June 10 to July 5. Rowe *Diary* 274–277. Arrival at Boston of sixty artillerymen from New York City, Gage to Dartmouth May 30, 1774, *Gage* I 356.

2. In Knollenberg *Origin* 87–96, I discussed various possible motives of the British government's decision in 1764 to increase greatly the pre-war force of British troops in North America even though the recent cession of Canada to Great Britain had minimized the threat of French invasion of the old British North American colonies. After the widespread opposition in the old colonies in 1765 to execution of the Stamp Act, one of the chief motives almost certainly was to ensure obedience of the old colonies to British rule.

3. Transfer of the regiments and companies of infantry named in the text from Halifax, Quebec, and elsewhere in North America to Boston, Aug. to Nov. 1774, Dartmouth to Gage Aug. 27 to Nov. 2, *Gage* I 368–383 *passim*. (There had been a brief transfer of the Forty-seventh from N.J. to N.Y. before its transfer to Boston, *same* 368, 371, 379.)

4. Gage wrote Dartmouth May 30, 1774, "General [Frederick] Haldimand took the Opportunity of a Vessel in the Service to send a Detachment of Sixty Artillerists and eight Pieces of Ordance from New-York . . . ," *same* I 356. Col. Lord Percy wrote from Boston to the Duke of Northumberland Aug. 15, "I have now . . . 22 pieces of cannon," *Percy* 34; and on Oct. 31, Capt. William Glanville Evelyn wrote the Reverend William Evelyn that "more artillery" had recently arrived, *Evelyn* 38.

5. Gage to Dartmouth Nov. 2, 1774, stating that on the landing of the Tenth and Fifty-second Regiments at Boston he would have "a Force of near three Thousand Men exclusive of a Regiment for the Defence of Castle William," *Gage* I 383. The authorized strength of a regiment was 484 men (Shy *Toward Lexington* 276), but some if not all the regiments evidently were much below their authorized strength. Gage's return of troops dated July 19, 1775, shows that his infantry regiments then ranged from 333 to 457 men, *Gage* II 690.

6. As noted in Chapter 27, Dartmouth wrote Gage Oct. 17, 1774, that he was sending him a detachment of marines to Boston that would "probably not fall much short of 600 Men," *same* II 174. The *Massachusetts Spy* of Dec. 16 reported that 500 marines were being landed, Clark *Naval Doc.* I 30, but Gage wrote

Admiral Samuel Graves March 23, that "not quite four Hundred" had in fact been landed, *Gage* II 158.

7. Admiral Graves' "List of the North American Squadron," Jan. 1, 1775, reports the *Preston, Somerset, Boyne, Asia, Mercury,* and *Glasgow,* ships of war, and the schooner *Diana,* as stationed at Boston, Clark *Naval Doc.* I 47.

8. Members of the Crown-appointed Mass. Council appointed pursuant to the Regulating Act held sessions in Boston on Aug. 16 and 31, 1774, Matthews "Mass. Royal Council" 471–472, 475–476. Matthews gives records of several more meetings (*same* 494–501), but not until after April, 1774. But Gage was unable even in Boston to secure execution of provisions of the Regulating Act concerning juries, since the judges of the court sitting there "could get neither Grand, nor petit Jury," Gage to Dartmouth, Sept. 2, *Gage* I 370.

9. Gage to Dartmouth Sept. 2 and Oct. 30, 1774, stating his policy was to avoid, if possible, a clash with the rebels, while awaiting instructions from the administration, *same* 371–372, 380.

10. Gage's seizure of powder at Quarry Hill, Sept. 1, 1774, John Andrews to William Barrell Sept. 1, "Andrews Letters" 350; Gage to Dartmouth Sept. 3, *Gage* I 373; Ezra Stiles' diary Nov. 17, *Stiles Diary* I 477; newspaper account Sept. 5, 4 *Force* IV 762. Estimates of the powder carried away varied from 250 half-barrels to nearly 300 barrels. The spreading of an erroneous report that this powder raid had been accomplished by a British cannonade of Boston and the killing of six of its inhabitants and the effect of this report in the First Continental Congress were described in Chapter 22.

11. The work on the fortifications on Boston neck, Andrews to Barrell Sept. 5 and 11, 1775, "Andrews Letters" 355, 359. Protests, beginning early in Sept. and continuing until late Oct., against the work on these fortifications, by the selectmen of Boston, the Suffolk County Convention of Sept., 1774, and the First Mass. Congress, as well as Gage's temperate replies can be followed in Gage to Dartmouth Sept. 12, Oct. 17 and 20, *Gage* I 374, 378, 381; *Mass. Journals* 18, 20, 42–45, 606; *Journals Cont. Cong.* I 55, 60–61; 4 *Force* I 939.

12. The threat of "the country people" to drive the British troops from Boston, Andrews to Barrell Sept. 2, 3, and 5, 1775, "Andrews Letters" 351–355; Gage to Dartmouth Sept. 12, *Gage* I 374.

13. Lieut. John Barker's last comment in his diary on work on the fortification is Dec. 4, 1774, *Barker* 10. His earlier comments on this are in *same* 5, 8. (The British officers who acted as "assistant engineers" on the project apparently were very inefficient as engineers, *same* 10; *Mackenzie* I 3.)

14. The detachment sent to Marshfield under Capt. Nisbet Balfour in Jan., 1775, and maintained there until after April 18, Gage to Dartmouth Jan. 27, *Gage* I 391 and documents from Jan. 27 to Apr. 11, Clark *Naval Doc.* 94–96, 114, 120, 162, 173, 178. Withdrawal of this detachment April 21, Graves to Gage Apr. 20, *same* 202 and Stiles' diary for April 24, *Stiles Diary* I 539.

15. Intelligence report to Gage Feb. 21, 1775, that "Twelve pieces of Brass Cannon mounted are att Salem & lodged near the North River, on the back of the Town," Clark *Naval Doc.* I 101.

16. Expedition to Salem, Feb. 25–26, 1775, Gage to Dartmouth March 4, *Gage* I 394; *Essex Gazette* Feb. 28 and *Boston Evening Post* March 6, reprinted

in Clark *Naval Doc.* I 114–116, 120–121; Ezra Stiles' diary for March 7, Stiles *Diary* I 522–524.

17. The successful expedition to Fort Pownall on the Penobscot in the present state of Maine, then part of Mass., launched April 8, 1775, correspondence and list of cannon and other military supplies secured by the expedition, Clark *Naval Doc.* I 168–169, 172, 173, 175, 178, 185–187.

18. Gage's shipment of arms and ammunition to Col. Thomas Gilbert at Freetown, Admiral Graves' "Narrative" March 7, 1775; *Rose*'s log ("Remarks") March 14; Gilbert to Capt. James Wallace, commander of the *Rose,* March 23; Gage to Graves March 31, Clark *Naval Doc.* I 130, 144, 159, 160, 165; Stiles' diary for March 30, Stiles *Diary* I 529. About 1,000 rebels surrounded Gilbert's men on April 10, and captured "about thirty" of them; Gilbert himself escaped, Stiles' diary for April 11, *same* 533.

19. Gage wrote Governor Gen. Guy Carleton, of Quebec, Sept. 4, 1774, "As I must look forward to the worst . . . I am to ask your Opinion, whether a Body of Canadians and Indians might be collected, and confided in, for the Service in this Country should matters come to Extremities . . . ," to which Carleton replied Sept. 20 that he could, with proper inducements, raise several dependable battalions of Canadians and that "the Savages of this Province, I hear, are in a very good Humor . . . but you know what [undependable] sort of People they are," S & D *Doc.* II 583–584.

20. Reports of Gage's informers from March 9 to April 18, 1775, are in French *Gage's Informers* 9–30; also Gage to Dartmouth Feb. 17, 20 and March 4, 28, *Gage* I 392–395.

21. Gage's instructions of Feb. 22, 1775, to Captain William Brown (Browne) and Ensign Henry De Berniere (Birniere) to "go through the Counties of Suffolk and Worcester, taking a sketch of the country as you pass . . . , [and] mark out the Roads and Distances from Town to Town . . . ," 4 *Force* I 1268. Berniere's undated report of his and Captain Brown's survey is in *same* 1263–1268. Gage had issued a call for volunteers for such service, Jan. 8, 1775, diaries of Lieuts. John Barker and Frederick Mackenzie for Jan. 8, *Barker* 18; *Mackenzie* I 3.

22. Detachments sent out frequently for marches in the vicinity of Boston, Dec. 13, 1774, to March 30, 1775, Andrews to Barrell "Andrews Letters" 390–391; Barker's diary, *Barker* 11, 18, 23, 25, 27; Mackenzie's diary, *Mackenzie* I 6, 7, 13; Letter from Boston, April 1, 4 *Force* II 253.

23. Gen. James Wolfe's disparagement of colonial troops quoted in the Introduction is matched by statements of other British officers who served in the French and Indian War. When British and colonial troops were serving together, British officers were prone to excuse defeats by unfairly attributing them exclusively to the misconduct of colonial officers and men, but letters of some colonial officers (e.g., Washington's in Fitzpatrick *Washington* II 1–97) indicate that British disparagement of colonial troops, particularly colonial militiamen, was not wholly unwarranted.

24. Capt. Evelyn to William Evelyn, July 6, 1774, calling the rebels "rascals and poltroons," *Evelyn* 27. Evelyn's career was cut short in Nov., 1776, by a fatal wound received in battle near New York City, *same* 11.

25. Evelyn to Mrs. Leveson-Gower, wife of Captain John Gower, R.N., Dec. 6, 1774, hoping for orders to chastise the villainous rebels, *same* 42–43.

26. Evelyn to William Evelyn Feb. 18, 1775, hoping for early orders to scourge "the upstart vagabonds . . . with rods of iron," *same* 51. Earlier in this letter Evelyn had written "We . . . consider it as the most fortunate opportunity for Great Britain to establish her superiority over this country; even to reduce it to that state of subjection which the right of conquest may now give her the fairest title to; at least, to keep it in that state of dependency which they are now avowedly trying to free themselves from . . . ," *same* 50.

27. Col. Lord Percy to the Duke of Northumberland July 27, 1774, and to Henry Reveley Aug. 8, expressing his contempt for the cruel and cowardly New Englanders, *Percy* 28, 31. Percy, dissatisfied with General William Howe's treatment of him, was given leave to come home and returned to England in June, 1777, Lewis *Walpole* 24 (1967) 309n.; Lord George Germain to the King June 7, 1777, *Geo. III* III 454.

28. Percy to Thomas Percy Nov. 25, 1774, and to Gen. Edward Harvey, Feb. 9, 1775, denouncing the rebels as "the most designing Artfull Villains in the World" and expressing his hope for "pointed and effectual" orders from England to strike at them, *Percy* 44, 48.

29. Maj. John Pitcairn to Lord Sandwich Feb. 14, 1775, hoping for orders to seize "the impudent rascals" in the Mass. Provincial Congress and "send them to England," *Sandwich* I 57–58. The resolves enclosed in Pitcairn's letter were those of the First Mass. Congress for the payment of taxes to the Receiver-General chosen by that Congress and for preparations for defense, which the Second Mass. Congress ordered on Feb. 3, to be published and distributed throughout the province, *Mass. Journals* 84.

30. Pitcairn to Sandwich March 4, 1775, predicting that "one active campaign," etc., would "set everything to rights" with the cowardly rebels, *Sandwich* I 60–61. (Pitcairn was killed at Bunker Hill the following June 17; Major John Tupper, Pitcairn's second in command, wrote Sandwich June 21 that Pitcairn "was wounded a few Minutes before the Attack was made on the Redoubt and he died about two or three hours after . . . ," Clark *Naval Doc.* 731.)

31. Gage wrote Barrington Feb. 10, 1775, "I have hitherto Observed a Conduct . . . by which . . . the hot headed Leaders [were] baffled in their Projects. Your next Dispatches will probably require a different Conduct, and I shall wait for them Impatiently . . . for to keep quiet in the Town of Boston only, will not terminate Affairs; the Troops must March into the Country," *Gage* II 669. To similar effect, Gage to Dartmouth Jan. 18 and 27, *same* I 390, 391.

32. Arrival per the *Nautilus* on April 14, 1775, of a copy of Dartmouth's letter of Jan. 27, and of the original per the *Falcon* two days later, Gage to Dartmouth April 22, *same* I 396. For further details, Alden's important essay "Why the March to Concord?" 449–450. The long delay in Dartmouth's letter reaching Gage is explained in a letter from Philip Stephens of the Admiralty to John Pownall Feb. 17, reporting that the *Falcon*, carrying Dartmouth's letter, had been "driven back to St. Helen's by contrary winds," *Dartmouth* (1895) 270.

CHAPTER 31

1. The proclamation referred to in Lord Dartmouth's letter was issued by Gage Nov. 10, 1774, forbidding the people of Mass. to comply with various measures proposed by the First Mass. Congress, 4 *Force* I 973–974.

2. Dartmouth's direction to arrest the principal rebels even though this might be "a signal for Hostilities" referred to a letter of Sept. 25, 1774, to him from Gage stating he had not acted on suggestions "to apprehend a certain number of people" because this "wou'd be the Signal for Hostilities, which they seem very ripe to begin," *Gage* I 376.

3. Dartmouth to Gage Jan. 27, 1775, quoted in the text, giving him carte blanche to strike and implying that he was expected to, *same* II 179–183 at 181–182. Gage had written privately to the Secretary at War, Lord Barrington, Aug. 27, 1774, proposing that the radical leaders in Mass. be arrested and sent to England for trial, Gage Papers, summarized and quoted in part, Alden *Gage* 212. (Barrington himself favored use of the British navy only, Barrington to Gage Nov. 22, Gage Papers, and to Dartmouth Nov. 12 and Dec. 24, Dartmouth Papers I:2:1071 and Barrington *Barrington* 150–157.)

4. The First Continental Congress had passed a resolution Oct. 21, 1774, "That the seizing, or attempting to seize, any person in America, in order to transport such person beyond the sea, for trial of offences, committed within the body of a county in America, being against law, will justify, and ought to meet with resistance and reprisal," *Journals Cont. Cong.* I 102. Gage's seizure of any Mass. rebels would doubtless be assumed by colonial Whigs to be in order to send them to Great Britain for trial.

5. Gage wrote Dartmouth Jan. 18, 1775, that "it's the opinion of most People, if a respectable Force is seen in the field, the most obnoxious of the Leaders seized and a Pardon proclaimed for all others that Government will come off Victorious, and with less Opposition than was expected a few Months ago," *Gage* I 390. However, this was written before the Mass. Congress had decided to remove its place of meeting from Cambridge, only a few miles from Boston, to Concord.

6. On April 15, 1775, the Mass. Congress adjourned until May 10, *Mass. Cong. Journals* 146–147. An undated message received by Gage on April 15, from one of his informers reported that the Congress was to rise on that date, French *Gage's Informers* 23.

7. Though spurred to action by Dartmouth's letter, Gage may also have learned and been influenced by criticism in London of his seeming timidity. Hutchinson's diary for Dec. 1, 1774, to Jan. 2, 1775, records such criticism by at least six persons, including Lord Chancellor Apsley and Gen. Lord Loudoun, Hutchinson *Diary* I 312, 325, 351, 354, 364. See also Secretary of State Lord Suffolk and Under Secretary John Pownall to Dartmouth Nov. 22 and Dec. 18, 1774, *Dartmouth* (1887) 370 and *Dartmouth* (1895) 240. Pressure from Mass. Tories also may have contributed to Gage's decision.

8. An informer writing on March 9 reported the concentration of provisions and military stores in Concord, and another, in an undated report, received by Gage on April 18, stated that the provisions and some of the military stores were still there, French *Gage's Informers* 11–12, 25–26.

9. Lieut. John Barker's diary for Apr. 15, 1775, records "Genl. Orders. 'The Grenadiers and Light Infantry in order to learn Grenadrs. Exercize and new evolutions are to be off all duties 'till further orders'," *Barker* 29.

10. I have found no official statement of the number of officers and men in the expedition. The estimate of probably around 700 men is from Boatner *Encyclopedia of the Am. Revolution* 621 and sources cited therein.

11. Gage's choice of Lieut.-Col. Francis Smith as commander of the expedition to Concord, with Major John Pitcairn second in command, Gage to Smith April 18, 1775, *same* and Lieut. William Sutherland's statement of April 26, *Sutherland* 13. I have found no evidence as to why Pitcairn, an officer of marines, was chosen second in command of a detachment which apparently included no marines. Perhaps the inclusion of the marines in the reserve to be sent to support Smith, if necessary, prompted this choice.

12. There were two good reasons for Gage not to include pieces of artillery, as distinguished from artillery men, in Smith's detachment. Inclusion of artillery would tend to slow up the ferrying and march of the detachment, and Gage had been informed by one of his informers in a message received April 3, 1775, of the Mass. Congress' resolution (described in Chapter 29) that the militia was not to attack Gage's troops on marches into the country unless they were accompanied by artillery, French *Gage's Informers* 18.

13. Gage's instructions to Smith Apr. 18, 1775, *same* 31-32. Gage's description to Smith of the stores at Concord tallies with the report from an informer, published in *same* 11–12, referred to in note 8.

14. Statements of Adm. Samuel Graves and Capts. Edward Le Cras, James Montagu, and James Robinson Apr. 18 and 19, 1775, concerning the British navy's ferrying of the detachment from Boston to Phipp's Farm on the night of April 18–19, Clark *Naval Doc.* I 192, 193, 195.

15. John Hancock to Elbridge Gerry Apr. 18, 1775, and minutes of meeting of Committees of Safety and Supplies April 18, as described in the text, *Gerry* 68 and *Mass. Cong. Journals* 515–518. Some of the resolutions at this meeting as to removal or hiding of supplies at Concord suggest that the committees had got wind of the intended expedition to Concord, but this is countered by other resolutions at this same meeting for transferring supplies to Concord, *same* 516–518.

16. Paul Revere to Jeremy Belknap Jan. 1, 1798, states that on April 18, 1775, Dr. Joseph Warren in Boston dispatched him and another messenger to Lexington to warn Hancock and Samuel Adams of the expedition, Goss *Revere* I 187. I am skeptical that Warren, one of the outstanding radical Whigs in Boston, should have risked being there as late as April 18; I have found no contemporary evidence of his presence there later than April 3, when he wrote letters headed "Boston," Frothingham *Warren* 447–448.

17. The best-known account by Revere of his ride as one of the messengers is in his letter to Belknap of Jan. 1, 1798, Goss *Revere* I 18–207, but Goss prints two other undated statements by Revere concerning the ride, *same* 213–229.

18. John Andrews to Joseph Barrell April 19, 1775, states that the preceding evening, "men appointed to alarm the country upon such occasions got over by stealth as early as they [could] and took different routes," "Andrews Letters" 404. Revere wrote Belknap Jan. 1, 1798, that William Dawes was one of the messengers, Goss *Revere* I 187. I have found no contemporary evidence supporting this statement, but have found none discrediting it. (For later statements as to Dawes, Holland (*Dawes passim.*)

19. Evidence of the messengers' successful activity is given in Chapter 32, and a statement by Lieut. William Sutherland Apr. 26, 1775, and a letter by an unidentified writer dated April 23, identify Revere as one of them, *Sutherland* 14

and Stiles *Diary* 549. Furthermore, the fact, established by contemporary evidence, e.g., Clark *Naval Doc.* I 19, 27, that Revere had often acted as messenger for the Boston Whig leaders would have made him a natural choice to act as a messenger on this occasion.

CHAPTER 32

1. The progress of the Mass. Committee of Safety's message of April 19, 1775, from the committee of one town to another—Worcester, Mass., Brooklyn, Norwich, New London, Lyme, Saybrook, Killingworth, East Guilford [now Madison], Guilford, Branford, New Haven, and Fairfield, Conn.; New York City; New Brunswick, N.J.; Philadelphia; Annapolis, Md.; and Williamsburg, Va. (April 28)—Scheide "The Lexington Alarm" 50, 64–69. A second account of April 19th, dated Wallingford, Conn., April 24, reached Williamsburg May 2, and Georgetown, S.C., May 10, 4 *Force* II 365–369.

2. The committee's message of April 15, 1775, Scheide "The Lexington Alarm" 49. Joseph Palmer, a leading Whig of Braintree, who, together with John Adams and Ebenezer Thayer, represented Braintree in the First Mass. Congress, was the town's sole representative to the Second. Adams wrote James Warren, March 15, 1775, that Palmer "is the best man they [Braintree] have," Adams *Works* IX 354. There is a "Biographical Sketch of Gen. Joseph Palmer" in *The New Englander* III (1845) 1–23.

3. The *Essex Gazette's* estimate of "8 or 900 Men" was apparently correct. On April 23, 1775, Lieut. John Bourmaster, commander of the transport *Empress of Russia,* wrote, "I conducted all the Boats of the Fleet (as well Men a War as Transports) to the back part of Boston where I received the Grenadiers and light Infantry amounting to 850 Officers and Men and Landed them on a point of Marsh . . . ," 3 *W. & M.Q.* X (1935) 104. The name of the writer is known from Clark *Nav. Doc.* 192, 1097. Some other estimates were lower, e.g., *Evelyn* 53.

4. Gen. Gage to Gov. Jonathan Trumbull April 29, 1775, says, "about two hundred armed men [were observed] drawn up on a green" at Lexington; and Major John Pitcairn wrote Gage Apr. 26, "I observed drawn up upon a Green, near 200 of the Rebels," French *Gage's Informers* 53. But Thomas Rice Willard, who was looking out of a window in a house near Lexington Green, swore in an affidavit dated Apr. 23, that "about an Hundred of the Militia of Lexington" were on the green when the British came up, *Journals Cont. Cong.* II 30.

5. A letter from Col. Smith to Gage Apr. 22, 1775, adds to the destroyed items mentioned in the *Gazette,* "some gun powder and musquet-balls, with other small articles thrown into the river," *M.H.S. Proc.* XIV (1876) 350. He also added that "we . . . were informed, when at Concord, that some cannon had been carried [away] three days before, which prevented our having an opportunity of destroying so much as might have been expected at our first setting off."

6. The *Gazette's* figure of 1,800 men is 300 more than the estimate in the diary for Apr. 19, 1775, of Lieut. Frederick Mackenzie of the Royal Welsh Fusiliers which states, "The whole of the King's troops did not exceed 1500," *Mackenzie* I 24. Based on various scattered statements, I think the correct figure is about 1,700. Whether there were 1,500, 1,700, or 1,800 seems unimportant.

7. Frank W. Coburn, who made an extensive study of the casualties suffered by the Americans, gives forty-nine killed, forty-two wounded, and five missing, Coburn *Battle* 157.

8. The *Gazette* here lists ten men from Lexington—Robert Munroe, James Parker, Samuel Hadley, Jonathan Harrington, Caleb Harrington, Isaac Muzzy, John Brown, John Raymond, Nathaniel Wyman, and Jedediah Munroe—as killed. The *Gazette* stated that eight were killed on the green at Lexington; the other two presumably were killed later. Among the nine listed as wounded at Lexington was "Prince Easterbrooks (a Negro-Man)." Thus, both in the Boston Massacre (Crispus Attucks) and on the day of Lexington and Concord, a black was among the casualties.

9. The British official figures of losses are 65 killed, 180 wounded, and 27 missing, Coburn *Battle* 159.

10. *Essex Gazette* Apr. 25, 1775; reprinted with perfect accuracy in Clark *Naval Doc.* I 218–221; and, with modernized capitalization and a few other unimportant changes (as usual with *Force*), in 4 *Force* II 391–393. Many interesting additional details based on contemporary accounts, such as that Apr. 19 was a cold, sunny day, with a brisk east wind, are given in Murdock "Concord" 70–94.

11. Gage's account is based, sometimes word for word, on five eyewitness accounts of the day: Col. Lord Percy April 20, 1775, and Lieut. Col. Smith April 22, *M.H.S. Proc.* XIV (1876) 349–351n.; Maj. Pitcairn and Capt. Walter Sloane Laurie April 26, French *Gage's Informers* 52–54, 95–98; and Lieut. William Sutherland April 26, *Sutherland* 15–24.

12. In making the curious statement that Pitcairn ordered the troops not "to fire nor even attempt it without orders," Gage repeated what Major Pitcairn had written to him April 26, 1775, French *Gage's Informers* 53. I do not understand what Pitcairn meant by "nor even attempt it."

13. As brought out earlier in this chapter, the British and American versions differed as to the number of men on Lexington Green, the former, about 200, the latter about 100.

14. Capt. Laurie to Gage April 26, 1775, has interesting additional details concerning the engagement at the bridge near the village of Concord, *same* 95–98.

15. It is curious that the Americans made no effort (so far as is known) to overwhelm and capture the three companies under Capt. Lawrence Parsons that had marched beyond the bridge.

16. Neither Gage nor the *Gazette* gave an estimate of the number of Americans engaged in the course of the day. Coburn estimates that "about thirty-seven hundred and sixty Americans" were engaged, Coburn *Battle* 158–159. Mackenzie estimated "not less than 4,000 . . . towards the latter part of the day," *Mackenzie* I 24.

17. Col. Lord Percy took the road to Charlestown, rather than the route through Cambridge by which he had come, thereby avoiding the risk that the bridge across the Charles at Cambridge had been removed or destroyed, Barker's and Mackenzie's diaries for Apr. 19, 1775, *Barker* 36; *Mackenzie* 20. The ferrying of the troops from Charlestown to Boston, Admiral Samuel Graves to Philip Stephens Apr. 22, Clark *Naval Doc.* I 206.

18. Gage to Gov. Trumbull April 29, 1775, enclosing the account quoted in the text, 4 *Force* II 434–436. Gage's letter was in reply to a letter of Trumbull (April 28) stating that "by the best intelligence that we have yet been able to obtain, the late transaction was a most unprovoked attack upon the lives and property of His Majesty's subjects; and . . . such barbarities have been committed as would disgrace even barbarians. . . . Be so good, therefore, as to explain yourself upon this most important subject, so far as is consistent with your duty to our common Sovereign . . . ," *same* 434.

19. Gage wrote from Boston to Lord Barrington April 22, 1775, "The whole Country was Assembled in Arms with Surprising expedition, and Several Thousand are now Assembled about this Town, threatening an Attack, and getting up Artillery . . . ," *Gage* II 674.

20. Percy to Gen. Edward Harvey Apr. 20, 1775, as to the conduct of the Americans, *Percy* 52–53.

FIRST APPENDIX (INTRODUCTION)

1. The rule laid down by the Crown from 1759 to 1761 that acts passed by Legislature of the royal colonies amending an act approved by the Crown must contain a clause suspending operation of the amending act until it was approved by the Crown was, so far as I know, not formally changed. But the rule was in practice disregarded. The Crown approved scores of acts passed by Legislatures of the royal colonies from 1766 to 1775 which, though amending existing acts approved by the Crown, did not contain a suspending clause.

2. Order of the Privy Council Dec. 3, 1766, sustaining the decision of the Virginia Council (the highest court in Va.) in favor of the validity of the Two-penny Act of 1758 in a suit for additional salary brought by the Reverend John Camm, Smith *Appeals* 621–624. In 1768 the Virginia Council followed its decision in the *Camm* case in another similar suit, *same* 624–625.

3. The unsuccessful revival by colonial Anglican clergyman in 1767 of the movement for the establishment of one or more Church of England bishoprics in the colonies is described in an appendix to Chapter 7.

4. The unsuccessful effort of British customs officers to secure general writs of assistance in colonies other than Mass. and N.H. is described in an appendix to Chapter 5.

5. The settlement by compromise of the controversy over the Kayaderosseras land grant is described in letters of Aug. 17, 1768 from Gov. Sir Henry Moore of N.Y. and Sir William Johnson to Lord Hillsborough, *N.Y. Col. Doc.* VIII 92, 94.

6. The Indian Treaties of Hard Labor and Lochaber of 1768 and 1770 clearing Indian title to large areas west of the Alleghenies and south of the Ohio River and the opening of these areas to settlement, Jensen *Founding* 387–388 and sources cited therein; Alden *Southern Frontier* 272–280. For a map showing the territory in Virginia and present West Virginia covered by these treaties, Abernethey *Western Lands* 65.

7. The controversy in 1772 over Crown control of colonial judges stemming immediately from a Crown order for payment by the Crown of the salaries of the judges of the Mass. Superior (Supreme) Court is described in Chapter 12.

8. Continuing enforcement of, and controversy over, the White Pine Acts after 1765, Mayo *John Wentworth* 49–60; Malone *Pine Trees passim.* A statement in 1778 by John Wentworth, Surveyor General of the King's Woods in North America since 1766, describing the excessive restrictiveness of the White Pine Acts which his office required him to enforce, is quoted in Knollenberg *Origin* 130.

9. The continuing contribution of the American Act of 1764 to colonial discontent is brought out in several later chapters of this book.

SECOND APPENDIX (INTRODUCTION)

1. There is a good statement of the extreme Tory creed in the address to the King of the Crown-appointed members of the Massachusetts Council, July 17, 1775, "We . . . beg leave in humble Address to approach the Throne . . . , chearfully acquiescing in the wisdom and goodness of Parliament and acknowledging its Authority to bind us in all cases whatsoever," Matthews "Mass. Royal Council" 494–495.

2. My preference for the term *Tory* is strengthened by the fact that *loyalists* did not come into general use until after the war. The earliest use of the term *loyalist* that I recall having seen is in a diary of Stephen Kemble of N.J. Jan. 26, 1775, "Kemble" 41. *Tory* was still used, for example, by Tory Daniel Leonard, as well as by Whig John Adams, in their famous newspaper debate of 1774–1775, *Novanglus and Massachusettensis* 10 (Adams) and 149 (Leonard).

3. The colonial pamphlets and other publications mentioned in the text are discussed in Chapter 21.

4. Those familiar with recent publications bearing on the Assemblies of the thirteen colonies know there is considerable conflict of opinion as to whether or not the Assemblies were truly representative of the people of the several colonies. I believe from my own study of the question that in general they were.

5. For example, following the British victories at Brooklyn and New York City more than 900 inhabitants of the City and County of New York signed a statement, dated Oct. 16, 1776, declaring their allegiance to George III, Dawson *New York City* 117–138, thereby now classifying themselves as Tories no matter what their former status might have been.

6. Benjamin Franklin and Robert Morris to Silas Deane Oct. 1, 1776, concerning Tories, quoted in the text, *Deane Papers* I 298.

7. Studies of loyalism before 1950 include Flick *Loyalism in N.Y.* (1901); Van Tyne *Loyalists* (1902); Stark *Loyalists of Mass.* (1910); Egerton *Loyalists* (1915); Harrell *Loyalism in Va.* (1926); Jones *Loyalists of N.J.* (1927) and *Loyalists of Mass.* (1930); De Mond *Loyalists in N.C.* (1940); Siebert *Loyalists of Pa.* (1920) and at least seventeen other books or articles by Siebert; articles on loyalists of various colonies cited under "Secondary Works, Political" relating to these colonies in Gipson *Guide.* Tyler *Lit. Hist. of Am. Revolution* (1897), Davidson *Propaganda,* Lundin *N.J.* (1940) 70–108; and Labaree *Conservatism* 144–146 also have valuable material on loyalism.

8. The recent studies on loyalists referred to in the text are Wright *Loyalists* (1955); Commager and Morris *Spirit of Seventy-Six* (1958) 325–366; Nelson *American Tory* (1961); Smith *Loyalists and Redcoats* (1964) and "American Loyalists"

(1968) 259–277; Brown *King's Friends* (1966) and *"Loyalists"* (1970) 25–47; Callahan *Flight* (1967); and Benton *Whig-Loyalism* (1969). Brown's footnotes and bibliography give a wide coverage of the literature in the field. Also, valuable articles on loyalism in particular colonies are cited by colony in Gipson *Guide* under "Secondary Works, Political."

9. Studies of the loyalists are in progress today as brought out in a recent study of the loyalist emigration to Canada in Fellows "Loyalist Source Material in Canada" 67–270. Two valuable articles recently published are Fingerhut "Loyalist Claims" 245–258 and Smith "Loyalists" 259–277.

10. A considerable number of colonists had valuable contracts for various supplies for the British troops and navy in the colonies and for masts, yards, spars, and bowsprits for the British navy in Great Britain.

11. There is an admirable statement of the position described in the text by one of those holding these views in Bryan Fairfax to George Washington July 11 and Aug. 5, 1774, Hamilton *Letters to Washington* V 23–26.

12. Col. William Stephens Smith (later the son-in-law of John Adams) to George Washington Aug. 26, 1783, concerning the impending fate of many New York "Tories," quoted in the text, *same* 144.

13. "Novanglus" (John Adams) in the Feb. 27, 1775, issue of the *Boston Gazette* as to one Tory to nineteen Whigs in Mass., *Novanglus and Massachusettensis* 77, with the editorial note in *Adams Papers* II 161.

14. John Adams to Jedediah Morse Dec. 22, 1815, concerning the percentage of loyalists, quoted in the text, *same* 193. To similar effect, Adams to Thomas McKean Nov. 26, 1813, and McKean's reply of Jan. 7, 1814, 5 *M.H.S. Coll.* IV (1878) 506.

15. Phineas Bond, a resident of Pa. before the war and British consul in Philadelphia after the war, wrote in 1789 of the loss of inhabitants "occasioned by the war" as "perhaps little short of 100,000 men," and then proceeded to discuss the emigration of the loyalists, American Historical Association *Annual Report* I (1896) 648. This statement can and has been interpreted as an estimate that perhaps almost 100,000 loyalists families left the colonies (e.g., Brown *King's Friends* 249) but Bond may have meant losses from all causes.

16. Nelson's estimate of the percentage of loyalists, quoted in the text, Nelson *American Tory* 92.

17. Smith's estimate of the percentage of loyalists, quoted in the text, Smith "Loyalists" 267, 269.

18. Brown's estimate of the percentage of loyalists quoted in the text, Brown *King's Friends* vi, 288, 250–251. (Palmer *Age of the Democratic Revolution* 188, estimates that loyalist emigrés constituted about 2.4 percent of the population of the colonies, but gives no estimate of the percentage of the colonists classifiable as loyalists.)

19. Of the 130 loyalist claimants in Va., 24 are identified as American born, 82 as of British birth, 6 of other European countries, and the nativity of 18 is not identified, Brown *King's Friends* 329.

20. Of the 313 loyalist claimants in Mass., 203 are identified as American born, 48 as of British birth, 13 of Irish, 4 of other European countries, and the nativity of 45 is not identified, *same* 294.

21. Statement as to influence of Va. planters' debts on weakness of loyalism in Va., Harrell *Loyalism in Virginia,* 4–29, 129–130. The quotation is at p. 29.

22. Gipson's suggestion similar to Harrell's, Gipson *British Empire* X 158–159 Tate "Coming of the Revolution in Virginia" 334–337, Evans "Planter Indebtedness" 511–533, and Brown *Virginia* 96–142 have valuable evidence or discussions, or both, relating to planter indebtedness and its possible relationship to the weakness of loyalism in Va.

23. Virginians owed almost half of the nearly 4 million pounds sterling, principal and interest, payable by the colonists to British merchants at the close of the Revolutionary War, Evans "Planter Indebtedness" 511. Evidence that many Virginians were very heavily in debt to British merchants and that the pressure for payment became exceptionally severe following a British credit crisis in 1772, *same* 519–525; Mays *Pendleton* I 144–147, 181–182, 327–328, 332; Rosenblatt "Significance of Credit in the Tobacco Trade" 394–398. The crisis is described in Sheridan "British Credit Crisis and the Colonies" 161–186.

24. Brown's suggested explanation of the relative weakness of loyalism in Va., quoted in the text, Brown *King's Friends* 190.

25. Refusal of the Virginia Council to concur, or concurrence by a bare majority in bills, or resolutions passed by the House of Burgesses in over forty instances from 1755 to 1773, *Va. Legislative Council Journals* III 1131–1487 *passim.*

26. Examples of divisions apparently of serious importance between the House of Burgesses and the Council: the controversy over the issue of additional paper money in 1765 and proposed removal of the capital from Williamsburg in 1772, *same* 1346, 1464. The vote in the House on the latter, one of the few recorded votes of the House, had been 43 for removal, 32 against, *Va. Journals* (for 1770–72) 268.

27. The statement in the text as to the families of members of the Council is based on attendance at Council meetings from May 1, 1755, to March 15, 1773, in *Va. Legislative Council Journals* III 1131–1486 *passim* and April 14, 1773, to June 17, 1774, in *Va. Executive Council Journals* VI 522–577 *passim.* For example, those attending the meeting of the Council March 27, 1772, at which the House bill for removing the capital was rejected, were William and Thomas Nelson, William Byrd, Philip Ludwell Lee, John Tayloe, Robert Carter, and John Page, all of outstanding Virginia families, *Va. Legislative Council Journals* III 1462, 1464.

28. Gov. Francis Bernard of Mass. to Lord Barrington May 1, 1762, *Barrington–Bernard* Corresp. 53 and Hutchinson *Hist. of Mass.* III 72 speak of the division into parties in 1762. See also Brennan *Massachusetts* 50–51. Very few votes of either the Mass. House of Representatives or the Mass. Council are recorded; but votes on two seemingly unrelated bills before the Mass. House in 1762 are recorded, and the alignment in both was so nearly the same as to indicate a division along party lines, *Mass. Journals* XXXVIII Part 2 224–225, 319–320.

29. The journals of the Mass. House do not give votes for and against the protests of the Mass. House in June and November, 1764, against British taxation of the colonies, *Mass. Journals* XLI 72–77, 129. The only record of the vote on any bill or motion in the House from June, 1764, through March, 1765, on a motion in Feb., 1765, to grant Thomas Hutchinson an additional salary as

Chief Justice, carried 42 to 41, *same* 206. Comparison of this vote with the vote on the bills in 1762 referred to in note 28 discloses that the alignment of members in 1764 differed materially from that in 1762, and James Otis, reputed leader of the so-called "country" or anti-Hutchinson, party in 1762, was among those voting in favor of the additional salary to Hutchinson in 1765.

30. The joint protest of the Va. House and Council incorporated in a Petition to the King, a Memorial to the House of Lords, and a Remonstrance to the House of Commons, adopted Dec. 18, 1764, is in *Va. Journals* (for 1761–1765) 302–304. The Council's concurrence, also on Dec. 18, is in *Va. Legislative Council Journals* III 1334.

31. The protest of the Mass. House against British taxation of the colonies was adopted Nov. 1, 1764, *Mass. Journals* XLI 129. I have found no evidence of the names of the members voting for or against the protest. The protest, incorporated in a joint petition of the Mass. Council and House to the British House of Commons, is not in the *Journals,* but is printed in *Bowdoin–Temple Papers* 32–36. (There is a garbled version of the petition and an erroneous editorial note concerning it in Bradford *Mass. Papers* 21–24.)

32. The influence of Thomas Hutchinson in securing a vote first by the Council and then by the House in favor of basing the colony's protest on the ground that British taxation of the colonies infringed merely a "privilege" previously enjoyed by the people of Massachusetts, Knollenberg *Origin* 200–201, 364, with sources cited therein and Hutchinson to Henry Seymour Conway, Mass. Arch. XXVI (*Mass. Journals* XLI 102) was based on a claim of "right," *M.H.S. Proc.* XX 49–154–156. The draft of the protest initially adopted by the House, Oct. 22, 1764, 52 and *Mauduit* 167n.

33. In studying Hutchinson's remarkable career as a politician and loyalist leader, I have found the typed copies of a mass of Hutchinson's correspondence in the Massachusetts Historical Society and the writings of Malcolm Freiberg described in my table of books, articles, and dissertations cited, the most valuable sources of information. The sketches of Hutchinson in *D.A.B.;* Shipton *Harvard Graduates* VIII 149–217; Hosmer *Hutchinson;* the third volume of Hutchinson *Hist. of Mass.,* with the supplement in Mayo *Additions;* and Hutchinson *Diary* throw much additional light on the life and character of this remarkable man.

34. Hutchinson retained his appointive offices of Chief Justice and judge of probate until he became Acting Governor on Bernard's return to England in 1769. The following year he acceded to the Governorship in which capacity he served until 1774. The Massachusetts charter gave the Governor absolute power to appoint all officers (hundreds of them) of the provincial militia, to reject the person elected Speaker of the House of Representatives and those elected to the Council, and to veto all bills passed by the House and Council; and the power, with the advice and consent of the Council, to appoint all sheriffs, justices of the peace, and judges of the provincial courts, *Mass. Acts* I 10–23.

35. There is a sketch of John Robinson in *D.A.B.* and additional information concerning him in Mays *Pendleton,* traceable by references to Robinson and his estate in the index, *same* II 456.

36. The members of the committee of the House of Burgesses to draft the protest against British taxation of the colonies were Peyton Randolph ("Mr. At-

torney"), Richard Henry Lee, Landon Carter, George Wythe, Edmund Pendleton, Benjamin Harrison, Archibald Cary, and John Fleming, *Va. Journals* (for 1761–1765) 257.

37. A letter of Aug. 5, 1774, from Bryan Fairfax to George Washington stating that many who attended a recent meeting of freeholders of Fairfax County had remained silent, though opposed to some of the strongly Whiggish resolutions adopted at the meeting, suggests that if there had been a leader of stature and influence to speak for their point of view, they might have openly opposed them, Hamilton *Letters to Washington* V 34–35.

APPENDIX (CHAPTER 1)

1. George Grenville's diary for March 18 and 25, 1765, recording his talks with the King concerning appointment of the Governor of Cork, *Grenville* III 122, 123. The Duke of Northumberland was Lord Lieutenant of Ireland.

2. Grenville's diary for March 25, Apr. 3, and Apr. 4, 1765, recording his talks with the King, pressing the appointment of "Mr. Duff" (probably Alexander Duff, later third Earl of Fife) and Registrar to the Order of the Thistle, *same* 124, 126, 126–127. James Stuart Mackenzie was Lord Privy Seal for Scotland.

3. The Duke of Cumberland's undated statement concerning negotiations in April, 1765, for a change of Ministry, *Rockingham* I 188–198; Duke of Newcastle to John White June 4, 1765, reporting what Cumberland and Lord Albemarle had told him, *Newcastle* 3–4; Cumberland wrote that until Apr. 7 he had not seen the King in private for over a year, *Rockingham* I 187.

4. There is a full account of the muddle (Apr. 29–May 13, 1765) over omission of George III's mother, Dowager Princess of Wales, from among those described in the Regency Bill of 1765 as eligible for the regency, in Horace Walpole to Horace Mann May 14, and explanatory editorial notes, Lewis *Walpole* XXII 294–299. The Regency Bill as enacted is 5 Geo. III ch. 27 (1765). See also Walpole to Lord Hertford May 5, and 12, Toynbee *Walpole* VI 219–224, 225–229.

5. Walpole to Lord Hertford May 5, 1765, as to setting fire "the old stubble of the Princess and Lord Bute" and in effect having "the worst of *North Britons* published by Act of Parliament!" *same* 220–223. The rumors concerning Bute and the Princess and their dissemination in the July 3, 1762, issue of John Wilkes' *North Briton* are discussed in Knollenberg *Origin* 293–294.

6. The Regency Bill as passed in the House of Lords amended in the House of Commons to include the Princess as one eligible for regent and the House of Lords acceptance of the amendment, May 9 and 13, 1765, Walpole to Mann May 14, and editorial notes, Lewis *Walpole* XXII 299. Report and covering letter of Grenville to the King May 9, reporting the day's debate on the bill in the House of Commons, *Grenville* III 25–34 and notes on 25–33.

7. Newcastle to John White June 4, 1765, relating Cumberland's report of a talk with Lord Northumberland on May 13, *Newcastle* 9.

8. Newcastle to White June 4, 1765, reporting Cumberland's account of his talk with the King on May 14 and the latter's complaint of the Ministry, *same* 10–11; Cumberland to Duke of Grafton May 14, *Grafton* 78. An undated memorandum of the King written after the death of Cumberland on Oct. 31, 1765,

gives a long list of actions of Grenville that had offended him, *Geo. III* I 170–171.

9. William Pitt and Lord Temple gave a number of reasons for declining, but apparently the chief one was that Cumberland would not assure them the King would cease consulting Bute, Walpole to Mann May 25, 1765, Lewis *Walpole* XXII 302; Mrs. Grenville's "Fragments" dated May 19, *Grenville* III 226; Newcastle to White June 4, *Newcastle* 14.

10. Newcastle to White June 4, 1765, reporting accounts by Cumberland and Albemarle of their talk with Pitt and Temple May 19, *same* 13–14; various correspondents May 19–22, *Grafton* 78–83; *Grenville* III 39; "Fragments" in Mrs. George Grenville's hand, May 19, *same* 226; Walpole to Hertford May 20, Toynbee *Walpole* VI 238.

11. "The points agreed upon" by Grenville, Lord Chancellor (Lord Northington), the Duke of Bedford, President of the Council, and Secretaries of State Lords Halifax and Sandwich to be laid before the King "as indispensably necessary . . . for carrying on the public business," May 22, 1765, *Grenville* III 41.

12. Grenville diary for May 23, 1765, describing the King's particular distress over the demand for the dismissal of Mackenzie, *same* 187. A memorandum of Lord Egmont, May 23, explains that the King considered that he would be dishonored by dismissing Mackenzie because when he gave Mackenzie the place of Lord Privy Seal for Scotland "he promised that he would never take it from him," *Geo. III* I 114.

13. The King yielded to the ultimatum on May 23, 1765, saying to Grenville, "I see I must yield. I do it for the good of my people," Grenville's diary for May 23, *Grenville* III 187.

14. The Duke of Bedford's complaints and threat at his audience with the King June 12, 1766, Bedford's memorandum of June 12, *Bedford* III 288–289, and the King to Lord Northington June 12, *Geo. III* I 116. According to Bedford, the King gave no answer other than "declaring Lord Bute was not consulted, and that he had never done me ill offices with the King," *Bedford* III 289–290. To same effect, Walpole to Mann June 25, Lewis *Walpole* XXII 307.

15. The King to Northington June 12, 1765, telling of his "indignation" over Bedford's "so very offensive a declaration," *Geo. III* I 116.

16. The King to Cumberland June 12, 1765, asking him to try again to form a new Ministry, *same*.

17. Cumberland's vain effort (June 16–25) to persuade Pitt and Temple to form a new Ministry, Newcastle to White June 29, 1765, *Newcastle* 21–24; Walpole to Mann June 26, Lewis *Walpole* XXII 307–308; Cumberland–Pitt Corresp. June 17–20, *Pitt II* 311–313; many documents of the King and others June 12–27, *Geo. III* I 117–125, *Grenville* III 52–64, *Bedford* III 290–303, and *Grafton* 83–86; Gilbert Elliot's undated memorandum covering June 18–26, Jucker *Jenkinson* 375–377; Cumberland to Albemarle June 26, *Rockingham* I 213–214.

18. Pitt was willing to take office if Temple would become First Lord of the Treasury, Cumberland to Albemarle June 26, 1765, *Rockingham* I 213–214; Charles Townshend to Lord Townshend July 3; *Grenville* III 65.

19. Temple refused to take office because of "the difficulty of forming a proper plan with regard to the House of Commons" and for an undisclosed reason of

"a tender and delicate nature," Grenville's diary June 25, 1765, *sa* The difficulty about the Commons—Pitt's ill health making his attenda uncertain—is explained in Newcastle to White June 29, *Newcastle* 24; as to the reason of "a tender and delicate nature" are in Walpole to Mann 26, and George Onslow to Newcastle June 27, Lewis *Walpole* XXII 308, 308n

20. Walpole wrote Mann July 12, 1765, "Cumberland has persuaded the Opposition to . . . form a ministry. Without Mr. Pitt they were unwilling, but, pressed, . . . they have submitted . . . ," *same* 310; also Albemarle to Newcastle June 29, and Newcastle to Duke of Portland July 1, *same* 310n. Newcastle to White, undated, but apparently soon after July 8, *Newcastle* 25–31; Newcastle's memorandum of June 30, *Rockingham* I 218–219.

APPENDIX (CHAPTER 2)

1. By the act of 7 and 8 William III ch. 7, passed in 1696. Lawrence Gipson's statement as to the Act of 1696 quoted in the text, Gipson *British Empire* XIII (1967) 196–199. Gipson quotes in support of his views a statement in Coke's *Institutes:* "The power and jurisdiction of parliament is so transcendent and absolute, that it cannot be confined, either for causes or persons, within any bounds [p. 196]." But Coke also wrote, "when an act of parliament is against right and reason . . . the common law will controul it and adjudge such act to be void," Corwin "Higher Law" 368; also on Coke's statements *same* 272n.

2. The proceedings of Parliament from Dec. 17, 1695, to March 28, 1696, collected in Stock *Proceedings* II 142–171 *passim,* with respect to the proposed Statute of Frauds of 1696 give no indication of any intention of dealing with the question of whether or not Parliament was bound by any constitutional limitations in legislating for the colonies. The discussion dealt exclusively with implementing the enforcement of English regulation of colonial trade, which was generally recognized as being within the scope of Parliament's authority.

3. The Act of 1696 (7 and 8 William III ch. 7) is entitled "An act for preventing frauds, and regulating abuses in the plantation trade." The preamble recites, "Whereas notwithstanding diverse acts made for the encouragement of the navigation of this kingdom, and for the better securing and regulating the plantation trade . . . great abuses are clearly committed . . . For remedy whereof for the future . . . Be it enacted," etc. All the other sections of the act, as well as section 9, quoted in the text, deal primarily with means of enforcing the regulation of colonial navigation and trade.

4. Gipson's statement as to colonial acceptance of the principle set forth in the Act of 1696, Gipson *Brit. Empire* XIII 198.

5. The Mass. House of Representatives, for example, in a message to Gov. Francis Bernard Jan. 27, 1761, stated, "Every Act we make repugnant to an Act of Parliament, extending to the Plantations [as the Act of 1696 expressly did] is (*ipso facto*) null and void," *Mass. Journals* XXXVII Part II 243. But, as clearly appears from the context of this statement, it was assumed that the Act of 1696 was constitutional; the question of whether an act of Parliament might itself be void because unconstitutional and, therefore, inoperative was not then under consideration.

ckstone (1770) 82–83 challenged Blackstone's state-
r of Parliament, quoted in the text. See, to similar
in the House of Lords in 1766, quoted in Chapter
it was not bound by constitutional limitations was
opinion in the *Wensleydale Peerage Case, House*

ment in the text concerning British and colonial
hority of the King in Parliament is given in
-350, and sources cited therein.

of the Mass. House, to Lord Shelburne Jan. 15,
the colonial concept of constitutional limitations on the authority of
Parliament quoted in the text, *Prior Doc.* 178.

9. Governor Stephen Hopkins' statement on colonial taxation by Parliament quoted in the text, *The Rights of Colonies Examined* (Providence, 1764 or 1765) 16–17, Bailyn *Pamphlets* 517.

10. The Act of 1778 as to taxation of the colonies, quoted in the text, is in Schuyler *Parliament* 254. An act of 1783, 23 Geo. III ch. 28, explicitly waived authority of Parliament to legislate in any way for Ireland, *same* 100.

11. Gipson's statement as to freedom of protest quoted in the text, Gipson *Brit. Empire* XIII 197.

12. Benjamin Franklin wrote Joseph Galloway Jan. 9, 1769, of the refusal of the House of Commons to accept petitions or remonstrances denying the right of Parliament to tax the colonies, in view of the Declaratory Act of 1766, *Franklin* IX 14–16. To same effect, evidence set forth in Kammen *Agents* 230–233, 238.

FIRST APPENDIX (CHAPTER 3)

1. The Act of 1663, 15 Chas. II ch. 7, restricting colonial imports and the associated Act of 1660, 12 Chas. II ch. 18, restricting colonial exports are discussed in Knollenberg *Origin* 168–172, 263–264, 352–355, 389–391. Even the exception in the Act of 1663 permitting importation of continental European salt directly into the colonies was limited to the northern and middle colonies, *same* 169.

2. The act made no provision for punishment by imprisonment for nonviolent infringement of the act, but forfeiture of the offending vessel, as well as all the goods on board, was of course, a serious penalty.

3. Article 4 of the Act of Union of 1707 (5 Anne ch. 8) provided that all the subjects of the "united kingdoms of Great Britain shall, from and after the union, have full freedom of intercourse of trade and navigation to and from any port or place within the said united kingdom and the dominions and plantations thereunto belonging. . . ."

4. Examples of the complaints by Crown officials in the colonies of the reluctance or refusal of colonial juries to find against the owners in suits for forfeiture under acts restricting colonial trade, Lieut.-Gov. George Clarke of N.Y. to B. of T. Dec. 15, 1739, *N.Y. Col. Doc.* VI 154; William Bollan, Advocate-General in Mass., to the Board of Trade Feb. 26, 1742/43, quoted later in this chapter, *Col. Soc. Public.* VI 301.

5. Opinions of Sir John Cooke, Advocate-General to the Crown, July 23, 1702, and of Attorney-General Edward Northey, Aug. 21, 1702, that the Act of 1696, 7 and 8 Wm. III ch. 22, gave colonial admiralty courts jurisdiction over suits for forfeiture arising under the Act of 1663, Chalmers *Opinions* 504–505, 500–501. (Though the colonial courts of admiralty are commonly called "vice-admiralty" courts, Cooke referred to them as "admiralty" courts, and I adopt this shorter name.)

6. Richard West's opinion of June 20, 1720, as to limited jurisdiction of colonial admiralty courts and issuance of writs of prohibition. Chalmers *Opinions* 515–520. See also Wroth "Mass. Vice-Admiralty Court" 46–48; Andrews "Col. Adm. Courts" 69–75; Towle *R.I. Admiralty* 297; Wiener "R.I. Adm." 34–35, 87; and Noble "Admiralty Jurisdiction" 166–169. The writ must, however, be requested before the admiralty court had proceeded to trial, *Kennedy Qui Tam against 32 Barrels of Gunpowder* and authorities therein cited.

7. Gov. William Shirley of Mass. to the Board of Trade Feb. 26, 1742/43, confirms the frequent violation of the Act of 1663 (15 Chas. II ch. 7), *Col. Soc. Public.* VI (1900) 298. Additional evidence of the widespread violation of this act, some of it winked at by the customs officers, sources cited in Knollenberg *Origin* 390 and Jensen *Philadelphia* 133–135, 268–269. The Act of 1721 relating to East Indian products was probably no better observed; indeed, East Indian tea seems to have been among the products most extensively imported into the colonies in violation of law.

8. Bollan [misprinted "Bolum"] to B. of T. Feb. 26, 1742 [1743, new style], concerning non-enforcibility of the Act of 1663, writs of prohibition, and proposed act of Parliament, *Col. Soc. Public.* VI (1900) 299–304. Bollan wrote of a recent condemnation of a ship, the *Hannah,* by the admiralty court at Boston, but explained this on the ground that counsel for the owner of the vessel apparently was unaware that he could have secured a writ of prohibition to prevent this, *same* 303.

9. A *qui tam* ("who as well") action was for a penalty to be divided by the plaintiff with others.

10. The opinion of Attorney-General Sir Philip Yorke (later Lord Chancellor Hardwicke) Nov. 2, 1726, that "importation" is "always accounted from the time of the ship's coming within the limits of the port, with intent to lay the goods on land," Chalmers *Opinions* (1858) 576, seems to have been unchallenged, and the port of New York unquestionably was within the body of a county, namely the City and County of New York.

11. The Act of 1391 (15 Richard II ch. 3) referred to in the text provided that "all manner of contracts, pleas and quarrels, and all other things rising within the bodies of the counties, as well by land as by water . . . shall be tried, determined, discussed and remedied by the laws of the land, and not before the admiral nor his lieutenant in any wise."

12. My account of the *Kennedy* case in the N.Y. Admiralty Court and the N.Y. Supreme Court is drawn from notes on the proceedings in the Admiralty Court Oct. 2 and 5, 1739, Hough *Cases* 16; Kennedy's undated memorandum in *N.Y. Col. Doc.* VI 154–155; record of proceedings, January, 1740, term of the N.Y. Supreme Court, in James Alexander Mss, Box 45, N.Y. Hist. Soc.; and the report

of "Lords of the Committee of Council for hearing Appeals from the Plantations" Feb. 10, 1742/3, in P.C.2:97:314–315 (P.R.O.), supplemented by Smith *Appeals* 515–517.

13. The legal skirmishing is described in the record of proceedings (sixteen foolscap pages) in the Alexander Mss cited in note 12.

14. Decision in the *Kennedy* case of the Governor and Council of N.Y. sitting as a Court of Error Apr. 17, 1741, referred to in report of the "Lords of the Committee of Council for hearing Appeals from the Plantations," Feb. 10, 1742/3, P.C.2:97:314–315 (P.R.O.).

15. The Privy Council as the final court of appeals in cases appealed from colonial courts of common law, its reference of such appeals to its "Committee for hearing Appeals from the Plantations," and the Council's formal adoption and issuance of orders embodying the committee's advice are discussed in Knollenberg *Origin* 46–47, 299. (Appeals from colonial admiralty courts in suits concerning the British acts of trade are fully discussed in Smith *Appeals* 187–191).

16. Report of the Committee to the Privy Council Feb. 10, 1742/3, advising affirmation of the decisions of the N.Y. Supreme Court ("Court of King's Bench") and the N.Y. Court of Error, P.C. 2:97:314–315 (P.R.O.). The report refers to the decision of the Court of King's Bench, i.e., the N.Y. Supreme Court, as based on seizure having been made "in the Body of the City of New York"; but the record in this court (Box 15, James Alexander Mss. N.Y. Hist. Soc.) makes clear that Fowles referred to New York City *and County,* thus establishing the basis for invoking the act of 15 Richard II ch. 3.

17. Privy Council's order of March 23, 1742/3, adopting and implementing the Committee's advice in the *Kennedy* case, P.C. 2:97:345–346, *Acts P.C.* III 720–721.

18. The act of 7 Geo. I, first session, Ch. 21 sec. 9 (1721) forbad importation of any product of the East Indies into the colonies except via Great Britain. The act of 9 and 10 Wm. III ch. 44 sec. 61 (1698) had defined "the East Indies" to include all "places of Asia, Africa and America . . . beyond the cape of Bona Esperanza to the streights of Magellan" i.e., the entire region from and including the East Coast of Africa to and including the West Coast of the Americas.

19. The bill proposed by the Admiralty Board to give colonial admiralty courts jurisdiction over all suits for forfeiture for alleged violations in the colonies of all British acts of trade and customs is described in the Admiralty Board to the Treasury Board Apr. 23, 1742, Adm. 7:298:88–96 (P.R.O.) and is quoted in Smith *Appeals* 189n.

20. Section 41 of the Act of 1764, quoted in the text, did not expressly amend the Act of 1391 to exclude the colonies, but apparently no one questioned that the Act of 1764 gave colonial admiralty courts jurisdiction over all suits involving violation in the colonies of British acts restricting colonial trade, including alleged violations of the Acts of 1663 and 1721, just as, so far as I have found, there was no challenge of the jurisdiction of colonial admiralty courts in cases involving the earlier act of 4 Geo. II ch. 13 (1733), containing a similar provision.

21. The Admiralty Board's memorandum quoted in the text is in P.C. 1:50, Unbound Papers, Part 2 (P.R.O.). This memorandum was in response to a

Treasury Board memorandum and an order of the Privy Council in Oct., 1763, *same* and *Acts. P.C.* IV 569–573.

22. Order in Council Apr. 18, 1764, for the establishment of a new court of admiralty having jurisdiction over "all America," *same* IV 663–664, VI 365. The Act of 1764 had been assented to by the King on April 5.

23. Letters Patent June 15, 1764, appointing Dr. William Spry judge of the new colonial admiralty court, T:28:1:16–17. As to appeals, Blackstone *Commentaries* III 69 states that "Appeals from the vice-admiralty courts in America . . . may be brought before the courts of admiralty in England . . . [or] before the king in council." Smith *Appeals* 88–95, 177–193 shows there was much confusion on this point. (The Stamp Act passed in 1765, but repealed in 1766, briefly gave Spry appellate jurisdiction, *same* 187.)

24. Establishment and opening session of the new court at Halifax, Nova Scotia, Oct. 2 and 9, 1764, *M.H.S. Proc.* XVII (1879–80) 291–293 and colonial newspapers in Oct. and Nov., 1764, cited in Ubbelohde *Vice-Admiralty Courts* 4n.

25. Halifax had a population of only about 1,400 in 1764, Brebner *New Eng. Outpost* 64.

26. Admiral Lord Colville to Philip Stevens Oct. 25, 1763, quoted in the text, Adm. 1:482:615–617 (P.R.O.).

27. Colonial alarm over the extensive jurisdiction conferred on the new admiralty court, Thacher *Sentiments* (Boston, 1764) 7–9; Hopkins *Rights* (Providence, 1765) 15.

28. Colonial admiralty judges received as a perquisite of office part of the proceeds from sales of condemned property, Thacher *Sentiments* 8; Root *Pa.* 118–119, 126n.; *Journals Cont. Cong.* I 116; Burke *Speeches* 129; whereas Spry was to receive a fixed salary, Admiralty Board memorandum of March 14, 1764, P.C. 1:50, Unbound Papers Part 2 (P.R.O.); Ubbelohde *Vice-Admiralty Courts,* 53. Customs officers may well have thought they had a better chance of securing condemnation of seizures by a judge who would share in the proceeds of the condemnation than by Spry.

29. The only recorded suit in the new admiralty court for forfeiture or other penalty for an offense committed outside Nova Scotia was against the *Polly,* seized in Mass. in 1765, *same* 67–69.

30. The new court was abolished in 1768, and four new admiralty courts were established at Halifax, Boston, Philadelphia, and Charleston, each with jurisdiction over a limited district, pursuant to an act of 8 Geo. III ch. 22 (1768).

SECOND APPENDIX (CHAPTER 3)

1. Section 1 of the Navigation Act of 1660, 12 Chas. II ch. 18, clarified by the act of 13 and 14 Chas. II ch. 11 sec. 7 (1662), prohibited vessels owned by foreigners or manned to the extent of more than one-fourth of the crew by foreigners, to trade with the English colonies except to import gold or silver, and this prohibition was extended by the act of 7 and 8 Wm. III ch. 22 sec. 2 (1696) to exclude foreign-built ships even if owned and manned by English subjects, Knollenberg *Origin* 168, 262, 352, 389.

2. The advantages of an act making Dominica a free port had been well presented in a letter from Lieut.-Col. Campbell Dalrymple writing from Guadeloupe to Lord Bute Feb. 27, 1963, *Geo. III* I 44–50. Countermeasures by the French are described in Goebel "West Indies" 335–371.

3. The collaboration of Rockingham's follower, Edmund Burke, with a consortium of British merchants and shipowners engaged in trade with British America in drafting and promoting the Free Port Act is brought out in Hoffman *Burke* 39–45, 332–351 *passim;* Burke *Corresp.* I 239–256 *passim;* Committee of British Merchants' Agreement March 10, 1766, Penson *Agents of West Indies* 284–285; printed in part in Adams *Rev. New Eng.* 340; Armytage *Free Port System* 28–51; Rockingham to George III March 12, 1766, *Geo. III* I 282; Charles Garth to S.C. Comm. of Corresp. Sept. 26, 1766, *So. Car. Hist. Mag.* XXVIII (1927) 47.

4. The Free Port Act of 1766, 6 Geo. III ch. 49, also gave leave for small foreign vessels to import some articles of foreign colonial produce (but not the most important, sugar) into four ports of Jamaica.

5. The trade of the British North American colonies with the French and other foreign West Indies, some illegal, some under hard-to-get licenses from local French officials, is discussed in Pitman *West Indies* 189–333, 414–430; Pares *Yankees and Creoles,* index under "Danish colonies," "Dutch colonies," "French colonies," "Spanish colonies," and "Surinam"; Knollenberg *Origin* 138–141, 338–340, sources cited therein; and Dalrymple to Bute Feb. 27, 1763, *Geo. III* I 44–45. The wartime trade of the northern British colonies with the French and Spanish West Indies is described in Beer *Brit. Col. Policy* 72–131.

6. Sec. 8 of the Free Port Act permitted the export of all other foreign colonial products to the British colonies and European ports south of Cape Finisterre, but not to any part of northern Europe except Great Britain.

APPENDIX (CHAPTER 5)

1. Quincy *Reports* 398–400 prints a form of general writs. Their provisions are well described in Opinion of Attorney-General William De Grey Aug. 20, 1768, *same* 454. A general writ of assistance issued in Mass. in Dec., 1761, closely following the form of the English writs, is in *same* 418–421.

2. The writs of assistance commonly issued by the Court of Exchequer to customs officers in England were general writs, Opinion of Attorney-General William De Grey Aug. 20, 1768, *same* 454. Supporting evidence is in *same* 398–399, 532, and *Adams Legal Papers* II 110.

3. In his otherwise admirable discussion of general writs of assistance in Mass. before 1767 in Gipson *Brit. Empire* X 113–129, Gipson states: "in the colonies such a writ could be legally granted by any court having powers comparable to that of the Court of Exchequer," and that "there was really nothing that the Superior Court could do but to grant the writs of assistance," *same* 118, 127. For reasons brought out in the text, I think these statements are erroneous.

4. Mass. Superior Court issues several general writs of assistance between 1756 and 1760, Quincy *Reports* 403–406.

5. The Mass. act giving the superior court cognizance of all matters as fully as the Court of Exchequer in England had, is Chapter 3 of the Laws of 1669–1700 passed June 26, 1699, *Mass. Acts* I 372–373. The application for the first writ

known to have been issued by the court (in 1756) was based on the court's being "vested with the Power of a Court of Exchequer for the Province," and apparently the court issued the writ on this ground, Quincy *Reports* 402–403.

6. Previous to 1701 writs of assistance apparently expired on the death of the sovereign during whose reign they were issued. The act of 1 Anne, first sess., ch. 8 sec. 5 (1701) provided that writs of assistance were to continue in force for six months after the sovereign's death.

7. The arguments of James Otis and Oxenbridge Thacher, representing a group of Mass. merchants, against the authority of the Mass. Superior Court to issue any writs of assistance and especially general writs, are discussed in Quincy *Reports* 51–59, 469–499; Knollenberg *Origin* 66–69, 307–308; *Adams Legal Papers* II 106–147; Gipson *Brit. Empire* X 120–128. The names of the merchants retaining Otis and Thacher are in Quincy *Reports* 413.

8. Decision of the Mass. Superior Court Nov. 18, 1761, that it had authority to issue general writs and issuance of such writs to numerous British customs officers in Mass. from Dec., 1761, to 1769, *same* 403–434. The decision was rendered following receipt of a copy of the kind of writs—general writs—commonly issued by the English Court of Exchequer, Wolkins "Bollan" 420. (Apparently the Superior Court of New Hampshire also issued a writ of assistance, soon afterward, but at some time before Oct., 1769, revoked it, Quincy *Reports* 500, 510–511.)

9. The Collector and Comptroller at New London, Conn., to British Customs Board May 14 or 24, 1766, as to the Conn. Superior Court's refusal to issue a writ of assistance, Wolkins "Malcom" 61. The New London officers indicated that the Conn. Court based its decision on the narrow ground that, unlike in Mass., there was no local act constituting the Conn. Superior Court a court of exchequer. But, as brought out later in this appendix, the Conn. Court later refused to grant general writs even after it was expressly authorized by a British statute to issue writs of assistance.

10. Opinion of Attorney-General De Grey Oct. 17, 1766, sustaining the position of the Conn. Superior Court, Wolkins "Malcom" 72–73. De Grey added that "the Court of Exchequer in England do not send their Process into the Plantations," from which it followed that, under existing law, no court was authorized to issue general writs of assistance to customs officers in the colonies.

11. De Grey's opinion of Oct. 17, 1766, was apparently confirmed by an opinion by him and the Solicitor-General in the Malcom case referred to in a Treasury minute dated Feb. 6, 1767, giving the opinion of the law officers that "no action can . . . be brought for obstructing the Officers of the Customs in execution of their office, inasmuch as the Writ of Assistance by Virtue of which they entered the House and Cellar, was not in this case a legal Authority," *same* 73.

12. I have not found the letters from the American Customs Board to the customs officers under their jurisdictions instructing them to apply for writs, but the officers' replies, mentioned in later footnotes, indicate that the Board's letters were sent in April, 1768.

13. Chief Justice Thomas Hutchinson of Mass. to Richard Jackson March 23, 1768, reporting the refusal of the Conn. Superior Court to grant "Writs of Assistance agreeable to the late Act of Parliament" because they were "un-

constitutional," Quincy *Reports* 501. To same effect, Collector and Comptroller of Customs at New Haven to the American Customs Board March 2, Wolkins "Malcom" 61n. Further details are in Dickerson "Writs" 52–54 and in Hickman "Writs" 97.

14. Chief Justice William Allen of Pa. to customs officers at Philadelphia May 10, 1768, declining to issue a writ of assistance (presumably a general writ) requested by them, Dickerson "Writs" 59.

15. The Superior Courts of R.I., Md., and S.C. took no action on the petitions in 1768 for issuance of writs of assistance under section 10 of the Townshend Act, as shown by the failure of the application by R.I. customs officers to R.I. Superior Court at its term beginning Apr. 12, 1768; and letters of the Collector at Patuxent, Md., to Am. Customs Board June 8, and customs officers at Charleston, S.C., to Am. Customs Board May 25, Dickerson "Writs" 50, 62, 66. But, as brought out later in the text, general writs were eventually issued in S.C.

16. Petitions from customs officers at N.Y. to N.Y. Supreme Court for general writs of assistance and the court's decision to grant the writs Apr. 28, 1768, Quincy *Reports* 507–508. Dickerson "Writs" 54–55, and copy of the N.Y. writ to Lambert Moore Apr. 28, 1768, show that the words quoted in the text were omitted in the writ, *same* 54–55.

17. De Grey's opinion dated Aug. 20, 1768, as to the effect of sec. 10 of the Townshend Act, 7 Geo. III ch. 46 (1767), Quincy *Reports* 552–554.

18. Hutchinson's collaboration is described by a letter from the American Customs Board to him Dec. 20, 1768, and his reply, *same* 455.

19. American Customs Board circular letter of March 16, 1769, enclosing form of writ to be obtained, *same* 506. I have not found a copy of the form of writ, but there is evidence that it was sent out in March, 1769, and that it closely followed the form of general writ granted by the Mass. Superior Court, *same* 455, 510; Dickerson "Writs" 56–58 and *Va. Journals* (for 1773–76) 135.

20. Conn. Court refers the petition for writs in March, 1769, to the Legislature, and apparently neither the Legislature nor the court takes any further action, Quincy *Reports* 503–504; Zeichner *Conn.* 83, 279; minutes of conference between Duncan Stewart, Collector of Customs at New London, and judges of the Conn. Superior Court March 31, 1769, *Pitkin* 184–187; *Conn. Courant* of Hartford July 31, 1769.

21. Report of the May and Oct., 1769, sessions of the Conn. Legislature, disclosing no action taken on the question of writs, *Conn. Records* (for 1768–1772) 168–282.

22. Proceedings of the N.Y. Supreme Court from April, 1769, to May, 1772, as to writs, Dickerson "Writs" 56–58.

23. Proceedings of the R.I., Md., and S.C. Courts in 1769 as to writs, Quincy *Reports* 506–507; Dickerson "Writs" 62, 66.

24. Collector John Swift at Philadelphia to Am. Customs Board May 5, 1769, as to writs in Pa., *same* 59–60, and sources cited in Jensen *Philadelphia* 148, 273.

25. Proceedings of the Va. Court in 1769 as to writs of assistance, *same* 68–70 and Quincy *Reports* 510.

26. Peyton Randolph, Robert Carter Nicholas, and Dudley Digges of the Va. Comm. of Corresp. Jan. 6, 1774, to the Conn. Comm. of Corresp. in response to

the latter's inquiry of Aug. 10, 1773, concerning writs of assistance, *Va. Journals* (for 1773–76) 55, 135–137. (Virginia's leadership in 1773 in establishing the important system of intercolonial Committees of Correspondence is brought out in Chapter 12.)

27. The views of Horace Gray and Joseph R. Frese are set forth in Gray "Notes," Quincy *Reports* 530–532 and in Frese "Writs of Assistance in the American Colonies" (Harvard dissertation, 1951) 97–106 and Frese "Legislation on Writs of Assistance" 318–359.

28. Opinion Aug. 31, 1771, as to writs by Attorney-General Edward Thurlow, Dickerson "Writs" 69–71, corrected as to the signature from original in Treasury Bundle 1:501 P.R.O. My view that Thurlow's opinion was sound is based on the fact that the act of 12 Chas. II ch. 19 (1662) authorized either the Lord Treasurer or the Court of Exchequer to issue particular writs and that the act of 13 and 14 Chas. II ch. 11 presumably was intended to give the Court of Exchequer, though not the Lord Treasurer, discretion to issue either general or particular writs. Had Parliament intended to limit the court to the kind of writ specified in the earlier act, it could easily, and presumably would, have said so.

29. In January and November, 1772, the Am. Customs Board ordered customs officers in Va. to petition again for general writs, Dickerson "Writs" 71–72; *Va. Journals* (for 1773–76) 135, and similar orders were given about the same time to customs officers in several other colonies, Dickerson "Writs" 50, 56–65.

30. Issuance of general writs by the S.C. Court of General Sessions in April, 1773, *same* 66–67. As to the replacement of native judges on the South Carolina Court of General Sessions (Supreme Court) by judges sent out from Great Britain, McCrady *South Carolina* 469; Smith *S.C.* 139.

31. Refusal of colonial courts other than the S.C. Court to issue general writs on renewed petitions for these in 1772 and 1773, Dickerson "Writs" 56–65, 71–72; *Va. Journals* (for 1773–76) 135; Frese "James Otis and Writs of Assistance" 506–507.

32. Thurlow's opinion Aug. 31, 1771, as to impracticability of compelling the courts to issue general writs, Dickerson "Writs" 70.

33. The Enoch Ilfley fracas at Falmouth, Mass. (now Portland, Maine), in Aug., 1766, is described in Gipson *Brit. Empire* XI 34–35.

34. A general writ of assistance was issued by the Superior Court of Mass. to Benjamin Hallowell March 22, 1765, *same* 434. Presumably it was under this writ that Hallowell was acting in demanding entrance into Daniel Malcom's cellar in 1766.

35. My account of the Malcom affair is based chiefly on the affidavits of Hallowell and Deputy Collector William Sheaffe dated Sept. 24, 1766, and of Stephen Greenleaf, Sheriff of Suffolk County, Oct. 1, and Malcom Oct. 21, Wolkins "Malcom" 26–29, 34–39, 39–42. Other affidavits in *same* 29–33, 43–58 give a somewhat, but not radically, different version.

36. De Grey's opinion dated Feb. 6, 1767, in the Malcom case, *same* 73.

37. Gov. Francis Bernard of Mass. to B. of T. Oct. 10, 1766, Quincy *Reports* 447, and Hallowell to the British Customs Board Nov. 14, Wolkins "Malcom" 77–80 giving detailed reports of the Malcom affair. John Temple, Surveyor-General of Customs for the Northern District of America, also wrote the Board

enclosing affidavits concerning the affair and criticizing local "Civil Authority" for lack of "Firmness," *same* 64. The Ilfley incident cited in note 33 above also was reported to officials in England by Bernard, Gipson *Brit. Empire* XI 35.

38. "Freeman" (William Henry Drayton) in a letter of Aug. 10, 1774, to the Continental Congress recited as one of the grievances of S.C. that, "no sooner was the bench filled with men who depended on the smiles of the crown for their daily bread, than . . . the general writ . . . was granted . . . ," Gibbes *Doc. Hist.* 21–22. As to the newly appointed judges in S.C., headed by Thomas Knox Gordon, Smith *S.C.* 139.

39. The Address (or Petition) to the King adopted by the First Continental Congress Oct. 25, 1774, reciting the grievance as to writs of assistance quoted in the text, *Journals Cont. Cong.* I 116.

APPENDIX (CHAPTER 7)

1. The unsuccessful project in 1740 for an Anglican episcopate in the colonies, Knollenberg *Origin* 81–83, 314. Earlier projects are described in sources cited in *same* 314 and in Perry *History* I 395–407; Cross *Anglican Episcopate* 21, 88–112; Bridenbaugh *Mitre and Sceptre* 27–31, 97–98. The last of these and Manning *Deputies* 417–418 bring out the important part played by English Dissenters in discouraging the 1750 and earlier projects.

2. Argument for an Anglican bishop in the colonies to confirm and ordain: Report of the Bishop of London (Thomas Sherlock) to the King, undated, read in the Privy Council Feb. 21, 1759; *N.Y. Col. Doc.* VII 364; Thomas Secker, Archbishop of Canterbury, to the Reverend Samuel Johnson, May 2, 1766, Schneider *Johnson* I 361.

3. The calm reception in America of bishops of the Protestant Episcopal Church after the Revolutionary War, sources cited in Knollenberg *Origin* 315.

4. Colonial fears of American episcopate: undated letter, probably in 1768, attributed to Roger Sherman of Conn., Boutell *Sherman* 66; instructions Jan. 12, 1768, from Mass. House of Representatives to Dennys De Berdt, Bradford *Mass. Papers* 132; The Reverend Francis Alison to the Reverend James Sproct, Nov. 15, 1766, and conventions of Conn., N.Y., N.J., and Pa. ministers to Dissenting Deputies in 1768, 1770, and 1771, *Minutes of the Convention* 14–16, 28, 66–67, 84; Thomas Gwatkin *Letter to the Clergy* (Williamsburg, 1772) 12; documents cited in note 5 below.

5. Josiah Willard to Spencer Phipps Dec. 12, 1750, as to Congregationalists' reason for fearing the settlement of Anglican bishops in America, Foote *King's Chapel* II 251. To similar effect, the Reverend Charles Chauncy and other Congregational ministers of Boston to the Corresponding Committee of the Protestant Dissenting Deputies in London Jan. 4, 1768, Manning *Deputies* 421.

6. No visits to the colonies from any of the forty-three Anglican bishops in England, Ireland, and the Isle of Man, Knollenberg *Origin* 83, 315.

7. Colonists' fear of taxation for support of colonial bishops, Mass. House of Rep. to Dennys De Berdt Jan. 12, 1768, Bradford *Mass. Papers* 132; Andrew Eliot's "Remarks" enclosed in Eliot to Thomas Hollis Dec. 7, 1767, 2 *M.H.S.*

Coll. II 209. A letter of Oct. 26, 1764, from the Reverend Samuel Auchmuty, rector of Trinity Church, New York City, to Johnson favoring an act of Parliament to tax the residents of the entire colony of New York to support an Anglican minister in every county of the colony (Bridenbaugh *Mitre and Sceptre* 246–247) indicates that there was some basis for this fear.

8. Sir William Johnson to Col. William Eyre Jan. 19, 1764, to Board of Trade Jan. 20, to Cadwallader Colden Jan. 27, and to Gen. Thomas Gage Jan. 27 suggesting confiscation of Jesuits' property in Canada to endow a bishopric in Canada, Pargellis *Military Affairs* 460; *N.Y. Col. Doc.* VII 600; *Johnson* IV 306, 309. To similar effect, the Reverend Thomas Barton of Pa. to Secretary of the Society Nov. 16, 1764. The Reverend George Craig of Pa. to the Secretary June 25, 1766, proposed to apply Crown lands in the colonies to support three colonial bishops, Perry *Pa.* 366, 405.

9. There is a sketch of Thomas Secker (1693–1768) in *D.N.B.*; see also Porteus *Secker* and Horace Walpole to Horace Mann, Lewis *Walpole* XX 133–134. Secker to Horatio Walpole Jan. 9, 1750–51, proposed that "two or three persons should be ordained Bishops and sent into our American colonies [primarily] to administer confirmation and give Deacons and Priests orders to proper candidates . . . ," *London Chronicle* June 29, 1769.

10. New York City convention to Secker June 22, 1758, appealing for a colonial bishop, quoted in the text, Jones *St. Peter's* 71–72, where it is misdated 1768. (The correct date is from the original ms. in Lambeth Papers, London.)

11. The distinguished career of Samuel Johnson (1696–1772), born in Conn., graduate of Yale, missionary of the Society at Stratford, Conn. (1724–54, 1764–72), first President of King's College (1754–63), is described in *D.A.B.*; Beardsley *Johnson;* and Johnson's autobiography in Schneider *Johnson* I 3–49.

12. Secker to Johnson Sept. 27, 1758, replying to the convention's letter of June 22, *same* III 246–60.

13. Johnson to Secker March 1, 1759, replying to his letter of Sept. 27, 1758, *same* I 282–287. Their subsequent correspondence from 1759 through 1763 is listed (with citations of where located) in *same* IV 326–338. Particularly interesting in this correspondence is Secker to Johnson Nov. 4, 1760, stating that Lord Halifax "is very earnest for bishops in America" and expressing the hope "we may have a chance to succeed in that great point, when it shall please God to give us a peace," *same* IV 73.

14. Secker to Johnson May 22, 1764, as to favorable prospect for an American episcopate, quoted in the text, Beardsley *Johnson* 280–283.

15. *D.A.B.* has a sketch of the Reverend Myles Cooper (1737–1785), an Englishman, graduate of Oxford, President of King's College (1763–1775), who returned to England during the Revolutionary War and never came back to America.

16. The convention at Perth Amboy, N.J., attended by twelve Anglican clergymen of New York and New Jersey, referred to in the text, was described in a letter from the convention to the Secretary of the Society, the Reverend Daniel Burton, Oct. 3, 1765, *St. Peter's* 69–70, and Thomas Bradbury Chandler, a participant in the convention, to Johnson Nov. 12, Schneider *Johnson* I 356. (As to Burton, Secretary of the Society from 1761 to 1773, Pascoe *Two Hundred Years of the S.P.G.* 836; Secker to Johnson Dec. 10, 1761, Schneider *Johnson* III 262.)

17. The history of the Society and its colonial missionary work, including the support of over thirty missionaries in the colonies, Pascoe *Classified Digest of Records of the Society*; Pascoe *Two Hundred Years of the S.P.G.*; Hawkins *Historical Notices;* Perry *Historical Collections of the American Colonial Church* (5 vols.); Hawks and Perry *Conn.*; Ellis *Sermon Preached before the Society* (1759) 45–50; Schneider *Johnson;* Cross *Anglican Episcopate;* Bridenbaugh *Mitre and Sceptre;* Knollenberg *Origin* 75–83, 311–316.

18. George II, as head of the Church of England, issued a commission, April 19, 1728, to Edmund Gibson, Bishop of London, authorizing him or his commissaries "to visit all Anglican churches in the colonies and the Rectors . . . by whatever name called belonging to said Churches . . . with all and every Sort of Jurisdiction, power, and Ecclesiastical coercion, requisite in the premises," *N.Y. Col. Doc.* V 849–854 at 850. This was not renewed to any of the successors of Gibson, who died in 1748.

19. Supervision of the Bishops of London after 1748, Thomas Sherlock to the King of Council, *same* VII 360–69, undated but about 1752 according to Sherlock to Board of Trade, Feb. 19, 1759, *N.C. Col. Rec.* VI 10–13; Richard Terrick to Lord Hillsborough, Jan. 11, 1771, C.O. 5:1349:25–31, summarized in Labaree *Royal Government* 117n.; correspondence of Sherlock, Terrick, and other Bishops of London from 1749 to 1776 with their commissaries in Va., Perry *Va.* 365–536 *passim;* Labaree *Royal Government* 115–117; Labaree *Instructions* II 484–487, 489–492, 504–505.

20. The shipwreck and death of the young men, Hugh Wilson and Samuel Giles, the Reverend Samuel Seabury (1729–1796) to the Secretary of the Society Apr. 17, 1766, *N.Y. Doc. Hist.* III 329; Lydekker *Inglis* 3n., 43.

21. Ordination other than by a bishop was unthinkable to a good Churchman. Chandler, for example, wrote indignantly to an unidentified correspondent April 6, 1761, that if the growing tolerance of Anglicans toward Dissenters was not curbed "we may come to think that . . . Episcopal is no better than the leathern mitten ordination; or in other Words, that the authority derived from Christ is no better than that which is given by the mob," Clark *St. John's Church* 83–84. As to the Congregationalists' "leathern mitten ordination," Hawks and Perry *Conn.* I 63–64.

22. Johnson to Secker May 2, 1766, for colonial bishops, quoted in the text, Schneider *Johnson* I 361. His plea, based on the recent death of Wilson and Giles, was supported by the Reverend Charles Inglis, assistant minister of Trinity Church, New York City, to the Secretary April 19 and May 1, Lydekker *Inglis* 53, 57; the Reverend Hugh Neill and George Craig of Pa. to the Secretary of the Society May 19 and June 25, Perry *Pa.* 404–406; and convention of clergy at New York City May 22, to the Secretary, Stowe "Minutes" 132, 141–142.

23. Settlement of an Anglican bishop at Quebec would, of course, have alleviated the hardship of colonial candidates for the Anglican clergy having to go to England for ordination, but would not have met other considerations—such as the hope among some of being chosen an American bishop, immediately or later, and the belief of many of the Anglican clergy that the colonial Anglican Church would be strengthened by the presence of a resident bishop.

24. Secker to Johnson July 31, 1766, concerning the proposal for a bishop in Canada, quoted in the text, Schneider *Johnson* III 286–287. Secker seems to have

been doing his best for the project; but Auchmuty wrote Johnson June 12, 1766, criticizing Secker for his supposed neglect to "push the affair," and expressing the wish that " we had a L——d" instead, *same* I 362–363. "L——d" was, of course, William Laud (1573–1645), Archbishop of Canterbury (1633–1645), notable for his extremely aggressive championship of compulsory uniformity.

25. Johnson to Secker Nov. 10, 1766, concerning bishops quoted in the text, *same* I 380. Johnson did not mention N.J. and Del., but presumably he would include these in the bishopric mentioned for New England, N.Y., and Pa. In stating there were few "Dissenters" at Albany, Johnson must have ignored members of the Dutch Reformed Church who were numerous there.

26. Chandler to Johnson July 7, 1768, scorning the proposal to settle an Anglican bishop in Canada, quoted in the text, *same* I 442. In an earlier letter to Johnson (Sept. 5, 1766) Chandler had written in similar vein of this proposal, *same* I 366.

27. "Holt," referred to in Johnson's letter, doubtless was John Holt, formerly of Williamsburg, Va., now settled in New York City as publisher of the *New-York Journal,* sketch in *D.A.B.* I have not found the letter to Holt mentioned by Johnson.

28. Johnson to the Reverend John Camm, April 10, 1767, appealing for support for at least three colonial bishops, quoted in the text, *same* I 398–399. I have found no reply from Camm. There is a sketch of Camm, later the President of the College of William and Mary, in *D.A.B.* Camm had taken a leading part in the attack by some of the Virginia clergy on the Virginia Twopenny Act of 1758, Knollenberg *Origin* 54–63, 303–305, 306.

29. Johnson's encouragement to Chandler to write and publish an appeal to the public in support of the establishment of an American episcopate, referred to in Chandler to Johnson Sept. 5, 1766, and Jan. 9, March 31 and June 9, 1767, Schneider *Johnson* I 366, 388, 396, 408. Johnson's letters to Chandler are missing. Also at this time, a convention of fourteen Anglican clergymen of Mass. and R.I. assembled at Boston, signed a letter (June 17, 1767) to the Secretary of the Society (Burton) asking the Society's support for "American Bishops," Perry *Mass.* 531.

30. Chandler's *Appeal* was advertised as "just published" in the *New-York Gazette* of Oct. 15, 1767, Nelson *Bibliography* unpaged. Correspondence of Johnson concerning the *Appeal,* Schneider *Johnson* I 402, 408, 415. Chandler to Terrick Oct. 21, enclosing a copy of the *Appeal,* has some interesting data concerning its origin, Cross *Anglican Episcopate* 345–346. Chandler (1726–1790), born in Conn., was a graduate of Yale and a former student in theology of Johnson, sketch of Chandler in *D.A.B.*

31. The sermon by the Bishop of Llandaff, John Ewer, was delivered at a meeting of the Society Feb. 20, 1767, and was published soon afterward under the title *A Sermon Preached before the Incorporated Society . . .* in London and reprinted at New York City in Apr., 1768, Nelson *Bibliography* unpaged. (Ewer's pamphlet carries the incorrect spelling "Landaff" on the title page, and the bishopric is listed as "Landaff" in Beatson *Pol. Index* I 142.)

32. The pamphlets concerning colonial bishops, with their authors or reputed authors and dates of publication, Nelson *Bibliography* unpaged; Bridenbaugh *Mitre and Sceptre* 264–310; and Cross *Anglican Episcopate* 161–194. The news-

paper war from March, 1768, to February, 1769, is well covered in Bridenbaugh 297–301 and Cross 195–210. William Livingston of N.Y. wrote the Reverend Samuel Cooper, April 18, 1768, that his aim was to arouse "an universal alarm" to induce "our superiors at home" not to support the project, Sedgwick *Livingston* 136–137.

33. Chauncy contributed pamphlets described in Nelson *Bibliography passim*. Livingston's bitter newspaper articles, reprinted in pamphlets, are described in *same*. Livingston later moved to New Jersey, and was elected one of the N.J. delegates to both the First and Second Continental Congresses and the first Governor of the State of New Jersey. There are sketches of Chauncy (1705–1787) and Livingston (1723–1790) in *D.A.B.*

34. The petition for a charter by the Presbyterian Church of New York City, the Anglican opposition and rejection of the petition by the Privy Council Aug. 26, 1767, Baird "Presbyterians" 608–610; Hastings *N.Y. Ecclesiastical Rec.* VI 4046–4048, 4067, 4081, 4083–4084, 4098–4099; Bridenbaugh *Mitre and Sceptre* 260–262, 330–331.

35. Inglis and Chandler to Johnson Nov. 10 and Dec. 14, 1770, concerning Cooper's recent trip to Md., Lydekker *Inglis* 117 and Schneider *Johnson* IV 352. For the genesis of this trip, minutes of N.Y. convention May 21 and 22, 1767, Stowe "Minutes" 159–161.

36. Md. convention's undated address to the King and other undated addresses referred to in the text, enclosed in an undated letter from the Reverend Robert Read, Secretary of the convention, to Governor Robert Eden, which he laid before the Md. Council Sept. 15, 1770, *Md. Archives* XXXII 379–384. There were forty-four Anglican clergymen in Md. in 1767, Perry *Md.* 336–337, and I suppose about the same number in 1770.

37. Eden's reply, Sept. 15, 1770, stating that a matter of such "momentous Concern" ought to have been presented "by the Subscription of the Clergy individually," *Md. Archives* XXXII 384–385. (Eden said he would lay the matter before the Assembly, but he did not do so in his opening address to the Assembly Sept. 25, *same* LXII 206–207, and I have found no evidence of his doing so at any later date.)

38. Henry Addison, Bennet Allen, and Jonathan Boucher to the Anglican clergy of Md. Sept. 16, 1770, requesting a report to Boucher of their approval or disapproval of the proposed move, *same* 388. As to Boucher (1738–1804), apparently the leader in Md. for an American episcopate, sketch in *D.A.B.*; Boucher *View of the American Revolution;* Boucher's autobiography in Bouchier *Reminiscence of an American Loyalist;* Boucher's letter in *Md. Hist. Mag.* VI–IX *passim;* correspondence between Boucher and George Washington, Knollenberg *Washington: The Virginia Period* 73–75, 174–175.

39. Md. Anglican clergy's address to the King opposed by ten members, Rev. John Rodgers to "Committee of Dissenters," Sept. 5, 1771, *Minutes of the Convention* 33.

40. Stiles' diary for Feb. 11, 1771, records "By the prints I find under the News of November last that the Episcopal Clergymen in Maryland had lately preferred a Petition to the King asking a Bishop for that province," Stiles *Diary* I 91. See also Rodgers' letter cited in note 39 above.

41. The circular letter from Anglican clergymen of N.Y., N.J., and Conn. to those in Va. and the Carolinas is described in Inglis to Johnson, Dec. 4, 1770, Lydekker *Inglis* 119. I have not found a copy of this letter or evidence of any action in the Carolinas in response to it.

42. The reply of the Reverend James Horrocks quoted in the text is known from Inglis to Johnson March 28, 1771, *same* 122. There is a sketch of Horrocks (1734–1772), rector of Bruton parish, President of William and Mary College (1764–1772) and the Bishop of London's commissary for Va., in *D.A.B.* Richard Bland to Thomas Adams, Aug. 1, 1771, further describes Horrocks, 1 *W and M Q* V (1897) 152–54.

43. Call made by Horrocks for a convention of the Anglican clergy of Va. to be held in Williamsburg June 4, 1771, Bridenbaugh *Mitre and Sceptre* 318.

44. The resolution of the convention quoted in the text, adopted June 4, 1771, is in a protest, undated, of the Reverends Samuel Henley and Thomas Gwatkin, professors at the College of William and Mary, in the *London Chronicle* of Aug. 31, 1771. Bland to Adams Aug. 1, 1771, states that Camm (to whom Johnson had written in 1767) was "the champion" in the project, 1 *W and M Q* V (1897) 152–154. Francis Fauquier, Acting Governor of Va., wrote the Reverend Samuel Nicholls, July 29, 1761, that Camm was one "whose Delight . . . is to raise a Flame and to live in it," Perry *Va.* 471.

45. Brydon *Mother Church* 608–613 lists 104 Anglican ministers of Va. in 1774, and states (p. 349) that there were "a hundred [or] more" in 1771. The attendance at the convention of June, 1771, was evidently very thin.

46. The protest of Henley and Gwatkin, printed in the *Va. Gazette* (Purdie) of June 6, 1771, and reprinted in the *London Chronicle* of Aug. 31. The other dissenters were William Bland and Richard Hewitt, Brydon *Mother Church* 363. The problem in Va. was complicated by a Va. act of March 2, 1642 (Hening *Va.* II 46) providing that no minister should be inducted in Va. unless "he hath received his ordination from some bishop in England," making it doubtful if a minister ordained by a bishop in America could be legally inducted in Va.

47. Resolution of thanks by the Va. House of Burgesses to the four dissenters, quoted in the text, July 12, 1771, *Va. Journals* (for 1770–1772) 122. Bland, a member of the House, wrote: "I profess myself a sincere son of the established church but I can embrace her Doctrines without approving of her Hierarchy, which I know to be a Relick of the Papal Encroachments upon the Common Law," 1 *W and M Q* V (1897) 152–154.

48. Brydon *Mother Church* 351 states that it is not known "whether or not they prepared it [the proposed Petition to the King]; or if copies were sent to all the clergy," and (pp. 352–353) presents evidence that later attempts (Sept., 1771, and Jan. 1, 1772) to assemble another convention to discuss the matter failed.

49. The report of Horrocks' presentation of a petition is in the Instructions of June, 1772, from the Conn. Association of Congregational ministers concerning counteracting a petition presented by Horrocks (misspelled "Horrax") to the Archbishop of Canterbury for an American episcopate, *Minutes of the Convention* 35.

50. The consecration of Inglis as Anglican bishop of Nova Scotia in 1787, sketch of Inglis in *D.A.B.* and Lydekker *Inglis* 249. His diocese included not only

Nova Scotia, but also New Brunswick, Quebec, Prince Edward Island, Newfoundland, and Bermuda, *same* 251. (The Reverend Samuel Seabury had previously [1784] been consecrated bishop for Conn. in the Protestant Episcopal Church by so-called non-juring bishops in Scotland, sketch of Seabury in *D.A.B.*)

51. Stiles' note in 1768 of a statement of the Reverend William Willard Wheeler quoted in the text, Stiles *Itineraries* 254.

52. Lowth to William Samuel Johnson, May 20, 1773, states that Lord Dartmouth is the only member of the Ministry sympathetic to the establishment of an American episcopate, Beardsley *W.S. Johnson* 98–99; and the Reverend George Berkeley wrote William Samuel Johnson Aug. 11, 1774, that he was convinced the administration would never settle a bishop in the colonies "though Lord Dartmouth wishes it sincerely," *same* 107.

53. Benjamin Franklin in London to John Ross in Pa., May 14, 1768, Smyth *Franklin* V 133–134, and the Reverend William Gordon in England to the Reverend Joseph Bellamy in Conn. in 1769, Baird "Presbyterians" 651, as to Ministry's reluctance to aggravate colonial unrest by settling bishops in the colonies. Also Robert Lowth, Bishop of Oxford, wrote Samuel Johnson's son, William Samuel Johnson, May 20, 1773, "As to the important object of our wishes, the American Episcopate . . . the Ministry seem determined to put a stop to every motion of this kind that . . . may hazard the least disturbance . . . ," Beardsley *W.S. Johnson* 99.

APPENDIX (CHAPTER 9)

1. Judge William Spry, appointed judge of the overall court of admiralty at Halifax, May 28, 1764, opened his court there Oct. 2, Ubbelohde *Vice-Admiralty Courts* 2, 53.

2. Expressions of fear of having to defend suits for forfeiture of property in a court far from the place of seizure or from the owner's home or place of business are, for example, in Thacher *Sentiments* (1764) and Hopkins *Rights of Colonies* (1765) reprinted in Bailyn *Pamphlets* 494, 514–515.

3. The records of Spry's court are missing, but colonial newspapers would almost certainly have commented on cases, if any, similar to that of the *Polly*, and I have found no such comment.

4. Thomas Whately, Secretary to the Treasury, wrote John Temple May 10, 1765, "It having been represented that the option of carrying all causes within that [admiralty] jurisdiction to Halifax might be made a great grievance, it is proposed to divide all North America into three districts . . . and confine all causes to the Court of the district . . . ," *Bowdoin-Temple Papers* 56. Why the proposed change was so long delayed I do not know. The establishment and work of the new courts are discussed at length in Ubbelohde *Vice-Admiralty Courts* 130–178.

5. The particular colonies and adjacent waters placed within the jurisdiction of each of the several district courts established in 1768 and the nature of the courts' jurisdiction were given in warrants issued by the High Court of Admiralty in London Sept. 22, 1768, Adm. 2:1057, P.R.O., quoted in part in *same* 131n. A typical commission is that issued Oct. 17, 1768, to Jared Ingersoll, judge of the

new court at Philadelphia, printed in full in the *Pennsylvania Journal* Jan. 26, 1773.

6. The extent of the courts' jurisdiction is given in the judges' commissions, e.g., Ingersoll's commission of Oct. 17, 1768, in the *Pennsylvania Journal* Jan. 26, 1773. (The statement in Gipson *Brit. Empire* XI 134 that the new district courts had broader power than the existing colonial admiralty courts because given jurisdiction over "all district cases concerned with breaches of the trade laws" is erroneous. As brought out in Chapter 3 of this volume, the provincial admiralty courts had had such jurisdiction since 1764.)

7. Ingersoll's commission, *Philadelphia Journal* for Jan. 26, 1773, granted a salary of £600 a year. Since the £600 was not stated in terms of some form of colonial currency, £600 sterling was doubtless meant. Colonial criticism of the high salaries will be found in newspaper items dated Nov. 17 and 29, 1768, Dickerson *Boston* 23, 28.

8. The appointment of Jared Ingersoll and Augustus Johnston as Stamp Distributors in 1765 and their enforced resignation, Knollenberg *Origin* 230–232, 377–378 and Morgan *Stamp Act* 145–151, 232–234.

9. Joseph Reed of Pa. wrote Lord Dartmouth Apr. 4, 1774, criticizing the choice of officers, such as the register and marshal, of the new court at Philadelphia and of dissatisfaction over the appointment of judges "who had made themselves obnoxious by their conduct at the time of the Stamp Act," Reed *Reed* I 57. Other criticisms are cited in Gipson *Ingersoll* 304–313 and Ubbelohde *Vice-Admiralty Courts* 182–189.

APPENDIX (CHAPTER 10)

1. George Mason to Richard Henry Lee June 7, 1770, concerning the planters' disregard of the Va. non-importation agreement of May, 1769, Rowland *Mason* I 144. (A letter from George Washington to Robert Cary & Co., July 23, 1769, *Washington* II 512 indicates that he wished to adhere to the agreement, but seems to have thought, erroneously, that only "Articles . . . which are taxed by Act of Parliament for the purpose of Raising a Revenue in America" were banned.)

2. Richard Henry Lee to William Lee July 7, 1770, stating, "You will observe some clauses therein [the modified Va. non-importation agreement of June, 1770], calculated to produce the operation of this scheme, which, being omitted before, occasioned the shameful neglect of the former Association among the Merchants here," Ballagh *Lee* I 45. Thomas Adams to Perkins, Buchanan & Brown June 16, 1770, Price "Glasgow" 199n. implies that the Scotch merchants were the most flagrant offenders. Further evidence of disregard of the Va. agreement, Jensen *Founding* 355–356, 369–370; *Norton* 101, 103, 105, 119–121, 124–126.

3. The official figures for exports given in the text are from *Historical Statistics* 757. The yearly figures in *same,* captioned "Imports from England," actually cover exports from England, *same* 744. McCusker "Exports" 610n. points out that the statistical year probably was Jan. 6 through Jan. 5, rather than Dec. 25 through Dec. 24, as stated in *Historical Statistics,* and that the figures there are based on an obsolete method of valuation. However, McCusker's

adjusted figures for 1767–1770 show the same *pattern* of decline as those in *Historical Statistics*.

4. Figures of exports from England to Md. and Va. in the text, *same* 757. The figures of exports from Scotland, which were very substantial to these two colonies, show a similar trend, McCusker "Exports" 625. (As to the extensive trade between Scotland and Va. and Md., Price "Glasgow" 180–181, 194–195; Soltow "Scottish Traders" 83–98.) The agreement probably was better observed in Md. than in Va., Rowland *Mason* I 146 and Schlesinger *Col. Merchants* 199–202; but other evidence in *same* 218 and in Jensen *Philadelphia* 193, 284 indicates poor observance in Md., too.

5. The several dates when agreements became operative are in Chapter 7, the dates of termination are given in Chapter 10.

6. Figures of exports from England to the Carolinas in 1769 and 1770 given in the text, *Historical Statistics* 757. Additional evidence as to strict enforcement in S.C., Schlesinger *Col. Merchants* 206–208; McCrady *South Carolina* 651–662; Sellers *Charleston* 213–216. Probably a large part of the exports in 1770 went to N.C., where, as indicated in a later footnote, the local government had not been well observed.

7. Exports from England to Pennsylvania given in the text, *same* 757. Measures to enforce the Philadelphia non-importation agreement are described in Jensen *Philadelphia* 181–183. Though the exports for 1768 were somewhat higher than in earlier years, 1768 was fairly representative; the exports in 1767 to the Pa. district, for example, were £371,880, compared with £432,107 in 1768, and a similar pattern obtained in the other districts, *Historical Statistics* 757. The figures probably include a negligible amount of exports to Delaware and western New Jersey.

8. Exports from England to New England in 1768 and 1769, *Historical Statistics* 757.

9. Exports from England to New York for 1768 and 1769 stated in the text, *same* 757. These figures probably include a negligible amount of exports to eastern New Jersey. The exports from Scotland to the thirteen colonies except Va. and Md. were almost negligible, as shown by the table of exports in McCusker "Exports" 625.

10. Supporting evidence as to N.Y. referred to in the text, correspondence of Sir William Johnson, *Johnson* VII 162–179 *passim;* VIII 223; XII 814; and of James Beekman, *Beekman* II 723, 724, 806, 809, 875, 877, 920. Some of the letters to Johnson charge certain N.Y. merchants with chicanery and profiteering, but the general picture is one of strict observance.

11. The Newport agreement, Andrews "Boston Merchants" 213–236; Ezra Stiles' diary for May 31, 1770, Stiles *Diary* I 53–54; letters in *Pa. Mag. Hist.* XIV (1890) 44 and *M.H.S. Proc.* (for 1885–86) 121–122; Lovejoy *R.I. Politics* 143, 212; Schlesinger *Col. Merchants* 154–155, 215–216. (Newport merchants entered into a new agreement on Aug. 20, 1770, Andrews "Boston Merchants" 247, but by that time, the non-importation movement was collapsing.)

12. Gov. Francis Bernard of Mass., in writing Lord Barrington June 27, 1769, against removing the British troops from Boston, pointed out that "if the Troops are removed, the importers of goods from England in defiance of the Combination must remove also," *Bernard–Barrington Corresp.* 205.

13. The refusal of several Boston merchants to subscribe and the efforts, only partially successful, to secure their adherence are brought out in Schlesinger *Col. Merchants* 156–159, 162–164, 172–181 *passim;* Andrews "Boston Merchants" 224–226, 244, and in Chapter 11 of this book.

14. John Mein, his important activities in 1768–1769, and the financial support received by him from British officials are described in Andrews "Boston Merchants" 226–230; Schlesinger *Col. Merchants* 159–170, 177–179; Schlesinger "Propaganda" 411–416; Schlesinger *Prelude* 104–108; Bolton "Circulating Libraries" 196–200; Alden "John Mein, Publisher" 199–214; Alden "John Mein" 571–599; Dickerson "British Control" 460–466; and *Adams Legal Papers* I 151–157, 199–210, 216–218; II 397–398. As to William Fleeming, Alden "John Mein" 580–592.

15. The bills of lading of imports into Boston referred to in the text were published in the *Boston Chronicle* Aug. 17–Oct. 19, 1769, and from Dec. 11, 1769 to March 1, 1770, Schlesinger *Col. Merchants* 165n. Pamphlets published in 1769 and 1770 reprinting the invoices are described in Adams *Bibliography* 54, 64 and Schlesinger "Propaganda" 414n.

16. Carriage of proscribed goods on ships belonging to John Hancock, Schlesinger *Col. Merchants* 168–169. The Boston agreement was amended July 29, 1769, explicitly to bar the carriage of proscribed goods, *Mass. Gazette* July 31, 1769, and on Sept. 6, Hancock wrote his principal London correspondents, Haley & Hopkins, of the amended agreement, instructing them to observe the new agreement and to inform his shipmasters to do the same, Brown *Hancock* 165–166.

FIRST APPENDIX (CHAPTER 11)

1. The prosecution tried to establish that Lieut. Henry Panton and his party from the *Rose* boarded the *Pitt Packet* merely to search for contraband, but the testimony showed clearly that Panton planned to impress at least two members of the crew, *Adams Legal Papers* II 293–322. The ship *Rose* had arrived at Boston in Nov., 1768, Commodore Samuel Hood to Philip Stephens Nov. 27, 1768, *Letters to Ministry* 112, and on April 3, 1769, Hood ordered her captain, Benjamin Caldwell, to impress, Zobel *Boston Massacre* 335.

2. The statement concerning the attempt to impress Michael Corbet and three other Irish sailors and the killing of Panton, *same,* 115–120, 335; *Adams Legal Papers* II 276–277, 293–322. The seizure and prompt release of the two members of the crew who were residents of Mass., testimony of Thomas Power, master of the *Pitt Packet, same* 314–315.

3. On Jan. 14, 1762, the British admiralty, pursuant to the act cited, issued a commission to a group of Crown officers, *ex officio,* or by name, in Mass., N.H., and R.I., to form courts for the trial of piracies and other felonies committed in Mass., R.I., or N.H. waters, to consist of at least seven members, three of whom must be members of the commission. Others (if needed) were to be chosen from a wide range of persons by any three of a group composed of the commissioners specified in the commission, "Book of Charters, Commissions, Proclamations, etc." II 231–238, Mass. Arch.

4. The names and offices of the members of the court, all of whom were persons named by office or in person in the commission of Jan. 14, 1762, which convened May 23, 1769, *Adams Legal Papers* II 279, and sources therein cited. Governor Francis Bernard of Mass. presided, Dickerson *Boston* 110, quoting a newspaper account of June 19.

5. John Adams and James Otis as counsel for the accused, Zobel *Boston Massacre* 125–126, 336. Adams wrote William Tudor Dec. 30, 1816, that "Mr. Otis . . . constantly and finally refused to appear publicly in the cause," *Adams Works* II 224n., but Adams' own minutes of the trial show that Otis participated in the public examination of witnesses, *Adams Legal Papers* II 305, 306, 307.

6. Plea demanding trial by jury under acts of 28 Henry VIII ch. 15 (1536) and 4 Geo. I ch. 11 (1717), *same* 288–292.

7. Plea for trial by jury denied, and special court proceeds to trial without a jury, *same* 293–322.

8. Adams' statement that "No trial had ever interested the community so much before, excited so much curiosity and compassion, or so many apprehensions of the fatal consequences of the supremacy of parliamentary jurisdiction, or the intrigues of parliamentary courts," *Adams Works* X 209–210, was not made until years later, but the copious contemporary evidence of bitter hostility in Mass. to impressment, and denial of trial by jury lend color to Adams' statement.

9. The decree of "justifiable homicide" and acquittal of the accused, June 17, 1769, Dickerson *Boston* 110, quoting a newspaper account of June 19.

10. Though there was no act of Parliament explicitly authorizing impressment, the general authority of the Crown to impress was firmly established, Blackstone *Commentaries* I 419–420.

11. The arguments for and against the view that section 9 of the act of 6 Anne ch. 37 (1708) was still currently in force, Knollenberg *Origin* 103–104, 362. The question was never finally determined; it became moot in 1775, when the section in question was repealed by 15 Geo. III ch. 31 sec. 19. Adams was prepared to argue in the *Corbet* case that sec. 9 was still in force, *Adams Legal Papers* II 323–325. Also, see discussion of the *Liberty* case in Chapter 8.

12. Gov. William Shirley to the Board of Trade Dec. 1, 1747, of the view throughout the colonies that impressment there was "illegal by virtue of a Clause in a statute of Queen Anne," *Shirley* I 417–418.

13. Instructions, prepared by a committee of which John Adams was a member, adopted at Boston town meeting June 17, 1768, condemning impressment in the colonies as illegal under the act of 6 Anne ch. 37 sec. 9 (1708), *Boston Town Records* (for 1758–1769) 259. Many years later, John Adams wrote several letters concerning the Corbet case, some of which are demonstrably inaccurate and others unsupported by contemporary evidence, *Adams Works* II 226n., *same* X 207–210; *M.H.S. Proc.* 44 (1911) 424.

14. Hutchinson's explanation of the court's action quoted in the text, Hutchinson *Hist. of Mass.* III 167n. As to the requirement for a warrant of impressment, Lords of the Admiralty to Captains of His Majesty's Ships in America Sept. 26, 1743, *Law* I 117; Clark "Impressment" 204–215; *Adams Legal Papers* II 323n.; Stout "Manning the Royal Navy" 174–185.

15. Hutchinson's diary for Oct. 22, 1778, records: "I finished the revisal of my History to the end of my Administration [the third volume], and laid it by," Hutchinson *Diary and Letters* II 218.

SECOND APPENDIX (CHAPTER 11)

1. Clashes between civilians, especially merchant seamen, and British troops in New York, Lemisch "Jack Tar vs. John Bull" *passim.*

2. The irritation caused by the soldiers' working in spare time for cut-rate wages, *same;* Lemisch "Jack Tar in the Streets" 400; Morris *Govt. and Labor* 190. According to a New York broadside signed "a Merchant," issued in February, 1770, quoted in Lemisch "Jack Tar vs. John Bull" 163, 227, soldiers would work for eighteen pence (a shilling and a half) to two shillings a day at jobs for which civilian workmen were paid four shillings.

3. Attack by British soldiers on the Liberty Pole in New York City, Stokes *Iconography* IV 802. Earlier attacks on the pole or its predecessor, are described in *same* 806.

4. The handbill dated Jan. 15, 1770, and signed "Brutus," quoted in the text *same* 802–803.

5. Tearing down of the Liberty Pole in "the dead Hour of Night . . . , one o'clock" Jan. 17, 1770, *same* 803.

6. The handbill signed "16th Regiment of Foot," quoted in the text, Dewson *Sons of Liberty* 113–114n.

7. Golden Hill, since leveled, was "That portion of John-street which is between Cliff-street and Burling Slip," *same* 114n.

8. The clash Jan. 19, 1770, described in the text, Stokes *Iconography* IV 803. A "Letter from New York" of Jan. 22, published in the *St. James Chronicle* (London) of March 15 and reprinted in Dewson *Sons of Liberty* 117–118n. states that a merchant sailor was killed by the soldiers. But contemporary New York City newspaper accounts report no death, and Cadwallader Colden to Lord Hillsborough Feb. 21, says "only a few wounds and bruises were received on each side," *N.Y. Col. Doc.* VII 208.)

APPENDIX (CHAPTER 14)

1. Gov. Hutchinson's statement in his "Narrative" as to the entry of the *Dartmouth,* Hutchinson *Diary and Letters* I 100–101. The narrative was written apparently some time after August 31, 1778, *same* 105.

2. Hutchinson's similar statement in his *History of Mass.* is at III 305, 307–308. The *History*, of which this is in the concluding part, was finished in October, 1778, Hutchinson *Diary and Letters* II 218.

3. Miller *Sam Adams* 289–90 quoted in the text. Sydney George Fisher's *The Struggle for American Independence* I 174–175 (1908) is in similar vein. Paraphrasing Hutchinson's retrospective account of the tea episode, Fisher states, "Governor Hutchinson followed the conciliatory policy of the home government. . . . But the radical patriots would not take this conservative and moderate course. . . ."

4. Shipton "Samuel Adams" in *Harvard Graduates* X 443 (1958).

5. *Dartmouth's* log for Nov. 27 and 28, 1773, says nothing of any order or request from the consignees or Hutchinson to remain outside the harbor or any order or request from Samuel Adams or any Boston committee to enter, but mentions the unusual circumstance of boarding by customs officers, *Traits of the Tea Party* 259–260.

6. No mention by James Hall in his testimony before the Privy Council Feb. 19, 1774, of any request or order from the consignees or Boston Whigs as to the *Dartmouth's* entering port, P.C. 1:56:Part I:Bundle 2.

7. Hutchinson to Gov. William Tryon Dec. 1, 1773, Mass. Arch. XXVII 576, and other contemporary letters of Hutchinson, referred to in the text, to one of his sons Nov. 30, 1773, Hutchinson *Diary and Letters* I 94–95; to Dartmouth Dec. 2, 14, 17, 18, 20, and 24, Mass. Arch. XXVII 577–578, 586–588, 589, 594; William Palmer Dec. 9, Directors of the East India Company Dec. 19, Israel Mauduit Dec. [no day], and Francis Bernard Jan. 1, 1774, *same* 584–585, 597–599, 604–607, 609. (Bernard was now Sir Francis, having been made a baronet on his return to England in 1769.)

8. Hutchinson wrote Bernard Jan. 1, 1774, "After the usurpers of government had tried every method they could think of to force the tea back to England, and all in vain, they . . . destroyed three hundred and fifty chests," Hutchinson *Diary and Letters* I 174. Truslow Adams' statement in *Rev. New England* 394 that the destruction of the tea was "an irresponsible piece of reckless bravado designed to precipitate a crisis" is in conflict with the evidence.

9. Hutchinson wrote Dartmouth on Jan. 4, 1774, that the owners and masters of the tea ships said "they were compelled to bring their ships to the wharffe and to keep them there unless the Teas imported were sent back to England without payment of the duty . . . ," Mass. Arch. XXVI 166 and "Papers relating to the Boston Tea Party" Harv. Coll. Lib. This is confirmed as to one of the ships, the *Eleanor,* in a diary entry of Dec. 3, 1773, by its owner John Rowe, *Rowe* 256–257.

10. The Tory writer "Massachusettensis" in a letter published Feb. 2, 1775, gives the impression, without explicitly saying so, that the so-called "body" meeting in Boston ordered the owner of the *Dartmouth* "to bring her to the wharf" while she was still outside the port, i.e., before the tea on board her had become liable to duty. The evidence shows clearly that this was not true.

11. Hutchinson to Gov. Tryon Dec. 1, 1773, as printed in Frothingham "Tea Party" 168.

12. Hutchinson's actual words were "The day before, one of the ships with 114 chests of tea arrived, and anchored below the castle," etc., Mass. Arch. XXVII 576.

FIRST APPENDIX (CHAPTER 20)

1. Instruction of the Philadelphia mass meeting of May 20, 1774, for the committee chosen at the meeting to ask Governor John Penn to call a special session of the Pa. Assembly, *same* 342. The Assembly had adjourned on Jan. 22, until Sept. 12, *Pa. Assembly* VIII 7085.

2. Petition of Philadelphia "Freeholders" to Gov. Penn to call a meeting of the Pa. Assembly to consider action on the Boston Port Act, 4 *Force* I 391–392. (I have found no evidence as to whether or not the committee chosen at the Philadelphia mass meeting of May 20, with instructions to petition the Governor to call the Assembly, had a hand in securing this petition.)

3. Penn's reply of June 8, 1774, *same* 391.

4. Resolutions of the Philadelphia mass meeting of June 18, 1774 and the names of the forty-four members of the committee chosen at this meeting, *same* 426–428. I have found no evidence as to why three of the members (Joseph Fox, John Gibson, and Thomas Penrose) of the original committee were dropped. The leading part played by John Dickinson in the meeting of June 18 and throughout the movement for bringing Pa. into union with the other colonies is detailed in Jacobson *Dickinson* 72–76.

5. On June 27, 1774, Gov. Penn, on news of the Indian outbreak, summoned a special session of the Pa. Assembly to meet in Philadelphia July 18, 4 *Force* I 454. (Perhaps Penn thought that an extralegal convention was inevitable unless the Assembly were convened, and he preferred the latter; however, I have found no evidence that the Indian threat was not the real reason for his decision.)

6. The Philadelphia committee's circular letter of June 28, 1774, calling for a convention to meet in Philadelphia July 15, Smith *Smith* I 496–497.

7. Though the Quakers now were a minority group in Pennsylvania, they retained great influence in the Assembly because the three old counties, Philadelphia, Bucks, and Chester, where they were chiefly concentrated, had twenty-four representatives, while the more populous City of Philadelphia and the eight newer counties combined had only sixteen, *Pa. Assembly* VIII 7024. (For the situation in 1764, which had not greatly changed in the intervening years, Knollenberg *Origin* 212–213, 370, and sources cited therein.)

8. On May 26, Thomas Mifflin wrote Samuel Adams that the Friends "universally" favored a Petition to the King before adoption of a non-importation agreement, Rossman *Mifflin* 24. The "Elders and Overseers" of the several Friends (Quaker) Meetings in Philadelphia had published a protest in the *Pa. Gazette* of June 1, 1774, against a statement in the *Pa. Packet* of May 30, that "the Members of all Societies in this city" had unanimously voted to suspend business on June 1, when the Boston Port Act was to take effect, Lincoln *Rev. Movement in Pa.* 168.

9. The meeting of the convention at Philadelphia July 15, 1774, with the names of the seventy-five delegates, 4 *Force* IV 555. The convention was called "The Committee for the Province of Pennsylvania," *same* 557–558. The place of meeting, Carpenters' Hall, Christopher Marshall's diary July 15, *Marshall* 8.

10. The Pa. convention's resolution of July 15, 1774, quoted in the text, 4 *Force* I 556.

11. Request from the Pa. convention to members of the Pa. Assembly July 21, 1774, quoted in the text, *same* 564. The convention's resolutions and a dissertation by Dickinson, *same* 558–593, were published soon afterward in a pamphlet entitled *An Essay on the Constitutional Power of Great Britain.* . . .

12. William Bradford of Philadelphia wrote James Madison Aug. 1, 1774, that Joseph Galloway and Charles Humphreys were "known to be inimical to the

Liberties of America," *Madison* I 118. The charge was almost certainly unfair to Humphreys and probably to Galloway, even though he did later become an active Tory.

13. Thomas Mifflin, an outstanding member of the Continental Congress, general in the Continental Army, and a member of the Congressional Board of War, has generally been given less credit than he deserves as a leader in the Revolution, probably because of his supposed complicity in the probably non-existent "Conway Cabal" against Washington, Knollenberg *Washington and the Revolution*, index under "Mifflin, Thomas." Also, Rossman *Mifflin* 29–183.

14. Pa. Assembly's election of delegates to the proposed Continental Congress and its instructions to them quoted in the text, July 22 and 23, 1774, 4 *Force* I 607–609.

SECOND APPENDIX (CHAPTER 20)

1. Nomination by the Committee of Fifty-One of Philip Livingston, John Alsop, Isaac Low, James Duane, and John Jay as delegates for N.Y. City and County, July 4, 1774, 4 *Force* I 308. Isaac Sears, Alexander McDougall, Peter Van Brugh Livingston, Leonard Lispenard, and eight other members of the committee voted for John Morin Scott and McDougall, instead of Jay and Alsop, but were defeated, *same.* A "Committee of Mechanics," meeting on July 5, proposed McDougall and Lispenard in place of Duane and Alsop, broadside of July 6, quoted in Becker *New York* 123n.

2. Vote of support by the N.Y. Committee of Mechanics, July 27, 1774. As to this committee, Lynd "Mechanics in N.Y." 225–246; Champagne "Liberty Boys and Mechanics" 115–135, and documents in 4 *Force* I 295, 308, 310, 317, 318, 320, 329, 330, 803, 804. Becker *New York* 120 states that this committee was "virtually a continuation of the N.Y. *Sons of Liberty*"; but, unlike the latter, the Committee of Mechanics apparently represented exclusively mechanics, such as carpenters, masons, coopers, tailors, shoemakers, butchers, and bakers, described in McKee *Labor in Col. N.Y.* 22–30; Bridenbaugh *Colonial Craftsman passim;* Walsh *Charleston's Sons passim.*

3. Proceedings for election of delegates for N.Y. City and County by all "inhabitants who pay taxes," and the election on July 28, 1774, of the slate nominated by the Committee of Fifty-One, notices from June 29 to July 28, 4 *Force* I 309, 310, 315, 318–321.

4. Circular letter from the New York City and County Committee of Fifty-One to other countries of the New York province proposing their Selection of delegates, *same* 322.

5. Albany, Westchester, Dutchess, and Ulster Counties authorized the delegates for New York City and County to act for them and Orange, Suffolk, and Kings Counties elected their own delegates, Becker *New York* 139–141. Six New York counties—Charlotte, Cumberland, Gloucester, Queens, Richmond (Staten Island), and Tryon—apparently did not choose delegates nor authorize those of New York City and County to act for them. (Gloucester County, in present northeastern Vermont, was so sparsely settled that it should perhaps not be counted.)

6. The names of the members of the N.Y. Assembly in 1774 are in Bonomi *Factious People* App. C, unpaged, and Werner *N.Y. Civil List* 112.

7. The offending resolutions referred to by Moore asserted the Assembly's right to petition the King and correspond with the Assemblies of other colonies as it saw fit, protested against any suspension of the N.Y. Assembly other than by the Crown's exercise of its prerogative to prorogue or dissolve the Assembly, and instructed the Speaker (Philip Livingston) to answer the Massachusetts House's circular letter of Feb., 1768, described in Chapter 7, inviting the Assemblies of other colonies to join in protesting against the Townshend Act, *same* 70–72.

8. Governor Sir Henry Moore's dissolution of the New York Assembly and statement of his reason for doing so, Jan. 2, 1769, *N.Y. Assembly Journal* Oct., 1768, session, 75–76.

9. There are sketches of Philip Livingston (1716–1778), a Signer of the Declaration of Independence, and James De Lancey (1732–1800), in *D.A.B.*, and of Jacob Walton (d. 1782) and James Jauncey (d. 1790) in Stevens *New York* Part 2 170.

10. William Smith to Robert R. Livingston Jan. 5, 1769, concerning the negotiations quoted in the text, Bonomi *Factious People* 251n. There is a sketch of Smith (1728–1793) in *D.A.B.* He was a member of the N.Y. Council and closely connected politically with Philip Livingston's brother, William (Dillon *New York Triumverate passim*), and by marriage with their nephew, Peter R. Livingston. (The wives of Smith and Peter R. Livingston were sisters, daughters of James Livingston, Livingston *Livingston* 76.)

11. The election in 1768 of New York City's representatives in the Assembly and the vote for John Morin Scott, Champagne "Liberty Boys and Mechanics" 132; Champagne "N.Y. Elections" 62–68; Bonomi *Factious People* 239–245. Scott tried unsuccessfully to persuade the Assembly to oust his successful opponent, James Jauncey, from the Assembly on the ground of having corrupted many of those who had voted for Jauncey, *N.Y. Assembly Journal* (for 1766–1776) Oct., 1768, session 7, 15, 52–53. As to Scott, sketch of him in *D.A.B.* and Dillon *New York Triumverate* (including Scott) *passim.*

12. There is a sketch of John Cruger, a leading merchant of New York City, former Mayor of the City (1756–1765) and one of the representatives of New York City and County in the Assembly (1759–1768, 1769–1775), in *D.A.B.*

13. Cruger's niece, Polly Cruger, was married to Walton, Wilson *New-York* IV xx, and his nephew, John Harris Cruger, was married to De Lancey's niece, Anne De Lancey, Stevens *New York* Part 2 128. De Lancey and Walton, too, were related by marriage: De Lancey's sister, Mary, was the wife of Walton's brother, William, *same* 60.

14. The church affiliations of De Lancey, Walton, Jauncey, and Cruger as stated in the text, "Philo-Patriae" in *New-York Gazette* Jan. 16, 1769. The unidentified writer pointed out that Cruger was a member of the "pure, Orthodox Dutch Church," not of the congregation of the Reverend Archibald Laidlie. Members of the Dutch Reformed Church in New York were at odds over various issues described in papers of July, 1767, to May, 1769, published in Hastings *N.Y. Ecclesiastical Records* VI 4094–4160 *passim.*

15. Philip Livingston was a member of the Great Consistory of the Dutch Reformed Church in New York, which in 1762 voted to consent to calling an English-speaking minister to serve as a collegiate pastor of the Church, Robert F. Williams, Clerk and Treasurer of Collegiate Reformed Protestant Dutch Church of the City of New York, to the author Jan. 5, 1973. No evidence is cited for the statement in the sketch of Livingston in *D.A.B.* that it was "the Presbyterians with whom he worshipped," and I have seen none.

16. Theodore (Theodorus) Van Wyck was a member of the congregation of the Dutch Reformed Church of which Laidlie was pastor, Hastings *N.Y. Ecclesiastical* Hist. VI 4088, 4100, 4202, 4209–10, 4240, 4243, 4245, 4252.

17. Membership of Peter Van Brugh Livingston and Scott in the Presbyterian Church, Osgood "Society of Dissenters" 500, 502. There is a sketch of P.V. Livingston in *D.A.B.*

18. The N.Y. Assembly election of Jan., 1769, Bonomi *Factious People* 248–257; Champagne "N.Y. Elections" 72–75; Champagne "Liberty Boys and Mechanics" 132. The vote was: De Lancey, 936; Walton, 931; Cruger, 882; Jauncey, 877; Philip Livingston, 666, Scott, 646; Peter Van Brugh Livingston 535; Van Wyck, 518; *same* 132. In 1768 the vote for the four successful candidates was: Philip Livingston, 1,320; De Lancey, 1,204; Walton, 1,175; and Jauncey 1,052; *same* 132.

19. The disgust of voters over the Dissenters' injection into the election campaign of the issue of Church v. Dissenters and other factors contributing to the victory of the De Lancey ticket, Bonomi *Factious People* 251–254 and sources cited therein.

20. Governor Moore wrote Secretary of State Lord Hillsborough June 3, 1769 that "a licentious set of Men who call themselves the Sons of Liberty" had had "great influence on the Elections of Members for this City . . . ," *N.Y. Col. Doc.* VIII 170.

21. The Sons of Liberty in New York City are discussed in Morais "Sons of Liberty in New York" 270–289; Champagne "The Sons of Liberty . . . in New York Politics" *passim;* Champagne "Sons of Liberty" 339–347; Champagne "Liberty Boys" 115–135; Champagne "Military Assoc. of the Sons of Liberty" 338–348; Friedman "Disruption of Family Politics" 4–24; Bonomi *Factious People* 234–276 *passim;* Maier *Resistance* 78–112, 297–303; Becker New York 41–50; Leake *Lamb* 3–14, 18–37. For a good account of the Sons of Liberties in other colonies, Maier *Resistance* 77–112, 297–312 *passim.*

22. Isaac Sears, John Lamb, and others wrote Nicholas Ray Oct. 10, 1766, of "the dissolution of our society [Sons of Liberty] . . . immediately upon the repeal of the Stamp Act," *same* 36. A new York City broadside dated July 7, 1769, announced the formation of a new Society, "the United Sons of Liberty," to support the non-importation agreement and secure repeal of the Townshend Act duties, *Am. Revolution in N.Y.* 310–311, but gave no evidence of who promoted or composed the Society.

23. There is a sketch of Sears (b. about 1730; d. 1786), outstanding leader of the more zealous Whigs in New York City from 1765 to 1775, when he retired to his native Conn., in *D.A.B.* and an unpublished dissertation, Robert Jay Christen "King Sears: Politician and Patriot . . ." (1968), in the Columbia U. Lib. Sears

was a member of the New York City Chamber of Commerce, composed of leading merchants of the city, Stevens *New York* Part 2 160–161, and of the important committee of merchants chosen to enforce the New York City merchants' non-importation agreement of 1768–1770, *Pitkin* 191, 194.

24. Sears' outstanding leadership of the Sons of Liberty in N.Y. against the Stamp Act, Capt. John Montresor's diary, Feb. 14 to Aug. 11, 1766, *Montresor* 349, 353, 361, 362, 382; Champagne "Military Assoc. of the Sons of Liberty" 343–348.

25. Sears' support of the De Lancey ticket in the 1769 election, Champagne "N.Y. Elections" 75 and sources cited therein. Sears was a vestryman of Trinity Church (Episcopal) 1784–1786, Dix *Trinity Church* IV 578, which suggests that he probably was an Anglican in 1769.

26. The *New-York Journal* of Nov. 17, 1768, reported: "On Monday last [Nov. 14] . . . Effigies of Governor Bernard and Sheriff Greenleaf of Boston . . . made their appearances in the Streets, hanging on a Gallows . . . attended by a vast Number of Spectators . . . after which they were publickly burnt. . . ."

27. Gov. Moore's proclamation offering a reward for the arrest and conviction of the ringleaders in the demonstration of Nov. 15, and his message to the Assembly Nov. 21, 1768, requesting a vote of funds to pay the offered reward, *N.Y. Assembly Journal* (for 1766–1776) Oct., 1768, session, 28.

28. Adoption Nov. 23, 1768, of a motion to grant funds to pay the reward, by a vote of 17 to 5, *same* 30.

29. The resolution against the N.Y. Suspending Act, presented to the Assembly Dec. 31, 1768, failed explicitly to name the act, *N.Y. Assembly Journal* (for 1766–1776) Oct., 1768, session, 70. De Lancey's motion was for an amendment explicitly to denounce the act. (Wilson *New York* II 396 and Becker *New York* 74 state that De Lancey's motion was designed "to cut out the [Assembly's] resolution with respect to the right of correspondence," i.e., was pro-British; but neither Wilson or Becker cites evidence to support the statement, which is discredited by the Assembly's minutes.)

30. De Lancey's motion was defeated 17 to 6, *N.Y. Assembly Journal* (for 1766–1776) Oct. 1768, session, 70.

31. Peter R. Livingston (1737–1794) was the son of Philip's oldest brother, Robert R. Livingston, Jr. (1708–1790), third and last lord of Livingston Manor. There is a sketch of Peter R., a Harvard drop-out, in Shipton *Harvard Graduates* XIV 183–190.

32. Abraham Ten Broeck was a brother of Philip Livingston's wife, born Christina Ten Broeck. Pierre Van Cortlandt's wife (born Joanna Livingston) and Philip Livingston had a common grandfather, Robert Livingston (1654–1728), first lord of Livingston Manor. Sketches of Philip Livingston, Ten Broeck, and Van Cortlandt are in *D.A.B.* and genealogical data in Livingston *Livingston passim.*

33. Peter R. Livingston wrote Philip Schuyler Feb. 6, 1769, that "for the sake of the Family, as Philip was Speaker, have given him up my Place," Bancroft transcripts, N.Y.P.L. The initial plan had been for Ten Broeck to step aside to permit Philip's election as member for Rensselaerwyck Manor; but this had miscarried, *same.*

34. Election of Cruger as Speaker of the Assembly, April 4, 1769, *N.Y. Assembly Journal* (for 1766–1776), April, 1769, session, 4.

35. Philip Livingston's ouster from the Assembly, May 12, 1769, by a vote of 17 to 6, *same* 61. The N.Y. Election Act of May 16, 1699, referred to in the text provided that representatives "shall be Dwelling & Resident within the Cittys, Countys & Manors" for which elected, *N.Y. Col. Laws* I 408. There apparently was no question that Philip Livingston was not a resident of the Manor. Non-residents had sometimes been permitted to sit, Bonomi *Factious People* 258–259, but improperly so in view of the Act of 1699.

36. After Philip Livingston's ouster, Robert R. Livingston, dsecribed in note 37 below, was repeatedly elected for the Manor, but each time was rejected by a majority in the Assembly on the ground of the impropriety of a judge of the N.Y. Supreme Court sitting in the Assembly, *same* 259–61. Finally, Peter R. Livingston was reelected member for the Manor and, on February 21, 1774, was accepted as its member by vote of the Assembly, *N.Y. Assembly Journal* (for 1766–1776) Jan., 1774, session, 60.

37. Judge Robert R. Livingston (1718–1775), a judge of the N.Y. Supreme Court and one of the two members in the Assembly for Dutchess County from 1761 to 1768, was defeated for election in 1768 and again in 1769, Bonomi *Factious People* 245, 255, 256n. There is a sketch of him in *D.A.B.* He was the father of the better-known Chancellor Robert R. Livingston (1746–1813) and a first cousin of Philip Livingston, Livingston, *Livingston* 541–543, 555.

38. The tenants of Henry Beekman and R. G. Livingston whose votes defeated Judge Livingston presumably had leases for life which, under a N.Y. Election Act of Oct. 18, 1701, put the leasee on the same footing in voting for representatives in the Assembly as an owner of land in fee, *N.Y. Col. Laws* I 453.

39. The Assembly's grant of supplies for the troops at the April, 1769, session was made without a division at any stage, minutes of the Assembly April 14 to May 12, *N.Y. Assembly Journal* (for 1766–1776) April, 1769, session, 27–28 *passim*.

40. Peter R. Livingston to Schuyler Feb. 27, 1769, concerning the defeat of Judge Livingston and the possibility by proper management of forcing a dissolution of the Assembly and a new election, Bancroft transcripts, N.Y.P.L.

41. Message of Acting Governor Cadwallader Colden to the Assembly Nov. 22, 1769, asking for the supplies for the British troops required by the British Quartering Act, *N.Y. Assembly Journal* (for 1766–1776) Nov., 1769, session, 4. Colden had succeeded Moore upon the latter's death Sept. 11. There are sketches of Moore (1713–1769) and Colden (1688–1766) in *D.A.B.*

42. The votes of supplies for the troops since 1767, without a single division, can be followed in *N.Y. Assembly Journal* (for 1766–1776) *passim*. The required supplies had been voted as recently as May 12, 1769, *same*, April, 1769, session, 61–62.

43. Vote of supplies for the troops out of proposed new issue of paper currency, Dec. 29, 1769, *same*, Nov., 1769, session, 54.

44. A motion for the bill to issue £120,000 in paper currency, effective April 1, 1770, was adopted Dec. 28, 1769, and the bill was passed Dec. 30, *same* 53, 55. It was concurred in by the provincial Council Jan. 4, 1770, *N.Y. Legislative Council Journal* II 1725–1726, and signed by Colden the next day, Colden to

Hillsborough Jan. 6, 1770, *N.Y. Col. Doc.* VIII 198. Colden pointed out in this letter that if the Crown disapproved the act, it could be disallowed before it was to take effect. The act is in *N.Y. Col. Laws* V 24–26.

45. Motion on Dec. 15, 1769, by William Nicoll of Suffolk County to supply the troops as described in the text, *N.Y. Assembly Journal* (for 1766–1776) Nov., 1769, session, 38. (Perhaps Colden intimated to Nicoll or other members of the Assembly that he would sign the proposed currency act only on condition that at least part of the money for the troops be voted from existing funds; but I have found no evidence of this.)

46. John De Lancey, member for Westchester Borough, was a first cousin of James De Lancey and a grandson of Colden, Jones *Hist. of N.Y.* I 661. But neither John De Lancey nor other members of the Assembly, except those from New York City, voted together with such consistency as to constitute a bloc. However, votes in the New York provincial Council, recorded in Smith *Memoirs* I 46–180, indicate that there was a group voting together in the Council, including James De Lancey's uncle, Oliver De Lancey, which might be considered a "De Lancey" bloc.

47. Vote on Nicoll's motion, *N.Y. Assembly Journal* (for 1766–1776) Nov., 1769, session, 38. All those voting in favor of the motion were from lower New York; those voting against it were about equally divided between upper and lower New York. Many residents of lower New York benefited directly from the sale of supplies to the British forces in New York City, headquarters of the British army in North America and were, therefore, particularly interested in having the Assembly grant the funds to pay for these supplies.

48. Gerlach *Schuyler* 199 gives evidence that Schuyler was incapacitated from gout in early December, 1769, and probably he was absent from the Assembly on December 15. When the bill for the proposed grant was presented for its second reading on Dec. 20, he voted against the bill, *N.Y. Assembly Journal* (for 1766–1776) Nov., 1769, session, 43.

49. The bill to grant funds to supply the troops passed Dec. 30, 1769, by a vote of 12 to 10, *same* 56. The act for the supplies, dated Jan. 5, 1770, is in *N.Y. Col. Laws* V 23–24. In subsequent grants of supplies, only George Clinton and Nathaniel Woodhull consistently opposed the grants, *N.Y. Assembly Journal* (for 1766–1776) *passim.*

50. The more zealous Whigs in New York, among whom Sears was most often named, were usually referred to as Sons of Liberty. In his journal, William Smith referred initially to radical Whigs as "Sons of Liberty," later (from December, 1773, onward) as "Liberty Boys," Smith *Memoirs* I 48–156; 157–256. A handbill of January, 1770, signed "16th Regiment of Foot," refers to the radical Whigs as "S—— of L——" in one place, as "L——B——" in another, Dawson *Sons of Liberty* 113–114n.

51. The handbill dated Dec. 17, 1769, signed "A Son of Liberty," addressed "To The Betrayed Inhabitants Of The City And Colony Of New York," is in *N.Y. Doc. Hist.* III 528–530. An undated handbill signed "Legion," published about this same time, called for a meeting of citizens "to avert the Destructive Consequences of the late *base inglorius* Conduct of our General Assembly . . . ," *same* 534–535. As to Colden's role in N.Y. politics, Shammas "Colden" 105–124.

52. Alexander McDougall's support of Philip Livingston in the election of 1769, Bonomi *Factious People* 253 and sources cited therein. There are sketches of McDougall (1732–1786), a merchant in New York City, later a general in the Revolutionary War, in *D.A.B.* and Bonomi *Factious People* 268–269, 271–272. Having been captain of a privateer in the Seven Years War, McDougall was commonly called "Captain." He was among the leading Presbyterian members in the founding of the Society for Dissenters in Feb., 1769, Osgood "Society of Dissenters" 502.

53. Petition of Jacobus Van Zandt, Sears, Joseph Bull, Joseph Drake, and Alexander McDougall to the Mayor of New York City (Whitehead Hicks) Jan. 30, 1770, asking for allotment of public land for erection of a new liberty pole, and refusal of the City Council to grant the petition, Stokes *Iconography* IV 804–805.

54. Peter R. Livingston to his father, Robert Livingston, Jr., Feb. 5, 1770, as to having provided the land for erection of a new liberty pole, Bonomi *Factious People* 276. The location of the new pole and the elaborate ceremony accompanying its erection are described in Stokes *Iconography* IV 806.

55. Colden's proclamation of Dec. 20, 1769, quoting the Assembly's resolution of Dec. 19, and offering a reward of £100 to anyone "who shall Discover" the author of the Sons of Liberty handbill, *N.Y. Doc. Hist.* III 532–534.

56. James Parker's identification, Feb. 7, 1770, of McDougall as having hired him to print the Sons of Liberty handbill, Stokes *Iconography* IV 806, Smith *Memoirs* I 74.

57. The build-up of McDougall as the American Wilkes, Dillon *New York Triumverate* 108–123; Jensen *Founding* 340–344; Bonomi *Factious People* 268–275. John Wilkes' career from 1763 to 1770 as the champion of liberty in England is described in Rudé *Wilkes & Liberty* 1748, his influence in the colonies in Maier "Wilkes" 373–395; and Maier *Resistance* 162–169, 172–177, 184–185, 192–204 *passim*. Maier "Popular Uprisings in America" 3–35 also is pertinent, though not dealing particularly with McDougall or Wilkes.

58. Philip Livingston and Nicholas Bayard each furnished bail of £250 for McDougall April 28, 1770, Dillon *New York Triumverate* 113, citing papers in *The King* v. *McDougall* in the minutes of the N.Y. Supreme Court of Judicature, Hall of Records, New York City.

59. Scott was McDougall's lawyer in his defense against the charge of criminal libel, Dillon *New York Triumverate* 113, citing the papers described in note 58 above and *New-York Gazette* May 7, 1770.

60. Peter R. Livingston to Oliver Wendell concerning his support of McDougall's cause, Feb. 19, 1770, Bonomi *Factious People* 274.

61. Philip and Peter Van Brugh Livingston are not included in the long list of names of those in New York City favoring dilution of the non-importation agreement published in the *Boston Gazette* of July 23, 1770; and I have found no other evidence that they favored the dilution. Alexander Colden to Anthony Todd, July 11, states that Sears and McDougall led the opposition to the dilution, but does not mention the Livingstons, *N.Y. Col. Doc.* VIII 219–220.

62. Application Dec. 10, 1773, by Philip Livingston, Sears, McDougall, and others to William Smith to use his influence with Governor Tryon not to assist in landing the East India Company's tea, Smith *Memoirs* I 157.

63. All four of the New York City members are included in the list of those in New York City favoring the dilution of the merchants' non-importation agreement, published in the *Boston Gazette* of July 23, 1770, and Colden to Hillsborough Oct. 5 confirms this, *N.Y. Col. Doc.* VIII 248. Launitz-Schürer "De Lanceys" 192 cites McDougall's diary for July 9 as stating that De Lancey and Walton were among the leaders in the movement for dilution.

64. I have found no evidence of any of the New York City members of the Assembly having taken part in opposition to the landing in New York of the East India Company's tea. One or more of them may, of course, have done so secretly.

65. The New York City delegation to the First Continental Congress included not only Philip Livingston, but two of his nephews by marriage—James Duane, married to a daughter of Philip's brother, Robert Livingston, Jr., and John Jay, married to a daughter of Philip's brother, William.

FOURTH APPENDIX (CHAPTER 20)

1. Thomas Hutchinson to Lord Dartmouth Oct. 9, 1773, concerning Samuel Adams' "defalcations." There is a similar, better-known later statement by Hutchinson in his *Hist. of Mass.* III 212, written during the war.

2. The statements of Peter Oliver in his *Origin* 41, written in 1781 and by William Gordon in his *History* I 229, published in England in 1788.

3. The assessors of taxes in Boston were authorized to abate the taxes of poor persons, bankrupts, and others found to be unable to pay the taxes assessed against them, and, if the assessors failed to make all permissible abatements, the Collectors could, on proper showing, secure additional abatements. As to these procedures, records of the town of Boston listed under "Taxes, abatement of" in the index to *Boston Records* (for 1758–1769) 342.

4. Statement by Boston town committee May 10, 1763, quoted in the text, *same* 91–92. The names of committee members, appointed March 14, by the moderator, James Otis, *same* 79, 85. (The figure "4178" on *same* 92 is a misprint for 4,718. I have made the correction in the text.)

5. The statement in the text as to the Boston Collectors collecting for the town, province, and county, each with its own treasurer, *same* 81.

6. Boston town committee chosen March 11, 1765, to examine the state of the town treasury and its report May 14, *same* 134, 143–144.

7. Boston town committee's report of March 16, 1767, on the state of the treasury and recommendation that the bonds of delinquent Collectors "be put in suit," *same* 200–203. I have found no evidence that the amounts due from the Collectors to Suffolk County as its share of the taxes collected in Boston were not paid in full.

8. Suit on Adams' bond as Collector for taxes for 1764–1765 and judgment against him by the Mass. Superior Court March 8, 1768, Goodell "Samuel Adams" 219. A copy of the bond dated Nov. 28, 1764, is in *same* 215n.

9. Adams' petition to the town of Boston March 14, 1768, for deferment of proceedings by the town treasurer on Adams' bond, Cushing *S. Adams* I 199–200, and the town's favorable action on the petition, *Boston Records* (for 1758–1769) 241.

10. Vote of Boston town meeting March 22, 1768, appointing a committee "to wait upon the Province Treasurer and Mr. Sheriff Greenleaf to desire that the Warrant of Distress or Execution issued by the Province Treasurer against the said Mr. Samuel Adams a defective Collector for this town 1764 be stayed for Six Months," *same* 243.

11. Reply quoted in the text of Harrison Gray, treasurer of Mass., March 23, 1768, to Boston town committee's request for deferment of proceedings against Adams, Goodell "Samuel Adams" 231.

12. Adams' undated petition, quoted in the text, presented to a Boston town meeting March 13, 1769, *New Eng. Hist. and Gen. Reg.* 45 (1891) 27–28.

13. Undated "List of subscribers towards Mr. Adams' debt," *New Eng. Hist. & Gen. Reg.* XIV 262.

14. Acceptance of Adams' offer of settlement at a Boston town meeting, March 13, 1769, *Boston Records* (for 1758–1769) 272. Robert Pierpont as surety on Adams' bond for 1764, Goodell "Samuel Adams" 215n. An act to enable Pierpont to enforce payment of tax debts owed to Adams was passed by the Mass. Legislature July 15, 1769, Chap. 3 of Acts of 1769–1770, *Mass. Acts* V 27 and editorial note concerning this, *same* 55–56.

15. Report of committee to Boston town meeting March 9, 1772, concerning the deficiencies referred to in the text, *Boston Records* (for 1770–1777) 69. The committee had been elected the preceding May, *same* 58. The committee's report dealt exclusively with Adams' accounts with "the town." I have found no evidence concerning the amounts, if any, still owed by him to the county and province as their shares of the taxes for the collection of which he was responsible.

16. Vote of March 16, 1774, quoted in the text, *Boston Records* (for 1770–1777) 161–162.

17. Under the terms of their employment, Boston Collectors of taxes were entitled to fees only if they turned over to the town, county, and province treasurers within specified times the amounts they were responsible for collecting— e.g., Boston town minutes for March 12, 1759, *same* (for 1758–1769) 21.

18. *Black's Law Dictionary* 653 discusses various legal definitions of "embezzlement."

19. Adams' election as one of Boston's four representatives in the Mass. House in 1765 and his reelection every subsequent year through 1774, *Boston Records* (for 1758–1769) 158, 177, 211, 245, 278; (for 1770–1777) 21, 53, 78, 129, 166, evidences his popularity with the voters at Boston town meetings. Adams was reelected nearly unanimously in every year after 1765, except in 1772, when he received 505 votes out of a total of 723, *same* (for 1770–1777) 78.

20. John Andrews to William Barrell Aug. 11, 1774, concerning the financial assistance to Samuel Adams quoted in the text, "Andrews Letters" 340.

21. John Adams' diary for Dec. 30, 1772, concerning Samuel Adams, quoted in the text, *Adams Papers* II 74. A letter of July 15, 1766, from Abigail Adams to her sister, Mary Smith Cranch, *Adams Family Corresp.* I 54, gives an impression of Adams different from that which one gets from the grim visage in Copley's famous portrait of him. "Mr. Saml Adams and wife," wrote Abigail, "are a charming pair. In them is to be seen the tenderest affection towards each other, without any ful-

some fondness, and the greatest Complasance, delicacy and good breeding that you can immagine...."

APPENDIX (CHAPTER 22)

1. James Duane seconded Galloway's motion, and John Jay and Edward Rutledge expressed their approval, John Adams' notes of debates [Sept. 28, 1774,] Burnett *Letters* I 53–54. A notation by Duane on a copy of the plan in his papers at the *N.Y. Hist. Soc.* states that it was "Seconded & supported by the New York Delegates," Boyd *Anglo-American Union* 112, meaning presumably all of those present. Gov. Cadwallader Colden to Lord Dartmouth Dec. 7 mentions Duane having seconded the motion, *Colden* 1877 374.

2. Galloway's motion Sept. 28, 1774, for the approval of his Plan of Union, *Journals Cont. Cong.* I 43, 48–49n. I use the word *approve,* rather than *adopt,* because there are two versions of the motion. One of these envisages adoption, but the other, the so-called Franklin version, states that the motion was not for the Congress to adopt the plan, but only to approve it and submit it to the several colonial Assemblies to be by them severally adopted and presented to the King and Parliament, *same* 48–49n.

3. Galloway's Plan of Union, undated, *same* 49–51.

4. Galloway's authorship of the *Candid Examination,* which was published without the author's name, is known from "Galloway's Letters 1774–1775" 481–482 and Gov. Cadwallader Colden of N.Y. to Lord Dartmouth March 1, 1775, *Colden* 1877 390–391, and the date of publication from Colden's speaking of the pamphlet as "lately publish'd."

5. Galloway's statements in his *Candid Examination* 394–395, as to the objections to his plan, quoted in the text. John Adams' notes of debates, probably of Sept. 28, 1774, record that Richard Henry Lee made the first objection and Patrick Henry the second, Burnett *Letters* I 53. I have found no evidence as to who made the third. The citation to the *Candid Examination* is to the reprint in Jensen *Tracts.*

6. The passage in the plan concerning choosing members of the General Council "in the following proportions," *Journals Cont. Cong.* I 50.

7. *Candid Examination* (in Jensen *Tracts* 390–391) intimating that Galloway proposed deferment of other action pending action on his plan by the King or Parliament or both.

8. Ezra Stiles' diary for Nov. 8, 1774, records that Samuel Ward had told him that day that Galloway's plan "was almost universally rejected," Stiles *Diary* I 475. Ward's diary for Oct. 22 recorded "Met, dismissed the plan for a union, etc., (Mr. Hopkins [Ward's fellow delegate from R.I.] for the plan), I against it," Burnett *Letters* I 80. I have found no contemporary evidence corroborating a statement by Galloway in his *Historical and Political Reflections* . . . (London, 1780), reprinted in *Journals Cont. Cong.* I 48n., that "all the men of property and most of the ablest speakers" supported the plan.

9. Statement in Galloway's *Candid Examination* 390–391, as to expunging, quoted in the text.

10. Committee chosen by the Congress Oct. 21, 1774, "to revise the minutes of the Congress," *Journals Cont. Cong.* I 101. Galloway was named to this committee, but I have found no evidence that he acted on it.

FIRST APPENDIX (CHAPTER 23)

1. The Council as an advisory, legislative (and also judicial) body, Labaree *Royal Government* 134–135; Labaree *Instructions* I 14–80. Also the text of a typical commission (in 1758) to the Governor of a royal colony, New Jersey, in Greene *Provincial Governor* 226–233.

2. The Governor's authority for appointment of councilors and suspension for "just cause" quoted in the text, *same* 227–228. Richard Henry Lee wrote Arthur Lee Dec. 20, 1766, that members of the Council of Virginia are "appointed by the Crown and their places [are] held by the precarious tenure of pleasure only," Ballagh *Lee* I 19, but he gives no evidence for his view that the Crown retained authority to remove members of the Council of Virginia with or without "just cause."

3. Instructions as to appointing to the Council persons of "good life," "good estates," etc., Labaree *Royal Instructions* I 55–56. (The instructions to the Governors of N.H., Nova Scotia, and S.C., for reason or reasons unknown to me, omitted the words "of good estates," *same* 56.)

4. There is no mention of tenure in what is probably a typical mandamus for the appointment of a councilor, the mandamus from the King to the Governor of N.Y. May 22, 1767, stating: "We being well satisfied of the Loyalty Integrity & Ability of our Trusty and well beloved William Smith Junr, Esqr have thought fit hereby to signify to you our Will and Pleasure that forth with upon Receipt hereof you swear and admit him . . . to be of our Council for our Colony of New York . . . ," Smith *Memoirs* I 40.

5. Richard Henry Lee to Arthur Lee Dec. 20, 1766, complained of the councilors holding their office "by the precarious tenure of pleasure only," Ballagh *Lee* I 19. See also the case of Councillor William Wragg of South Carolina, Sirmans "S.C. Royal Council" 388–389.

6. Conflicts between the Council and the Assembly in the Carolinas and Georgia are described in Main *Upper House* 8–11, 14–21, 23–28, 249–254; and in South Carolina in McCrady *South Carolina* 172–176, 281–292, 717–723; Smith *S.C.* 295–324 *passim*, 387–388; Sirmans *South Carolina passim;* and Greene "Bridge to Revolution" 19–52.

7. Resolution of S.C. Assembly in December, 1769, for payment to be made by the provincial treasurer, quoted in the text, Smith *S.C.* 369. The Speaker was Peter Manigault, *same* 415. The other six members named in the resolution included Christopher Gadsden and John Rutledge, who were later delegates from S.C. to the First Continental Congress. The £10,500 in S.C. currency was the equivalent of £1,500 sterling.

8. The money was to be paid by the assemblyman designated to receive it to the Supporters of the Bill of Rights Society, Committee of the Assembly to correspondents in London, Dec. 9, 1769, "Garth" XXX (1930) 132–133. John Wilkes' struggle to be seated in the House of Commons and the Society's part in this, Rudé *Wilkes & Liberty* 41–62.

9. Payment of the money by the treasurer as directed by the Assembly's resolution and its passage in April, 1770, of a bill to repay the treasurer the money paid by him, Smith *S.C.* 371; Greene "Bridge to Revolution" 21–22.

10. Passage by the Assembly at subsequent sessions from August, 1770, to 1773 of bills containing this item, *same* 26–49. The controversy over the Wilkes item had been intensified by issuance of an instruction of April 14, 1770, from the Crown to Gov. Bull not to assent to any bill appropriating money "for defraying any expense incurred for services or purposes not immediately arising within or incident to our said province unless upon special order from us," Labaree *Instructions* I 209.

11. Appointment of "placemen"—men holding places at the pleasure of the Crown—to the Council of South Carolina, Main *Upper House* 19–21, 251–252; Sirmans "S.C. Royal Council" 389–393; Weir "S.C. Politics" 490–493.

12. Appointment of numerous placemen to the Council in Georgia and North Carolina, Main *Upper House* 6, 22–23, 247, 252.

13. Sec. 2 of the Massachusetts Regulating Act of 1774, 14 Geo. III 45, provided that members of the council were to hold office only "for and during the pleasure of his Majesty. . . ."

14. Statements expressing fear over growing Crown control over the Council, had been made in 1769, 1770, and 1773 by Richard Henry Lee of Va., William Henry Drayton of S.C., and George Mason of Va., Greene *Quest for Power* 441. The Crown's intention to ensure Crown control of the provincial Councils was soon further indicated by a Crown instruction to the Governor of Quebec, Jan. 3, 1775, to appoint councilors in Quebec to serve "during Our Will and Pleasure . . . and not otherwise," *S &D Doc.* II 595.

APPENDIX (CHAPTER 26)

1. Resolutions of Boston town meetings of May 13 and May 30, 1774, described in the text, *Boston Records* (for 1770–1777) 173, 176.

2. Circular letter of June 8, 1774, of the Boston Comm. of Corresp. enclosing forms of covenant, Matthews "Solemn League" 104–107. Two forms apparently were circulated, but each called for non-importation of all kinds of British goods after Aug. 31, 1774, *same* 107–109. This gives both forms, one of which also is in 4 *Force* I 397–398.

3. The term "Solemn League and Covenant" had a special significance because this was the title of the key document of 1643 in the revolution that overthrew Charles I. A copy of the covenant of Sept. 25, 1643, signed by many members of the English House of Commons, is in Adams *Select. Doc.* 383–386.

4. A protest signed by 129 Boston merchants and others, dated June 27, 1774, is in 4 *Force* I 490–491 and another signed by John Andrews and eight others in the *Mass. Gazette & Post-Boy* of July 4. For additional evidence, Schlesinger *Col. Merchants* 321; Samuel Adams to Comm. of Corresp. of Colrain July 18, Cushing *S. Adams* III 145; Rowe's diary for June 28, *Rowe* 277.

5. Forms of covenant somewhat similar to the Boston Committee's were approved by conventions of Berkshire, Worcester, Suffolk, Bristol, and Plymouth

Counties, July 6 to Sept. 28, 1774, *Mass. Congress Journals* 604, 625, 627, 630, 653.

6. Schlesinger *Col. Merchants* 323, 323n. names Worcester and thirteen other towns in Mass. that adopted non-consumption agreements; Gov. Thomas Gage was sufficiently worried over the movement to issue a proclamation June 29 ordering the prosecution of anyone signing or abetting signing of the covenant, 1 *M.H.S. Proc.* XII (1871–1873) 48; and on July 22, Andrews wrote Barrell of the "amazing progress the non-consumption agreement has made through this country [Mass.] . . . ," "Andrews Letters" 332.

7. Action of Boston town meeting of June 27 and 28, 1774, described in the text, *Boston Records* (for 1770–1777) 178.

8. Salem Comm. of Corresp. to Falmouth Comm. July 12, 1774, rejecting the proposed covenant, quoted in the text, Matthews "Solemn League" 120–121.

9. Marblehead and at least six other towns took action similar to Salem's, Schlesinger *Col. Merchants* 323–324.

FIRST APPENDIX (CHAPTER 27)

1. Benjamin Franklin to Joseph Galloway concerning John Jay and Joseph Galloway Feb. 25, 1775, quoted in the text, Smyth *Franklin* VI 311.

2. William Lee to Francis Lightfoot Lee Feb. 25, 1775, concerning Jay, quoted in the text, Jensen *Founding* 571n. I agree with Jensen's supposition that F. L. Lee was the addressee. There is a sketch of William Lee, former sheriff of London and in May, 1775, elected an Alderman of the City, in *D.A.B.*

3. John Vardill's statement concerning Jay, James Duane, and others, quoted in the text, Einstein *Divided Loyalties* 412. *D.A.B.* has a sketch of Vardill (1749–1811), a Church of England clergymen, who left New York late in 1773 or early in 1774 and thereafter lived in England.

4. Vardill to Duane Sept. 15, 1774, inviting a statement of his "sentiments," quoted in the text, Alexander *Duane* 105n.

5. Jay to Vardill Sept. 24, 1774, while Jay was at the First Continental Congress, quoted in the text, Jay Papers, Columbia U. Lib. Jay had been corresponding with Vardill concerning the possibility of securing a Crown appointment for Jay as a judge in N.Y., Monaghan *Jay* 53–54. When Vardill left N.Y., Jay had been a member of the "Protestant" (Anglican) party, but he had later joined the "Blue Skin" (Presbyterian) party, as William Laight disgustedly wrote Vardill March 27, 1775, *same* 65–66. Matthews *Dictionary* I 146, II 1321 gives the interpolated meanings.

6. To his letter to Vardill of Sept. 24, 1775, quoted in the text, Jay added a postscript, "Pray inform me whether you ever see or hear of my Brother James; . . . we have received no Letters from him for some time past; be so kind as to forward the enclosed to him," Jay Papers, Columbia U. Lib.

7. Thomas Hutchinson's diary entry of Nov. 19, 1774, concerning his talk with John Pownall, states that, in speaking of "the proceedings of the Congress," Pownall said "there was a private correspondence, and every step had been communicated," Hutchinson *Diary* I 296.

SECOND APPENDIX (CHAPTER 27)

1. The activities of London merchants for a peaceful solution, including their petition to the House of Commons, Dec., 1774–March, 1775, Sosin *Agents* 196–199, 218–221. David Barclay (1729–1809), grandson of Robert Barclay, the famous apologist for the Quakers, and son of David Barclay (1682–1769) of D. Barclay and Company, merchants and bankers, had long been active in business with Pa., Labaree *Franklin* IX 190n., XI 543n.

2. Benjamin Franklin's appointment in 1770, as London Agent for the Mass. House of Representatives, Thomas Cushing to Franklin Oct. 31, 1770, *Mass. Papers* 168; his appointment as London Agent for the Pa. Assembly in 1764, for Ga. in 1768, and for N.J. in 1768, Sosin *Agents,* 111–112.

3. Barclay's talk with Franklin, Dec. 1, 1774, described in the text, Franklin to William Franklin March 22, 1775, hereafter cited as *Letter to W.F.,* Smyth *Franklin* VI 325–326.

4. Dr. John Fothergill and Barclay to Franklin Dec. 3, 1774, proposing a meeting of the three, *same* 326. As to Fothergill, *D.N.B.* and Lettsom *Fothergill passim.*

5. Franklin's talk with Barclay and Fothergill Dec. 4, 1774, *Letter to W.F.* 327–328.

6. Franklin's "Hints" described in the text, presented by him to Barclay and Fothergill Dec. 6, 1774, *same* 328–340.

7. Conference of Franklin with Barclay and Fothergill Dec. 6, 1774, described in the text, *same* 341. Fox *Fothergill* 327 states that Fothergill visited Lord Dartmouth "daily at this time in his medical capacity" and, though Fox gives no source for his statement, I suppose it is substantially true. As to Lord Hyde (Thomas Villiers), a member of the House of Lords and of the Privy Council and Chancellor of the Duchy of Cornwall, *D.N.B.* and Namier and Brooke *Commons* III 587–588.

8. Franklin sends Barclay a copy of his "Hints," revised to incorporate suggestions of Barclay and Fothergill, Dec. 8, 1775, *Letter to W.F.* 341–342.

9. Barclay tells Franklin Dec. 22, 1774, that Hyde thinks his "Hints" are "too hard," *same* 344.

10. Fothergill tells Franklin, probably in Jan., 1775, that Dartmouth thought some articles of Franklin's "Hints" "appear'd reasonable, but others were unreasonable or impracticable," *same* 359. Both Hyde and Fothergill had reviewed the "Hints" with Dartmouth, Donoughue *Brit. Politics* 215; *Dartmouth* (1895) 236; *Letter to W.F.* 359.

11. Barclay and Fothergill on Feb. 4, 1775, present Franklin with a paper of "Observations," which Franklin tells them is unacceptable, *same* 371–374; and Fothergill to Dartmouth Feb. 6, *Fothergill* 442–443. Sosin *Agents* 214n. calls attention to discrepancies between Franklin's and Dartmouth's versions of the ministerial reaction to Franklin's "Hints," indicating that the Ministry and Franklin were even further apart than he understood.

12. Barclay and Fothergill ask Franklin for another conference, and on Feb. 16, 1775, present him with a counterplan; the counterplan and Franklin's commitment as to payment for the destroyed tea, *Letter to W.F.* 375–378.

13. Fruitless final meeting of Barclay, Fothergill, and Franklin Feb. 17, 1775, *same* 383–384. Franklin had drafted some further papers, *same* 379–383, but did not present them, *same* 384.

14. Fothergill's letter to Franklin condemning the Ministry, quoted in the text, delivered to him just before he sailed for America in the latter part of March, 1775, *same* 399.

15. Franklin to Joseph Galloway Feb. 25, 1775, quoted in the text, opposing a closer union with Great Britain, Smyth *Franklin* VI 312. The passage quoted by Franklin is from Book VIII of the *Aeneid*, which Dryden, in his translation of the *Aeneid*, renders: "Till choak'd with stench, in loath'd embraces ty'd, The ling'ring wretches pin'd away and dy'd."

16. Franklin and the Honorable Mrs. Caroline Howe meet through a common acquaintance Dec. 2, 1774, and Franklin's parties of chess with her, *same* 324, 326–327. There is a note on Mrs. Howe, sister of the Howe brothers and widow of John Howe, in Lewis *Walpole* XVII 209n.

17. Sketch of Col. George Augustus Howe, *D.A.B.;* sketches of Admiral Richard Lord Howe and Gen. William Howe, *D.N.B.*

18. Mrs. Howe brings Lord Howe and Franklin together at her home Christmas night, and Howe's statement to Franklin as to disposition of "some of the Ministry" for "any reasonable Accommodation," *Letter to W.F.* 345–348.

19. Franklin's conference with Howe Dec. 28, 1774, and statements of Howe quoted in the text, *same* 352–354, 357.

20. Franklin's revised plan given by him to Mrs. Howe "a Day or two" after Dec. 28, 1774, for delivery to Lord Howe, *same* 354–356. The Albany Congress of 1754 referred to by Franklin is described in Labaree *Franklin* V 344–418.

21. Howe's message of Jan. 2, 1775, to Franklin as to the "difficulty" concerning his plan, quoted in the text, *Letter to W.F.* 357.

22. Howe's conference with Franklin Feb. 17, 1775, at which he suggested that Franklin confer with Hyde, *same* 383, 384–386.

23. Statements by Franklin and Hyde, quoted in the text, at their conference March 1, 1775, terminating the negotiations, *same* 391–394.

APPENDIX (CHAPTER 28)

1. The New York Assembly, summoned to meet by Acting Governor Cadwallader Colden, met on Jan. 13, 1775, 4 *Force* I 1281–1282. The last general election for the Assembly was in 1769; it had last convened in Jan.–March, 1774. The names of the members of the Assembly, 1769–1775, their constituencies, and dates of sitting, Bonomi *Factious People* App. C, unpaged.

2. Defeat of motion of Abraham Ten Broeck, Jan. 26, 1775, concerning the Continental Congress, quoted in the text, 4 *Force* I 1286–1287. The vote was 11 to 10.

3. Defeat of motions of Feb. 17 and 23, 1775, concerning the Continental Congress, described in the text, by votes of 15 to 9 and 15 to 10, respectively, *same* 1289, 1290.

4. Vote on John Thomas' motion, Feb. 23, 1775, concerning election of delegates to the proposed Second Continental Congress, *same* 1290. Tryon, Charlotte,

and Gloucester Counties and the district of Schenectady apparently had no members in attendance at this session, and Cortlandt Manor apparently not before March 8, 1775, *same* 1287–1324. Livingston Manor, long unrepresented, had regained representation by the admission of Peter R. Livingston in Feb., 1774, Bonomi *Factious People* App. C, unpaged. John Cruger of N.Y. City and County, presiding as Speaker, did not vote.

5. An exchange of letters in July, 1774, between a committee of N.Y. citizens and four of the five delegates to the Congress from the City indicates that the delegates expected, and were expected, to support an agreement for non-importation only, 4 *Force* I 319.

6. The Suffolk Resolves and the proceedings of the First Continental Congress concerning them (Sept., 1774) are in *Journals Cont. Cong.* I 31–40.

7. There is a copy of Sauthier's map of N.Y. (1779) showing the county and manor boundaries of the colony in 1775 in the large (1750) edition of *N.Y. Doc. Hist.* I facing p. 526 and a tracing in Brown *King's Friends* 76. The Highlands of the Hudson ran from east to west through Westchester and Orange Counties. The other counties mentioned in the text are wholly south of the Highlands.

8. The pamphlets referred to in the text (reprinted in Vance *Letters of a Westchester Farmer*) are *Free Thoughts on the Proceedings of the Continental Congress* . . . (1774); *The Congress Canvassed* . . . (1774); *A View of the Controversy* . . . (1774); and *An Alarm to the Legislature* . . . *of New York* . . . (1775).

9. I follow the introduction to Vance *Letters of a Westchester Farmer passim* and Adams *Bibliography* 106, 107, 116, 131, for the reasons given there, in attributing the pamphlets to Samuel Seabury, rector of West Chester parish (N.Y.), despite his statement, in a petition in 1775 for release from confinement, that he had not "written pamphlets and newspapers against the liberties of America," Beardsley *Seabury* 38. As to the life and writings of Seabury, first bishop of the Protestant Episcopal Church in Conn., Vance, Beardsley, and Seabury *Seabury*.

10. Appointment Jan. 31, 1775, of a committee of the N.Y. Assembly to prepare a statement of grievances, 4 *Force* I 1286–1287. The committee's statement presented March 3, 1775, *same* 1298.

11. The solution quoted in the text, Philip Schuyler's proposed amendment, and the vote on this, *same* 1301.

12. The steps taken by the New York City Committee of Fifty-One in March, 1775, to convene a N.Y. provincial convention, *same* II 4, 138–139.

13. Convening of the N.Y. provincial convention April 20–22, 1775, and election by it of delegates to the Second Continental Congress on April 21, *same* II 351–355. The N.Y. delegation comprised all the delegates to the First Congress except Isaac Low, with the addition of Philip Schuyler, George Clinton, Lewis Morris, Francis Lewis, and Robert R. Livingston, Jr.

APPENDIX (CHAPTER 29)

1. [Samuel Johnson] *Taxation no Tyranny* (London, 1775), 4 *Force* I 1449, "how is it that we hear the loudest yelps for liberty among the drivers of negroes?"

2. Examples of the outcry of leading colonial Whigs against alleged British attempts to enslave the colonies are in Jefferson *A Summary View of the Rights of*

British America (Williamsburg, 1774), draft in Boyd *Jefferson* I 134; Quincy *Observations On . . . The Boston Port-Bill* (Boston, 1774), in Quincy *Memoirs* 363; and John Adams' letter of Jan. 30, 1775, in *Novanglus and Massachusettensis* 22–23.

3. John Camm's *Critical Remarks* (Williamsburg, 1765) 19. Camm's statement was in reply to Richard Bland's *The Colonel Dismounted* (Williamsburg, 1764) 21. The pamphlet controversy between Camm and Bland and Landon Carter is discussed in Knollenberg *Origin* 58–59, 305.

4. The movements before 1775 of individual Quakers and Quaker meetings in England and the colonies against Negro slavery and the slave trade are described in Weeks *Southern Quakers and Slavery*, 198–208 and sources cited therein; Drake *Quakers and Slavery in America passim;* and Klingberg *Anti-Slavery Movement in England passim.*

5. Anthony Benezet's comment on colonial slaveholding quoted in the text, Benezet *Caution and Warning* (Philadelphia, 1767) 3. Benezet wrote Elias Boudinot April 17, 1775, "how strange it is to see the southern Colonies take such a lead in what they call the cause of liberty, while the most horrible oppressions, even under the Sanction of their Laws, is continually practiced among them . . . ," Bruns "Benezet" 104. There is a sketch of Benezet in *D.A.B.* and a good biography, Brooke *Benezet.*

6. The efforts of the Mass. Legislature to "free themselves from *Slavery,*" referred to in the passage quoted in the text probably was the protest in resolutions adopted by the Mass. House July 10, 1772, against the payment by the Crown of the Governor's salary from duties imposed by Parliament on the colonies, Bradford *Mass. Papers* 325–329.

7. Circular letter of April 20, 1773, from Peter Bestes, Sambo Freeman, Felix Holbrook, and Chester Joie to members of the Mass. House of Representatives in John Allen's *Oration upon the Beauties of Liberty . . . Delivered at the Second Baptist Church in Boston . . . Dec. 3d 1772* 4th ed. (Boston, 1773) appendix 78–80. I have found no record of the slaves' letter in the proceedings of the House or any evidence as to who, if anyone, helped them prepare it.

8. *Brief Considerations on Slavery* (Burlington [N.J.], 1773) 6, quoted in the text. I have not identified the author but I think he probably was a New Jersey Quaker. Additional passages in writings at this period pointing out the irony of the outcry of colonial Whigs against British enslavement of the colonies and their continuing ownership of black slaves, Bailyn *Pamphlets* I 145–149.

9. For facts concerning Allen, a wandering Baptist preacher who came to America from England about 1770, *same* 17n. Love *Fast Days* 544 quotes the *New-London Gazette* of Dec. 18, 1772, as reporting "Last Thanksgiving P.M., Mr. Allen, a British Bostonian, preached a sermon [the *Oration*] at the Rev. Mr. Davis's [Baptist] Meeting House. . . ." (Weiss *New Eng. Col. Clergy* 70, 188 gives information concerning the regular ministers at this period, but none concerning Allen.)

10. Allen *The Watchman's Alarm* (Salem [Mass.], 1774) quoted in Bailyn *Pamphlets* I 146. I follow Adams *Bibliography* 103, 98 in ascribing this pamphlet and the earlier *Oration* to John Allen. (The ascription in Heimert *Religion* 401 of the *Oration* to "Joseph" Allen is almost certainly erroneous.)

11. Granville Sharp *Declaration* (New York, 1774) quoted in Bailyn *Pamphlets* I 146. The numerous reprints of this popular pamphlet, published first in Lon-

don, are described in Adams *Bibliography* 108–110. There is a sketch of Sharp in *D.N.B.*

12. Abigail Adams to John Adams Sept. 22, 1774, concerning slavery quoted in the text, *Adams Family Corresp.* I 162.

13. Adams to Abigail Adams Oct. 7, 1774, acknowledging and replying in part to her "kind favours," but not referring to her remarks on slavery, *same* I 164–166.

14. Even the ban on the importation of slaves in the Continental Association adopted by the First Continental Congress Oct. 20, 1774, *Journals Cont. Congress* I 77, 79–80, like all the other prohibitions in the Association, was to remain in force only so long as colonial grievances were unredressed.

15. Patrick Henry to Robert Pleasants Jan. 18, 1773, quoted in the text, Meade *Henry* 299–300. Thomas Jefferson, too, was very outspoken in condemnation of slavery, but he manumitted only a few of his slaves, Freehling "Slavery" 81–93 at 85 and Jordan *White over Black, passim.* As to the related question of discouragment of the slave trade in Va., Wax "Negro Import Duties" 29–44.

16. The development of George Washington's attitude toward Negro slavery is well described in Flexner *Washington* IV 112–125, 260–261, 432–448. Numerous details concerning the slaves of Washington and his stepson, John Parke Custis, will be found in Knollenberg *Washington* 75, 82–84, 86, 103, 127–132, 178, 180.

17. Washington's will, dated July 9, 1799, is in Fitzpatrick *Washington* XXXVII 275–303. The provisions for manumission of and support for his slaves are in *same* 276–277.

18. Resolution of Providence, R.I., town meeting May 17, 1774, for gradual emancipation of slaves, quoted in the text, 4 *Force* I 334.

19. The four Providence representatives in the Rhode Island General Assembly in June, 1774, headed by Stephen Hopkins, are listed in *R.I. Col. Rec.* VII 240.

20. *Hist. Statistics* 756 gives R.I. a Negro population in 1770 of 3,761, most of whom probably were slaves.

21. The act quoted in the text prohibiting importation of slaves into R.I. was passed at the June, 1774, session of the R.I. General Assembly, *R.I. Col. Rec.* VII 251–253. The act provided that slaves illegally imported were to have their freedom.

APPENDIX (CHAPTER 32)

1. Mass. Committee of Safety's undated circular letter to the towns of Mass. concerning the events of April 19, 1775, and calling for troops, *Mass. Journals* 518. (The editor of the *Journals* dates the letter April 20, but the reference to the murders committed "Wednesday, the 19th instant," rather than "yesterday," suggests that the letter was written later.) The Committee of Safety also sent (April 20) an appeal for help to N.H. and Conn., *same* 518–519n.

2. Depositions dated April 23 and 25, 1775, concerning the killing of members of the Lexington militia and other events of April 19th, and the accompanying account sent by the Mass. Congress to London Agent for publication, *Journals Cont. Cong.* II 26–44. The swift voyage to England of the schooner *Quero,* John Derby of Salem, captain, and delivery of the papers to Arthur Lee (Benjamin Franklin's successor as London Agent for the Mass. House of Representatives)

two weeks before Gen. Gage's version reached the British Ministry, Rantoul "Cruise of the Quero" 4–19.

3. The Mass. Congress' statement of April 26, 1775, including the passage concerning alleged British atrocities quoted in the text, *Journals Cont. Cong.* II 42–43. This statement and accompanying depositions were presented by John Hancock, leader of the Mass. delegation to the Second Continental Congress, to the Congress on May 11, *same* 24. On May 22, the Mass. Congress ordered the publication of a somewhat similar statement for home consumption, "A Narrative Of The Excursion And Ravages Of The King's Troops," with accompanying depositions, *Mass. Journals* 660–678.

4. Murdock *Nineteenth of April* (1923); Tourtellot *William Diamond's Drum* 112–113, 125–127 (1959); and Barton "Lexington" 385–390 (1959) suggest that Parker stationed his men in the path of the British advance by the direction or advice of Samuel Adams, who wished to provoke bloodshed as a means of uniting the colonies against the British. Parker's deposition gives no hint of this, and, as brought out in Knollenberg "Samuel Adams" 10–12 (1961), no substantial evidence to support this sensational hypothesis has been adduced.

5. Captain John Parker's deposition April 25, 1775, quoted in the text, *Journals Cont. Cong.* II 31. It will be observed that Parker describes himself as "Commander of the Militia in Lexington," not as commander of a company of "minute men." All the contemporary statements concerning the incident at Lexington refer to this company simply as the "Lexington company," "Captain Parker's company," or the "Company of Militia at Lexington"; the description by later writers of the company as "minute men" apparently is unwarranted.

6. The list of members of the Lexington company present on April 19, in Coburn *Battle*, unnumbered page following page 60, gives William Diamond as the company drummer. His name is not among those signing any of the depositions concerning the Lexington affair, presumably because he was under "lawful age."

7. Deposition of Nathaniel Mulliken and thirty-three other members "of lawful age" of the Lexington company of militia April 25, 1775, *Journals Cont. Cong.* II 32–33.

8. Maj. John Pitcairn to Gage April 26, 1775, concerning the firing at Lexington, French *Gage's Informers* 53.

9. Lieut. William Sutherland's statement of April 26, 1775, concerning the firing at Lexington, *Sutherland* 13–24 at 17. (Sutherland's statement which I follow is from the papers of Sir Henry Clinton at the Clements Library in Ann Arbor, Mich. Another version, dated April 29, differing somewhat but not substantially as to this point, in the Gage Papers in the same library, is printed in French *Gage's Informers* 42–46, 85–92, 111–112.)

10. Lieut. John Barker's diary entry for April 19, 1775, concerning the firing at Lexington, *Barker* 32. Col. Lord Percy, who was not an eyewitness, wrote his father, the Duke of Northumberland, April 20, that "there can now surely be no doubt of their being in open Rebellion, for *they* fired first upon the King's Troops, as they were marching quietly along . . . ," *Percy* 54–55.

11. George Leonard is frequently referred to in the minutes of Boston town meetings 1770 to March, 1775, as a miller in Boston and thereafter as "lately" a

miller there, *Boston Town Records* (for 1770–1777) 11, 43, 68, 114, 156, 171, 232, 273. He was a signer of fulsome addresses to Thomas Hutchinson May 30, 1774, and Gage Oct. 6, 1775; he went to Halifax, Nova Scotia, on the British evacuation of Boston in March, 1776, and was banished from Mass. in Sept., 1778, Stark *Loyalists of Mass.* 125, 132, 135, 137. His subsequent career, Jones *Loyalists of Mass.* 191–194, 229, 311.

12. Statement of George Leonard of Boston May 4, 1775, as to the firing at Lexington, French *Gage's Informers* 57–58.

13. Deposition of Nathan Barrett and others of Concord, April 23, 1775, that the British fired first there, *Journals Cont. Cong.* II 37.

14. Supporting depositions Apr. 23, 1775, of American eyewitnesses; of Lieut. Edward Gould, a British officer, dated April 25; and of James Marr, a British soldier, dated April 23, as to British firing first at Concord, *same* 36–37, 38–39, 40–41.

15. Conflicting statements dated April 26, 1775, as to the British firing first at Concord, Capt. Walter S. Laurie, French *Gage's Informers* 97 and Lieut. Sutherland, *Sutherland* 21.

16. British accounts of American atrocities: Gage to Lord Dartmouth April 22, 1775, *Gage* I 396, enclosing Col. Francis Smith's account, *M.H.S. Proc.* XIV (1876) 350n.; Percy to Gage Apr. 20, *same* 349n.; Anne Hulton to Mrs. Adam Lightbody April [no day], *Hulton Letters* 77.

17. Rev. William Gordon to an unidentified correspondent May 17, 1775, concerning the mangled British soldier at Concord, 4 *Force* II 630. As to Gordon, who later wrote a well-known history of the American Revolution, *D.A.B.* The Reverend William Emerson (grandfather of Ralph Waldo Emerson) was pastor of the First Congregational parish of Concord, Shipton *Harvard Graduates* XV 39–47.

18. "Narrative" published by the Second Mass. Congress in May, 1775, *Mass. Congress Journals* 660–662.

19. Letters in the English newspapers as to alleged British atrocities, quoted in the text, Williard *Letters* 85, 89, 92–93, and letter of April 23, 1775, from Wethersfield, Conn., as to British atrocities, quoted in the text, 4 *Force* II 362. The *New-York Journal* of May 5 carried a similar story of the slaughter of children.

20. *Plundering of houses:* Frederick Mackenzie diary for April 19, 1775, *Mackenzie* I 22; Barker diary for April 25, *Barker* 39; Lieut. Col. James Abercrombie to Cadwallader Colden May 2, 2 *M.H.S. Proc.* XI 301, all contemporary accounts by British officers.

21. *Burning of houses:* Intercepted letters of British officers, April 25, 28, and 30 1775, *Journals Mass. Congress* 682–684; deposition of sixteen inhabitants of Concord, *Journals Cont. Cong.* II 37–38.

22. *Firing on the British troops from houses along the road:* Barker 35; Mackenzie 21; Percy 50; Sutherland 23; Evelyn 54; all contemporary accounts by British officers who were on the expedition, and Boston letter of April 23, 1775, in *The Gazetteer and New Daily Advertiser* (London) June 16.

23. Killing in a house along the line of march of "two aged gentlemen . . . unarmed," who were "most barbarously and inhumanly murdered . . . , being stabbed through in many places, their heads mauled, skulls broke, and their brains dashed

out . . . ," deposition of Benjamin and Rachel Cooper, May 10, 1775, *Mass. Congress Journals* 678.

24. Deposition of Hannah Adams May 16, 1775, "I then was laid on my bed, . . . not having been from my chamber door . . . since being delivered in childbirth." A soldier, she continued, had "pointed a bayonet" at her; another said "we will not hurt the woman, if she will go out of the house, but we will surely burn it." She then fled, carrying her infant but leaving five children behind. The house was set afire, but "the fire was happily extinguished," *same* 677.

25. A statement in the deposition concerning the killing of the old men that more than 100 bullets were fired into the house in which they were killed, suggests that it was one of those from which the British soldiers had been fired upon, in which case the killing of the men is, of course, understandable.

BIBLIOGRAPHY

LIST OF PUBLICATIONS AND DOCUMENTS CITED

A.A.S. Proc.—*Proceedings of the American Antiquarian Society.*

A.H.A. Ann. Rep.—*Annual Report of the American Historical Association.*

A.H.R.—*The American Historical Review.*

Abbott *Governors of Ga.*—William W. Abbott *The Royal Governors of Georgia 1754–1775* (1959).

Abernethy *Western Lands*—Thomas P. Abernethy *Western Lands and the American Revolution* (1937).

Acts P.C.—William L. Grant and James Munro (eds.) *Acts of the Privy Council of England, Colonial Series* [1613–1783] 6 vols. (1908–1912).

Adair *Peter Oliver's American Revolution*—Douglass Adair and John A. Schutz (eds.) *Peter Oliver's Origin & Progress of the American Revolution: A Tory View* (1961).

Adams *Bibliography*—Thomas R. Adams *American Independence . . . A Bibliographical Study . . .* (1965).

Adams *Familiar Letters*—Charles Francis Adams (ed.) *Familiar Letters of John Adams and His Wife Abigail . . .* (1876).

Adams Family Corresp.—Lyman Butterfield et al. (eds.) *Adams Family Correspondence* I (1963).

Adams Legal Papers—*The Adams Papers* Ser. 3: Laurence Kinvin Wroth and Hiller B. Zobel (eds.) *Legal Papers of John Adams* 3 vols. (1965).

Adams *New Light*—Randolph G. Adams *New Light on the Boston Massacre,* reprint from *Am. Antiq. Soc. Proc.* new ser. XLVII 259–354.

Adams "Novanglus"—A series of letters by John Adams signed "Novanglus" published in the *Boston Gazette* Jan. 23 to April 17, 1775.

Adams *Novanglus and Massachusettensis*—John Adams *Novanglus and Massachusettensis . . . Political Essays . . . in 1774 and 1775* (1819).

Adams Papers—Lyman H. Butterfield et al. (eds.) *The Adams Papers* Ser. 1, I–IV (1961) entitled *Diary and Autobiography of John Adams.*

Adams Portraits—Andrew Oliver *Portraits of John and Abigail Adams* (1967).

Adams *Rev. New Eng.*—James Truslow Adams *Revolutionary New England 1691–1776* (1939).

Adams, Samuel—See Wells *Adams* and Miller *Sam Adams.*

Adams *Select Doc.*—George B. Adams and H. Morse Stephens (eds.) *Select Documents of English Constitutional History* (1910).

Adams–Warren Letters—See *Warren–Adams.*

Adams *Works*—Charles Francis Adams (ed.) *The Works of John Adams* 10 vols. (1850–1856).

Agricultural Hist.—*Agricultural History* (magazine).

Alden *Gage*—John R. Alden *General Gage in America . . .* (1948).

Alden "John Mein"—John E. Alden "John Mein, Scourge of Patriots" *Col. Soc. Publ.* XXXIV 571–599.

Alden "John Mein, Publisher"—John E. Alden "John Mein, Publisher: An Essay in Bibliographical Detection" *Bibliographical Soc. of America Public.* XXXVI (1942) 199–214.

Alden *Stuart*—John R. Alden *John Stuart and the Southern Colonial Frontier* . . . (1944).

Alden "Why the March"—John R. Alden "Why the March to Concord" *A.H.R.* XLIX (1944) 446–454.

Allan *Hancock*—Herbert S. Allan *John Hancock Patriot in Purple* (1953).

Allen *Oration Upon the Beauties of Liberty*—[John Allen] *An Oration, upon the Beauties of Liberty, or the Essential Rights of the Americans* . . . (4th ed., Boston, 1773).

Allen *The Watchman's Alarm*—[John Allen] *The Watchman's Alarm to Lord N——H* . . . *by the British Bostonian, Author of the Oration on the Beauties of Liberty* . . . (Salem [Mass.], 1994).

Almon *Biographical Anecdotes*—[John Almon] *Biographical, Literary and Political Anecdotes of Several of the Most Eminent Persons* 3 vols. (1797).

Almon *Pitt*—John Almon *Anecdotes of the Life of* . . . *Pitt* 3 vols. (7th ed., 1810).

Almon *Prior Documents*—See *Prior Documents.*

Almon *Remembrancer*—[John Almon] *The Remembrancer, or Impartial Depository of Public Events* (3rd London ed., 1775).

Alvord *Mississippi Valley*—Clarence W. Alvord *The Mississippi Valley in British Politics* . . . 2 vols. (1917).

Alvord "Virginia and the West"—Clarence W. Alvord "Virginia and the West: An Interpretation" *Miss. Val. H.R.* III (1917) 19–38.

Alvord and Carter *New Regime*—Clarence W. Alvord and Clarence E. Carter (eds.) *The New Regime 1765–1767* (1916).

Am. Antiq. Soc. Proc.—*Proceedings of the American Antiquarian Society.*

American Gazette—*The American Gazette, Being a Collection of* . . . *Addresses* . . . *which relate to the Present Disputes between Great Britain and her Colonies* (London, 1768).

Am. Hist. Assoc. Rep.—*Annual Report of the American Historical Association.*

Am. Neptune—*The American Neptune* (journal).

Am. Phil. Soc. Proc.—*Proceedings of the American Philosophical Society.*

Am. Revolution in N.Y.—*The American Revolution in New York* (1926) published by The University of the State of New York.

Andrews "Boston Merchants"—Charles M. Andrews "The Boston Merchants and the Non-Importation Movement" *Col. Soc. Publ.* XIX (1917) 159–259.

Andrews "Col. Adm. Courts"—Charles M. Andrews "Vice Admiralty Courts in the Colonies" in Towle *R.I. Admiralty* 1–79 (1936).

Andrews *Col. Period*—Charles M. Andrews *The Colonial Period* . . . 4 vols. (1934–1938).

Andrews "Commissions"—Charles M. Andrews "List of the Commissions and Instructions Issued to the Governors . . . 1609 to 1784" *Am. Hist. Assoc. Rep.* for 1911, I 393–528.

Andrews *Guide to P.R.O.*—Charles M. Andrews (ed.) *Guide to the Materials* . . . *in the Public Record Office of Great Britain* 2 vols. (1912–1914).

"Andrews Letters"—Winthrop Sargent (ed.) "Letters of John Andrews, Esq. of Boston 1772–1776" *Mass. Hist. Soc. Proc.* for 1864–1865, 316–412.

Andrews "State of Trade"—Charles M. Andrews "State of the Trade" *Col. Soc. Publ.* XIX (1918) 379–390.

Annual Register—The Annual Register, Or a View of the History, Politics and Literature (for each year from 1766 to 1775).

*Appleton's Cyclopaedia—*James G. Wilson and John Fiske (eds.) *Appleton's Cyclopaedia Of American Biography* 6 vols. (1887–1889).

A.P.S. Proc.—Proceedings of the American Philosophical Society.

Armytage *Free Port System—*Frances Armytage *The Free Port System in the British West Indies . . . 1766–1822* (1953).

Ashe, *N.C.—*Samuel A. Ashe *History of North Carolina* I (1584–1783) (1908).

Aspinwall I and II—*The Aspinwall Papers* 4 *M.H.S. Coll.* IX and X.

Bailyn *Ideological Origins—*Bernard Bailyn *The Ideological Origins of the American Revolution* (1967).

Bailyn *Origins of American Politics—*Bernard Bailyn *The Origins of American Politics* (1968).

Bailyn, *Pamphlets—*Bernard Bailyn (ed.) *Pamphlets of the American Revolution . . . 1750–1765* (1965).

Bailyn "Political Experience"—Bernard Bailyn "Political Experience and Enlightenment Ideas in Eighteenth-Century America" *A.H.R.* LXVII (1962) 339–351.

Baird "Presbyterians"—Charles W. Baird "Civil Status of the Presbyterians in the Province of New York" *Mag. Am. Hist.* III (1879) 593–628.

Baldwin *British Customs—*Samuel Baldwin *A Survey of the British Customs . . .* (1770).

Baldwin "Galloway"—Ernest H. Baldwin "Joseph Galloway" *Pa. Mag. Hist.* XXVI (1902) 161–191, 289–321, and 417–442.

Baldwin *New England Clergy—*Alice M. Baldwin *The New England Clergy and the American Revolution* (1928).

Ballagh *Lee—*James C. Ballagh (ed.) *The Letters of Richard Henry Lee* 2 vols. (1914).

Bancroft *History—*George Bancroft *History of the United States . . .* 10 vols. (1857–1874).

Bargar *Dartmouth—*B. D. Bargar *Lord Dartmouth and the American Revolution* (1965).

Bargar, "Dartmouth"—B. D. Bargar "Lord Dartmouth's Patronage, 1772–1775" 3 *W. & M.Q.* XV (1958) 191–200.

*Barker—*Elizabeth E. Dana (ed.) *The British in Boston . . . Being the Diary of Lieutenant John Barker . . .* (1924).

Barker *Md.—*Charles A. Barker *The Background of the Revolution in Maryland* (1940).

*Barrington—*Shute Barrington *The Political Life of William Wildman Viscount Barrington . . .* (1815).

*Barrington–Bernard Corresp.—*Edward Channing and Archibald C. Coolidge (eds.) *The Barrington–Bernard Correspondence and Illustrative Matter 1760–1770* (1912).

Barrow "American Revolution"—Thomas C. Barrow "The American Revolution as a Colonial War for Independence" 3 *W. & M.Q.* XXV (1968) 452–464.

Barrow "Background to the Grenville Program"—Thomas C. Barrow "Background to the Grenville Program, 1757–1763" 3 *W. & M.Q.* XXIII (1965) 93–104.

Barrow "English Point of View"—Thomas C. Barrow "The Old Colonial System from an English Point of View" in Olson and Brown *Anglo-American Relations* 125–139.

Barrow *Trade—*Thomas C. Barrow *Trade and Empire: The British Customs Service in Colonial America 1660–1775* (1967).

Barry *Mass.—*John S. Barry *The History of Massachusetts* 3 vols. (1855–57).

Barton "Lexington"—John A. Barton "Lexington the End of a Myth" *History Today* IX (June, 1959) 382–391.

Bassett "Regulators"—John S. Bassett "The Regulators of North Carolina" (1765–1771) *Am. Hist. Assoc. Rep.* for 1894 141–212.

Basye *Board of Trade*—Arthur H. Basye *The Lords Commissioners of Trade* . . . (1925).

Basye "Secretary of State"—Arthur H. Basye "The Secretary of State for the Colonies, 1768–1782" *A.H.R.* XXVIII (1923) 13–23.

Baxter *Hancock*—W. T. Baxter *The House of Hancock: Business in Boston 1724–1775* (1945).

Beardsley *Seabury*—Eben Edwards Beardsley *Life and Correspondence of . . . Samuel Seabury* . . . (1881).

Beardsley *W. S. Johnson*—Eben Edwards Beardsley *Life and Times of William Samuel Johnson L.L.D.* . . . (1876).

Beatson *Pol. Index*—Robert Beatson *A Political Index* . . . 2 vols. (1788).

Beaven *Aldermen*—Alfred B. Beaven *The Aldermen of the City of London* 2 vols. (1913).

Becker *New York*—Carl L. Becker *The History of Political Parties in . . . New York, 1760–1776* (1909).

Bedford—John Russell (ed.) *Correspondence of John, Fourth Duke of Bedford* 3 vols. (1842–1846).

Beekman—See White *Beekman Papers.*

Belcher *First Am. Civil War*—Henry Belcher *The First American Civil War* 2 vols. (1911).

Benedict *American Admiralty*—Erastus C. Benedict *The American Admiralty: Its Jurisdiction and Practice* . . . (1870).

Benezet *Caution and Warning*—Anthony Benezet *A Caution and Warning to Great Britain; and Her Colonies* . . . [concerning] *the Enslaved Negroes in the British Dominions* (Philadelphia, 1767).

Benton *Whig-Loyalism*—William A. Benton *Whig-Loyalism: An Aspect of Political Ideology* . . . (1969).

Bernard—See *Barrington–Bernard Corresp.*

[Bernard] *Letters to Hillsborough*—See *Letters to Hillsborough.*

[Bernard] *Letters to Ministry*—See *Letters to Ministry.*

Bernard *Select Letters*—[Francis Bernard] *Select Letters on the Trade and Government of America* . . . (London, 1774).

Bezanson *Prices*—Anne Bezanson, Robert D. Gray, and Miriam Hussey *Prices in Colonial Philadelphia* (1935).

Bibliographical Soc. of America Public.—*Publications of the Bibliographical Society of America.*

Bigelow *Franklin*—John Bigelow (ed.) *The Works of Benjamin Franklin* 10 vols. (1887–1888).

Billias *Law in Col. America*—George A. Billias (ed.) *Selected Essays: Law and Authority in Colonial America* (1965).

Billias *Mass. Land Bankers*—George A. Billias *The Massachusetts Land Bankers of 1740* (1959).

Black's Law Dictionary—Henry C. Black *Black's Law Dictionary* . . . (1933).

Blackstone *Analysis*—Wliliam Blackstone *An Analysis of the Laws of England* . . . [1756], references to 3rd ed., 1758.

Blackstone *Commentaries*—William Blackstone *Commentaries on the Laws of England* (4 books 1765–1769). Unless noted, my citations are to the book and page number of the first edition as given in Thomas Cooley *Blackstone Commentaries* 2 vols. (1884).

Bland *The Colonel Dismounted*—[Richard Bland] *The Colonel Dismounted . . . in a Letter . . . Containing a Dissertation upon the Constitution of the Colony by Common Sense* (Williamsburg, 1764).

Bleackley *Wilkes*—Horace Bleackley *Life of John Wilkes* (1917).

Boardman *Sherman*—Roger S. Boardman *Roger Sherman Singer and Statesman* (1938).

Boatner *Encyclopedia of the Am. Revolution*—Mark Boatner *Encyclopedia of the American Revolution* (1966).

Bolingbroke *Parties*—Henry St. John, Viscount Bolingbroke *A Dissertation upon Parties . . .* (Dublin, 1735).

Bolton "Circulating Libraries"—Charles K. Bolton "Circulating Libraries in Boston, 1765–1865" *Col. Soc. Public.* XI (1910) 196–207.

Boorstin *Americans*—Daniel J. Boorstin *The Americans: The Colonial Experience* (1958).

Boston Chronicle—The Boston Chronicle (John Mein and John Fleeming, publishers) Dec., 1767–June, 1770.

Boston Evening-Post—The Boston Evening-Post 1735–1775.

Boston Gazette—The Boston-Gazette, and Country Journal 1719–1775 (fervently Whig paper, after 1755 published by Benjamin Edes and John Gill).

Boston Massacre—See Adams "New Light"; *Short Narrative;* Zobel *Boston Massacre.*

Boston News-Letter—The Boston News-Letter (1757–1762), continued under various titles to 1776.

Boston Post-Boy—The Boston Post-Boy & Advertiser.

Boston Records—A Report of the Record Commissioners of the City of Boston, containing the Boston Town Records.

Boston Selectmen's Minutes—A Report of the Record Commissioners of the city of Boston Containing the Selectmen's Minutes from 1769 through April, 1775 (1893).

Boucher *View of the American Revolution*—Jonathan Boucher *A View of the Causes and Consequences of the American Revolution . . .* (1797).

Bouchier *Reminiscences of an American Loyalist*—Jonathan Bouchier (ed.) *Reminiscences of an American Loyalist . . . Jonathan Boucher* (1925).

Boutell *Sherman*—Lewis H. Boutell *The Life of Roger Sherman* (1896).

Bowdoin–Temple—The Bowdoin and Temple Papers, 6 *M.H.S. Coll.* IX (1897).

Bowman "Va. Committees"—Larry Bowman "The Virginia County Committees of Safety, 1774–1776" *Va. Mag. Hist.* LXXIX (1971) 322–337.

Boyd *Anglo-American Union*—Julian P. Boyd *Anglo-American Union Joseph Galloway's Plans . . .* (1941).

Boyd *Jefferson*—Julian P. Boyd (ed.-in-chief) *The Papers of Thomas Jefferson; Volume I: 1760–1776* (1950).

Boyd *Susquehannah Co. Papers*—Julian P. Boyd (ed.) *The Susquehannah Company Papers* 4 vols. (1930–1933).

Boyd *Union*—Julian P. Boyd *Anglo-American Union: Joseph Galloway's Plans . . . 1774–1788* (1941).

"Boyles Journal"—"[John] Boyle's Journals of Occurrences in Boston [1766–71]" *New Eng. Hist. and Gen. Reg.* LXXXIV (1930) 248–272.

Bradford *Mass. Papers*—Alden Bradford (ed.) *Speeches of the Governors of Massachusetts . . . and Other Public Papers . . .* (1818).

Brebner *New Eng. Outpost*—John B. Brebner *New England's Outpost: Acadia before the Conquest of Canada* (1927).

Brennan *Massachusetts*—Ellen E. Brennan *Plural Office-Holding in Massachusetts 1760–1780* . . . (1945).

Brennan "Otis"—Ellen E. Brennan "James Otis: Recreant and Patriot" *New England Q.* XII (1939) 691–725.

Bridenbaugh *Cities in Revolt*—Carl Bridenbaugh *Cities in Revolt: Urban Life in America, 1743–1776* (1935).

Bridenbaugh *Colonial Craftsman*—Carl Bridenbaugh *The Colonial Craftsman* (1950).

Bridenbaugh *Mitre and Sceptre*—Carl Bridenbaugh *Mitre and Sceptre: Transatlantic Faiths, Idea, Personalities, in Politics 1689–1775* (1962).

Bridenbaugh *Rebels and Gentlemen*—Carl and Jessica Bridenbaugh *Rebels and Gentlemen: Philadelphia in the Age of Franklin* (1942).

Brief Considerations on Slavery—[anonymous] *Brief Considerations on Slavery and the Expediency of Its Extinction* (Burlington [N.J.], 1773).

Brigham *Am. Newspapers*—Clarence S. Brigham *History and Bibliography of American Newspapers 1690–1820* 2 vols. (1947). The titles and dates of publication of the newspapers given in this list are drawn from this monumental work.

Brigham *British Proclamations*—Clarence S. Brigham (ed.) *British Royal Proclamations Relating to America 1603–1783* (1911).

Brooke *Chatham Administration*—John Brooke *The Chatham Administration 1766–1768* (1956).

Brookes *Benezet*—George Brookes *Friend Anthony Benezet* (1937).

Brown *The American Secretary . . . Germain*—Gerald Saxon Brown *The American Secretary: The Colonial Policy of Lord George Germain, 1775–1778* (1963).

Brown *Democracy in Mass.*—Robert E. Brown *Middle-Class Democracy and the Revolution in Massachusetts, 1691–1780* (1955).

Brown *Hancock*—Abram English Brown *John Hancock His Book* (1893).

Brown *Hawley*—E. Francis Brown *Joseph Hawley Colonial Radical* (1931).

Brown "Hawley's Law Career"—E. Francis Brown "The Law Career of Major Joseph Hawley" *New Eng. Q.* IV (1931) 482–508.

Brown *King's Friends*—Wallace Brown *The King's Friends: The Composition and Motives of the American Loyalist Claimants* (1966).

Brown "Loyalists"—Wallace Brown "The View at Two Hundred Years: The Loyalists . . ." *A.A.S. Proc.* LXXX part 1 (1970) 25–47.

Brown "Mass. Convention of 1768"—Richard D. Brown "The Massachusetts Convention of Towns, 1768" 3 *W. & M.Q.* XXVI (1969) 94–104.

Brown "Mass. Loyalists"—Richard D. Brown "The Confiscation and Disposition of Loyalists' Estates in Suffolk County, Massachusetts" 3 *W. & M.Q.* XXI (1964) 534–560.

Brown *Virginia*—Robert E. and B. Katherine Brown *Virginia 1705–1786: Democracy Or Aristocracy?* (1964).

Brunhouse "Townshend Acts"—R. L. Brunhouse "The Effect of the Townshend Acts in Pennsylvania" *Pa. Mag. Hist.* LIV (1930) 355–366.

Bruns "Benezet"—Roger A. Bruns "Anthony Benezet and the Natural Rights of the Negro" *Pa. Mag. Hist.* XCVI (1972) 104–113.

Bryant "R. I. Justice"—Samuel W. Bryant "Rhode Island Justice—1772 Vintage" *R.I. Hist.* XXVI (1967) 65–71.

Brydon *Mother Church*—George M. Brydon *Virginia's Mother Church* . . . *1727–1814* 2 vols. (1952).

Buel "Democracy and the Am. Revolution"—Richard Buel "Democracy and the American Revolution: A Frame of Reference" 3 *W. & M.Q.* XXI (1964) 165–190.

Bullock *Williamsburg Art of Cookery* Helen Bullock *The Williamsburg Art of Cookery* . . . (1938).

Bumstead and Clark "John Allen"—John M. Bumstead and Charles E. Clark "New England's Tom Paine: John Allen and the Spirit of Liberty" 3 *W. & M.Q.* XXI (1964) 561–570.

Burke—Thomas W. Copeland et al. (eds.) *The Correspondence of Edmund Burke* vols. I–III (1958, 1960, 1961).

Burke *Speeches*—Edmund Burke *Speeches and Letters on American Affairs* (Everyman's Library ed., 1942).

Burke's Works—The Works of the Right Honourable Edmund Burke C. Rivington, printer (1801).

Burnett *Continental Congress*—Edmund C. Burnett *The Continental Congress* (1941).

Burnett *Letters*—Edmund C. Burnett (ed.) *Letters of Members of the Continental Congress.* 8 vols. (1921–1938).

Burt *Quebec*—Alfred L. Burt *The Old Province of Quebec* (1933).

Burton *Letters to Hume*—John H. Burton *Letters of Eminent Persons Addressed to David Hume* (1849).

Butterfield—See *Adams Papers* and *Adams Family Corresp.*

Cadbury "Quaker Relief"—Henry J. Cadbury "Quaker Relief during the Siege of Boston" *Col. Soc. Public.* XXIV (1943) 39–179.

Calder *Stiles*—Isabel M. Calder (ed.) *Letters and Papers of Ezra Stiles* (1933).

Caldwell—William Mure (ed.) *Selections from the Family Papers at Caldwell* 2 parts in 3 vols. (1854); see also *Mure.*

Calendar H.O. Papers—Joseph Redington and Richard A. Roberts (eds.) *Calendar of Home Office Papers . . . 1760–1775* 4 vols. (1878–1899).

Callahan *Flight*—North Callahan *Flight from the Republic* (1967).

Camm *Critical Remarks*—[John Camm] *Critical Remarks on a Letter Ascribed to Common Sense . . .* (Williamsburg, 1765).

Can. H.R.—The Canadian Historical Review.

Canadian *Doc.*—See S. & D. *Doc.*

Cappon *Va. Gazette Index*—Lester J. Cappon and Stella F. Duff (eds.) *Virginia Gazette Index 1736–1780* 2 vols. (1950).

Care *English Liberties*—Henry Care *English Liberties Or the Free-born Subject's Inheritance . . .* (Providence, R.I., reprint of the 6th ed., 1774).

Carroll Letters—Thomas Meagher Field (ed.) *Unpublished Letters of Charles Carroll of Carrollton . . .* (1902).

Carroll and Ashworth *Washington*—John A. Carroll and Mary W. Ashworth *George Washington: First in Peace* (1957), vol. 7 in the continuation of Freeman *Washington.*

Carter "Commander in Chief"—Clarence E. Carter "The Office of Commander in Chief [in North America] . . ." in Morris *Era* 170–213.

Cary *Warren*—John Cary *Joseph Warren: Physician, Politician, Patriot* (1961).

"Cato" (Litto)—Fredric Litto "Addison's *Cato* in the Colonies" 3 *W. & M.Q.* XXIII (1966) 431–449.

Cavendish *Debates*—John Wright (ed.) *Sir Henry Cavendish's Debates of the House of Commons . . . [1768–1771]; Letters . . . etc.* 2 vols. (1841–1843).

Cavendish *Quebec Bill*—John Wright (ed.) *Debates of the House of Commons in the Year 1774 . . . on the Bill for . . . Quebec . . . from the Note of . . . Sir Henry Cavendish* (1839).

Chaffin "Townshend Acts"—Robert J. Chaffin "The Townshend Acts of 1767" 3 *W. & M.Q.* XXVII (1970) 90–121.

Chalmers *Opinions*—George Chalmers (ed.) *Opinions of Eminent Lawyers* . . . (1858).

Champagne "Liberty Boys and Mechanics"—Roger J. Champagne "Liberty Boys and Mechanics of New York City, 1764–1774" *Labor History* VIII (1967) 115–135.

Champagne "Military Assoc. of the Sons of Liberty"—Roger J. Champagne "The Military Association of the Sons of Liberty" *N.Y.H.S.A.* XLI (1957) 338–350.

Champagne "N.Y."—Roger Champagne "New York and the Intolerable Acts, 1774" *N.Y.H.S.Q.* XLV (1961) 195–207.

Champagne "N.Y. Elections"—Roger J. Champagne "Family Politics . . . ; The New York Assembly Elections of 1768 and 1769" 3 *W. & M.Q.* XX (1903) 57–79.

Chandler *Appeal*—Thomas Bradbury Chandler *An Appeal to the Public in Behalf of the Church of England in America* . . . (New York City, 1767).

Channing "American Board of Customs"—Edward Channing "The American Board of the Commissioners of the Customs" *M.H.S. Proc.* XLVII 477–490.

Channing "Commissioners"—Edward Channing "Commissioners of the Customs, 1767" *M.H.S. Proc.* XLIII (1910) 477–491.

Channing *History*—Edward Channing *A History of the United States* II and III (1924).

Chatham—See *Pitt*.

Chesterfield—Lord Mahon (Philip Henry Stanhope) *The Letters of Philip Dormer Stanhope, Earl of Chesterfield* . . . 5 vols. (1892).

Chitwood *Lee*—Oliver P. Chitwood *Richard Henry Lee: Statesman of the Revolution* (1967).

Christelow "Contraband Trade"—Allan Christelow "Contraband Trade . . . and the Free Port Act of 1766" *Hisp. Am. Hist. Rev.* XXII (1942) 309–343.

Christen "Sears"—Robert Jay Christen "King Sears: Politician and Patriot . . ." Dissertation (1968) Columbia U. Library.

Clark "American Customs Board"—Dora Mae Clark "The American Board of Customs, 1767–1783" *A.H.R.* XLV (1940) 777–806.

Clark *British Treasury*—Dora Mae Clark *The Rise of the British Treasury: Colonial Administration in the Eighteenth Century* (1960).

Clark "Impressment"—Dora Mae Clark "The Impressment of Seamen in the American Colonies" *Essays in Colonial History* 198–224.

Clark *Naval Doc.*—William Bell Clark (ed.) *Naval Documents of the American Revolution* vol. I [Dec., 1774–Sept., 1775] (1964).

Clark *St. John's Church*—Samuel A. Clark *The History of St. John's Church Elizabeth Town, New Jersey* . . . (1857).

"Clarke Papers"—Denison R. Slade "Papers of Richard Clarke" *Col. Soc. Public.* VIII 78–89.

Coburn *Battle*—Frank W. Coburn *The Battle of April 19, 1775* . . . (1922).

Coburn *Muster Rolls*—Frank W. Coburn *Muster Rolls of the Participating Companies* . . . *in the Battle of April 19, 1775* . . . (1922).

Coffin *Quebec*—Victor Coffin *The Province of Quebec and the Early American Revolution* (1896).

Coke *Institutes*—Edward Coke *Institutes of the Laws of England* (four books), the first, the famous *Commentary upon Lyttleton* (1628–1644) and several later editions by 1765.

Coke *Letters and Journals*—J. A. Home (ed.) *The Letters and Journals of Lady Mary Coke* 4 vols. (1889–1896).

Colbourn "Dickinson"—H. Trevor Colbourn "The Historical Perspective of John Dickinson" in *Early Dickinsoniana The Boyd Lee Spahr Lectures in Americana 1957–1961* (1961).

Colbourn "Dickinson, Historical Revolutionary"—H. Trevor Colbourn "John Dickinson, Historical Revolutionary" *Pa. Mag. Hist.* LXXIII (1959) 271–292.

Colbourn "Dickinson's London Letters"—H. Trevor Colbourn "A Pennsylvania Farmer . . . John Dickinson's London Letters, 1754–1756" *Pa. Mag. Hist.* LXXXVI (1962) 241–286.

Colbourn *Lamp of Experience*—H. Trevor Colbourn *The Lamp of Experience: Whig History and the Intellectual Origins of the American Revolution* (1965).

Colden—N.Y. Hist. Soc. Coll. for 1876, 1877, 1920, 1922, 1923, 1924.

Colden *Conduct*—Cadwallader Colden *The Conduct of Cadwallader Colden* . . . (New York, 1767), reprinted *Colden* (1877) 435–467.

Coleman *Ga.*—Kenneth Coleman *The American Revolution in Georgia* (1958).

Collins "Committees"—Edward D. Collins "Committees of Correspondence of the American Revolution" *Am. Hist. Assoc. Rep.* for 1901 I 243–271.

Col. Soc. Publ.—Publications of the Colonial Society of Massachusetts.

Commager and Morris *Spirit of Seventy-Six*—Henry Steele Commager and Richard B. Morris *The Spirit of Seventy-Six: The Story . . . by Participants* I (1958).

Conduct of the Late Administration—The Conduct of the Late Administration Examined . . . (dated 1767, but actually published in Dec., 1766).

Congressional Biographies—Ansel Wold, compiler *Biographical Directory of the American Congress 1774–1927* (1928).

Conn. Col. Rec.—Charles J. Hoadly (ed.) *The Public Records of the Colony of Connecticut* XI–XIV (1880–1887).

Conn. Hist. Soc. Bull.—The Connecticut Historical Society Bulletin.

Conn. Hist. Soc. Coll.—Collections of the Connecticut Historical Society.

Conn. Journal—The Connecticut Journal, and the New-Haven Post-Boy New Haven, 1772–1775.

Cook *Literary Influences*—Elizabeth C. Cook *Literary Influences in Colonial Newspapers, 1704–1750* (1912).

Cooke *A Sermon*—Samuel Cooke *A Sermon Preached at Cambridge in the Audience of His Honor Thomas Hutchinson* . . . (Boston, 1770).

Cooper—See Tuckerman "Cooper Diary" and "Cooper Letters."

Cooper *S.C. Statutes*—Thomas Cooper and David J. McCord (eds.) *The Statutes at Large of South Carolina* 10 vols. (1846–1841).

Copley *Letters—Letters and Papers of John Singleton Copley and Henry Pelham 1739–1776, M.H.S. Coll.* LXXI (1814).

Corwin "Higher Law"—Edward S. Corwin "The 'Higher Law' Background of American Constitutional Law" *Harv. Law Rev.* XLII (1929) 148–185, 365–409.

Coupland *Quebec Act*—Reginald Coupland *The Quebec Act: A Study in Statesmanship* (1925).

Crane *Franklin's Letters to Press*—Verner W. Crane *Benjamin Franklin's Letters to the Press 1758–1775* (1950).

Croker *Letters of Mary Lepel*—John Wilson Croker (ed.) *Letters of Mary Lepel, Lady Hervey* . . . (1821).

Cross *Anglican Episcopate*—Arthur L. Cross *The Anglican Episcopate and the American Colonies* (1902).

Cross "Benefit of Clergy"—Arthur Lyon Cross "Benefit of Clergy in American Criminal Law" *M.H.S. Proc.* LXIII 154–181.

Curry *Franklin*—Cecil B. Curry *Road to Revolution: Benjamin Franklin in England, 1765–1775* (1958).

"Cushing Letters"—"Letters of Thomas Cushing from 1767 to 1775" *M.H.S. Coll.* IV 347–366.

"Cushing Letters" (*Mass. Papers*)—Letters of Thomas Cushing, 1765–1770, in *Mass. Papers* 14–177 *passim.*

Cushing *S. Adams*—Harry A. Cushing (ed.) *The Writings of Samuel Adams* 4 vols. (1904–1908).

Cushing *Transition in Mass.*—Harry A. Cushing *History of the Transition from Provincial to Commonwealth Government in Massachusetts* (1896).

D.A.B.—*Dictionary of American Biography* 21 vols. (1943), Supplement One (1944).

D.N.B.—*Dictionary of National Biography* (English) 21 vols. (1908–1909), Supplement One (1909).

Dartmouth Papers—*The Manuscripts of the Earl of Dartmouth* 4 vols. *H.M.C.* 11th Rep., App., Part V (1887); *H.M.C.* 13th Rep., App., Part IV (1892) 499–503; *H.M.C.* 14th Rep., App., Part X (1895); *H.M.C.* 15th Rep., App., Part I (1896). In citing these, I identify the volume by the year of publication; e.g., *Dartmouth* (1887).

Davidson *Propaganda*—Philip Davidson *Propaganda and the American Revolution 1763–1783* (1941).

Dawson *New York City*—Henry B. Dawson (ed.) *New York City during the American Revolution* . . . (1861).

Dawson *Sons of Liberty*—Henry B. Dawson *The Sons of Liberty in New York* (1859).

Dawson "The Park"—Henry B. Dawson "The Park and Its Vicinity" in David T. Valentine *Manual of the Corporation of the City of New-York for 1855* 433–485.

Deane Corresp.—*Correspondence of Silas Deane* . . . *1774–1776* in *Conn. Hist. Soc. Coll.* II 129–368 (1870).

"Deane Notes"—Christopher Collins (ed.) "Silas Deane Reports on the Continental Congress . . ." *Conn. Hist. Soc. Bull.* XXIX (1964) 1–8.

Deane Papers—*The Deane Papers, 1774–1790* (*N.Y. Hist. Soc. Coll.* for 1886–1890) 5 vols. (1887–1891).

De Berdt—See Matthews "De Berdt"; "Cushing Letters"; and *Mass. Papers.*

Delaplaine *Johnson*—Edward S. Delaplaine *The Life of Thos. Johnson* (1927).

De Mond *Loyalists in N.C.*—Robert O. De Mond *The Loyalists in North Carolina during the Revolution* (1940).

Dexter *Yale Biographies*—Franklin Bowditch Dexter *Biographical Sketches of the Graduates of Yale College* [from 1701 to 1778] 3 vols. (1885–1903).

Diamond "Experiment in Feudalism"—Sigmund Diamond "An Experiment in Feudalism: French Canada in the Seventeenth Century" 3 *W. & M.Q.* XVIII (1961) 1–35.

Dickerson *Boston*—Oliver M. Dickerson (ed.) *Boston under Military Rule 1768–1769* . . . (1936).

Dickerson "British Control"—Oliver M. Dickerson "British Control of American Newspapers on the Eve of the Revolution" *New Eng. Q.* XXIV (1951) 435–468.

Dickerson "Commissioners of Customs"—Oliver M. Dickerson "The Commissioners of Customs and the 'Boston Massacre'" *New Eng. Q.* XXVII (1954) 307–325.

Dickerson "Hancock"—Oliver M. Dickerson "John Hancock: Notorious Smuggler or Victim of British Revenue Racketeers?" *Miss. Vall. H.R.* XXXII (1946) 517–540.

Dickerson *Navigation Acts*—Oliver M. Dickerson *The Navigation Acts and the American Revolution* (1951).

Dickerson "Opinion of Sewall"—Oliver M. Dickerson "Opinion of Attorney General Sewall . . . in the Case of the *Lydia*" 3 *W. & M.Q.* IV (1947) 499–504.

Dickerson "Revenue"—Oliver M. Dickerson "Use Made of the Revenue from the Tax on Tea" *New Eng. Q.* XXXI (1958) 232–243.

Dickerson "Writs"—Oliver M. Dickerson "Writs of Assistance . . ." in Morris *Era* 40–75.

Dickinson *Essay on Constitutional Power*—John Dickinson *An Essay on the Constitutional Power of Great-Britain over the Colonies* . . . (Philadelphia, 1774). My citations are to the reprint in 4 *Force* I 564–593.

Dickinson *Late Regulations*—John Dickinson *The Late Regulations Respecting the British Colonies* . . . (Philadelphia, 1765).

Dickinson *Letters from a Farmer*—John Dickinson *Letters from a Farmer in Pennsylvania to the Inhabitants of the British Colonies* (Philadelphia, 1768). Ford *Dickinson* I 277–406.

Dillon *New York Triumverate*—Dorothy R. Dillon *The New York Triumverate* . . . (1949).

Dix *Trinity Church*—Morgan Dix (ed.) *A History of the Parish of Trinity Church in the City of New York* (4 vols., 1898–1906).

Dodington—Henry P. Wyndham (ed.) *The Diary of the Late Bubb Dodington* . . . (1785).

"Donations"—Richard Frothingham "Correspondence of the Boston Committee of Donations" 4 *M.H.S. Coll.* IV (1858) 1–278.

Donoughue *British Politics*—Bernard Donoughue *British Politics and the American Revolution* . . . *1773–75* (1964).

Downes *Council Fires*—Randolph C. Downes *Council Fires on the Upper Ohio* (1940).

Drake *Boston*—Samuel G. Drake *The History and Antiquities of Boston* . . . *to the Year 1770* (1856).

Drake *Quakers and Slavery*—Thomas Drake *Quakers and Slavery in America* (1950).

Drake *Tea Leaves*—Francis Drake *Tea Leaves; Being a Collection of Letters and Documents* . . . (1884).

Drayton *Memoirs of the Revolution*—John Drayton *Memoirs of the American Revolution . . . as Relating to . . . South-Carolina* 2 vols. (1824).

Duff "Case Against the King"—Stella F. Duff "The Case Against the King . . ." 3 *W. & M.Q.* VI (1949) 383–397.

Dulany *Considerations*—Daniel Dulany *Considerations on the Propriety of Imposing Taxes* . . . (Annapolis, Maryland, 1765).

E.H.R.—*The English Historical Review.*

Eardly-Wilmot *Historical View*—John Eardly-Wilmot *Historical View of the Commission for Enquiry into . . . the American Loyalists* (1815).

Econ. Hist. Rev.—*The Economic History Review.*

Eddis *Letters*—William Eddis *Letters from America . . . 1769 to 1777 inclusive* (London, 1792).

Edes "Young"—Henry H. Edes "Memoir of Dr. Thomas Young, 1731–1777" *Col. Soc. Publ.* XI (1910) 2–54.

Egerton *Loyalists*—Hugh E. Egerton *The Royal Commission on the Losses and Services of American Loyalists* XXX (1915).

Egnal and Ernst "Economic Interpretation of the Am. Revolution"—Marc Egnal and Joseph A. Ernst "An Economic Interpretation of the American Revolution" 3 *W. & M.Q.* XXIX (1972) 3–32.

Einstein *Divided Loyalties*—Lewis Einstein *Divided Loyalties: Americans in England during the War of Independence* (1933).

"Eliot Letters"—"Letters from Andrew Eliot to Thomas Hollis" 4 *M.H.S.* Coll. IV 398–461.

Elliot—George F. S. Elliot *The Border Elliots* . . . (1897).

Ellis—Henry Ellis *Original Letters Illustrative of English History* . . . 2nd ser. (1827); 3rd ser. (1846).

Ellis *Sermon Preached before the Society*—Anthony Ellis, Bishop of St. David's, *A Sermon Preached before the Incorporated Society* . . . (London, 1759).

Elsey "Wilkes"—George M. Elsey "John Wilkes and William Palfrey" *Col. Soc. Publ.* XXXIV (1943) 411–428.

Elwyn *Mass. Papers*—A. L. Elwyn *Papers Relating to Public Events in Massachusetts Preceding the American Revolution* (1856).

English Reports—The English [*Law*] *Reports* (1900–1930).

Ernst "Currency Act Repeal"—Joseph A. Ernst "The Currency Act Repeal Movement . . . 1764–1767" 3 *W. & M.Q.* XXV (1968) 177–211.

Essays in Colonial History—*Essays in Colonial History Presented to Charles McLean Andrews* . . . (1931).

Essex Gazette—The *Essex Gazette* of Salem Mass., June, 1774–April, 1775.

Essex Inst. Hist. Coll.—*Historical Collections* of the Essex Institute (Salem, Mass.).

Evans *Am. Bibliography*—Charles Evans *American Bibliography* . . . *1639–1880* vols. 4 and 5 (1941).

Evans "Planter Indebtedness"—Emory G. Evans "Planter Indebtedness and the Coming of the Revolution in Virginia" 3 *W. & M.Q.* XIX (1962) 511–533.

Evelyn—G. D. Scull (ed.) *Memoir and Letters of Captain W. Glanville Evelyn* . . . (1879).

Everett "Last Royal Veto"—William Everett "The Last Royal Veto" 2 *M.H.S.* Proc. V 156–164.

Ewer *A Sermon Preached before the Incorporated Society*—John Ewer, Bishop of Landaff *A Sermon Preached before the Incorporated Society* . . . *on Friday, February 20, 1767* (London, 1767).

Fair Account—*A Fair Account of the Late Unhappy Disturbances at Boston* . . . (London, 1770).

Farmer's Letters—See Dickinson *Letters from a Farmer.*

Farrand "Taxation of Tea"—Max Farrand "The Taxation of Tea, 1767–1773" *A.H.R.* III (1898) 266–269.

Feiling *Second Tory Party*—Keith G. Feiling *The Second Tory Party 1714–1832* (1951).

Fellows "Loyalist Source Material"—Jo-Ann Fellows (ed.) "A Bibliography of Loyalist Source Material in Canada" *Am. Antiq. Soc. Proc.* LXXXVI, Part 1 (1972) 67–270.

Ferguson "Currency Finance"—E. James Ferguson "Currency Finance: An Interpretation of Colonial Monetary Practices" 3 *W. & M.Q.* X (1953) 153–180.

Fingerhut "Loyalist Claims"—Eugene R. Fingerhut "Uses and Abuses of the American Loyalists' Claims . . ." 3 *W. & M.Q.* XXV (1968) 245–258.

Fisher *Struggle for Independence*—*The Struggle for American Independence* 2 vols. (1908).

Fitch—Albert C. Bates (ed.) *The Fitch Papers* . . . *Conn. Hist. Soc. Coll.* XVII, XVIII (1918, 1920).

Fitzpatrick *Washington*—John C. Fitzpatrick (ed.) *The Writings of George Washington* 38 vols. (1931–1940).

Fitzpatrick *Washington Diaries*—John C. Fitzpatrick *The Diaries of George Washington, 1748–1799* 4 vols. (1925).

Flexner *Washington*—James T. Flexner *George Washington* 4 vols. (1965–1972).

Flick *Loyalism in N.Y.*—Alexander C. Flick *Loyalism in New York during the American Revolution* (1901).

Foote *King's Chapel*—Henry Wilder Foote *Annals of King's Chapel from the Puritan Age of New England to the Present Day* 2 vols. (1882, 1896).

Forbes *Diaries*—Harriette M. Forbes *New England Diaries, Orderly Books, and Sea Journals* (1923).

Force *Am. Archives* (or *Force*)—Peter Force (ed.) *American Archives* . . . 4th series 6 vols. (1837–1846).

Ford *Dickinson*—Paul Leicester Ford (ed.) *The Writings of John Dickinson* (1895).

Ford *Webb*—Worthington C. Ford (ed.) *Correspondence and Journals of Samuel Blachley Webb* 3 vols. (1893–1894).

Ford "Wilkes and Boston"—Worthington C. Ford "John Wilkes and Boston" *M.H.S. Proc.* LXVII 190–215.

Ford *William Lee*—Worthington C. Ford (ed.) *Letters of William Lee* 2 vols. (1891).

Fortescue *History*—John W. Fortescue *A History of the British Army* III (1911).

Fothergill—Betsy C. Corner and Christopher C. Booth (eds.) *Chain of Friendship: Selected Letters of Dr. John Fothergill* . . . (1971).

Fox *Fothergill*—Richard Hingston Fox *Dr. John Fothergill and His Friends* . . . (1919).

Francis *Letters*—Beata Francis and Eliza Keary (eds.) *The Francis Letters* . . . 2 vols. (1901).

Franklin, Benjamin—See Bigelow, Crane, Labaree, Smyth, Sparks.

Franklin—Leonard W. Labaree et al. (eds.) *The Papers of Benjamin Franklin* (1959–1972).

"Franklin's Accounts"—Worthington C. Ford "Franklin's Accounts against Massachusetts" *M.H.S. Proc.* LVI (1926) 64–120.

Freehling "Founding Fathers and Slavery"—William W. Freehling "The Founding Fathers and Slavery" *A.H.R.* LXXVII (1972) 81–93.

Freeman *Washington*—Douglas Southall Freeman *George Washington* . . . *Planter and Patriot* (1951) vol. 3 of Freeman *Washington*.

Freiberg "Bollan"—Malcolm Freiberg "William Bollan, Agent of Massachusetts" *More Books: The Monthly Bulletin of the Boston Public Library* XIII (1948) 43–220 *passim*.

Freiberg "Footnote"—Malcolm Freiberg "Footnote to a Riot . . ." *Old-Time New England* col. 48 (1958) 105–106.

Freiberg "Governor Hutchinson"—Malcolm Freiberg "How to Become a Colonial Governor: Thomas Hutchinson of Massachusetts" *The Review of Politics* XXI (1959) 646–656.

Freiberg "Hutchinson and the Currency"—Malcolm Freiberg "Thomas Hutchinson and the Province Currency" *New Eng. Q.* XXX (1957) 190–208.

Freiberg "Letter"—Malcolm Freiberg "Missing: One Hutchinson Autograph Letter" *Manuscripts* VIII (1956) 179–184.

Freiberg "Thomas Hutchinson"—Malcolm Freiberg "Thomas Hutchinson: The First Fifty Years (1711–1761)" 3 *W. & M.Q.* XV (1958) 35–55.

French *Day of Concord*—Allen French *The Day of Concord and Lexington* . . . (1925).

French *Gage*—Allen French *General Gage's Informers* . . . (1932).

Frese "Legislation on Writs of Assistance"—Joseph R. Frese "Early Parliamentary Legislation on Writs of Assistance . . ." *Col. Soc. Public.* XXXVIII 318–359.

Frese "Otis"—Joseph R. Frese "James Otis and Writs of Assistance" *New Eng. Q.* XXX (1957) 496–508.

Friedman "Disruption of Family Politics"—Bernard Friedman "The New York Assembly Elections of 1768 and 1769: The Disruption of Family Politics" *N.Y. History* XLVI (1965) 3–24.

Frothingham *Rise of the Republic*—Richard Frothingham *The Rise of the Republic of the United States* (1910).

Frothingham "Tea Party"—Richard Frothingham "Tea-Party Anniversary" *M.H.S. Proc.* for 1873–1875, 155–183.

Frothingham *Warren*—Richard Frothingham *Life and Times of Joseph Warren* (1865).

Furneaux *Letters to Blackstone*—Philip Furneaux *Letters to the Honourable Mr. Justice Blackstone* . . . (London, 1770). My citations are to the Philadelphia, 1773, edition.

Ga. Col. Rec.—Allen D. Candler (ed.) *The Colonial Records of the State of Georgia* 26 vols. (1904–1916).

Ga. Hist. Q.—*The Georgia Historical Quarterly.*

Ga. Rev. Records—Allen D. Candler (ed.) *The Revolutionary Records of the State of Georgia* 3 vols. (1908).

Gadsden—Richard Walsh (ed.) *The Writings of Christopher Gadsden 1746–1805* (1966).

Gage—See Alden *Gage* and French *Gage.*

Gage—Clarence E. Carter (ed.) *The Correspondence of General Thomas Gage* . . . *1763–1775* 2 vols. (1931, 1933).

"Galloway" (Baldwin)—Ernest H. Baldwin "Joseph Galloway, The Loyalist Politician" *Pa. Mag. Hist.* XXVI (1902) 161–191, 289–321, 417–442.

Galloway *Candid Examination*—Joseph Galloway *A Candid Examination of the Mutual Claims of Great Britain and the Colonies* (New York, 1775), reprinted in Jensen *Tracts* 350–399.

"Galloway's Letters"—"Some Letters of Joseph Galloway, 1774–1775" *Pa. Mag. Hist.* XXI (1897) 481–482.

Gimbel *Common Sense*—Richard Gimbel *Thomas Paine a Bibliographical Check List of Common Sense* . . . (1956).

Gipson *Brit. Empire*—Lawrence H. Gipson *The British Empire before the American Revolution* 9 vols. (1936–1956).

Gipson *Coming of Revolution*—Lawrence H. Gipson *The Coming of the Revolution, 1763–1775* (1954).

Gipson *Guide*—Lawrence H. Gipson *A Bibliographical Guide to the History of the British Empire 1748–1776* (1959) vol. XIV of Gipson *Brit. Empire.* (indispensable).

Gipson *Ingersoll*—Lawrence H. Gipson *Jared Ingersoll* . . . (1920).

Gipson "The Great Debate"—Lawrence H. Gipson "The Great Debate . . . on the Stamp Act, 1766, as Reported by Nathaniel Ryder" *Pa. Mag. Hist.* LXXXVI (1962) 10–41.

Gipson "Virginia Planter Debts"—Lawrence H. Gipson "Virginia Planter Debts before the American Revolution" *Va. Mag.* LXIX (1961) 259–277.

Goebel "French West Indies"—Dorothy Burne Goebel "The 'New England Trade' and the French West Indies, 1763–1774 . . ." 3 *W. & M.Q.* XX (1963) 331–372.

Good Humour or a Way with the Colonies—*Good Humour or a Way with the Colonies; wherein Mr. P—tt's popularity is enquired into* (London, 1766) by an unidentified author. Benjamin Franklin's annotations of it are in Sparks *Franklin* IV 212—215.

"Garth"—Joseph W. Barnwell and Theodore D. Jervey (eds.) "Garth Correspondence" *So. Car. Hist. Mag.* XXVIII–XXXIII *passim.*

"Gaspee Doc."—"Gaspee Documents" *Proceedings of the Rhode Island Historical Society 1890–91* (1891).

"Gaspee Papers"—*Publications of the Rhode Island Historical Society* New series VII (1900) 238–240.

Gentleman's Mag.—*The Gentlemen's Magazine and Historical Chronicle* (London, 1731–1775).

Geo. III—Sir John Fortescue *The Correspondence of King George the Third* . . . 6 vols. (1927–1928). Volume I, covering the years 1760–1767, of this wretchedly edited work has been corrected in Namier *Additions,* which should be consulted constantly in using this volume.

Gerlach *Schuyler*—Don R. Gerlach *Philip Schuyler . . . 1733–1777* (1964).

Gerry—James T. Austin *The Life of Elbridge Gerry* . . . (1828).

Gibbs *Doc. Hist.*—Robert W. Gibbes *Documentary History of the American Revolution . . . in South Carolina* . . . (1855).

Gibbon (Norton)—James E. Norton *The Letters of Edward Gibbon* 3 vols. (1956).

Giesecke *Am. Col. Legis. before 1789*—Albert A. Giesecke *American Commercial Legislation before 1789* (1910).

Goodell "Samuel Adams"—A. G. Goodell "Charges Against Samuel Adams" *M.H.S. Proc.* XX (1883) 213–226.

Goodman *Am. Overture*—Abram V. Goodman *American Overture: Jewish Rights in Colonial Times* (1947).

"Gordon"—William Gordon's letter of May 17, 1775, 4 *Force* II 625–631.

Gordon *History*—William Gordon *The History of the Rise, Progress and Establishment of the Independence of the United States* . . . 3 vols. (1794), first published in 1788.

Goss *Revere*—Elbridge H. Goss *The Life of Colonel Paul Revere* . . . 2 vols. (1906).

Grace *Johnson*—George C. Grace, Jr. *William Samuel Johnson a Maker of the Constitution* (1937).

Grafton—William R. Anson (ed.) *Autobiography and Political Correspondence of Augustus Henry Third Duke of Grafton* (1898).

Grant *James Grant*—Alistair Macpherson Grant *General James Grant of Ballindalloch, 1720–1806* . . . [1930].

Gray "Notes"—Horace Gray "Notes and Appendix" in Quincy *Reports* 395–540.

Green *Short History*—John R. Green *A Short History of the English People* 4 vols. (1895).

Greene "Bridge to Revolution"—Jack P. Greene "Bridge to Revolution: The Wilkes Fund Controversy in South Carolina, 1769–1775" *Journal So. Hist.* XXIX (1963) 19–52.

Greene "Not to be Governed"—Jack P. Greene "Not to be Governed Or Taxed but by . . . Our Representatives, Four Essays by Landon Carter" *Va. Mag.* LXXVI (1968) 259–300.

Greene "Political Mimesis"—Jack P. Greene "Political Mimesis: A Consideration of the Historical and Cultural Roots of Legislative Behavior in the British Colonies in the Eighteenth Century" *A.H.R.* LXXV (1969) 337–360.

Greene *Provincial Governor*—Evarts B. Greene *The Provincial Governor* . . . (1898).

Greene *Quest for Power*—Jack P. Greene *The Quest for Power* . . . *Southern Colonies 1689–1776* (1963).

Greene and Jellison "Currency Act of 1764"—Jack P. Greene and Richard M. Jellison "The Currency Act of 1764 in Imperial–Colonial Relations, 1764–1766" 3 *W. & M.Q.* XVIII (1961) 485–518.

Greenough *New Eng. Almanacs*—Chester N. Greenough *New England Almanacs 1776–1775* . . . (1936) reprint from *Am. Antiq. Soc. Proc.* for Oct., 1935.

Grenville—William James Smith (ed.) *The Grenville Papers* . . . 4 vols. (1852–1853).

Grenville Papers (Tomlinson)—John R. G. Tomlinson *Additional Grenville Papers 1763–1765* (1962).

Griffin *Junius*—Frederick Griffin *Junius* [Thomas Pownall] *Discovered* (1854).

Guttridge *Champion*—George H. Guttridge *The American Correspondence* . . . *1766–1776* . . . *of Richard Champion* (1934).

Guttridge *Hartley*—George H. Guttridge *David Hartley, M.P. an Advocate of Conciliation 1774–1783* (1926).

Guttridge "Pownall's *Administration of the Colonies*"—George H. Guttridge "Thomas Pownall's *The Administration of the Colonies*: the Six Editions" 3 *W. & M.Q.* XXVI (1969) 31–46.

Guttridge *Rockingham*—George H. Guttridge *The Early Career of Lord Rockingham 1730–1765* (1952).

Gwatkin *Letter to the Clergy*—Thomas Gwatkin *A Letter to the Clergy of New York and New Jersey* . . . (Williamsburg, 1762).

H. & L. Dict.—*Dictionary of Anonymous and Pseudonymous English Literature* (Samuel Halkett and John Laing, eds.) 7 vols. (1926–1934).

H.M.C.—*Historical Manuscripts Commission.* See Pargellis and Medley *Bibliography* 507–529 for full description of this series.

Hamilton *Letters to Washington*—Stanislaus M. Hamilton (ed.) *Letters to Washington* . . . 5 vols. (1898–1902).

Hancock, John—See Allan *Hancock;* Brown *Hancock;* and Baxter *Hancock.*

Hancock *Oration*—John Hancock *An Oration; Delivered March 5, 1774* . . . (Boston, 1774).

Handlin "Burgh"—Oscar and Mary Handlin "James Burgh and American Revolutionary Theory" *M.H.S. Proc.* LXXIII (1963) 38–57.

Hanks and Perry *Conn.*—Frances L. Hanks and William Stevens Perry (eds.) *Documentary History of the Protestant Episcopal Church* . . . *Connecticut* 2 vols. (1863, 1864).

Harper "Mercantilism"—Lawrence A. Harper "Mercantilism and the American Revolution" *Can. H.R.* XXIII (1942) 1015.

Harper *Navig. Laws*—Lawrence A. Harper *The English Navigation Laws* . . . (1919).

Harrell *Loyalism in Va.*—Isaac S. Harrell *Loyalism in Virginia: Chapters in the Economic History of the Revolution.*

Harrington *N.Y. Merchant*—Virginia D. Harrington *The New York Merchant on the Eve of the Revolution* (1935).

Hartley (Guttridge)—George H. Guttridge *David Hartley, M.P. an Advocate of Conciliation 1774–1783* (1926).

Harv. Law Rev.—*Harvard Law Review.*

Harvard Quinquennial Catalogue—*Harvard Quinquennial Catalogue* . . . *1636–1930* (1930).

Hassam "Register of Probate"—John T. Hassam "Register of Probate for the County of Suffolk, Massachusetts 1639–1799" 2 *M.H.S. Proc.* XVI (1903) 23–125.

Hastings *N.Y. Ecclesiastical Records*—Hugh Hastings (ed.) *Ecclesiastical Records State of New York* vol. VI (1905).

Hawkins *Historical Notices*—Ernest Hawkins *Historical Notices of the Missions of the Church of England in the North American Colonies* (1845).

Heimert *Religion*—Alan Heimert *Religion and the American Mind from the Great Awakening to The Revolution* (1966).

Heneker *Seignioral Regime*—Dorothy Heneker *The Seignioral Regime in Canada* (1927).

Hening *Va.*—William W. Hening (ed.) *The Statutes at Large of Virginia* 13 vols. (1809–1823).

Hersey "Malcom"—Frank W. C. Hersey "Tar and Feathers: . . . John Malcom" *Col. Soc. Publ.* XXXIV 429–473.

Hickman "Writs"—Emily Hickman "Colonial Writs of Assistance" *New Eng. Q.* V (1932) 83–104.

Hicks *Parl. Power*—William Hicks *The Nature and Extent of Parliamentary Power* . . . (New York, 1768) in Jensen *Tracts* 164–184.

Hildeburn *A Century of Printing in Pa.*—Charles R. Hildeburn *A Century of Printing . . . in Pennsylvania 1685–1784* 2 vols. (1885).

Hinkhouse *Preliminaries*—Fred J. Hinkhouse *The Preliminaries of the American Revolution as Seen in the English Press 1763–1775* (1926).

Hinsdale *Old Northwest*—Burke A. Hinsdale *The Old Northwest . . . As Constituted by the Royal Charters* (1888).

Hisp. Am. Hist. Rev.—*The Hispanic American Historical Review.*

Hist. Mag. Prot. Episc. Church—*Historical Magazine (Quarterly) of the Protestant Episcopal Church.* . . .

Hist. Statistics—*Historical Statistics of the United States, Colonial Times to 1957* (U.S. Bureau of the Census, 1960).

History Today (published monthly in London).

Hoffman *Burke*—Ross J. S. Hoffman *Edmund Burke, New York Agent with His Letters to the New York Assembly and Intimate Correspondence with Charles O'Hara, 1761–1776* (1956).

Holdsworth *Hist. of Eng. Law*—William Holdsworth *A History of English Law* 13 vols. (1922–1952).

Holland *Dawes*—Henry W. Holland *William Dawes and His Ride with Paul Revere* (1878).

Home Office Pap.—Joseph Redington and Richard A. Roberts (eds.) *Calendar of Home Office Papers . . . for 1760 to 1775* 4 vols. (1878–1899).

Honeyman's Journal—Philip Padelford (ed.) *Colonial Panorama 1775: Dr. Robert Honeyman's Journal for March and April* (1939).

Hooker "Wine Glass"—Richard J. Hooker "The American Revolution Seen Through a Wine Glass" 3 *W. & M.Q.* XI (1954) 52–77.

Hopkins *Rights of Colonies*—Stephen Hopkins *The Rights of Colonies Examined* (Providence, R.I., 1765 [actually December, 1764]).

Horsman *Elliott*—Reginald Horsman *Matthew Elliott, British Indian Agent* (1964).

Hosack *Williamson*—David Hosack *A Biographical Memoir of Hugh Williamson* (1820).

Hosmer *Hutchinson*—James K. Hosmer *The Life of Thomas Hutchinson* . . . (1896).

Hough *Cases*—Charles M. Hough (ed.) *Reports of Cases in . . . Admiralty . . . New York* (1925).

Hulton Letters—*Letters of a Loyalist Lady . . . Anne Hulton . . . at Boston . . . 1767–1776* (1927).

Hume *History of England*—David Hume *The History of England* . . . 6 vols. (1754–1761 and two other editions by 1765).

Humphreys "Shelburne and Brit. Col. Policy" R. A. Humphreys "Lord Shelburne and British Colonial Policy 1766–1768" *E.H.R.* L (1935) 257–277.

Hunt. Lib. Q.—_Huntington Library Quarterly._

Huntley "Seaborne Trade of Va."—Francis C. Huntley "The Seaborne Trade of Virginia in Mid-Eighteenth Century: Port Hampton" _Va. Mag. Hist._ (July, 1951) 298–305.

Hutchinson _Diary_—Peter Orlando Hutchinson (ed.) _The Diary and Letters of His Excellency Thomas Hutchinson_ 2 vols. (1884, 1886).

Hutchinson _Hist. of Mass._—Lawrence S. Mayo (ed.) _The History of the Colony and Province of Massachusetts-Bay_ by _Thomas Hutchinson_ . . . (1936) reprint of earlier editions (I—1764, II—1767, III—1828).

Hutchinson _Letters to Great Britain_—Copy of Letters sent to Great-Britain by . . . Thomas Hutchinson and . . . Other Persons . . . (Boston, 1773).

Hutson "Investigation of the Inarticulate"—James H. Hutson "An Investigation of the Inarticulate: Philadelphia's White Oaks" 3 _W. & M.Q._ XXVIII (1971) 3–25.

Hutson "Pennsylvania"—James H. Hutson "The Campaign to Make Pennsylvania a Royal Province, 1764–1770" _Pa. Mag. Hist._ XCIV (1970) 427–463 and XCV (1971) 28–49.

Ilchester _Fox_—Lord Ilchester _Henry Fox, First Lord Holland_ . . . 2 vols. (1920).

Ill. State Hist. Lib. Coll.—_Collections of the Illinois State Historical Library._

"Ingersoll Letters"—Franklin B. Dexter (ed.) "A Selection from the Correspondence and Miscellaneous Papers of Jared Ingersoll" _New Haven Hist. Soc. Papers_ IX 201–472.

Iredell (McRee)—Griffith J. McRee _Life and Correspondence of James Iredell_ . . . 2 vols. in one (1949).

Izard—Anne Izard Deas (compiler) _Correspondence of Mr. Ralph Izard of South Carolina_ . . . _1774 to 1804_ . . . I (1844).

_J.A.H._—_The Journal of American History_ (continuation of the _Miss. Vall. H.R._).

Jackson—Carl Van Doren (ed.) _Letters and Papers of Benjamin Franklin and Richard Jackson_ (1947).

Jacobson _Dickinson_—David L. Jacobson _John Dickinson and the Revolution in Pennsylvania 1764–1776_ (1965).

James "Irish Colonial Trade"—Francis G. James "Irish Colonial Trade in the Eighteenth Century" 3 _W. & M.Q._ XX (1963) 544–584.

Jameson _American Revolution_—J. [John] Franklin Jameson _The American Revolution Considered as a Social Movement_ (1926).

Jefferson (Boyd)—See Boyd _Jefferson._

Jefferson _Summary View_—[Thomas Jefferson] _A Summary View of the Rights of British America_ . . . (Williamsburg [1774]), in 4 _Force_ I 690–699. (As to date and authorship, Boyd _Jefferson_ I 669–676.)

Jenkinson—Ninetta S. Jucker (ed.) _The Jenkinson Papers, 1760–1766_ (1949).

Jensen _Articles of Confederation_—Merrill Jensen _The Articles of Confederation_ . . . _1774–1781_ (1948).

Jensen "Democracy"—Merrill Jensen "Democracy and the American Revolution" _Hunt Lib. Q._ XX (1957) 321–341.

Jensen _Founding_—Merrill Jensen _The Founding of a Nation_ . . . _1763–1776_ (1968).

Jensen _Hist. Doc._—Merrill Jensen (ed.) _American Colonial Documents to 1776_ (1955) vol. 9 of _English Historical Documents._

Jensen _Philadelphia_—Arthur L. Jensen _The Maritime Commerce of Colonial Philadelphia_ (1963).

Jensen _Tracts_—Merrill Jensen (ed.) _Tracts of the American Revolution 1763–1776_ (1967).

Jervey "Trecothick"—Theodore D. Jervey "Barlow Trecothick" _So. Car. Hist. Mag._ XXXII (1931) 157–169.

Jesse *Selwyn*—John H. Jesse *George Selwyn and His Contemporaries* . . . 4 vols. (1843–1884).

Johnson—*The Papers of Sir William Johnson* (various editors) 13 vols. (1921–1962).

Johnson *Taxation no Tyranny*—[Samuel Johnson] *Taxation no Tyranny: An Answer to the Resolutions and Address of the American Congress* (London, 1775) in 4 *Force* I 1431–1449.

Johnson and Syrett "The *New York Affair*"—Herbert A. Johnson and David Syrett "Some Nice Sharp Quillets . . . The *New York* Affair, 1763–1767" 3 *W. & M.Q.* XXV (1968) 432–451.

Jones *Hist. of N.Y.*—Edward F. DeLancey (ed.) *History of New York during the Revolutionary War . . . by Thomas Jones* . . . 2 vols. (1879).

Jones *Loyalists of N.J.*—E. [Edward] Alfred Jones *The Loyalists of New Jersey* (1927).

Jones *Loyalists of Mass.*—E. [Edward] Alfred Jones *The Loyalists of Massachusetts* . . . (1930).

Jones *St. Peter's*—William Northey Jones *The History of St. Peter's Church in Perth Amboy, New Jersey* . . . (1924).

Jordan *White over Black*—Winthrop D. Jordan *White over Black: American Attitudes Towards the Negro, 1550–1812* (1968).

Journal Am. Hist.—The *Journal of American History* (formerly *The Mississippi Valley Historical Review*).

Journal B. of T.—*Journal of the Commissioners for Trade and Plantations* [1704–1782] 14 vols. (1920–1938).

Journal Economic Hist.—The *Journal of Economic History*.

Journal So. Hist.—The *Journal of Southern History*.

Journals Cont. Cong.—Worthington C. Ford (ed.) *Journals of the Continental Congress* . . . vols. 1–3 (1904–1905).

Journals H. of C.—*Journals of the House of Commons*.

Journals H. of L.—*Journals of the House of Lords*.

Judd *Members*—Gerrit P. Judd *Members of Parliament, 1734–1832* (1955).

Junius—*Junius* (London, 1772), collection of Junius' letters published by Henry Sampson Woodfall.

Kaestle "Farmer's Letters"—Carl F. Kaestle "The Public Reaction to John Dickinson's Farmer's Letters" *Am. Antiq. Soc. Proc.* LXXVIII part 2 (1969) 323–359.

Kammen *Agents*—Michael G. Kammen *A Rope of Sand: The Colonial Agents* . . . (1968).

"Kemble"—"Journals of Lieut.-Col. Stephen Kemble" *N.Y.H.S. Coll.* for 1883 1–247.

Kemmerer *N.J.*—Donald L. Kemmerer *Path to Freedom . . . N.J. 1703–1776* (1940).

Keppel—Thomas Keppel *The Life of Augustus Viscount Keppel* (1842).

Kerr "Newfoundland"—Wilfred B. Kerr "Newfoundland in the Period before the American Revolution" *Pa. Mag. Hist.* LXV (1941) 56–78.

Kidder *Boston Massacre*—Frederic Kidder *History of the Boston Massacre* . . . (1870).

Kimball *R.I.*—Gertrude Selwyn Kimball (ed.) *The Correspondence of the Colonial Governors of Rhode Island 1723–1775* 2 vols. (1902–1903).

Kirtland *Letters*—Frederick R. Kirtland *Letters on the American Revolution* . . . (1941).

Klein "Democracy"—Milton M. Klein "Democracy and Politics in Colonial New York" *N.Y. History* XL (1959) 221–246.

Klein *Independent Reflector*—Milton M. Klein *The Independent Reflector* . . . (1963).

Klein "Prelude to Revolution in N.Y."—Milton M. Klein "Prelude to Revolution in New York: Jury Trials and Judicial Tenure" 3 *W. & M.Q.* XVII (1960) 439–462.

Klingberg *Anti-Slavery Movement in England*—Frank Klingberg *The Anti-Slavery Movement in England* (1926).

Knollenberg "Dickinson vs. Adams"—Bernhard Knollenberg "John Dickinson vs. John Adams: 1774–1776" *Am. Phil. Soc. Proc.* CI (1963) 138–144.

Knollenberg "Franklin and the Hutchinson Letters"—Bernhard Knollenberg "Benjamin Franklin and the Hutchinson and Oliver Letters" *Yale Lib. Gazette* XLVII (1972) 1–9.

Knollenberg *Franklin, Williams and Pitt*—Bernhard Knollenberg *Franklin, Jonathan Williams and William Pitt, A Letter of January 21, 1775* (1949).

Knollenberg "Hollis and Mayhew"—Bernhard Knollenberg (ed.) "Thomas Hollis and Jonathan Mayhew, Their Correspondence, 1759–1766" *M.H.S. Proc.* LXIX 102–193.

Knollenberg *Origin*—Bernhard Knollenberg *Origin of the American Revolution: 1759–1765* (1960), reprinted, with a few changes in 1961 and in later paperback editions. Unless otherwise noted, citations are to the original (1960) edition.

Knollenberg "Sage Brush Rule"—Bernhard Knollenberg "Sage Brush Rule" *Atlantic Monthly* CXLIX (1932) 289–295.

Knollenberg "Samuel Adams"—Bernhard Knollenberg "Did Samuel Adams Provoke the Boston Tea Party and the Clash at Lexington?" *Am. Antiq. Soc. Proc.* LXX (1960) 493–503.

Knollenberg "Stiles"—Bernhard Knollenberg "Ezra Stiles on British Taxation of the Colonies" *Yale Lib. Gazette* XXI (1947) 18–27.

Knollenberg *Ward*—Bernhard Knollenberg (ed.) *Correspondence of Governor Samuel Ward, May 1775–March 1776* (1952).

Knollenberg *Washington*—Bernhard Knollenberg *George Washington, The Virginia Period, 1732–1775* (1964).

Knollenberg *Washington and the Revolution*—*Washington and the Revolution: A Reappraisal* (1940).

Knox—*H.M.S. Various Reports* VI (1909) including many letters to William Knox 1766–1775.

Knox *Controversy*—William Knox *The Controversy between Great Britain and Her Colonies Reviewed* . . . (London, 1769).

Kuntzleman *Galloway*—Oliver C. Kuntzleman *Joseph Galloway, Loyalist* (1941).

Labaree [Benjamin] *Patriots and Partisans*—Benjamin W. Labaree *Patriots and Partisans The Merchants of Newburyport 1764–1815* (1962).

Labaree [Benjamin] *Tea Party*—Benjamin W. Labaree *The Boston Tea Party* (1964).

Labaree [Leonard] *Conservatism*—Leonard Labaree *Conservatism in Early American History* (1948).

Labaree [Leonard] *Franklin*—See *Franklin*.

Labaree [Leonard] *Instructions*—Leonard W. Labaree *Royal Instructions* . . . 2 vols. (1935).

Labaree [Leonard] *Royal Government*—Leonard W. Labaree *Royal Government in America* (1930).

Lanctot *Canada*—Gustave Lanctot *Canada and the American Revolution 1744–1783* (1967).

Land *The Dulanys*—Aubrey C. Land *The Dulanys of Maryland* . . . (1955).

Laprade *Robinson*—William T. Laprade *Parliamentary Papers of John Robinson 1774–1784* (1922).

Launitz-Schurer "De Lanceys"—Leopold S. Launitz-Schurer "Whig-Loyalists: The De Lanceys of New York" *N.Y.H.S.Q.* LVI (1972) 179–198.

Law—Albert C. Bates (ed.) *The Law Papers Conn. Hist. Soc. Coll.* XI, XIII, XV (1907–1914).

Leake *Lamb*—Isaac K. Leake *Memoir of the Life and Times of General John Lamb* (1850).

Lee *Arthur Lee*—Richard Henry Lee *Life of Arthur Lee LL.D.* 2 vols. (1829).

Lee Papers—The [Charles] Lee Papers, Vol. I 1754–1776, N.Y. Hist. Soc. Coll. for 1871 (1872).

Lee *Richard H. Lee*—Richard Henry Lee *Memoir of the Life of Richard Henry Lee and His Correspondence* . . . 2 vols. (1825).

Lemisch "Jack Tar in the Streets"—Jesse Lemisch "Jack Tar in the Streets: Merchant Seaman in the Politics of Revolutionary America" 3 *W. & M.Q.* XXV (1968) 371–407.

Lemisch "White Oaks"—Jesse Lemisch, John and K. Alexander "The White Oaks, Jack Tar and the Concept of the 'Inarticulate'" with a Note by Simeon J. Crowthea and a Rebuttal by James H. Hutson" 3 *W. & M.Q.* XXIX (1972) 109–142.

Leslie "Gaspee Affair"—William R. Leslie "The Gaspee Affair: A Study of Its Constitutional Significance" *Miss. Vall. H.R.* XXXIX (1953) 233–256.

Letter to W. F.—Benjamin Franklin to William Franklin March 22, 1775, in Smyth *Franklin* VI 318–399.

Letters to Hillsborough—Letters to the Right Honorable the Earl of Hillsborough from Governor Bernard . . . (Boston, 1769).

Letters to Ministry—Letters to the Ministry from Governor Bernard . . . (London, 1769).

Lettsom *Fothergill*—John C. Lettsom *Memoirs of John Fothergill M.D.* (1876).

Lewis *Walpole*—Wilmarth S. Lewis (ed.-in-chief) *The Yale Edition of Horace Walpole's Correspondence* (1937–).

"Lexington" (Tyler)—J. E. Tyler "An Account of Lexington" 3 *W. & M.Q.* X (1953) 99–107.

Lincoln *Rev. Movement in Pa.*—Charles H. Lincoln *The Revolutionary Movement in Pennsylvania 1760–1776* (1901).

Lincoln *Shirley*—Charles H. Lincoln (ed.) *Correspondence of William Shirley* . . . *1731–1760* 2 vols. (1912).

List of Voters in Commons Against Repeal—A List of the Members of the House of Commons Who Voted Against the Bill to Repeal the American Stamp Act (1766).

Litto "Cato"—Fredric M. Litto "Addison's *Cato* in the Colonies" 3 *W. & M.Q.* XXIII (1966) 431–449.

Livingston (Dangerfield)—George Dangerfield *Chancellor Robert R. Livingston of New York 1746–1813* (1960).

Livingston *Livingston*—Edwin B. Livingston *The Livingstons of Livingston Manor* . . . (1910).

Lloyd *Conduct of the Late Administration*—Charles Lloyd *The Conduct of the Late Administration Examined. With an Appendix Containing Original and Authentic Documents* London, dated 1767 (but published Dec. 20, 1766, as advertised in the *London Chronicle* of that date).

Locke *Two Treatises of Government*—John Locke *Two Treatises of Government*. My citations are to the London (1887) edition.

Lockmiller *Blackstone*—David A. Lockmiller *Sir William Blackstone* (1938).

London Chronicle—The London Chronicle: or, Universal Evening Post (1757–1775).

London Gazetteer—Gazetteer and New Daily Advertiser (London).

London Mag.—The London Magazine; or, Gentleman's Monthly Intelligencer (1732–1775).

Long *Amherst*—John C. Long *Lord Jeffery Amherst a Soldier of the King* (1933).

Lonn *Agents of Southern Colonies*—Ella Lonn *The Colonial Agents of the Southern Colonies* (1945).

Lord *Industrial Experiments*—Eleanor L. Lord *Industrial Experiments in the British Colonies of North America* (1896).

Lord and Calhoun "Removal of the Mass. General Court"—Donald C. Lord and Robert M. Calhoun "The Removal of the Massachusetts General Court from Boston 1769–1772" *Journ. Am. Hist.* LV (1969) 735–755.

Lothian—H.M.C. *Report on the Manuscripts of the Marquess of Lothian* (1905).

Love *Fast Days*—William DeLoss Love *The Fast and Thanksgiving Days of New England* (1895).

Lovejoy "Case Against Admiralty Jurisdiction" David S. Lovejoy "Rights Imply Equality: The Case Against Admiralty Jurisdiction in America, 1774–1776" 3 *W. & M.Q.* XVI (1959) 459–484.

Lovejoy *R.I. Politics*—David S. Lovejoy *Rhode Island Politics and the American Revolution 1760–1776* (1958).

Lucas *Lord North*—Reginald Lucas *Lord North, Second Earl of Guilford, K.G., 1732–1792* (1913).

Lundin *N.J.*—Leonard Lundin *Cockpit of the Revolution: The War . . . in New Jersey* (1940).

Lydekker *Inglis*—John Wolfe Lydekker *The Life and Letters of Charles Inglis . . . 1759 to 1787* (1936).

Lynd *Dutchess County*—Staughton Lynd *Anti-Federalism in Dutchess County, New York* (1962).

Lynd "Mechanics in N.Y."—Staughton Lynd "The Mechanics in New York Politics, 1774–1801" *Labor History* V (1964) 225–246.

Lynd "Who Should Rule at Home"—Staughton Lynd "Who Should Rule at Home? Dutchess County, New York, in the American Revolution" 3 *W. & M.Q.* XVIII (1961) 330–339.

Lynd and Young "After Carl Becker"—Staughton Lynd and Alfred Young "After Carl Becker: The Mechanics and New York City Politics, 1774–1801" *Labor History* V (1964) 213–224.

Lynde Diaries—*The Diaries of Benjamin Lynde and of Benjamin Lynde Jr.* (1880).

Lyttelton—Robert J. Phillimore *Memoirs and Correspondence of George, Lord Lyttelton* 2 vols. (1845).

M.H.S. (Mass. Hist. Soc. Coll.)—*Collections of the Massachusetts Historical Society.*

M.H.S. Proc. (Mass. Hist. Soc. Proc.)—*Proceedings of the Massachusetts Historical Society.*

Macalpine and Hunter "The 'Insanity' of George III"—Ida Macalpine and Richard Hunter "The 'Insanity' of King George III: a Classic Case of Porphyria" *Br. Med. Journal.*

Maccoby *English Radicalism*—Simon Maccoby *English Radicalism 1762–1785, the Origins* (1955).

Macdonald *Documentary Source Book*—William Macdonald (ed.) *Documentary Source Book of American History 1606–1898* (1908).

Mackenzie—*Diary of Frederick Mackenzie . . . of Royal Welsh Fusiliers* 2 vols. (1930).

Macpherson *Annals*—David Macpherson *Annals of Commerce . . .* 4 vols. (1805).

Macpherson *Hist. of Commerce with India*—David Macpherson *The History of the European Commerce with India . . .* (1812).

Madison—Irving Brant *James Madison: The Revolutionist* (1941).

Madison—William T. Hutchinson and William M. E. Rachal (eds.) *The Papers of James Madison* vol. I (1962).

Mag. Am. Hist.—*The Magazine of American History with Notes and Queries.*

Mahon *Chesterfield*—Philip H. Stanhope, Lord Mahon, *The Letters of Philip Dormer Stanhope, Earl of Chesterfield* . . . 5 vols. (1892).

Mahon *Hist. of Eng.*—Lord Mahon (Philip H. Stanhope) *History of England 1713–1783* 7 vols. (1892).

Maier "Popular Uprisings in America"—Pauline Maier "Popular Uprisings and Civil Authority in Eighteenth-Century America" 3 *W. & M.Q.* XXVII (1970) 3–35.

Maier *Resistance*—Pauline Maier *From Resistance to Revolution* . . . *1765–1776* (1972).

Maier "Wilkes"—Pauline Maier "John Wilkes and American Disallusionment with Britain" 3 *W. & M.Q.* XX (1963) 373–395.

Main *Social Structure*—Jackson Turner Main *Social Structure of Revolutionary America* (1965).

Main *Upper House*—Jackson T. Main *The Upper House in Revolutionary America: 1763–1788* (1967).

Malone *Pine Trees*—Joseph J. Malone *Pine Trees and Politics: The Naval Stores and Forest Policy in Colonial New England, 1691–1775* (1964).

Manning *Dissenting Deputies*—Bernard Lord Manning *The Protestant Dissenting Deputies* (1952).

Mark *Agrarian Conflicts*—Irving Mark *Agrarian Conflicts in New York 1711–1775* (1940).

Marshall—*Passages from the Remembrancer of Christopher Marshall* William Duane, ed. (1877).

Martin *Empire*—Chester Martin *Empire & Commonwealth* . . . *Canada* (1929).

Martin "King's Customs"—Alfred S. Martin "The King's Customs, Philadelphia 1763–1774" 3 *W. & M.Q.* V (1948) 201–216.

Mason "Becker"—Bernard Mason "The Heritage of Carl Becker: The Historiography of the Revolution in New York" *N.Y.H.S.Q.* LIII (1969) 127–147.

Mason *Road to Independence*—Bernard Mason *The Road to Independence: The Revolutionary Movement in New York, 1773–1777* (1966).

Mason (Rutland)—Robert A. Rutland (ed.) *The Papers of George Mason 1725–1792* vol. I (*1749–1778*) (1970).

Mass. Acts—*Acts and Resolves of the Province of the Massachusetts Bay* 5 vols. (1869–1886).

Mass. Broadsides—*Broadsides, Ballads, etc. Printed in Massachusetts 1639–1800* M.H.S. *Coll.* LXXV (1922).

Mass. Civil List—William H. Whitmore (ed.) *The Massachusetts Civil List for the Colonial and Provincial Periods 1630–1774* . . . (1870).

Mass. Congress Journals—William Lincoln (ed.) *The Journals of Each Provincial Congress of Massachusetts in 1774 and 1775* . . . (1838).

Mass. Gazette (Draper)—*The Massachusetts Gazette, and Boston News-Letter* published by Richard Draper April 7, 1763–1775. For various changes of name: Brigham *Am. Newspapers* I 328.

Mass. Gazette (Mills and Hicks)—*The Massachusetts Gazette; and the Boston Post-Boy and Advertiser* published by Nathaniel Mills and John Hicks (1773–1775); Brigham *Am. Newspapers* I 335.

Mass. Journals—*Journals of the Honourable House of Representatives of His Majesty's Province of the Massachusetts-Bay in New-England* the Massachusetts Society reprint for 1715–1756 32 vols. (1919–1958).

Mass. Papers—*Papers Relating to Public Events in Massachusetts Preceding the American Revolution* (1856).

Mass. Spy—*The Massachusetts Spy* (later with the addition *Or Thomas's Boston Journal*) Boston, July 17, 1770–Apr. 6, 1775.

Mass. Spy (Worcester)—*The Massachusetts Spy Or, American Oracle of Liberty,* Worcester, Mass., May 3, 1775–1820.

Mathews *Dictionary*—Milford M. Mathews (ed.) *A Dictionary of Americanisms* . . . 2 vols. (1951).

Matthews "Book of America"—Albert Matthews "The Book of America" *Mass. Hist. Soc. Proc.* LXII (1930) 171–197.

Matthews "De Berdt"—Albert Matthews "Letters of Dennys De Berdt, 1757–1770" *Col. Soc. Publ.* XIII (1912) 293–461.

Matthews "Mass. Royal Council"—Albert Matthews "Documents Relating to the Last Meetings of the Massachusetts Royal Council, 1774–1776" *Col. Soc. Publ.* XXXII (1931) 460–504.

Matthews "Preston"—Albert Matthews "Capt. Thomas Preston and the Boston Massacre" *Col. Soc. Publ.* VII (1906) 2–21.

Matthews "Solemn League"—Albert Matthews "The Solemn League and Covenant, 1774" *Col. Soc. Publ.* XVIII (1917) 103–122.

Mauduit—Worthington C. Ford (ed.) *Jasper Mauduit, Agent in London* . . . *for Massachusetts-Bay M.H.S. Coll.* LXXIV (1918).

Mauduit *Franklin*—[Israel Mauduit] *Franklin before the Privy Council* . . . [on] *the Removal of Hutchinson and Oliver* (1860).

Mayo *Additions*—Catherine B. Mayo (ed.) *Additions to Thomas Hutchinson's 'History'* . . . (1949).

Mayo *Amherst*—Lawrence Shaw Mayo *Jeffery Amherst a Biography* (1916).

Mayo *Langdon*—Lawrence S. Mayo *John Langdon of New Hampshire* (1937).

Mayo *Wentworth*—Lawrence S. Mayo *John Wentworth, Governor of New Hampshire 1767–1775* (1921).

Mays *Pendleton*—David J. Mays *Edmund Pendleton, 1721–1803: A Biography* 2 vols. (1952).

Mays *Pendleton Letters*—David J. Mays (ed.) *The Letters and Papers of Edmund Pendleton 1734–1803* 2 vols. (1967).

McCrady *South Carolina*—Edward McCrady *The History of South Carolina under the Royal Government 1719–1776* (1901).

McCusker "Exports"—John J. McCusker "The Current Value of English Exports 1697 to 1800" 3 *W. & M.Q.* XXVIII (1971) 607–628.

McDougall *Papers*—Papers of Alexander McDougall, N.Y. Hist. Soc.

McKee *Labor in Col. N.Y.*—Samuel McKee *Labor in Colonial New York 1664–1776* (1933).

McKinley *Suffrage*—Albert E. McKinley *The Suffrage Franchise in the English Colonies* (1905).

Md. Arch.—Jacob Hall Pleasants (ed.) *Archives of Maryland.*

Md. Hist. Mag.—*Maryland Historical Magazine.*

Meade *Henry*—Robert D. Meade *Patrick Henry: Patriot in the Making* (1957).

Mein—See Alden *John Mein, Publisher* and Alden "John Mein."

Meredith *Amory*—Gertrude E. Meredith *The Descendants of Hugh Amory 1605–1805* (1901).

Merritt "Loyalism in Deerfield Mass."—Bruce G. Merritt "Loyalism and Social Conflict in Revolutionary Deerfield, Massachusetts" *Journal Am. Hist.* LVII (1970) 277–289.

Bibliography

Metzger *The Quebec Act*—Charles H. Metzger *The Quebec Act:* *American Revolution* (1936).

Middleton *Tobacco Coast*—Arthur P. Middleton *Tobacco Coast . . .* (1953).

Miller "Mass. Convention 1768"—John C. Miller "The Massachusetts C॒ *New Eng. Q.* VII (1934) 445–474.

Miller *Origins*—John C. Miller *Origins of the American Revolution* (1943).

Miller *Sam Adams*—John C. Miller *Sam Adams Pioneer in Propaganda* (1936).

Minchinton *Politics*—Walter E. Minchinton *Politics and the Port of Bristol ॒n the Eighteenth Century* (1963).

Minchinton "Stamp Act Crisis"—Walter E. Minchinton "The Stamp Act Crisis: Bristol and Virginia" *Va. Mag.* LXXIII (1965) 145–155.

Minutes of the Convention—*Minutes of the Convention from the Synod of New York and from the Association of Connecticut . . . 1766 to 1775 . . .* David D. Field, ed. (1843).

Miss. Vall. H.R. (or *Hist. Rev.*)—*The Mississippi Valley Historical Review.*

Monaghan *Jay*—Frank Monaghan *John Jay . . . Defender of Liberty* (1935).

Montesquieu (or Secondat) *Spirit of Laws*—Charles Louis de Secondat, Baron de la Brède et de Montesquieu *De l'Esprit des lois* (1748).

Montresor—G. D. Scull (ed.) *The Montresor Journals, N.Y. Hist. Soc. Coll.* for 1881.

Morais "Sons of Liberty in N.Y."—Herbert M. Morais "The Sons of Liberty in New York" in Morris *Era* 269–289.

Morgan "Col. Ideas of Parl. Power"—Edmund S. Morgan "Colonial Ideas of Parliamentary Power, 1764–1766" 3 *W. & M.Q.* V (1948) 311–341.

Morgan *Declaration of 1764*—Edmund S. Morgan (ed.) *The New York Declaration of 1764, Old South Leaflets* No. 224 (1948).

Morgan "Hutchinson"—Edmund S. Morgan "Thomas Hutchinson and the Stamp Act" *New Eng. Q.* XXI (1948) 459–462.

Morgan *Prologue*—Edmund S. Morgan (ed.) *Prologue to Revolution Sources and Documents on the Stamp Act Crisis, 1764–1766* (1959).

Morgan "Puritan Ethic and the American Revolution"—Edmund S. Morgan "The Puritan Ethic and the American Revolution" 3 *W. & M.Q.* (1967) 3–43.

Morgan *Stamp Act*—Edmund S. and Helen M. Morgan *The Stamp Act Crisis: Prologue to Revolution* (1953).

Morgan *Stiles*—Edmund S. Morgan *The Gentle Puritan: A Life of Ezra Stiles, 1727–1795* (1962).

Morison *Sources*—Samuel E. Morison (ed.) *Sources and Documents Illustrating the American Revolution 1764–1788 . . .* (1948).

Morris *Era*—Richard B. Morris (ed.) *The Era of the American Revolution . . .* (1939).

Morris *Govt. and Labor*—Richard B. Morris *Government and Labor in Early America* (1946).

Mui "Smuggling"—Hoh-chung Mui and Lorna H. Mui "Smuggling and the British Tea Trade before 1784" *A.H.R.* LXXIV (1968–69) 44–73.

Mulkearn *Mercer Papers*—Lois Mulkearn (ed.) *George Mercer Papers Relating to the Ohio Company of Virginia* (1954).

Mullett "Classical Influences"—Charles F. Mullett "Classical Influences on the American Revolution" *Classical Journal* XXXV (1940) 92–104.

Mullett "Coke"—Charles F. Mullett "Coke and the American Revolution" *Economica* XII (1932) 457–471.

Mullett *Colonial Claims*—Charles F. Mullett *Colonial Claims to Home Rule (1764–1775)* ... (1927).

Mullett *Fundamental Law*—Charles F. Mullett *Fundamental Law and the American Revolution, 1760–1776* (1933).

Mullett *Writings of Otis*—Charles F. Mullett (ed.) *Some Political Writings of James Otis* 2 vols. (1929).

Munro *Documents*—William B. Munro (ed.) *Documents Relating to Seignioral Tenure* ... (1908).

Munro *Seignioral System*—William B. Munro *The Seignioral System in Canada* ... (1907).

Murdock *British in Boston*—Harold Murdock *The British in Boston, Being the Diary of Lieutenant John Barker 1774–1776* ... (1924).

Murdock *Nineteenth of April*—Harold Murdock *The Nineteenth of April, 1775* (1923).

Mure—See *Caldwell*, which includes the correspondence of Baron Mure of Caldwell from 1733 to 1776.

Namier *Additions*—Lewis (now Sir Lewis) B. Namier *Additions and Corrections to Sir John Fortescue's Edition of the Correspondence of King George The Third* Vol. I (1937).

Namier *England*—Lewis B. Namier *England in the Age of the American Revolution* (1930).

Namier *"Garth"*—Lewis B. Namier "Charles Garth Agent for South Carolina" *E.H.R.* LIV (1939) 632–652.

Namier *Townshend*—Sir Lewis Namier *Charles Townshend His Character and Career* (1959).

Namier and Brooke *Commons*—Lewis Namier and John Brooke *The House of Commons 1754–1790* 3 vols. (1964).

Namier and Brooke *Townshend*—Lewis Namier and John Brooke *Charles Townshend* (1964).

N.C. Col. Rec.—William L. Saunders (ed.) *The Colonial Records of North Carolina* vols. 1–11 and 23 (1886–1904).

Nelson *American Tory*—William H. Nelson *The American Tory* (1961).

Nelson *Bibliography*—William Nelson *The Controversy over the Proposition for an American Episcopate 1767–1774, A Bibliography* ... (1909).

New Eng. Hist. and Gen. Reg.—*The New England Historical and Genealogical Register.*

New Eng. Q.—*The New England Quarterly.*

New Haven Hist. Soc. Papers—*Papers of the New Haven Colony Historical Society.*

Newcastle—Mary Bateson (ed.) *A Narrative of the Changes in the Ministry 1765–1767 Told by the Duke of Newcastle* ... (1898).

Newcomer *Embattled Farmers*—Lee N. Newcomer *The Embattled Farmers: A Massachusetts Countryside in the American Revolution* (1953).

"Newell Diary"—"Diary for 1773 to the End of 1774, of Mr. Thomas Newell, Boston" *M.H.S. Proc.* XV 335–363.

New-London Gazette—*The New-London [Connecticut] Gazette* (1763–1773).

New-York Gazette—*The New-York Gazette; and the Weekly Mercury* (1769–1775).

New-York Gazette or Post-Boy—*The New-York Gazette or, the Weekly Post-Boy* (1766–1775).

New-York Gazette (Weyman's)—*The New-York Gazette* (1766–1767).

New-York Journal—*The New-York Journal; or, the General Advertiser* (1766–1776), published by John Holt.

N.H. Papers—Nathaniel Bouton and Isaac W. Hammond (eds.) *Provincial and State Papers of New Hampshire* 7 vols. (1867–1873).

Niles *Principles*—Hezekiah Niles (ed.) *Republication of the Principles and Acts of the Revolution in America* (1876).

N.J. Archives—Frederick W. Ricord and William Nelson (eds.) *New Jersey Archives, First Series, Documents Relating to the Colonial History of the State* 10 vols., (1880–1886).

Noble "Admiralty Jurisdiction"—John Noble "A Few Notes on Admiralty Jurisdiction . . . in . . . Massachusetts Bay" *Col. Soc. Public.* VIII (1906) 150–186.

Noble "Fifth of March Papers"—John Noble "Papers [concerning] . . . the Night of the Fifth of March 1770" *Col. Soc. Publ.* V 68–77 and 82.

Norris *Shelburne*—John Norris *Shelburne and Reform* (1963).

North "North"—Lord North "Lord North, the Prime Minister: A Personal Memoir" *North American Review* CLXXVI (1902) 778–791 and CLXXVII (1903) 260–277.

Norton—Frances Norton Mason (ed.) *John Norton & Sons Merchants of London and Virginia . . . Papers . . . 1750 to 1795* (1937).

Norton Gibbon—J. E. Norton (ed.) *Edward Gibbon, Letters* vol. II (1956).

"Novanglus" [John Adams]—"Novanglus" letters of Jan. 23–April 17, 1775, *Adams Works* IV 11–177.

Novanglus and Massachusettensis—[John Adams and Daniel Leonard] *Novanglus and Massachusettensis; Or Political Essays . . . 1774 and 1775* (1819).

N.Y. Assembly Journal (1691–1765)—*Journal of the Votes and Proceedings of the General Assembly of the Colony of New-York* 3 vols. (1764, 1766, 1820).

N.Y. Col. Doc.—Edmund B. O'Callaghan (ed.) *Documents Relative to the Colonial History . . . of New-York* 15 vols. (1853–1887).

N.Y. Col. Laws—*The Colonial Laws of New-York from the Year 1664 to the Revolution* 5 vols. (1894).

N.Y. Doc. Hist.—Edmund B. O'Callaghan (ed.) *The Documentary History of the State of New York* 4 vols. (1849–1851)—the small page edition.

N.Y.H.S. Coll.—*Collections of the New-York Historical Society.*

N.Y.H.S.Q.—*The New-York Historical Society Quarterly.*

N.Y. History—*New York History, Quarterly Journal of New York State Historical Association.*

N.Y. Legislative Council Journal—*Journal of the Legislative Council of . . . New-York . . .* 2 vols. (1861).

Observations—*Observations on Several Acts of Parliament . . . and Also, on the Conduct of . . . the Board of Commissioners. . . . Published by the Merchants of Boston* (Boston, 1769).

O'Callaghan *N.Y. Commissions*—Edmund B. O'Callaghan *Calendar of New York Colonial Commissions 1680–1770* (1929).

O.E.D.—*The Oxford English Dictionary . . .* 13 vols. (1933).

Oliver *Origin*—Douglass Adair and John A. Schutz (ed.) *Peter Oliver's Origin & Progress of the American Revolution . . .* (1961).

Olson and Brown *Anglo-American Relations*—Alison G. Olson and Richard Maxwell Brown (eds.) *Anglo-American Political Relations, 1675–1775* (1970).

Olton "Philadelphia's Mechanics"—Charles S. Olton "Philadelphia's Mechanics in the First Decade of Revolution 1765–1775" *Journal Am. Hist.* LIX (1972) 311–326.

Orations—Orations Delivered at the Request of the Inhabitants of the Town of Boston to Commemorate . . . the Fifth of March 1770 (1807).

Orations at Boston—Peter Edes (compiler) *Orations . . . at Boston . . . to Commemorate . . . [the Boston Massacre]* (1807).

Origin—See Knollenberg *Origin*.

Osgood "Society of Dissenters"—Herbert L. Osgood "The Society of Dissenters Founded at New York in 1769" *A.H.R.* VI (1901) 498–507.

Ostrander "Col. Molasses Trade"—Gilman M. Ostrander "The Colonial Molasses Trade" *Agricultural Hist.* XXX (1956) 77–84.

Otis *Considerations* [James Otis]—*Considerations on Behalf of the Colonists in a Letter to a Noble Lord* (London, 1765), Mullett *Writings of Otis* II 109–125.

Otis *Rights*—James Otis *The Rights of the British Colonies Asserted and Proved* (Boston, 1764) reprinted in Bailyn *Pamphlets* I 418–552.

Otis *Vindication*—James Otis *A Vindication of the British Colonies . . .* (Boston, 1765) reprinted in Bailyn *Pamphlets* I 553–579.

Pa. Archives—Pennsylvania Archives.

Pa. Assembly—Pennsylvania Archives, 8th series, "Votes of Assembly" Charles F. Hoban, ed. (1935).

Pa. Mag. Hist.—The Pennsylvania Magazine of History and Biography.

Palfrey *New Eng.*—John G. Palfrey *History of New England* 5 vols. (1890).

Palfrey *Palfrey*—John G. Palfrey *Life of William Palfrey . . .* (1845) in Jared Sparks (ed.) *The Library of American Biography* 2 VII 335–448.

Palmer *Age of the Democratic Revolution 1760–1800*—Robert R. Palmer *The Age of the Democratic Revolution: . . . Europe and America, 1760–1800* 2 vols. (1959, 1965).

Pares *Geo. III*—Richard Pares *King George III and the Politicians . . .* (1953).

Pares *War and Trade*—Richard Pares *War and Trade in the West Indies 1748–1763* (1936).

Pares *West India*—Richard Pares *A West India Fortune* (1950).

Pares *Yankees and Creoles*—Richard Pares *Yankees and Creoles; the Trade between North America and the West Indies before the American Revolution* (1956).

Pargellis *Bibliography*—Stanley M. Pargellis and J. D. Medley (eds.) *Bibliography of British History, The Eighteenth Century, 1714–1789* (1951).

Pargellis *Military Affairs*—Stanley M. Pargellis (ed.) *Military Affairs in North America, 1748–1765 . . .* (1936).

Parkman *The Old Régime*—Francis Parkman *The Old Régime in Canada* (1922).

Parl. Hist.—William Cobbett and Thomas C. Hansard (eds.) *The Parliamentary History of England . . . to 1803* 36 vols. (1806–1820).

Pascoe *Classified Digest of Records of the Society*—Charles F. Pascoe *Classified Digest of Records of the Society . . . 1701–1892* (1893).

Pascoe *Two Hundred Years of the S.P.G.*—Charles F. Pascoe *Two Hundred Years of the S.P.G.: . . . the Society for the Propagation of the Gospel in Foreign Parts, 1701–1900* 2 vols. (1901).

Pemberton *North*—W. Baring Pemberton *Lord North* (1938).

Pennsylvania Chronicle—The Pennsylvania Chronicle and Universal Advertiser (William Goddard, publisher, 1767–1774).

Pennsylvania Gazette—The Pennsylvania Gazette Philadelphia, 1728–1775 (B. Franklin and David Hall publishers).

Pennsylvania Journal—The Pennsylvania Journal and Weekly Advertiser Philadelphia, 1742–1775 (William and Thomas Bradford publishers).

Penson *Agents of West Indies*—Lillian M. Penson *The Colonial Agents . . . West Indies* (1924).

Percy—Charles K. Bolton (ed.) *Letters of Hugh Earl Percy . . . 1774–1776* (1902).

Perry *Del.*—William Stevens Perry (ed.) *Historical Collections Relating to the American Colonial Church* V Delaware (1878).

Perry *Historical Collections of the American Colonial Church*—See Perry *Del.*, *Md.*, *Mass.*, *Pa.*, and *Va.*

Perry *History*—William Stevens Perry *The History of the American Episcopal Church 1587–1883* 2 vols. (1885).

Perry *Md.*—William Stevens Perry (ed.) *Historical Collections . . . Church* IV Maryland (1878).

Perry *Mass.*—William S. Perry (ed.) *Historical Collections . . . Church* III Massachusetts (1873).

Perry *Pa.*—William S. Perry (ed.) *Historical Collections . . . Church* II Pennsylvania (1871).

Perry *Va.*—William S. Perry (ed.) *Historical Collections . . . Church* I Virginia (1870).

Peters *History*—Samuel Peters *A General History of Connecticut . . .* (London, 1781).

Peterson "Historic Philadelphia"—Charles E. Peterson "Historic Philadelphia" in *American Philosophical Society Transactions* XLIII (1953) 96–128.

Pickering *Statutes*—Danby Pickering *The Statutes at Large* (1762–1775).

Pitkin—Albert C. Bates (ed.) *The Pitkin Papers Conn. Hist. Soc. Coll.* XIX (1921).

Pitman *West Indies*—Frank Pitman *The Development of the British West Indies, 1704–1763* (1917).

Pitt—William Stanhope Taylor and John H. Pringle (eds.) *Correspondence of William Pitt, Earl of Chatham* 4 vols. (1838–1840).

Plutarch—Thomas North's popular English translation *The Lives of the Noble Grecians and Romans compared together by . . . Plutarche of Chaeronea* (1579) and several later English editions had been published by 1765.

Pocock "English Political Ideologies"—J. G. A. Pocock "Machiavelli, Harrington, and English Political Ideologies in the Eighteenth Century" 3 *W. & M.Q.* XXII (1965) 549–583.

Pocock *The Ancient Constitution*—J. G. A. Pocock *The Ancient Constitution and the Feudal Law* (1957).

Pole *Political Representation*—J. R. Pole *Political Representation in England and the Origins of the American Republic* (1966).

Porter *Jacksons and Lees*—Kenneth W. Porter *The Jacksons and the Lees . . . 1765–1844* 2 vols. (1937).

Porteus *Secker*—Beilby Porteus *The Works of . . . Thomas Secker . . .* 6 vols. (1825).

Pownall *Administration*—Thomas Pownall *The Administration of the Colonies* (3rd ed., 1766).

Pownall *Pownall*—Charles A. W. Pownall *Thomas Pownall . . . Governor of Massachusetts Bay . . .* (1908).

Price "Glasgow"—Jacob M. Price "The Rise of Glasgow in the Chesapeake Tobacco Trade 1707–1775" 3 *W. & M.Q.* XI (1954) 179–199.

"Price Letters"—"Letters to and from Richard Price, 1767–1790" in 2 *M.H.S. Proc.* XVII 263–378.

Prior Documents—[John Almon] *A Collection of Interesting, Authentic Papers relative to the Dispute between Great Britain and America . . . from 1764 to 1775* (London, 1777).

Proc. Am. Phil. Soc.—See *A.P.S. Proc.*

Providence Gazette—The Providence Gazette; and Country Journal 1762–1775.

Public Advertiser—The Public Advertiser (London newspaper).

Quarles, Benjamin—*The Negro in the American Revolution* (1961).

"Quincy Journal"—Mark A. DeWolfe Howe (ed.) "Journal of Josiah Quincy, Junior, 1773" *M.H.S. Proc.* XLIX 424–481.

Quincy *Memoir*—Josiah Quincy (1772–1864) *Memoir of the Life of Josiah Quincy, Jun., of Massachusetts: 1744–1775* (1874).

Quincy *Observations*—Josiah Quincy *Observations on . . . the Boston Port-Bill . . .* (Boston, 1774). My citations are to the reprint in Quincy *Memoirs* 293–376.

Quincy *Reports*—Samuel M. Quincy (ed.) *Reports of Cases . . . in the Superior Court of Massachusetts Bay between 1761 and 1772 by Josiah Quincy, Junior* (1865).

Rae *Smith*—John Rae *Life of Adam Smith* (1895).

Ragatz *Fall of the Planter Class*—Lowell J. Ragatz *The Fall of the Planter Class in the British Caribbean, 1763–1833* (1928).

Rantoul "Cruise of the Quero"—Robert S. Rantoul "The Cruise of the 'Quero' . . ." *Essex Inst. Hist. Coll.* XXXVI (1900).

Reed *De Berdt*—William B. Reed *The Life of Esther De Berdt . . .* (1853).

Reed *Reed*—William B. Reed *Life and Correspondence of Joseph Reed . . .* 2 vols. (1847).

Remembrancer—The Remembrancer, or Important Repository of Public Events 13 vols. (London, 1775–1782).

R.I. Col. Rec.—John R. Bartlett (ed.) *Records of the Colony of Rhode Island . . .* 9 vols. (1856–1864).

R.I. Commerce—Commerce of Rhode Island 1726–1774 *M.H.S. Coll.* LXIX (1914).

R.I. Hist.—Rhode Island History (a quarterly).

R.I. Hist. Soc. Proc.—Proceedings of the Rhode Island Historical Society.

Ritcheson *British Politics*—Charles R. Ritcheson *British Politics and the American Revolution* (1954).

Ritcheson "Pitt"—Charles R. Ritcheson "The Elder Pitt and an American Department" *A.H.R.* LVII (1952) 376–383.

Rivington's New-York Gazetteer—[beginning Dec. 16, 1773, name changed to *Gazette*] New York City (Apr., 1773–Nov., 1775).

Robbins *Eighteenth-Century Commonwealthman*—Caroline Robbins *The Eighteenth-Century Commonwealth Man* (1959).

Robbins "Hollis"—Caroline Robbins "The Strenuous Whig, Thomas Hollis of Lincoln's Inn" 3 *W. & M.Q.* VII (1950) 406–453.

Robbins "Sidney"—Carolina Robbins "Algernon Sidney's *Discourses Concerning Government:* Textbook of Revolution" 3 *W. & M.Q.* IV (1947) 267–296.

Robinson-Morris *Considerations*—Matthew Robinson-Morris (later Baron Rokeby) *Considerations on the Measures Carrying on with Respect to the British Colonies in North America . . .* (London, 1774).

Roche *Reed*—John F. Roche *Joseph Reed a Moderate in the American Revolution* (1957).

Rockingham—Earl of Albemarle (George Thomas Keppel) *Memoirs of the Marquis of Rockingham . . .* 2 vols. (1852).

Rodd *Charlemont*—Thomas Rodd *Original Letters Principally from Lord Charlemont . . .* (1820).

Root *Pa.*—Winfred T. Root *The Relations of Pennsylvania with the British Government, 1696–1765* (1912).

Rosenblatt "Significance of Credit in the Tobacco Trade"—Samuel M. Rosenblatt "The Significance of Credit in the Tobacco Consignment Trade: A Study of John Norton and Sons, 1768–1775" 3 *W. & M.Q.* XIX (1962) 383–399.

Rossiter *Seedtime*—Clinton Rossiter *Seedtime of the Republic: The Origin of the American Tradition of Political Liberty* (1953).

Rossman *Mifflin*—Kenneth R. Rossman *Thomas Mifflin and the Politics of the American Revolution* (1952).

Rothney "Case of Bayne"—Gordon O. Rothney "The Case of Bayne and Brymer . . ." *Can. H.R.* XV (1934) 264–275.

Rowe (or *Rowe Diary*)—Anne R. Cunningham (ed.) *Letters and Diary of John Rowe, Boston Merchant 1759–1762; 1764–1779* (1903).

Rowland *Carroll*—Kate M. Rowland *The Life of Charles Carroll of Carrollton* . . . 2 vols. (1898).

Rowland *Mason*—Kate M. Rowland *The Life of George Mason, 1725–1792* 2 vols. (1892).

Rudé *Wilkes and Liberty*—George Rudé *Wilkes and Liberty, A Social Study of 1763 to 1774* (1962).

Rush *Address . . . on the Slavery of the Negroes in America*—"A Pennsylvanian" [Benjamin Rush] *An Address to the Inhabitants of the British Settlements, on the Slavery of the Negroes in America* (2nd ed., Philadelphia, 1773).

Rush—Lyman H. Butterfield (ed.) *Letters of Benjamin Rush* 2 vols. (1951).

S & D *Doc.*—Adam Shortt and Arthur G. Doughty (eds.) *Documents Relating to the Constitutional History of Canada 1759–1791* 2 vols. (1918).

Sabine *Loyalists*—Lorenzo Sabine *Biographical Sketches of Loyalists of the American Revolution with an Historical Essay* 2 vols. (1864).

St. James Chronicle—*The St. James Chronicle; or the British Evening Post* London.

Sallust—Gaius Sallustius Cresputo *Bellum Coniuratio* and *Bellum lugurthinum* (English translation by Thomas Gordon 1728).

Sandwich—George R. Barnes and J. H. Owens (eds.) *The Private Papers of John, Earl of Sandwich . . . 1771–1782* (1932).

Savelle *Morgan*—Max Savelle *George Morgan Colony Builder* (1932).

Savelle—*Seeds of Liberty*—Max Savelle *Seeds of Liberty: The Genesis of the American Mind* (1948).

Saxby *The British Customs*—Henry Saxby *The British Customs containing an Historical and Practical Account of each Branch of that Revenue . . .* (London, 1757).

Scharf *Philadelphia*—John Thomas Scharf and Thompson Wescott *History of Philadelphia 1609–1884* 3 vols. (1884).

Scheide "The Lexington Alarm"—John H. Scheide "The Lexington Alarm" *A.A.S. Proc.* L Part 1 (1940) 49–79.

Schlesinger *Col. Merchants*—Arthur M. Schlesinger *The Colonial Merchants and the American Revolution 1763–1776* (1918).

Schlesinger "Colonial Newspapers"—Arthur M. Schlesinger "Colonial Newspapers and the Stamp Act" *New Eng. Q.* VIII (1935) 63–83.

Schlesinger "Politics"—Arthur M. Schlesinger "Politics, Propaganda and the Philadelphia Press, 1767–1770" *Pa. Mag. Hist.* LX (1936) 309–322.

Schlesinger *Prelude*—Arthur M. Schlesinger *Prelude to Independence The Newspaper War on Britain 1764–1776* (1958).

Schlesinger "Propaganda"—Arthur M. Schlesinger "Propaganda of the Boston Newspaper Press 1767–1770" *Col. Soc. Public.* XXXII (1937) 396–416.

Schlesinger "Songs"—Arthur M. Schlesinger "A Note on Songs as Patriot Propaganda 1765–1776" 3 *W. & M.Q.* XI (1954) 78–88.

Schlesinger "Uprising"—Arthur M. Schlesinger "The Uprising Against the East India Company" *Political Science Quarterly* (1917) 60–79.

Schneider *Johnson*—Herbert and Carol Schneider (eds.) *Samuel Johnson President of King's College: His Career and Writings* 4 vols. (1929).

Schutz *Pownall*—John A. Schutz *Thomas Pownall, British Defender of American Liberty* . . . (1951).

Schutz *Shirley*—John A. Schutz *William Shirley, King's Governor of Massachusetts* (1961).

Schuyler *Parliament*—Robert Livingston Schuyler *Parliament and the British Empire* . . . (1929).

Seabury, Samuel—Four pamphlets listed in notes to the appendix to Chapter 28 of this volume.

Seabury, Samuel—Pamphlets of 1774 and 1775 reprinted in Vance *Letters of a Westchester Farmer*.

Seabury *Seabury*—William J. Seabury *Memoir of Bishop Seabury* (1908).

Sedgwick *Livingston*—Theodore Sedgwick *A Memoir of the Life of William Livingston* . . . (1833).

Sellers *Charleston*—Leila Sellers *Charleston Business on the Eve of the American Revolution* (1934).

Selwny—John Heneage Jesse *George Selwyn and His Contemporaries* . . . 4 vols. (1843–1844).

Shalhope "Toward a Republican Synthesis"—Robert E. Shalhope "Toward a Republican Synthesis . . ." 3 *W. & M.Q.* XXIX (1972) 49–80.

Shammas "Colden"—Carole Shammas "Cadwallader Colden and the Role of the King's Prerogative" *N.Y.H.S.Q.* LIII (1969) 103.

Sharp *Declaration*—Granville Sharp *A Declaration of the People's Natural Right to a Share in the Legislature* . . . (New York, 1774).

Sharpe—William H. Browne (ed.) *Correspondence of Governor Horatio Sharpe, Archives of Maryland* 1888, 1890, 1895.

Sharpless *Quakers in the Revolution*—Isaac Sharpless *The Quakers in the Revolution* (1902).

Shelburne—Edmond Fitzmaurice *Life of William, Earl of Shelburne afterwards First Marquess of Lansdowne* . . . 3 vols. (1875–1876).

Shepherd *Pa.*—William R. Shepherd *History of Proprietary Government in Pennsylvania* (1896).

Sheridan "British Credit Crisis and the Colonies"—Richard B. Sheridan "The British Credit Crisis of 1772 and the American Colonies" *Journ. Economic Hist.* XX (1960) 161–186.

Shipley *Sermon*—Jonathan Shipley, Bishop of St. Asaph, *A Sermon Preached before the Incorporated Society* . . . (London, 1773).

Shipley *Speech*—Jonathan Shipley, Bishop of St. Asaph, *A Speech Intended to Have Been Spoken* . . . (London, 1774).

Shipton *Harvard Graduates*—Clifford K. Shipton *Sibley's Harvard Graduates Biographical Sketches of Those Who Attended Harvard College* . . . vols. 4–10 (1933–1968).

Shirley—Charles H. Lincoln (ed.) *Correspondence of William Shirley, Governor of Massachusetts* . . . *1731–1760* 2 vols. (1912).

Short Narrative—*A Short Narrative of the Horrid Massacre in Boston* . . . (Boston, 1770; 1849 reprint).

Shurtleff *Boston*—Nathaniel B. Shurtleff *A Topographical and Historical Description of Boston* (1890).

Shy "Pownall"—John Shy "Thomas Pownall, Henry Ellis, and the Spectrum of Possibilities" Olson and Brown (eds.) *Anglo–American Relations* 155–186.

Shy *Toward Lexington*—John Shy *Toward Lexington, The Role of the British Army in the Coming of the American Revolution* (1965).

Siebert *Loyalists of Pa.*—Wilbur H. Siebert *The Loyalists of Pennsylvania* (1920).

Sirmans "S.C. Royal Council"—M. Eugene Sirmans "The South Carolina Royal Council, 1720–1763" 3 *W. & M.Q.* XVIII (1961) 373–391.

Sirmans *South Carolina*—M. Eugene Sirmans *Colonial South Carolina: A Political History, 1663–1763* (1966).

Smith *Appeals*—Joseph Henry Smith *Appeals to the Privy Council from the American Plantations* (1950).

Smith *Hist. of N.Y.*—William Smith *History of New-York* . . . (New York City, 1756). My citations are to the 1814 edition.

Smith "Loyalists"—Paul H. Smith "The American Loyalists: Notes on Their Organization and Numerical Strength" 3 *W. & M.Q.* XXV (1968) 259–277.

Smith *Loyalists and Redcoats*—Paul H. Smith *Loyalists and Redcoats* (1964).

Smith *Memoirs*—William H. M. Sabine (ed.) *Historical Memoirs* . . . *of William Smith* . . . *of New York* . . . *1763–1776* (1956); *1776–1778* (1958), cited respectively as I and II.

Smith *S.C.*—William Roy Smith *South Carolina as a Royal Province 1719–1776* (1903).

Smith *William Smith*—Horace Wemyss Smith *Life and Correspondence of the Rev. William Smith, D.D.* . . . 2 vols. (1879, 1880).

Smyth *Franklin*—Albert Henry Smyth (ed.) *The Life and Writings of Benjamin Franklin* 10 vols. (1907).

So. Hist. Assoc. Public.—*Publications of the Southern History Association.*

Soltow "Scottish Traders"—James H. Soltow "Scottish Traders in Virginia, 1750–1775" 2 *Econ. Hist. Rev.* XII (1959) 83–98.

Sosin *Agents*—Jack M. Sosin *Agents and Merchants: British Colonial Policy and the Origins of the American Revolution, 1763–1775* (1965).

Sosin "Mass. Acts of 1774"—Jack M. Sosin "The Massachusetts Acts of 1774: Coercive or Preventive?" *Hunt. Lib. Q.* XXVI (1963) 235–252.

Sosin "Paper Money"—Jack M. Sosin "Imperial Regulation of Colonial Paper Money, 1764–1773" *Pa. Mag. Hist.* LXXXVIII (1964) 174–198.

Sosin *Rev. Frontier*—Jack M. Sosin *The Revolutionary Frontier 1763–1783* (1967).

Sosin *Whitehall and Wilderness*—*Whitehall and the Wilderness: The Middle West in British Colonial Policy, 1760–1775* (1961).

South-Carolina Gazette—*The South-Carolina Gazette* (Charleston, 1732–1775).

South-Carolina Gazette; and Country Journal—*The South-Carolina Gazette; and Country Journal* (Charleston, 1765–1775).

South-Carolina and American General Gazette—*The South-Carolina and American General Gazette* (Charleston, 1764–1781).

So. Car. Hist. Mag.—*The South Carolina Historical and Genealogical Magazine.*

Southern Hist. Assoc. Public.—*Publications of the Southern History Association.*

Sparks *Franklin*—Jared Sparks (ed.) *The Works of Benjamin Franklin* . . . 10 vols. (1840).

Spector *American Department*—Margaret M. Spector *The American Department of the British Government 1768–1782* (1940).

Staples *Rhode Island*—William R. Staples *Rhode Island in the Continental Congress . . . 1765–1790* (1870).

Stark *Loyalists of Mass.*—James H. Stark *The Loyalists of Massachusetts . . .* (1910).

State Papers—William Noel Sainsbury et al. (eds.) *Calendar of State Papers, Colonial Series, America and West Indies.*

Statutes at Large (English and British). Unless otherwise noted, my references to English or British acts are to the Danby Pickering edition of 1762–1775, vols. 1–31.

Stevens *Facsimiles*—Benjamin F. Stevens *Facsimiles of Manuscripts in European Archives Relating to America 1773–1784 . . .* (1889–1898).

Stevens *New York*—John A. Stevens (ed.) *Colonial Records of the New York Chamber of Commerce 1768–1784 . . .* (1867).

Stiles Diary—Franklin B. Dexter (ed.) *The Literary Diary of Ezra Stiles . . .* 3 vols. (1901).

Stiles *Discourse*—Ezra Stiles *A Discourse on the Christian Union . . .* (Boston, 1761).

Stiles *Itineraries*—Franklin B. Dexter (ed.) *Extracts from the Itineraries . . . of Ezra Stiles . . . with a selection from his Correspondence* (1916).

Stillé *Dickinson*—Charles J. Stillé *The Life and Times of John Dickinson 1732–1808* (1891).

Stock *Proceedings*—Leo Francis Stock (ed.) *Proceedings and Debates of the British Parliaments Respecting North America* 5 vols. (1924–1941).

Stokes *Iconography*—Isaac N. P. Stokes *The Iconography of Manhattan Island . . .* 6 vols. (1915–1928).

Stone "Philadelphia"—Frederick D. Stone "How the Landing of Tea Was Opposed in Philadelphia . . ." *Pa. Mag. Hist.* XV (1891) 385–393.

Stopford—H.M.C.—Report on the Manuscripts of Mrs. Stopford-Sackville I (1904).

Stout "Manning the Royal Navy"—Neil R. Stout "Manning the Royal Navy in North America 1763–1775" *Am. Neptune* XXIII (1963) 174–195.

Stowe "Minutes"—Walter H. Stowe "The Seabury Minutes of the New York Clergy Conventions of 1766 and 1767" *Hist. Mag. Prot. Episc. Church* IX (1940) 124–162.

Sullivan—Otis G. Hammond (ed.) *Letters and Papers of Major-General John Sullivan, Continental Army* 2 vols. (1930–1931).

Sutherland—Harold Murdock (ed.) *Late News . . . The Narratives of Lieut. William Sutherland . . .* (1927). Another slightly different copy from the papers of Gen. Thomas Gage, French *Gage* 42–46, 58–61, 85–92, 111–112.

Sutherland "Burke"—Lucy Stuart Sutherland "Edmund Burke and the First Rockingham Ministry" *E.H.R.* XLVII (1932) 46–72.

Sutherland *East India Co.*—Lucy Stuart Sutherland *The East India Company in Eighteenth-Century Politics* (1952).

Swem *Va. Hist. Index*—Earl Gregg Swem (ed.) *Virginia Historical Index* 2 vols. (1934–1936).

Tacitus—Cornelius Tacitus *Historiae* (English translation by Thomas Gordon 1744).

Tate "Coming of the Revolution in Virginia"—Thad W. Tate "The Coming of the Revolution in Virginia: Britain's Challenge to Virginia's Ruling Class, 1763–1776" 3 *W. & M.Q.* XIX (1962) 323–343.

Taylor "Philadelphia Tea Party"—Thomas B. Taylor "The Philadelphia Counterpart of the Boston Tea Party . . ." with an additional letter *Bulletin of Friends' Historical Society of Pennsylvania* II (1908) 86–110, III (1909) 21–49 and X (1921) 68–70.

Tea Leaves—See Drake *Tea Leaves.*

Thacher *Sentiments*—Oxenbridge Thacher *The Sentiments of a British American* (Boston, 1764), Bailyn *Pamphlets* 489–498.

Thayer *Pa. Politics*—Theodore Thayer *Pennsylvania Politics and the Growth of Democracy 1740–1776* (1953).

Thomas "Townshend"—P. D. C. Thomas "Charles Townshend and American Taxation in 1767" *E.H.R.* LXXXIII (1968) 33–51.

"Thomson" [Zimmerman]—John J. Zimmerman "Charles Thomson 'The Sam Adams of Philadelphia'" *Miss. Vall. H.R.* XLV (1958) 464–480.

Thomson Papers—The Papers of Charles Thomson . . . 1765–1816 N.Y. Hist. Soc. Coll. 1878, 1–186.

Thorpe *Charters*—Francis N. Thorpe (ed.) *The Federal and State Constitutions, Colonial Charters and Other Organic Laws . . .* 7 vols. (1909).

Tourtellot *William Diamond's Drum*—Arthur B. Tourtellot *William Diamond's Drum: The Beginning of the War of the American Revolution* (1959).

Towle *R.I. Admiralty*—Dorothy S. Towle (ed.) *Records of the Vice-Admiralty Court of Rhode Island 1716–1752* (1936).

Toynbee *Walpole*—Mrs. Paget Toynbee (ed.) *The Letters of Horace Walpole* 16 vols. (1903–1905) with 3 supplementary vols. (1918–1925).

Traits of the Tea Party—[Benjamin B. Thatcher] *Traits of the Tea Party; Being a Memoir of George R. T. Hewes . . .* (1835).

Trenchard and Gordon *Cato's Letters*—[John Trenchard and Thomas Gordon] *Cato's Letters; Or, Essays on Liberty, Civil and Religious . . .* 4 vols. (1748).

Trial of the Soldiers—The Trial of the British Soldiers . . . (1807).

Trial of William Wemms—The Trial of William Wemms and Seven Other Soldiers . . . Taken in Short-Hand by John Hodgson (Boston, 1770).

Trumbull—The Trumbull Papers 5 *M.H.S. Coll.* IX (1885).

Tucker *Letter from a Merchant in London*—Josiah Tucker *A Letter from a Merchant in London to His Nephew in America* (London, 1766). Reprinted with Benjamin Franklin's notes in *Pa. Mag. Hist.* XXV (1901) 307–322 and 516–526 and XXVI (1902) 81–90 and 255–264.

Tuckerman "Cooper Diary"—Frederick Tuckerman "Diary of Samuel Cooper, 1775–1776" *A.H.R.* VI (1901) 301–341.

Tuckerman "Cooper Letters"—Frederick Tuckerman "Letters of Samuel Cooper to Thomas Pownall 1769–1777" *A.H.R.* VIII (1903) 301–330.

Tunstall *Pitt*—Brian Tunstall *William Pitt, Earl of Chatham* (1938).

Tyler *Lit. Hist. of Am. Revolution*—Moses Coit Tyler *The Literary History of the American Revolution 1763–1783* (2 vols. in one, 1905).

Ubbelohde *Vice-Admiralty Courts*—Carl Ubbelohde *The Vice-Admiralty Courts and the American Revolution* (1960).

Upton *Diary of William Smith*—L. F. S. Upton (ed.) *The Diary and Selected Papers of Chief Justice William Smith* I (1963).

Upton *Revolutionary New Hampshire*—Richard F. Upton *Revolutionary New Hampshire An Account of the Social and Political Forces . . .* (1936).

Va. Executive Council Journals—Benjamin J. Hillman (ed.) *Executive Journals of the Council of Colonial Virginia* VI [1754–1775] (1966).

Va. Gazette (Hunter)—The Virginia Gazette (Hunter etc.) Williamsburg (1765–1775).

Va. Gazette (Purdie)—The Virginia Gazette Williamsburg (1766–1775) published by Alexander Purdie and John Dixon.

Va. Gazette (Rind)—The Virginia Gazette Williamsburg (1766–1775) published by William Rind and his heirs.

Va. Journals—John P. Kennedy (ed.) *Journals of the House of Burgesses of Virginia* 4 vols. [1761–1776] (1905–1907).

Va. Legislative Council Journals—Henry R. McIlwaine (ed.) *Legislative Journals of the Council of Colonial Virginia* III [1754–1775] (1919).

Va. Mag.—*The Virginia Magazine of History and Biography*.

Van Alstine "Parliamentary Supremacy"—Richard W. Van Alstyne "Parliamentary Supremacy versus Independence . . ." *Hunt. Lib. Q.* XXVI (1963) 201–233.

Vance *Letters of a Westchester Farmer*—Clarence H. Vance *Letters of a Westchester Farmer . . . Samuel Seabury* (1930).

Van Doren *Franklin*—Carl Van Doren *Benjamin Franklin* (1938).

Van Doren *Franklin and Jackson*—Carl Van Doren (ed.) *The Letters and Papers of Benjamin Franklin and Richard Jackson 1753–1785* (1947).

Van Doren *Franklin–Mecom Letters*—Carl Van Doren (ed.) *The Letters of Benjamin Franklin and Jane Mecom* (1950).

Van Doren *Franklin's Writings*—Carl Van Doren (ed.) *Benjamin Franklin's Autobiographical Writings* (1945).

Valentine *North*—Alan Valentine *Lord North* 2 vols. (1967).

Van Schaack—Henry C. Van Schaack (ed.) *The Life of Peter Van Schaack . . .* (1842).

Van Tyne *Causes*—Claude H. Van Tyne *The Causes of the War of Independence . . .* (1922).

Van Tyne *Loyalists*—Claude H. Van Tyne *The Loyalists in the American Revolution* (1902).

Varga "N.Y. Restraining Act"—Nicholas Varga "The New York Restraining Act: Its Passages and Some Effects, 1766–1768" *N.Y. History* XXXVII (1956) 233–258.

W. & M.Q.—*The William and Mary Quarterly*.

Wade *Junius*—John Wade (ed.) *Junius: Including Letters by the Same Author under Other Signatures* 2 vols. (1850, 1860).

Wainwright *Croghan*—Nicholas B. Wainwright *George Croghan Wilderness Diplomat* (1959).

Walett "Bowdoin"—Francis G. Walett "James Bowdoin, Patriot Propagandist" *New Eng. Q.* XXIII (1950) 320–338.

Walett "Mass. Council"—Francis G. Walett "The Massachusetts Council 1766–1774 . . ." 3 *W. & M.Q.* VI (1949) 605–627.

Walker *Burd Papers*—Lewis Burd Walker (ed.) *The Burd Papers, Extracts from Chief Justice William Allen's Letter Book* (1897).

Wallace "Chapter of S.C. History"—David Duncan Wallace "A Chapter of South Carolina Constitutional History" *Publications of the Vanderbilt Southern Historical Society* #4 (1900) 3–8.

Wallace *Const. Hist. of S.C.*—David D. Wallace *Constitutional History of South Carolina from 1725 to 1775* (1899).

Wallace *Laurens*—David Duncan Wallace *The Life of Henry Laurens with a Sketch of Lieutenant-Colonel John Laurens* (1915).

Wallace *Maseres Letters*—William Stewart Wallace (ed.) *The Maseres Letters 1766–1768* (1919).

Walpole "Journal of Events"—Horace Walpole "Journal of the Most Remarkable Events of the Reign of King George the Third" Collection of W. S. Lewis, Farmington, Conn.

Walpole *Last Journal*—Horace Walpole *Journal of the Reign of King George the Third . . . 1771 to 1783 (Last Journals)* 2 vols. (1859) John Doran ed.

Walpole *Memoirs of Geo. III*—Horace Walpole *Memoirs of the Reign of King George the Third* 4 vols. (1845), edited by Denis LeMarchant.

Walsh *Charleston's Sons*—Richard Walsh *Charleston's Sons of Liberty: A Study of the Artisans 1763–1789* (1959).

Warren–Adams—*Warren–Adams Letters Being Chiefly a Correspondence among John Adams, Samuel Adams, and James Warren* 2 vols. *M.H.S. Coll.* LXXII and LXXIII (1917, 1925).

Warren "Colonial Customs Service"—Winslow Warren "The Colonial Customs Service in Massachusetts . . ." *M.H.S. Proc.* XLVI 440–474.

Washington—See Fitzpatrick *Washington*.

Washington Diaries—John C. Fitzpatrick (ed.) *The Diaries of George Washington 1748–1799* 4 vols. (1925).

Waters *Otis Family*—John Waters *The Otis Family in Provincial and Revolutionary Massachusetts* (1968).

Watson "Baker"—D. H. Watson "William Baker's Account of the Debate on the Repeal of the Stamp Act" 3 *W. & M.Q.* XXVI (1969) 259–265.

Watson "Harrison"—D. H. Watson "Joseph Harrison and the Liberty Incident" 3 *W. & M.Q.* XX (1963) 585–595.

Watson *Tea-Party*—Henry C. Watson *The Yankee Tea-Party* . . . (1852). (A collection of yarns about the Revolution).

Wax "Negro Import Duties"—Darold D. Wax "Negro Import Duties in Colonial Virginia . . ." *Va. Mag. Hist.* LXXIX (1971) 29–44.

Weeks *Southern Quakers and Slavery*—Stephen B. Weeks *Southern Quakers and Slavery: A Study in Institutional History* (1896).

Weir "S.C. Politics"—Robert M. Weir " 'The Harmony We Were Famous For': . . . South Carolina Politics" 3 *W. & M.Q.* XXVI (1969) 473–501.

Weiss *New Engl. Col. Clergy*—Frederick L. Weiss *The Colonial Clergy and the Colonial Churches of New England* (1936).

Wells *Political Reflections*—[Richard Wells] *A Few Political Reflections Submitted to the Consideration of the British Colonies* . . . (Philadelphia, 1774).

Wells *S. Adams*—William V. Wells *The Life and Public Services of Samuel Adams* . . . 3 vols. (1865).

Werner *N.Y. Civil List*—Edgar A. Werner *Civil List and Constitutional History of the Colony and State of New York* (1884).

Wertenbaker *Father Knickerbocker*—Thomas J. Wertenbaker *Father Knickerbocker Rebels: New York City during the Revolution* (1948).

"Wharton Letters"—"Selections from the Letter-Books of Thomas Wharton . . ." (from Nov., 1773, to Jan., 1775) *Pa. Mag. Hist.* (1909) XXXIII 319–339, 432–453.

Wheately *London*—Henry B. Wheately *London Past and Present* . . . 3 vols. (1891).

Wheeler "Calvin's Case"—Harvey Wheeler "Calvin's Case (1608) and the McIlwain-Schuyler Debate" *A.H.R.* LXI (1956) 587–597.

White *Beekman Papers*—Philip L. White (ed.) *The Beekman Mercantile Papers 1746–1799* 2 vols. (1956).

White *Beekmans of N.Y.*—Philip L. White *The Beekmans of New York* . . . *1647–1877* (1956).

Whitmore *Civil List*—William H. Whitmore *The Massachusetts Civil List* . . . *1630–1774* . . . (1870).

Wickwire *British Subministers*—Franklin B. Wickwire *British Subministers and Colonial America 1763–1783* (1966).

Wickwire "John Pownall"—Franklin B. Wickwire "John Pownall and British Colonial Policy" 3 *W. & M.Q.* XX (1963) 543–554.

Wiener "R.I. Adm."—Frederick B. Wiener "The Rhode Island Admiralty" *Harv. Law Rev.* XLVI (1933) 44–90.

Wiener "R.I. Merchants"—Frederick B. Wiener "The Rhode Island Merchants and the Sugar Act" *New Eng. Q.* III (1930) 464–500.

Wigmore *Evidence*—John H. Wigmore *A Treatise on the Anglo-American System of Evidence . . .* (1940).

Wilkes—See Bleackley *Wilkes;* Rudé *Wilkes and Liberty;* Elsey "Wilkes and Boston"; Palfrey *Palfrey* 358–362.

Willard *Letters*—Margaret Wheeler Willard (ed.) *Letters on the American Revolution: 1774–1776* (1925).

Williams *Pitt*—Basil Williams *The Life of William Pitt, Earl of Chatham* 2 vols. (1913).

Wilson *New-York*—James Grant Wilson *The Memorial History of the City of New-York* 4 vols. (1892–1893).

Winstanley *Chatham*—Denys A. Winstanley *Lord Chatham and the Whig Opposition* (1912).

Winstanley *Government*—Denys A. Winstanley *Personal and Party Government . . . 1760–1766* (1910).

Wolf "Authorship"—Edwin Wolf "The Authorship of the 1774 Address to the King Restudied" 3 *W. & M.Q.* XXII (1965) 189–224.

Wolff *Pa. Col. Agency*—Mabel P. Wolff *The Colonial Agency of Pennsylvania, 1712–1757* (1933).

Wolkins "Boston Customs District"—George G. Wolkins "The Boston Customs District in 1768" *M.H.S. Proc.* LVIII 418–445.

Wolkins "Bollan"—George G. Wolkins "Bollan on Writs of Assistance" *M.H.S. Proc.* LIX 414–421.

Wolkins "Liberty" (or Wolkins "Hancock")—George G. Wolkins "The Seizure of John Hancock's Sloop 'Liberty' " *M.H.S. Proc.* LV 239–284.

Wolkins "Malcom"—George G. Wolkins "Daniel Malcom and Writs of Assistance" *M.H.S. Proc.* LVIII 5–84 amended and supplemented in Wolkins "Writs of Assistance in England" *M.H.S. Proc.* LXVI 357–364.

Wolkins "Paxton"—George G. Wolkins "Letters of Charles Paxton" *M.H.S. Proc.* XLVI 345–352.

Wood *Creation of the American Republic*—Gordon S. Wood *The Creation of the American Republic 1776–1787* (1969).

Wood "Mobs in the American Revolution"—Gordon S. Wood "A Note on Mobs in the American Revolution" 635–642.

Wood "Rhetoric"—Gordon S. Wood "Rhetoric and Reality in the American Revolution" 3 *W. & M.Q.* XXIII (1966) 3–32.

Wright *Am. Negotiator*—John Wright *The American Negotiator . . .* (London, 1765).

Wright *Cavendish Debates*—See *Cavendish*.

Wright *Loyalists*—Esther Clark Wright *The Loyalists of New Brunswick* [i.e., those settling New Brunswick] (1955).

Wroth "Mass. Vice-Admiralty Court"—Lawrence Kinvin Wroth "The Massachusetts Vice-Admiralty Court" in Billias *Law in Col. America* 32–91.

Wulsin, Eugene—"The Political Consequences of the Burning of the Gaspee" *R.I. Hist.* III (1944) 1–11, 55–64.

Yale Lib. Gazette—The Yale University Library Gazette.

Yoshpe *Disposition*—Harry B. Yoshpe *The Disposition of Loyalist Estates in . . . New York* (1939).

Zeichner *Conn.*—Oscar Zeichner *Connecticut's Years of Controversy, 1750–1776* (1949).

Zobel "Boston Massacre"—Hiller B. Zobel "Newer Light on the Boston Massacre" *Am. Antiq. Soc. Proc.* LXXVIII Part I (1968) 119–128.

Zobel *Boston Massacre*—Hiller B. Zobel *The Boston Massacre* (1970).

COLLECTIONS OF DOCUMENTS CITED

Adams—See Samuel Adams.

Adm.—Admiralty Papers, Public Record Office, London.

Am. Phil. Soc.—American Philosophical Society, Philadelphia, Pa.

Arthur Lee Papers—Papers of Arthur Lee, Sparks Transcripts, Harvard College Library.

B.M.—British Museum (library), London.

Bancroft Papers—Papers of George Bancroft, New York Public Library.

Bernard Papers—Papers of Francis Bernard, Governor of Massachusetts, Harvard College Library.

Boston Committee of Correspondence minutes and related papers in Bancroft Papers, New York Public Library.

Boston Comm. of Corresp. Papers—New York Public Library.

Brickdale "Debates"—Matthew Brickdale's notes of debates in House of Commons, 1770–1774, University of Bristol Library.

C.R.O.—Commonwealth Relations Office, London.

Cavendish "Debates"—Henry Cavendish's unpublished notes of debates in the House of Commons in 1772–1774, long-hand transcript in University of London Institute of short-hand notes in Egerton Mss. in B.M.

Chatham Papers—Public Record Office, London.

Clements Lib.—William L. Clements Library, University of Michigan, Ann Arbor, Michigan.

Columbia U. Lib.—Columbia University Library, New York, N.Y.

Conway Papers—Papers of Henry Seymour Conway, Library of W. S. Lewis, Farmington, Conn.

Customs Papers—The Library, H.M. Customs and Excise, King Beam House, London.

Dartmouth Papers—William Salt Library, Stafford, Staffordshire, Eng.

Dowdeswell Papers—Clements Library, University of Michigan.

Gage Papers—Clements Library.

Garth Papers—South Carolina Historical Society.

Gay Transcripts—Massachusetts Historical Society, Boston, Mass.

Grafton Mss.—Bury St. Edmunds and West Suffolk Record Office, Bury St. Edmunds.

Grenville Pap.—Papers of George Grenville, Huntington Library.

Haldimand Papers—Canadian Archives, Ottawa, Canada.

Harris "Debates"—Copy of James Harris notes of debates in the House of Commons 1761–1766, University of London Institute.

Harv. Coll. Lib.—Harvard College Library, Cambridge, Mass.

Hist. Soc. of Pa.—The Historical Society of Pennsylvania, Philadelphia, Pa.

Hollis Diary—Diary of Thomas Hollis, The Institute, Williamsburg, Va.

Huntington Lib.—Henry E. Huntington Library, San Marino, Cal.

Hutchinson Corresp.—Mass. Archives, State House, Boston, Mass.

India Office Library—London (also called Commonwealth Relations Office).

Institute—Institute of Early American History and Culture, Williamsburg, Va.

L.C.—Library of Congress, Washington, D.C.

Lamb Papers—Papers of John Lamb, New-York Historical Society.

Lambeth Papers—Papers at Lambeth Palace, London, England.

Lee—See Arthur Lee Papers.

Lewis Coll.—Collection of Manuscripts of W. S. Lewis, Farmington, Conn.

M.H.S.—See Mass. Hist. Soc.

Mass. Arch.—Massachusetts Archives, State House, Boston, Mass. (Most of Thomas Hutchinson's letters cited as in Mass. Arch. are available in typed copies at the Mass. Hist. Soc.)

Mass. Hist. Soc.—Massachusetts Historical Society, Boston, Mass.

Newdigate "Debates"—Roger Newdigate, notes of debates in House of Commons 1754–1768, Warwickshire County Rec. Office, Warwick.

Newport Hist. Soc. Mss.—Newport Historical Society, Newport, R.I.

N.Y. Hist. Soc.—The New-York Historical Society, New York, N.Y.

N.Y. Pub. Lib.—New York Public Library, New York City.

P.C.—Privy Council Register, in P.R.O.

P.R.O.—Public Record Office, London.

Paine Papers—Robert Treat Paine Papers, Massachusetts Historical Society, Boston.

Price Papers—Massachusetts Historical Society, Boston.

Record Office, House of Lords—The Record Office of the House of Lords, London.

Rockingham Papers—Sheffield City Libraries, Sheffield, England.

Salt Lib.—William Salt Library, Stafford, Staffordshire, England.

Samuel Adams Papers—In Bancroft Papers, New York Public Library.

Sandwich Papers—Hinchinbrooke, Huntingdonshire, England.

S.C. Arch.—South Carolina Archives Department, Columbia, S.C.

S.C. Hist. Soc.—South Carolina Historical Society, Charleston, South Carolina.

S.C. Transcripts—Transcripts in South Carolina Archives of papers relating to South Carolina in P.R.O.

Shelburne Papers—Papers of Lord Shelburne in Clements Library.

Stiles Papers—Papers of Ezra Stiles, Yale Library.

T.—Treasury Papers in P.R.O.

Townshend Papers—At Dalkeith House, Edinburgh, Scotland.

Transcripts of Instructions to Provincial Governors VIII—Mass. Hist. Soc.

U. of London Institute—Institute of Historical Research, University of London.

Va. U. Mss. Dept.—University of Virginia, Manuscripts Department.

Yale U. Lib.—Yale University Library, New Haven, Conn.

UNPUBLISHED DISSERTATIONS CITED

Barrow "Customs Service"—Thomas Barrow "The Colonial Customs Service, 1660–1775," Ph.D. dissertation, Harvard University Library (1961).

Champagne, Roger J. "The Sons of Liberty and the Aristocracy in New York Politics, 1765–1790," University of Wisconsin (1960).

Currie, Harold W. "Massachusetts Politics and the Colonial Agency, 1762–1770," University of Michigan (1960).

Ernst, Joseph A. "Currency in the Era of the American Revolution," University of Wisconsin (1962).

Frese "Writs of Assistance"—Joseph R. Frese "Writs of Assistance in the American Colonies, 1660–1776," dissertation, Harvard University (1951).

Freiberg "Hutchinson"—Freiberg, Malcolm "Prelude to Purgatory: Thomas Hutchinson in Massachusetts Politics, 1760–1770," Ph.D. thesis, Brown University Library, Providence, R.I. (1950).

Lemisch "Jack Tar vs John Bull"—L. Jesse Lemisch "Jack Tar vs John Bull: The Role of New York Seamen in Precipitating the Revolution," dissertation, Yale University Library (1962).

Olm, Elmer "The Chatham Ministry and the American Colonies, 1766–1768," University of Michigan (1960).

Sachs, William T. "The Business Outlook in the Northern Colonies, 1770–1775," Columbia University (1957).

Yoder, Peyton W. "Paper Currency in Colonial Pennsylvania," Indiana University (1941).

Zimmerman, John J. "Benjamin Franklin: A Study of Pennsylvania Politics and the Colonial Agency, 1755–1775," University of Michigan (1956).

INDEX

This index is intended to give specific references, and is to serve as a supplement to, not a replacement for, the Table of Contents. The reader wishing to research specific broad issues will find the synopsis offered in the Introduction, as well as the Chronology, most useful.

Act of 1391, 209, 451–452
Act of 1660, 211, 215, 450, 453
Act of 1663, 44, 208–210, 390, 450–452
Act of 1696, 206–207, 390, 449, 451
Act of 1698, 6
Act of 1715 (Septennial Act), 170, 422
Act of 1721, 90, 451–452
Act of 1758, *see* Twopenny Act
Act of 1764, *see* American Act
Act of 1766, 31–33, 39, 44, 58, 147, 206–207, *see also* Declaratory Act
Act of 1768, 147
Act of 1772, 5, 6, 147
Act of 1778, 207, 450
Act of Union (1707), 208, 450
Adams, Abigail, 262, 394
Adams, Hannah, 492
Adams, John, 87, 128, 181, 201–202, 225, 262, 269, 319, 321, 377, 387, 389, 468; Boston "Massacre" and, 78–80, 338; Boston Tea Party and, 100; as delegate to First Continental Congress, 137–142, 239, 392–415 *passim;* Statement of Rights and, 146–147; Suffolk Resolves and, 150; impressions of other delegates, 139–140; Petition to the King and, 156–158, 411; revision of minutes of Congress by, 160; on Dickinson, 130; at First Massachusetts Congress, 179; on Johnson, 161; as "Novanglus," 201, 443
Adams, Samuel, 6, 88, 136, 156, 229, 286, 288, 308, 349–350, 384, 434, 490; Boston "Massacre" and, 81, 332–340 *passim;* Boston Port Act and, 165, 250, 365, 419; Boston Tea Party and, 93, 97, 99–100, 104, 356–361 *passim,* 470; as delegate to

First Continental Congress, 126, 128, 131, 136, 138–139, 142, 239, 287, 289, 398, 404, 411; at First Massachusetts Congress, 179; as tax collector, 242–245, 479–480
Adams, Thomas, 465
Addison, Henry, 462
Address to the King (Petition to the King; 1774), 9–10, 156–162, 173, 410–414
Address to the People of Great Britain (1774), 155, 409
Administration of Justice Act (1774), 119, 147, 379
Admiralty Courts, 9, 31, 66, 157–158, 209–210, 222, 254, 411, 451–453, 464–465
Albany Congress (1754), 130, 389
Allen, Bennet, 462
Allen, James, 143, 399
Allen, Rev. John, 261, 347, 488
Allen, William, 456
Alsop, John, 129, 138, 233, 240, 472
American Act of 1764, 24, 28–32, 39, 58, 64, 198, 209–210, 406, 452–453; demands for repeal of, 2, 147; enforcement provisions of, 29–32
American Customs Board, 47, 75, 109, 213–215, 287, 301, 307, 316–319, 324, 340–341, 357–361 *passim,* 364, 369, 371, 417, 455–457; *Liberty* riot and, 61–65
Amherst, Gen. Sir Jeffrey, 171–172, 284, 323, 379, 424
Andrews, John, 100, 163, 244, 389, 393, 417, 439, 483–484
Angelican episcopate, attempted establishment in colonies, 60, 217–221, 442, 458–464

Anthony, Theophilus, 427

Appleton, Dr. Nathaniel, 431

Apsley, Baron (Henry Bathurst), 103, 121, 169, 364, 424, 438

Articles of Confederation (1777), 142, 398

Association, the, *see* First Continental Congress

Astley, Sir Edward, 118

Attucks, Crispus, 79, 337–338

Auchmuty, Robert, 79, 338

Auchmuty, Rev. Samuel, 359

Aufrère, George, 17

Austin, Samuel, 359

Ayres, Samuel, 101

Baker, Sir William, 17, 279–280, 383

Baltimore, non-importation agreements in (1768), 73, 330; support of Boston (1774), 165, 418

Balfour, Capt. Nisbet, 435

Barber, Major Nathaniel, 356

Barbour, Peter, 334

Barclay, David, 254–257, 485–486

Barker, Lieut. John, 265–266, 438

Barré, Col. Isaac, 21, 71, 106, 118, 172, 276, 329, 367

Barrell, William, 100, 389

Barrett, Capt. Nathan, 266–267, 491

Barrington, 2nd Viscount (William Wildman Barrington), 71–72, 109–110, 169, 187, 195, 298, 299, 318, 324, 328–329, 371–373, 438

Battle of the Golden Hill, 227, 469

Bayard, Nicholas, 478

Beaver (ship), 84, 358

Beckford, William, 21, 40, 276, 299

Bedford, 4th Duke of (John Russell), 23–24, 66, 205, 218, 273, 278, 289, 292, 297, 309, 322

Beekman, Henry, 476

Beers, Isaac, 138

Belknap, Jeremiah, 334

Benezet, Anthony, 261, 488

Bernard, Francis, 41, 48, 53, 119, 155, 234, 272, 278, 308, 315–316, 370–372, 457, 466, 468, 470; Boston "Massacre" and, 75–76, 79, 331–335; *Liberty* riot and, 61–63, 65, 317–321; Townshend Act and, 53, 56,

304, 310; treason resolution and, 67, 324, 326

Bernard, John, 335

Bestes, Peter, 488

Biddle, Edward, 130, 157, 232, 240

Bigelow, Joshua, 427

Billop, Christopher, 259–260

Blackstone, Sir William, 85, 276, 279, 294

Blair, John, 54, 309

Blake, Jonathan, 385, 427

Bland, Richard, 129, 139, 142–143, 157, 178, 240, 261, 393, 397, 412, 430, 488

Bland, William, 463

Blowers, Sampson S., 339

Boerum, Simon, 129, 233, 240, 259

Bollan, William, 94, 107, 208–209, 272, 367, 375, 412

Bond, Joshua, 192

Bond, Phineas, 201, 444

bond on colonial vessels, 30, 32

Boston, Boston Port Act and, *see* below; committee to enforce Association in, 175; Gage fortifies (December, 1775), 185; judges' salaries controversy in, 88; *Liberty* riot in, 61–65, 69, 76, 109, 317–321, 331, 366; non-importation agreements in (1768), 57–58, 72, 77, 223–224, 329–330, 466–467; Stamp Act (1765) and, 48, 100, 362; troops sent to, 8, 75–76, 103–109, 118–119, 163, 169, 184–187, 331–333, 417, 434; troops removed as gesture of conciliation, 81, 173, 341; treason resolution and, 69

Boston Committee of Correspondence, 88, 97–98, 126, 150, 166, 250, 357, 384, 387, 389, 483; attempted censure of, 164, 418; controversy over judges' salaries and, 88, 349–350

Boston "Massacre" (1770), 75–81, 334–341 *passim,* 359, 366

Boston Port Act (1774), 6–7, 9, 103–108, 126–131, 164, 250, 367–368, 384, 407, 416; proposals for suspension of, 156, 174, 231, 249, 254–255; enforcement of, 118–119, 163, 165–166, 184, 416–421; foundations of, 81, 103; Quebec Act compared with, 121

Boston Tea Party (1773), 6–7, 90, 95–
102, 104, 107, 112, 121, 162, 354–
365 *passim*, 469–470
Botetourt, Baron de (Norborne
Berkeley), 59, 214, 314
Boucher, Rev. Jonathan, 220, 462
Bourgatte, Charlotte, 340
Bourmaster, John, 440
Bourne, Sylvanus, 349
Bowdoin, James, 128, 316, 318, 387
Bowen, Ephraim, 344
Braddock, Gen. Edward, 140
Bradford, William, 471
Bradshaw, Thomas, 317
Brasher, Abraham, 427
Brattle, William, 377
Breckdale, Matthew, 366
Briggs, Aaron, 83–85, 344
Bristol, 3rd Earl of (Augustus John
Hervey), 67, 272, 323
British Board of Trade, 197, 208
British Customs, 30, 283–284, 301, 317,
366, 457, *see also* American Customs
Board
British East India Company, *see* East
India Company
Brown, John, 84, 441
Brown, Capt. William, 346
Brush, Crean, 259
"Brutus," 227
Buckinghamshire, 2nd Earl of (John
Hobart), 364–365
Bull, Joseph, 478
Bull, William, 282
Burch, William, 61–62, 316
Burgoyne, Gen. John, 171
Burke, Edmund, 23, 40, 276–282
passim, 291–292, 360, 376, 412, 454;
Boston Port Act opposed by, 106–
107, 366–368; denounces North's
attempts at conciliation, 172, 173;
Massachusetts Regulating Act op-
posed by, 118; peace efforts of
(March 1775), 174; repeal of
Townshend Act and, 93, 118, 352,
378
Burton, Rev. Daniel, 459
Bute, 3rd Earl of (John Stuart), 23,
34–35, 37, 70, 186, 204, 278, 280,
288–292, 447–448

Butler, Lieut. Joseph, 266–267
Byng, George, 107, 367
Byrd, William, 445

Caldwell, Benjamin, 467
Caldwell, James, 79, 337
Camden, 1st Earl (Sir Charles Pratt),
21, 70, 275, 277, 291, 300; Boston
Port Act opposed by, 107, 368; in
Chatham Ministry, 35, 37; in
Grafton Ministry, 67, 70; Massachu-
setts Regulating Act opposed by,
378; revision of Townshend Act
and, 68, 324–327; treason resolu-
tion opposed by, 67, 326
Camm, Rev. John, 219, 261, 442, 461,
463, 488
Canadian role in war preparations,
see Carleton
Carleton, Gen. Guy, 123–124, 185, 380–
384, 433, 436
Carr, Patrick, 79, 332, 337
Carroll, Charles, of Carrollton, Md.,
133, 389
Carter, Landon, 44
Carter, Robert, 445
Cary, Archibald, 447
Castle William, 76, 108, 163, 324
Caswell, Richard, 130, 241, 389, 393–
394
Cavendish, Lord John, 106, 366
Chambers, John, 348
Champion, Richard, 172
Chandler, Rev. Samuel, 218
Chandler, Rev. Thomas Bradbury, 219,
459
Charleston, non-importation agree-
ments in, 60, 73, 223, 330–331;
opposition to Tea Act in, 6, 96;
outbreaks against colonial trade
restrictions in, 61; Stamp Riots in
(1765), 48, 304
Chase, Samuel, 129, 153, 240
Chatham, Earl of (William Pitt), 55,
67, 71, 204–205, 288–295, 298, 300,
310; Boston Port Act and, 107;
conciliation plan of (1775), 10–11,
173–174, 425–427; denounces North's
conciliation attempts, 172, 423–424;
Grafton opposed by, 70; illness of,

Chatham, Earl of (*cont.*)
  39, 42–43, 66, 321; problems inherited by, 34–42; Quartering Act and, 39–40, 379; Quebec Act and, 121, 380; replacement of, 66, 321, 323; Rockingham Ministry and, 204–205; Stamp Act and, 15–19, 21, 23, 271–276, 280; Townshend Act and, 42–43, 45, 327, 329
Chauncy, Rev. Charles, 220, 458
Cheever, Ezekiel, 356
Church, Benjamin, 104, 179–180, 341, 356–357
circular orders and instructions to colonial governors, 10, 31, 56, 67–68, 107, 163, 169, 198, 285, 311, 324–326, 366–367, 417–418
Clarke, Jonathan, 96–97, 104, 356–357
Clarke, Richard, 96–97, 314, 354, 356
classical authors, influence of, 135
Cleveland, Aaron, 398
Clinton, George, 176, 259, 477, 487
Clinton, Gen. Henry, 171
Coffin, Hezekiah, 358
Colbourne, H. Trevor, 135
Colden, Cadwallader, 161, 236–238, 278, 283, 295, 394, 397, 405, 415, 423–424, 476–478
Colonial Currency Act (1764), 27, 236, 282, 353
Committee of Safety (Second Massachusetts Congress; February 1775), 181–182, 191, 431–433, 439–440, 489
Concord (Mass.; April 19, 1775, British raid), 174, 178, 185, 264, 441–442, 491–492; conflict of evidence, 264–268; description, 12–13, 191–196; Gage's preparations for, 188–189
Connecticut Colony, First Continental Congress and, 128–130, 150, 158, 239; non-importation agreements in (1768), 58, 313; dilution of non-importation agreements (1770), 72; petition to repeal Townshend Act, 55, 57, 309; population of (1770), 5; protests resolution of stamp tax, 2; response of, to closing of port of

Boston, 164, 386; war preparations in, 176, 429
Continental Congresses, *see* First Continental Congress and Second Continental Congress
Conway, Henry Seymour, Boston Port Act supported by, 106, 367; formation of Pitt Ministry and, 34–37, 288–293, 295, 298; in Grafton Ministry, 66–67, 205, 322, 324; revision of Townshend Act and, 68, 71, 325, 329; Stamp Act and, 15–17, 19, 21, 23, 271–273, 275–276, 279–280; trade provisions of American Act and, 31, 211; trade relief promised by, 31, 33, 211; treason resolution opposed by, 67
Cooke, Sir John, 451
Cooper, Benjamin, 492
Cooper, Grey, 325
Cooper, Rev. Myles, 459
Cooper, Rachel, 492
Cooper, William, 88, 99, 333, 335, 359, 419
Copley, John Singleton, 97
Corbet, Michael, 77, 225–226, 467–468
Corner, Capt. John, 63–65, 319, 321
Cornwall, Charles Wolfram, 92, 352
Cornwallis, 1st Marquis (Charles Cornwallis), 21, 276
Cornwallis, Frederick, 198
Correspondence, Committees of, creation of, 86–88
Cramahé, Hector, 122
Cranch, Mary Smith, 394
Crane, Stephen, 130, 240
Cruger, Henry, Jr., 22, 277, 279
Cruger, Henry, Sr., 277, 279
Cruger, John, 234–260 *passim*, 473–476, 487 *passim*
Cumberland, Duke of (William Augustus), 15, 204–205, 271–272, 426, 447–449
Cummins, Anne, 335
Cummins, Elizabeth, 335
Cunningham, Peter, 337
Cushing, John, 337, 339, 349
Cushing, Thomas, as delegate to First Continental Congress, 128, 136, 138–

139, 143–144, 151, 159, 239, 330,
387–388, 392, 400, 405–406; at
First Massachusetts Congress, 179;
Massachusetts Petition of 1773 and,
113–116, 374–376; at Second Massachusetts Congress, 182

Dalrymple, Col. William, 77, 81, 331,
334, 341, 359
Danforth, Samuel, 420
Dartmouth, 2nd Earl of (William
Legge), 11–12, 17, 107, 143, 160–161,
171, 188, 255, 267, 273, 277, 350,
423–424, 434–438 *passim,* 485;
Boston Port Act and, 103–104, 107–
108, 364–369; conciliation attempts
and (1775), 174, 427; enforcement
of Intolerable Acts, 165–169, 184,
416–421; Franklin on, 107, 368;
Gaspee affair and, 84–86, 346–347;
Massachusetts Petition of 1773 and,
115; Quebec Act and, 121–124
passim, 381–384 *passim*
Dartmouth (ship), 7, 96–99, 229–230,
357–360, 470
Dawes, William, 439
Deane, Silas, 130, 138–141, 199, 239,
394–402 *passim*
De Berdt, Dennys, 143, 275–276, 296–
297, 309–318 *passim,* 332, 458
De Berniere, Ensign Henry, 436
Declaratory Act (1766), 1, 21–25, 27,
33, 37, 111, 206–207, 273–274, 277,
287–288, 300–301, 307, 392, 450
De Grey, William, 213–215, 321, 455
Dehart, John, 130, 240
De Lancey, Stephen, 233–238, 259–
260, 348, 473–479 *passim*
Delaware Colony, delegation to First
Continental Congress, 129–130, 136,
158, 240; non-importation agree-
ments in (1768), 58, 313; petition for
repeal of Townshend Act by, 57,
311–312; population of (1770), 5;
response of, to First Continental
Congress, 178; Second Continental
Congress and, 178
Dempster, George, 106, 367
Derby, John, 489
Devens, Richard, 180

Devonshire, 4th Duke of (William
Cavendish), 15, 271
De Witt, Charles, 235–237, 239
Diamond, William, 490
Dickinson, John, 176, 231, 313, 389,
430, 471; biography of, 49–50, 306;
as delegate to First Continental
Congress, 130, 139, 158–160, 240,
388–389, 411–412; *Farmer's Letters*
of, 3, 50–54, 56, 58, 306–308
Dickinson, William, 344
Digges, Dudley, 456
Dissenters, 218–219, 233–234, 458,
474
Dockyards Act (1772), 84, 345
Dominica, 211, 286, 295, 406–407
Dowdeswell, William, 16–17, 19, 21,
40, 70, 90, 106, 300, 327, 366; Stamp
Act and, 21, 272, 273; Tea Act of
1773 and, 93–94, 352
Drake, Joseph, 478
Drayton, William Henry ("Freeman"),
458, 483
Duane, James, as delegate to First
Continental Congress, 129, 138, 140,
148–160 *passim,* 233, 240, 246, 252,
396–398, 403–410 *passim,* 415, 472,
479, 481; as delegate to Second Con-
tinental Congress, 178
Duché, Rev. Jacob, 142, 398
Dudingston, Lt. William, 82–83, 86
Duff, Alexander, 204, 447
Dulany, Daniel, 33, 307
Dunmore, 4th Earl of (John Murray),
127, 175, 386, 429
Dunning, John, 115–116, 119, 172,
323–324, 375
Dupuis, Abraham & Co., 354
Du Simitière, Eugène, 414
Duyckinck, Christopher, 427
Dyer, Eliphalet, 130–146, 154, 157,
160, 239, 401, 411
Dyer, Samuel, 414

East India Company, 42, 228, 230, 299,
328, 354–363 *passim,* 367, 406; consignees of, 93–94, 96, 100, 229–230,
354; indemnifying, 105–106, 156,
163–164; losses suffered by, 71, 100;
refund of tea duty requested by, 90,

East India Company (*cont.*)
228, 351; Tea Act and, 90–96, 350–354

"Easterbrooks, Prince," 441

Eckley (barber), 100, 362

Eden, Robert, 220, 462

Edson, Josiah, 420

Egmont, 2nd Earl (Sir John Perceval), 15–17, 34, 37, 273, 288–289, 291

Eleanor (ship), 97, 358

Ellis, Welbore, 71, 329

Emerson, Rev. William, 491

Erskine, Sir Henry, 204

Erving, George, 163

Erving, John, 420

Evelyn, Capt. William Glanville, 186–187, 190, 434, 436–437

Ewer, John (Bishop of Llandaff), 220, 461

Fairfax, Bryan, 132, 392, 447

Fairfax County Resolves, 136–137, 392

Farmer's Letters (Dickinson), 3, 50–54, 56, 58; *see also* Dickinson

Farrar, Lt. Jonathan, 266–267

Fauquier, Francis, 463

Fawkes, Guy, 62

Finch, Thomas, 292

First Continental Congress (1774), 3–4, 124, 169, 170, 173, 176, 252–253, 258–260, 262, 393–401, 432, 489; Address to the inhabitants of Quebec, 156; Address to the People of Great Britain, 155; Association plan, 9, 151–154, 160–162; 175; call for, 9, 126–131, 384–389 *passim;* circular letter, 156, 159; colonial response to, 175–178; Committee for the Statement of Rights, 142, 146–149, 398–399; delegates to, listed, 239–241; dissolution of, 161–162; first steps of, 138–145; information furnished to British Ministry about, 252–253; Memorial to colonists, 154–155, 161; Petition to the King, 9–10, 156–162, 173, 216; reprisal resolution, 160; Suffolk Resolves, 142, 146–150, 179, 249, 404–405;

unifying and divisive elements in, 132–137, 390–392

First Massachusetts Congress, *see* Massachusetts Provincial Congress

Fisher, Jabez, 432

Fisher, John, 336

Fisher, Miers, 146

Fleeming, William, 224

Fleming, John, 447

Floyd, William, 233, 240

Folsom, John, 239

Folsom, Nathaniel, 130, 176, 429

Fortune (ship), 319

Foster, Col. Jedediah, 182

Fothergill, Dr. John, 254–257, 485–486

Fowles, Thomas, 209

Fox, Charles James, 106, 118, 354, 423

Fox, Joseph, 471

Francis, Philip, 327

Franklin, Benjamin, 2, 172, 174, 252, 270, 273–274, 278, 281, 298, 300–301, 311, 325, 352, 372–373, 404, 429, 450; on Dartmouth, 107; dismissal from Crown office, 116, 376; Hutchinson-Oliver letters and, 113–116 *passim;* Massachusetts Petition of 1773 and, 113–116; peace negotiations of, 254–257, 485–486; in Quaker Party, 50; Second Continental Congress and, 199; Stamp Act and, 3, 22, 26, 45–46, 281, 283; Townshend Act and, 50, 304–305, 328–331 *passim*

Franklin, William, 107, 270, 273, 294, 399

Free Port Act (1766), 33, 39, 211–212, 294, 454

Freeman, Sambo, 488

French and Indian War (Seven Years' War, 1756–1763), 11–12, 171, 184

Fuller, Rose, 40, 106–107, 118, 366–367, 378

Gadsden, Christopher, 130, 140–145 *passim,* 154–156, 393–401 *passim,* 408, 482

Gage, Gen. Thomas, 41, 55, 75, 119, 150, 173, 182–183, 264–267, 272, 293, 296, 298–299, 304, 332–341 *passim,* 431–434, 484; Administration of Justice Act and, 379; biography of, 370; as Governor of Massachusetts, 10, 12, 107–110, 163–171, 174, 181–189, 381, 384; enforcement of Intolerable Acts by, 163–169, 179, 181, 416–421; launches expedition on Concord, 188–189, 193–195; military activities and, 170–171, 182, 184–187, 405, 434–442 *passim;* tightening reins on Massachusetts, 109–110, 369–371

Galloway, Joseph, 26, 130, 140–160 *passim,* 176, 232, 240, 246, 252, 255, 281, 298, 389, 394–400 *passim,* 405, 415, 428, 471–472, 481–482

Gardner, Henry, 341

Gardner, Col. Thomas, 182

Garrick, Edward, 79, 336–337

Garth, Charles, 40, 92, 272, 274–279, 286, 298, 352–354, 390, 412

Gaspee affair (1772), 6, 82–87

George III, Administration of Justice Act and, 379; Boston Port Act and, 104–105, 107, 365–368 *passim;* conciliation attempt of (1775), 171–172, 424–425; declares New England governments in state of rebellion (June 1774), 169, 422; dissolves thirteenth Parliament (June 1774), 170; *Gaspee* affair and, 84; Grafton Ministry and, 67, 321–322; Massachusetts Petition of 1773 and, 115–116; New York Restraining Act and, 40; Pitt Ministry and, 34–37, 288–292; political power of, 204; Quebec Act and, 121, 123; Rockingham Ministry and, 204–205; Stamp Act and, 14, 16–20, 23, 273–281; taxation of colonies and, 1; Tea Act and, 93; tightening reins on Massachusetts and, 67, 119, 170; treason resolution and, 67, 323–324; Townshend Act and, 45, 300, 326

Georgia Colony, 8, 14; Continental Congress and, 129, 196, 388, 429; non-importation agreements (1768) in, 60, 315; dilution of non-importation agreements (1770), 73; petition for repeal of Townshend Act by, 57,

311–312; population of (1770), 5; response to treason resolution in, 69, 325

Germain, Lord George, *see* Sackville

Gerry, Elbridge, 179

Gibbon, Edward, 423

Gibson, Edmund, 460

Gibson, John, 471

Gifford, Capt. James, 338

Gilbert, Thomas, 185

Gilman, Peter, 326

Gloucester, Duke of (George Augustus Frederick; later George IV), 23, 380

Goldfinch, Capt. John, 336

Goldsborough, Robert, 129, 146, 154, 156, 160, 240, 409

Gordon, Thomas Knox, 458

Gordon, Rev. William, 242, 244, 267, 464, 491

Gore, John, 336

Gould, Lt. Edward, 491

Gower, 2nd Earl of (Granville Leveson-Gower), 66–67, 186, 273, 290, 424; Boston Port Act and, 103, 364; revision of Townshend Act and, 68, 325; tightening reins on Massachusetts and, 110

Grafton, 3rd Duke of (Augustus Henry Fitzroy), 134, 271–273, 275, 280, 288, 309; becomes First Minister, 66–67, 322; formation of Pitt Ministry and, 34–35, 37, 291, 295, 299–300; opposition faced by, 70; Townshend Act and, 42–43, 45, 68, 103

Granby, Marquis of (John Manners), 37, 67–68, 70, 205, 291, 325, 327

Grant, Col. James, 12, 270

Grantham, Lord, 16, 272

Graves, Adm. Samuel, 169, 421, 439

Gray, Harrison, 243, 480

Gray, Samuel, 19, 338

Greenleaf, Stephen, 234, 243, 334–335, 457

Grenville, George, 34, 39, 70–71, 111, 113, 204–205, 281, 288, 290, 295–296, 298, 300–301, 317–318, 448; Act of 1764 passed under, 2; colonial trade under, 287; cost of maintaining troops in the colonies and, 42; death of, 103; Grafton Ministry

Grenville, George (*cont.*)
and, 66, 322; Hillsborough's friendship for, 55, 310; N.Y. Restraining Act and, 40; Stamp Act and, 14,
16, 19, 23–24, 270, 272–274, 278–
279, 281
Guilford, 1st Baron (Francis North),
66, 70, 424
Gwatkin, Thomas, 221, 463

Hadley, Samuel, 441
Haldimand, Gen. Frederick, 357, 434
Halifax, Admiralty Court at, 210, 222,
464–465
Halifax, 2nd Earl of (George Montagu
Dunk), 34, 205, 288, 310, 459
Hall, David, 49, 205
Hall, Capt. James, 99, 230, 359–360,
470
Hall, John, 176
Hallowell, Benjamin, 64, 215, 320, 457
Hamersely, Hugh, 273–279 *passim*
Hancock, John, 58, 130, 183, 190, 224,
244, 308, 324, 350, 365, 370, 439, 467;
Boston "Massacre" and, 81, 332, 341;
Boston Tea Party and, 96, 98, 100,
104, 358–359, 362; as delegate to
Second Continental Congress, 176,
490; *Liberty* riot and, 62, 64–65,
317, 320; Massachusetts Provincial
Congress and, 179–180, 388, 432
Hannah (ship), 451
Hardwicke, 1st Earl of (Philip Yorke),
21, 275, 280–281, 358, 434, 451
Haring, John, 176, 233, 240, 409, 428
Harrington, Caleb, 441
Harrington, Jonathan, 441
Harrison, Benjamin, 129, 136, 139, 141,
157, 178, 240, 393, 397, 412, 447
Harrison, Joseph, 64, 307
Hartigan, James, 339
Hartley, David, 174, 426
Harvey, Gen. Edward, 187
Hawke, Sir Edward, 37, 67–68, 103,
291, 325
Hawley, Joseph, 179, 182, 297, 350,
432
Hayley, George, 173, 426
Hayley (ship), 365
Heath, Gen. William, 179–180, 182

Henderson, Benjamin, 356
Henley, Rev. Samuel, 221, 463
Henry, Patrick, 86, 262, 314, 385, 430;
as delegate to First Continental
Congress, 129, 136, 139, 141, 150,
156–157, 240, 393–400 *passim*, 409,
411–412, 481; war preparations and,
178, 430
Henry VIII, 67, 69
Hertford, 1st Earl of (Francis Seymour
Conway), 15, 23
Hewes, George R. T., 362
Hewes, Joseph, 130, 241, 389, 393
Hewitt, James, 21, 276
Hewitt, Richard, 463
Hillsborough, 1st Earl and 2nd Vis-
count of (Wills Hill), 155, 278, 298–
299, 310; controversy over judges'
salaries and, 87; *Farmer's Letters*
and, 55–56, 58; *Gaspee* affair and,
83; in Grafton Ministry, 66–67, 321;
role of, in Boston "Massacre," 75;
tightening reins on Massachusetts
and, 110–111, 371–373; Townshend
Act and, 56–57, 68–69, 309, 323–326;
treason resolution and, 67
Hitchborn, Thomas, 362
Hobby, Charles, 338
Holbrook, Felix, 488
Hollis, Thomas, 23, 278, 316
Holroyd, John Baker, 423
Holt, John, 461
Hood, Commodore Samuel, 63, 225,
317, 319, 467
Hooper, Richard, 225
Hooper, William, 130, 157, 160, 241,
389, 393
Hooten, Joseph, Jr., 338
Hopkins, Stephen, 128, 132, 136, 146,
207, 239, 262, 389–390, 392, 403, 416
Horrocks, Rev. James, 220–221, 463
Horsmanden, Daniel, 345–348 *passim*
Hovering Act (1763), 28–29, 283
Howe, Adm. (Lord Richard Howe),
174, 256
Howe, Caroline (Mrs. John), 256, 486
Howe, Col. George Augustus, 256
Howe, William, 171, 256, 437
Hulton, Ann(e), 267, 316, 361–362, 371
Hulton, Henry, 61–62, 316, 317

Humphreys, Charles, 130, 232, 240, 471–472

Hutchinson, Thomas, 107, 163, 169, 202, 213–214, 225, 242, 244, 252, 272, 278, 297, 304, 311–312, 372, 417–418, 421, 445–446, 468–469, 484; biography, 203; Boston "Massacre" and, 77, 79, 81, 335–341; Boston Tea Party and, 96–100, 229–230, 355–363 *passim,* 470; controversy over judges' salaries and, 88–89, 349–350; *Liberty* riot and, 63–64, 217–221; Massachusetts Petition of 1773 and, 113–114, 116, 374–376; tightening reins on Massachusetts and, 111–112, 119, 369, 373; writs of assistance and, 213–214

Hyde, Lord (Thomas Villiers), 255, 257, 485–486

Ilfley, Enoch, 457–458

impressment, 63, 77, 225–226, 319 467–468

Ingersoll, Jared, 222, 464–465

Inglis, Charles, 221, 463–464

instructions, Crown, *see* circular orders and instructions

Intolerable Acts, *see* Administration of Justice Act; Boston Port Act; Massachusetts Regulating Act; Quebec Act

Ireland, colonial trade with, 28, 39, 133, 286, 390–391

Irving, Thomas, 65

Izard, Ralph, 73, 143

Jackson, Edward, 334

Jackson, Joseph, 370

Jackson, Richard, 2, 22, 53, 111, 278, 287, 294, 297, 319, 320

Jackson, William, 334–335

James, Maj. Thomas, 23, 278

Jauncey, James, 233–236, 259–260, 473

Jay, Sir James, 252–253

Jay, John, 129, 138, 148, 150, 154, 156, 233, 240, 246, 252–253, 398, 409, 410, 472, 479, 481, 484

Jefferson, Thomas, 86, 178, 314, 385–386, 489

Jeffries, David, 243

Johnson, Rev. Samuel, 218–219, 261, 459

Johnson, Thomas, 129, 146, 151, 154, 156, 161, 240

Johnson, William Samuel, 71, 275, 310, 316, 318, 325, 327–329, 404, 411, 415, 464

Johnston, Augustus, 222, 465

Johnstone, George, 92, 106, 352

Johnstone, William, 92

Johonnot ("Johonat"), Gabriel, 104, 356

Joie, Chester, 488

Kayaderossas patent, 198, 442

Kennedy, Archibald, 209

Keppel, Frederick (Bishop of Exeter), 426

Kilroy, Matthew, 80, 339–340

Kinsey, James, 130, 240, 415

Kirk, Thomas, 320

Kissam, David, 235, 237, 260

Knox, William, 124, 310, 383–384, 423

Laidlie, Rev. Archibald, 473–474

Laight, William, 252, 484

Lamb, John, 474

Langdon, John, 176

Laud, William, 461

Laurens, Henry, 58, 61, 342

Laurie, Capt. Walter Sloane, 194, 267, 441, 491

Le Cras, Capt. Edward, 439

Lee, Arthur, 93, 115, 368, 374–375, 489

Lee, Gen. Charles, 414

Lee, Francis Lightfoot, 484

Lee, John, 115–116

Lee, Philip Ludwell, 445

Lee, Richard Henry, 86, 124, 223, 313, 374, 383–394 *passim,* 415, 447, 465, 481–484 *passim;* as delegate to First Continental Congress, 128–129, 136, 139, 142, 145, 148, 151–161 *passim,* 240, 397, 399, 407, 411–412; war preparations and, 178, 430

Lee, William, 252–253, 365, 368, 484

Leonard, Daniel (*penname* "Massachusettsensis"), 420, 443, 470

Leonard, George, 226, 490–491
Leslie, Lt. Col. Alexander, 99, 357–360
Levison-Gower, Mrs. John, 186
Lewis, Francis, 176, 487
Lexington (Mass.; April 19, 1775, skirmish), 12–13, 178, 185, 191–196, 264–268, 440–441, 490–491
Liberty pole, 227, 237–238
Liberty riot (1768), 61–65, 69, 76, 109, 317–321, 331, 366
Life, Thomas, 115, 375, 412
Lillie, Thomas, 77–78, 335
Lincoln, Benjamin, 179, 432
Linzee, Capt. John, 84–86, 344–346
Lispenard, Leonard, 472
Livingston, Peter R., 235–238, 475–476, 478, 487
Livingston, Peter Van Brugh, 234, 472, 474, 478
Livingston, Philip, 129, 138, 233–238, 312, 389, 472–479 *passim*
Livingston, Robert R., 176, 233–236, 473–479 *passim,* 487
Livingston, William, 130, 154, 220, 240, 388–389, 409, 462
Lockyer, Benjamin, 102, 363
London (ship), 101
Loring, Dr. John, 334
Loring, Joseph, 192
Loring, Joshua, 420
Lovell, James, 341
Low, Isaac, 129, 151–158 *passim,* 176, 233, 240, 330, 385, 396, 405, 428, 470, 487
Lowell, John, 356, 362
Lowth, Robert, 464
Luttrell, Col. Henry, 70, 326
Lynch, Thomas, 130, 140–141, 153, 156–157, 241, 393–397, 410–411
Lynde, Benjamin, 339
Lyttelton of Frankley, 1st Baron (George Lyttelton), 24, 280, 290
Lyttelton of Frankley, 2nd Baron (Thomas Lyttelton), 125, 240

McDougall, Alexander, 237–238, 472, 477
McKean, Thomas, 130, 146, 154, 160, 240

Mackay, Maj. Gen. Alexander, 333
Mackenzie, Lt. Frederick, 440–441
Mackenzie, James Stuart, 34, 37, 204–205, 291, 447–448
Madison, James, 471
Maidstone (ship), 342
Malcom, Daniel, 58, 61, 215, 320, 457
Malcom, John, 361–362, 366
Manigault, Peter, 482
Mansfield, Earl of (William Murray), 20, 24, 107, 424
Manwaring, Edward, 338, 340
Marchant, Henry, 346
Marlborough, 4th Duke of (George Spencer), 15, 380, 426
Marshall, Thomas, 359
Mary & Margaret (ship), 209
Maryland Colony, Anglican clergy in, 220; delegation to First Continental Congress from, 129, 139, 158, 161, 240, 388, 404; non-importation agreements in, 57, 60, 315; outbreaks against trade restrictions in (1765), 61; population of (1770), 5; war preparations in, 177
Maseres, Francis, 121
Mason, George, 27, 59, 127–128, 223, 281, 287, 313–314, 385, 483
"Massachusettensis," 443, 470, *see also* Leonard, Daniel
Massachusetts Charter (1691), 7, 117
Massachusetts Colony, 202–203, 445–446; circular letter (1773), 54–60 *passim,* 355; First Continental Congress and, 128–129, 136, 138–140, 148–149, 158, 161–162, 239, 387, 404; developments in (May to September 1774), 163–168, 415–421; judges' salaries controversy in, 87–89, 348–349; negro slavery and, 261–263, 488; non-importation agreements in (1768), 54, 56–58, 312, 314; dilution of non-importation agreements, 73; petitions to the King, 54, 114–116; population of (1770), 5; proposals for tightening reins on, 109–112, 119; protests against Stamp Act, 2–3; Quartering Act opposed by, 41, 60, 76; treason resolution and, 67–69, 323–326; war preparations

in, 176, 179–183, 434–439; writs of
assistance in, 47, 212–216

Massachusetts Indemnity Act, 297

Massachusetts Provincial Congress, 10,
179–182, 190, 431–443 *passim*, 489–
490

Massachusetts Regulating Act (1774),
6–8, 60, 81, 89, 108–109, 117–119,
121, 248–257, 376–377, 407, 416–421
passim, 483; demand for repeal of,
at First Continental Congress, 131,
147; enforcement of, 10, 163, 166–
167, 179, 184, 435; factors contributing to enactment of, 60, 81

Mauduit, Israel, 424

Maverick, Samuel, 79

Mawney, Dr. John, 344

Mechanics, Committee or Body of,
385, 427, 472

Mein, John, 224, 335, 467

Memorial to the colonists (1774; prepared at the First Continental Congress), 154–155, 161

Memorial to the House of Lords
(Virginia; 1768), 54

Meredith, Sir William, 426

Middleton, Henry, 130, 241, 389, 393,
412, 415

Mifflin, Charles, 232

Mifflin, Thomas (*penname* "Scaevola"),
95, 130, 139, 143, 151, 232, 240, 400,
405, 407, 412, 471–472

Mitchell, Andrew, 370

Mitchell, Col. Edward, 182

Molesworth, Capt. Ponsonby, 334

Molineux, William, 96, 104, 356–358,
364–365

Montagu, Capt. James, 439

Montagu, Adm. John, *see* Sandwich

Montgomery, Hugh, 80, 339–340

Moore, Sir Henry, 38–40, 233–236
passim, 293–294, 304, 312, 473–476

Moore, James, 418

Moore, Will, 100

Morris, Corbyn, 362

Morris, John, 362

Morris, Lewis, 176, 209

Morris, Robert, 199

Morton, John, 130, 232, 240

Muhlenberg, Frederick A. C., 389

Munroe, Jedediah, 441

Munroe, Robert, 441

Mure, Baron (William Mure), 23, 275–
276, 279, 289, 298

Murray, Daniel, 166–167

Murray, James, 382

Murray, John, 166–167, 420

Muzzy, Isaac, 441

Myndertse, Jacobus, 235, 237

Nancy (ship), 101, 363

Navigation Acts, 22–33, 44, 282–286
passim

Nelson, Thomas, 445

Nelson, William, 445

Ness, Ensign (Lt.) John, 77, 334

New England Governments declared
to be in state of rebellion (June
1774), 169–170

New Hampshire Colony, delegation to
First Continental Congress from,
129–130, 136, 158, 239; Massachusetts war preparations and, 183;
non-importation agreements in
(1768), 57–58, 314; population of
(1770), 5; treason resolution and, 69;
war preparations in, 177

New Jersey Colony, delegation to
First Continental Congress from,
129–130, 158, 240; non-importation
agreements in (1768), 55, 57–58, 314,
400; population of (1770), 5; war
preparations in, 178

New York City, clashes between
British troops and civilians in (1770),
227; Committee of Fifty-One, 126–
127, 175, 260, 385, 387, 472; committee to enforce Association plan
in, 175; non-importation agreements in, 57–58, 72, 342; opposition
to Tea Act in, 96, 101–102; Stamp
Act riots in (1765), 48, 100; Tories
in, 199, 443

New York Colony, controversy over
judges' salaries in, 87; delegation to
First Continental Congress from,
129–131; 141, 158, 233–240; 428;
effects of Massachusetts Regulating
Act on, 8; non-importation agreements in (1768), 57–58; 312–313;

New York Colony (*cont.*)
dilution of non-importation agreements (1770), 72–73; population of (1770), 5; Quartering Act and, 38–39, 41, 45, 60; response of, to First Continental Congress, 176, 258–260; war preparations in, 178

New York Restraining (or Suspending) Act (1767), 40–41, 43, 50, 112, 233, 235, 295–300 *passim*, 307, 312

Newcastle, 1st Duke of (Thomas Pelham-Holles), 37, 55, 70, 204–205, 272–274, 370, 414; and formation of Pitt Ministry, 34, 36, 288–292; Stamp Act and, 15–18, 24, 271–273, 279–280

Newdigate, Sir Roger, 298, 390

Newell, Timothy, 359

Nicholas, Robert Carter, 178, 430, 456

Nicholls, Rev. Samuel, 463

Nicoll, William, 236–237, 259–260, 477

non-importation agreements (1768), as response to Townshend Act, 54–60, 250–251, 304, 312–315, 328–331; uneven observance of, 223–224, 465–467

non-importation agreements, dilution of (1770), 70–74, 77, 82

non-importation, non-exportation agreements (1774), 9, 126–128, 135–136, 143–144, 151–154, 160–162, 175, 384, 386, 399–401, 405, 410–411

North, Frederick (*later* 2nd Earl of Guilford), 7, 10, 117, 134, 169, 246, 254, 270, 299, 391; Administration of Justice Act and, 379; becomes First Minister, 70; biography of, 70–71; Boston Port Act and, 103, 105, 108; conciliation attempts (February, 1775) of, 172–173; formation of Pitt Ministry and, 34, 299; Grafton Ministry and, 66–67, 322–325; Quebec Act and, 121, 381; Tea Act and, 91, 93, 95, 352–354; tightening reins on Massachusetts and, 110, 112; Townshend Act and, 68, 71–72, 118, 134; treason resolution and, 67, 324–325

North Carolina Colony, delegation to First Continental Congress from, 129–130, 158, 241, 389; effects of

Massachusetts Regulating Act on, 8; insurrections in, 82; non-importation agreements in (1768), 60, 315; dilution of non-importation agreements (1770), 73; petition for repeal of Townshend Act in, 57, 311–312; population of (1770), 5; war preparations in, 178

North End Caucus (Boston), 96, 101, 356, 385

Northey, Atty.-Gen. Edward, 451

Northington, 1st Earl (Robert Henley), formation of the Pitt Ministry and, 34–36, 288–291, 295; Quartering Act and, 39; replacement of, 37, 66; Stamp Act and, 15–16, 21, 24, 272–273, 275

Northumberland, 1st Duke of (Sir Hugh Percy), 11, 34, 186, 204, 270, 447

"Novanglus," *see* John Adams

Nugent, Robert, 18, 274

Oliver, Andrew, 113–114, 116, 349, 374–375

Oliver, Peter, 80, 87, 163

Orne, Azor, 180

Otis, James, 6, 48, 54, 77, 133, 213, 215, 225, 304, 308, 324, 332, 334, 340, 349, 368

Paca, William, 129, 240, 404

Page, John, 445

Paine, Robert Treat, 79, 128, 138–139, 146, 179, 239, 339, 387, 402, 409

Paine, Thomas, 49, 306

Paine, Timothy, 427

Palfrey, John, 62–63, 317, 339

Palmer, Joseph, 440

Palmer, Norton, 180

Palmer, William, 353, 355–356

Panton, Lt. Henry, 225–226, 467

Parker, James, 49, 178, 205, 248, 430, 441, 478

Parker, Capt. John, 264–266

Parsons, Capt. Lawrence, 194, 441

Patten, Matthew, 420

Paulet, Harry (6th Duke of Bolton), 21

Paxton, Charles, 61–62, 113–114, 316, 319, 373–374

Payson, Jonathan, 242

Pemberton, Samuel, 370

Pendleton, Edmund, 136, 139, 153, 156–157, 240, 393, 412

Penn, John, 231

Pennsylvania Colony, First Continental Congress and, 129–130, 136, 158, 231–232, 240, 430; non-importation agreements in (1768), 57–58, 313–314, 342; dilution of non-importation agreements (1770), 72–74; opposition to Tea Act in, 95–96, 101; population of (1770), 5; treason resolution in, 69, 325; war preparations in, 178

Penrose, Thomas, 471

Pepperell, William, 420

Percy, Col. Lord (Sir Hugh Percy; 2nd Duke of Northumberland), 11, 186–187, 190, 192, 195, 266–267, 270, 434, 437, 441, 490

Percy, Rev. Thomas, 187

"Petition of the Merchants and Traders of the City of London trading to North America" (1770), 71

Petition to the King (Address to the King; 1774), 9–10, 156–162, 173, 410–415

Philadelphia, committee for enforcement of the Association in, 175; meetings against Tea Act in, 6; non-importation agreements in (1768), 58, 72, 74, 126, 223, 329–331; opposition to Tea Act in, 96, 101; Stamp Act riots in (1765), 48

Philipse, Frederick, 259–260

Phillips, William, 98, 359

Phipps, Spencer, 217

Pierpont, Robert, 77, 224, 334, 480

Pigeon, John, 180

Pitcairn, Maj. John, 12, 181, 187–194 *passim*, 265, 437–441 *passim*

Pitkin, William, 309–310

Pitt, William, *see* Chatham, Earl of

Pitt Packet (ship), 225, 467

Pitts, John, 359

Platt, Jeremiah, 427

Pomeroy, Col. John, 333

Pomeroy, Seth, 180

Porteous, Capt. John, 366

Potter, Simeon, 84

Powell, Samuel, 146

Power, Thomas, 467

Pownall, John, 100, 111–112, 121, 252–253, 308, 325, 438, 484

Pownall, Thomas, 40, 67–68, 71–72, 118, 328–329, 335, 340, 377–378

Preble, Jedediah, 180, 341

Prescott, Col. Richard, 424

Preston, Capt. Thomas, 79–80, 119, 334–339 *passim*

Proctor, Capt. Edward, 97, 104, 356, 365

Providence, 126

Pulteney, William, 352

Purviance, Robert and Samuel, 418

Putnam, Israel, 398

Quakers, 200, 231, 418, 471, 488

Quartering Act (1765), 38–41, 45, 60, 76, 227, 235, 259, 282, 293–298, 307, 315, 324–325; extensions (1767–1774), 66, 119–120, 379

Quebec Act (1774), 121–125, 143, 154–155, 380–384, 399, 407, 409

Quebec Revenue Act (1774), 122, 125, 384

Quero (ship), 489–490

Quincy, Edmund, 334

Quincy, Josiah, Jr., 79–80, 361

Quincy, Norton, 180, 432

Quincy, Samuel, 79

Randolph, John, 214

Randolph, Peyton, 54, 86, 127, 129, 136, 139, 141, 154, 160, 214, 240, 309, 314, 326, 347, 392–396 *passim*, 409, 412, 415, 446, 456

Rapalje, John, 259–260

Rawson, Edward, 427

Ray, Nicholas, 474

Read, George, 130, 157, 240, 410

Read, Rev. Robert, 462

Reed, Joseph, 124, 143, 355, 368, 399, 465

Regency Bill of 1765, 204, 447

Regulator Insurrection (1774), 82

Remonstrance to the House of Commons (Virginia; 1768), 54

Reveley, Henry, 186

Revere, Paul, 97, 126, 190, 356, 362, 385, 404, 439–440

Rhoads, Samuel, 130, 154, 160, 176, 232, 240, 409, 428

Rhode Island Colony, First Continental Congress and, 128, 136, 140, 148, 158, 161, 239, 387; *Gaspee* affair in, 6, 82–87; non-importation agreement in (1768), 57–58, 313; dilution of non-importation agreement, 72; population of (1770), 5; negro slavery and, 262–263, 489; war preparations and, 176, 183, 429

Richardson, Ebenezer, 78, 335–336

Richmond, 3rd Duke of (Charles Lennox), 34, 36–37, 107, 119, 270, 288, 294, 353, 368, 379, 426

Riley, John, 77, 334

Robinson, Capt. James, 439

Robinson, John, 61, 77, 203, 292, 317, 334

Rochford, 4th Earl of (William Henry Zuylestein), 67–68, 103, 325, 364, 424

Rockingham, 2nd Marquis of (Charles Watson Wentworth), 45, 92, 287, 317, 378; Administration of Justice Act opposed by, 119, 379; Declaratory Act and, 300; followers of, 1, 106, 118, 172, 423–424, 426; formation of Pitt Ministry and, 34–37, 288–291, 293; Free Port Act and, 33, 211; George III and Ministry of, 204–205; Grafton Ministry and, 66, 70, 322–323; Quartering Act and, 40; Stamp Act and, 14–23, 271–277, 279–281; Townshend Act and, 300, 329

Rodney, Caesar, 130, 140, 146, 240, 394–397 *passim,* 409

Rogers, Nathaniel, 335

Romney (ship), 61, 63, 65, 319–320

Rose (ship), 77, 225, 436, 467

Ross, George, 145, 153–154, 156, 232, 240

Rotch, Francis, 97–98, 100, 357–361 *passim*

Rouet, William, 23, 275–276, 279, 289, 298

Rowe, John, 98, 318–319, 330, 335–341 *passim,* 354–359 *passim,* 370

Royal Proclamation (1763), 121, 198

Ruddock, Abiel, 356, 362

Ruddock, John, 242, 370

Ruggles, Timothy, 171, 420, 424

Rush, Benjamin, 354–355

Rutledge, Edward, 130, 140, 143–145, 154, 156–157, 241, 246, 393, 400–401, 408–409, 415

Rutledge, John, 130, 140, 148, 150, 156–157, 241, 393, 411, 415, 482

Rynell, John, 313

Sackville, 1st Viscount (George Sackville, Lord George Germain), 11, 45, 270, 274–275, 280, 288, 300, 377

St. John (ship), 342

Sandwich, 4th Earl of (John Montagu), 12, 24, 103, 169, 181, 187, 189, 270, 273, 280, 288, 310, 364, 379, 421, 424

Sardoine (ship), 61

Saunders, Adm. Sir Charles, 37, 291

Saville, Sir George, 118

Sawbridge, John, 106

"Scaevola", *see* Mifflin, Thomas

Schuyler, Philip, 176, 235, 237, 260, 487

Scollay, John, 357–359

Scott, James, 104, 365

Scott, John Morin, 234, 237, 472–478 *passim*

Seabury, Rev. Samuel, 260, 464, 487

Sears, Isaac, 234, 238, 472–478 *passim*

Secker, Thomas (Archbishop of Canterbury), 197–198, 217–218, 221, 280, 458–461

Second Continental Congress (1776), 142, 161–162, 174, 176, 180, 196, 256–260 *passim,* 395, 400, 415–416, 423, 428–429

Second Massachusetts Congress, *see* Massachusetts Provincial Congress

Septennial Act of 1715, 170

Sessions, Darius, 83

Seven Years' War (French and Indian War), 11–12, 171, 184

Sewall, Atty.-Gen. Jonathan, 286

Shaeffe, William, 215, 457

Sharp, Granville, 261, 488–489

Sharpe, Horatio, 273, 276–277, 279, 310

Shelburne, 2nd Earl of (Sir William Petty; Eng. Wycombe), 21, 38–40, 206, 294–295, 316; Boston Port Act opposed by, 107, 368; Hillsborough's appointment and, 55, 309–310; *Liberty* riot and, 62–63, 317, 319–320; Massachusetts Regulating Act opposed by, 378; in Pitt Ministry, 37, 273, 276, 280, 291–299; resignation of, 67, 323; Townshend Act and, 42, 45, 298–299

Sherman, Roger, 130, 137–138, 146, 157, 239, 275, 392, 401

Shipley, Jonathan, 378

Shirley, William, 226, 451, 468

slavery, negro, 132, 141, 153, 261–263, 408, 488–489

Smith, Col. Francis, 189, 191, 194, 439, 441

Smith, Richard, 130, 240

Smith, William, 473, 478, 482

smuggling 90, 350, 451

Smythe, Frederick, 345

Snider, Christopher, 77–78

Society for the Propagation of the Gospel in Foreign Parts (the Society), 201, 218, 460

Solemn League and Covenant (May 1774), 164, 250–251, 483

Sons of Liberty, 101, 227, 229, 234–235, 238, 363, 474–478

South Carolina Colony, Committee of Correspondence, 92; First Continental Congress and, 130, 140, 158, 161, 241, 388, 408; effects of Massachusetts Regulating Act on, 8; government of, 247–248, 313; non-importation agreement in (1768), 57, 60, 315; dilution of non-importation agreement (1770), 73; opposition to Tea Act in, 101–102; population of (1770), 5; war preparations in, 177

Spencer, *see* Marlborough

Spry, Dr. William, 210, 453, 464

Stamp Act (1765), 2–3, 14–33 *passim*, 103, 222; colonial opposition to, 33, 48–49, 100, 197–198, 297, 304, 362; repeal of (1776), 21–33, 62, 96, 222, 227, 282, 287, 293, 310, 327, 330, 355; crisis averted by repeal of, 1;

Franklin and, 3, 22, 45–46, 49; repeal of, opposed by North, 71; supporters of, in Pitt Ministry, 37–38; Townshend Act compared with, 48–49, 51, 213, 305–306

Stamp Act Congress (1765), 3, 21, 50–51, 130, 385, 389, 413, 410

Stanhope, Philip, 290, 298, 426

Statement of Rights, Committee for the (First Continental Congress; Committee on Rights), 142, 146–149, 398–399, 402–403, 413

Statement of Rights and Grievances (1774), 146–149, 156, 161, 247–248

Stephens, Philip, 210, 345, 360

Stiles, Rev. Ezra, 344, 396, 399

Stone, Thomas, 176

Strahan, William, 46

Strange, Sir John, 23, 280

Suffolk, 12th Earl of (Henry Howard), 16, 103, 273, 364, 424, 438

Suffolk County Resolves (1774), 142, 146–150, 179, 249, 259, 404–405, 487

Sullivan, John, 124, 130, 141, 153, 239, 383, 397, 411

Sutherland, Lt. William, 265, 267, 439, 441, 490–491

Swift, John, 456

taxes, "internal" and "external," 2, 3; Dickinson on, 50; Franklin on, 46; Townshend on, 43

Tayloe, John, 445

Taylor, John, 335

Tea Act (1773), 6–7, 81, 90–94, 229, 354–363 *passim, see also* Boston Tea Party and East India Company

Temple, 1st Earl of (Richard Grenville), 18, 36, 204–205, 290

Temple, John, 61, 316, 318, 457

Temple, William, 73

Ten Broeck, Abraham, 235, 258–259, 428, 475, 486

Ten Eyck, Jacob, 235, 237

Thacher, Oxenbridge, 213, 215

Thatcher, Benjamin, 362

Thayer, Ebenezer, 440

Thomas, John, 180, 235, 237, 258–260

Thomas, Nathaniel Roy, 426

Thomson, Charles, 141, 269, 282, 395–396, 411–412

Thurlow, Atty.-Gen. Edward, 103–104, 215, 345–346, 364–369 *passim,* 457

Tilghman, Matthew, 129, 240

Tompkins, Samuel, 344

Townshend, Charles, 16, 19, 40, 42, 133; American Customs Board and, 61, 316–317, 319; death of, 66, 322; in Pitt Ministry, 37, 291–293, 295; Stamp Act supported by, 37–38, 272–274

Townshend, Charles ("Spanish Charles"), 354

Townshend, Thomas, 17–18, 106

Townshend Act (1767), 2, 103, 118, 133–134, 155, 214–215, 298–303, 316, 318, 378, 403, 406; passage of, 42–47; petitions for repeal of, 54–57, 300, 308–312; reactions to, 48–58 *passim,* 304–308, *see also* Dickinson's *Farmer's Letters,* and non-importation agreements; revision of, 5, 66–82 *passim,* 324–331 *passim;* Stamp Act compared with, 48–49, 51, 305–306; tea duty under, 91–95, 301, 350–354 *passim,* 368

Treason Act (1543), 84, 254

treason resolution (1768), 66–69, 325–326; attempts to try participants of *Gaspee* affair under, 85–87

Trecothick, Barlow, 17, 92, 277–278, 352

Trelawney, Gen. Edward, 63, 319

Trowbridge, Edmund, 80

Trumbull, Jonathan, 162, 193, 213–214, 440

Tryon, William, 238, 330

Tudor, William, 142, 150, 397

Tupper, Major John, 437

Twopenny Act (1758), 197–198, 442, 461

Tyler, Dr. William, 361

Van, Charles, 106, 367

Van Cortlandt, Pierre, 235

Van Dyck, Francis, 427

Van Kleeck, Leonard, 259

Van Wyck, Theodorus, 234, 474

Van Zandt, Jacobus, 478

Vardill, Rev. John, 252–253, 484

Venner, Samuel, 317

Virginia Colony, Committee of Correspondence, 86–87, 386; First Continental Congress and, 128–129, 136, 139–140, 150, 158, 161, 240; government of, 202, 443, 482; non-importation agreements in (1768), 54–55, 57, 59–60, 73, 214–215, 223, 330, 400; petitions to the King (1768), 54, 57, 221, 309; population of (1770), 5; response to Boston Port Act, 385–386; treason resolution and, 69, 325, 347; war preparations in, 177–178

Virginia Convention (1774), 129, 153, 388

Wallace, Charles, 313

Wallace, Capt. James, 436

Walpole, Horace, 288–292

Walton, Jacob, 233–235, 259, 473–474, 479

Wanton, Joseph, 82–84, 86

Ward, Col. Artemas, 179–180

Ward, Samuel, 275, 416; First Continental Congress and, 128, 140–141, 145–146, 153–154, 156, 239, 393, 397, 403, 408–409, 481; war preparations and, 176–177

Warren, James, 179–183, 356–358, 432–433, 440

Warren, Joseph, 81, 104, 179, 190, 341, 349, 389, 417, 439

Washington, George, 27, 127, 201, 313–314, 386; as delegate to First Continental Congress, 129, 132, 139–140, 146, 240, 392, 401–402, 412–413; non-importation agreements and, 59, 313–314, 465; negro slavery and, 262, 489; war preparations and, 177–178

Watson, Abraham, 180

Weaver, Ralph, 336

Wedderburn, Alexander, 103–104, 116, 345–346, 364–369 *passim,* 376, 381, 383

Wells, Samuel, 260

Wendell, Oliver, 359, 478

Wentworth, John, 63, 317

West, Richard, 208

West, William, 313

Weymouth, 3rd Viscount (Thomas Thynne), 66–68, 325

Wharton, Thomas, 355

Whately, Thomas, 113–114, 281, 298, 317–318, 320–321, 373–374, 464

Wheeler, Lt. Francis, 266–267

Wheeler, Joseph, 431

Wheeler, Rev. William Willard, 464

White, Benjamin, 180

White, Henry, 102

White, Hugh, 79, 336–339 *passim*

White Pine Acts, 198, 443

Whitworth, John Dean, 100, 360

Wilkes, John, 70, 110, 134, 238, 248, 289, 326, 391, 447, 478, 483

Wilkins, Isaac, 260

Willard, Josiah, 217, 258

Willard, Thomas Rice, 440

William (ship), 97, 358–359

Williams, John, 63–64, 317

Williams, Jonathan, 104, 358, 365, 425

Williams, Robert F., 474

Williamsburg, Committee of Corre-
spondence, 127; receives news of Lexington, 191; response to Boston Port Act in, 127

Willing, Thomas, 231, 429

Wilson, James, 429

Winchilsea, 9th Earl of (George Finch-Haddon), 15–16, 34, 37, 272, 288

Winship, Jonathan, 77, 334

Wisner, Henry, 129, 233, 240

Witherspoon, Rev. John, 138

Wolfe, Gen. James, 11, 270, 412

Wood, Abiel, 362

Woodhull, Nathaniel, 259, 477

writs of assistance, 46–47, 197–198, 212–216, 316, 454–458

Wyat, William, 337–338

Wyman, Nathaniel, 441

Yard, Sarah, 138

York, Duke of (Frederick Augustus; son of George III), 23, 278

Yorke, Charles, 17, 19–21, 272–275

Yorke, Philip, *see* Hardwick, 1st Earl of

Young, Dr. Thomas, 99, 317, 357–360